PHILOSOPHY OF RELIGION

PHILOSOPHY OF RELIGION:

Selected Readings

MICHAEL PETERSON
WILLIAM HASKER
BRUCE REICHENBACH
DAVID BASINGER

New York Oxford
OXFORD UNIVERSITY PRESS
1996

OXFORD UNIVERSITY PRESS

Oxford New York
Athens Auckland Bangkok Bombay
Calcutta Cape Town Dar es Salaam Delhi
Florence Hong Kong Istanbul Karachi
Kuala Lumpur Madras Madrid Melbourne
Mexico City Nairobi Paris Singapore
Taipei Tokyo Toronto

and associated companies in
Berlin Ibadan

Published by Oxford University Press, Inc.,
198 Madison Avenue, New York, NY 10016

Library of Congress Cataloging-in-Publication Data
Philosophy of religion : selected readings / Michael Peterson . . . [et al.].
p. cm. Includes bibliographical references.
ISBN 0–19–508909–X
1. Religion—Philosophy.
2. Christianity—Philosophy.
I. Peterson, Michael L., 1950–
BL51.P545 1996 210—dc20
95-11561

9 8 7 6 5 4 3 2 1

Printed in the United States of America
on acid-free paper

CONTENTS

PHILOSOPHY OF RELIGION

INTRODUCTION

For many centuries, the philosophy of religion has been a major area of philosophical inquiry. In the Western world, philosophers have had a long-standing interest in classical theism, the view that there exists a Supreme Spiritual Being, transcendent from the world, who is omnipotent, omniscient, and perfectly good. The major theistic religions (Judaism, Christianity, and Islam) basically share this view of God. While most of the readings in this text focus on issues pertaining to classical general theism, some readings consider issues or themes pertaining specifically to Christian theism.

Actually, the philosophy of religion fell on lean times during the first portion of the twentieth century. During this period, the widespread acceptance of the verifiability principle of meaning led many thinkers to conclude that religious claims, which are nonempirical and thus not verifiable, are cognitively meaningless. This certainly made it difficult for any self-respecting intellectual to take religious claims seriously. In the 1960s and 1970s about the only energetic work in the philosophy of religion was being done by philosophers who had discovered that the work of the later Wittgenstein might, on the one hand, rebut the positivistic critique of religious language and, on the other hand, lead to fruitful insights into the nature of religious language. About the only exceptions to these trends were Roman Catholic philosophers, most of whom had roots in more ancient ideas, making them less susceptible to the impact of twentieth-century trends on religious language.

In the last few decades, the overall situation has changed dramatically. Now philosophers know that the positivistic principle of verifiability must be rejected as not adequate even for science, let alone religion. It is virtually impossible anymore to find any self-respecting philosopher who will call himself or herself a positivist. The situation also seems to be changing because there has been a noticeable increase in the number of practicing philosophers who not only espouse some form of personal religious faith but also address issues regarding religious faith from within their professional discipline. Even opponents of religious faith are coming to respect its rational integrity. All of this has made for a virtual explosion of high-quality publications in the philosophy of religion—produced by philosophers who affirm religious faith as well as by those who do not.

It is therefore an exciting time in the field of philosophy of religion. This renewal has exposed us to some very fine work in the field, past and present, inviting us to be listeners and even participants in the great, ongoing dialogue. We are seeing more and more discussions of the eminent medieval philosophers such as Augustine, Anselm, and Aquinas. We are learning of the careful analysis of key concepts and rigorous examination of major arguments provided by the celebrated thinkers of the modern period such as Leibniz, Hume, and Kant. And we are invigorated by the efforts of recent philosophers to bring the latest insights and methods to bear on familiar issues. The names of John Hick, Alvin Plantinga, J. L. Mackie, and others will long be remembered for helping shape the current discussions in the philosophy of religion.

The present anthology has been assembled in an effort to represent some of the best primary works on most of the important themes in the philosophy of religion today. It includes key essays from writers in the medieval, modern, and contemporary periods. Employing a method of organization that is very comprehensive, this collection of readings can be used as the sole text or in conjunction with a secondary text in appropriate courses. Readers who are already familiar with our own secondary text, *Reason and Religious Belief,* will notice a particularly close fit.

The structure of the present text is straightforward. It consists of sixty-two selections organized into thirteen different parts: religious experience, faith and reason, divine attributes, theistic arguments, the problem of evil, knowing God without arguments, religious language, miracles, life after death, religion and science, religious diversity, religious ethics, and philosophy and theological doctrines. To maximize the pedagogical value of this anthology, we have included a general introduction to each of the thirteen major parts of the book as well as a brief synopsis with each selection. We have also placed a list of suggested readings at the end of each major part.

PART ONE RELIGIOUS EXPERIENCE

In almost every religion some believers not only claim to experience something transcendent or divine, but think that such experiences provide meaning and direction to their lives. Some believers even take these experiences to help justify their beliefs. They report diverse experiences, from the experiences of God mediated through public, common things like icons or the sunset to experiences of unusual objects, like weeping statues or faces in clouds; to inner experiences where the divine is mediated through objects only they experience: ultimately to experiences of God or Ultimate Reality not mediated by anything describable in sensory language, According to William James, these experiences form the root of religion.

Philosophers of religion have several concerns about these experiences. First, what kind of event is a religious experience? Some philosophers understand religious experience as a feeling, or better, as a complex of feelings. In his classic work, *The Idea of the Holy,* Rudolph Otto speaks of three types of feelings: the feeling of dependence [that we are mere creatures "submerged and overwhelmed by (our) own nothingness"], the feeling of religious dread or awe, and the feeling of longing for the transcendent being that fascinates us.

Others see religious experience as a type of perception. It has a structure similar to sense experience (perceiver, object perceived, and appearance). One line of argument they take rests on the fact that the experience of God might be neither a common nor a sensory experience should not count against understanding it as a type of perception.

Other philosophers view religious experiences as interpretative accounts of our experience. It is true that in order for an experience to be a religious one, persons must take or describe the experience as being of something transcendent. Purely naturalistic accounts are inadequate. However, some would caution that it is important to distinguish the description of the experience from its explanation. The fact that the believer describes the experience to be of the transcendent tells us nothing about whether it is in fact so.

This brings us to the second issue, namely, can they employ religious experience to justify religious beliefs, such as the belief that God exists? On the one hand, if the experience is an ineffable feeling, little that is cognitive follows from it. It could scarcely function as the basis for religious truths. On the other hand, those who understand religious experiences as a type of perceptual experience might use such experiences to argue for God's existence, much as one would use the visual experience of a cat as evidence for the existence of a cat. This view, however, must face the challenge of philosophers who maintain that it is more likely that religious experiences have a psychological or natural explanation than that they truly report an encounter with the divine.

What bothers many philosophers is the diversity of religious experiences. Religious experiences can be found in monotheistic, polytheistic and atheistic religions alike. If experiences are prima facie reliable, how can one explain this diversity? What beliefs could they establish if the religious claims they apparently support radically differ? Of course, merely noting that religious experiences involve interpretation will not allow us to dispose of such experiences, for all experiences involve interpretation.

Instead of asking what religious experience justifies, phenomenologists argue that the most profitable approach is to provide a phenomenological description of the experience. The experiences in question are best understood as the opening of oneself to the transcendent Other. Whether this self-transcendence is an authentic experience of God is not easily decidable, for self-deception is always possible.

Clearly, many points—the nature of religious experience, the role of interpretation in experience, whether there is a common core that underlies all religious experience, whether a prima facie trust in experiential reports should be maintained—need clarification and defense, and thus provide opportunity for philosophical reflection on the issue of religious experience.

SAINT TERESA OF JESUS

Religious Experiences

Saint Teresa (1515–1582) describes two different types of religious experience. In reporting her experience of the first type, she claims to have been conscious of Jesus Christ appearing and speaking to her. Though she did not see him with either her physical eyes or the eyes of her soul, she is certain by an internal illumination that he is beside her. She goes on to describe an experience of the second type in which she gradually comes to see the resurrected Jesus and his glory and majesty with the eyes of her soul. Though this vision is imaginary (i.e., accompanied by images) and hence subject to deception, she believes that she can be sure it comes from God and not the devil because of its characteristics and the changes for the better it made in her life.

⌘

I

At the end of two years, during the whole of which time both other people and myself were continually praying for what I have described—that the Lord would either lead me by another way or make plain the truth: and these locutions which, as I have said, the Lord was giving me were very frequent—I had the following experience. I was at prayer on a festival of the glorious Saint Peter when I saw Christ at my side—or, to put it better, I was conscious of Him, for neither with the eyes of the body nor with those of the soul did I see anything. I thought He was quite close to me and I saw that it was He Who, as I thought, was speaking to me. Being completely ignorant that visions of this kind could occur, I was at first very much afraid, and did nothing but weep, though, as soon as He addressed a single word to me to reassure me, I became quiet again, as I had been before, and was quite happy and free from fear. All the time Jesus Christ seemed to be beside me, but, as this was not an imaginary vision, I could not discern in what form: what I felt very clearly was that all the time He was at my right hand, and a witness of everything that I was doing, and that, whenever I became slightly recollected or was not greatly distracted, I could not but be aware of His nearness to me.

Sorely troubled, I went at once to my confessor, to tell him about it. He asked me in what form I had seen Him. I told him that I had not seen Him at all. Then he asked me how I knew it was Christ. I told him that I did not know how, but that I could not help realizing that He was beside me, and that I saw and felt this clearly; that when in the Prayer of Quiet my soul was now much more deeply and continuously recollected; that the effects of my prayer were very different from those which I had previously been accustomed to experience; and that the thing was quite clear to me. I did nothing, in my efforts to make myself understood, but draw comparisons—though really, for describing this kind of vision, there is no comparison which is very much to the point, for it is one of the highest kinds of vision possible. . . .

II

One day, when I was at prayer, the Lord was pleased to reveal to me nothing but His hands, the beauty of which was so great as to be indescribable. This made me very fearful, as does every new experience that I have when the Lord is beginning to grant me some supernatural favour. A few days later I also saw that Divine face, which seemed to leave me completely absorbed. I could not understand why the Lord revealed Himself gradually like this since He was later to grant me the favour of seeing Him wholly, until at length I realized that His Majesty was leading me according to my natural weakness. May He be blessed for ever, for so much glory all at once would have been more than so base and wicked a person could bear: knowing this, the compassionate Lord prepared me for it by degrees.

Your Reverence may suppose that it would have needed no great effort to behold those hands and that beauteous face. But there is such beauty about glorified bodies that the glory which illumines them throws all who look upon such supernatural loveliness into confusion. I was so much afraid, then, that I was plunged into turmoil and confusion, though later I began to feel such certainty and security that my fear was soon lost.

One year, on Saint Paul's Day, when I was at Mass, I saw a complete representation of this most sacred Humanity, just as in a picture of His resurrection body, in very great beauty and majesty; this I described in detail to Your Reverence in writing, at your very insistent request. It distressed me terribly to have to do so, for it is impossible to write such a description without a disruption of one's very being, but I did the best I could and so there is no reason for me to repeat the attempt here. I will only say that, if there were nothing else in Heaven to delight the eyes but the extreme beauty of the glorified bodies there, that alone would be the greatest bliss. A most especial bliss, then, will it be to us when we see the Humanity of Jesus Christ; for, if it is so even on earth, where His Majesty reveals Himself according to what our wretchedness can bear, what will it be where the fruition of that joy is complete? Although this vision is imaginary, I never saw it, or any other vision, with the eyes of the body, but only with the eyes of the soul.

Those who know better than I say that the type of vision already described is nearer perfection than this, while this in its turn is much more so than those which are seen with the eyes of the body. . . .

I will describe, then, what I have discovered by experience. How the Lord effects it, Your Reverence will explain better than I and will expound everything obscure of which I do not know the explanation. At certain times it really seemed to me that it was an image I was seeing; but on many other occasions I thought it was no image, but Christ Himself, such was the brightness with which He was pleased to reveal Himself to me. Sometimes, because of its indistinctness, I would think the vision was an image, though it was like no earthly painting, however perfect, and I have seen a great many good ones. It is ridiculous to think that the one thing is any more like the other than a living person is like his portrait: however well the portrait is done, it can never look completely natural: one sees, in fact, that it is a dead thing. But let us pass over that, apposite and literally true though it is.

I am not saying this as a comparison, for comparisons are never quite satisfactory: it is the actual truth. The difference is similar to that between something living and something painted, neither more so nor less. For if what I see is an image it is a living image—not a dead man but the living Christ. And He shows me that He is both Man and God—not as He was in the sepulchre, but as He was when He left it after rising from the dead. Sometimes He comes with such majesty that no one can doubt it is the Lord Himself; this is especially so after Communion, for we know that He is there, since the Faith tells us so. He reveals Himself so completely as the Lord of that inn, the soul, that it feels as though it were wholly dissolved and consumed in Christ. O my Jesus, if one could but describe the majesty with which Thou dost reveal Thyself! . . .

The soul is now a new creature: it is continuously absorbed in God; it seems to me that a new and living love of God is beginning to work within it to a very high degree; for, though the former type of vision which, as I said, reveals God without presenting any image of Him, is of a higher kind, yet, if the memory of it is to last, despite our weakness, and if the thoughts are to be well occupied, it is a great thing that so Divine a Presence should be presented to the imagination and should remain within it. These two kinds of vision almost invariably occur simultaneously, and, as they come in this way, the eyes of the soul see the excellence and the beauty and the glory of the most holy Humanity. And in the other way which has been described it is revealed to us how He is God, and that He is powerful, and can do all things, and commands all things, and rules all things, and fills all things with His love.

This vision is to be very highly esteemed, and, in my view, there is no peril in it, as its effects show that the devil has no power over it. . . .

Of all impossibilities, the most impossible is that these true visions should be the work of the imagination. There is no way in which this could be so: by the mere beauty and whiteness of a single one of the hands which we are shown the imagination is completely transcended. In any case, there is no other way in which it would be possible for us to see in a moment things of which we have no recollection, which we have never thought of, and which, even in a long period of time, we could not invent with our imagination, because, as I have already said, they far transcend what we can comprehend on earth. . . .

I used to put forward this argument together with others, when they told me, as they often did, that I was being deceived by the devil and that it was all the work of my imagination. I also drew such comparisons as I could and as the Lord revealed to my understanding. . . .

I once said to the people who were talking to me in this way that if they were to tell me that a person whom I knew well and had just been speaking to was not herself at all, but that I was imagining her to be so, and that they knew this was the case, I should certainly believe them rather than my own eyes. But, I added, if that person left some jewels with me, which I was actually holding in my hands as pledges of her great love, and if, never having had any before, I were thus to find myself rich instead of poor, I could not possibly believe that this was delusion, even if I wanted to. And, I said, I could show them these jewels—for all who knew me were well aware how my soul had changed: my confessor himself testified to this, for the difference was very great in every respect, and no fancy, but such as all could clearly see. As I had previously been so wicked, I concluded, I could not believe that, if the devil were doing this to delude me and drag me down to hell, he would make use of means which so completely defeated their own ends by taking away my vices and making me virtuous and strong; for it was quite clear to me that these experiences had immediately made me a different person.

WILLIAM JAMES

Religious Experience as the Root of Religion

William James (1842–1910) first notes four characteristics of mystical experience and then illustrates these by appealing to mystical experiences from diverse traditions. He concludes that though a mystical experience is authoritative for those who experience it, it need not be authoritative for others. However, he also argues that nonmystical (rationally cognitive) states are not the sole mediators of reality. This is particularly true for religion, whose deeper source, James believes, is feeling; philosophical and theological formulas are secondary, derived from religious experience.

⌘

From *Varieties of Religious Experience*, copyright © 1923. New York: Longmans, Green, and Co.

One may say truly, I think, that personal religious experience has its root and centre in mystical states of consciousness; so for us, who in these lectures are treating personal experience as the exclusive subject of our study, such states of consciousness ought to form the vital chapter from which the other chapters get their light. . . .

First of all, then, I ask, What does the expression 'mystical states of consciousness' mean? How do we part off mystical states from other states? . . . I propose to you four marks which, when an experience has them, may justify us in calling it mystical for the purpose of the present lectures.

1. *Ineffability.* The handiest of the marks by which I classify a state of mind as mystical is negative. The subject of it immediately says that it defies expression, that no adequate report of its contents can be given in words. It follows from this that its quality must be directly experienced; it cannot be imparted or transferred to others. In this peculiarity mystical states are more like states of feeling than like states of intellect. No one can make clear to another who has never had a certain feeling, in what the quality or worth of it consists. . . .

2. *Noetic quality.* Although so similar to states of feeling, mystical states seem to those who experience them to be also states of knowledge. They are states of insight into depths of truth unplumbed by the discursive intellect. They are illuminations, revelations, full of significance and importance, all inarticulate though they remain; and as a rule they carry with them a curious sense of authority for after-time.

These two characters will entitle any state to be called mystical, in the sense in which I use the word. Two other qualities are less sharply marked, but are usually found. These are:

3. *Transiency.* Mystical states cannot be sustained for long. Except in rare instances, half an hour, or at most an hour or two, seems to be the limit beyond which they fade into the light of common day. Often, when faded, their quality can but imperfectly be reproduced in memory; but when they recur it is recognized; and from one recurrence to another it is susceptible of continuous development in what is felt as inner richness and importance.

4. *Passivity.* Although the oncoming of mystical states may be facilitated by preliminary voluntary operations, as by fixing the attention, or going through certain bodily performances, or in other ways which manuals of mysticism prescribe; yet when the characteristic sort of consciousness once has set in, the mystic feels as if his own will were in abeyance, and indeed sometimes as if he were grasped and held by a superior power. This latter peculiarity connects mystical states with certain definite phenomena of secondary or alternative personality, such as prophetic speech, automatic writing, or the mediumistic trance. When these latter conditions are well pronounced, however, there may be no recollection whatever of the phenomenon, and it may have no significance for the subject's usual inner life, to which, as it were, it makes a mere interruption. Mystical states, strictly so called, are never merely interruptive. Some memory of their content al-

ways remains, and a profound sense of their importance. They modify the inner life of the subject between the times of their recurrence. Sharp divisions in this region are, however, difficult to make, and we find all sorts of gradations and mixtures.

These four characteristics are sufficient to mark out a group of states of consciousness peculiar enough to deserve a special name and to call for careful study. Let it then be called the mystical group.

Our next step should be to gain acceptance with some typical examples. Professional mystics at the height of their development have often elaborately organized experiences and a philosophy based thereupon. . . .

The simplest rudiment of mystical experience would seem to be that deepened sense of the significance of a maxim or formula which occasionally sweeps over one. "I've heard that said all my life," we exclaim, "but I never realized its full meaning until now." "When a fellow-monk," said Luther, "one day repeated the words of the Creed: 'I believe in the forgiveness of sins,' I saw the Scripture in an entirely new light; and straightway I felt as if I were born anew. It was as if I had found the door of paradise thrown wide open." This sense of deeper significance is not confined to rational propositions. Single words, and conjunctions of words, effects of light on land and sea, odors and musical sounds, all bring it when the mind is tuned aright. Most of us can remember the strangely moving power of passages in certain poems read when we were young, irrational doorways as they were through which the mystery of fact, the wildness and the pang of life, stole into our hearts and thrilled them. The words have now perhaps become mere polished surfaces for us; but lyric poetry and music are alive and significant only in proportion as they fetch these vague vistas of a life continuous with our own, beckoning and inviting, yet ever eluding our pursuit. We are alive or dead to the eternal inner message of the arts according as we have kept or lost this mystical susceptibility.

A more pronounced step forward on the mystical ladder is found in an extremely frequent phenomenon, that sudden feeling, namely, which sometimes sweeps over us, of having 'been here before,' as if at some indefinite past time, in just this place, with just these people, we were already saying just these things. . . .

Somewhat deeper plunges into mystical consciousness are met with in yet other dreamy states. Such feelings as these which Charles Kingsley describes are surely far from being uncommon, especially in youth:

> When I walk the fields, I am oppressed now and then with an innate feeling that everything I see has a meaning, if I could but understand it. And this feeling of being surrounded with truths which I cannot grasp amounts to indescribable awe sometimes. . . . Have you not felt that your real soul was imperceptible to your mental vision, except in a few hallowed moments? . . .

Certain aspects of nature seem to have a peculiar power of awakening such mystical moods. Most of the striking cases which I have collected have occurred out of doors. . . .

Here is a . . . record from the memoirs of that interesting German idealist, Malwida von Meysenbug:

> I was alone upon the seashore as all these thoughts flowed over me, liberating and reconciling; and now again, as once before in distant days in the Alps of Dauphiné, I was impelled to kneel down, this time before the illimitable ocean, symbol of the Infinite. I felt that I prayed as I had never prayed before, and knew now what prayer really is: to return from the solitude of individuation into the consciousness of unity with all that is, to kneel down as one that passes away, and to rise up as one imperishable. Earth, heaven, and sea resounded as in one vast world-encircling harmony. It was as if the chorus of all the great who had ever lived were about me. I felt myself one with them, and it appeared as if I heard their greeting: "Thou too belongest to the company of those who overcome.". . .

We have now seen enough of this cosmic or mystic consciousness, as it comes sporadically. We must next pass to its methodical cultivation as an element of the religious life. Hindus, Buddhists, Mohammedans, and Christians all have cultivated it methodically.

In India, training in mystical insight has been known from time immemorial under the name of yoga. Yoga means the experimental union of the individual with the divine. It is based on persevering exercise; and the diet, posture, breathing, intellectual concentration, and moral discipline vary slightly in the different systems which teach it. The yogi, or disciple, who has by these means overcome the obscurations of his lower nature sufficiently, enters into the condition termed *samâdhi*, "and comes face to face with facts which no instinct or reason can ever know." He learns

> That the mind itself has a higher state of existence, beyond reason, a superconscious state, and that when the mind gets to that higher state, then this knowledge beyond reasoning comes. . . . All the different steps in yoga are intended to bring us scientifically to the superconscious state or samâdhi. . . . Just as unconscious work is beneath consciousness, so there is another work which is above consciousness, and which, also, is not accompanied with the feeling of egoism. . . . There is no feeling of *I*, and yet the mind works, desireless, free from restlessness, objectless, bodiless. Then the Truth shines in its full effulgence, and we know ourselves—for Samâdhi lies potential in us all—for what we truly are, free, immortal, omnipotent, loosed from the finite, and its contrasts of good and evil altogether, and identical with the Atman or Universal Soul.

The Vedanists say that one may stumble into superconsciousness sporadically, without the previous discipline, but it is then impure. Their test of its purity, like our test of religion's value, is empirical: its fruits must be good for life. When a man comes out of Samâdhi, they assure us that he remains "enlightened, a sage, a prophet, a saint, his whole character changed, his life changed, illumined."

The Buddhists use the word 'samâdhi' as well as the Hindus; but 'dhyâna' is their special word for higher states of contemplation. There seem to be four stages recognized in dhyâna. The first stage comes through concentration of the mind upon one point. It excludes desire, but not discernment or judgment: it is still intellectual. In the second state the intellectual functions drop off, and the satisfied sense of unity remains. In the third stage the satisfaction departs, and indifference begins, along with memory and self-consciousness. In the fourth stage the indifference, memory, and self-consciousness are perfected. [Just what 'memory' and 'self-consciousness' mean in this connection is doubtful. They cannot be the faculties familiar to us in the lower life.] Higher stages still of contemplation are mentioned—a region where there exists nothing, and where the meditator says: "There exists absolutely nothing," and stops. Then he reaches another region where he says: "There are neither ideas nor absence of ideas," and stops again. Then another region where, "having reached the end of both idea and perception, he stops finally." This would seem to be, not yet Nirvâna, but as close an approach to it as this life affords.

In the Mohammedan world the Sufi sect and various dervish bodies are the possessors of the mystical tradition. The Sufis have existed in Persia from the earliest times, and as their pantheism is so at variance with the hot and rigid monotheism of the Arab mind, it has been suggested that Sufism must have been inoculated into Islam by Hindu influences. We Christians know little of Sufism, for its secrets are disclosed only to those initiated. To give its existence a certain liveliness in your minds, I will quote a Moslem document, and pass away from the subject.

Al-Ghazzali, a Persian philosopher and theologian, who flourished in the eleventh century, and ranks as one of the greatest doctors of the Moslem church, has left us one of the few autobiographies to be found outside of Christian literature.

"The Science of the Sufis," says the Moslem author, "aims at detaching the heart from all that is not God, and at giving to it for sole occupation the meditation of the divine being. . . . What pertains most exclusively to their method is just what no study can grasp, but only transport, ecstasy, and the transformation of the soul.

"The first condition for a Sufi is to purge his heart entirely of all that is not God. The next key of the contemplative life consists in the humble prayers which escape from the fervent soul, and in the meditations on God in which the heart is swallowed up entirely. But in reality this is only the beginning of the Sufi life, the end of Sufism being total absorption in God. The intuitions and all that precede are, so to speak, only the threshold for those who enter. From the beginning, revelations take place in so flagrant a shape that the Sufis see before them, whilst wide awake, the angels and the souls of the prophets. They hear their voices and obtain their favors. Then the transport rises from the perception of forms and figures to a degree which escapes all expression, and which no man may seek to give an account of without his words involving sin.

"The chief properties of prophetism are perceptible only during the transport, by those who embrace the Sufi life. The prophet is endowed with qualities to which you possess nothing analogous, and which consequently you cannot possibly understand. How should you know their true nature, since one knows only what one can comprehend? But the transport which one attains by the method of the Sufis is like an immediate perception, as if one touched the objects with one's hand."

This incommunicableness of the transport is the keynote of all mysticism. Mystical truth exists for the individual who has the transport, but for no one else. In this, as I have said, it resembles the knowledge given to us in sensations more than that given by conceptual thought. Thought, with its remoteness and abstractness, has often enough in the history of philosophy been contrasted unfavorably with sensation. It is a commonplace of metaphysics that God's knowledge cannot be discursive but must be intuitive, that is, must be constructed more after the pattern of what in ourselves is called immediate feeling, than after that of proposition and judgment. But *our* immediate feelings have no content but what the five senses supply; and we have seen and shall see again that mystics may emphatically deny that the senses play any part in the very highest type of knowledge which their transports yield.

In the Christian church there have always been mystics. Although many of them have been viewed with suspicion, some have gained favor in the eyes of the authorities. The experiences of these have been treated as precedents, and a codified system of mystical theology has been based upon them, in which everything legitimate finds its place. The basis of the system is 'orison' or meditation, the methodical elevation of the soul towards God. Through the practice of orison the higher levels of mystical experience may be attained.

The first thing to be aimed at in orison is the mind's detachment from outer sensations, for these interfere with its concentration upon ideal things. Such manuals as Saint Ignatius's Spiritual Exercises recommend the disciple to expel sensation by a graduated series of efforts to imagine holy scenes. The acme of this kind of discipline would be a semi-hallucinatory monoideism—an imaginary figure of Christ, for example, coming fully to occupy the mind. Sensorial images of this sort, whether literal or symbolic, play an enormous part in mysticism. But in certain cases imagery may fall away entirely, and in the very highest raptures it tends to do so. The state of consciousness becomes then insusceptible of any verbal description. Mystical teachers are unanimous as to this. Saint John of the Cross, for instance, one of the best of them, thus describes the condition called the 'union of love,' which, he says, is reached by 'dark contemplation.'...

I have now sketched with extreme brevity and insufficiency, but as fairly as I am able in the time allowed, the general traits of the mystic range of consciousness. *It is on the whole pantheistic and optimistic, or at least the opposite of pessimistic. It is anti-naturalistic, and harmonizes best with twice-bornness and so-called otherworldly states of mind.*

My next task is to inquire whether we can invoke it as authoritative. Does it furnish any *warrant for the truth* of the twice-bornness and supernaturality and pantheism which it favors? I must give my answer to this question as concisely as I can.

In brief my answer is this, and I will divide it into three parts:

(1) Mystical states, when well developed, usually are, and have the right to be, absolutely authoritative over the individuals to whom they come.

(2) No authority emanates from them which should make it a duty for those who stand outside of them to accept their revelations uncritically.

(3) They break down the authority of the non-mystical or rationalistic consciousness, based upon the understanding and the senses alone. They show it to be only one kind of consciousness. They open out the possibility of other orders of truth, in which, so far as anything in us vitally responds to them, we may freely continue to have faith.

I will take up these points one by one.

1

As a matter of psychological fact, mystical states of a well-pronounced and emphatic sort *are* usually authoritative over those who have them. They have been 'there,' and know. It is vain for rationalism to grumble about this. If the mystical truth that comes to a man proves to be a force that he can live by, what mandate have we of the majority to order him to live in another way? We can throw him into a prison or a madhouse, but we cannot change his mind—we commonly attach it only the more stubbornly to its beliefs. It mocks our utmost efforts, as a matter of fact, and in point of logic it absolutely escapes our jurisdiction. Our own more 'rational' beliefs are based on evidence exactly similar in nature to that which mystics quote for theirs. Our senses, namely, have assured us of certain states of fact; but mystical experiences are as direct perceptions of fact for those who have them as any sensations ever were for us. The records show that even though the five senses be in abeyance in them, they are absolutely sensational in their epistemological quality, if I may be pardoned the barbarous expression—that is, they are face to face presentations of what seems immediately to exist.

The mystic is, in short, *invulnerable*, and must be left, whether we relish it or not, in undisturbed enjoyment of his creed. Faith, says Tolstoy, is that by which men live. And faith-state and mystic state are practically convertible terms.

2

But I now proceed to add that mystics have no right to claim that we ought to accept the deliverance of their peculiar experiences, if we are ourselves outsiders and feel no private call thereto. The utmost they can ever ask of us in this life is to admit that they establish a presumption. They form a consensus and have an unequivocal outcome; and it would be odd, mystics might say, if such a unanimous type of experience should prove to be altogether wrong. At bottom, however, this would only be an appeal to numbers, like the appeal of rationalism the other way; and the appeal to numbers has no logical force. If we acknowledge it, it is for 'suggestive,' not for logical reasons: we follow the majority because to do so suits our life.

But even this presumption from the unanimity of mystics is far from being strong. In characterizing mystic states as pantheistic, optimistic, etc., I am afraid I over-simplified the truth. I did so for expository reasons, and to keep the closer to the classic mystical tradition. The classic religious mysticism, it now must be confessed, is only a 'privileged case.' It is an *extract*, kept true to type by the selection of the fittest specimens and their preservation in 'schools.' It is carved out from a much larger mass; and if we take the larger mass as seriously as religious mysticism has historically taken itself, we find that the supposed unanimity largely disappears. To begin with, even religious mysticism itself, the kind that accumulates traditions and makes schools, is much less unanimous than I have allowed. It has been both ascetic and antinomianly self-indulgent within the Christian church. It is dualistic in Sankhya, and monistic in Vedanta philosophy. I called it pantheistic; but the great Spanish mystics are anything but pantheists. They are with few exceptions non-metaphysical minds, for whom 'the category of personality' is absolute. The 'union' of man with God is for them much more like an occasional miracle than like an original identity. . . . The fact is that the mystical feeling of enlargement, union, and emancipation has no specific intellectual content whatever of its own. It is capable of forming matrimonial alliances with material furnished by the most diverse philosophies and theologies, provided only they can find a place in their framework for its peculiar emotional mood. We have no right, therefore, to invoke its prestige as distinctively in favor of any special belief, such as that in absolute idealism, or in the absolute monistic identity, or in the absolute goodness, of the world. It is only relatively in favor of all these things—it passes out of common human consciousness in the direction in which they lie.

So much for religious mysticism proper. But more remains to be told, for religious mysticism is only one half of mysticism. The other half has no accumulated traditions except those which the text-books on insanity supply. Open any one of these, and you will find abundant cases in which 'mystical ideas' are cited as characteristic symptoms of enfeebled or deluded states of mind. In delusional insanity, paranoia, as they sometimes call it, we may have a *diabolical* mysticism, a sort of religious mysticism turned upside down. The same sense of ineffable importance in the smallest events, the same texts and words coming with new meanings, the same voices and visions and leadings and missions, the same controlling by extraneous powers; only this time the emotion is pessimistic: instead of consolations we have desolations; the meanings are dreadful; and the powers are enemies to life. It is evident that from the point of view of their psychological mechanism, the classic mysticism and these lower mysticisms spring from the same mental level, from that great subliminal or transmarginal region of which science is beginning to admit the existence, but of which so little is really known. That region contains every kind of matter: 'seraph and snake' abide there side by side. To come from thence is no infallible credential. What comes must be sifted and tested, and run the gauntlet of confrontation with the total context of experience, just like what comes from the outer world of sense. Its value must be ascertained by empirical methods, so long as we are not mystics ourselves.

3

Yet, I repeat once more, the existence of mystical states absolutely overthrows the pretension of non-mystical states to be the sole and ultimate dictators of what we may believe. As a rule, mystical states merely add a supersensuous meaning to the ordinary outward data of consciousness. They are excitements like the emotions of love or ambition, gifts to our spirit by means of which facts already objectively before us fall into a new expressiveness and make a new connection with our active life. They do not contradict these facts as such, or deny anything that our senses have immediately seized. It is the rationalistic critic rather who plays the part of denier in the controversy, and his denials have no strength, for there never can be a state of facts to which new meaning may not truthfully be added, provided the mind ascend to a more enveloping point of view. It must always remain an open question whether mystical states may not possibly be such superior points of view, windows through which the mind looks out upon a more extensive and inclusive world. The difference of the views seen from the different mystical windows need not prevent us from entertaining this supposition. The wider world would in that case prove to have a mixed constitution like that of this world, that is all. . . . The counting in of that wider world of meanings, and the serious dealing with it, might, in spite of all the perplexity, be indispensable stages in our approach to the final fullness of the truth.

In this shape, I think, we have to leave the subject. Mystical states indeed wield no authority due simply to their being mystical states. But the higher ones among them point in directions to which the religious sentiments even of non-mystical men incline. They tell of the supremacy of the ideal, of vastness, of union, of safety, and of rest. They offer us *hypotheses*, hypotheses which we may voluntarily ignore, but which as thinkers we cannot possibly upset. The supernaturalism and optimism to which they would persuade us may, interpreted in one way or another, be after all the truest of insights into the meaning of this life. . . .

The subject of Saintliness left us face to face with the question, Is the sense of divine presence a sense of anything objectively true? We turned first to mysticism for an answer, and found that although mysticism is entirely willing to corroborate religion, it is too private (and also too various) in its utterances to be able to claim a universal authority. But philosophy publishes results which claim to be universally valid if they are valid at all, so we now turn with our question to philosophy. Can philosophy stamp a warrant of veracity upon the religious man's sense of the divine? . . .

I do believe that feeling is the deeper source of religion, and that philosophic and theological formulas are secondary products, like translations of a text into another tongue. But all such statements are misleading from their brevity, and it will take the whole hour for me to explain to you exactly what I mean.

When I call theological formulas secondary products, I mean that in a world in which no religious feeling had ever existed, I doubt whether any philosophic theology could ever have been framed. I doubt if dispassionate intellectual contemplation of the universe, apart from inner unhappiness and need of deliverance on the one hand and mystical emotion on the other, would ever have resulted in religious philosophies such as we now possess. Men would have begun with animistic explanations of natural fact, and criticised these away into scientific ones, as they actually have done. In the science they would have left a certain amount of 'psychical research,' even as they now will probably have to re-admit a certain amount. But high-flying speculations like those of either dogmatic or idealistic theology, these they would have had no motive to venture on, feeling no need of commerce with such deities. These speculations must, it seems to me, be classed as over-beliefs, buildings-out performed by the intellect into directions of which feeling originally supplied the hint.

But even if religious philosophy had to have its first hint supplied by feeling, may it not have dealt in a superior way with the matter which feeling suggested? Feeling is private and dumb, and unable to give an account of itself. It allows that its results are mysteries and enigmas, declines to justify them rationally, and on occasion is willing that they should even pass for paradoxical and absurd. Philosophy takes just the opposite attitude. Her aspiration is to reclaim from mystery and paradox whatever territory she touches. To find an escape from obscure and wayward personal persuasion to truth objectively valid for all thinking men has ever been the intellect's most cherished ideal. To redeem religion from unwholesome privacy, and to give public status and universal right of way to its deliverances, has been reason's task.

I believe that philosophy will always have opportunity to labor at this task. We are thinking beings, and we cannot exclude the intellect from participating in any of our functions. Even in soliloquizing with ourselves, we construe our feelings intellectually. Both our personal ideals and our religious and mystical experiences must be interpreted congruously with the kind of scenery which our thinking mind inhabits. The philosophic climate of our time inevitably forces its own clothing on us. Moreover, we must exchange our feelings with one another, and in doing so we have to speak, and to use general and abstract verbal formulas. Conceptions and constructions are thus a necessary part of our religion; and as moderator amid the clash of hypotheses, and mediator among the criticisms of one man's constructions by another, philosophy will always have much to do. It would be strange if I disputed this, when these very lectures which I am giving are (as you will see more clearly from now onwards) a laborious attempt to extract from the privacies of religious experience some general facts which can be defined in formulas upon which everybody may agree.

Religious experience, in other words, spontaneously and inevitably engenders myths, superstitions, dogmas, creeds, and metaphysical theologies, and criticisms of one set of these by the adherents of another.

WILLIAM P. ALSTON

Religious Experience as Perception of God

After noting that he wants to consider direct rather than indirect awareness of God, William Alston (1921–) briefly sketches his "Theory of Appearing" model of perception, according to which perception consists of something presenting itself to me in a certain way, apart from my conceptualizing it or making judgments about it. Alston then applies this model to direct religious experience, showing that many who have religious experiences understand their experiences along similar lines, saying that it is possible to have a direct, genuine perception of God. To the objection that the properties by which God presents himself to us are very different from those presented by sensory objects, Alston replies that we often report appearances by using comparative concepts, which is what we use to report how God presents himself to our experience. Finally he notes that the problems that arise when one attempts to establish the veridicality of religious experience are in principle no different from those that arise from ordinary perceptual experience.

⌘

I

I pick out what I am calling "experience of God" by the fact that the subject takes the experience (or would take it if the question arose) to be a direct awareness of God. Here is a clear example cited in William James's *The Varieties of Religious Experience.*

> (1) . . . all at once I . . . felt the presence of God—I tell of the thing just as I was conscious of it—as if his goodness and his power were penetrating me altogether. Then, slowly, the ecstasy left my heart; that is, I felt that God had withdrawn the communion which he had granted. . . . I asked myself if it were possible that Moses on Sinai could have had a more intimate communication with God. I think it well to add that in this ecstasy of mine God had neither form, color, odor, nor taste; moreover, that the feeling of his presence was accompanied by no determinate localization. . . . But the more I seek words to express this intimate intercourse, the more I feel the impossibility of describing the thing by any of our usual images. At bottom the expression most apt to render what I felt is this: God was present, though invisible; he fell under no one of my senses, yet my consciousness perceived him.

Note that I do not restrict "experience of God" to cases in which it is really God of whom the subject is aware. The term, as I use it, ranges over all experiences that the subject *takes* to have this status. Thus the general category would be more exactly termed '*supposed* experience of God,' where calling it 'supposed' does not prejudice the question of whether it is genuine or not. However, I will generally omit this qualification. Note too that my category of "experience of God" is much narrower than "religious experience," which covers a diverse and ill-defined multitude of experiences.

In restricting myself to *direct* awareness of God I exclude cases in which one takes oneself to be aware of God through the beauties of nature, the words of the Bible or of a sermon, or other natural phenomena. For example:

> (2) I feel him [God] in the sunshine or rain; and awe mingled with a delicious restfulness most nearly describes my feelings.

My reason for concentrating on direct experience of God, where there is no other object of experience in or through which God is experienced, is that these experiences are the ones that are most plausibly regarded as *presentations* of God to the individual, in somewhat the way in which physical objects are presented to sense perception, as I will shortly make explicit.

Within this territory I will range over both lay and professional examples, both ordinary people living in the world and monastics who more or less devote their lives to attaining union with God. The category also embraces both focal and background experiences; though in order to discern the structure of the phenomenon we are well advised to concentrate on its more intense forms.

There is also the distinction between experiences with and without sensory content. In (1) the subject explicitly denies that the experience was sensory in character. Here is an example that does involve sensory content.

> (3) During the night . . . I awoke and looking out of my window saw what I took to be a luminous star which gradually came nearer, and appeared as a soft slightly blurred white light. I was seized with violent trembling, but had

> no fear. I knew that what I felt was great awe. This was followed by a sense of overwhelming love coming to me, and going out from me, then of great compassion from this Outer Presence. (Cited in T. Beardsworth, *A Sense of Presence.*)

In this discussion I will concentrate on nonsensory experiences. The main reason for this choice is that since God is purely spiritual, a nonsensory experience has a greater chance of presenting Him as He is than any sensory experience. If God appears to us as bearing a certain shape or as speaking in a certain tone of voice, that is a long way from representing Him as He is in Himself. I shall refer to nonsensory experience of God as "mystical experience," and the form of perception of God that involves that experience as "mystical perception." I use these terms with trepidation, for I do not want them to carry connotations of the merging of the individual subject into the One, or any of the other salient features of what we may term "classical mystical experience." (See William James.) They are to be understood simply as shorthand for "supposed nonsensory experience (perception) of God."

Many people find it incredible, unintelligible, or incoherent to suppose that there could be something that counts as *presentation,* that contrasts with abstract thought in the way sense perception does, but is devoid of sensory content. However, so far as I see, this simply evinces lack of speculative imagination or perhaps a mindless parochialism. Why should we suppose that the possibilities of experiential givenness, for human beings or otherwise, are exhausted by the powers of *our* five senses. Surely it is possible, to start with the most obvious point, that other creatures should possess a sensitivity to other physical stimuli that play a role in their functioning analogous to that played by our five senses in our lives. And, to push the matter a bit further, why can't we also envisage presentations that do not stem from the activity of any physical sense organs, as is apparently the case with mystical perception?

II

As the title indicates, I will be advocating a "perceptual model" of mystical experience. To explain what I mean by that, I must first say something about sense perception, since even if we suppose, as I do, that perception is not restricted to its sensory form, still that is the form with which we are far and away most familiar, and it is by generalizing from sense perception that we acquire a wider concept of perception.

As I see the matter, at the heart of perception (sensory or otherwise) is a phenomenon variously termed *presentation, appearance,* or *givenness.* Something is presented to one's experience (awareness) *as* so-and-so, as blue, as acrid, as a house, as Susie's house, or whatever. I take this phenomenon of *presentation* to be essentially independent of conceptualization, belief, or judgment. It is possible, in principle, for this book to visually present itself to me as blue even if I do not *take* it to be blue, *think* of it as blue, *conceptualize* it as blue, *judge* it to be blue, or anything else of the sort. No doubt, in mature human perception presentation is intimately intertwined with conceptualization and belief, but presentation does not *consist* in anything like that. The best way to see this is to contrast actually seeing the book with thinking about the book, or making judgments about it, in its absence. What is involved in the former case but not in the latter that makes the difference? It can't be anything of a conceptual or judgmental order, for anything of that sort can be present in the latter case when the book is not seen. Reflection on this question leads me to conclude that what makes the difference is that when I see the book it is *presented* to my awareness; it occupies a place in my visual field. This crucial notion of presentation cannot be analyzed; it can be conveyed only by helping another to identify instances of it in experience, as I have just done.

On the view of perception I favor, the "Theory of Appearing," perceiving X simply consists in X's appearing to one, or being presented to one, as so-and-so. That's all there is to it, as far as what perception is, in contrast to its causes and effects. Where X is an external physical object like a book, to perceive the book is just for the book to appear to one in a certain way.

In saying that a direct awareness that does not essentially involve conceptualization and judgment is at the heart of perception, I am *not* denying that a person's conceptual scheme, beliefs, cognitive readinesses, and so on, can affect the *way* an object presents itself to the subject, what it presents itself *as*. Things do look and sound differently to us after we are familiar with them, have the details sorted out, can smoothly put everything in its place without effort. My house presents a different appearance to me now after long habituation than it did the first time I walked in. Whereas Stravinski's *The Rite of Spring* sounded like a formless cacophony the first time I heard it, it now presents itself to me as a complex interweaving of themes. In saying this I am not going back on my assertion that X's presenting itself to one's awareness as P is not the same as S's *taking* S to be P. The latter involves the application of the concept of P to X, but the former does not, even though the character of the presentation can be influenced by one's conceptual repertoire and one's beliefs. But though my conceptual capacities and tendencies can affect the *way* objects appear to me, they have no power over *what object it is* that looks (sounds . . .) that way. When I look at my living room, the same objects present themselves to my visual awareness as when I first saw it. It is essential not to confuse *what* appears with what it appears *as*.

Even if to perceive X is simply for X to appear to one in a certain way, there can be further necessary conditions for someone to perceive X, for there can be further conditions for X's appearing to one. First, and this is just spelling out one thing that is involved in X's appearing to one, X must exist. I can't (really) perceive a tree unless the tree is there to be perceived. Second, it seems to be necessary for X's appearing to me (for my perceiving X) that X make an important *causal* contribution to my current experience. If there is a thick concrete wall between me and a certain house, thereby preventing light reflected from the house from striking my retina, then it couldn't be that that house is visually presented to me. I will assume such a causal condition in this discussion. Third, I will also assume a doxastic condition, that perceiving X at least tends to give rise to beliefs about X. This is much more questionable than the causal condition, but in any event we are concerned here with cases in which perception does give rise to beliefs about what is perceived.

III

Now we are ready to turn to the application of the perceptual model to mystical experience. In this essay I will not try to show that mystical experience (even sometimes) constitutes (genuine) perception of God. Remembering the necessary conditions of perception just mentioned, this would involve showing that God exists and that He makes the right kind of causal contribution to the experiences in question. What I will undertake here is the following. (1) I will argue that mystical experience is the right sort of experience to constitute a genuine perception of God if the other requirements are met. (2) I will argue that there is no bar in principle to these other requirements being satisfied if God does exist. This adds up to a defence of the thesis that it is quite possible that human beings do sometimes perceive God if God is "there" to be perceived. In other words, the thesis defended is that if God exists, then mystical experience is quite properly thought of as mystical perception.

If mystical experience is not construed perceptually, how can it be understood? The most common alternative is to think of it as made up of purely subjective feelings and sensations, to which is added an *explanation* according to which the experience is due to God. A recent example of this approach is the important book, *Religious Experience*, by Wayne Proudfoot. Proudfoot goes so far as to identify the "noetic" quality that James and many others have noted in mystical experience with the supposition by the subject that the experience must be given a theological rather than a naturalistic explanation.

It is not difficult to show that the people I have quoted and countless others take their mystical experiences to be perceptual, to involve what I have been calling a direct presentation of God to their awareness, though they do not typically use this terminology. They take their experience to contrast with thinking about God, calling up mental images, entertaining propositions, reasoning, or remembering something about God, just as seeing a tree contrasts with these other cognitive relations to it. They take it that

God has been *presented* or *given* to their consciousness in generically the same way as that in which objects in the environment are *presented* to one's consciousness in sense perception. They emphasize the difference between *presence* to consciousness and absence. Saint Teresa says that God "presents Himself to the soul by a knowledge brighter than the sun." Again she contrasts a "consciousness of the presence of God" with "spiritual feelings and effects of great love and faith of which we become conscious," and with "the fresh resolutions which we make with such deep emotion." Although she takes it that the latter is a "great favour" that "comes from God," still it does not amount to God's actually being present. Another writer who clearly makes this distinction is Angela of Foligno.

> (4) At times God comes into the soul without being called; and He instills into her fire, love, and sometimes sweetness; and the soul believes this comes from God, and delights therein. But she does not yet know, or see, that He dwells in her; she perceives His grace, in which she delights. . . . And beyond this the soul receives the gift of seeing God. God says to her, 'Behold Me!' and the soul sees Him dwelling within her. She sees Him more clearly than one man sees another. For the eyes of the soul behold a plenitude of which I cannot speak: a plenitude which is not bodily but spiritual, of which I can say nothing. And the soul rejoices in that sight with an ineffable joy; and this is the manifest and certain sign that God indeed dwells in her.

Thus it is quite clear that the people cited, who are representative of a vast throng, take their experiences to be structured the way, on my view, perception generally is structured. In fact, it may be thought that it is too easy to show this, too much like shooting fish in a barrel. For haven't I chosen my cases on the basis of the subjects' taking themselves to be directly aware of God? They are tailor-made for my purpose. I must plead guilty to picking cases that conform to my construal. But the significant point is that it is so easy to find such cases and that they are so numerous, given the fact that most mystical experiences are not reported at all. As pointed out earlier, I do not wish to deny that there are other forms of "religious experience" and even other forms of experience of God, such as the indirect experiences of God mentioned earlier. My contention is that there is a large body of experiences of God that are perceptual in character, and that they have played a prominent role in Christianity and other religions.

I don't know what could be said against this position except to claim that people who report such experiences are all confused about the character of their experience. Let's consider the following charge.

> These people were all having strongly affective experiences that, because of their theological assumptions and preoccupations, they confused with a direct experience of God. Thus (1) was in an unusual state of exaltation that he interpreted as the power and goodness of God penetrating him. In (4) the "ineffable joy" that Angela says to be "the manifest and certain sign that God indeed dwells in her" is simply a state of feeling that her theological convictions lead her to *interpret* as an awareness of the presence of God. Another possibility is

> that the person is suddenly seized with an extremely strong conviction of the presence of God, together with sensations and feelings that seem to confirm it. Thus Teresa says that she "had a most distinct feeling that He was always on my right hand, a witness of all I did."

It is conceivable that one should suppose that a purely affective experience or a strongly held conviction should involve the experiential presentation of God when it doesn't, especially if there is a strong need or longing for the latter. But, even if an individual's account of the character of his/her own experience is not infallible, it must certainly be taken seriously. Who is in a better position to determine whether S is having an experience as of something's presenting itself to S as divine than S? We would need strong reasons to override the subject's confident report of the character of her experience. And where could we find such reasons? I suspect that most people who put forward these alternative diagnoses do so because they have general philosophical reasons for supposing either that God does not exist or that no human being could perceive Him, and they fail to recognize the difference between a *phenomenological* account of object presentation, and the occurrence of veridical perception. In any event, once we get straight about all this, I cannot see any reason for doubting the subjects' account of the character of their experience, whatever reasons there may be for doubting that God Himself does in fact appear to them.

If these cases are to conform to our account of perceptual consciousness, they must seem to involve God's appearing to the person as being and/or doing so-and-so. And our subjects do tell us this. God is experienced as good, powerful, loving, compassionate, and as exhibiting "plenitude." He is experienced as speaking, forgiving, comforting, and strengthening. And yet how can these be ways in which God presents Himself to experience? Power and goodness are complex dispositional properties or bases thereof, dispositions to act in various ways in various situations. And to forgive or to strengthen someone is to carry out a certain intention. None of this can be read off the phenomenal surface of experience. This is quite different from something's presenting itself to one's sensory consciousness as red, round, sweet, loud, or pungent. Isn't it rather that the subject is *interpreting*, or *taking*, what she is aware of as being good or powerful, as forgiving or strengthening? But then what is God *experienced* as being or doing? We seem to still lack an answer.

But that charge misconstrues the situation. The basic point is that we have different sorts of concepts for specifying how something looks, sounds, tastes, or otherwise perceptually appears. There are *phenomenal* concepts that specify the felt qualities that objects present themselves as bearing—round, red, acrid, etc. But there are also *comparative* concepts that specify a mode of appearance in terms of the sort of objective thing that typically appears in that way. In reporting sensory appearances we typically use comparative concepts whenever the appearances involve something more complex than one or two basic sensory qualities. Thus we say, "She looks like Susie," "It tastes like a pineapple," "It sounds like Bach." In these cases there undoubtedly is some complex pattern of simple sensory qualities, but it is beyond our powers to analyze the appearance into its simple components. We are thrown back on the use of comparative concepts to report how something looks, sounds, or tastes. And so it is in our religious cases. Our subjects tell us that God presented Himself to their experience as a good, powerful, compassionate, forgiving being could be expected to appear. In reporting modes of divine appearance in this way, they are proceeding just as we typically do in reporting modes of sensory appearance.

IV

Now for the task of showing that if God exists there is no bar to the (not infrequent) satisfaction of the causal and doxastic conditions by the subject of mystical experience. First consider the doxastic condition. It is clear that mystical experience typically gives rise to beliefs about God. To be sure, those who perceive God as loving, powerful, and so on, usually believed that God is that way long before they had that experience. But the same is true of sense perception. My 50,000th look at my house doesn't generate any important new beliefs. I knew just what my house looks like long before that 50,000th look. That is why I put the doxastic condition in terms of a "tendency" to engender beliefs about what is perceived. However, in both sensory and mystical cases some kinds of new beliefs will almost always be produced. Even if I don't see anything new about my house on that umpteenth look, I at least learn that it is blue and tall *today*. When what we perceive is a person the new beliefs will be more interesting. On my 50,000th look at my wife I not only learn that she is still beautiful today, but I learn what she is doing right now. And similarly with God. One who perceives God will thereby come to learn that God is strengthening her or comforting her *then*, or telling her so-and-so *then*. There is, if anything, even less of a problem with the doxastic condition here.

The causal condition calls for a bit more discussion. First, there is no reason to think it impossible that God, if He exists, does causally contribute to the occurrence of mystical experiences. Quite the contrary. If God exists and things are as supposed by classical theism, God causally contributes to everything that occurs. That follows just from the fact that nothing would exist without the creative and sustaining activity of God. And with respect to many things, including mystical experiences, God's causality presumably extends farther than that, though the precise story will vary from one theology to another. To fix our thoughts let us say that it is possible (and remember that we are concerned here only with whether this causal condition *can* be satisfied) that at least some of these experiences occur only because God intentionally presents Himself to the subject's awareness as so-and-so.

It may well be pointed out that not every causal contributor to an experience is perceived via that experience. When I see a house, light waves and goings on in my nervous system form parts of the causal chain leading to the visual experience, but I don't see them. Thus it is not enough that God figures somehow or other in the causes of the experience; He would have to make the right kind of causal contribution. But what is the right kind? There is no one answer to this question for all perceptual modalities. The causal contribution a seen object makes to the production of visual experience (transmitting light to the retina) is different from the causal contribution a felt object makes to tactile experience, and different from the causal contribution a heard object makes to aural experience. And how do we tell, for each modality, what the crucial causal contribution is? We have no a priori insight into this. We cannot abstract from everything we have learned from perception and still ascertain how an object must be causally related to a visual experience in order to be what is seen in that experience. Quite the contrary. We learn this by first determining in many cases *what* is seen, felt, or heard in those cases, and then looking for some causal contribution that is distinctive of the object perceived. That is, we have first to be able to determine *what is seen*; then on the basis of that we determine how an entity has to be causally related to the visual experience to be seen therein. We have no resources for doing it the other way around, first determining the specific causal requirement and then picking out objects seen on the basis of what satisfies that requirement.

The application of this to divine perception is as follows. We will have a chance of determining how God has to be causally related to an experience in order to be perceived only if we can first determine in a number of cases that it is God who is being perceived. And since that is so, we can't rule out the possibility of perceiving God on the grounds that God can't be related to the relevant experience in the right way. For unless we do sometimes perceive God we are unable to determine what the right way is. Hence, so long as God does make some causal contribution to the relevant experiences, we can't rule out God's being perceived in those experiences on the grounds that He isn't causally related to them in the right way. To be sure, by the same token we cannot show that we do perceive God by showing that God is causally related to the experiences in the right way. But showing that is no part of our purpose here. It will be sufficient to show that, so far as we can see, there is no reason to doubt that it is possible that God should satisfy an appropriate causal requirement for being perceived in at least some of the cases in which people take themselves to be directly aware of Him.

V

If my arguments have been sound, we are justified in thinking of the experience of God as a mode of perception in the same generic sense of the term as sense perception. And if God exists, there is no reason to suppose that this perception is not sometimes veridical rather than delusory. I will conclude by mentioning a couple of respects in which this conclusion is of importance.

First, the main function of the experience of God in theistic religion is that it constitutes a mode, an avenue of communion between God and us. It makes it possible for us to enter into personal interaction with God. And if it involves our directly perceiving God in a sense generically the same as that in which we perceive each other, this can be personal intercourse in a literal sense, rather than some stripped down, analogical or symbolic reconception thereof. We can have the real thing, not a metaphorical substitute.

Second, there are bearings on the cognitive significance of this mode of experience. If it is perceptual in character, and if it is possible that the other requirements should be satisfied for it to be a genuine perception of God, then the question of whether it is genuine is just a question of whether it is what it seems to its subject to be. Thus the question of genuineness arises here in just the same way as for sense perception, making possible a uniform treatment of the epistemology of the two modes of experience. This is not to beg the question of the genuineness of mystical perception. It could still be true that sense perception is the real thing, whereas mystical perception is not. And it could still be true that sense perception provides knowledge about its objects, whereas mystical perception yields no such results. The point is only that the *problems*, both as to the status of the perception and as to the epistemic status of perceptual beliefs, arise in the same form for both. This contrasts with the situation on the widespread view that "experience of God" is to be construed as purely subjective feelings and sensations to which supernaturalistic causal hypotheses are added. On that view the issues concerning the two modes of experience will look very different, unless one is misguided enough to treat sense perception in the same fashion. For on this subjectivist construal the subject is faced with the task of justifying a causal hypothesis before he can warrantedly claim to be perceiving God. Whereas if the experience is given a perceptual construal from the start, we will at least have to take seriously the view that a claim to be perceiving God is prima facie acceptable on its own merits, pending any sufficient reasons to the contrary.[1]

NOTE

1. See my *Perceiving God* (Cornell University Press, 1991) for a development of this last idea.

WAYNE PROUDFOOT

Religious Experiences as Interpretative Accounts

Wayne Proudfoot (1939–) holds that a description of a religious experience must include reference to the experiencer's belief system, which it is not belief-neutral. Since religious experience has this connection with beliefs, it is similar to perceptual experience in that it includes reference to the cause or origin of the experience. It differs from perception, however, in that perceiving a tree, for example, requires that a tree be present and perceived by the person. To place this same requirement on religious experience would be to impose too narrow a restriction, for to admit that others had a religious experience we would have to grant that the object of their experience (e.g., Jesus, Krishna, Nirvana) existed. Rather, a religious experience is an experience that the subject takes as religious; that is, as being incapable of being accounted for or explained without reference to religious beliefs. According to Proudfoot, the remaining task is that of understanding why persons explain their experiences in terms of the particular beliefs and concepts that they use. Here an appeal to historical and social factors may be helpful.

⌘

We have seen that James describes the common core of religious experience as a sense or consciousness of the presence of a reality of power that transcends the self and its ordinary world. This sense or consciousness is said to be more like a sensation than like an intellectual operation. It is formative of, rather than consequent upon, religious belief. But the examples James gives of a sense of reality or consciousness of a presence suggest that intellectual operations are involved, and that what he has called a sense is really a thought or belief. He proposes that questions of origin and questions of evaluation be radically separated in the study of religious experience. But his observation that that experience is characterized by a noetic quality similar to that of sense perception suggests that matters of assessment and explanation cannot be kept as clearly distinct as he would like. To that question we now turn.

SENSIBLE AUTHORITY

The analogy James draws between mystical experience and sense perception is weakened by his assumption that perceptual experience is unmediated by concepts and beliefs, but his observation is accurate. The contrast he makes between the authority of the experience for the subject and its authority for an observer is important, and it does parallel the case of ordinary perception. There is a noetic quality to the experience, a sense of authority that distinguishes the attitude of the subject of the experience from that of an observer. An analysis of this characteristic of the experience will demonstrate the impossibility of following James in his proposal to exclude questions about the cause or origin of the experience.

An important distinction that will help to capture the noetic quality or the authority of perceptual experience is that drawn by Chisholm . . . between the epistemic and comparative uses of what he calls "appear words."[1] When I say that the table across the room appears to be round, I am using *appears* to report what I am inclined to believe on the basis of my present sensory experience. I believe that the table is round even though its image on my retina is elliptical. When I say that the tree in the distance appears to be as tall as the one under which I am standing, I am reporting my belief about the actual size of the tree. In both cases I have already made corrections for parallax and distance, and I am stating what appears to me to be the case. Such adjustments have become habitual in my learning to use the relevant words and to report what I see. Now I am making a judgment and a claim. When, however, I report that the table appears elliptical even though I believe it really to be round, or that the stick I have just dropped into the water appears to be bent, I am employing what Chisholm calls the comparative use of *appears*. I am stating that the table looks to me as it would look if it were an ellipse and were viewed under standard conditions, or the stick appears as it would if it were out of the water and bent. I am not making a judgment about the actual characteristics of the table or the stick; I am reporting an image by comparing it with other known images. The epistemic use is a report of what the subject is inclined to believe on the basis of the present experience, and thus it assumes habits of inference and of explanation which are relevant for arriving at beliefs on the basis of this data. The comparative use is a report of how the image appears to the subject, despite what he may believe about the actual state of affairs. The epistemic use assumes a theoretical interest and an inference to the best explanation, whereas the comparative use does not. Ordinary perceptual judgments include an epistemic component. This is what James refers to as the noetic quality of religious experience. . . .

James understands that the religious consciousness is more than a way of seeing, that it includes a claim about the nature of things. . . . Religious experience includes a judgment about how things actually are. Stephen Bradley's accelerated heart rate appeared to him to be the result of the operation of the Holy Spirit. His belief that it was to be explained that way was a constitutive part of his experience. Schleiermacher's pious theist experiences every event in the light of the sense of absolute dependence. For him, every event is a miracle. It is to be ascribed to a power on which the entire nexus of natural causes is dependent. . . .

A noetic quality is an essential part of the experience. Once we recognize this noetic or epistemic quality in the religious experience, it is not possible to maintain the sharp separation James proposes between inquiry into its significance or value. When he introduces this distinction, James says that it is drawn in recent books on logic. His reference here is probably to Peirce. . . . Peirce argues that the origin of a hypothesis is altogether irrelevant to the issue of its truth or falsity. A physicist might arrive at a novel hypothesis in a dream, by painstaking calculation, or he might derive it from some mystical interpretation of ancient texts. But the hypothesis must be assessed only according to the results of an experiment designed to test it, without regard for its origin. The justification of a belief and the explanation of how one came to hold it must be kept distinct. The criteria for empirical inquiry are orthogonal to the criteria appropriate for the causal explanation of a belief. The scientist is and should be indifferent to the origin of his hypotheses. . . .

Granted Peirce's point that the evaluation of a belief should be independent of its origin, does this apply to religious experience as well? Were religious experience a matter of a simple feeling more akin to a physiological sensation than to an intellectual process, it is possible that it could be evaluated without reference to its origin. A particular shade of blue, the taste of honey, the scent of eucalyptus, or a lowered body temperature or accelerated heart rate can each be described and, for some purposes, assessed without attention to their causes. A high body temperature may be desirable in order to combat a particular virus, and that judgment can be made independently of the means used to achieve that end. A certain shade of blue might be preferred to another. . . .

If we consider, not a particular shade of blue or a taste of honey, but the perceptual judgment that this sample is blue and this liquid contains honey, then the situation is different. Beliefs can ordinarily be assessed without regard to the origin or cause of the experience that gave rise to those beliefs. But an exception must be made in the case of beliefs that include claims about the cause of an experience. Perceptual beliefs and judgments are of this kind. A perceptual judgment includes an embedded claim about the cause or origin of the perceptual experience. What are the conditions under which we identify an experience as a perception? My having a visual image of a tree, believing that I see a tree, and possessing evidence to justify my belief are not jointly sufficient to constitute a perception of the tree. My belief may be mistaken; perhaps there is no tree there at all. More surprisingly, my having a visual image of a tree, believing that I see that tree, having evidence to justify my belief, and the actual existence of a tree at the point at which I think I see one are not sufficient for the conclusion that I am seeing the tree. Each of these conditions could be fulfilled and yet the circumstances be such that we would not call it a perception.

Consider the following example: I have a visual image of a tree, and on the basis of that image, my beliefs about my visual capacities, my waking state, and other background assumptions, I believe I see a tree thirty yards ahead. It is possible that a tree exactly matching the description of the tree I think I see does stand at that point thirty yards away, thus that my belief is both justified and true, and yet that I have not perceived the tree. Suppose that, unknown to me, halfway between where I stand and the tree is a large mirror. This mirror blocks my vision of the tree but reflects a tree of exactly the same description placed off to the side at such a distance that the reflected image exactly simulates the image I would have received had the mirror not been interposed. I have not actually perceived the tree because the relevant causal conditions have not been fulfilled. The tree has not entered in the requisite way into my coming to believe there is a tree at that spot. Most important, were the tree that I think I perceive not there, I would have the same experience I now have. Should I come to know the actual conditions that have produced my visual image of the tree and my belief, I would conclude that I had not perceived the tree that I had supposed, but that I did perceive another tree. Reflection on such examples has led to the recent revival of the causal theory of perception.

The authority of the perceptual judgment is dependent on an assumed causal relation. It is the assumption of such a relation which gives the perceptual experience its noetic quality. If James is correct in saying that the noetic quality and the authority of religious experience are analogous to that of sense perception, then a similar assumption about the cause of the experience may be embedded in reports of religious experience. Consider religious conversion. . . .

For the subject, the identification of an experience as religious assumes an embedded causal claim; consequently the experience has an epistemic quality, as in the case of sense perception. But what are the conditions under which an observer would identify an experience as religious? Here the cases of sense perception and religious experience diverge in an important way. *To perceive* is what Ryle[2] calls an achievement verb. The criteria for saying that someone has perceived an object include the assumption that the object is really there to be perceived and that he has perceived it. If you claim you see a table, and I think there is no table there to be seen and you are hallucinating, I will not identify your experience as a perception of the table. I will say that you think (wrongly) that you see the table. The identification by an observer of a subject's experience as a perception includes an endorsement by the observer of the subject's perpetual claims. The subject believes the tree or table is there and he has seen it, and the observer identifies the experience as a perception only if he endorses that belief. If a person erroneously believes he has seen a table, or if he has been to Rouen and is confusing that town with Chartres, we would not claim he has seen the table or the cathedral at Chartres.

One could follow a similar policy with respect to the identification of a religious experience, but the result would be too restrictive. Were we to require the existence of the object or the accuracy of the subject's embedded claim as a criterion for the identification of an experience as religious, then the very existence of religious experiences would depend on the existence of God, Krishna, or other objects people have claimed to experience. Edwards did require that an affection be caused by the operation of the Holy

Spirit for it to be identified as a religious affection. By that criterion, the identification of an experience as religious presupposes belief in God and his Spirit. We want to admit, however, that there are religious experiences. Reports of them abound in religious literature. People identify their experiences as religious, though, as we shall see, not often in those terms. But we want to identify certain experiences as religious without committing ourselves to endorsing the claims that are constitutive of those experiences. Perceptual experience and religious experience are similar in that the experience is constituted by certain embedded claims. The subject assumes certain beliefs in identifying his experience as perceptual or religious. But they differ in that the observer's identification of a perceptual experience does, and his identification of a religious experience does not, imply an endorsement of the claims assumed by the subject which constitute the experience.

RELIGIOUS EXPERIENCE

We can now return to the question with which we began this chapter: What are the distinguishing marks of a religious experience? The aim of the question is not to arrive at a definition that will capture the real essence of religious experience. There is no such essence to capture. Our aim is rather to explicate the concept. . . .

The concept of religious experience is a difficult one to make precise, as much because of the term *experience* as because of anything to do with religion. *Experience* covers a wide variety of phenomena, from ordinary sense experience to dreams, fantasies, and extraordinary states that may be either spontaneously induced or highly contrived. This is not the place to enter into an elaborate analysis of the term. We might agree, however, that anything that is described as an experience must be specified under a description that is given from the subject's point of view. . . .

Religious experience must be characterized from the perspective of the one who has that experience. It is an experience that the subject apprehends as religious. . . .

Even from the subject's perspective, religious content is not enough to identify an experience as religious. The intellectual or imagistic content of an experience does not suffice to identify it as religious. . . . One would not want to characterize religious experience in this way. Were we to do so, visiting Borobodur, listening to Bach, admiring a painting by Piero della Francesca, wishing there were a God, and tracing the history of the concept of nirvana would all be religious experiences. Any of these might be a religious experience, but it is not made such by the fact that the person attends to concepts or images that derive from a religious tradition. The experience must be one that the subject takes to have religious significance or import.

What does it mean to say that an experience has religious import, if this is to be identified with the subject matter of the experience? This is the noetic quality or authority described above, the basis for the analogy with perception. . . . Religion refers to the feelings, acts, and experiences of persons "so far as they apprehend themselves to stand in relation to whatever they may consider the divine." "Apprehend" includes a judgment about what is real and its relation to the subject. In order to do justice to the authority of the experience, the subject must be convinced that the experience could not be accounted for without reference to religious beliefs. This does not mean only that it could not be described without reference to religious concepts or beliefs. That would be true of Borobodur, of a performance of the Bach B-minor Mass, or of an exhibition of Islamic calligraphy. It must also be the case that the experience cannot be explained without such a reference. We saw that the noetic quality of sense perception and of mystical experience assumes a judgment about the proper explanation of that experience. The subject matter on which attention is focused might not be distinctively religious at all, . . . but the one who has the experience must be convinced that it cannot be exhaustively accounted for without reference to religious beliefs. . . .

A religious experience is an experience that is identified by its subject as religious, and this identification must be based not on the subject matter or content of the experience, but on its noetic quality or its significance for the truth of religious beliefs. . . .

We have discovered that our concept of religious experience includes a noetic quality or epistemic element, and that that component is best analyzed as an assumed claim about the proper explanation of the experience. We have found this in various guises in Schleiermacher, Otto, and James, and in accounts of mystical experiences. More specifically, we have seen that Otto includes among the criteria for the identification of the religious moment the condition that it cannot be explained exhaustively in natural terms. Schleiermacher describes the experience as one of the utter dependence of oneself and the nexus of natural causes on some other power. James includes in his description of the common element in all religious experience a consciousness of a "More" that is operative in the universe beyond the self and its ordinary world. He thinks it is best understood as a straightforward supernaturalism, though he says this is an overbelief that goes beyond the data. In the discussion of mystical experience, we saw that the noetic quality of the experience seems to derive from an assumption that naturalistic explanations are insufficient. This assumption accords with the way in which the concept of religious experience is ordinarily used. We would think it odd if someone claimed to have had a religious experience and then argued that the experience could be exhaustively explained as the effect of a pill he had ingested. It would be strange for someone to report a religious experience and to subscribe to a psychoanalytic or sociological explanation as providing a complete account of that experience. The words *exhaustive* and *complete* are important here. Mystical regimens and other disciplines for prayer and meditation do prescribe exercises and conditioning that powerfully affect both mind and body, and the meditator is normally aware of such effects. But in the doctrine that governs those practices, and in the beliefs of the adept, those manipulations are viewed as catalysts. They are required for the experience, but they don't constitute a sufficient explanation. If it was thought that an experience could be exhaustively explained by these manipulations, then it could not be apprehended by the subject as religious.

EXPLAINING RELIGIOUS EXPERIENCE

The term *experience* is ambiguous. When I inquire about what a person has experienced at a certain moment, my question is ambiguous between two meanings: (1) how it seemed to that person at that time; and (2) the best explanation that can be given of the experience. This ambiguity is present in our ordinary talk about perception. I may have been frightened by the bear that I saw up ahead on the trail. My friend points out to me that it is not a bear but a log, and my fear subsides. What did I really see up ahead? By one interpretation of the word *see*, I saw a bear. That is the way I apprehended it, and that apprehension accounts for my fear and behavioral response. By another interpretation, what I really saw was a log, and I took it for a bear. I was wrong about what I experienced, and now that I can explain what happened I can correct my mistake.

This distinction is similar to, but differs from, Chisholm's distinction between the comparative and epistemic uses of "appear" words. It differs because Chisholm suggests that the comparative use, the description of how it appears to the subject, is a report of an immediate experience that is independent of interpretation or other beliefs. No such unmediated experience is possible. The distinction drawn here is between one interpretation, which presupposes a particular explanation of the experience, and another interpretation, also assuming an explanation, which is adopted by another person or by the same person at a later time. The perception of the object ahead as a bear was one explanation, and that was replaced by a better explanation when more information became available. That better explanation led to a reinterpretation of the experience.

It is important to note that both senses of *experience* assume explanations. It is not the case that explanation enters only into the second sense. The first, the description of his or her experience as assumed by the subject at the time of the experience, presupposes an explanation. If the distinguishing mark of the religious is that it is assumed to elude natural explanation, then the labeling of the experience as religious by the subject includes the belief that it cannot be exhaustively explained in naturalistic terms. . . .

The distinction we have drawn between descriptive and explanatory reduction is tailored to meet this ambiguity. Descriptive reduction is inappropriate because the experience must be identified under a description that can be ascribed to the subject at the time of the experience. The experience must be described with reference to its intentional object. In the example given above, my fright was the result of noticing a bear ahead of me. The fact that the analyst must attempt to formulate a description of the experience which captures the way it was apprehended by the subject does not mean that no explanation is incorporated into the subject's description, nor does it mean that the analyst is not engaged in an inference toward the best explanation in his attempt to arrive at that formulation.

The identification of an experience under a description that can be ascribed to the subject is required before any explanation of the experience can be proposed. Every explanation assumes a description of that which is to be explained. One cannot explain phenomena as such but only phenomena under a description. . . . An event, action, emotion, or experience can be identified only under a certain description, and reference must be made to that description in any explanation that is offered. If the relevant description is not acknowledged, it will be tacitly assumed. The analyst's choice of the appropriate description of an experience or action is not entirely independent of the explanation he goes on to offer. If a practice is completely baffling to me under a certain description, and would be recognizable as a practice common to the culture in which it is ensconced if the description were altered slightly, then I will be tempted to alter it and to ascribe the discrepancy to defects in my observation or in the reports from which I am working. If the evidence for the original description is compelling, I must accept the anomaly and search further for an explanation; if it is weak, I may adjust the description in the interest of overall plausibility. This is the proper point at which to invoke Quine's principle of charity. I want my total account, with its descriptive and explanatory components, to be the most plausible of the available alternatives. I adjust each until I reach a reflective equilibrium.

The recognition that religious experience is constituted by concepts and beliefs permits an optimism with respect to the descriptive task which would not otherwise be possible. There is no reason, in principle, to despair about the possibility of understanding the experience of persons and communities that are historically and culturally remote from the interpreter. The difficulty is not posed by an unbridgeable gap between an experience that can only be known by acquaintance and the concepts in which that experience is expressed. Because the concepts and beliefs are constitutive of the experience, careful study of the concepts available in a particular culture, the rules that govern them, and the practices that are informed by them will provide access to the variety of experiences available to persons in that culture. Though it may be difficult to reconstruct, the evidence required for understanding the experience is public evidence about linguistic forms and practices. We attempt to formulate a description of the experience from the perspective of the subject, but the evidence is, in principle, accessible to us.

This conception of religious experience also shows that the variety of that experience is much greater and richer than has been suggested by those who claim that a single experience of the numinous or sacred, or a few such types, underlie all the diverse reports in different traditions. Just as the experiences of nirvana and devekuth differ because they are informed by different concepts and beliefs, so the often rather subtle doctrinal differences between religious communities, or subgroups of the same community, will give rise to different experiences. . . . The catalogue of varieties can never be completed.

If explanation is as central to the study of religious experience as this account suggests, then why has it not been recognized as such? Why is the explanatory component so often disguised or ignored in favor of appeals to a sense or a consciousness that is contrasted with belief? There are two motivations for this procedure: phenomenological accuracy and a protective strategy adopted for apologetic purposes. The first arises from the fact that those who report religious experiences typically take them to be independent of and more fundamental than beliefs or theories. The sense of the infinite or the consciousness of finitude is not apprehended as a theoretical commitment but as an inchoate sense that provides a practical orientation. It seems to the subject to be inaccurate to classify it with inference, inquiry, and hypothesis. Since an understanding of the experience requires that it be identified under a description that accords with that of the subject, it is tempting to assimilate it to the case of sensations, and to assume that sensations are independent of practices and beliefs. For these reasons, phenomenological accuracy appears to some to require that the experience be described so as to make it independent of beliefs.

The appeal to a sense of consciousness that is allegedly innocent of explanatory commitments has an apologetic advantage. If such an appeal could be made, it would be unaffected by any developments in science or other kinds of inquiry. It would, as Schleiermacher said, leave one's physics and psychology unaffected. Religious belief and practice could be seen as derived from this independent experience, and the difficult questions that have been raised for religion by changes in our other beliefs could be circumvented. Rather than seeing the experience as constituted by the beliefs, one could view the beliefs as expressive of the experience. The direction of derivation would be reversed, and that would serve the task of apologetics. If it did not provide a way of justifying religious beliefs and practices, it would at least protect them from the criticism that they conflict with ordinary and scientific beliefs. . . .

A consequence of such strategies is that language that appears to be descriptive may be intended to evoke or reproduce the experience that is purportedly described.

Such terms as *numinous, holy,* and *sacred* are presented as descriptive or analytical tools but in conjunction with warnings against reductionism, they function to preclude explanation and evoke a sense of mystery or awe. They are used to persuade the reader that the distinguishing mark of the religious is some quality that eludes description and analysis in nonreligious terms. Otto's use of *numinous* is an example of how one can employ the term to create a sense of mystery and present it as analysis. Such approaches to the study of religion are offered as neutral descriptions, but they assume not only a theory of religion but also religious theory.

We have distinguished the tasks of description and explanation and have argued that explanation is central both to religious experience and to its study. What kind of explanation, then, might we expect to construct for religious experience? An experience or an event can be explained only when it is identified under a description. And we have concluded that the distinguishing mark of religious experience is the subject's belief that the experience can only be accounted for in religious terms. It is this belief, and the subject's identification of his or her experience under a particular description, which makes it religious. If the concepts and beliefs under which the subject identifies his or her experience determine whether or not it is a religious experience, then we need to explain why the subject employs those particular concepts and beliefs. We must explain why the subject was confronted with this particular set of alternative ways of understanding his experience and why he employed the one he did. In general, what we want is a historical or cultural explanation.

This holds both for discrete, datable religious experiences, of the sort on which James concentrates, and for the identification of an underlying and pervasive religious moment in experience. Why did Stephen Bradley identify his accelerated heart rate as the work of the Holy Spirit? What caused Astor to regard what he saw as a miracle whereas Bingham remained skeptical? Why did Schleiermacher apprehend the moment that precedes thought as a sense of the infinite and discern a feeling of absolute dependence which accompanies all consciousness of the polarity of self and world? For Bradley, we would need to know something about Methodist revivalism in early nineteenth-century New England, about the particular meeting he attended earlier in the evening, and about the events in his life up to that moment. To explain Astor's beliefs about what he saw it would be necessary to acquaint oneself with Roman Catholic teachings on miracles, the significance of the shrine at Lourdes, and the details of Astor's background. To explain Schleiermacher's sense of the infinite, his feeling of absolute dependence, and his apprehension of all events as miracles one would need to know more about his early years among the Moravians, his study of Spinoza, and the circle of friends in Berlin for whom he wrote *On Religion.* Each of these instances requires acquaintance with the Christian tradition and with the particular forms of that tradition which shaped the person and his experience.

For experiences sought in highly manipulative settings, as in meditative traditions where the training is carefully prescribed and a person is guided by a spiritual director in the interpretation of the states of mind and body achieved by the regimen, explanations of the sort suggested by Schachter's experiment seem clearly relevant. The novice learns to make attributions that accord with the tradition, and he engages self-consciously in manipulations to attain states that confirm those attributions. For seemingly more spontaneous but still relatively discrete and datable experiences in less contrived settings, one would still look to explain the experience by accounting for why the subject makes these particular attributions. Just as Schachter's experiment sheds light on the experience of emotions in natural settings, attention to the meditative traditions may provide insight into the allegedly natural, spontaneous examples of religious experience. The phenomenologist of religion has often claimed that elaborately contrived ritualistic settings are expressions of the pervasive sense of the sacred or the infinite in human experience, but it seems more likely that the supposedly natural and spontaneous experiences are derived from beliefs and practices in much the same way that an experience is produced in the more disciplined traditions of meditative practice. How did Schleiermacher and others come to think that the sense of the infinite or the sense of finitude was independent of and prior to the beliefs and practices of a culture shaped by theism? His identification of what he takes to be a universal moment in human experience seems clearly to reflect the concept of God as Creator and Governor derived from the Hebrew Bible and the traditions it formed. The consciousness Schleiermacher accurately describes may, upon investigation, turn out to be the product of prior religious beliefs and practices. . . .

It seems quite likely that the feeling of absolute dependence and Otto's sense of the numinous are legacies of belief in the God of the Hebrew Bible and Christian tradition and of the practices informed by that belief. These experiences now appear to be autonomous and independent of that belief and that tradition. At a time in which belief in a transcendent Creator and associated metaphysical doctrines have been rejected by many, the habits of interpretation informed by those beliefs remain firmly entrenched in cultural patterns of thought, action, and feeling. Belief in God as Creator once provided the justifying context for these affections and practices. Now the direction of justification is reversed, and attempts are made to defend the beliefs by appeal to the affective experiences and practices. The sense of finitude, the feeling of absolute dependence, the practice of worship, and the grammar that governs the use of the word *God* are appealed to in order to justify the traditional religious statements without which this sense, feeling, practice, and grammar would not be intelligible.

These are only some suggestions of the kind of explanation that might be offered of religious experience. While one might venture a hypothesis to account for Bradley's accelerated heart rate or the recovery that Astor witnessed, that approach will not yield an explanation of their experiences. What must be explained is why they understood what happened to them or what they witnessed in religious terms. This requires a mapping of the concepts and beliefs that were available to them, the commitments they brought to the experience, and the contextual conditions that might have supported their identification of their experiences in religious terms. Interest in explanations is not an alien element that is illegitimately introduced into the study of religious experience. Those who identify their experiences in religious terms are seeking the best explanations for what is happening to them. The analyst should work to understand those explanations and discover why they are adopted.

NOTES

1. Roderick Chisholm, *Perceiving: A Philosophical Study* (Ithaca, N.Y.: Cornell University Press, 1957), pp. 43–55.

2. Gilbert Ryle, *The Concept of God* (London: Hutchinson & Co., Ltd., 1949), pp. 130–154.

MICHAEL MARTIN

Critique of Religious Experience

After briefly describing the argument for God's existence from religious experience, Michael Martin (1932–) proceeds to criticize its first premise. For Martin, it is just as likely that the experience has a psychological explanation as that it has an external cause. He notes that even the experience of a public physical object is open to different interpretations, and maintains that mystical experiences fare no better. Considering Swinburne's Principle of Credulity, Martin suggests a parallel negative principle of credulity such that the absence of any experience of God would count against there being a God. He also points out that applying an unqualified Principle of Credulity to diverse and incompatible religious experiences actually proves too much.

⌘

I. RELIGIOUS EXPERIENCE DEFINED

Down through the ages religious believers have had a variety of religious experiences and have used these to justify their belief in God. What is the religious experience? Although the notion is difficult to define, for my purpose here a religious experience is understood as an experience in which one senses the immediate presence of some supernatural entity.[1] But what does this involve?

As I am using the term "senses," if someone senses the immediate presence of some entity, this does *not* entail that it exists. It does entail that the person either believes or is inclined to believe that the entity exists, at least partly on the basis of the person's experience.[2] For example, if Jones senses the immediate presence of the angel Gabriel, this does not entail that the angel Gabriel exists, but it does entail that Jones believes or is inclined to believe that the angel Gabriel exists, at least in part on the basis of his experience. However, the entailment cannot be reversed. One may believe that an entity is present or be inclined to believe that it is present and yet not do so on the basis of one's religious experience if, for example, one's belief is based entirely on faith or indirect evidence. Furthermore, by "some supernatural entity" I mean to include more than God, in the sense of an all-good, all-knowing, all-powerful being. For example, one could sense the immediate presence of an angel or a finite god. In addition, by sensing the immediate presence of some supernatural being I do not mean to imply that the being whose immediate presence is sensed is experienced as distinct or separate from the person who is having the experience. I mean rather to include phenomena in which the person experiences a union or a merging with the divine.

II. TYPES OF RELIGIOUS EXPERIENCE

There are several types of religious experience in the sense defined above. It is useful to consider Swinburne's classification of religious experience, which is one of the most extensive and illuminating schemes to appear in recent literature.[3]

Type 1 One can experience an ordinary nonreligious object *as* a supernatural being—for example, a dove as an angel. The experience is of a public object, an object that ordinary observers would experience under normal conditions. For example, ordinary observers under normal conditions would experience the dove, although they would not experience it as an angel.

Type 2 One can experience some supernatural being that is a public object and use ordinary vocabulary to describe the experience. This experience would not be of some ordinary object *as* a supernatural being but of a supernatural being in its normal guise. Thus a person P can experience an angel in its normal guise as a beautiful being with wings, and the object of P's experience can be such that any ordinary observer would experience what P would experience under ordinary circumstances. For example, Joseph Smith, the founder of the Mormon Church, had an experience of the angel Moroni "standing in the air" by his bedside on September 21, 1823.[4] If we assume that any normal observer who had been in Joseph Smith's bedroom on the night of September 21, 1823, would have experienced the angel Moroni standing in the air near Smith's bed, then Smith's experience would be of type 2.

Type 3 This is like type 2 experiences except that the experience is not of a public object. One can experience some supernatural being in its standard guise, not some ordinary object as a supernatural being, and use ordinary vocabulary to describe the experience, although this being could not be experienced by ordinary observers under normal conditions. . . .

Type 4 Another kind of experience entails sensations that are not describable by the normal vocabulary. Mystical experiences, for example, are sometimes so difficult to describe that the mystic is forced to use paradoxical and negative terms. . . .

Type 5 The experience of a supernatural being can involve no sensations at all. A person may experience God and not claim to have had any particular sensations either of the typical sort or of some sort that is difficult to describe.[5] For example, it is likely that one of the experiences of St. Teresa of Avila, a Spanish nun of the sixteenth century, was of this kind, for she described it in this way:

> I was at prayer on a festival of the glorious Saint Peter when I saw Christ at my side—or, to put it better, I was conscious of Him, for neither with the eyes of the body nor with those of the soul did I see anything. I thought He was quite close to me and I saw that it was He Who, as I thought, was speaking to me.[6]

This last type of experience is also of a nonpublic object. Her nonsensory experience of Christ is not something that ordinary people could have had.

The Argument in Brief

Although religious experiences have been used to justify religious belief, such as belief in the existence of God, it is sometimes maintained that this use does not constitute an *argument* for the existence of God because when one senses the presence of God, no inference is involved. Religious belief based on religious experience, it is said, is like a perceptual belief of tables and chairs; because it is immediate and noninferential, it cannot be construed as being based on an argument. Consequently, there is no argument from religious experience.

However, the thesis that appeals to religious experience to justify religious belief does not constitute an argument is much less compelling than it may seem. Its apparent plausibility rests on a confusion between how a belief is arrived at—that is, the genesis of the belief—and how it is justified. For it may well be true that a person who arrives at his or her beliefs by means of religious experience or ordinary perceptual experience does so without using inferences or arguments, but it is not obviously true that this person could justify those beliefs without using inferences or arguments.[7] For example, in order to be able to justify my spontaneous perceptual belief that there is a brown table in front of me, it would seem to be necessary in principle to be able to argue thus: Spontaneous beliefs of a certain sort occurring under certain conditions are usually true, and my belief that there is a brown table in front of me is of this sort and occurs under these conditions. Consequently, my belief is probably true. . . .

Given that religious beliefs based on religious experiences need to be justified by an argument, what kind would be appropriate? I suggest that the following sort is basic to justifying belief in God on the basis of religious experience:

(1′) Under certain conditions C_1, religious beliefs of type K_1—that is, beliefs generated by religious experience—are likely to be true.

(2′) Condition C_1 obtains.

(3′) My religious belief that God exists is of type K_1.

(4′) Hence my religious belief that God exists is likely to be true.

Evaluation of the Argument

Clearly the crucial premise of the argument is premise (1′). What reason can we have for supposing the religious beliefs generated by certain types of religious experiences under certain conditions are likely to be true? One general problem with the several types of experience considered above is that they are concerned with nonpublic objects. In order for us to suppose that beliefs generated by these experiences are likely to be true, we must assume that each experience is caused by a reality external to the person who is having it, a reality that does not cause ordinary persons to experience something similar. Let us call this supposition the external cause Hypothesis (H_1).

The problem arising in relation to premise (1′) is that there is a rival hypothesis. One might suppose that a person's religious experience is caused not by some external reality but by the workings of the person's own mind. On this theory, a religious experience would have an origin similar to that of delusion and delirium. But then religious experience would have no objective import and would not be trustworthy at all. Let us call this the psychological hypothesis (H_2).

Which hypothesis should be accepted? Consider first the reasons why we do not use the external cause hypothesis (H_1) to explain the experiences that result from the use of certain drugs, from mental illness, and from going without sleep for long periods of time. Why could not one argue that these experiences are caused by some external reality and that they provide evidence of the nature of such a reality? It may be suggested that when one takes certain drugs, has a mental illness, or goes without sleep the mind is opened to this reality and ordinary perception is unable to make contact with it. Certainly, people who have such experiences often interpret then as experiences of objects external to their minds. We have good reasons to suppose, however, that such an interpretation is mistaken and thus good reason not to use (H_1) to explain these experiences. Why? The primary reason is that experiences induced by drugs, alcohol, sleep deprivation, and mental illness tell no uniform or coherent story of a supposed external reality that one can experience only in these extraordinary ways. . . .

Religious experiences are like those induced by drugs, alcohol, mental illness, and sleep deprivation: They tell no uniform or coherent story, and there is no plausible theory to account for discrepancies among them. Again the situation could be different. Imagine a possible world where part of reality can only be known through religious experiences. There religious experiences would tend to tell a coherent story. Not only would the descriptions of each religious experience be coherent, but the descriptions of the experiences of different people would tend to be consistent with one another. Indeed, a religious experience in one culture would generally corroborate a religious experience in another culture. When there was a lack of corroboration, there would be a plausible explanation for the discrepancy. For example, it might be known that the experiences of a person who had not performed certain spiritual exercises for at least three months would be untrustworthy. Moreover, if first-hand descriptions of religious experience made no sense, there would be a ready explanation. For instance, the person might not be properly trained to describe such experiences but, once trained, would be able to provide coherent descriptions. Indeed, there might be independent reason to suppose that the incoherent descriptions could be translated into coherent terms. In this possible world the external cause hypothesis might well be the best explanation of religious experiences.

Once again, this possible world is not ours. In our world, descriptions of religious experience sometimes make no sense, yet we have no ready explanation of this incoherence and no reason to suppose that some suggested coherent translation captures the meaning of the description. Furthermore, religious experiences in one culture often conflict with those in another. One cannot accept all of them as veridical, yet there does not seem to be any way to separate the veridical experiences from the rest. With the possible exception of mystical experiences in our world, the psychological hypothesis is therefore the best explanation of these experiences. In a moment I will take up the claim made by some scholars that mystical experience is uniform over cultures and time. Even if it is correct, other types of religious experience of nonpublic objects tell no uniform or coherent story.

But is there really no way to determine which religious experiences should be considered trustworthy and which should be rejected? St. Teresa suggested several ways of ruling out deceptive religious experiences. These techniques have been adopted by other religious believers,[8] and two of them are especially important. If the content of a religious experience is incompatible with Scripture, she says, it should be considered nonveridical. She also maintained that if a religious experience has a bad effect on one—for example, if a person becomes less humble or loving or fervent in faith after the experience—then the experience is deceptive.

Unfortunately, these tests for separating deceptive from trustworthy religious experiences will not do. Since the test of scriptural compatibility already presumes that the Bible is the revealed word of God and therefore that the Christian God exists, it cannot be used to support an argument from religious experience for the existence of God. Further, it would hardly be surprising on the psychological hypothesis (H_2) that people raised in the Christian tradition should tend to have religious experiences that are compatible with Christian Scripture. This hypothesis, combined with plausible auxiliary hypotheses such as that people's delusions tend to be strongly influenced by their training and culture, predicts that in general people raised in a certain religious tradition tend to have religious experiences compatible with the religious literature of this tradition. This is exactly what one finds. Divergences from this prediction are rare and in any case can be accounted for in terms of individual psychological factors and the influence of other traditions.

Unless we grant large and dubious assumptions about the relations between religious experience and conduct, St. Teresa's test of conduct will not work either. Why should one assume that a vision of ultimate reality will always or even usually make a person better? One could have a vision of God and yet, on account of weakness of will or the overpowering and dreadful nature of the vision, degenerate morally. Furthermore, there is no *a priori* reason why a person might not show moral improvement after an illusory religious experience. It might just be the catalyst needed to change the person's life. St. Teresa wrongly seemed to think that the only deception possible in a religious experience is brought about by the devil. But the deceptive nature of such experience could have purely psychological causes, and the moral improvement that results could have such causes as well. In addition to these problems, the test of conduct surely proves too much. Since religious experiences occur in the context of different religions, it would not be surprising to discover that, for example, Christian, Islamic, and Hindu religious experiences have all resulted in improved conduct. However, since they seem to be incompatible, it can hardly be claimed that all these experiences are trustworthy. I must conclude, therefore, that St. Teresa's tests of veridical religious experience are unsatisfactory.

As we have seen, two kinds of religious experience, type 1 and type 2, are of public objects. Could these provide the corroboration needed to claim that some religious experience is trustworthy? Although this is possible in principle, as a matter of fact the ingredients necessary for the experience of a public object are missing. Consider, for example, a type 1 experience of a black cat as the devil. We have here the same problem as in the case of nonpublic objects. There is no agreement among observers and no plausible theory to explain disagreement. To be sure, there is agreement among observers that a black cat is seen. However, there is no agreement that the devil is seen and no plausible theory to account for discrepancies. Because of this, the experience of seeing the black cat as the devil is better explained by the psychological hypothesis (H_2) than by the external cause hypothesis (H_1). . . .

Turning now to experiences of type 2, we must distinguish two different cases. In the first, several people experience some supernatural being at the same time. In the second, some lone individual P experiences a supernatural being, but it is claimed that if other normal people had been with P, they would have experienced what P did. Since the second case can for all practical purposes be treated as a type 3 experience, it can be ignored here.

The first kind of type 2 experience seems important, however. For it may be maintained that if there were clear and uncontroversial cases of type 2 religious experiences, there would be strong evidence for the existence of God. Furthermore, it might be claimed by religious believers that there have been such cases. One example that could be cited is the appearance of Jesus to several of his disciples after his resurrection. It could be maintained that Jesus was a public object capable of being observed by all normal observers. Furthermore, he was surely a supernatural being, since he arose from the dead. Moreover, religious believers could claim that this case provides evidence for the existence of God, since Jesus' appearance after his resurrection is best explained by the hypothesis that he was God incarnate.

But have there been clear and uncontroversial cases of type 2 religious experience? Certainly the case of Jesus' alleged resurrection is not one of them. Indeed, there is little reason to accept this story as true. The accounts of Jesus' resurrection in different gospels contradict each other.[9]; the story is not supported by Paul's letters, which many scholars believe were written earlier[10]; and the story is not supported by Jewish and Roman sources.[11] Furthermore, I know of no clear and uncontroversial cases of type 2 religious experiences.

However, suppose that there were good grounds to suppose that Jesus appeared to several of his disciples after his death on the cross. Would this be strong evidence that God, an all-powerful, all-knowing, all-good being, exists? This would, indeed, be strong evidence that Jesus was a supernatural being, but it would not be strong evidence for the existence of an all-good, all-powerful, all-knowing being. This is because Jesus' appearance is compatible with many different supernatural explanations. For example, Jesus may have been the incarnation of a finite god or one of many gods or even of the devil. This is a basic problem in appealing to any religious experience—even type 2 religious experiences—as evidence for the existence of God. Even if one has good grounds for supposing a religious experience cannot be explained by (H_2) and must be explained by (H_1), this is compatible with various alternative supernatural explanations.

So although type 2 religious experiences could in principle provide support for belief in *some* supernatural being, in fact it remains to be shown that they do. And in any case it remains dubious that, even if such experience supported the belief that some supernatural being exists, it could provide more support for the existence of an all-good, all-powerful, all-knowing God than for the existence of some other supernatural being.

III. MYSTICAL EXPERIENCE

Mystical experiences are typically type 4 religious experiences in which a person has sensations that are not describable by our normal vocabulary. Some scholars of mysticism maintain that there is a common core of mysticism. They maintain that, although there are cultural differences among mystics, mystical experiences in different times and in different religions have important and fundamental similarities. If these scholars are correct, then perhaps these similarities provide the basis for a sound argument from mystical experiences to the existence of God.

Consider the following argument:

(1) All mystical experiences are basically the same.

(2) This similarity is better explained in terms of the external cause hypothesis (H_1) than of the psychological hypothesis (H_2).

(3) The most adequate version of (H_1) is that God causes the mystical experience (H_1').

---

(4) Therefore, mystical experiences provide inductive support for (H_1').

Walter Stace has argued for premise (1). According to Stace, all mystical experiences "involve the apprehension of *an ultimate nonsensuous unity of all things,* a oneness or a One to which neither the senses or the reason can penetrate."[12] He distinguishes two kinds of mysticism: extrovertive and introvertive. In extrovertive mysticism the mystic "looks outward and through the physical sense into the external world and finds the One there. The introvertive way turns inward, introspectively, and finds the One at the bottom of the self, at the bottom of the human personality."...

Stace's view is not shared by all scholars of mysticism. For example, Steven Katz maintains that there is no clear way of distinguishing the mystical experience itself from the interpretation of it.[13] Consequently, the meaning of the experience and even the meaning of the language used to describe the experience vary from context to context. For example, Katz argues that although all mystics claim that they experience a sense of objective reality (characteristic 3), what they mean differs radically from context to context and, indeed, their interpretations are often mutually incompatible.... Fortunately, we do not have to settle the debate between Stace and his defenders on the one hand[14] and his critics on the other, for whether the critics are correct or not, the argument fails. Suppose that critics such as Steven Katz are correct that mystics in different religious traditions experience different realities. Then the first premise of the above argument fails, and in order to argue from mystical experiences to the existence of God, a new one would have to be constructed. Suppose now that Stace's critics are mistaken and that mystical experiences in different religious traditions show significant similarities. Then premise (1) would be true. What about premise (2)? It is possible that the similarity of mystical experience in different religious traditions can be explained in terms of the psychological hypothesis. There have been attempts, for example, to explain mystical experiences in terms of sexual repression and to show that mystical experiences are similar to ones that are caused by psychedelic drugs.[15] But even if these explanations are valid, given the alleged striking similarity of all mystical experiences, the external cause hypothesis is not ruled out. Sexual repression may be necessary if certain individuals are to have access to ultimate reality; and psychedelic drugs, as we have already argued, may provide this access.

The problem with the external cause hypothesis in the case of mystical experiences, and the reason for preferring the psychological hypothesis over the external cause hypothesis, is the difficulty of making sense of these experiences. As we have seen, for the external cause hypothesis to apply, not only must the experiences of different people usually cohere with one another, and not only must there be a plausible theory to explain cases where there are discrepancies, but the individual experiences themselves must be coherent or else there must be some plausible way to account for the incoherence. According to Stace, mystics claim that their experience is ineffable and yet describe it. . . . So his characteristics of mystical experience seem prima facie contradictory. Further, according to Stace, the mystical experience itself has paradoxicality. By this he means that many mystics describe their experience in seemingly paradoxical language. For example, Dionysius the Aeropagite described his experience of God as "the dazzling obscurity of the Secret Silence, outshining all brilliance with the intensity of their darkness.[16] Taken literally, descriptions of this sort are nonsense. The mystic who gives them cannot be interpreted as making any factual claims.[17] Further, there is no widely accepted theory to account for the incoherences[18] and no objective way of translating such nonsensical statements into statements that are not. Without such a theory and method of translation, the external cause hypothesis is not to be preferred to the psychological hypothesis.

However, let us suppose that there is some good reason to prefer the external cause hypothesis to the psychological hypothesis. This would establish premise (2) in the above argument but not premise (3) (the most adequate version of (H_1) is that God causes the mystical experience (H_1'). However, it is difficult to see why God should be postulated as the external cause rather than the Tao, nirvana, or nature.[19] Indeed, if the paradoxical language of mystical experience points beyond itself to some external cause, this external cause would have to be very obscure and difficult to understand. To suppose that this external cause is God, an all-good, all-powerful, all-knowing being, is surely unwarranted. Thus there seems to be no good reason to suppose that (H_1') is the most plausible version of (H_1). Consequently, even if the argument is successful in providing evidence for an external cause of mystical experience, it fails as an argument for God.

IV. SWINBURNE'S PRINCIPLE OF CREDULITY AND RELIGIOUS EXPERIENCE

. . . In his argument from religious experience Swinburne makes use of what he calls the principle of credulity, which allows one to infer from the fact that it seems to a person that something is present to the probability that it is present. Let us evaluate this principle and the use Swinburne makes of it.

The Principle of Credulity and Its Limitations

Traditionally, critics of the argument from religious experience have maintained that it is a fallacy to argue from a psychological experience of x to x—for example, from the fact that it appears to you that God is present to the probability that God is present.[20] Maintaining, however, that the way things seem is indeed good grounds for belief about the way things are, Swinburne calls the general principle that guides our inferences the principle of credulity. It can be formulated as follows:

> (PC) If it seems (epistemically) to a subject S that x is present, then probably x is present.

By the expression "seems (epistemically)" Swinburne means that the subject S is inclined to believe what appears to S on the basis of his or her present sensory experience. Swinburne contrasts this sense of "seems" with the comparative sense in which one compares the way an object looks with the way other objects normally look. Thus when S says, "It seemed that the Virgin Mary was talking to me," S is using "seemed" epistemically. But if S says, "The figure seemed like a beautiful lady bathed in a white light," S is using "seemed" comparatively.

Swinburne gives two basic reasons for advocating (PC). The first one is that without such a means of arguing, we would land in a "skeptical bog."[21] Unfortunately, he does not expand on this reason, but one can assume he means something like this: Without (PC) we would be unable ever to get outside our own experiences and make justified judgments about how things really are; we would be restricted to how things appear to us. However, if we are restricted to how things appear to us, skepticism about the world is the only justified position to take. But with (PC) we can say how things really are and avoid skepticism.

The second reason Swinburne gives for advocating (PC) is that the attempt to restrict it so that it does not apply to religious experience is arbitrary. He considers only two attempts to restrict the range of application. First one might argue that (PC) is not an ultimate principle of rationality but must itself be justified on inductive grounds; in other words, by showing that appearances have in general proved reliable in the past. But, the argument continues, although this reliability has been demonstrated in the case of the appearance of ordinary things, it has not been in the case of religious experience. So (PC) should be restricted to ordinary appearances. Swinburne rejects this restriction on two grounds. He maintains that people are justified in taking what looks like a table to be a table "even if they do not recall their past experience with tables,"[22] and in any case this attempt to restrict the range of application would not allow us to deal with cases where the subject has no experience of x's but does have experiences of the properties in terms of which x is defined.

Another objection to the use of (PC) with respect to religious experiences that Swinburne discusses is based on the distinction between experience and the interpretation of experience. One might argue, he says, that (PC) should be used only when one is experiencing certain properties—for example, the so-called sensible properties of red, brown, soft, hard, left, right—but that it should not be used when one makes interpretations. Thus if it seems that x is red, one can infer that probably it is red since the inference entails no interpretation. But if it seems x is a Russian ship, then one cannot infer that it probably is since one is interpreting. Using this argument one could argue that (PC) cannot be used to infer from the appearance of God that probably God exists, since interpretation is involved. Swinburne rejects this line of argument, maintaining that it rests on the dubious distinction between experience and interpretation. There is no way, he claims, of making this distinction without being arbitrary.

Swinburne of course believes that (PC) is limited in its application by some special considerations. On his view there are in fact four special considerations that limit (PC). First, one can show that the subject S was unreliable or that the experience occurred under conditions that in the past have been unreliable. For example, if S was subject to hallucinations or delusions or was under the influence of a drug such as LSD, this would limit the application of (PC). Second, one can show that the perceptual claim was to have perceived an object of a certain kind in circumstances where similar perceptual claims have proved false. For example, one might show that the perceiver did not have the experience necessary to make reliable perceptual claims in these circumstances. Swinburne argues, however, that what experiences are necessary in order to recognize something is often unclear, and in any case the ability to recognize something, given certain experiences, varies widely from person to person. . . .

A third circumstance in which (PC) would be limited is one in which there was strong evidence that x did not exist. Because he believes that S's experience has a very strong evidential force, Swinburne emphasizes that this evidence would have to be very, very strong. Finally, a fourth way to limit (PC) would be to show that although x is present, the appearance of x can be accounted for in other ways.

Swinburne believes that these four special considerations do not apply to religious experiences. Although the first special consideration may rule out some religious experience, most religious experiences are not affected, he says. Thus most people who claim that they have had a religious experience are not subject to hallucinations or delusions and are not on drugs such as LSD. Swinburne also argues that the second special consideration does not apply. He maintains that one cannot argue that someone who claims to experience God could not recognize God; nor can one argue that many religious experiences are incompatible. For example, it may be argued that in order to recognize God one would have to have previously perceived

God or been given a detailed description of Him. But since people have not previously experienced God and do not have a detailed description of Him, they could not recognize Him. Swinburne rejects this contention and argues that the description of God as an omnipotent, omniscient, and perfectly free person may be sufficient for S to recognize God "by hearing his voice, or feeling his presence, or seeing his handiwork or by some sixth sense."[23]. . .

The Negative Principle of Credulity

One obvious critical question that can be raised about Swinburne's argument is this: Since experiences of God are good grounds for the existence of God, are not experiences of the absence of God good grounds for the nonexistence of God? After all, many people have tried to experience God and have failed. Cannot these experiences of the absence of God be used by atheists to counter the theistic argument based on experience of the presence of God? Swinburne thinks they cannot be so used.

In ordinary life we suppose that the experience of a chair is a good ground for believing that the chair is present. But we also believe that the experience of the absence of a chair is a good ground for supposing that a chair is absent. If Swinburne is correct that the way things appear is good ground for the way they are, then surely the way things do not seem is good ground for the way they are not. Indeed, if (PC) is a legitimate principle of inference, then one would suppose that there is a negative principle of credulity that can be formulated as follows:

> (NPC) If it seems (epistemically) to a subject S that x is absent, then probably x is absent. . . .

Swinburne does not explicitly formulate a negative credulity principle. Whether he would be opposed to one as such or merely to the applications I have made of it is unclear. But let us try to understand his objection to the use of (NPC) to argue that probably God does not exist.

His objection to the use of (NPC) in showing the nonexistence of God based on the experience of God's absence turns on the alleged disanalogy between ordinary perceptual claims that can legitimately be made about the absence of something, such as the absence of a chair, and a perceptual claim in the context of religion that cannot be made, such as the absence of God. Swinburne sees the difference in this way: In the case of a chair one can know under what conditions one would see a chair if a chair was there. But in the case of God one cannot know under what conditions one would see God if God existed. Swinburne seems to believe that since we do not know under what conditions God would appear if He existed, experience of the absence of God cannot be used as evidence that God does not exist. But he maintains that this lack of knowledge only "*somewhat* lessens" the evidential value of perceptual claims of God's presence.[24]

It is difficult to understand why, if there were this difference, it would affect the evidential value of perceptual claims in religious contexts in the way Swinburne says. One would suppose that if one did not know under what conditions a subject could expect to see x if x existed, this would affect both the evidential value of S's claim that it seemed that x is present and S's claim that it seemed that x is not present, and to the same extent. Yet Swinburne maintains that since we do not know under what conditions someone would see God if God existed, this only somewhat lessens the evidential value of a perceptual claim that it seems to S that God is present, but it completely negates the evidential value of the perceptual claim that it seems to S that God is not present. Perceptual judgments of both the absence and the presence of God seem equally suspect, yet Swinburne finds a great disanalogy. . . .

The Reliability of Religious Experiences

As I have indicated, Swinburne does not believe it possible to show that religious experience is unreliable by arguing that different religious experiences are incompatible. He maintains that religious experiences stemming from non-Christian traditions are of a being who is supposed to have "similar properties to those of God" or "experiences of apparently lesser beings."[25] Swinburne admits that if there were religious experiences of an all-powerful devil, they would conflict with religious experiences of God. But he argues that no such experiences exist.

However, it is not necessary to have experiences of an all-powerful devil to claim that religious experiences are systematically incompatible. Swinburne must do more than argue that the beings described in the religious experience of non-Western cultures have properties similar to those of God in the Western tradition in order to show no incompatibility. He must show that these beings do not have *any* properties that are incompatible with properties of God.

Prima facie there does seem to be a remarkable incompatibility between the concept of God in the Western tradition and the concept of Brahma, the absolute, and so on in Eastern thought. In the Western tradition, God is a person distinct from the world and from His creatures. Not surprisingly, many religious experiences within the Western tradition, especially nonmystical ones such as the experience of God speaking to someone and giving advice and counsel, convey this idea of God. On the other hand, mystical religious experience within the Eastern tradition tends to convey a pantheistic and impersonal God. The experience of God in this tradition typically is not that of a caring, loving person but of an impersonal absolute and ultimate reality. To be sure, this difference is not uniform: There are theistic trends in Hinduism and pantheistic trends in Christianity. But the differences between East and West are sufficiently widespread to be noted by scholars, and they certainly seem incompatible. A God that transcends the world seemingly cannot be identical with the world; a God that is a person can apparently not be impersonal. Indeed, Christians who have held pantheistic and impersonal views about God have typically been thought to be heretics by Christian orthodoxy. So there do seem to be incompatible differences in the religious experiences of different cultures. . . .

V. CONCLUSION

I do not wish to deny that (PC) operates in ordinary life and science. But there are more limitations on its use than Swinburne imagines, and they need to be more tightly drawn. If without PC we might land in a skeptical bog, without tighter restrictions on (PC) we would find ourselves in a cluttered ontological landscape. Given Swinburne's version of (PC), there would indeed be more things in heaven and earth than are dreamt of in anyone's philosophy.

NOTES

1. I am indebted here to William Rowe's illuminating discussion of the meaning of religious experience. See William L. Rowe, *Philosophy of Religion: An Introduction* (Belmont, Calif.: Wadsworth, 1978), pp. 63–64.

2. Cf. R. M. Chisholm, *Perception* (Ithaca, N.Y.: Cornell University Press, 1957), chap. 4.

3. See Richard Swinburne, *The Existence of God* (Oxford: Clarendon Press, 1979), pp. 249–253.

4. Quoted in Paul Kurtz, *The Transcendental Temptation* (Buffalo, N.Y.: Prometheus Books, 1986), p. 237.

5. See also Gary Gutting, *Religious Belief and Religious Skepticism* (Notre Dame, Ind.: University of Notre Dame Press, 1982), chap. 5, for further discussion of this type of experience.

6. St. Teresa, *The Life of Teresa of Jesus*, trans. and ed. by E. Allison Peers (Garden City, N.Y.: Image Books, 1960), p. 249. Quoted by George Mavrodes in "Real v. Deceptive Mystical Experiences," *Mysticism and Philosophical Analysis* (New York: Oxford University Press, 1978), p. 238.

7. See Laurence BonJour, *The Structure of Empirical Knowledge* (Cambridge, Mass.: Harvard University Press, 1985), p. 112.

8. Cf. Mavrodes, "Real v. Deceptive Mystical Experiences."

9. Kurtz, *Transcendental Temptation*, pp. 153–159.

10. G. A. Wells, *The Historical Evidence for Jesus* (Buffalo, N.Y.: Prometheus Books, 1982), pp. 22–25.

11. R. Joseph Hoffman, *Jesus Outside the Gospels* (Buffalo, N.Y.: Prometheus Books, 1984).

12. Stace, *Teachings of the Mystics*, p. 14.

13. Steven Katz, "Language, Epistemology and Mysticism," *Mysticism and Philosophical Analysis*, pp. 22–74.

14. See, for example, Gary E. Kessler and Normal Prigge, "Is Mystical Experience Everywhere the Same?" *Sophia*, 21, 1982, pp. 39–55. They argue against Katz, maintaining that mystical experience is contentless consciousness, and such experience is found in all cases of introvertive mysticism. See also Agehananda Bharati, *The Light at the Center* (Santa Barbara, Calif.: Ross-Erikson, 1976), chap. 2. Bharati maintains that his mystical experience and that of others are a "zero experience," by which he means an experience that has zero cognitive content.

15. See, for example, Kurtz, *Transcendental Temptation*, pp. 97–102.

16. Stace, *Teachings of the Mystics*, p. 135. Whether this means that the experience seems to the mystic to have contradictory features or whether, as Katz has suggested, the paradoxical language cloaks the content, we need not decide here. We are assuming for the sake of argument that the experience seems contradictory. See also Katz, "Language, Epistemology and Mysticism," *Mysticism and Philosophical Analysis*, p. 54.

17. Robert Hoffman, "Logic, Meaning and Mystical Intuition," *Philosophical Studies*, 5, 1960, pp. 65–70.

18. For one interesting attempt to account for the incoherence of the descriptions of mystical experiences, see Paul Henle, "Mysticism and Semantics," *Philosophy and Phenomenological Research*, 9, 1948–1949, pp. 416–422.

19. In *Teachings of the Mystics*, p. 27, Stace admits that mystical experiences can be interpreted in terms of many religious traditions.

20. Indeed, I have argued something similar above: In order to justify my spontaneous perceptual belief, for example, that there is a brown table in front of me, it is necessary to give some sort of argument. Moreover, as my criticism of Swinburne's argument makes clear, I do not believe that the way things appear is *by itself* good grounds for believing how they are. A sound argument is needed that enables one to infer from the appearance of x to x.

21. Swinburne, *Existence of God*, p. 254, n. 1.

22. *Ibid.*, p. 255.

23. *Ibid.*, p. 268.

24. *Ibid.*, p. 263.

25. *Ibid.*, p. 267.

SUGGESTED READING

Alston, William. *Perceiving God*. Ithaca, New York: Cornell University Press, 1991.

Brakenhielm, Carl. *Problems of Religious Experience*. Uppsala, Sweden: University of Uppsala, 1985.

Clark, Ralph W. "The Evidential Value of Religious Experiences." *International Journal for the Philosophy of Religion* 16 (1984): 189–202.

Davis, Caroline Franks. *The Evidential Force of Religious Experience*. Oxford: Clarendon Press, 1989.

Hardy, Alister. *The Spiritual Nature of Man: A Study of Contemporary Religious Experience*. Oxford: Clarendon Press, 1979.

James, William. *The Varieties of Religious Experience*. New York: New American Library, 1958.

Katz, Steven T., ed. *Mysticism and Philosophical Analysis*. Oxford: Oxford University Press, 1978.

Lewis, H. D. *Our Experience of God*. London: Allen and Unwin, 1959.

Miles, T. R. *Religious Experience*. London: Macmillan, 1972.

Otto, Rudolph. *The Idea of the Holy*. London: Oxford University Press, 1958.

Proudfoot, Wayne. *Religious Experience*. Berkeley: University of California Press, 1985.

Rowe, William L. "Religious Experience and the Principle of Credulity." *International Journal for the Philosophy of Religion* 13 (1982): 85–92.

Stace, W. T. *Mysticism and Philosophy*. New York: Macmillan, 1960.

Swinburne, Richard. *The Existence of God*. London: Oxford University Press, 1979, ch. 13.

Underhill, Evelyn. *Mysticism*. Cleveland: Meridian Books, 1955.

Wainwright, William. *Mysticism: A Study of Its Nature, Cognitive Value, and Moral Implications*. Madison: University of Wisconsin Press, 1981.

Yandell, Keith. *The Epistemology of Religious Experience*. Cambridge: Cambridge University Press, 1993.

PART TWO FAITH AND REASON

Questions about the relation of faith and reason are nearly as old as religion itself. Is faith reasonable or unreasonable? Can the truth of religious beliefs be proved? Even if religious beliefs can be proved true, is proving them important to religion? If these beliefs cannot be proved, is that bad or good? What is the relationship between religious beliefs and the knowledge we think we have about all sorts of other things?

One approach to these matters may be labeled "strong rationalism." On this view, one cannot be fully rational in accepting religious beliefs unless they can be shown by convincing reasons to be true. Precisely what it takes for reasons to be convincing is controversial, but it is clear that the reasons must be available to any rational, well-informed person, and must at least strongly indicate the truth of the religious belief in question. Important thinkers line up on both sides of this issue: some who are assured that belief in God meets these criteria and therefore endorse theism, and others who disagree and therefore reject theism.

Contrasting with strong rationalism is "fideism" (literally, "faith-ism"). According to fideism, faith can and must stand on its own, without support from rational arguments. For most fideists, to subject one's faith to independent rational evaluation is in effect to elevate reason above God. Fideists typically say that the "truth," which is essential in religious faith, is more a matter of subjective, inner commitment than an objective matter of reasoned argument.

Somewhat similar to the fideistic approach is the "pragmatic" approach, which has different variations. This approach justifies religious belief by arguing that it is reasonable to accept belief in God because of its practical "payoff"—even when the belief lacks convincing rational support. Of course, this payoff has been envisioned differently by different thinkers (e.g., as heavenly bliss or increased psychological sense of meaning).

Finally, there is the approach sometimes known as "critical rationalism" or "soft rationalism." This view agrees with strong rationalism against fideism in holding that it is reasonable, appropriate, and necessary to subject religious beliefs to rational assessment. But it recognizes that when there is disagreement on matters of fundamental importance, issues are not likely to be settled by conclusive arguments that convince all persons regardless of their previous state of belief or disbelief. Because no single argument or piece of evidence is able to bear the full weight of either supporting or refuting belief, some are exploring a "cumulative case" to show that one's belief-system does a better job than its rivals of explaining the "total evidence" provided by life in all its complexity.

THOMAS AQUINAS

The Harmony of Reason and Revelation

In this selection, Thomas Aquinas (1224–1274) articulates a classical position concerning the relationship between reason and revelation. He says that there are some truths about God that can be learned through human reasoning, and other truths that can only be known because God has disclosed them through revelation. Both kinds of truths are worthy of our belief, and even the truths knowable by reason may and should be accepted on faith by those who lack the time, opportunity, or ability to verify them for themselves. Though the sources of the two kinds of truth are different, they are not and cannot be in disagreement with each other, since "only the false is opposed to the true."

⌘

There is a twofold mode of truth in what we profess about God. Some truths about God exceed all the ability of the human reason. Such is the truth that God is triune. But there are some truths which the natural reason also is able to reach. Such are that God exists, that He is one, and the like. In fact, such truths about God have been proved demonstratively by philosophers, guided by the light of natural reason.

That there are certain truths about God that totally surpass man's ability appears with the greatest evidence. . . . For the human intellect is not able to reach a comprehension of the divine substance through its natural power. For, according to its manner of knowing in the present life, the intellect depends on the sense for the origin of knowledge; and so those things that do not fall under the senses cannot be grasped by the human intellect except in so far as the knowledge of them is gathered from sensible things. Now, sensible things cannot lead the human intellect to the point of seeing in them the nature of the divine substance; for sensible things are effects that fall short of the power of their cause. Yet, beginning with sensible things, our intellect is led to the point of knowing about God that He exists, and other such characteristics that must be attributed to the First Principle. There are, consequently, some intelligible truths about God that are open to the human reason; but there are others that absolutely surpass its power. . . .

Sacred Scripture also gives testimony to this truth. We read in Job: "Peradventure thou wilt comprehend the steps of God, and wilt find out the Almighty perfectly?" (11:7). And again: "Behold, God is great, exceeding our knowledge" (Job 36:26). And St. Paul: "We know in part" (I Cor. 13:9).

From *Summa Contra Gentiles* by Thomas Aquinas, trans. A. C. Pegis. Notre Dame: University of Notre Dame Press, 1975.

We should not, therefore, immediately reject as false, following the opinion of the Manicheans and many unbelievers, everything that is said about God even though it cannot be investigated by reason.

Since, therefore, there exists a twofold truth concerning the divine being, one to which the inquiry of the reason can reach, the other which surpasses the whole ability of the human reason, it is fitting that both of these truths be proposed to man divinely for belief. This point must first be shown concerning the truth that is open to the inquiry of the reason; otherwise, it might perhaps seem to someone that, since such a truth can be known by the reason, it was uselessly given to men through a supernatural inspiration as an object of belief.

Yet, if this truth were left solely as a matter of inquiry for the human reason, three awkward consequences would follow. The first is that few men would possess the knowledge of God. For there are three reasons why most men are cut off from the fruit of diligent inquiry which is the discovery of truth. Some do not have the physical disposition for such work. As a result, there are many who are naturally not fitted to pursue knowledge; and so, however much they tried, they would be unable to reach the highest level of human knowledge which consists in knowing God. Others are cut off from pursuing this truth by the necessities imposed upon them by their daily lives. For some men must devote themselves to taking care of temporal matters. Such men would not be able to give so much time to the leisure of contemplative inquiry as to reach the highest peak at which human investigation can arrive, namely, the knowledge of God. Finally, there are some who are cut off by indolence. In order to know the things that the reason can investigate concerning God, a knowledge of many things must already be possessed. For almost all of philosophy is directed towards the knowledge of God, and that is why metaphysics, which deals with divine things, is the last part of philosophy to be learned. This means that we are able to arrive at the inquiry concerning the aforementioned truth only on the basis of a great deal of labor spent in study. Now, those who wish to undergo such a labor for the mere love of knowledge are few, even though God has inserted into the minds of men a natural appetite for knowledge.

The second awkward effect is that those who would come to discover the abovementioned truth would barely reach it after a great deal of time. . . . If the only way open to us for the knowledge of God were solely that of the reason, the human race would remain in the blackest shadows of ignorance. For then the knowledge of God, which especially renders men perfect and good, would come to be possessed only by a few, and these few would require a great deal of time in order to reach it.

The third awkward effect is this. The investigation of the human reason for the most part has falsity present within it, and this is due partly to the weakness of our intellect in judgment, and partly to the admixture of images. The result is that many, remaining ignorant of the power of demonstration, would hold in doubt those things that have been most truly demonstrated. This would be particularly the case since they see that, among those who are reputed to be wise men, each one teaches his own brand of doctrine. Furthermore, with the many truths that are demonstrated, there sometimes is mingled something that is false, which is not demonstrated but rather asserted on the basis of some probable or sophistical argument, which yet has the credit of being a demonstration. That is why it was necessary that the unshakeable certitude and pure truth concerning divine things should be presented to men by way of faith.

Beneficially, therefore, did the divine Mercy provide that it should instruct us to hold by faith even those truths that the human reason is able to investigate. In this way, all men would easily be able to have a share in the knowledge of God, and this without uncertainty and error. . . .

Now, perhaps some will think that men should not be asked to believe what the reason is not adequate to investigate, since the divine Wisdom provides in the case of each thing according to the mode of its nature. We must therefore prove that it is necessary for man to receive from God as objects of belief even those truths that are above the human reason.

No one tends with desire and zeal towards something that is not already known to him. But, as we shall examine later on in this work, men are ordained by the divine Providence towards a higher good than human fragility can experience in the present life. That is why it was necessary for the human mind to be called to something higher than the human reason here and now can reach, so that it would thus learn to desire something and with zeal tend towards something that surpasses the whole state of the present life. This belongs especially to the Christian religion, which in a unique way promises spiritual and eternal goods. And so there are many things proposed to men in it that transcend human sense. The Old Law, on the other hand, whose promises were of a temporal character, contained very few proposals that transcended the inquiry of the human reason. Following this same direction, the philosophers themselves, in order that they might lead men from the pleasure of sensible things to virtue, were concerned to show that there were in existence other goods of a higher nature than these things of sense, and that those who gave themselves to the active or contemplative virtues would find much sweeter enjoyment in the taste of these higher goods.

It is also necessary that such truth be proposed to men for belief so that they may have a truer knowledge of God. For then only do we know God truly when we believe Him to be above everything that it is possible for man to think about Him; for, as we have shown, the divine substance surpasses the natural knowledge of which man is capable. Hence, by the fact that some things about God are proposed to man that surpass his reason, there is strengthened in man the view that God is something above what he can think.

Another benefit that comes from the revelation to men of truths that exceed the reason is the curbing of presumption, which is the mother of error. For there are some who have such a presumptuous opinion of their own ability that they deem themselves able to measure the nature of everything; I mean to say that, in their estimation, everything is true that seems to them so, and everything is false that does not. So that the human mind, therefore, might be freed from this presumption and come to a humble inquiry after truth, it was necessary that some things should be proposed to man by God that would completely surpass his intellect. . . . From all these considerations it is clear that even the most imperfect knowledge about the most noble realities brings the greatest perfection to the soul. Therefore, although the human reason cannot grasp fully the truths that are above it, yet, if it somehow holds these truths at least by faith, it acquires great perfection for itself. . . .

Those who place their faith in this truth, however, "for which the human reason offers no experimental evidence," do not believe foolishly, as though "following artificial fables" (II Peter 1:16). For these "secrets of divine Wisdom" (Job 11:6) the divine Wisdom itself, which knows all things to the full, has deigned to reveal to men. It reveals its own presence, as well as the truth of its teaching and inspiration, by fitting arguments; and in order to confirm those truths that exceed natural knowledge, it gives visible manifestation to works that surpass the ability of all nature. Thus, there are the wonderful cures of illnesses, there is the raising of the dead, and the wonderful immutation in the heavenly bodies; and what is more wonderful, there is the inspiration given to human minds, so that simple and untutored persons, filled with the gift of the Holy Spirit, come to possess instantaneously the highest wisdom and the readiest eloquence. When these arguments were examined, through the efficacy of the abovementioned proof, and not the violent assault of arms or the promise of pleasures, and (what is most wonderful of all) in the midst of the tyranny of the persecutors, an innumerable throng of people, both simple and most learned, flocked to the Christian faith. In this faith there are truths preached that surpass every human intellect; the pleasures of the flesh are curbed; it is taught that the things of the world should be spurned. Now, for the minds of mortal men to assent to these things is the greatest of miracles, just as it is a manifest work of divine inspiration that, spurning visible things, men should seek only what is invisible. Now, that this has happened neither without preparation nor by chance, but as a result of the disposition of God, is clear from the fact that through many pronouncements of the ancient prophets God had foretold that He would do this. The books of these prophets are held in veneration among us Christians, since they give witness to our faith. . . .

This wonderful conversion of the world to the Christian faith is the clearest witness of the signs given in the past; so that it is not necessary that they should be further repeated, since they appear most clearly in their effect. For it would be truly more wonderful than all signs if the world had been led by simple and humble men to believe such lofty truths, to accomplish such difficult actions, and to have such high hopes. Yet it is also a fact that, even in our own time, God does not cease to work miracles through His saints for the confirmation of the faith. . . .

Now, although the truth of the Christian faith which we have discussed surpasses the capacity of the reason, nevertheless that truth that the human reason is naturally endowed to know cannot be opposed to the truth of the Christian faith. For that with which the human reason is naturally endowed is clearly most true; so much so, that it is impossible for us to think of such truths as false. Nor is it permissible to believe as false that which we hold by faith, since this is confirmed in a way that is so clearly divine. Since, therefore, only the false is opposed to the true, as is clearly evident from an examination of their definitions, it is impossible that the truth of faith should be opposed to those principles that the human reason knows naturally.

BLAISE PASCAL

The Wager

In his famous Wager, Blaise Pascal (1623–1662) poses the question: If you had to decide for or against belief in the Christian God with no evidence whatsoever—no reason either to believe God exists or to believe that he does not—what should you choose? Basing his case on probability theory, Pascal argues that the only rational choice under such circumstances is to believe. Note, however, that Pascal does not think it really is in our power simply to "decide to believe." On the contrary, he thinks that our desires will keep us from believing even when we can clearly see that this is the rational choice; thus, we must purify our hearts so as to be able to believe. Nor does he really think the believer has no good reasons in support of his or her faith; Pascal's *Pensées* as a whole constitutes a forceful defense of the truth of Christianity.

⌘

If there is a God, He is infinitely incomprehensible, since, having neither parts nor limits, He has no affinity to us. We are then incapable of knowing either what He is or if He is. This being so, who will dare to undertake the decision of the question? Not we, who have no affinity to Him.

Who then will blame Christians for not being able to give a reason for their belief, since they profess a religion for which they cannot give a reason? They declare, in expounding it to the world, that it is a foolishness, *stultitiam*; and then you complain that they do not prove it! If they proved it, they would not keep their word; it is in lacking proofs that they are not lacking in sense. "Yes, but although this excuses those who offer it as such, and takes away from them the blame of putting it forward without reason, it does not excuse those who receive it." Let us then examine this point, and say, "God

From *Penses,* in *Pensées and the Provincial Letters* by Blaise Pascal, trans. W. F. Trotter. New York: Modern Library, 1941.

is, or He is not." But to which side shall we incline? Reason can decide nothing here. There is an infinite chaos which separated us. A game is being played at the extremity of this infinite distance where heads or tails will turn up. What will you wager? According to reason, you can do neither the one thing nor the other; according to reason, you can defend neither of the propositions.

Do not then reprove for error those who have made a choice; for you know nothing about it. "No, but I blame them for having made, not this choice, but a choice; for again both he who chooses heads and he who chooses tails are equally at fault, they are both in the wrong. The true course is not to wager at all."

Yes; but you must wager. It is not optional. You are embarked. Which will you choose then? Let us see. Since you must choose, let us see which interests you least. You have two things to lose, the true and the good; and two things to stake, your reason and your will, your knowledge and your happiness; and your nature has two things to shun, error and misery. Your reason is no more shocked in choosing one rather than the other, since you must of necessity choose. This is one point settled. But your happiness? Let us weigh the gain and the loss in wagering that God is. Let us estimate these two chances. If you gain, you gain all; if you lose, you lose nothing. Wager, then, without hesitation that He is.—"That is very fine. Yes, I must wager; but I may perhaps wager too much."—Let us see. Since there is an equal risk of gain and of loss, if you had only to gain two lives, instead of one, you might still wager. But if there were three lives to gain, you would have to play (since you are under the necessity of playing), and you would be imprudent, when you are forced to play, not to chance your life to gain three at a game where there is an equal risk of loss and gain. But there is an eternity of life and happiness. And this being so, if there were an infinity of chances, of which one only would be for you, you would still be right in wagering one to win two, and you would act stupidly, being obliged to play, by refusing to stake one life against three at a game in which out of an infinity of chances there is one for you, if there were an infinity of an infinitely happy life to gain. But there is here an infinity of an infinitely happy life to gain, a chance of gain against a finite number of chances of loss, and what you stake is finite. It is all divided; wherever the infinite is and there is not an infinity of chances of loss against that of gain, there is no time to hesitate, you must give all. And thus, when one is forced to play, he must renounce reason to preserve his life, rather than risk it for infinite gain, as likely to happen as the loss of nothingness.

For it is no use to say it is uncertain if we will gain, and it is certain that we risk, and that the infinite distance between the *certainty* of what is staked and the *uncertainty* of what will be gained, equals the finite good which is certainly staked against the uncertain infinite. It is not so, as every player stakes a certainty to gain an uncertainty, and yet he stakes a finite certainty to gain a finite uncertainty, without transgressing against reason. There is not an infinite distance between the certainty staked and the uncertainty of the gain; that is untrue. In truth, there is an infinity between the certainty of gain and the certainty of loss. But the uncertainty of the gain is proportioned to the certainty of the stake according to the proportion of the chances of gain and loss. Hence it comes that, if there are as many risks on one side as on the other, the course is to play even; and then the certainty of the stake is equal to the uncertainty of the gain, so far is it from fact that there is an infinite distance between them. And so our proposition is of infinite force, when there is the finite to stake in a game where there are equal risks of gain and of loss, and the infinite to gain. This is demonstrable: and if men are capable of any truths, this is one.

"I confess it, I admit it. But, still, is there no means of seeing the faces of the cards?"—Yes, Scripture and the rest, etc. "Yes, but I have my hands tied and my mouth closed; I am forced to wager, and am not free. I am not released, and am so made that I cannot believe. What, then, would you have me do?"

True. But at least learn your inability to believe, since reason brings you to this, and yet you cannot believe. Endeavour then to convince yourself, not by increase of proofs of God, but by the abatement of your passions. You would like to attain faith, and do not know the way; you would like to cure yourself of unbelief, and ask the remedy for it. Learn of those who have been bound like you, and who now stake all their possessions. These are people who know the way which you would follow, and who are cured of an ill of which you would be cured. Follow the way by which they began; by acting as if they believed, taking the holy water, having masses said, etc. Even this will naturally make you believe, and deaden your acuteness.—"But this is what I am afraid of."—And why? What have you to lose?

But to show you that this leads you there, it is this which will lessen the passions, which are your stumbling-blocks.

WILLIAM CLIFFORD The Ethics of Belief

What moral obligations pertain to our decisions about what to believe and what not to believe? Although many people think that moral obligations are irrelevant to belief, Clifford argues that "it is wrong always, everywhere, and for anyone, to believe anything upon insufficient evidence." This is true, first of all, because if we act on poorly supported beliefs we are very likely to harm others as well as ourselves. But also, and more fundamentally, by habitually accepting beliefs not supported by evidence, we make ourselves and other people credulous, so that we and they will more easily be seduced by falsehood in the future.

From *Lectures and Essays*. New York: Macmillan, 1974.

⌘

A shipowner was about to send to sea an emigrant ship. He knew that she was old, and not over-well built at the first; that she had seen many seas and climes, and often had needed repairs. Doubts had been suggested to him that possibly she was not seaworthy. These doubts preyed upon his mind, and made him unhappy; he thought that perhaps he ought to have her thoroughly overhauled and refitted, even though this should put him to great expense. Before the ship sailed, however, he succeeded in overcoming these melancholy reflections. He said to himself that she had gone safely through so many voyages and weathered so many storms that it was idle to suppose she would not come safely home from this trip also. He would put his trust in Providence, which could hardly fail to protect all these unhappy families that were leaving their fatherland to seek for better times elsewhere. He would dismiss from his mind all ungenerous suspicions about the honesty of builders and contractors. In such ways he acquired a sincere and comfortable conviction that his vessel was thoroughly safe and seaworthy; he watched her departure with a light heart, and benevolent wishes for the success of the exiles in their strange new home that was to be; and he got his insurance money when she went down in mid-ocean and told no tales.

What shall we say of him? Surely this, that he was verily guilty of the death of those men. It is admitted that he did sincerely believe in the soundness of his ship; but the sincerity of his conviction can in no wise help him, because *he had no right to believe on such evidence as was before him.* He had acquired his belief not by honestly earning it in patient investigation, but by stifling his doubts. And although in the end he may have felt so sure about it that he could not think otherwise, yet inasmuch as he had knowingly and willingly worked himself into that frame of mind, he must be held responsible for it.

Let us alter the case a little, and suppose that the ship was not unsound after all; that she made her voyage safely, and many others after it. Will that diminish the guilt of her owner? Not one jot. When an action is once done, it is right or wrong for ever; no accidental failure of its good or evil fruits can possibly alter that. The man would not have been innocent, he would only have been not found out. The question of right or wrong has to do with the origin of his belief, not the matter of it; not what it was, but how he got it; not whether it turned out to be true or false, but whether he had a right to believe on such evidence as was before him.

There was once an island in which some of the inhabitants professed a religion teaching neither the doctrine of original sin nor that of eternal punishment. A suspicion got abroad that the professors of this religion had made use of unfair means to get their doctrines taught to children. They were accused of wresting the laws of their country in such a way as to remove children from the care of their natural and legal guardians; and even of stealing them away and keeping them concealed from their friends and relations. A certain number of men formed themselves into a society for the purpose of agitating the public about this matter. They published grave accusations against individual citizens of the highest position and character, and did all in their power to injure these citizens in the exercise of their professions. So great was the noise they made, that a Commission was appointed to investigate the facts; but after the Commission had carefully inquired into all the evidence that could be got, it appeared that the accused were innocent. Not only had they been accused on insufficient evidence, but the evidence of their innocence was such as the agitators might easily have obtained, if they had attempted a fair inquiry. After these disclosures the inhabitants of that country looked upon the members of the agitating society, not only as persons whose judgment was to be distrusted, but also as no longer to be counted honourable men. For although they had sincerely and conscientiously believed in the charges they had made, yet *they had no right to believe on such evidence as was before them.* Their sincere convictions, instead of being honestly earned by patient inquiring, were stolen by listening to the voice of prejudice and passion.

Let us vary this case also, and suppose, other things remaining as before, that a still more accurate investigation proved the accused to have been really guilty. Would this make any difference in the guilt of the accusers? Clearly not; the question is not whether their belief was true or false, but whether they entertained it on wrong grounds. They would no doubt say, "Now you see that we were right after all; next time perhaps you will believe us." And they might be believed, but they would not thereby become honourable men. They would not be innocent, they would only be not found out. Every one of them, if he chose to examine himself *in foro conscientiæ,* would know that he had acquired and nourished a belief, when he had no right to believe on such evidence as was before him; and therein he would know that he had done a wrong thing.

It may be said, however, that in both of these supposed cases it is not the belief which is judged to be wrong, but the action following upon it. The shipowner might say, "I am perfectly certain that my ship is sound, but still I feel it my duty to have her examined, before trusting the lives of so many people to her." And it might be said to the agitator, "However convinced you were of the justice of your cause and the truth of your convictions, you ought not to have made a public attack upon any man's character until you had examined the evidence on both sides with the utmost patience and care."

In the first place, let us admit that, so far as it goes, this view of the case is right and necessary; right, because even when a man's belief is so fixed that he cannot think otherwise, he still has a choice in regard to the action suggested by it, and so cannot escape the duty of investigating on the ground of the strength of his convictions; and necessary, because those who are not yet capable of controlling their feelings and thoughts must have a plain rule dealing with overt acts.

But this being premised as necessary, it becomes clear that it is not sufficient, and that our previous judgment is required to supplement it. For it is not possible so to sever the belief from the action it suggests as to condemn the one without condemning the other. No man holding a strong belief on one side of a question, or even wishing to hold a belief on one side, can investigate it with such fairness and completeness as if he were really in doubt and unbiassed; so that the existence of a belief not founded on fair inquiry unfits a man for the performance of this necessary duty.

Nor is that truly a belief at all which has not some influence upon the actions of him who holds it. He who truly believes that which prompts him to an action has looked upon the action to lust after it, he has committed it already in his heart. If a belief is not realized immediately in open deeds, it is stored up for the guidance of the future. It goes to make a part of that aggregate of beliefs which is the link between sensation and action at every moment of all our lives, and which is so organized and compacted together that no part of it can be isolated from the rest, but every new addition modifies the structure of the whole. No real belief, however trifling and fragmentary it may seem, is ever truly insignificant; it prepares us to receive more of its like, confirms those which resembled it before, and weakens others; and so gradually it lays a stealthy train in our inmost thoughts, which may some day explode into overt action, and leave its stamp upon our character for ever.

And no one man's belief is in any case a private matter which concerns himself alone. Our lives are guided by that general conception of the course of things which has been created by society for social purposes. Our words, our phrases, our forms and processes and modes of thought, are common property, fashioned and perfected from age to age; an heirloom which every succeeding generation inherits as a precious deposit and a sacred trust to be handed on to the next one, not unchanged but enlarged and purified, with some clear marks of its proper handiwork. Into this, for good or ill, is woven every belief of every man who has speech of his fellows. An awful privilege, and an awful responsibility, that we should help to create the world in which posterity will live.

In the two supposed cases which have been considered, it has been judged wrong to believe on insufficient evidence, or to nourish belief by suppressing doubts and avoiding investigation. The reason of this judgment is not far to seek: it is that in both these cases the belief held by one man was of great importance to other men. But forasmuch as no belief held by one man, however seemingly trivial the belief, and however obscure the believer, is ever actually insignificant or without its effect on the fate of mankind, we have no choice but to extend our judgment to all cases of belief whatever. Belief, that sacred faculty which prompts the decisions of our will, and knits into harmonious working all the compacted energies of our being, is ours not for ourselves, but for humanity. It is rightly used on truths which have been established by long experience and waiting toil, and which have stood in the fierce light of free and fearless questioning. Then it helps to bind men together, and to strengthen and direct their common action. It is desecrated when given to unproved and unquestioned statements, for the solace and private pleasure of the believer; to add a tinsel splendour to the plain straight road of our life and display a bright mirage beyond it; or even to drown the common sorrows of our kind by a self-deception which allows them not only to cast down, but also to degrade us. Whoso would deserve well of his fellows in this matter will guard the purity of his belief with a very fanaticism of jealous care, lest at any time it should rest on an unworthy object, and catch a stain which can never be wiped away.

It is not only the leader of men, statesman, philosopher, or poet, that owes this bounden duty to mankind. Every rustic who delivers in the village alehouse his slow, infrequent sentences, may help to kill or keep alive the fatal superstitions which clog his race. Every hard-worked wife of an artisan may transmit to her children beliefs which shall knit society together, or rend it in pieces. No simplicity of mind, no obscurity of station, can escape the universal duty of questioning all that we believe.

It is true that this duty is a hard one, and the doubt which comes out of it is often a very bitter thing. It leaves us bare and powerless where we thought that we were safe and strong. To know all about anything is to know how to deal with it under all circumstances. We feel much happier and more secure when we think we know precisely what to do, no matter what happens, than when we have lost our way and do not know where to turn. And if we have supposed ourselves to know all about anything, and to be capable of doing what is fit in regard to it, we naturally do not like to find that we are really ignorant and powerless, that we have to begin again at the beginning, and try to learn what the thing is and how it is to be dealt with—if indeed anything can be learnt about it. It is the sense of power attached to a sense of knowledge that makes men desirous of believing, and afraid of doubting.

The sense of power is the highest and best of pleasures when the belief on which it is founded is a true belief, and has been fairly earned by investigation. For then we may justly feel that it is common property, and holds good for others as well as for ourselves. Then we may be glad, not that *I* have learned secrets by which I am safer and stronger, but that *we men* have got mastery over more of the world; and we shall be strong, not for ourselves, but in the name of Man and in his strength. But if the belief has been accepted on insufficient evidence, the pleasure is a stolen one. Not only does it deceive ourselves by giving us a sense of power which we do not really possess, but it is sinful, because it is stolen in defiance of our duty to mankind. That duty is to guard ourselves from such beliefs as from a pestilence, which may shortly master our own body and then spread to the rest of the town. What would be thought of one who, for the sake of a sweet fruit, should deliberately run the risk of bringing a plague upon his family and his neighbours?

And, as in other such cases, it is not the risk only which has to be considered; for a bad action is always bad at the time when it is done, no matter what happens afterwards. Every time we let ourselves believe for unworthy reasons, we weaken our powers of self-control, of doubting, of judicially and fairly weighing evidence. We all suffer severely enough from the maintenance and support of false beliefs and the fatally wrong actions which they lead to, and the evil born when one such belief is entertained is great and wide. But a greater and wider evil arises when the credulous character is maintained and supported, when a habit of believing for unworthy reasons is fostered and made permanent. If I steal money from any person, there may be no harm done by the mere transfer of possession; he may not feel the loss, or it may prevent him from using the money badly. But I cannot help doing this great wrong towards Man, that I make myself dishonest. What hurts society is not that it should lose its property, but that it should become a den of thieves; for then it must cease to be society. This is why we ought not to do evil that good may come; for at any rate this great evil has come, that we have done evil and are made wicked thereby. In like manner, if I let myself believe anything on insufficient evidence, there may be no great harm done by the mere belief; it may be true after all, or I may never have occasion to exhibit it in outward acts. But I cannot help doing this great wrong towards Man, that I make myself credulous. The danger to society is not merely that it should believe wrong things, though that is great enough; but that it should become credulous, and lose the habit of testing things and inquiring into them; for then it must sink back into savagery.

The harm which is done by credulity in a man is not confined to the fostering of a credulous character in others, and consequent support of false beliefs. Habitual want of care about what I believe leads to habitual want of care in others about the truth of what is told to me. Men speak the truth to one another when each reveres the truth in his own mind and in the other's mind; but how shall my friend revere the truth in my mind when I myself am careless about it, when I believe things because I want to believe them, and because they are comforting and pleasant? Will he not learn to cry, "Peace," to me, when there is no peace? By such a course I shall surround myself with a thick atmosphere of falsehood and fraud, and in that I must live. It may matter little to me, in my cloud-castle of sweet illusions and darling lies; but it matters much to Man that I have made my neighbours ready to deceive. The credulous man is father to the liar and the cheat; he lives in the bosom of this his family, and it is no marvel if he should become even as they are. So closely are our duties knit together, that whoso shall keep the whole law, and yet offend in one point, he is guilty of all.

To sum up: it is wrong always, everywhere, and for anyone, to believe anything upon insufficient evidence.

If a man, holding a belief which he was taught in childhood or persuaded of afterwards, keeps down and pushes away any doubts which arise about it in his mind, purposely avoids the reading of books and the company of men that call in question or discuss it, and regards as impious those questions which cannot easily be asked without disturbing it—the life of that man is one long sin against mankind.

If this judgment seems harsh when applied to those simple souls who have never known better, who have been brought up from the cradle with a horror of doubt, and taught that their eternal welfare depends on *what* they believe, then it leads to the very serious question, *Who hath made Israel to sin?*

It may be permitted me to fortify this judgment with the sentence of Milton:[1]

"A man may be a heretic in the truth; and if he believe things only because his pastor says so, or the assembly so determine, without knowing other reason, though his belief be true, yet the very truth he holds becomes his heresy."

And with this famous aphorism of Coleridge:[2]

"He who begins by loving Christianity better than Truth, will proceed by loving his own sect or Church better than Christianity, and end in loving himself better than all."

Inquiry into the evidence of a doctrine is not to be made once for all, and then taken as finally settled. It is never lawful to stifle a doubt; for either it can be honestly answered by means of the inquiry already made, or else it proves that the inquiry was not complete.

"But," says one, "I am a busy man; I have no time for the long course of study which would be necessary to make me in any degree a competent judge of certain questions, or even able to understand the nature of the arguments." Then he should have no time to believe.

NOTES

1. *Areopagitica.*
2. *Aids to Reflection.*

WILLIAM JAMES

The Will to Believe

In an essay that responds directly to Clifford William James (1842–1910) argues for the "will to believe"—or, more accurately, the *right* to believe—in some cases in which we lack the strong supporting evidence Clifford considers essential. In the case of "genuine options"—choices which are "living, forced and momentous"—we may and indeed must make our decisions to believe or disbelieve with our "passional nature." It should be noted, however, that James endorses this course only when clear-cut, objective evidence is unavailable; he does not advocate ignoring or defying the evidence.

From *Essays in Pragmatism.* New York: Hafner, 1969.

⌘

Let us give the name of *hypothesis* to anything that may be proposed to our belief; and just as the electricians speak of live and dead wires, let us speak of any hypothesis as either *live* or *dead*. A live hypothesis is one which appeals as a real possibility to him to whom it is proposed. If I ask you to believe in the Mahdi, the notion makes no electric connection with your nature—it refuses to scintillate with any credibility at all. As an hypothesis it is completely dead. To an Arab, however (even if he be not one of the Mahdi's followers), the hypothesis is among the mind's possibilities: it is alive. This shows that deadness and liveness in an hypothesis are not intrinsic properties, but relations to the individual thinker. They are measured by his willingness to act. The maximum of liveness in an hypothesis means willingness to act irrevocably. Practically, that means belief; but there is some believing tendency wherever there is willingness to act at all.

Next, let us call the decision between two hypotheses an *option*. Options may be of several kinds. They may be—first, *living* or *dead*; secondly, *forced* or *avoidable*; thirdly, *momentous* or *trivial*; and for our purposes we may call an option a *genuine* option when it is of the forced, living, and momentous kind.

1. A living option is one in which both hypotheses are live ones. If I say to you: "Be a theosophist or be a Mohammedan," it is probably a dead option, because for you neither hypothesis is likely to be alive. But if I say: "Be an agnostic or be a Christian," it is otherwise: trained as you are, each hypothesis makes some appeal, however small, to your belief.

2. Next, if I say to you: "Choose between going out with your umbrella or without it," I do not offer you a genuine option, for it is not forced. You can easily avoid it by not going out at all. Similarly, if I say, "Either love me or hate me," "Either call my theory true or call it false," your option is avoidable. You may remain indifferent to me, neither loving nor hating, and you may decline to offer any judgment as to my theory. But if I say, "Either accept this truth or go without it," I put on you a forced option, for there is no standing place outside of the alternative. Every dilemma based on a complete logical disjunction, with no possibility of not choosing, is an option of this forced kind.

3. Finally, if I were Dr. Nansen and proposed to you to join my North Pole expedition, your option would be momentous; for this would probably be your only similar opportunity, and your choice now would either exclude you from the North Pole sort of immortality altogether or put at least the chance of it into your hands. He who refuses to embrace a unique opportunity loses the prize as surely as if he tried and failed. *Per contra*, the option is trivial when the opportunity is not unique, when the stake is insignificant, or when the decision is reversible if it later proves unwise. Such trivial options abound in the scientific life. A chemist finds an hypothesis live enough to spend a year in its verification: he believes in it to that extent. But if his

experiments prove inconclusive either way, he is quit for his loss of time, no vital harm being done.

It will facilitate our discussion if we keep all these distinctions well in mind.

The next matter to consider is the actual psychology of human opinion. . . . Evidently . . . our non-intellectual nature does influence our convictions. There are passional tendencies and volitions which run before and others which come after belief, and it is only the latter that are too late for the fair; and they are not too late when the previous passional work has been already in their own direction. . . . The state of things is evidently far from simple; and pure insight and logic, whatever they might do ideally, are not the only things that really do produce our creeds.

Our next duty, having recognized this mixed-up state of affairs, is to ask whether it be simply reprehensible and pathological, or whether, on the contrary, we must treat it as a normal element in making up our minds. The thesis I defend is, briefly stated, this: *Our passional nature not only lawfully may, but must, decide an option between propositions, whenever it is a genuine option that cannot by its nature be decided on intellectual grounds; for to say, under such circumstances, "Do not decide, but leave the question open," is itself a passional decision—just like deciding yes or no—and is attended with the same risk of losing the truth.* The thesis thus abstractly expressed will, I trust, soon become quite clear. . . .

There are two ways of looking at our duty in the matter of opinion—ways entirely different, and yet ways about whose difference the theory of knowledge seems hitherto to have shown very little concern. *We must know the truth*; and *we must avoid error*—these are our first and great commandments as would-be knowers; but they are not two ways of stating an identical commandment, they are two separable laws. Although it may indeed happen that when we believe the truth *A*, we escape as an incidental consequence from believing the falsehood *B*, it hardly ever happens that by merely disbelieving *B* we necessarily believe *A*. We may in escaping *B* fall into believing other falsehoods, *C* or *D*, just as bad as *B*; or we may escape *B* by not believing anything at all, not even *A*.

Believe truth! Shun error!—these, we see, are two materially different laws; and by choosing between them we may end by coloring differently our whole intellectual life. We may regard the chase for truth as paramount, and the avoidance of error as secondary; or we may, on the other hand, treat the avoidance of error as more imperative, and let truth take its chance. Clifford . . . exhorts us to the latter course. Believe nothing, he tells us, keep your mind in suspense forever, rather than by closing it on insufficient evidence incur the awful risk of believing lies. You, on the other hand, may think that the risk of being in error is a very small matter when compared with the blessings of real knowledge, and be ready to be duped many times in your investigation rather than postpone indefinitely the chance of guessing true. I myself find it impossible to go with Clifford. We must remember that these feelings of our duty about either truth or error are in any case only expressions of our passional life. Biologically considered, our minds are as ready to grind out falsehood as veracity, and he who says, "Better go without belief forever than believe a lie!" merely shows his own preponderant private horror of becoming a dupe. He may be critical of many of his desires and fears, but this fear he slavishly obeys. He cannot imagine any one questioning its binding force. For my own part, I have also a horror of being duped; but I can believe that worse things than being duped may happen to a man in this world: so Clifford's exhortation has to my ears a thoroughly fantastic sound. It is like a general informing his soldiers that it is better to keep out of battle forever than to risk a single wound. Not so are victories either over enemies or over nature gained. Our errors are surely not such awfully solemn things. In a world where we are so certain to incur them in spite of all our caution, a certain lightness of heart seems healthier than this excessive nervousness on their behalf. At any rate, it seems the fittest thing for the empiricist philosopher.

And now, after all this introduction, let us go straight at our question. I have said, and now repeat it, that not only as a matter of fact do we find our passional nature influencing us in our opinions, but that there are some options between opinions in which this influence must be regarded both as an inevitable and as a lawful determinant of our choice.

I fear here that some of you my hearers will begin to scent danger, and lend an inhospitable ear. Two first steps of passion you have indeed had to admit as necessary—we must think so as to avoid dupery, and we must think so as to gain truth; but the surest path to those ideal consummations, you will probably consider, is from now onwards to take no further passional step.

Well, of course, I agree as far as the facts will allow. Wherever the option between losing truth and gaining it is not momentous, we can throw the chance of *gaining truth* away, and at any rate save ourselves from any chance of *believing falsehood*, by not making up our minds at all till objective evidence has come. In scientific questions, this is almost always the case; and even in human affairs in general, the need of acting is seldom so urgent that a false belief to act on is better than no belief at all. Law courts, indeed, have to decide on the best evidence attainable for the moment, because a judge's duty is to make law as well as to ascertain it, and (as a learned judge once said to me) few cases are worth spending much time over: the great thing is to have them decided on *any* acceptable principle, and got out of the way. But in our dealings with objective nature we obviously are recorders, not makers, of the truth; and decisions for the mere sake of deciding promptly and getting on to the next business would be wholly out of place. Throughout the breadth of physical nature facts are what they are quite independently of us, and seldom is there any such hurry about them that the risks of being duped by believing a premature theory need be faced. The questions here are always trivial options, the hypotheses are hardly living (at any rate not living for us spectators), the choice between believing truth or falsehood is seldom forced. The attitude of sceptical balance is therefore the absolutely wise one if we would escape mistakes. What difference, indeed, does it make to most of us whether we have or have not a theory of the Röntgen rays, whether we believe or not in mind-stuff, or have a conviction about the causality of conscious states? It makes no difference. Such options are not forced on us. On every account it is better not to make them, but still keep weighing reasons *pro et contra* with an indifferent hand.

I speak, of course, here of the purely judging mind. For purposes of discovery such indifference is to be less highly recommended, and science would be far less advanced than she is if the passionate desires of individuals to get their own faiths confirmed had been kept out of the game. See for example the sagacity which Spencer and Weismann now display. On the other hand, if you want an absolute duffer in an investigation, you must, after all, take the man who has no interest whatever in its results: he is the warranted incapable, the positive fool. The most useful investigator, because the most sensitive observer, is always he whose eager interest in one side of the question is balanced by an equally keen nervousness lest he become deceived. Science has organized this nervousness into a regular *technique*, her so-called method of verification; and she has fallen so deeply in love with the method that one may even say she has ceased to care for truth by itself at all. It is only truth as technically verified that interests her. The truth of truths might come in merely affirmative form, and she would decline to touch it. Such truth as that, she might repeat with Clifford, would be stolen in defiance of her duty to mankind. Human passions, however, are stronger than technical rules. *"Le cœur a ses raisons,"* as Pascal says, *"que la raison ne connaît pas"*; and however indifferent to all but the bare rules of the game the umpire, the abstract intellect, may be, the concrete players who furnish him the materials to judge of are usually, each one of them, in love with some pet "live hypothesis" of his own. Let us agree, however, that wherever there is no forced option, the dispassionately judicial intellect with no pet hypothesis, saving us, as it does, from dupery at any rate, ought to be our ideal.

The question next arises: Are there not somewhere forced options in our speculative questions, and can we (as men who may be interested at least as much in positively gaining truth as in merely escaping dupery) always wait with impunity till the coercive evidence shall have arrived? It seems *a priori* improbable that the truth should be so nicely adjusted to our needs and powers as that. In the great boarding-house of nature, the cakes and the butter and the syrup seldom come out so even and leave the plates so clean. Indeed, we should view them with scientific suspicion if they did.

Moral questions immediately present themselves as questions whose solution cannot wait for sensible proof. A moral question is a question not of what sensibly exists, but of what is good, or would be good if it did exist. Science can tell us what exists; but to compare the *worths*, both of what exists and of what does not exist, we must consult not science, but what Pascal calls our heart. Science herself consults her heart when she lays it down that the infinite ascertainment of fact and correction of false belief are the supreme goods for man. Challenge the statement, and science can only repeat it oracularly, or else prove it by showing that such ascertainment and correction bring man all sorts of other goods which man's heart in turn declares. The question of having moral beliefs at all or not having them is decided by our will. Are our moral preferences true or false, or are they only odd biological phenomena, making things good or bad for *us*, but in themselves indifferent? How can your pure intellect decide? If your heart does not *want* a world of moral reality, your head will assuredly never make you believe in one. Mephistophelian scepticism, indeed, will satisfy the head's play-instincts much better than any rigorous idealism can. Some men (even at the student age) are so naturally cool-hearted that the moralistic hypothesis never has for them any pungent life, and in their supercilious presence the hot young moralist always feels strangely ill at ease. The appearance of knowingness is on their side, of *naïveté* and gullibility on his. Yet, in the inarticulate heart of him, he clings to it that he is not a dupe, and that there is a realm in which (as Emerson says) all their wit and intellectual superiority is no better than the cunning of a fox. Moral scepticism can no more be refuted or proved by logic than intellectual scepticism can. When we stick to it that there *is* truth (be it of either kind), we do so with our whole nature, and resolve to stand or fall by the results. The sceptic with his whole nature adopts the doubting attitude; but which of us is the wiser, Omniscience only knows.

Turn now from these wide questions of good to a certain class of questions of fact, questions concerning personal relations, states of mind between one man and another. *Do you like me or not?*—for example. Whether you do or not depends, in countless instances, on whether I meet you half-way, am willing to assume that you must like me, and show you trust and expectation. The previous faith on my part in your liking's existence is in such cases what makes your liking come. But if I stand aloof, and refuse to budge an inch until I have objective evidence, until you shall have done something apt, as the absolutists say, *ad extorquendum assensum meum*, ten to one your liking never comes. How many women's hearts are vanquished by the mere sanguine insistence of some man that they *must* love him! He will not consent to the hypothesis that they cannot. The desire for a certain kind of truth here brings about that special truth's existence; and so it is in innumerable cases of other sorts. Who gains promotions, boons, appointments, but the man in whose life they are seen to play the part of live hypotheses, who discounts them, sacrifices other things for their sake before they have come, and takes risks for them in advance? His faith acts on the powers above him as a claim, and creates its own verification.

A social organism of any sort whatever, large or small, is what it is because each member proceeds to his own duty with a trust that the other members will simultaneously do theirs. Wherever a desired result is achieved by the co-operation of many independent persons, its existence as a fact is a pure consequence of the precursive faith in one another of those immediately concerned. A government, an army, a commercial system, a ship, a college, an athletic team, all exist on this condition, without which not only is nothing achieved, but nothing is even attempted. A whole train of passengers (individually brave enough) will be looted by a few highwaymen, simply because the latter can count on one another, while each passenger fears that if he makes a movement of resistance, he will be shot before any one else backs him up. If we believed that the whole car-full would rise at once with us, we should each severally rise, and train-robbing would never even be attempted. There are, then, cases where a fact cannot come at all unless a preliminary faith exists in its coming. *And where faith in a fact can help create the fact,* that would be an insane logic which should say that faith running ahead of scientific evidence is the "lowest kind of immorality" into which a thinking being can fall. Yet such is the logic by which our scientific absolutists pretend to regulate our lives!

In truths dependent on our personal action, then, faith based on desire is certainly a lawful and possibly an indispensable thing.

But now, it will be said, these are all childish human cases, and have nothing to do with great cosmical matters, like the question of religious faith. Let us then pass on to that. Religions differ so much in their accidents that in discussing the religious question we must make it very generic and broad. What then do we now mean by the religious hypothesis? Science says things are; morality says some things are better than other things; and religion says essentially two things.

First, she says that the best things are the more eternal things, the overlapping things, the things in the universe that throw the last stone, so to speak, and say the final word. "Perfection is eternal"—this phrase of Charles Secrétan seems a good way of putting this first affirmation of religion, an affirmation which obviously cannot yet be verified scientifically at all.

The second affirmation of religion is that we are better off even now if we believe her first affirmation to be true.

Now, let us consider what the logical elements of this situation are *in case the religious hypothesis in both its branches be really true.* (Of course, we must admit that possibility at the outset. If we are to discuss the question at all, it must involve a living option. If for any of you religion be a hypothesis that cannot, by any living possibility, be true, then you need go no farther. I speak to the "saving remnant" alone.) So proceeding, we see, first, that religion offers itself as a *momentous* option. We are supposed to gain, even now, by our belief, and to lose by our non-belief, a certain vital good. Secondly, religion is a *forced* option, so far as that good goes. We cannot escape the issue by remaining sceptical and waiting for more light, because, although we do avoid error in that way *if religion be untrue,* we lose the good, *if it be true,* just as certainly as if we positively chose to disbelieve. It is as if a man should hesitate indefinitely to ask a certain woman to marry him because he was not perfectly sure that she would prove an angel after he brought her home. Would he not cut himself off from that particular angel-possibility as decisively as if he went and married some one else? Scepticism, then, is not avoidance of option; it is option of a certain particular kind of risk. *Better risk less of truth than chance of error*—that is your faith-vetoer's exact position. He is actively playing his stake as much as the believer is; he is backing the field against the religious hypothesis, just as the believer is backing the religious hypothesis against the field. To preach scepticism to us as a duty until "sufficient evidence" for religion be found, is tantamount therefore to telling us, when in presence of the religious hypothesis, that to yield to our fear of its being error is wiser and better than to yield to our hope that it may be true. It is not intellect against all passions, then; it is only intellect with one passion laying down its law. And by what, forsooth, is the supreme wisdom of this passion warranted? Dupery for dupery, what proof is there that dupery through hope is so much worse than dupery through fear? I, for one, can see no proof; and I simply refuse obedience to the scientist's command to imitate his kind of option, in a case where my own stake is important enough to give me the right to choose my own form of risk. If religion be true and the evidence for it be still insufficient, I do not wish, by putting your extinguisher upon my nature (which feels to me as if it had after all some business in this matter), to forfeit my sole chance in life of getting upon the winning side—that chance depending, of course, on my willingness to run the risk of acting as if my passional need of taking the world religiously might be prophetic and right.

All this is on the supposition that it really may be prophetic and right, and that, even to us who are discussing the matter, religion is a live hypothesis which may be true. Now, to most of us religion comes in a still further way that makes a veto on our active faith even more illogical. The more perfect and more eternal aspect of the universe is represented in our religions as having personal form. The universe is no longer a mere *It* to us, but a *Then,* if we are religious; and any relation that may be possible from person to person might be possible here. For instance, although in one sense we are passive portions of the universe, in another we show a curious autonomy, as if we were small active centres on our own account. We feel, too, as if the appeal of religion to us were made to our own active good-will, as if evidence might be forever withheld from us unless we met the hypothesis half-way. To take a trivial illustration: just as a man who in a company of gentlemen made no advances, asked a warrant for every concession, and believed no one's word without proof, would cut himself off by such churlishness from all the social rewards that a more trusting spirit would earn—so here, one who should shut himself up in snarling logicality and try to make the gods extort his recognition willy-nilly, or not get it at all, might cut himself off forever from his only opportunity of making the gods' acquaintance. This feeling, forced on us we know not whence, that by obstinately believing that there are gods (although not to do so would be so easy both for our logic and our life) we are doing the universe the deepest service we can, seems part of the living essence of the religious hypothesis. If the hypothesis *were* true in all its parts, including this one, then pure intellectualism, with its veto on our making willing advances, would be an absurdity; and some participation of our sympathetic nature would be logically required. I, therefore, for one, cannot see my way to accepting the agnostic rules for truth-seeking, or wilfully agree to keep my willing nature out of the game. I cannot do so for this plain reason, that *a rule of thinking which would absolutely prevent me from acknowledging certain kinds of truth if these kinds of truth were really there, would be an irrational rule.* That for me is the long and short of the formal logic of the situation, no matter what the kinds of truth might materially be.

I confess I do not see how this logic can be escaped. But sad experience makes me fear that some of you may still shrink from radically saying with me, *in abtracts,* that we have the rights to believe at our own risk any hypothesis that is live enough to tempt our will. I suspect, however, that if this is so, it is because you have got away from the abstract logical point of view altogether, and are thinking (perhaps without realizing it) of some particular religious hypothesis which for you is dead. The freedom to "believe what we will" you apply to the case of some patent superstition; and the faith you think of is the faith defined by the schoolboy when he said, "Faith is when you believe something that you know ain't true." I can only repeat that this is misapprehension. *In concreto,* the freedom to believe can only cover living options which the intellect of the individual cannot by itself resolve; and living options never seem absurdities to him who has them to consider. When I look at the religious question as it really puts itself to concrete men, and when I think of all the possibilities which both practically and theoretically it involves, then this command that we shall put a stopper on our hearts, instincts, and courage, and *wait*—acting of course meanwhile more or less as if religion were *not* true[1]—till doomsday, or till such time as our intellect and senses working together may have raked in evidence enough—this command, I say, seems to me the queerest idol ever manufactured in the philosophic cave. Were we scholastic absolutists, there might be more excuse. If we had an infallible intellect with its objective certitudes, we might feel ourselves disloyal to such a perfect organ of knowledge in not trusting to it exclusively, in not waiting for its releasing word. But if we are empiricists, if we believe that no bell in us tolls to let us know for certain when truth is in our grasp, then it seems a piece of idle fantasticality to preach so solemnly our duty of waiting for the bell. Indeed we *may* wait if we will—I hope you do not think that I am denying that—but if we do so, we do so at our peril as much as if we believed. In either case we *act,* taking our life in our hands. No one of us ought to issue vetoes to the other, nor should we bandy words of abuse. We ought, on the contrary, delicately and profoundly to respect one another's mental freedom: then only shall we bring about the intellectual republic; then only shall we have that spirit of inner tolerance without which all our outer tolerance is soulless, and which is empiricism's glory; then only shall we live and let live, in speculative as well as in practical things.

NOTE

1. Since belief is measured by action, he who forbids us to believe religion to be true, necessarily also forbids us to act as we should if we did believe it to be true. The whole defence of religious faith hinges upon action. If the action required or inspired by the religious hypothesis is in no way different from that dictated by the naturalistic hypothesis, then religious faith is a pure superfluity, better pruned away, and controversy about its legitimacy is a piece of idle trifling, unworthy of serious minds. I myself believe, of course, that the religious hypothesis gives to the world an expression which specifically determines our reactions, and makes them in a large part unlike what they might be on a purely naturalistic scheme of belief.

SØREN KIERKEGAARD

Truth Is Subjectivity

In this selection, Søren Kierkegaard (1813–1855) strongly emphasizes the deeply subjective and personal nature of religious faith. While he does not deny that there is a difference between truth and falsehood, he insists that an attitude of detached, objective inquiry is totally inappropriate in religious matters. In religious matters, he maintains, what is critical is the *way in which one is related* to the truth that one believes. Interestingly, Kierkegaard stresses that in order to have a vital *faith* it is essential that one should *not* be able to prove that one's belief is true.

⌘

In an attempt to make clear the difference of way that exists between an objective and a subjective reflection, I shall now proceed to show how a subjective reflection makes its way inwardly in inwardness. Inwardness in an existing subject culminates in passion; corresponding to passion in the subject the truth becomes a paradox; and the fact that the truth becomes a paradox is rooted precisely in its having a relationship to an existing subject. Thus the one corresponds to the other. By forgetting that one is an existing subject, passion goes by the board and the truth is no longer a paradox; the knowing subject becomes a fantastic entity rather than a human being, and the truth becomes a fantastic object for the knowledge of this fantastic entity.

When the question of truth is raised in an objective manner, reflection is directed objectively to the truth, as an object to which the knower is related. Reflection is not focussed upon the relationship, however, but upon the question of whether it is the truth to which the knower is related. If only the object to which he is related is the truth, the subject is accounted to be in the truth. When the question of the truth is raised subjectively, reflection is directed subjectively to the nature of the individual's relationship; if only the mode of this relationship is in the truth, the individual is in the truth even if he should happen to be thus related to what is not true. Let us take as an example the knowledge of God. Objectively, reflection is directed to the problem of whether this object is the true God; subjectively, reflection is directed to the question whether the individual is related to a something *in such a manner* that his relationship is in truth a God-relationship. On which side is the truth now to be found? Ah, may we not here resort to a mediation, and say: It is on neither side, but in the mediation of both? Excellently well said, provided we might have it explained how an existing individual manages to be in a state of mediation. For to be in a state of mediation is to be finished, while to exist is to become. Nor can an existing individual be in two places at the same time—he cannot be an identity of subject and object. When he is nearest to being in two places at the same time he is in passion; but passion is momentary, and passion is also the highest expression of subjectivity.

The existing individual who chooses to pursue the objective way enters upon the entire approximation process by which it is proposed to bring God to light objectively. But this is in all eternity impossible, because God is a subject, and therefore exists only for subjectivity in inwardness. The existing individual who chooses the subjective way apprehends instantly the entire dialectical difficulty involved in having to use some time, perhaps a long time, in finding God objectively; and he feels this dialectical difficulty in all its painfulness, because every moment is wasted in which he does not have God. That very instant he has God, not by virtue of any objective deliberation, but by virtue of the infinite passion of inwardness. The objective inquirer, on the other hand, is not embarrassed by such dialectical difficulties as are involved in devoting an entire period of investigation to finding God—since it is possible that the inquirer may die tomorrow; and if he lives he can scarcely regard God as something to be taken along if convenient, since God is precisely that which one takes *a tout prix*, which in the understanding of passion constitutes the true inward relationship to God.

It is at this point, so difficult dialectically, that the way swings off for everyone who knows what it means to think, and to think existentially; which is something very different from sitting at a desk and writing about what one has never done, something very different from writing *de omnibus dubitandum* and at the same time being as credulous existentially as the most sensuous of men. Here is where the way swings off, and the change is marked by the fact that while objective knowledge rambles comfortably on by way of the long road of approximation without being impelled by the urge of passion, subjective knowledge counts every delay a deadly peril, and the decision so infinitely important and so instantly pressing that it is as if the opportunity had already passed.

Now when the problem is to reckon up on which side there is most truth, whether on the side of one who seeks the true God objectively, and pursues the approximate truth of the God-idea; or on the side of one who, driven by the infinite passion of his need of God, feels an infinite concern for his own relationship to God in truth (and to be at one and the same time on both sides equally, is as we have noted not possible for an existing individual, but is merely the happy delusion of an imaginary I-am-I): the answer cannot be in doubt for anyone who has not been demoralized with the aid of science. If one who lives in the midst of Christendom goes up to the house of God, the house of the true God, with the true conception of God in his knowledge, and prays, but prays in a false spirit; and one who lives in an idolatrous community prays with the entire passion of the infinite, although his eyes rest upon the image of an idol: where is there most truth? The one prays in truth to God though he worships an idol; the other prays falsely to the true God, and hence worships in fact an idol.

When one man investigates objectively the problem of immortality, and another embraces an uncertainty with the passion of the infinite: where is there most truth, and who has the greater certainty? The one has entered upon a never-ending approximation, for the certainty of immortality lies precisely in the subjectivity of the individual; the other is immortal, and fights for his immortality by struggling with the uncertainty. Let us consider Socrates. Nowadays everyone dabbles in a few proofs; some have several such proofs, other fewer. But Socrates! He puts the question objectively in a problematic manner: *if* there is an immortality. He must therefore be accounted a doubter in comparison with one of our modern thinkers with the three proofs? By no means. On this "if" he risks his entire life, he has the courage to meet death, and he has with the passion of the infinite so determined the pattern of his life that it must be found acceptable—*if* there is an immortality. Is any better proof capable of being given for the immortality of the soul? But those who have the three proofs do not at all determine their lives in conformity therewith; if there is an immortality it must feel disgust over their manner of life: can any better refutation be given of the three proofs? The bit of uncertainty that Socrates had, helped him because he himself contributed the passion of the infinite; the three proofs that the others have do not profit them at all, because they are dead to spirit and enthusiasm, and their three proofs, in lieu of proving anything else, prove just this. A young girl may enjoy all the sweetness of love on the basis of what is merely a weak hope that she is beloved, because she rests everything on this weak hope; but many a wedded matron more than once subjected to the strongest expressions of love, has in so far indeed had proofs, but strangely enough has not enjoyed *quod erat demonstrandum*. The Socratic ignorance, which Socrates held fast with the entire passion of his inwardness, was thus an expression for the principle that the eternal truth is related to an existing individual, and that this truth must therefore be a paradox for him as long as he exists; and yet it is possible that there was more truth in the Socratic ignorance as it was in him, than in the entire objective truth of the System, which flirts with what the times demand and accommodates itself to *Privatdocents*.

The objective accent falls on WHAT is said, the subjective accent on HOW it is said. This distinction holds even in the aesthetic realm, and receives definite expression in the principle that what is in itself true may in the mouth of such and such a person become untrue. In these times this distinction is particularly worthy of notice, for if we wish to express in a single sentence the difference between ancient times and our own, we should doubtless have to say: "In ancient times only an individual here and there knew the truth; now all know it, except that the inwardness of its appropriation stands in an inverse relationship to the extent of its dissemination. Aesthetically the contradiction that truth becomes untruth in this or that person's mouth, is best construed comically: In the ethico-religious sphere, accent is again on the "how." But this is not to be understood as referring to demeanor, expression, or the like; rather it refers to the relationship sustained by the existing individual, in his own existence, to the content of his utterance. Objectively the interest focussed merely on the thought-content, subjectively on the inwardness. At its maximum this inward "how" is the passion of the infinite, and the passion of the infinite is the truth. But the passion of the infinite is precisely subjectivity, and thus subjectivity becomes the truth. Objectively there is no infinite decisiveness, and hence it is objectively in order to annul the difference between good and evil, together with the principle of contradiction, and therewith also the infinite difference between the true and the false. Only in subjectivity is there decisiveness, to seek objectivity is to be in error. It is the passion of the infinite that is the decisive factor and not its content, for its content is precisely itself. In this manner subjectivity and the subjective "how" constitute the truth.

But the "how" which is thus subjectivity accentuated precisely because the subject is an existing individual, is also subject to a dialectic with respect to time. In the passionate moment of decision, where the road swings away from objective knowledge, it seems as if the infinite decision were thereby realized. But in the same moment the existing individual finds himself in the temporal order, and the subjective "how" is transformed into a striving, a striving which receives indeed its impulse and a repeated renewal from the decisive passion of the infinite, but is nevertheless a striving.

When subjectivity is the truth, the conceptual determination of the truth must include an expression for the antithesis to objectivity, a memento of the fork in the road where the way swings off; this expression will at the same time serve as an indication of the tension of the subjective inwardness. Here is such a definition of truth: *An objective uncertainty held fast in an appropriation-process of the most passionate inwardness is the truth*, the highest truth attainable for an *existing* individual. At the point where the way swings off (and where this is cannot be specified objectively, since it is a matter of subjectivity), there objective knowledge is placed in abeyance. Thus the subject merely has, objectively, the uncertainty; but it is this which precisely increases the tension of that infinite passion which constitutes his inwardness. The truth is precisely the venture which chooses an objective uncertainty with the passion of the infinite. I contemplate the order of nature in the hope of finding God, and I see omnipotence and wisdom; but I also see much else that disturbs my mind and excites anxiety. The sum of all this is an objective uncertainty. But it is for this very reason that the inwardness becomes as intense as it is, for it embraces this objective uncertainty with the entire passion of the infinite. In the case of a mathematical proposition the objectivity is given, but for this reason the truth of such a proposition is also an indifferent truth.

But the above definition of truth is an equivalent expression for faith. Without risk there is no faith. Faith is precisely the contradiction between the infinite passion of the individual's inwardness and the objective uncertainty. If I am capable of grasping God objectively, I do not believe, but precisely because I cannot do this I must believe. If I wish to preserve myself in faith I must constantly be intent upon holding fast the objective uncertainty, so as to remain out upon the deep, over seventy thousand fathoms of water, still preserving my faith.

WILLIAM J. ABRAHAM

Soft Rationalism

In advocating "soft rationalism," William J. Abraham (1947–) mediates in a certain way between the more extreme and opposing views represented in the two preceding selections. He rejects the "hard rationalism" of Clifford and (to a certain extent) Aquinas, which holds that there must be rationally conclusive evidence for what one believes. On the other hand, Abraham also rejects the "fideism" of Kierkegaard (and, to a lesser extent, of Pascal and William James), according to which the truth-claims of religion are not subject to rational adjudication. He maintains that there are ways in which "global metaphysical systems" such as those found in religious belief can be rationally assessed, and that it is appropriate and desirable to engage in such assessment. At the same time, he acknowledges that such assessment is quite difficult and that it may sometimes be impossible in practice for those with different starting-points to reach agreement.

⌘

Soft rationalism is essentially a claim about the kind of argument that should take place in debates about significant religious beliefs. It attempts to lay bare the general character of the arguments which really make sense of the kind of disputes which take place between believers and nonbelievers. The central tenets of soft rationalism can be laid out as follows.

There are three main points. First, religious belief should be assessed as a rounded whole rather than taken in stark isolation. Christianity, for ex-

From William J. Abraham, *An Introduction to the Philosophy of Religion.* Copyright © 1985, pp. 104–113. Reprinted by permission of Prentice Hall, Englewood Cliffs, N.J.

ample, like other world faiths, is a complex, large-scale system of belief which must be seen as a whole before it is assessed. To break it up into disconnected parts is to mutilate and distort its true character. We can, of course, distinguish certain elements in the Christian faith, but we must still stand back and see it as a complex interaction of these elements. We need to see it as a metaphysical system, as a world view, that is total in its scope and range. We can develop this viewpoint by briefly schematizing the content of the Christian religion. Consider the following minimal outline of the Christian faith.

Christians believe that the whole universe is created and sustained by God, a transcendent, invisible, personal agent who is omnipotent, omniscient, and all good. Thus it attempts to say why the world exists and why it is partly as it is by saying that it is the effect of the action of God. Along with these beliefs about the natural world, Christians hold certain beliefs about human beings. Human beings are made in the image of God, and their fate depends on their relationship with God. They are free to respond to or reject God and they will be judged in accordance with how they respond to him. This judgment begins now but finally takes place beyond death in a life to come. Christians furthermore offer a diagnosis of what is wrong with the world. Fundamentally, they say, our problems are spiritual: we need to be made anew by God. Human beings have misused their freedom; they are in a state of rebellion against God; they are sinners. These conclusions lead to a set of solutions to this ill. As one might expect, the fundamental solution is again spiritual: in Israel and in Jesus of Nazareth God has intervened to save and remake mankind. Each individual needs to respond to this and become part of Christ's body, the church, where they are to grow in grace and become more like Christ. This in turn generates a certain vision of the future. In the coming of Jesus, God has inaugurated his kingdom, but it will be consummated at some unspecified time in the future when Christ returns and becomes all in all. All of these elements taken together generate a characteristically Christian ethic, which differs in key respects from other rival systems of morality.

We see here an overall theory about life with several dimensions which can be isolated but need to be seen as a whole. Christianity is one such theory. It offers an account of the world as a whole; a theory of human nature; a diagnosis of the world's ills; a prescription for those ills; a vision of the future; and a vision of morality which is intimately connected with these elements taken as a whole.

It might, of course, be questioned whether this is a fair account of the Christian faith. Clearly it is ridiculously brief, and it is much tidier than the rich vision which is passed on in the media of transmission within Christianity. However, if this account is rejected, some other account will have to be substituted. Otherwise we invite the charge of being obscurantist. Religion is inescapably a creedal affair, and fideists exaggerate if they insist it is impossible to summarize the faith. After all, that is what a creed is: it is a summary of the faith intended to fix its central reference points so that believers know what they believe. Fideists also exaggerate if they insist that such summaries become remote and lifeless. That can happen but it need not. Moreover, there is no objection in principle to articulating as clearly as possible the central concepts of religion. Clarity is not enough, nor is it essential to holiness of life; but neither are the pure in heart given special grace to become muddle-headed. Therefore soft rationalists are right to insist that the Christian tradition does offer an overall theory about life as a whole.

Much could be said about such overall theories. To begin with, there are many on the market. Marxism, humanism, existentialism are but three examples. Moreover, no one can avoid having some such theory. Here we vote with our feet; we may move from one to another, or live in accordance with elements of one one day and elements of another the next, but choice is inescapable. Therefore the only issue facing us is not, Shall we choose a theory of life as a whole?, but, Shall we choose as wisely as possible between the various options? With this we arrive at the second tenet of soft rationalism.

Assessment of such global theories is never a matter of simple demonstration or strict probabilistic reasoning. On the contrary, one appeals to various considerations which taken together lead one to say that one is true and another false. One develops what Basil Mitchell calls a cumulative case.[1] The different pieces of evidence taken in isolation are defective, but taken together they reinforce one another and add up to a substantial case. What is vital to realize is that there is no formal calculus into which all the evidence can be fitted and assessed. There is an irreducible element of personal judgment, which weighs up the evidence taken as a whole. Moreover, there is no agreed starting point, and there may well be dispute about what is to count as evidence, but this does not vitiate the process. What matters is not where you start but the total case you make out. Dispute about what is to count as evidence is to be weighed by sensitive personal judgment.

Philosophers and some theologians tend to become uneasy at this point. They fear a lurking subjectivism behind this appeal to personal judgment. They want hard evidence that is beyond doubt and dispute. It is precisely this that the soft rationalist rejects as irrational. Hard rationalists set the standards for rationality far too high for the subject matter. By so doing they pave the way for fideistic brands of theists and atheists. Fideistic theists are just hard rationalists who opt for theism. Hard rationalists appear the more rational because they seem tough-minded and are always insisting on clear, precise evidence which will fit into some sort of formal calculus. But this appearance of being more rational is an illusion, for hard rationalism is open to the following objection: hard rationalism cannot make sense of a whole range of debates which depend for their existence on cumulative case arguments. This objection constitutes a *reductio ad absurdum* of the position of hard rationalism. We can develop this objection into a third positive thesis of soft rationalism.

The kind of assessment proposed by soft rationalism is a genuine rational assessment because cumulative-case arguments are generally accepted as reliable. Without such arguments we could make no sense of the disputes that go on in fields as diverse as jurisprudence, literary exegesis, history, philosophy, and science. Some of these may involve strict demonstration and strict probability arguments, but that is not the whole story. All of these arguments often involve what we might call informal reasoning. They require judgments of plausibility. They involve an irreducible element of personal judgment, which cannot be measured by a formal calculus but which can be trained and rendered more sensitive. Hard rationalism would eliminate this, which is one reason why it needs to be attacked with a fair degree of vigor. It destroys the sensitivity for dialectic and dialogue; it inhibits the commitment to fair and sympathetic understanding to both sides in the argument.

That such arguments as soft rationalists appeal to exist is surely obvious. Theologians should be the first to recognize them, for work in exegesis, in the history of Israel, and in the history of the church depends crucially on such arguments. Consider, for example, the question of the priority of Mark. Was Mark the first gospel to be written? On this issue there is no demonstration and there is no strict probability argument. Yet there is surely a rational discussion; it is not a matter of blind opting; and the arguments are typically cumulative case arguments. So there can be no denying that they do exist and that they are a genuine expression of rationality.

What might be denied is that this type of reasoning can apply to global metaphysical systems. Thus it might be thought that cumulative-case arguments have a restricted role and only work in the field, say, of history or literary criticism but do not apply outside such areas. This, however, cannot be assumed in advance. We have to look and see if this type of reasoning does apply to disputes about metaphysical or religious systems. Let us explore this further and see if it is a fruitful way to consider the rationality of the Christian faith. We can helpfully approach this by sketching an imaginary intellectual pilgrimage from unbelief to belief.

SOFT RATIONALISM ILLUSTRATED

Rachel has been brought up on the edge of the Christian tradition. She knows enough about it to reject it as lacking credibility. Then one day a close friend is converted and begins taking the Christian faith in earnest. Initially Rachel accepts this as entirely normal; through time, however, she notices a profound change in her friend's life. What especially impresses her is the love which has come to characterize her friend. Casting around for an explanation of this change, she asks her friend what has happened. Her friend's reply is that any change for the better is due entirely to the grace of God in her life. When she explores this further, she understands it to mean that God has acted in her friend's life, giving her a deep sense of forgiveness and self-acceptance and filling her with love. In other words the change is due to the activity of God in her life. At first, Rachel was tempted to dismiss this as pious rambling, but somehow the explanation had a faint ring of truth about it. For a while she thought that the change could best be explained psychologically. However, these alternative explanations tended to be as debatable as the theistic alternative or were more on the level of hypothetical possibilities lacking specific backing for the case in hand. Thus the faint ring of truth in her friend's initial explanation remained, and she decided to explore the matter further.

She went to the library and began delving into the lives of such figures as Augustine, Luther, and Mother Teresa. Here she found her friend's experience vividly confirmed to a degree that amazed her. Those whose lives exhibited conspicuous sanctity invariably insisted that this was entirely due to the grace of God. In addition, she found that Augustine, for example, laid bare, in his *Confessions*, an incisive and penetrating analysis of evil and temptation which spoke very powerfully to her own condition, illuminating and exposing concealed corridors which she would have preferred remain closed. In other words, he presented an account of human nature and a diagnosis of its fragile and broken condition which found a very clear echo in her own experience.

That diagnosis was matched by a proposed solution which involved two distinct dimensions. On the one side, it involved a complex story of what God had done in Israel, in Jesus Christ, and in the church to bring liberation and new life to those caught in a web of self-service and spiritual indifference. In other words, Rachel found substantial claims about special revelation which fitted and illuminated her reading of the Christian scriptures and the historical events which lay behind them. The Christian creed, that is, made intelligible events and experiences which otherwise were puzzling and inexplicable. The other dimension to the solution was human. It called for a change of heart, a radical openness to God's Spirit, and a total trust in God for one's life and future. Rachel found this disturbing and shattering, yet attractive and adventurous. She found, for example, that the gospel story of God's sacrificial love deeply enriched her natural moral sense and inspired a measure of concern for others in herself which surprised and delighted her.

These experiences, in turn, led her to raise some old cosmic questions which had been hibernating since adolescence. She found herself at times overwhelmed by a sense of finitude and contingency. It puzzled her why there should be a world at all. Moreover, she found herself in pursuit of an explanation which would render intelligible the existence of order, beauty, and seeming design in nature. As she pondered these questions, in some detail, she sensed a fresh ring of truth in the overall vision proposed by the Christian tradition. That vision had immense explanatory power, as it made intelligible the fact and nature of the world by viewing these as effects of the activity of God.

All this led Rachel to embark on her own personal search for God. She continued reading in the Christian scriptures and attendant literature. She began participating in a local Christian community. She haltingly began to pray and make use of other means of grace. She found herself vividly aware of God in nature and at worship. She sensed God speaking intimately to her as she listened to the Gospel story and the call to commitment. She eventually gave herself over to God in faith and found a peace of soul which was profoundly authentic and long lasting.

At no point in this process is there any deductive proof nor is there any argument which could be formally set in a probability calculus. Rather a whole series of considerations come together over time to provide a cumulative case for the Christian creed. At every step objections of a rational character can arise. However, when examined they do not prove to be decisive, and the various elements provide mutual support and give credibility to commitment and faith.

This point has been succinctly made in a parable by Basil Mitchell.

> Two explorers find a hole in the ground, little more, perhaps than a slight depression. One of them says, "There is something funny about that hole; it doesn't look natural to me." The other says, "It's just an ordinary hole, and can be explained in a hundred and one different ways." Shortly afterwards they come upon a number of smaller holes in the same area as the first. The first explorer thinks they must be related to it: indeed he fancies that they have the same *sort* of oddness about them. The other pooh-poohs the idea. He sees nothing in any way remarkable about the holes—anything could have caused them, they are probably just natural depressions. Later, to their surprise, they find in a neighbouring cave a papyrus containing fragments of the plan of a building. "Ah," says the first explorer, "now I see what was odd about those holes; the big one was made to make the centre post of a wooden building, the smaller ones took the other posts."
>
> "All right," says the other, "we can soon test your theory. Let us take the fragments of your plan and piece them together on the site. If they fit, well and good, but they probably won't." So they take them to the site. The first explorer says he can see how the plan fits the site, and arranges the fragments accordingly, with what might be the centre of the roof over the largest hole. Then he sketches his reconstruction out on paper and shows it to his companion. "This is all very well," says the latter, "but you haven't accounted for all the holes or all the features shown in the fragments. The way the remainder fit is purely coincidental." The first explorer replies that he doesn't claim to know precisely what the original building was like, or how all the details fitted in. Moreover he thinks he can explain why some of the features mentioned in the plan should be missing in what remains on the site. If his impression of the character of the complete building is right, then these would be the first to be stolen or to disintegrate. "But," says the other, "the facts as we have them are compatible with a number of quite different interpretations. Each of them taken by itself can be explained away without much difficulty. And as for the fragmentary plan in the papyrus, of which you make such extensive use, it could well be an imaginative construction with no reference to the real world at all."

In the parable the original large hole represents the intellectual demand for ultimate explanation to which natural theology appeals. The smaller holes represent private religious experiences of sin, grace, etc. The fragmentary plan represents the concepts of the Christian revelation.[2]

THE VIRTUES OF SOFT RATIONALISM

This approach to the rationality of religious belief shows considerable promise. To begin, it would seem to capture and articulate the kind of reasoning which has a clear place in disputes between different belief systems. Thus it shows how interminable religious disputes can be, for they range over a whole network of phenomena and thus require great patience if they are to be understood and resolved. Moreover, it brings out the self-involving nature of religious belief by highlighting the crucial place of a person's religious experience in the total set of considerations which convince the believer. It also explains why becoming a believer is often a matter of conversion. Radical changes in one's metaphysical and religious commitments may have been brewing for a long time, but the actual change may take place quite quickly and dramatically. Exposure to revelation or a vivid awareness of the presence of God may be enough to lead one to reassess all the other strands in the case. One comes to organize one's world in a wholly new way and to develop a completely different perspective on life.

Furthermore, it does justice to the internal content of the Christian faith. The God in whom one comes to trust is not some idol invented by a philosopher; he is the God and father of Jesus Christ. The evidence which has been accumulating undergirds the total theistic vision rather than some isolated element within it. To be sure, that comprehensive vision is never static, for there are rival accounts of what the Christian faith is. But the tradition in its classical form, at least, has sufficient stability to bear adequate scrutiny. Also this account of the rationality of faith is entirely compatible with the emphasis on proclamation and call to repentance which is such a central feature of the Christian Gospel. Indeed these are elements which have to be weighed and taken into account in the deeply personal judgment which must ultimately be made.

This approach also attempts to do justice to those subjective elements which matter so much to religious believers. Clearly not just any experience leads to Christian commitment, but some characteristically do, and I have sought to acknowledge their proper epistemic significance. Note that this means that there is no question of the believer's relying on abstract philosophical evidence. The philosopher's task is more modest. He or she seeks to clarify the informal logic which operates in the life of faith. Some philosophers may well want to attempt to quantify the whole process and thus bring the matter within the domain of inductive logic. This is entirely laudatory so long as it is recognized that it is not essential to the rationality of informal reasoning. In recent years Richard Swinburne has attempted to a limited degree to achieve this end.[3]

Another feature of soft rationalism which commends it is its ability to make sense both of tenacity in believing and the certainty which often accompanies it. The latter stems from the believer's vivid sense of divine love commonly described as the witness of the Spirit. The former derives from the need to exercise patience in order to allow all the evidence to play its part. Equally it derives from the fact that, once believers commit themselves, they need to examine any counterevidence very carefully before concluding that it requires modification of their beliefs. Well-established convictions about matters of religious significance should not be abandoned at the first sign of trouble but should be weighed sensitively over time.

RESOLVING PROBLEMS IN SOFT RATIONALISM

Whatever the virtues in soft rationalism there are several problems within it that have to be faced.

First, when the soft rationalist speaks of, say, Marxism or traditional Christian theism as a metaphysical system or world view, it is clear that these terms are not simply descriptive in character. In fact it is very difficult to specify what they mean. World views are complex, dynamic traditions which interact with their intellectual environments, hence even to specify their content is to enter into a heated debate about what they actually embody. They tend to be elusive and subject to interpretation and reinterpretation in the light of new knowledge. This means that it is extremely difficult to pin them down and then proceed to determine whether they are rationally acceptable or not by appeal to a cumulative case argument. If this is so it becomes difficult to judge on the merits of a particular world view. For if understanding their claims is elusive and difficult, so too must their rationality, for until they are properly understood, they cannot be properly judged to be rational or irrational.

Secondly, there are several problems related to the crucial notion of personal judgment which need to be resolved. We can agree that the soft rationalist has drawn attention to something very important. In everyday disputes and scholarly debate, we do speak of a piece of evidence or a body of accumulated evidence as being beyond reasonable doubt, reasonable, persuasive, plausible, convincing, possessing rational force, intuitively compelling, and the like. However it is worth asking what kind of necessity such informal judgment has in rational evaluation. Is it logical or psychological necessity? Rod Sykes has raised the issue pointedly in this way.

> The epistemic Scrooge can admit that informal judgement is a psychological reality, that as a matter of fact we do usually depend on intuition and rarely consciously apply rules of thought. It is heuristically necessary, since adequate rules of good reasoning would be tediously complex to use: efficiency favours

> the use of intuition. Flying by feel is usually preferable to flying by the book, and the reason for this is that the former is more flexible and thus better able to meet sudden changes in conditions. But it must also be noted that flying by feel can quickly degenerate into flying by the seat of our pants, and that is where the book is the only thing that saves us. Similarly, intuition is useful in matters of rationality, even suggestive perhaps, but theoretically—and when things go wrong, pragmatically—dispensable. The difference must be noticed between a description of the psychology of an evaluative judgement (or its phenomenology—what it feels like to make such a judgement) and a description of its logical structure, which is to say of the justificational relations among propositions that underpin it. Soft Rationalism must argue that intuitive judgement is adequate as such a *logical* description.[4]

A legitimate worry behind Sykes's challenge is the fear that a person's judgment is liable to serious error. There is the danger of personal whim, bias, emotional involvement, and other non-rational factors adversely influencing the weighing of evidence. This is less likely where the canons or rules of critical thinking are objectively specified and deliberately followed. To rebut this the soft rationalist can reply that there is such a danger but it can be offset by an appeal not just to personal judgment but to *trained* personal judgment. Thus, as Mitchell points out, the ability to exercise rationality depends on having "appropriate intellectual, moral, and spiritual values."[5] One must be well educated in the relevant fields, be committed to the search for truth, be sensitive to any relevant moral, aesthetic, or spiritual possibilities, and the like. This is surely correct but it generates its own problems.

To begin it is not clear where or how one can receive such training to develop the appropriate skill to judge between world views. Such training is available, say, for debates about the meaning of disputed texts, the strength of a particular case presented in a court of law, the elegance of a particular scientific theory, and so on. However such training is not available for deciding between competing metaphysical interpretations of the universe.

Moreover, mastering all the relevant data and warrants needed to exercise the required personal judgment seems remote and impractical. For example, to arrive at a proper historical estimate of the scriptures of the world religions is a matter of heated debate between rival schools of experts. Yet this cannot be ignored if considerations from putative revelation are to be weighed as part of a cumulative case. Matters only become more elusive when one is invited to add up considerations derived from religious experience, classical natural theology, the existence of moral and natural evil, the existence of conspicuous sanctity, and so on. This is surely beyond the capabilities of most ordinary mortals.

Lastly, there is the danger that the process of weighing the rationality of world views is thoroughly circular. Training in personal judgment would seem to involve training in a tradition. One is initiated into a way of life where skills, virtues, and dispositions which enable one to judge correctly are inculcated. But a way of life, in the soft rationalist's view, is itself intimately related to a world or metaphysical system. Hence the appeal to personal judgment presupposes commitment to a deeper vision of things and cannot be used to test the rationality of that deeper vision. If one does appeal to personal judgment to support the metaphysical system that helped to create it then that appeal is patently circular.

It is open to the soft rationalist to attempt to rebut these objections, if necessary modifying the details of his or her position yet without abandoning its essential elements. Thus one could fully accept that the articulating of a world view and the weighing of all the relevant data and warrants is an elusive affair. From a practical standpoint one will have to rely to some extent on the intellectual labors of others both in the interpretation of the pertinent metaphysical system and its justification by appeal to a cumulative case. But this is not something that the soft rationalist has ever denied. It is admitted that the process of justification is difficult and must be done over time. For a time much may have to be taken on faith. Moreover, the appeal to personal judgment is not necessarily circular. All the soft rationalist requests is that all sides be open to their opponents, competing ontological claims and explanations. Thus religious believers, for example, must seriously consider the possibility that alternative, secular explanations can be given of what they take to be the experiences of the divine. Equally nonbelievers must explore sensitively the possibility of genuine experience of the divine. Such openness, although it is clearly intellectually demanding, does not necessarily depend on initiation into a particular metaphysical tradition. Therefore the appeal to personal judgment is not circular.

Furthermore, even though there is no simple way to acquire training in the exercise of personal judgment in metaphysical disputes, this is not a decisive consideration. Learning to judge and weigh evidence is a general skill which can be informally developed. For example, in voting in an election one has to exercise personal judgment in weighing up the merits of competing candidates even though it is difficult to receive formal training in this area. One simply has to proceed, often in an ad hoc fashion, and work through the issues as honestly and rigorously as possible. Finally, it seems difficult to eliminate an element of personal judgment or intuition from many rational procedures. For example, even the foundations of logic depend upon an intuitive grasp of the truth of certain basic premises. Codifying such intuitions does not establish the rationality of such judgments; it simply describes them more clearly and conveniently. If this is the case then the appeal to personal judgment is not in itself epistemically reprehensible.

It is clear by now that the soft rationalist must admit that the actual justification of religious and metaphysical beliefs is in practice a very elusive affair. Much is taken on faith in the articulation of the metaphysical position under review, in the gathering and weighing of the relevant evidence, and in the use of personal judgment. So soft rationalism could perhaps be equally well described as soft fideism. What label we use at this point is a matter of verbal convenience. What really matters is to emphasize the relevance of various considerations in the debate about the merits of rival interpretive systems. The soft rationalist wants to insist that, *logically* speaking, there are relevant data and warrants. That data and warrants may be contested and elusive does not destroy this fact. Equally the soft rationalist wants to insist that there is little point in craving more rigorous standards of rationality in this domain. Arguments may at times appear elusive when compared to what is available in science, mathematics, or some other favored paradigm. But if such standards are not available, the best course is to examine the relevant evidence as best one can, learning in the process to cultivate as much wisdom as one can muster.

NOTES

1. Basil Mitchell, *The Justification of Religious Belief* (London: Macmillan, 1973), pp. 39–57. By permission of Macmillan, London and Basingstoke.
2. Ibid., pp. 43–44.
3. Richard Swinburne, *The Existence of God* (Oxford: Clarendon Press, 1979).
4. Rod Sykes, "Soft Rationalism," *International Journal for Philosophy of Religion* 11 (1980), pp. 60–61.
5. Mitchell, *The Justification of Religious Belief,* p. 126.

SUGGESTED READING

Abraham, William. *An Introduction to the Philosophy of Religion.* Englewood Cliffs, N.J.: Prentice-Hall, 1985, chaps. 7, 8, 9, and 10.
Allen, Diogenes. *Christian Belief in a Postmodern World: The Full Wealth of Conviction.* Louisville: Westminster/John Knox Press, 1989.
Evans, C. Stephen. *Philosophy of Religion: Thinking About Faith.* Downers Grove, Ill.: InterVarsity Press, 1985, chap. 1.
———. *Kierkegaard's "Fragments" and "Postscript": The Religious Philosophy of Johannes Climacus.* Atlantic Highlands, N.J.: Humanities Press, 1983.
Kierkegaard, Søren. *Concluding Unscientific Postscript*, trans. David P. Swenson and Walter Lowrie. Princeton, N.J.: Princeton University Press, 1941.
Hick, John. *Faith and Knowledge.* London: Macmillan, 1966, 2d ed.
Mavrodes, George I. *Belief in God.* New York: Random House, 1970.
———, ed. *The Rationality of Belief in God.* Englewood Cliffs, N.J.: Prentice-Hall, 1970.
Mitchell, Mitchell. *The Justification of Religious Belief.* Oxford: Oxford University Press, 1981.
Pascal, Blaise. *Pensées*, trans. W. F. Trotter. *The Provincial Letters*, trans. Thomas M'Crie. New York: Random House, 1941, p. 83.
Penelhum, Terence. *God and Skepticism.* Dordrecht: D. Riedel, 1983.
Phillips, D. Z. *Religion without Explanation.* Oxford: Basil Blackwell, 1976.
Placher, William C. *Unapologetic Theology: A Christian Voice in a Pluralistic Conversation.* Louisville, Ky.: Westminster/John Knox Press, 1989.
Pojman, Louis P. *Religious Belief and the Will.* New York: Routledge and Kegan Paul, 1986.
Swinburne, Richard. *The Existence of God.* Oxford: Oxford University Press, 1979.
———. *Faith and Reason.* Oxford: Oxford University Press, 1981.
(See also suggested readings for chap. 7.)

PART THREE

THE DIVINE ATTRIBUTES

Who, or what, is God? Although there are many differences, the major theistic religions of Judaism, Christianity, and Islam generally agree on the broad outlines of a common understanding of God. God is a personal being (not an impersonal "something," as held in some varieties of Hinduism). God has created the entire universe, not because of any need of his own but out of his sheer generosity and goodness. God is all-powerful (omnipotent), all-knowing (omniscient), and perfectly morally good. God exercises providential control and guidance over the affairs of the world, though the extent to which God directly controls everything that happens is controversial. God desires to bring human beings into friendship with himself, and his purposes include bringing the world's history to a culmination in which human life will find its ultimate fulfillment. (Although God is not actually a sexual being, we follow the theistic traditions in using masculine pronouns in referring to deity.)

As the theistic picture of God has been discussed and refined over time, a number of important controversies have surfaced. One controversy surrounds the claim that God possesses the attribute of *necessary existence*—that unlike everything else it is impossible that he fail to exist. Some thinkers to the contrary have maintained that the theistic concept of God's necessary existence is conceptually incoherent and thus proves the nonexistence of God.

Another set of issues regards what it means to say that God is omnipotent. The classic Thomistic definition of omnipotence, is that God has the power to bring about any state of affairs the description of which is logically possible. Historically, a number of important puzzles have surfaced concerning the classic definition and prodded theistic thinkers to search for solutions.

Another puzzle is based on the apparent incompatibility between God's comprehensive knowledge of the future and the freedom of human beings to choose for themselves how to conduct their lives. Still, another cluster of problems arises from the view that God is "eternal." One body of opinion maintains that God's eternity is "timelessness"—that his existence is entirely outside the realm of time and change inhabited by human beings. Another body of opinion insists that God is "everlasting"—that he exists and lives and acts *in time*. An increasing number of thinkers also say that failure to affirm that God is everlasting undermines the biblical message of God's working in history on behalf of human beings.

In addition to the various issues pertaining to the classical conception of deity, there are issues relating to whether an alternative conception of deity is viable. "Process theism" has become popular in both Christian and Jewish circles as an alternative to "classical theism." Process theism sees God as *guiding* the world but not *controlling* it, and differs from traditional theism in a number of other important ways.

J. N. FINDLAY

God's Necessary Existence Is Impossible

One of the things often said about God by reflective religious people is that God exists necessarily—that God "cannot not exist." Citing the attitude of worship that believers have toward their God, J. N. Findlay (1903–) argues that this attribute is essential to their concept of God. That is, they must think that God, if he exists at all, must have necessary existence. But Findlay then argues that necessary existence is impossible. Thus, neither God nor anything else can exist necessarily. His basis for this argument is the Kantian thesis that existence implies contingency and not necessity. Thus, the notion of necessary existence is incoherent. If one accepts both parts of Findlay's argument, the conclusion is inescapable: God does not exist. Indeed, God necessarily does not exist.

⌘

The course of philosophical development has been full of attempted proofs of the existence of God. Some of these have sought a basis in the bare necessities of thought, while others have tried to found themselves on the facts of experience. And, of these latter, some have founded themselves on *very general facts,* as that something exists, or that something is in motion, while others have tried to build on *highly special facts,* as that living beings are put together in a purposive manner, or that human beings are subject to certain improbable urges and passions, such as the zeal for righteousness, the love for useless truths and unprofitable beauties, as well as the many specifically religious needs and feelings. The general philosophical verdict is that none of these 'proofs' is truly compelling. The proofs based on the necessities of thought are universally regarded as fallacious: it is not thought possible to build bridges between mere abstractions and concrete existence. The proofs based on the general facts of existence and motion are only felt to be valid by a minority of thinkers, who seem quite powerless to communicate this sense of validity to others. And while most thinkers would accord weight to arguments resting on the special facts we have mentioned, they wouldn't think such arguments successful in ruling out a vast range of counter-possibilities. Religious people have, in fact, come to acquiesce in the total absence of any cogent proofs of the Being they believe in: they even find it positively satisfying that something so far surpassing clear conception should also surpass the possibility of demonstration. And non-religious people willingly mitigate their rejection with a tinge of agnosticism: they don't so much deny the existence of a God, as the existence of good reasons for believing in him.

We shall, however, maintain in this essay that there isn't room, in the case we are examining, for all these attitudes of tentative surmise and doubt. For we shall try to show that the Divine Existence can only be conceived, in a religiously satisfactory manner, if we also conceive it as something inescapable and necessary, whether for thought or reality. From which it follows that our modern denial of necessity or rational evidence for such an existence amounts to a demonstration that there cannot be a God.

Before we develop this argument, we must, however, give greater precision to our use of the term 'God.' For it is possible to say that there are nearly as many 'Gods' as there are speakers and worshippers, and while existence may be confidently asserted or denied of *some* of them, we should feel more hesitant in the case of others. It is one thing, plainly, to pronounce on God's existence, if he be taken to be some ancient, shapeless stone, or if we identify him with the bearded Father of the Sistine ceiling, and quite another matter, if we make of him an 'all-pervasive, immaterial intelligence,' or characterize him in some yet more negative and analogical manner. We shall, however, choose an indirect approach, and pin God down for our purposes as the 'adequate object of religious attitudes.' Plainly we find it possible to gather together, under the blanket term 'religious,' a large range of cases of possible action, linked together by so many overlapping[1] affinities that we are ready to treat them as the varying 'expressions' of a single 'attitude' or 'policy.' And plainly we find it possible to indicate the character of that attitude by a number of descriptive phrases which, though they may err individually by savouring too strongly of particular cases, nevertheless permit us, in their totality, to draw a rough boundary round the attitude in question. Thus we might say, for instance, that a religious attitude was one in which we tended to abase ourselves before some object, to defer to it wholly, to devote ourselves to it with unquestioning enthusiasm, to bend the knee before it, whether literally or metaphorically. These phrases, and a large number of similar ones, would make perfectly plain the sort of attitude we were speaking of, and would suffice to mark it off from cognate attitudes which are much less unconditional and extreme in their tone. And clearly similar phrases would suffice to fix the boundaries of religious *feeling*. We might describe religious frames of mind as ones in which we felt ready to abase ourselves before some object, to bend the knee before it, and so forth. Here, as elsewhere, we find ourselves indicating the *felt* character of our attitudes, by treating their inward character as, in some sense, a concentrated and condensed substitute for appropriate lines of action, a way of speaking that accords curiously with the functional significance of the inward.[2] But not only do we incorporate, in the meanings of our various names for attitudes, a reference to this readiness for appropriate lines of action: we also incorporate in these meanings a reference to *the sorts of things or situations to which these attitudes are the normal or appropriate responses*. For, as a matter of fact, our attitudes are not indifferently evoked in *any* setting: there is a range of situations in which they normally and most readily occur. And though they may at times arise in circumstances which are not in this range, they are also readily dissipated by the consciousness that such circumstances *are* unsuitable or unusual. Thus fear is an attitude very readily evoked in situations with a character of menace or potential injury, and it is also an attitude very readily allayed by the clear perception that a given situation isn't really dangerous. And anger, likewise, is an attitude provoked very readily by perverse resistance and obstructive difficulty in some object, and is also very readily dissipated, even in animals, by the consciousness that a given object is innocent of offence. All attitudes, we may say, *presume* characters in their objects, and are, in consequence, strengthened by the discovery that their objects *have* these characters, as they are weakened by the discovery that they really haven't got them. And not only do we find this out empirically: we also incorporate it in the *meanings* of our names for attitudes. Thus attitudes are said to be 'normal,' 'fully justified' and so forth, if we find them altered in a certain manner (called 'appropriate') by our knowledge of the actual state of things, whereas we speak of them as 'queer' or 'senseless' or 'neurotic,' if they aren't at all modified by this knowledge of reality. We call it abnormal, from this point of view, to feel a deep-seated fear of mice, to rage maniacally at strangers, to greet disasters with a hebephrenic giggle, whereas we think it altogether normal to deplore deep losses deeply, or to fear grave dangers gravely. And so an implicit reference to some standard object—which makes an attitude either normal or abnormal—is part of what we ordinarily mean by all our names for attitudes, and can be rendered explicit by a simple study of usage. We can consider the circumstances in which ordinary speakers would call an attitude 'appropriate' or 'justified.' And all that philosophy achieves in this regard is merely to push further, and develop into more considered and consistent forms, the implications of such ordinary ways of speaking. It can inquire whether an attitude would still seem justified, and its object appropriate, after we had reflected long and carefully on a certain matter, and looked at it from every wonted and unwonted angle. And such consideration may lead philosophers to a different and more reasoned notion of the appropriate objects of a given attitude, than could be garnered from our unreflective ways of speaking. And these developments of ordinary usage will only seem unfeasible to victims of that strange modern confusion which thinks of attitudes exclusively as hidden processes 'in our bosoms,' with nothing but an adventitious relation to appropriate outward acts and objects.

How then may we apply these notions to the case of our religious attitudes? Plainly we shall be following the natural trends of unreflective speech if we say that religious attitudes presume *superiority* in their objects, and such superiority, moreover, as reduces us, who feel the attitudes, to comparative nothingness. For having described a worshipful attitude as one in which we feel disposed to bend the knee before some object, to defer to it wholly, and the like, we find it natural to say that such an attitude can only be fitting where the object reverenced *exceeds* us very vastly, whether in power or wisdom or in other valued qualities. And while it is certainly possible to worship stocks and stones and articles of common use, one does so usually on the assumption that they aren't merely stocks and stones and ordinary articles, but the temporary seats of 'indwelling presences' or centres of extraordinary powers and virtues. And if one realizes clearly that such things *are* merely stocks and stones or articles of common use, one can't help suffering a total vanishing or grave abatement of religious ardour. To feel religiously is therefore to presume surpassing greatness in some object: so much characterizes the attitudes in which we bow and bend the knee, and enters into the ordinary meaning of the word 'religious.' But now we advance further—in company with a large number of theologians and philosophers, who have added new touches to the portrait of deity, pleading various theoretical necessities, but really concerned to make their object worthier of our worship—and ask whether it isn't wholly anomalous to worship anything *limited* in any thinkable manner. For all limited superiorities are tainted with an obvious relativity, and can be dwarfed in thought by still mightier superiorities, in which process of being dwarfed they lose their claim upon our worshipful attitudes. And hence we are led on irresistibly to demand that our religious object should have an *unsurpassable* supremacy along all avenues, that it should tower *infinitely* above all other objects. And not only are we led to demand for it such merely quantitative superiority: we also ask that it shouldn't stand surrounded by a world of *alien* objects, which owe it no allegiance, or set limits to its influence. The proper object of religious reverence must in some manner be *all-comprehensive*: there mustn't be anything capable of existing, or of displaying any virtue, without owing all of these absolutely to this single source. All these, certainly, are difficult requirements, involving not only the obscurities and doubtful significance of the infinite, but also all the well-worn antagonisms of the immanent and transcendent, of finite sinfulness and divine perfection and preordination, which centuries of theological brooding have failed to dissipate. But we are also led on irresistibly to a yet more stringent demand, which raises difficulties which make the difficulties we have mentioned seem wholly inconsiderable: we can't help feeling that the worthy object of our worship can never be a thing that merely *happens* to exist, nor one on which all other objects merely *happen* to depend. The true object of religious reverence must not be one, merely, to which no *actual* independent realities stand opposed: it must be one to which such opposition is totally *inconceivable.* God mustn't merely cover the territory of the actual, but also, with equal comprehensiveness, the territory of the possible. And not only must the existence of *other* things be unthinkable without him, but his own non-existence must be wholly unthinkable in any circumstances. There must, in short, be no conceivable alternative to an existence properly termed 'divine': God must be wholly inescapable, as we remarked previously, whether for thought or reality. And so we are led on insensibly to the barely intelligible notion of a Being in whom Essence and Existence lose their separateness. And all that the great medieval thinkers really did was to carry such a development to its logical limit.

We may, however, approach the matter from a slightly different angle.

Not only is it contrary to the demands and claims inherent in religious attitudes that their object should *exist* 'accidentally': it is also contrary to those demands that it should *possess its various excellences* in some merely adventitious or contingent manner. It would be quite unsatisfactory from the religious standpoint, if an object merely *happened* to be wise, good, powerful and so forth, even to a superlative degree, and if other beings had, *as a mere matter of fact*, derived their excellences from this single source. An object of this sort would doubtless deserve respect and admiration, and other quasi-religious attitudes, but it would not deserve the utter self-abandonment peculiar to the religious frame of mind. It would deserve the δουλεία canonically accorded to the saints, but not the λατρεία that we properly owe to God. We might respect this object as the crowning instance of most excellent qualities, but we should incline our head before the qualities and not before the person. And wherever such qualities were manifested, though perhaps less eminently, we should always be ready to perform an essentially similar obeisance. For though such qualities might be intimately characteristic of the Supreme Being, they still wouldn't be in any sense inalienably his own. And even if other beings had, in fact, derived such qualities from this sovereign source, they still would be *their own* qualities, possessed by them in their own right. And we should have no better reason to *adore* the author of such virtues, than sons have reason to adore superior parents, or pupils to adore superior teachers. For while these latter may deserve deep deference, the fact that we are coming to *participate* in their excellences renders them unworthy of our *worship*. Plainly a being that possesses and imparts desirable qualities—which other things might nevertheless have manifested though this source were totally absent—has all the utter inadequacy as a religious object which is expressed by saying that it would be *idolatrous* to worship it. Wisdom, kindness and other excellences deserve respect wherever they are manifested, but no being can appropriate them as its personal perquisites, even if it does possess them in a superlative degree. And so we are led on irresistibly, by the demands inherent in religious reverence, to hold that an adequate object of our worship must possess its various qualities *in some necessary manner*. These qualities must be intrinsically incapable of belonging to anything except in so far as they belong primarily to the object of our worship. Again we are led on to a queer and barely intelligible Scholastic doctrine, that God isn't merely good, but is in some manner indistinguishable from his own (and anything else's) goodness.

What, however, are the consequences of these requirements upon the possibility of God's existence? Plainly, (for all who share a contemporary outlook), they entail not only that there isn't a God, but that the Divine Existence is either senseless[3] or impossible. The modern mind feels not the faintest axiomatic force in principles which trace contingent things back to some necessarily existent source, nor does it find it hard to conceive that things should display various excellent qualities without deriving them from a source which manifests them supremely. Those who believe in necessary truths which aren't merely tautological, think that such truths merely connect the *possible* instances of various characteristics with each other: they don't expect such truths to tell them whether there *will* be instances of any characteristics. This is the outcome of the whole medieval and Kantian criticism of the Ontological Proof. And, on a yet more modern view of the matter, necessity in propositions merely reflects our use of words, the arbitrary conventions of our language. On such a view the Divine Existence could only be a necessary matter if we had made up our minds to speak theistically *whatever the empirical circumstances might turn out to be*. This, doubtless, would suffice for some, who speak theistically, much as Spinoza spoke monistically, merely to give expression to a particular way of looking at things, or of feeling about them. And it would also suffice for those who make use of the term 'God' to cover whatever tendencies towards righteousness and beauty are actually included in the make-up of our world. But it wouldn't suffice for the full-blooded worshipper, who can't help finding our actual world anything but edifying, and its half-formed tendencies towards righteousness and beauty very far from adorable. The religious frame of mind seems, in fact, to be in a quandary; it seems invincibly determined both to eat its cake and have it. It desires the Divine Existence both to have that inescapable character which can, on modern views, only be found where truth reflects an arbitrary convention, and also the character of 'making a real difference' which is only possible where truth doesn't have this merely linguistic basis. We may accordingly deny that modern approaches allow us to remain agnostically poised in regard to God: they force us to come down on the atheistic side. For if God is to satisfy religious claims and needs, he must be a being in every way inescapable, One whose existence and whose possession of certain excellences we cannot possibly conceive away. And modern views make it self-evidently absurd (if they don't make it ungrammatical) to speak of such a Being and attribute existence to him. It was indeed an ill day for Anselm when he hit upon his famous proof. For on that day he not only laid bare something that is of the essence of an adequate religious object, but also something that entails its necessary non-existence.[4]

The force of our argument must not, however, be exaggerated. We haven't proved that there aren't beings of all degrees of excellence and greatness, who may deserve attitudes approximating indefinitely to religious reverence. But such beings will at best be instances of valued qualities which we too may come to exemplify, though in lesser degree. And not only would it be idolatrous for us to worship them, but it would also be monstrous for them to exact worship, or to care for it. The attitude of such beings to our reverence would necessarily be deprecating: they would prefer cooperative atheists to adoring zealots. And they would probably hide themselves like royal personages from the anthems of their worshippers, and perhaps the fact that there are so few positive signs of their presence is itself a feeble evidence of their real existence. But whether such beings exist or not, they are not divine, and can never satisfy the demands inherent in religious reverence. And the effect of our argument will further be to discredit generally such forms of religion as attach a uniquely sacred meaning to existent things, whether these things be men or acts of institutions or writings.

But there are other frames of mind, to which we shouldn't deny the name 'religious,' which acquiesce quite readily in the non-existence of their objects. (This non-existence might, in fact, be taken to be the 'real meaning' of saying that religious objects and realities are 'not of this world.') In such frames of mind we give ourselves over unconditionally and gladly to the task of indefinite approach toward a certain imaginary focus where nothing actually is, and we find this task sufficiently inspiring and satisfying without demanding (absurdly) that there should be something actual at that limit. And the atheistic religious attitude we have mentioned has also undergone reflective elaboration by such philosophers as Fichte and Erigena and Alexander. There is, then, a religious atheism which takes full stock of our arguments, and we may be glad that this is so. For since the religious spirit is one of reverence before things greater than ourselves, we should be gravely impoverished and arrested if this spirit ceased to be operative in our personal and social life. And it would certainly be better that this spirit should survive, with all its fallacious existential trimmings, than that we should cast it forth merely in order to be rid of such irrelevances.

NOTES

1. This word is added to avoid the suggestion that there must be *one* pervasive affinity linking together all the actions commonly called 'religious.'
2. Whatever the philosophical 'ground' for it may be, this plainly is the way in which we do describe the 'inner quality' of our felt attitudes.
3. I have included this alternative, of which I am not fond, merely because so many modern thinkers make use of it in this sort of connection.
4. Or 'non-significance,' if this alternative is preferred.

THOMAS MORRIS

God's Necessary Existence

Taking up Findlay's challenge, Thomas Morris (1952–) explains what it means to say that God exists necessarily, and why the claim that no being (including God) could exist necessarily should be rejected. In the process, Morris explains the idea of a "possible world," and how this idea relates to possibility and necessity—concepts that have been extremely prominent in recent philosophical discussions of the nature of God.

⌘

God is necessarily good. God is necessarily omnipotent. Got is necessarily omniscient. Each of these claims can be taken to be the expression of a necessity in more than one sense, as we have seen. They can be understood as expressing necessities *de dicto*:

(1) Necessarily, God is good,

(2) Necessarily, God is omnipotent,

(3) Necessarily, God is omniscient,

where the necessity is, roughly speaking, a conceptual necessity, or a propositional necessity resulting from the unpacking of a concept, the concept of God. In this sense the necessity of God's being good consists in no more than the impossibility of an individual's counting as God, or properly instantiating the concept of God, without that individual's being good. Goodness is a conceptual requirement of deity.

The claims that God is necessarily good, omnipotent and omniscient, can also be understood as the expression of necessities *de re*:

(4) God is necessarily good,

(5) God is necessarily omnipotent,

(6) God is necessarily omniscient,

where the necessity in each case is one holding true of the individual who in fact is God, and is the expression of one of his essential properties, a property without which he could not exist. These *de re* necessities tie goodness, omnipotence and omniscience to the very existence of the divine being. And, as we have noted, the modally most exalted form of perfect being theology will go on to express the even more stringent conceptual requirement of deity that, in order to count as literally divine, an individual must have goodness, omnipotence and omniscience essentially:

(7) Necessarily, God is essentially good,

(8) Necessarily, God is essentially omnipotent,

(9) Necessarily, God is essentially omniscient,

for a being who was ultimately vulnerable to evil, weakness or ignorance in any possible circumstance would not be a greatest possible being.

From this modally exalted conception of the requirements of deity, it follows that any individual who is God has that status essentially. To spell this out most fully, and to extend this idea of deity to the utmost, it will be convenient to employ something like the idea, previously mentioned, of a "possible world." Consider the possible situation of my sitting with a fountain pen in my hand. This possible situation, or possible state of affairs, happens to be actual as I write these words. But there are many states of affairs which are possible but not actual, such as the state of affairs of my having lived my entire life as a rock guitarist, never having taken up philosophy. Now consider the idea of a collection or array of states of affairs, each in itself possible and together compossible. The idea of a possible world is just the idea of a very big collection of states of affairs, as complete an array as is possible. Think of the sum total of all the states of affairs which have been, are and will be included in the entire history of everything that ever exists. Now pause and catch your breath. This is a possible world—the one which happens to have the special status of being actual. But, as philosophers say, there are many other possible worlds which could have been actual instead. There are possible worlds in which I never touch a fountain pen. There are some possible worlds in which I exist and never become a philosopher. So the property of being a philosopher is not one of my essential properties, it is not one of the properties necessary for my existence. I have that property only in some possible worlds, not in all, so we say that I have it *contingently* or *accidentally*.

Many of my properties I have contingently. But some I have *essentially*—in every possible world in which I exist. The property of having a mind, or the related property of being at least potentially conscious, is one of my essential properties. There is no possible world in which I exist utterly devoid of a mind or the potentiality for consciousness.

On the conception of deity we are considering, part of what it means to be God is to have the properties of goodness, omnipotence and omniscience, and to have them essentially. That is to say, it is a conceptual requirement of deity that any individual who is God is God in every possible world in which he exists, and at any and every time at which he might exist. There is no ascending to, or abdicating, this throne. A being whose properties, and ultimate status, were not this stable could not be a greatest possible being.

And we are now in a position to make one further step. Theists who work in the tradition of perfect being theology, and those whose perspective is captured by the precise form of creation theology we have considered want to make one more claim. The further claim is that any individual who is God has this status in and perfectly throughout every possible world. But in order for this to be true, such an individual must of course exist in every possible world. This is what is known as *necessary existence*, the pinnacle of divine necessity. Necessary existence is just existence in all possible circumstances, in all possible worlds. A necessarily existent being is a being whose nonexistence is strictly, metaphysically impossible.

Why have theists endorsed the necessary existence of God? The reasoning from the side of perfect being theology is simple. We live in a world where many things have a very fragile and tenuous existence. Things come to be, things pass away. Many things that could have been never are, and most things that do exist could have failed ever to appear on the stage of reality. We live in a world of contingent beings. But contingency is not the greatest mode of existence imaginable. We can at least conceive of a being who could not possibly cease to exist, whose existence could not have appeared "from nothing," and whose anchorage in reality is so great that it is not even possible for the being to have failed to exist. Surely it is only this necessary existence, this firmest possible foothold in reality, which is appropriate for a maximally perfect being. This, in brief, is the argument from perfect being theology.[1]

The reasoning from creation theology is even simpler. If God is thought of as necessarily the creator, or ultimate cause, of any being which could exist distinct from himself, in the sense that there is no possible world in which anything distinct from God exists without deriving its existence from God, it follows straightforwardly that God must be conceived of as existing in every possible world. And this is the picture of creation required by any thoroughly theistic ontology, or world view. Anything less would not portray the ultimate in creator-creation relations.[2]

So the idea we have before us, from both perfect being theology and creation theology, is the idea of God as necessarily existent, existent in all possible worlds, in all possible circumstances. Although this idea connects up so naturally with both these methods for thinking about deity, it has been a controversial claim in recent years, yet perhaps not quite as controversial as the other metaphysical attributes we shall be examining in this chapter and the next. In each case, however, the controversy among Christian philosophers can be understood as a disagreement over whether a being characterized as necessary, or atemporal, or in some other esoterically metaphysical way, can possibly be the God of the Bible, an utterly free person, creator, sustainer and savior of all. In each case, an important aspect of the controversy turns on how different from human beings God can be and still exist as a personal being.

Critics of the claim that God enjoys necessary existence often reason like this. The most plausible candidates for necessary existence are abstract objects like numbers, properties, and propositions. For try to imagine a possible world in which nothing exists. If there could be such a world, it would be a world, or state of affairs, in which the number of things that exist would be properly numbered by the number 0. The number 0 would be instantiated, or exemplified, precisely by the absence of anything else. But then *it* would have to exist to be exemplified, or to number the things that exist. Moreover, it is one number, so it, itself, would properly be numbered by the number 1, and so on. In other words, it is impossible that there be a state of affairs or world in which literally nothing exists. At least the numbers would have to exist in any world. And the different numbers have different properties, so properties would have to exist. Likewise, in our attempted specification of a null world, the proposition "Nothing exists" would have to be true; but then, it would have to exist in order to be true of such a circumstance. The net result of such reasoning is that it is plausible to suppose that such abstract objects as numbers, properties, and propositions necessarily exist as a sort of formal framework of reality, providing necessary conditions for the possibility of any world. But it is another thing altogether, the critic of divine necessity alleges, to suppose that God exists necessarily. The paradigms of necessary existence, as we have seen, are *abstract objects*. But God is a person, and persons, like tables, chairs and planets, are *concrete objects*. Now, the philosophical distinction between abstract and concrete objects is a difficult one to draw precisely, but the critic here thinks it is clear enough to undermine the belief in God's necessity. For God is surely more like tables, chairs, planets, you and me than he is like numbers, properties and propositions. And we are contingent things.

If God is a person, then indeed in *most* respects he is more like you and me than he is like a number or a property. It just doesn't follow at all that he is unlike numbers and properties in any distinctive respect. In particular, there is no compelling argument here at all for the thesis that God could not exist necessarily unless he were an abstract object. One main distinction between concrete and abstract objects may be that only concrete objects can cause changes in other objects, or initiate causal chains in the world. On this ground, God would clearly stand on the side of concrete objects, regardless of the sweep of his existence across possible worlds. So this form of objection seems to go nowhere.

It may be tempting for critics to argue rather like this: From our experience, we know that

(1) Persons begin to exist and cease to exist.

Thus,

(2) Persons exist contingently.

But

(3) God is a person.

So

(4) God exists contingently.

And thus

(5) God does not exist necessarily.

If a being exists contingently, he exists only in some possible worlds and not in others, thus (5) follows from (4). Theists are committed to (3). Line (2) follows from line (1), in the sense that *if* (1) is true, then (2) is also. But *is* the first premise of this argument something we know to be true from our experience?

We see human persons born. We don't clearly see them begin to exist in any simple, straightforward sense. But if we are Christian theists, we believe that all created human persons begin to exist at one time or another. We see human beings die. We do not see them cease to exist. We see their bodies cease to function. But if we are Christian theists, we believe that all created human persons exist beyond bodily death. In fact, we never know that any intersubjectively experienceable object ceases to exist by sense experience alone. For that sort of knowledge, experience must be supplemented by theory. Otherwise, what seems to be the annihilation of such an object could just be its local disappearance, and it could continue to exist relocated in some other region of space-time. Recognizing this, we must recognize that our experience of human birth and death must be augmented by some theory of human existence before we can draw conclusions about ontological coming-to-be and ceasing-to-be. And the theory of human nature compatible with Christian theology will recognize our contingency as persons only as an implication of the fact that we are *created* persons. So we must judge that, from a theistic perspective, (1) is flawed as it stands, and so is (2). *Created* persons begin to be, and thus created persons exist contingently. But then the conclusions of (4) and (5) would follow only if it could be maintained that, in this sense of contingent creation,

(3′) God is a created person,

which is completely contrary to a Christian world-view, and so will be rejected as false. This argument against the necessity of God's existence is thus also a failure.

Some philosophers seem to think that the modalities of necessity, possibility and impossibility always have to do with simple logical consistency or inconsistency. On this view, the proposition that

(G) God exists

could not be a necessary truth, true in all possible worlds, unless

(GN) God does not exist

were somehow formally inconsistent, like

(I) I am both over six feet tall and not over six feet tall,

and impossible for that reason. But I see no good reason to be so restrictive about the grounds of necessity and impossibility. Some critics, like the philosopher J. N. Findlay, have thought that there are no necessities or impossibilities except for those which are established by human linguistic convention or agreement. It is absurd to suppose that the existence of any being in all possible worlds, or even in any world at all, could be a result of some linguistic convention. So, Findlay concludes, the existence of a necessary God is nonsense, an utter impossibility.[3]

Findlay really seems to think that it is *impossible* that there be any necessities or impossibilities not established by or resulting from some convention of linguistic usage. But what convention of linguistic usage establishes this alleged impossibility? None that I know of. Findlay offers no argument for his view that necessity and impossibility can only be the result of linguistic convention. And no one else has succeeded in making such a case. There seems to be no good reason to be restrictive in this way concerning the realm of modality. The theist who endorses the necessity of God's existence has an entirely sensible, and even, as we shall see in the chapter on creation, metaphysically powerful view of necessity and impossibility. Thus, I think it is entirely reasonable to follow the straightforward arguments from both perfect being theology and creation theology for the claim that God exists necessarily in all possible worlds.

NOTES

1. This reasoning also provides one basis for the famous ontological argument for the existence of God: The idea of God is that of a necessary being. If such a being is possible (i.e., existent in some possible world), it follows from his necessity that he exists in every possible world, and hence in the actual world. It is at least possible that there is a God. Thus, there is a God. It can be argued, however, that it is possible to incorporate into one's idea of God something like the property of necessary existence without endorsing any version of the ontological argument. To do this, for example, one could hold it to be required by the concept of God only that no individual could count as God unless that individual were such that if he existed in any possible world, he would exist in all possible worlds.

2. Many theistic philosophers have also argued that a fully adequate explanatory account of our world requires the postulation of a necessarily existent Creator. This is the core of one famous version of the cosmological argument for the existence of God.

3. J. N. Findlay, "Can God's Existence Be Disproved?" in *New Essays in Philosophical Theology*, ed. Antony Flew and Alasdair MacIntyre (New York: MacMillan, 1955), pp. 47–56. (Reprinted as the previous selection in this anthology.)

THOMAS AQUINAS

God Is Omnipotent

In affirming that God is omnipotent, Aquinas (1224–1274) is careful to explain exactly what it means to say this about God. It should be noted especially that God's omnipotence does not imply that God can do what is "impossible absolutely" because that is to do something that is contradictory (such as making a square circle). Nor does omnipotence imply that God can do evil, for to do evil would imply imperfection in God.

From *Summa Theologica* by Thomas Aquinas, trans. Fathers of the English Dominican Province. London: R. and T. Washbourne, 1911.

⌘

We proceed thus to the Third Article:

Objection 1. It seems that God is not omnipotent. For movement and passiveness belong to everything. But this is impossible for God, since He is immovable, as was said above. Therefore He is not omnipotent.

Obj. 2. Further, sin is an act of some kind. But God cannot sin, nor *deny Himself,* as it is said 2 *Tim.* ii. 13. Therefore He is not omnipotent.

Obj. 3. Further, it is said of God that He manifests His omnipotence *especially by sparing and having mercy.* Therefore the greatest act possible to the divine power is to spare and have mercy. There are things much greater, however, than sparing and having mercy; for example, to create another world, and the like. Therefore God is not omnipotent.

Obj. 4. Further, upon the text, *God hath made foolish the wisdom of this world* (*I Cor.* i. 20), the *Gloss* says: *God hath made the wisdom of this world foolish* by showing those things to be possible which it judges to be impossible. Whence it seems that nothing is to be judged possible or impossible in reference to inferior causes, as the wisdom of this world judges them; but in reference to the divine power. If God, then were omnipotent, all things would be possible; nothing, therefore, impossible. But if we take away the impossible, then we destroy also the necessary; for what necessarily exists cannot possibly not exist. Therefore, there would be nothing at all that is necessary in things if God were omnipotent. But this is an impossibility. Therefore God is not omnipotent.

On the contrary, It is said: *No word shall be impossible with God* (*Luke* i. 37).

I answer that, All confess that God is omnipotent; but it seems difficult to explain in what His omnipotence precisely consists. For there may be a doubt as to the precise meaning of the word "all" when we say that God can do all things. If, however, we consider the matter aright, since power is said in reference to possible things, this phrase, *God can do all things,* is rightly understood to mean that God can do all things that are possible; and for this reason He is said to be omnipotent. Now according to the Philosopher a thing is said to be possible in two ways. First, in relation to some power; thus whatever is subject to human power is said to be possible to man. Now God cannot be said to be omnipotent through being able to do all things that are possible to created nature; for the divine power extends farther than that. If, however, we were to say that God is omnipotent because He can do all things that are possible to His power, there would be a vicious circle in explaining the nature of His power. For this would be saying nothing else but that God is omnipotent because He can do all that He is able to do.

It remains, therefore, that God is called omnipotent because He can do all things that are possible absolutely; which is the second way of saying a thing is possible. For a thing is said to be possible or impossible absolutely, according to the relation in which the very terms stand to one another: possible, if the predicate is not incompatible with the subject, as that Socrates sits; and absolutely impossible when the predicate is altogether incompatible with the subject, as, for instance, that a man is an ass.

It must, however, be remembered that since every agent produces an effect like itself, to each active power there corresponds a thing possible as its proper object according to the nature of that act on which its active power is founded; for instance, the power of giving warmth is related, as to its proper object, to the being capable of being warmed. The divine being, however, upon which the nature of power in God is founded, is infinite; it is not limited to any class of being, but possesses within itself the perfection of all being. Whence, whatsoever has or can have the nature of being is numbered among the absolute possible, in respect of which God is called omnipotent.

Now nothing is opposed to the notion of being except non-being. Therefore, that which at the same time implies being and non-being is repugnant to the notion of an absolute possible, which is subject to the divine omnipotence. For such cannot come under the divine omnipotence; not indeed because of any defect in the power of God, but because it has not the nature of a feasible or possible thing. Therefore, everything that does not imply a contradiction in terms is numbered among those possibles in respect of which God is called omnipotent; whereas whatever implies contradiction does not come within the scope of divine omnipotence, because it cannot have the aspect of possibility. Hence it is more appropriate to say that such things cannot be done, than that God cannot do them. Nor is this contrary to the word of the angel, saying: *No word shall be impossible with God* (*Luke* i. 37). For whatever implies a contradiction cannot be a word, because no intellect can possibly conceive such a thing.

Reply Obj. 1. God is said to be omnipotent in respect to active power, not to passive power, as was shown above. Whence the fact that He is immovable or impassible is not repugnant to His omnipotence.

Reply Obj. 2. To sin is to fall short of a perfect action; hence to be able to sin is to be able to fall short in action, which is repugnant to omnipotence. Therefore it is that God cannot sin, because of His omnipotence. Now it is true that the Philosopher says that *God can deliberately do what is evil.* But this must be understood either on a condition, the antecedent of which is impossible—as, for instance, if we were to say that God can do evil things if He will. For there is no reason why a conditional proposition should not be true, though both the antecedent and consequent are impossible: as if one were to say: *If man is an ass, he has four feet.* Or he may be understood to mean that God can do some things which now seem to be evil: which, however, if He did them, would then be good. Or he is, perhaps, speaking after the common manner of the pagans, who thought that men became gods, like Jupiter or Mercury.

Reply Obj. 3. God's omnipotence is particularly shown in sharing and having mercy, because in this it is made manifest that God has supreme power, namely, that He freely forgives sins. For it is not for one who is bound by laws of a superior to forgive sins of his own free choice. Or, it is thus shown because by sparing and having mercy upon men, He leads them to the participation of an infinite good; which is the ultimate effect of the divine power. Or it is thus shown because, as was said above, the effect of the divine mercy is the foundation of all the divine works. For nothing is due anyone, except because of something already given him gratuitously by God. In this way the divine omnipotence is particularly made manifest, because to it pertains the first foundation of all good things.

Reply Obj. 4. The absolute possible is not so called in reference either to higher causes, or to inferior causes, but in reference to itself. But that which is called possible in reference to some power is named possible in reference to its proximate cause. Hence those things which it belongs to God alone to do immediately—as, for example, to create, to justify, and the like—are said to be possible in reference to a higher cause. Those things, however, which are such as to be done by inferior causes, are said to be possible in reference to those inferior causes. For it is according to the condition of the proximate cause that the effect has contingency or necessity, as was shown above. Thus it is that the wisdom of the world is deemed foolish, because what is impossible to nature it judges to be impossible to God. So it is clear that the omnipotence of God does not take away from things their impossibility and necessity.

GEORGE I. MAVRODES

Some Puzzles Concerning Omnipotence

In this article, George Mavrodes (1926–) explores the "paradox of the stone," one of a number of puzzles which have been devised by philosophers attempting to clarify the concept of omnipotence. Can God make a stone that he is unable to lift? If he cannot, then there is something he is unable to do. On the other hand, if God can do this, then there is still something he cannot do; namely lift the stone in question once he has made it. Mavrodes argues that this dilemma fails to show that God is not omnipotent.

⌘

The doctrine of God's omnipotence appears to claim that God can do anything. Consequently, there have been attempts to refute the doctrine by giv-

Originally published in *Philosophical Review*, vol. 72 (1963).

ing examples of things which God cannot do; for example, He cannot draw a square circle.

Responding to objections of this type, St. Thomas pointed out that "anything" should be here construed to refer only to objects, actions, or states of affairs whose descriptions are not self-contradictory.[1] For it is only such things whose nonexistence might plausibly be attributed to a lack of power in some agent. My failure to draw a circle on the exam may indicate my lack of geometrical skill, but my failure to draw a square circle does not indicate any such lack. Therefore, the fact that it is false (or perhaps meaningless) to say that God could draw one does no damage to the doctrine of His omnipotence.

A more involved problem, however, is posed by this type of question: can God create a stone too heavy for Him to lift? This appears to be stronger than the first problem, for it poses a dilemma. If we say that God can create a stone, then it seems that there might be such a stone. And if there might be a stone too heavy for Him to lift, then He is evidently not omnipotent. But if we deny that God can create such a stone, we seem to have given up His omnipotence already. Both answers lead us to the same conclusion.

Further, this problem does not seem obviously open to St. Thomas' solution. The form "x is able to draw a square circle" seems plainly to involve a contradiction, while "x is able to make a thing too heavy for x to lift" does not. For it may easily be true that I am able to make a boat too heavy for me to lift. So why should it not be possible for God to make a stone too heavy for Him to lift?

Despite this apparent difference, this second puzzle *is* open to essentially the same answer as the first. The dilemma fails because it consists of asking whether God can do a self-contradictory thing. And the reply that He cannot does no damage to the doctrine of omnipotence.

The specious nature of the problem may be seen in this way. God is either omnipotent or not.[2] Let us assume first that He is not. In that case the phrase "a stone too heavy for God to lift" may not be self-contradictory. And then, of course, if we assert either that God is able or that He is not able to create such a stone, we may conclude that He is not omnipotent. But this is no more than the assumption with which we began, meeting us again after our roundabout journey. If this were all that the dilemma could establish it would be trivial. To be significant it must derive this same conclusion *from the assumption that God is omnipotent*; that is, it must show that the assumption of the omnipotence of God leads to a *reductio*. But does it?

On the assumption that God is omnipotent, the phrase "a stone too heavy for God to lift" becomes self-contradictory. For it becomes "a stone which cannot be lifted by Him whose power is sufficient for lifting anything." But the "thing" described by a self-contradictory phrase is absolutely impossible and hence has nothing to do with the doctrine of omnipotence. Not being an object of power at all, its failure to exist cannot be the result of some lack in the power of God. And, interestingly, it is the very omnipotence of God which makes the existence of such a stone absolutely impossible, while it is the fact that I am finite in power which makes it possible for me to make a boat too heavy for me to lift.

But suppose that some die-hard objector takes the bit in his teeth and denies that the phrase "a stone too heavy for God to lift" is self-contradictory, even on the assumption that God is omnipotent. In other words, he contends that the description "a stone too heavy for an omnipotent God to lift" is self-coherent and therefore describes an absolutely possible object. Must I then attempt to prove the contradiction which I assume above as intuitively obvious? Not necessarily. Let me reply simply that if the objector is right in this contention, then the answer to the original question is "Yes, God can create such a stone." It may seem that this reply will force us into the original dilemma. But it does not. For now the objector can draw no damaging conclusion from this answer. And the reason is that he has just now contended that such a stone is compatible with the omnipotence of God. Therefore, from the possibility of God's creating such a stone it cannot be concluded that God is not omnipotent. The objector cannot have it both ways. The conclusion which he himself wishes to draw from an affirmative answer to the original question is itself the required proof that the descriptive phrase which appears there is self-contradictory. And "it is more appropriate to say that such things cannot be done, than that God cannot do them."[3]

The specious nature of this problem may also be seen in a somewhat different way.[4] Suppose that some theologian is convinced by this dilemma that he must give up the doctrine of omnipotence. But he resolves to give up as little as possible, just enough to meet the argument. One way he can do so is by retaining the infinite power of God with regard to lifting, while placing a restriction on the sort of stone He is able to create. The only restriction required here, however, is that God must not be able to create a stone too heavy for Him to lift. Beyond that the dilemma has not even suggested any necessary restriction. Our theologian has, in effect, answered the original question in the negative, and he now regretfully supposes that this has required him to give up the full doctrine of omnipotence. He is now retaining what he supposes to be the more modest remnants which he has salvaged from that doctrine.

We must ask, however, what it is which he has in fact given up. Is it the unlimited power of God to create stones? No doubt. But what stone is it which God is now precluded from creating? The stone too heavy for Him to lift, of course. But we must remember that nothing in the argument required the theologian to admit any limit on God's power with regard to the lifting of stones. He still holds that to be unlimited. And if God's power to lift is infinite, then His power to create may run to infinity also without outstripping that first power. The supposed limitation turns out to be no limitation at all, since it is specified only by reference to another power which is itself infinite. Our theologian need have no regrets, for he has given up nothing. The doctrine of the power of God remains just what it was before.

Nothing I have said above, of course, goes to prove that God is, in fact, omnipotent. All I have intended to show is that certain arguments intended to prove that He is not omnipotent fail. They fail because they propose, as tests of God's power, putative tasks whose descriptions are self-contradictory. Such pseudo-tasks, not falling within the realm of possibility are not objects of power at all. Hence the fact that they cannot be performed implies no limit on the power of God, and hence no defect in the doctrine of omnipotence.

NOTES

1. St. Thomas Aquinas, *Summa Theologiae*, Ia, q. 25, a. 3.
2. I assume, of course, the existence of God, since that is not being brought in question here.
3. St. Thomas Aquinas, *Summa Theologiae.*
4. But this method rests finally on the same logical relations as the preceding one.

NELSON PIKE

Divine Omniscience and Voluntary Action

If God knows the future completely, can human beings be free in deciding what to do? In a widely discussed article, Nelson Pike (–xxxx) argues for a negative answer to this question. His argument is based on certain widely held assumptions concerning the nature of God and the nature of knowledge. While Pike does not assume that theologians are obliged to accept these assumptions, he puts forward the problem of foreknowledge and freedom as one requiring much further study.

⌘

In Book V, sec. 3 of his *Consolatio Philosophiae*, Boethius entertained (though he later rejected) the claim that if God is omniscient, no human action is voluntary. This claim seems intuitively false. Surely, given only a doctrine describing God's *knowledge*, nothing about the voluntary status of human actions will follow. Perhaps such a conclusion would follow from a doctrine of divine omnipotence or divine providence, but what connection could there be between the claim that God is *omniscient* and the claim that human

Originally published in *Philosophical Review* 74 (1965).

actions are determined? Yet Boethius thought he saw a problem here. He thought that if one collected together just the right assumptions and principles regarding God's knowledge, one could derive the conclusion that if God exists, no human action is voluntary. Of course, Boethius did not think that all the assumptions and principles required to reach this conclusion are true (quite the contrary), but he thought it important to draw attention to them nonetheless. If a theologian is to construct a doctrine of God's knowledge which does not commit him to determinism, he must first understand that there is a way of thinking about God's knowledge which would so commit him.

In this paper, I shall argue that although his claim has a sharp counterintuitive ring, Boethius was right in thinking that there is a selection from among the various doctrines and principles clustering about the notions of knowledge, omniscience, and God which, when brought together, demand the conclusion that if God exists, no human action is voluntary. Boethius, I think, did not succeed in making explicit all of the ingredients in the problem. His suspicions were sound, but his discussion was incomplete. His argument needs to be developed. This is the task I shall undertake in the pages to follow. I should like to make clear at the outset that my purpose in re-arguing this thesis is not to show that determinism is true, nor to show that God does not exist, nor to show that either determinism is true or God does not exist. Following Boethius, I shall not claim that the items needed to generate the problem are either philosophically or theologically adequate. I want to concentrate attention on the implications of a certain set of assumptions. Whether the assumptions are themselves acceptable is a question I shall not consider. . . .

Last Saturday afternoon, Jones mowed his lawn. Assuming that God exists and is (essentially) omniscient in the sense outlined above, it follows that (let us say) eighty years prior to last Saturday afternoon, God knew (and thus believed) that Jones would mow his lawn at that time. But from this it follows, I think, that at the time of action (last Saturday afternoon) Jones was not *able*—that is, it was not *within Jones's power*—to refrain from mowing his lawn.[1] If at the time of action, Jones had been able to refrain from mowing his lawn, then (the most obvious conclusion would seem to be) at the time of action, Jones was able to do something which would have brought it about that God held a false belief eighty years earlier. But God cannot in anything be mistaken. It is not possible that some belief of His was false. Thus, last Saturday afternoon, Jones was not able to do something which would have brought it about that God held a false belief eighty years ago. To suppose that it was would be to suppose that, at the time of the action, Jones was able to do something that would have brought it about that one of God's beliefs was false. Hence, given that God believed eighty years ago that Jones would mow his lawn on Saturday, if we are to assign Jones the power on Saturday to refrain from mowing his lawn, this power must not be described as the power to do something that would have rendered one of God's beliefs false. How then should we describe it vis-à-vis God and His belief? So far as I can see, there are only two other alternatives. First, we might try describing it as the power to do something that would have brought it about that God believed otherwise than He did eighty years ago; or, secondly, we might try describing it as the power to do something that would have brought it about that God (Who, by hypothesis, existed eighty years earlier) did not exist eighty years earlier—that is, as the power to do something that would have brought it about that any person who believed eighty years ago that Jones would mow his lawn on Saturday (one of whom was, by hypothesis, God) held a false belief, and thus was not God. But again, neither of these latter can be accepted. Last Saturday afternoon, Jones was not able to do something that would have brought it about that God believed otherwise than He did eighty years ago. Even if we suppose (as was suggested by Calvin) that eighty years ago God knew Jones would mow his lawn on Saturday in the sense that He "saw" Jones mowing his lawn as if this action were occurring before Him, the fact remains that God knew (and thus believed) eighty years prior to Saturday that Jones would mow his lawn. And if God held such a belief eighty years prior to Saturday, Jones did not have the power on Saturday to do something that would have made it the case that God did not hold this belief eighty years earlier. No action performed at a given time can alter the fact that a given person held a certain belief at a time prior to the time in question. This last seems to be an a priori truth. For similar reasons, the last of the above alternatives must also be rejected. On the assumption that God existed eighty years prior to Saturday, Jones on Saturday was not able to do something that would have brought it about that God did not exist eighty years prior to that time. No action performed at a given time can alter the fact that a certain person existed at a time prior to the time in question. This, too, seems to me to be an a priori truth. But if these observations are correct, then, given that Jones mowed his lawn on Saturday, and given that God exists and is (essentially) omniscient, it seems to follow that at the time of action, Jones did not have the power to refrain from mowing his lawn. The upshot of these reflections would appear to be that Jones's mowing his lawn last Saturday cannot be counted as a voluntary action. Although I do not have an analysis of what it is for an action to be *voluntary*, it seems to me that a situation in which it would be wrong to assign Jones the *ability* or *power* to do *other* than he did would be a situation in which it would also be wrong to speak of his action as voluntary. As a general remark, if God exists and is (essentially) omniscient in the sense specified above, no human action is voluntary.[2]

As the argument just presented is somewhat complex, perhaps the following schematic representation of it will be of some use.

1. "God existed at t_1" entails "If Jones did X at t_2, God believed at t_1 that Jones would do X at t_2."
2. "God believes X" entails " 'X' is true."
3. It is not within one's power at a given time to do something having a description that is logically contradictory.

4. It is not within one's power at a given time to do something that would bring it about that someone who held a certain belief at a time prior to the time in question did not hold that belief at the time prior to the time in question.
5. It is not within one's power at a given time to do something that would bring it about that a person who existed at an earlier time did not exist at that earlier time.
6. If God existed at t_1 and if God believed at t_1 that Jones would do X at t_2, then if it was within Jones's power at t_2 to refrain from doing X, then (1) it was within Jones's power at t_2 to do something that would have brought it about that God held a false belief at t_1, or (2) it was within Jones's power at t_2 to do something which would have brought it about that God did not hold the belief He held at t_1, or (3) it was within Jones's power at t_2 to do something that would have brought it about that any person who believed at t_1 that Jones would do X at t_2 (one of whom was, by hypothesis, God) held a false belief and thus was not God—that is, that God (who by hypothesis existed at t_1) did not exist at t_1.
7. Alternative 1 in the consequent of item 6 is false. (from 2 and 3)
8. Alternative 2 in the consequent of item 6 is false. (from 4)
9. Alternative 3 in the consequent of item 6 is false. (from 5)
10. Therefore, if God existed at t_1 and if God believed at t_1 that Jones would do X at t_2, then it was not within Jones's power at t_2 to refrain from doing X. (from 6 through 9)
11. Therefore, if God existed at t_1, and if Jones did X at t_2, it was not within Jones's power at t_2 to refrain from doing X. (from 1 and 10)

In this argument, items 1 and 2 make explicit the doctrine of God's (essential) omniscience with which I am working. Items 3, 4, and 5 express what I take to be part of the logic of the concept of ability or power as it applies to human beings. Item 6 is offered as an analytic truth. If one assigns Jones the power to refrain from doing X at t_2 (given that God believed at t_1 that he would do X at t_2), so far as I can see, one would have to describe this power in one of the three ways listed in the consequent of item 6. I do not know how to argue that these are the only alternatives, but I have been unable to find another. Item 11, when generalized for all agents and actions, and when taken together with what seems to me to be a minimal condition for the application of "voluntary action," yields the conclusion that if God exists (and is essentially omniscient in the way I have described) no human action is voluntary.

It is important to notice that the argument given in the preceding paragraphs avoids use of two concepts that are often prominent in discussions of determinism.

In the first place, the argument makes no mention of the *causes* of Jones's action. Say (for example, with St. Thomas)[3] that God's foreknowledge of

Jones's action was, itself, the cause of the action (though I am really not sure what this means). Say, instead, that natural events or circumstances caused Jones to act. Even say that Jones's action had no cause at all. The argument outlined above remains unaffected. If eighty years prior to Saturday, God believed that Jones would mow his lawn at that time, it was not within Jones's power at the time of action to refrain from mowing his lawn. The reasoning that justifies this assertion makes no mention of a causal series preceding Jones's action.

Secondly, consider the following line of thinking. Suppose Jones mowed his lawn last Saturday. It was then *true* eighty years ago that Jones would mow his lawn at that time. Hence, on Saturday, Jones was not able to refrain from mowing his lawn. To suppose that he was would be to suppose that he was able on Saturday to do something that would have made false a proposition that was *already true* eighty years earlier. This general kind of argument for determinism is usually associated with Leibniz, although it was anticipated in chapter ix of Aristotle's *De Interpretatione*. It has been used since, with some modification, in Richard Taylor's article, "Fatalism."[4] This argument, like the one I have offered above, makes no use of the notion of causation. It turns, instead, on the notion of its being *true eighty years ago* that Jones would mow his lawn on Saturday.

I must confess that I share the misgivings of those contemporary philosophers who have wondered what (if any) sense can be attached to a statement of the form "It was true at t_1 that E would occur at t_2."[5] Does this statement mean that had someone believed, guessed, or asserted at t_2 that E would occur at t_2, he would have been right?[6] (I shall have something to say about this form of determinism later in this paper.) Perhaps it means that at t_1 there was sufficient evidence upon which to predict that E would occur at t_2.[7] Maybe it means neither of these. Maybe it means nothing at all.[8] The argument presented above presupposes that it makes a straightforward sense to suppose that God (or just anyone) held a true belief eighty years prior to Saturday. But this is not to suppose that *what* God believed *was true eighty years prior to Saturday*. Whether (or in what sense) it was true eighty years ago that Jones would mow his lawn on Saturday is a question I shall not discuss. As far as I can see, the argument in which I am interested requires nothing in the way of a decision on this issue. . . .

To conclude: I have assumed that any statement of the form "*A* knows *X*" entails a statement of the form "*A* believes *X*" as well as a statement of the form " '*X*' is true." I have then supposed (as an analytic truth) that if a given person is omniscient, that person (1) holds no false beliefs, and (2) holds beliefs about the outcome of human actions in advance of their performance. In addition, I have assumed that the statement "If a given person is God that person is omniscient" is an a priori statement. (This last I have labeled the doctrine of God's essential omniscience.) Given these items (plus some premises concerning what is and what is not within one's power), I have argued that if God exists, it is not within one's power to do other than he does. I have inferred from this that if God exists, no human action is voluntary.

As emphasized earlier, I do not want to claim that the assumptions underpinning the argument are acceptable. In fact, it seems to me that a theologian interested in claiming both that God is omniscient and that men have free well could deny any one (or more) of them. For example, a theologian might deny that a statement of the form "*A* knows *X*" entails a statement of the form "*A* believes *X*" (some contemporary philosophers have denied this) or, alternatively, he might claim that this entailment holds in the case of human knowledge but fails in the case of God's knowledge. This latter would be to claim that when knowledge is attributed to God, the term "knowledge" bears a sense other than the one it has when knowledge is attributed to human beings. Then again, a theologian might object to the analysis of "omniscience" with which I have been working. Although I doubt if any Christian theologian would allow that an omniscient being could believe something false, he might claim that a given person could be omniscient although he did not hold beliefs about the outcome of human actions *in advance* of their performance. (This latter is the way Boethius escaped the problem.) Still again, a theologian might deny the doctrine of God's essential omniscience. He might admit that if a given person is God that person is omniscient, but he might deny that this statement formulates an a priori truth. This would be to say that although God is omniscient, He is not *essentially* omniscient. So far as I can see, within the conceptual framework of theology employing any one of these adjustments, the problem of divine foreknowledge outlined in this paper could not be formulated. There thus appears to be a rather wide range of alternatives open to the theologian at this point. It would be a mistake to think that commitment to determinism is an unavoidable implication of the Christian concept of divine omniscience.

But having arrived at this understanding, the importance of the preceding deliberations ought not to be overlooked. There is a pitfall in the doctrine of divine omniscience. That knowing involves believing (truly) is surely a tempting philosophical view (witness the many contemporary philosophers who have affirmed it). And the idea that God's attributes (including omniscience) are essentially connected to His nature, together with the idea that an omniscient being would hold no false beliefs and would hold beliefs about the outcome of human actions in advance of their performance, might be taken by some theologians as obvious candidates for inclusion in a finished Christian theology. Yet the theologian must approach these items critically. If they are embraced together, then if one affirms the existence of God, one is committed to the view that no human action is voluntary.

NOTES

1. The notion of someone being *able* to do something and the notion of something being *within one's power* are essentially the same. Traditional formulations of the problem of divine foreknowledge (e.g., those of

Boethius and Augustine) made use of the notion of what is (and what is not) *within one's power*. But the problem is the same when framed in terms of what one is (and one is not) *able* to do. Thus, I shall treat the statements "Jones was able to do X," "Jones had the ability to do X," and "It was within Jones's power to do X" as equivalent. Richard Taylor, in "I Can," *Philosophical Review*, 69 (1960): 78–89, has argued that the notion of ability or power involved in these last three statements is incapable of philosophical analysis. Be this as it may, I shall not here attempt such an analysis. In what follows I shall, however, be careful to affirm only those statements about what is (or is not) within one's power that would have to be preserved on any analysis of this notion having even the most distant claim to adequacy.

2. In Bk. II, ch. xxi, secs. 8–11 of *An Essay*, Locke says that an agent is not *free* with respect to a given action (e.g., that an action is done "under necessity") when it is not within the agent's power to do otherwise. Locke allows a special kind of case, however, in which an action may be *voluntary* though done under necessity. If a man chooses to do something without knowing that it is not within his power to do otherwise (e.g., if a man chooses to stay in a room without knowing that the room is locked), his action may be voluntary though he is not free to forbear it. If Locke is right in this (and I shall not argue the point one way or the other), replace "voluntary" with (let us say) "free" in the above paragraph and throughout the remainder of this paper.

3. Aquinas, *Summa Theologicae*, Pt. I, q. 14, a. 8.

4. Richard Taylor, "Fatalism," *Philosophical Review*, 71 (1962): 56–66. Taylor argues that if an event *E* fails to occur at *t*, then at *t*, it was true that *E* would fail to occur at *t*. Thus, at *t*, no one could have the power to perform an action that would be sufficient for the occurrence of *E* at *t*. Hence, no one has the power at *t* to do something sufficient for an event that is not going to happen. The parallel between this argument and the one recited above can be seen very clearly if one reformulates Taylor's argument, pushing back the time at which it was true that *E* would not occur at *t*.

5. For a helpful discussion of difficulties involved here, see Rogers Albritton's "Present Truth and Future Contingency," a reply to Richard Taylor's "The Problem of Future Contingency," both in *Philosophical Review*, 66 (1957): 1–28.

6. Gilbert Ryle interprets it this way. See "It Was to Be," in *dilemma* (Cambridge, Engl., 1954).

7. Richard Gale suggests this interpretation in "Endorsing Predictions," *Philosophical Review*, 70 (1961): 376–85.

8. This view is held by John Turk Saunders in "Sea Fight Tomorrow?," *Philosophical Review*, 67 (1958): 367–78.

BOETHIUS

God Is Timeless

In this selection, Boethius (c. 480–524) presents the most widely accepted view of God's eternity in Christian theology: God lives completely outside of time, in a changeless "eternal Now" which contains all of time within itself. Boethius argues that this view of divine timelessness affords an answer to the dilemma of foreknowledge and freedom discussed in the previous selection. God, according to this view, does not know *beforehand* what humans will do, for this would place God in the time-sequence, and God is not in time. Rather, God knows what humans do *eternally*, in his "eternal Now," which is simultaneous with every moment of time at which they act. And just as our freedom is not taken away by others knowing what we do when we do it, neither is it taken away by God knowing this in his "eternal present."

The Consolation of Philosophy, ed. James T. Buchanan. New York: Frederick Ungar, 1957.

⌘

"Since . . . everything that is known is apprehended not according to its own nature but according to that of the knower, let us examine now, so far as we lawfully may, what is the state of the divine substance, so that we may be able to learn also what its knowledge is. The common opinion, according to all men living, is that God is eternal. Let us therefore consider what eternity is, for this will make clear to us at the same time the divine nature and the divine knowledge. Now, eternity is the complete possession of an endless life enjoyed as one simultaneous whole; this will appear clearer from a comparison with temporal things. For whatever is living in time proceeds in the present from times past to times future; and nothing existing in time is so constituted as to embrace the whole span of its life at once, but it has not yet grasped tomorrow, while it has already lost yesterday. In this life of today you are living in no more than a fleeting, transitory moment. And so it is with everything that is subject to the condition of time: even if it should never have begun and would never cease to be—which Aristotle believed of the universe—even if its life were to be co-extensive with the infinity of time, yet it could not rightly be held to be eternal. For, even granted that it has an infinite lifetime, it does not embrace this life as a simultaneous whole; it does not now have a grasp of the future, which is yet to be lived through. What is rightly called eternal is that which grasps and possesses simultaneously the entire fullness of an unending life, a life which lacks nothing of the future and has lost nothing of the fleeting past. Such a being must necessarily always be its whole self, unchangingly present to itself, and the infinity of changing time must be as one present before him. Wherefore they are mistaken who, hearing that Plato thought this world had no beginning in time and would have no end, think that in this way the created universe is co-eternal with the Creator. For to pass step by step through an unending life, a process ascribed by Plato to the universe, is one thing; to embrace simultaneously the whole of an unending life in one present, an act manifestly peculiar to the divine mind, is quite another thing. And, further, God should not be regarded as older than His creations by any quantity of time but rather by the peculiar quality of simplicity in His nature. For the infinite motion of temporal things tries to imitate the ever present immobility of His life, does not succeed in copying or equalling it, sinks from immobility into motion, and falls from the simplicity of the present to the infinite stretch of future and past; and since it cannot possess its life completely and simultaneously it seems to emulate, by the very fact that it somehow exists forever without ceasing, what it cannot fully attain and express, clinging as it does to the so-called present of this short and fleeting moment, which, inasmuch as it bears a certain resemblance to that abiding present, makes those to whom it comes appear to exist. But, since this present could not be abiding, it took to the infinite journey through time, and so it has come to pass that, by journeying on, it continues that life the fullness of which it could not grasp by staying. Thus if we would apply proper epithets to these subjects we would say, following Plato, that God is eternal, while the universe is perpetual.

"Since, then, every judgment comprehends the objects of its thought according to its own nature, and since God has an ever present and eternal state, His knowledge also, surpassing every temporal movement, remains in the simplicity of its own present and, embracing infinite lengths of past and future, views with its own simple comprehension all things as if they were taking place in the present. If you will weigh the foresight with which God discerns all things, you will rightly esteem it to be the knowledge of a never fading instant rather than a foreknowledge of the 'future.' It should therefore rather be called *pro*vision than *pre*vision because, placed high above lowly things, it looks out over all as from the loftiest mountain top. Why then do you demand that those things which are translucent to the divine mind's light be necessary if not even men make necessary the things they see? Because you can see present things, does your sight impose upon them any necessity?"

"Surely not."

"Yet, if one may not unworthily compare the human present with the divine, just as you see certain things in this, your temporal present, so God sees all things in His eternal present. Wherefore this divine foreknowledge does not change the nature or properties of things: it sees things present to its contemplation just as they will turn out some time in the future. Neither is there any confusion in its judgment of things: with one glimpse of the mind it distinguishes what will happen necessarily and what will happen non-necessarily. For example, when you observe at the same time a man walking on the earth and the sun rising in the sky, although you see both sights simultaneously, nevertheless you distinguish between them and judge that the one is moving voluntarily, the other necessarily; in like manner the intuition of God looks down upon all things without at all disturbing their nature, yet they are present to Him and future in relation to time. Wherefore it is not opinion but knowledge grounded in truth when He knows that something will occur in the future and knows as well that it will not occur of necessity. If you say at this point that what God sees as about to happen cannot but happen and that what cannot but happen happens, and you pin me down to this definition of necessity, I will confess a matter of the firmest truth but one which scarcely any one save a contemplator of the divine can reach: i.e., I shall answer that one and the same future event is necessary with respect to God's knowledge of it but absolutely free and unrestrained when it is examined in its own nature.

"For there are two kinds of necessity. One is simple: for instance, it is necessary that all men are mortal. The other is conditional: for instance, if you really know that a man is walking, he must be walking. For what a man really knows cannot be otherwise than it is known to be. But the conditional kind of necessity by no means implies the simple kind, for the former is not based on the very nature of the thing called necessary but on the addition of an 'if.' For example, no necessity compels a man who is walking of his own accord to proceed, though it is necessary that, *if* he is walking, he should be proceeding. In the same way, if Providence sees any thing as present, that thing must be, though it has no necessity of its own nature; and, of course, God sees as present those future things which come to pass through free will. Therefore free acts, when referred to the divine intuition, become necessary in the conditional sense because God's knowledge provides that condition; on the other hand, viewed by themselves, they do not lose the perfect freedom of their nature. Without doubt, then, all things which God foreknows do come to pass, but certain of them proceed from free will. And these free acts, though they come to pass, do not by actually occurring lose their proper nature, because of which, before they come to pass, they could also not have come to pass. . . .

" 'But,' you will say, 'if it is within my power to change my mind I can make Providence void, for I may change what she foreknows.' To this I will answer that you can indeed change your mind but, since Providence truly sees in her present that you can change it, whether you will change it, and whither you may change it, you cannot avoid the divine foreknowledge any more than you can avoid the glance of an eye which is present, though you may by your free will turn yourself to various different actions. You will then say, 'Will the divine foreknowledge be altered by my own disposition, so that when I choose now one thing, now another, it too will seem to undergo alternations in its own cognition?' By no means; for the divine insight precedes the future and recalls it to the one present of its own proper cognition. It does not alternate, as you suppose, between this and that in its foreknowledge, but it is constantly preceding and grasping with one glance all mutations. This presence of comprehending and witnessing all things is not based on the actual occurrence of future events but on God's own peculiar simplicity—which fact also resolves that problem which you posed a little while ago when you said that it is shameful to maintain that our future acts are the cause of God's knowledge. For this power of knowledge to take cognizance, with one ever present glance, of all things has itself determined for each thing its mode of existence and owes nothing more to future things. Since this is so, mortal man's freedom of judgment remains inviolate and, because his will is free from any necessity, the laws which propose rewards and punishments are not unjust. God is the ever prescient spectator of all things, and the eternity of His vision, which is ever present, runs in unison with the future nature of our acts, dispensing rewards to the good, punishments to the evil. Hopes are not vainly put in God nor prayers vainly offered which, if they be right, cannot be ineffective. Therefore turn from vice, cultivate virtue, raise your heart to legitimate hope, direct humble prayers to the heavens. If you will only take notice and not dissemble, a great necessity for righteousness is laid upon you, since you live under the eyes of a Judge who discerns all."

NICHOLAS WOLTERSTORFF

God Is Everlasting

In this essay, Nicholas Wolterstorff (1932–) argues that, rather than existing timelessly—as Boethius, Aquinas, and many others have asserted—God exists *in time* without beginning or end. The belief in timeless divine eternity, he argues, is the result of excessive reliance by the early church fathers on ancient Greek philosophy. Presenting various facets of the picture of God's nature and actions found in the Bible, Wolterstorff maintains that these aspects of biblical teaching cannot be explained adequately on the assumption that God is timeless. For example, God conceived as a redeemer in classical theology is a God who *changes* and therefore cannot technically be eternal.

⌘

All Christian theologians agree that God is without beginning and without end. The vast majority have held, in addition, that God is *eternal*, existing outside of time. Only a small minority have contended that God is *everlasting*, existing within time.[1] In what follows I shall take up the cudgels for that minority, arguing that God as conceived and presented by the biblical writers is a being whose own life and existence is temporal.

The biblical writers do not present God as some passive factor within reality but as an agent in it. Further, they present him as acting within *human* history. The god they present is neither the impassive god of the Oriental nor the nonhistorical god of the Deist. Indeed, so basic to the biblical writings is their speaking of God as agent within history that if one viewed God as only an impassive factor in reality, or as one whose agency does not occur within human history, one would have to regard the biblical speech about God as at best one long sequence of metaphors pointing to a reality for which they are singularly inept, and as at worst one long sequence of falsehoods.

More specifically, the biblical writers present God as a redeeming God. From times most ancient, man has departed from the pattern of responsibilities awarded him at his creation by God. A multitude of evils has followed. But God was not content to leave man in the mire of his misery. Aware of what is going on, he has resolved, in response to man's sin and its resultant evils, to bring about renewal. He has, indeed, already been acting in accord with that resolve, centrally and decisively in the life, death, and resurrection of Jesus Christ.

What I shall argue is that if we are to accept this picture of God as acting for the renewal of human life, we must conceive of him as everlasting rather than eternal. God the Redeemer cannot be a God eternal. This is so because God the Redeemer is a God who *changes*. And any being which changes is a being among whose states there is temporal succession. Of course, there is an important sense in which God as presented in the Scriptures is changeless: he is steadfast in his redeeming intent and ever faithful to his children. Yet, *ontologically*, God cannot be a redeeming God without there being changeful variation among his states.

If this argument proves correct the importance of the issue here confronting us for Christian theology can scarcely be exaggerated. A theology which opts for God as eternal cannot avoid being in conflict with the confession of God as redeemer. And given the obvious fact that God is presented in the Bible as a God who redeems, a theology which opts for God as eternal cannot be a theology faithful to the biblical witness.

Our line of argument will prove to be neither subtle nor complicated. So the question will insistently arise, why have Christian theologians so massively contended that God is eternal? Why has not the dominant tradition of Christian theology been that of God everlasting?

Our argument will depend heavily on taking with seriousness a certain feature of temporality which has been neglected in Western philosophy. But the massiveness of the God eternal tradition cannot, I am persuaded, be attributed merely to philosophical oversight. There are, I think, two factors more fundamental. One is the feeling, deep-seated in much of human culture, that the flowing of events into an irrecoverable and unchangeable past is a matter for deep regret. Our bright actions and shining moments do not long endure. The gnawing tooth of time bites all. And our evil deeds can never be undone. They are forever to be regretted. Of course, the philosopher is inclined to distinguish the mere fact of temporality from the actual pattern of the events in history and to argue that regrets about the latter should not slosh over into regrets about the former. The philosopher is right. The regrettableness of what transpires in time is not good ground for regretting that there is time. Yet where the philosopher sees the possibility and the need for a distinction, most people have seen none. Regrets over the pervasive pattern of what transpires within time have led whole societies to place the divine outside of time—freed from the "bondage" of temporality.

But I am persuaded that William Kneale is correct when he contends that the most important factor accounting for the tradition of God eternal within Christian theology was the influence of the classical Greek philosophers on the early theologians.[2] The distinction between eternal being and everlasting being was drawn for the first time in history of thought by Plato (*Timaeus* 37–38), though the language he uses is reminiscent of words used still earlier by Parmenides. Plato does not connect eternity and divinity, but he does make clear his conviction that eternal being is the highest form of reality. This was enough to influence the early Christian theologians, who did their thinking within the milieu of Hellenic and Hellenistic thought, to assign eternity to God. Thus was the fateful choice made.

A good many twentieth-century theologians have been engaged in what one might call the dehellenization of Christian theology. If Kneale's contention is correct, then in this essay I am participating in that activity. Of course, not every bit of dehellenization is laudatory from the Christian standpoint, for not everything that the Greeks said is false. What is the case, though, is that the patterns of classical Greek thought are incompatible with the pattern of biblical thought. And in facing the issue of God everlasting versus God eternal we are dealing with the fundamental pattern of biblical thought. Indeed, I am persuaded that unless the tradition of God eternal is renounced, fundamental dehellenizing will perpetually occupy itself in the suburbs, never advancing to the city center. Every attempt to purge Christian theology of the traces of incompatible Hellenic patterns of thought must fail unless it removes the roadblock of the God eternal tradition. Around this barricade there are no detours. . . .

It might seem obvious that God, as described by the biblical writers, is a being who changes, and who accordingly is fundamentally noneternal. For God is described as a being who *acts*—in creation, in providence, and for the renewal of mankind. He is an agent, not an impassive factor in reality. And from the manner in which his acts are described, it seems obvious that many of them have beginnings and endings, that accordingly they stand in succession relations to each other, and that these successive acts are of such a sort that their presence and absence on God's time-strand constitutes changes thereon. Thus it seems obvious that God is fundamentally noneternal.

God is spoken of as calling Abraham to leave Chaldea and later instructing Moses to return to Egypt. So does not the event of *God's instructing Moses* succeed that of *God's calling Abraham*? And does not this sort of succession constitute a change on God's time-strand—not a change in his "essence," but nonetheless a change on his time-strand? Again, God is spoken of as leading Israel through the Red Sea and later sending his Son into the world. So does not his doing the latter succeed his doing the former? And does not the fact of this sort of succession constitute a change along God's time-strand?

In short, it seems evident that the biblical writers regard God as having a time-strand of his own on which actions on his part are to be found, and that some at least of these actions vary in such a way that there are changes along the strand. It seems evident that they do not regard changes on time-strands as confined to entities in God's creation. The God who acts, in the way in which the biblical writers speak of God as acting, seems clearly to change.

Furthermore, is it not clear from how they speak that the biblical writers regarded many of God's acts as bearing temporal order-relations to events which are not aspects of him but rather aspects of the earth, of ancient human beings, and so forth? The four cited above, for example, seem all to be described thus. It seems obvious that God's actions as described by the biblical writers stand in temporal order-relations to all the other events in our own time-array.

However, I think it is not at all so obvious as on first glance it might appear that the biblical writers do in fact describe God as changing. Granted that the language they use suggests this. It is not at once clear that this is what they wished to say with this language. It is not clear that this is how they were describing God. Let us begin to see why this is so by reflecting on the following passage from St. Thomas Aquinas:

> Nor, if the action of the first agent is eternal, does it follow that His effect is eternal, . . . God acts voluntarily in the production of things, . . . God's act of understanding and willing is, necessarily, His act of making. Now, an effect follows from the intellect and the will according to the determination of the intellect and the command of the will. Moreover, just as the intellect determines every other condition of the thing made, so does it prescribe the time of its making; for art determines not only that this thing is to be such and such, but that it is to be at this particular time, even as a physician determines that a dose of medicine is to be drunk at such and such a particular time, so that, if his act of will were of itself sufficient to produce the effect, the effect would follow anew from his previous decision, without any new action on his part. Nothing, therefore, prevents our saying that God's action existed from all eternity, whereas its effect was not present from eternity, but existed at that time when, from all eternity, He ordained it (*SCG* II.35; cf. II.36, 4).

Let us henceforth call an event which neither begins nor ends an *everlasting* event. And let us call an event which either begins or ends, a *temporal* event. In the passage above, St. Thomas is considering God's acts of bringing about temporal events. So consider some such act; say, that of God's bringing about Israel's deliverance from Egypt. The temporal event in question, Israel's deliverance from Egypt, occurred (let us say) in 1225 B.C. But from the fact that what God brought about occurred in 1225 it does not follow, says Aquinas, that God's act of bringing it about occurred in 1225. In fact, it does not follow that this act had any beginning or ending whatsoever. And in general, suppose that God brings about some temporal event *e*. From the fact that *e* is temporal it does not follow, says Aquinas, that God's act of bringing about *e*'s occurrence is temporal. The temporality of the event which God brings about does not infect God's act of bringing it about. God's act of bringing it about may well be everlasting. This can perhaps more easily be seen, he says, if we remember that God, unlike us, does not have to "take steps" so as to bring about the occurrence of some event. He need only will that it occur. If God just wants it to be the case that *e* occur at *t*, *e* occurs at *t*.

Thus God can bring about changes in our history without himself changing. The occurrence of the event of Israel's deliverance from Egypt constitutes a change in our history. But there is no counterpart change among God's aspects by virtue of his bringing this event about.

Now let us suppose that the four acts of God cited above—instructing Moses, calling Abraham, leading Israel through the Red Sea, and sending his Son into the world—regardless of the impression we might gain from the biblical language used to describe them, also have the structure of God's bringing about the occurrence of some temporal event. Suppose, for example, that God's leading Israel through the Red Sea has the structure of God's bringing it about that Israel's passage through the Red Sea occurs. And suppose Aquinas is right that the temporality of Israel's passage does not infect with temporality God's act of bringing about this passage. Then what is strictly speaking the case is not that God's leading Israel through the Red Sea occurs during 1225. What is rather the case is that Israel's passage through the Red Sea occurs during 1225, and that God brings this passage about. And the temporality of the passage does not entail the temporality of God's bringing it about. This latter may be everlasting. So, likewise, the fact that the occurrence of this passage marks a change in our history does not entail that God's bringing it about marks a change among God's aspects. God may unchangingly bring about historical changes.

It is natural, at this point, to wonder whether we do not have in hand here a general strategy for interpreting the biblical language about God acting. Is it not perhaps the case that all those acts of God which the biblical writers speak of as beginning or as ending really consist in God performing the everlasting event of bringing about the occurrence of some temporal event?

Well, God does other things with respect to temporal events than bringing about their occurrence. For example, he also *knows* them. Why then should it be thought that the best way to interpret all the temporal-event language used to describe God's actions is by reference to God's action of bringing about the occurrence of some event? May it not be that the best way to interpret what is said with some of such language is by reference to one of those other acts which God performs with respect to temporal events? But then if God is not to change, it is not only necessary that the temporality of *e* not infect God's act of *bringing about* the occurrence of *e*, but also that *every* act of God such that he performs it with respect to *e* not be infected by the temporality of *e*. For example, if God *knows* some temporal event *e*, his knowledge of *e* must not be infected by the temporality of *e*.

So the best way of extrapolating from Aquinas' hint would probably be along the lines of the following theory concerning God's actions and the biblical speech about them. All God's actions are everlasting. None has either beginning or ending. Of these everlasting acts, the structure of some consists in God's performing some action with respect to some event. And at least some of the events that God acts with respect to are temporal events. However, in no case does the temporality of the event that God acts with respect to infect the event of his acting. On the contrary, his acting with respect to some temporal event is itself invariably an everlasting event. So whenever the biblical writers use temporal-event language to describe God's actions, they are to be interpreted as thereby claiming that God acts with respect to some temporal event. They are not to be interpreted as claiming that God's acting is itself a temporal event. God as described by the biblical writers is to be interpreted as acting, and as acting with respect to temporal events. But he is not to be interpreted as changing. All his acts are everlasting.

This, I think is a fascinating theory. If true, it provides a way of harmonizing the fundamental biblical teaching that God is a being who acts in our history, with the conviction that God does not change. How far the proposed line of biblical interpretation can be carried out, I do not know. I am not aware of any theologian who has ever tried to carry it out, though there are a great many theologians who might have relieved the tension in their thought by developing and espousing it. But what concerns us here is not so much what the theory can adequately deal with as what it cannot adequately deal with. Does the theory in fact provide us with a wholly satisfactory way of harmonizing the biblical presentation of God as acting in history with the conviction that God is fundamentally eternal? . . .

To refute the . . . Thomistic theory we would have to do one or the other of two things. We would have to show that some of the temporal-event language the biblical writers use in speaking of God's actions cannot properly be construed in the suggested way—that is, cannot be construed as used to put forth the claim that God acts in some way with respect to some temporal events. Or, alternatively, we would have to show that some of the actions that God performs with respect to temporal events are themselves temporal, either because they are infected by the temporality of the events or for some other reason.

One way of developing this latter alternative would be to show that some of God's actions must be understood as a response to the free actions of human beings—that what God does he sometimes does in response to what some human being does. I think this is in fact the case. And I think it follows, given that all human actions are temporal, that those actions of God which are "response" actions are temporal as well. But to develop this line of thought would be to plunge us deep into questions of divine omniscience and human freedom. So I shall make a simpler, though I think equally effective objection to the theory, arguing that in the case of certain of God's actions the temporality of the event that God acts on infects his own action with temporality.

Three such acts are the diverse though similar acts of knowing about some temporal event that it is occurring (that it is *present*), of knowing about some temporal event that it was occurring (that it is *past*), and of knowing about some temporal event that it will be occurring (that it is *future*). Consider the first of these. No one can know about some temporal event *e* that it is occurring except when it is occurring. Before *e* has begun to occur one cannot know that it is occurring, for it is not. Not after *e* has ceased to occur can one know that it is occurring, for it is not. So suppose that *e* has a beginning. Then P's knowing about *e* that it is occurring cannot occur until *e* begins. And suppose that *e* has an ending. Then P's knowing about *e* that it is occurring cannot occur beyond *e*'s cessation. But every temporal event as (by definition) either a beginning or an ending. So every case of knowing about some temporal event that it is occurring itself either begins or ends (or both). Hence the act of knowing about *e* that it is occurring is infected by the temporality of *e*. So also, the act of knowing about *e* that it *was* occurring, and the act of knowing about *e* that it *will be* occurring, are infected by the temporality of *e*.

But, God, as the biblical writers describe him, performs all three of these acts, and performs them on temporal events. He knows what is happening in our history, what has happened, and what will happen. Hence, some of God's actions are themselves temporal events. But surely the nonoccurrence followed by the occurrence followed by the nonoccurrence of such knowings constitutes a change on God's time-strand. Accordingly, God is fundamentally noneternal. . . .

God is also described by the biblical writers as planning that he would bring about certain events which he does. This, too, is impossible if God does not change. For consider some event which someone brings about, and suppose that he planned to bring it about. His planning to bring it about must occur before the planned event occurs. For otherwise it is not a case of planning.

So in conclusion, if God were eternal he could not be aware, concerning any temporal event, that it is occurring nor aware that it was occurring nor aware that it will be occurring; nor could he remember that it has occurred; nor could he plan to bring it about and do so. But all of such actions are presupposed by, and essential to, the biblical presentation of God as a redeeming God. Hence God as presented by the biblical writers is fundamentally noneternal. He is fundamentally in time.

As with any argument, one can here choose to deny the premises rather than to accept the conclusion. Instead of agreeing that God is fundamentally noneternal because he changes with respect to his knowledge, his memory, and his planning, one could try to save one's conviction that God is eternal by denying that he knows what is or was or will be occurring, that he remembers what has occurred, and that he brings about what he has planned. It seems to me, however, that this is clearly to give up the notion of God as a redeeming God; and in turn it seems to me that to give this up is to give up what is central to the biblical vision of God. . . .

I have been arguing that God as described by the biblical writers is a being who changes. That, we have seen, is not self-evidently and obviously so, though the mode of expression of the biblical writers might lead one to think it was. Yet it is so nonetheless.

But are there not explicit statements in the Bible to the effect that God does not change? If we are honest to the evidence, must we not acknowledge that on this matter the biblical writers contradict each other? Let us see.

Surprisingly, given the massive Christian theological tradition in favor of God's ontological immutability, there are only two passages (to the best of my knowledge) in which it is directly said of God that he does not change. One of these is Malachi 3:6. The prophet has just been saying to the people that God is wearied by their hypocrisy; however (he goes on), God will send his messenger to clear a path before him; and "he will take his seat, refining and purifying." As a result of this cleansing, the "offerings of Judah and Jerusalem shall be pleasing to the Lord as they were in days of old." And then comes this assurance: "I am the Lord, unchanging; and you, too, have not ceased to be sons of Jacob. From the days of your forefathers you have been wayward and have not kept my laws. If you will return to me, I will return to you, says the Lord of Hosts" (NEB).

Surely it would be a gross misinterpretation to treat the prophet here as claiming that God is ontologically immutable. What he says, on the contrary, is that God is faithful to his people Israel—that he is unchanging in his fidelity to the covenant he has made with them. All too often theologians have ontologized the biblical message. Malachi 3:6 is a classic example of a passage which, cited out of context, would seem to support the doctrine of God's ontological immutability. Read in context, however, it supports not that but rather the doctrine of God's unswerving fidelity. No ontological claim whatever is made.

The other passage in which it is said of God that he is unchanging is to be found in Psalm 102:27. Again we must set the passage in its context:

> My strength is broken in mid course;
> the time allotted me is short.
> Snatch me not away before half my days are done,
> for thy years last through all generations.
> Long ago thou didst lay the foundations of the earth,
> and the heavens were thy handiwork.
>
> They shall pass away, but thou endurest;
> like clothes they shall all grow old;
> thou shalt cast them off like a cloak,
> and they shall vanish;
> but thou art the same and thy years shall have no end;
> thy servants' children shall continue,
> and their posterity shall be established in thy presence (NEB).

Here, too, it would be a gross misinterpretation to regard the writer as teaching that God is ontologically immutable. The Psalmist is making an ontological point of sorts, though even so the ontological point is set within a larger context of religious reflection. He is drawing a contrast between God on the one hand and his transitory creation on the other. And what he says about God is clearly that God is without end—"Thy years shall have no end." He does not say that God is ontologically immutable.

In short, God's ontological immutability is not a part of the explicit teaching of the biblical writers. What the biblical writers teach is that God is faithful and without beginning or end, not that none of his aspects is temporal. The theological tradition of God's ontological immutability has no explicit biblical foundation.[3]

The upshot of our discussion is this: the biblical presentation of God presupposes that God is everlasting rather than eternal. God is indeed without beginning and without end. But at least some of his aspects stand in temporal order-relations to each other. Thus God, too, has a time-strand. His life and existence is itself temporal. (Whether his life and existence always was and always will be temporal, or whether he has taken on temporality, is a question we have not had time to consider.) Further, the events to be found on God's time-strand belong within the same temporal array as that which contains our time-strands. God's aspects do not only bear temporal order-relations to each other but to the aspects of created entities as well. And the aspects and succession of aspects to be found on God's time-strand are such that they constitute *changes* thereon. God's life and existence incorporates changeful succession.

Haunting Christian theology and Western philosophy throughout the centuries has been the picture of time as bounded, with the created order on this side of the boundary and God on the other. Or sometimes the metaphor has been that of time as extending up to a horizon, with all creaturely reality on this side of the horizon and God on the other. All such metaphors, and the ways of thinking that they represent, must be discarded. Temporality embraces us along with God.

This conclusion from our discussion turns out to be wholly in accord with that to be found in Oscar Cullmann's *Christ and Time*. From his study of the biblical words for time Cullmann concluded that, in the biblical picture, God's "eternity" is not qualitatively different from our temporality. Cullmann's line of argument (though not his conclusion) has been vigorously attacked by James Barr on the ground that from the lexicographical patterns of biblical language we cannot legitimately make inferences as to what was being said by way of that language.[4] Verbal similarities may conceal differences in thought, and similarities in thought may be clothed with verbal differences. Barr's objection is *apropos*. But though we have traveled a very different route from Cullmann's we have come out at the same place. We have not engaged in any word studies. Yet, by seeing that God's temporality is presupposed by the biblical presentation of God as redeemer, we too have reached the conclusion that we share time with God. The lexicographical and philosophical cases coincide in their results.

Though God is within time, yet he is Lord of time. The whole array of contingent temporal events is within his power. He is Lord of what occurs. And that, along with the specific pattern of what he does, grounds all authentically biblical worship of, and obedience to, God. It is not because he is outside of time—eternal, immutable, impassive—that we are to worship and obey God. It is because of what he can and does bring about within time that we mortals are to render him praise and obedience.

NOTES

1. The most noteworthy contemporary example is Oscar Cullmann, *Christ and Time* (Philadelphia, 1950).

2. William Kneale, "Time and Eternity in Theology," *Proceedings of the Aristotelian Society* (1961).

3. "I am that I am" (Exod. 3:13) has also sometimes been used to support the doctrine of God's immutability. However, this is one of the most cryptic passages in all of Scripture; and—to understate the point—it is not in the least clear that what is being proclaimed is God's ontological immutability. There is a wealth of exe-

getical material on the passage, but see especially the comments by J. D. Murray, *The Problem of God* (New Haven, 1967), ch. 1.

4. *Biblical Words for Time* (London, 1962).

JOHN B. COBB and DAVID RAY GRIFFIN

God Is Creative-Responsive Love

In contrast with the "classical" conception of God assumed in previous selections, John Cobb (1925–   ) and David Ray Griffin (1939–   ) here present the conception of God developed in the "process theology" that stemmed from the philosophy of Alfred North Whitehead. They stress especially that God's love for human beings is "responsive" as well as "creative"—that God not only actively initiates "creative action" in the world, but also feelingly and sufferingly responds to what happens in the lives of the beings he loves. Furthermore, God's action is not accomplished by "coercive power" which overrides the power of creatures in order to accomplish his will unilaterally. Rather, God accomplishes his purposes by "persuasive power," which shows to human beings the "initial aim" he wishes them to fulfill, but leaves them free to follow or reject his will for them.

⌘

GOD AS RESPONSIVE LOVE

Whitehead noted that whereas in a primitive religion "you study the will of God in order that He may preserve you," in a universal religion "you study his goodness in order to be like him."[1] The Taoist tries to live in harmony with the Tao; the Hindu Vedantist seeks to realize the identity of Atman with Brahman; the Moslem bows to the will of Allah; the Marxist aligns with the dialectical process of history. Accordingly, the statement in Matt. 5:48, "You, therefore, must be perfect, as your heavenly Father is perfect," is a particular expression of the universal religious aspiration of humanity to participate in or be in harmony with perfection. By definition the divine reality is perfect. The question concerns the nature of this perfection.

From *Process Theology: An Introductory Exposition*, by John B. Cobb, Jr., and David Ray Griffin.

Christian faith has held that the basic character of this divine reality is best described by the term "love." However, the meaning of the statement "God is love" is by no means self-evident. Whitehead helps us to recover much of the meaning of that phrase as it is found in the New Testament.

We are told by psychologists, and we know from our own experience, that love in the fullest sense involves a sympathetic response to the loved one. Sympathy means feeling the feelings of the other, hurting with the pains of the other, grieving with the grief, rejoicing with the joys. The "others" with whom we sympathize most immediately are the members of our own bodies. When the cells in our hands, for example, are in pain, we share in the pain; we do not view their condition impassively from without. When our bodies are healthy and well exercised, we feel good with them. But we also feel sympathy for other human beings. We would doubt that a husband truly loved his wife if his mood did not to some extent reflect hers.

Nevertheless, traditional theism said that God is completely impassive, that there was no element of sympathy in the divine love for the creatures. The fact that there was an awareness that this Greek notion of divine impassibility was in serious tension with the Biblical notion of divine love for the world is most clearly reflected in this prayer of the eleventh-century theologian Anselm:

> Although it is better for thee to be . . . compassionate, passionless, than not to be these things; how art thou . . . compassionate, and, at the same time, passionless? For, if thou art passionless, thou does not feel sympathy; and if thou dost not feel sympathy, thy heart is not wretched from sympathy for the wretched; but this it is to be compassionate.[2]

Anselm resolved the tension by saying: "Thou art compassionate in terms of our experience, and not compassionate in terms of thy being."[3] In other words, God only *seems* to us to be compassionate; he is not *really* compassionate! In Anselm's words: "When thou beholdest us in our wretchedness, we experience the effect of compassion, but thou dost not experience the feeling."[4] Thomas Aquinas in the thirteenth century faced the same problem. The objection to the idea that there is love in God was stated as follows: "For in God there are no passions. Now love is a passion. Therefore love is not in God."[5] Thomas responds by making a distinction between two elements within love, one which involves passion and one which does not. He then says, after quoting Aristotle favorably, that God "loves without passion."[6]

This denial of an element of sympathetic responsiveness to the divine love meant that it was entirely creative. That is, God loves us only in the sense that he does good things for us. In Anselm's words:

> Thou art both compassionate, because thou dost save the wretched, and spare those who sin against thee; and not compassionate, because thou art affected by no sympathy for wretchedness.[7]

In Thomas' words: "To sorrow, therefore, over the misery of others belongs not to God, but it does most properly belong to Him to dispel that misery."[8]

Accordingly, for Anselm and Thomas the analogy is with the father who has no feeling for his children, and hence does not feel their needs, but "loves" them in that he gives good things to them. Thomas explicitly states that "love" is to be understood in this purely outgoing sense, as active goodwill: "To love anything is nothing else than to will good to that thing." He points out that God does not love as we love. For our love is partly responsive, since it is moved by its object, whereas the divine love is purely creative, since it creates its object.[9]

This notion of love as purely creative has implications that are in tension with the Biblical idea of God's equal love for all persons. All persons are obviously not equal in regard to the "good things of life" (however these be defined) that they enjoy (especially in the context of traditional theism, where the majority are consigned to eternal torment). And yet, if God's love is purely creative, totally creating the goodness of the beings loved, this implies that God loves some persons more than others. As Thomas said: "No one thing would be better than another if God did not will greater good for one than for another."[10] This is one of the central ways in which the acceptance of the notion of divine impassibility undercuts the Biblical witness to the love of God.

Since we mold ourselves partly in terms of our image of perfect human existence, and this in turn is based upon our notion of deity, the notion of God as an Impassive Absolute whose love was purely creative could not help but have practical consequences for human existence. Love is often defined by theologians as "active goodwill." The notion of sympathetic compassion is missing. Indeed, one of the major theological treatises on the meaning of agape, or Christian love, portrays it as totally outgoing, having no element of responsiveness to the qualities of the loved one.[11] This notion of love has promoted a "love" that is devoid of genuine sensitivity to the deepest needs of the "loved ones." Is this not why the word "charity," which is derived from *caritas* (the Latin word for agape), today has such heavily negative connotations? Also, the word "do-gooder" is a word of reproach, not because we do not want people to do good things, but because people labeled "do-gooders" go around trying to impose their own notions of the good that needs doing, without any sensitive responsiveness to the real desires and needs of those they think they are helping. This perverted view of love as purely active goodwill is due in large part to the long-standing notion that this is the kind of love which characterizes the divine reality.

This traditional notion of love as solely creative was based upon the value judgment that independence or absoluteness is unqualifiedly good, and that dependence or relativity in any sense derogates from perfection. But, as suggested in Chapter 1, while perfection entails independence or absoluteness in some respects, it also entails dependence or relativity in other respects. It entails ethical independence, in the sense that one should not be deflected by one's passions from the basic commitment to seek the greatest good in all situations. But this ethical commitment, in order to be actualized in concrete situations, requires responsiveness to the actual needs and desires of others. Hence, to promote the greatest good, one must be informed by, and thus relativized by, the feelings of others. Furthermore, we do not admire someone whose enjoyment is not in part dependent upon the condition of those around them. Parents who remained in absolute bliss while their children were in agony would not be perfect—unless there are such things as perfect monsters!

In other words, while there is a type of independence or absoluteness that is admirable, there is also a type of dependence or relativity that is admirable. And, if there is an example of absoluteness that is *unqualifiedly* admirable, this means that there is a divine absoluteness; and the same holds true of relativity. Process thought affirms that both of these are true. While traditional theism spoke only of the divine absoluteness, process theism speaks also of "the divine relativity" (this is the title of one of Hartshorne's books).

Process theism is sometimes called "dipolar theism," in contrast to traditional theism with its doctrine of divine simplicity. For Charles Hartshorne, the two "poles" or aspects of God are the abstract essence of God, on the one hand, and God's concrete actuality on the other. The abstract essence is eternal, absolute, independent, unchangeable. It includes those abstract attributes of deity which characterize the divine existence at every moment. For example, to say that God is omniscient means that in every moment of the divine life God knows everything which is knowable at that time. The concrete actuality is temporal, relative, dependent, and constantly changing. In each moment of God's life there are new, unforeseen happenings in the world which only then have become knowable. Hence, God's concrete knowledge is dependent upon the decisions made by the worldly actualities. God's knowledge is always relativized by, in the sense of internally related to, the world.

Whitehead's way of conceiving the divine dipolarity was not identical with Hartshorne's. Whitehead distinguished between the Primordial Nature of God and the Consequent Nature. The former will be discussed in the following section. The latter is largely identical with what Hartshorne has called God's concrete actuality. Since the Consequent Nature is God as fully actual,[12] the term "consequent" makes the same point as Hartshorne's term "relative," that God as fully actual is responsive to and receptive of the worldly actualizations.

This divine relativity is not limited to a "bare knowledge" of the new things happening in the world. Rather, the responsiveness includes a sympathetic feeling with the worldly beings, all of whom have feelings. Hence, it is not merely the content of God's knowledge which is dependent, but God's own emotional state. God enjoys our enjoyments, and suffers with our sufferings. This is the kind of responsiveness which is truly divine and belongs to the very nature of perfection. Hence it belongs to the ideal for human existence. Upon this basis, Christian agape can come to have the element of sympathy, of compassion for the present situation of others, which it should have had all along.

GOD AS CREATIVE LOVE

If sympathetic responsiveness is an essential aspect of Christian love, creative activity is no less essential. Whether it be considered a theme or a presupposition, the notion that God is active in the world, working to overcome evil and to create new things, is central to the Biblical tradition. To be in harmony with the God of Israel and of Jesus is to be involved in the struggle to overcome the various impediments to the fullness of life. In Luke 4:18, Jesus quotes from Isaiah, who indicates that the Spirit of the God he worships impels one to "set at liberty those who are oppressed."

The impetus in Western civilization for individual acts and social programs aimed at alleviating human misery and injustice has come in large part from the belief that God not only loves all persons equally, and hence desires justice, but also is directly acting in the world to create just conditions. The reason is that the basic religious drive of humanity is not only to be in harmony with deity, it is also to be in contact with this divine reality. It is because God is personally present and active in the world that contact with the sacred reality does not necessitate fleeing from history. Our activity aimed at creating good puts us in harmony and contact with God. Indeed, this activity can be understood in part as God's acting through us.

Accordingly, the loss of belief in the creative side of God's love would tend to undermine the various liberation movements that have been originally inspired by belief in divine providence, since it is largely this belief which has lent importance to these movements. Cultures in which the sacred is not understood as involved in creating better conditions for life in the world have had difficulty in generating the sustained commitments necessary to bring about significant change.

It is precisely this notion of divine creative activity in the world which has been most problematic in recent centuries, both within theological circles and in the culture at large. In traditional popular Christian thought, God was understood as intervening here and there in the course of the world. The notion of "acts of God" referred to events which did not have natural causes, but were directly caused by God. In traditional theological thought, all events were understood to be totally caused by God, so all events were "acts of God." However, most events were understood to be caused by God through the mediation of worldly or natural causes. God was the "primary cause" of these events, while the natural antecedents were called "secondary causes." However, a few events were thought to be caused directly by God, without the use of secondary causes. These events were "miracles." Accordingly, while all events were in one sense acts of God, these miracles were acts of God in a special sense. Thus, both in popular and theological circles, there was meaning to be given to the idea that God was creatively active in the world.

However, there are two major problems with this notion. First, it raises serious doubt that the creative activity of God can be understood as *love*, since it creates an enormous problem of evil by implying that *every* event in the world is *totally* caused by God, with or without the use of natural causes. Second, since the Renaissance and Enlightenment, the belief has grown that there are no events which happen without natural causes. Accordingly, the notion of "acts of God" has lost all unambiguous referents. Every event termed an act of God was said also, from another perspective, to be totally explainable in terms of natural causation. This rendered the notion of "act of God" of doubtful meaning. If an event can be totally explained in terms of natural forces, i.e., if these provide a "sufficient cause" for it, what justification is there for introducing the idea of "another perspective?" This seems like special pleading in order to retain a vacuous idea. . . .

In Western culture generally, the problem of evil, and the widespread belief that the nexus of natural cause and effect excludes divine "intervention," have combined to render the notion of divine creative love problematic. When the leading secular thinkers then see that the leading theologians have provided no intelligible means for speaking of God's activity in the world, they are confirmed in their suspicion that this belief belongs to the myths of the past. Process theology provides a way of recovering the conviction that God acts creatively in the world and of understanding this creative activity as the expression of divine *love* for the world. The notion that there is a creative power of love behind and within the worldly process is no longer one which can only be confessed in spite of all appearances to the contrary. Instead it illuminates our experience.

DIVINE CREATIVE LOVE AS PERSUASIVE

Traditional theism portrayed God as the Controlling Power. The doctrine of divine omnipotence finally meant that God controlled every detail of the world process. Some traditional theologians, such as Thomas Aquinas, muted this implication of their thought as much as possible (in order to protect the doctrine of human freedom). Others, such as Luther and Calvin, proclaimed the doctrine from the housetops (in order to guard against both pride and anxiety). But, in either case, the doctrine followed logically from other doctrines that were affirmed. The notion that God knows the world, and that this knowledge is unchanging, suggests that God must in fact determine every detail of the world, lest something happen which was not immutably known. The doctrine that God is completely independent of the world implies that the divine knowledge of it cannot be dependent upon it, and this can only be if the world does nothing which was not totally determined by God. The doctrine of divine simplicity involves the assertion that all the divine attributes are identical; hence God's knowing the world is identical with God's causing it. The Biblical record is quite ambivalent on the question of whether God is in complete control of the world. There is much in the Bible which implies that divine providence is not all-determining. But the interpretation of the Biblical God in terms of valuations about perfection derived from Greek philosophy ruled out this side of the Biblical witness, thereby making creaturely freedom vis-à-vis God merely apparent.

Process thought, with its different understanding of perfection, sees the divine creative activity as based upon responsiveness to the world. Since the very meaning of actuality involves internal relatedness, God as an actuality is essentially related to the world. Since actuality as such is partially self-creative, future events are not yet determinate, so that even perfect knowledge cannot know the future, and God does not wholly control the world. Any divine creative influence must be persuasive, not coercive.

Whitehead's fundamentally new conception of divine creativity in the world centers around the notion that God provides each worldly actuality with an "initial aim." This is an impulse, initially felt conformally by the occasion, to actualize the best possibility open to it, given its concrete situation. But this initial aim does not automatically becomes the subject's own aim. Rather, this "subjective aim" is a product of its own decision. The subject may choose to actualize the initial aim; but it may also choose from among the other real possibilities open to it, given its context. In other words, God seeks to persuade each occasion toward that possibility for its own existence which would be best for it; but God cannot control the finite occasion's self-actualization. Accordingly, the divine creative activity involves risk. The obvious point is that, since God is not in complete control of the events of the world, the occurrence of genuine evil is not incompatible with God's beneficence toward all his creatures.

A less obvious but equally important consequence is that, since persuasion and not control is the divine way of doing things, this is the way we should seek to accomplish our ends. Much of the tragedy in the course of human affairs can be attributed to the feeling that to control others, and the course of events, is to share in divinity. Although traditional theism said that God was essentially love, the divine love was subordinated to the divine power. Although the result of Jesus' message, life, and death should have been to redefine divine power in terms of the divine love, this did not happen. Power, in the sense of controlling domination, remained the *essential* definition of deity. Accordingly, the control of things, events, and other persons, which is to some extent a "natural" human tendency, took on that added sense of satisfaction which comes from participating in an attribute understood (more or less consciously) to be divine.

Process theology's understanding of divine love is in harmony with the insight, which we can gain both from psychologists and from our own experience, that if we truly love others we do not seek to control them. We do not seek to pressure them with promises and threats involving extrinsic rewards and punishments. Instead we try to persuade them to actualize those possibilities which they themselves will find intrinsically rewarding. We do this by providing ourselves as an environment that helps open up new, intrinsically attractive possibilities.

Insofar as the notion that divine love is persuasive is accepted, the exercise of persuasive influence becomes intrinsically rewarding. It takes on that aura of extra importance that has too often been associated with the feeling of controlling others. This change has implications in all our relations, from one-to-one I-thou encounters to international relations. It does not mean that coercive control could be eliminated, but it does mean that such control is exercised as a last resort and with a sense of regret rather than with the thrill that comes from the sense of imitating deity.

NOTES

1. Alfred North Whitehead, *Religion in the Making* (New York: Macmillan, 1926), p. 40.
2. Anselm, *Proslogium*, VI and VII, in *Proslogium; Monologium; An Appendix, In Behalf of the Fool, by Gaunilon; and Cur Deus Homo*, trans. S. N. Deane (The Open Court Publishing Company, 1903, 1945), pp. 11, 13.
3. Ibid., p. 13.
4. Ibid.
5. *Summa Theologica* I, Q. 20, art. 1, obj. 1.
6. Ibid., ans. 1.
7. *Proslogium*, VII, *loc. cit.*, pp. 13–14.
8. *Summa Theologica* I, Q. 21, art. 3, ans.
9. *Summa Theologica* I, Q. 20, art. 2, ans.
10. *Summa Theologica* I, Q. 20, art. 3, ans.
11. Anders Nygren, *Agape and Eros* (Philadelphia: Westminster Press, 1953), pp. 77–78.
12. Alfred North Whitehead, *Process and Reality* (New York: Macmillan, 1929), pp. 524, 530.

SUGGESTED READING

Basinger, David. *Divine Power in Process Theism: A Philosophical Critique*. Albany: SUNY Press, 1988.

Basinger, David, and Randall Basinger, eds. *Predestination and Free Will: Four Views of Divine Sovereignty and Human Freedom*. Downers Grove, Ill.: InterVarsity Press, 1986.

Cobb, John B., and David Ray Griffin. *Process Theology: An Introductory Exposition*. Philadelphia: Westminster Press, 1976.

Craig, William Lane. *The Only Wise God: The Compatibility of Divine Foreknowledge and Human Freedom*. Grand Rapids, Mich.: Baker, 1987.

Davis, Stephen T. *Logic and the Nature of God*. Grand Rapids: Eerdmans, 1983.

Gale, Richard M. *On the Nature and Existence of God*. New York: Cambridge University Press, 1991.

Hartshorne, Charles. *Omnipotence and Other Theological Mistakes*. Albany: SUNY Press, 1984.

Hasker, William. *God, Time, and Knowledge*. Ithaca, N.Y.: Cornell University Press, 1989.

Kenny, Anthony. *The God of the Philosophers*. Oxford: Oxford University Press, 1979.

Kvanvig, Jonathan L. *The Possibility of an All-Knowing God*. New York: St. Martin's, 1986.

Leftow, Brian. *Time and Eternity*. Ithaca: Cornell University Press, 1991.

Morris, Thomas V. *Our Idea of God: An Introduction to Philosophical Theology*. Downers Grove, Ill.: InterVarsity Press, 1991.

Pinnock, Clark, Richard Rice, John Sanders, William Hasker, and David Basinger. *The Openness of God*. Downers Grove, Ill.: InterVarsity Press, 1994.

Stump, Eleonore, and Norman Kretzmann. "Eternity." *Journal of Philosophy* 79 (1981), pp. 444–445.

Swinburne, Richard. *The Coherence of Theism*. Oxford: Oxford University Press, 1979.

Urban, Linwood, and Douglas Walton, eds. *The Power of God*. New York: Oxford University Press, 1978.

Wierenga, Edward R. *The Nature of God: An Inquiry into Divine Attributes*. Ithaca: Cornell University Press, 1989.

Zagzebski, Linda. *The Dilemma of Freedom and Foreknowledge*. New York: Oxford University Press, 1991.

PART FOUR THEISTIC ARGUMENTS

The question of whether there is any reason to believe that God exists is central to philosophy of religion. Throughout the centuries, numerous proofs or arguments for God's existence have been developed and subsequently critiqued. Contemporary philosophers of religion have come to about arguments or evidence rather than proofs in the strict sense, for there is very little about reality that can be proven. Indeed, we commonly see inductive reasoning replacing deductive arguments for God's existence. Oxford philosopher Richard Swinburne has certainly been influential in advancing inductive arguments for God's existence. Basil Mitchell and a number of other contemporary theists are interested in seeing whether a cumulative case, similar to what might be given in support of theories in science or history, can be constructed for God's existence. Nontheists, on the other hand, contend that the evidence presented by the arguments, individually or collectively, is quite weak. Antony Flew contends that ten leaky buckets, even stacked together, cannot hold their water.

Traditionally, two broad types of arguments for God's existence have been proposed: a priori arguments and a posteriori arguments. The ontological and moral arguments are a priori arguments. This type of reasoning moves from premises about concepts—for example, from an idea of what God must be like if God existed—to a claim about what really exists. The category of a posteriori arguments includes, most notably, the cosmological and teleological arguments, which commerce from analyses of the universe, asking why it exists or has order, and concludes with a claim that God exists. Each of these argument types comes in many versions, only a few of which can be presented in this anthology.

The ontological argument owes its intriguing formulation to the eleventh century theologian Anselm. The basic idea is that from an understanding of God's nature, for example, that God is a being that which none greater can be conceived, or that necessary existence is a property of God, one can show that God exists. Critics have long maintained that any move from pure concepts to a claim about reality is suspect. The critical and heavily debated issue is whether existence or necessary existence is properly understood to be a property of things.

The cosmological argument likewise comes in many forms. Traditional formulations of this argument are deductive in form and purport to identify the ultimate cause of motion or of contingent beings. Since a timeless infinite series of contingent causal conditions cannot account for any effect, he concludes that a first cause or necessary being must exist now to explain why things exist or are caused now. A different form of the argument looks for a first cause of the universe in time. Since the universe began to exist, the Kalam argument holds, it must have a cause outside itself. Critics of both arguments worry that the principle of causation is neither necessarily true nor applicable to the universe as a whole.

Different versions of the teleological argument have been presented over the centuries. Thomas Aquinas developed a deductive version in the thirteenth century. In the late century William Paley presented an analogical version that likened the universe to a machine with means-end ordering. Since a machine cannot come into being by chance but must have a cause, so must the universe. Contemporary versions take into account Darwin's thesis that nature can organize itself and argue that, though Darwin is generally correct in regard to particular biological phenomena, chance fails to provide the best explanation for certain features such as the origin of DNA out of nonliving things, the ordering principles themselves, or the narrow window that is necessary for humans to witness the universe.

Some non-theists, for example, Stephen Jay Gould, argue that the fact that we as conscious beings witness the universe is not very remarkable. Something—no matter how improbable it was—had to happen. The point simply is that the universe has evolved to its present state, but this fails to establish anything about why the present rather than another state resulted.

There are many versions of the moral argument, both deductive (Thomas Aquinas) and postulational (Immanuel Kant) in orientation. C. S. Lewis argues that there is an objective moral law that must be grounded in a being who commands and not grounded in physical nature. Nature tells us what must be the case, whereas morality deals with what ought to be the case. The argument raises important questions concerning whether there is an objective moral law and what is required to ground such a moral law.

A final issue concern whether the being the arguments affirm to exist in their conclusion—whether a necessary being, first cause, or mind that commands morality—is to be identified with the God of religion. To what extent can the detached, objective metaphysical description of the divine being correlate with the involved religious believer's idea of an accessible God? Some sort of process correlating the properties of each must be invoked to assess any claims of identity.

Students of philosophy must evaluate for themselves whether the arguments are successful. Clearly, they are not convincing to everyone, and perhaps not even to most. Yet there is a significant number of intelligent people who take them seriously and believe that they have a point. Lack of universal consent to any thesis should not deter the inquirer from investigating the claims. It is obvious, however, that the theistic arguments have evolved over the centuries as new models of the universe and new philosophical categories have gained preeminence. Accordingly, those who work with the arguments must pay attention to the broader intellectual milieu in which arguments are found.

SAINT ANSELM

The Classical Ontological Argument

Anselm (1033–1109) argues that we can conceive of God as "a being than which none greater can be conceived." Yet, if we conceive of such a being as existing only in the understanding, a greater being could be conceived, namely, one that also exists in reality. Anselm's strategy, then, is to move from the admission that we have the concept of "a being than which none greater can be conceived" to the conclusion that God cannot be conceived not to exist.

⌘

Truly there is a God, although the fool hath said in his heart, There is no God.

And so, Lord, do thou, who dost give understanding to faith, give me, so far as thou knowest it to be profitable, to understand that thou art as we believe; and that thou art that which we believe. And, indeed, we believe that thou art a being than which nothing greater can be conceived. Or is there no such nature, since the fool hath said in his heart, there is no God? (Psalms xiv. I). But, at any rate, this very fool, when he hears of this being of which I speak—a being than which nothing greater can be conceived—understands what he hears, and what he understands is in his understanding; although he does not understand it to exist.

For, it is one thing for an object to be in the understanding, and another to understand that the object exists. When a painter first conceives of what he will afterwards perform, he has it in his understanding, but he does not yet understand it to be, because he has not yet performed it. But after he has made the painting, he both has it in his understanding, and he understands that it exists, because he has made it.

Hence, even the fool is convinced that something exists in the understanding, at least, than which nothing greater can be conceived. For, when he hears of this, he understands it. And whatever is understood, exists in the understanding. And assuredly that, than which nothing greater can be conceived, cannot exist in the understanding alone. For, suppose it exists in the understanding alone: then it can be conceived to exist in reality; which is greater.

Therefore, if that, than which nothing greater can be conceived, exists in the understanding alone, the very being, than which nothing greater can be conceived, is one, than which a greater can be conceived. But obviously this is impossible. Hence, there is no doubt that there exists a being, than which nothing greater can be conceived, and it exists both in the understanding and in reality.

From *Proslogium*, in *St. Anselm: Basic Writings*, ed. S. N. Deane. LaSalle, Ill.: Open Court, 1962.

God cannot be conceived not to exist.—God is that, than which nothing greater can be conceived.—That which can be conceived not to exist is not God.

And it assuredly exists so truly, that it cannot be conceived not to exist. For, it is possible to conceive of a being which cannot be conceived not to exist; and this is greater than one which can be conceived not to exist. Hence, if that, than which nothing greater can be conceived, can be conceived not to exist, it is not that, than which nothing greater can be conceived. But this is an irreconcilable contradiction. There is, then, so truly a being than which nothing greater can be conceived to exist, that it cannot even be conceived not to exist; and this being thou art, O Lord, our God.

So truly, therefore, dost thou exist, O Lord, my God, that thou canst not be conceived not to exist; and rightly. For, if a mind could conceive of a being better than thee, the creature would rise above the Creator; and this is most absurd. And, indeed, whatever else there is, except thee alone, can be conceived not to exist. To thee alone, therefore, it belongs to exist more truly than all other beings, and hence in a higher degree than all others. For, whatever else exists does not exist so truly, and hence in a less degree it belongs to it to exist. Why, then, has the fool said in his heart, there is no God (Psalms xiv. I), since it is so evident, to a rational mind, that thou dost exist in the highest degree of all? Why, except that he is dull and a fool?

How the fool has said in his heart what cannot be conceived.—A thing may be conceived in two ways: (1) when the word signifying it is conceived; (2) when the thing itself is understood As far as the word goes, God can be conceived not to exist; in reality he cannot.

But how has the fool said in his heart what he could not conceive; or how is it that he could not conceive what he said in his heart? since it is the same to say in the heart, and to conceive.

But, if really, nay, since really, he both conceived, because he said in his heart; and did not say in his heart, because he could not conceive; there is more than one way in which a thing is said in the heart or conceived. For, in one sense, an object is conceived, when the word signifying it is conceived; and in another, when the very entity, which the object is, is understood.

In the former sense, then, God can be conceived not to exist; but in the latter, not at all. For no one who understands what fire and water are can conceive fire to be water, in accordance with the nature of the facts themselves, although this is possible according to the words. So, then, no one who understands what God is can conceive that God does not exist; although he says these words in his heart, either without any, or with some foreign, signification. For, God is that than which a greater cannot be conceived. And he who thoroughly understands this, assuredly understands that this being so truly exists, that not even in concept can it be non-existent. Therefore, he who understands that God so exists, cannot conceive that he does not exist.

I thank thee, gracious Lord, I thank thee; because what I formerly believed by thy bounty, I now so understand by thine illumination, that if I were unwilling to believe that thou dost exist, I should not be able to understand this to be true.

GAUNILO

Critique of Anselm's Argument

The monk Gaunilo (11th century) raises a number of objections to Anselm's argument. First, we cannot reason from the existence of something in my understanding to the fact that it exists in extramental reality, for by such reasoning we could show that unreal objects exist. According to Gaunilo, Anselm has not shown how the concept of "a being than which none greater can be conceived" differs from concepts of unreal objects. Second, Gaunilo charges that Anselm has confused the forming of a concept of something with discovering whether that thing exists. Third, he states that Anselm wrongly presupposed that we are able to conceive of or understand God himself. Finally, Gaunilo distinguishes between understanding something and proving it to exist. Otherwise by merely conceiving things like islands more excellent than any other we could prove that they exist.

⌘

The fool might make this reply:

This being is said to be in my understanding already, only because I understand what is said. Now could it not with equal justice be said that I have in my understanding all manner of unreal objects, having absolutely no existence in themselves, because I understand these things if one speaks of them, whatever they may be?

Unless indeed it is shown that this being is of such a character that it cannot be held in concept like all unreal objects, or objects whose existence is uncertain: and hence I am not able to conceive of it when I hear of it, or to hold it in concept; but I must understand it and have it in my understanding; because, it seems, I cannot conceive of it in any other way than by understanding it, that is, by comprehending in my knowledge its existence in reality.

From "On Behalf of the Fool," in *St. Anselm: Basic Writings*, ed. S. N. Deane. LaSalle, Ill.: Open Court, 1962.

But if this is the case, in the first place there will be no distinction between what has precedence in time—namely, the having of an object in the understanding—and what is subsequent in time—namely, the understanding that an object exists; as in the example of the picture, which exists first in the mind of the painter, and afterwards in his work.

Moreover, the following assertion can hardly be accepted: that this being, when it is spoken of and heard of, cannot be conceived not to exist in the way in which even God can be conceived not to exist. For if this is impossible, what was the object of this argument against one who doubts or denies the existence of such a being?

Finally, that this being so exists that it cannot be perceived by an understanding convinced of its own indubitable existence, unless this being is afterwards conceived of—this should be proved to me by an indisputable argument, but not by that which you have advanced: namely, that what I understand, when I hear it, already is in my understanding. For thus in my understanding, as I still think, could be all sorts of things whose existence is uncertain, or which do not exist at all, if some one whose words I should understand mentioned them. And so much the more if I should be deceived, as often happens, and believe in them: though I do not yet believe in the being whose existence you would prove. . . .

Let us notice also the point touched on above, with regard to this being which is greater than all which can be conceived, and which, it is said, can be none other than God himself. I, so far as actual knowledge of the object, either from its specific or general character, is concerned, am as little able to conceive of this being when I hear of it, or to have it in my understanding, as I am to conceive of or understand God himself: whom, indeed, for this very reason I can conceive not to exist. For I do not know that reality itself which God is, nor can I form a conjecture of that reality from some other like reality. For you yourself assert that that reality is such that there can be nothing else like it.

For, suppose that I should hear something said of a man absolutely unknown to me, of whose very existence I was unaware. Through that special or general knowledge by which I know what man is, or what men are, I could conceive of him also, according to the reality itself, which man is. And yet it would be possible, if the person who told me of him deceived me, that the man himself, of whom I conceived, did not exist; since that reality according to which I conceived of him, though a no less indisputable fact, was not that man, but any man.

Hence, I am not able, in the way in which I should have this unreal being in concept or in understanding, to have that being of which you speak in concept or in understanding, when I hear the word *God* or the words, *a being greater than all other things*. For I can conceive of the man according to a fact that is real and familiar to me: but of God, or a being greater than all others, I could not conceive at all, except merely according to the word. And an object can hardly or never be conceived according to the word alone.

For when it is so conceived, it is not so much the word itself (which is, indeed, a real thing—that is, the sound of the letters and syllables) as the signification of the word, when heard, that is conceived. But it is not conceived as by one who knows what is generally signified by the word; by whom, that is, it is conceived according to a reality and in true conception alone. It is conceived as by a man who does not know the object, and conceives of it only in accordance with the movement of his mind produced by hearing the word, the mind attempting to image for itself the signification of the word that is heard. And it would be surprising if in the reality of fact it could ever attain to this.

Thus, it appears, and in no other way, this being is also in my understanding, when I hear and understand a person who says that there is a being greater than all conceivable beings. So much for the assertion that this supreme nature already is in my understanding.

But that this being must exist, not only in the understanding but also in reality, is thus proved to me:

If it did not so exist, whatever exists in reality would be greater than it. And so the being which has been already proved to exist in my understanding, will not be greater than all other beings.

I still answer: if it should be said that a being which cannot be even conceived in terms of any fact, is in the understanding, I do not deny that this being is, accordingly, in my understanding. But since through this fact it can in no wise attain to real existence also, I do not yet concede to it that existence at all, until some certain proof of it shall be given.

For he who says that this being exists, because otherwise the being which is greater than all will not be greater than all, does not attend strictly enough to what he is saying. For I do not yet say, no, I even deny or doubt that this being is greater than any real object. Nor do I concede to it any other existence than this (if it should be called existence) which it has when the mind, according to a word merely heard, tries to form the image of an object absolutely unknown to it.

How, then, is the veritable existence of that being proved to me from the assumption, by hypothesis, that it is greater than all other beings? For I should still deny this, or doubt your demonstration of it, to this extent, that I should not admit that this being is in my understanding and concept even in the way in which many objects whose real existence is uncertain and doubtful, are in my understanding and concept. For it should be proved first that this being itself really exists somewhere; and then, from the fact that it is greater than all, we shall not hesitate to infer that it also subsists in itself.

For example: it is said that somewhere in the ocean is an island, which, because of the difficulty, or rather the impossibility, of discovering what does not exist, is called the lost island. And they say that this island has an inestimable wealth of all manner of riches and delicacies in greater abundance than is told of the Islands of the Blest; and that having no owner or inhabitant, it is more excellent than all other countries, which are inhabited by mankind, in the abundance with which it is stored.

Now if some one should tell me that there is such an island, I should easily understand his words, in which there is no difficulty. But suppose that he went on to say, as if by a logical inference: "You can no longer doubt that this island which is more excellent than all lands exists somewhere, since you have no doubt that it is in your understanding. And since it is more excellent not to be in the understanding alone, but to exist both in the understanding and in reality, for this reason it must exist. For if it does not exist, any land which really exists will be more excellent than it; and so the island already understood by you to be more excellent will not be more excellent."

If a man should try to prove to me by such reasoning that this island truly exists, and that its existence should no longer be doubted, either I should believe that he was jesting, or I know not which I ought to regard as the greater fool: myself, supposing that I should allow this proof; or him, if he should suppose that he had established with any certainty the existence of this island. For he ought to show first that the hypothetical excellence of this island exists as a real and indubitable fact, and in no wise as any unreal object, or one whose existence is uncertain, in my understanding.

ALVIN PLANTINGA

A Contemporary Modal Version of the Ontological Argument

Alvin Plantinga (1932–) first reviews and rejects Gaunilo's objections to Anselm's argument. He then proceeds to evaluate several versions of the ontological argument before developing his own version. According to Plantinga, it is possible that some being has maximal greatness. However, if a being has this property, then it has it in every possible world. So, reasons Plantinga, if it is possible that God exists with this property, it is necessary that God exists. Using the techniques and insights of contemporary modal logic, Plantinga fashions a widely discussed rendition of the ontological argument.

⌘

I wish to discuss the famous "ontological argument" first formulated by Anselm of Canterbury in the eleventh century. This argument for the existence of God has fascinated philosophers ever since Anselm first stated it. . . .

Although the argument certainly looks at first sight as if it ought to be unsound, it is profoundly difficult to say what, exactly, is wrong with it. Indeed, I do not believe that any philosopher has ever given a cogent and conclusive refutation of the ontological argument in its various forms. . . .

How can we outline Anselm's argument? It is best construed, I think, as a *reductio ad absurdum* argument. In a *reductio* you prove a given proposition *p* by showing that its denial, *not-p*, leads to (or more strictly, entails) a contradiction or some other kind of absurdity. Anselm's argument can be seen as an attempt to deduce an absurdity from the proposition that there is no God. If we use the term "God" as an abbreviation for Anselm's phrase "the being than which nothing greater can be conceived," then the argument seems to go approximately as follows: Suppose

(1) God exists in the understanding but not in reality.

(2) Existence in reality is greater than existence in the understanding alone. (premise)

(3) God's existence in reality is conceivable. (premise)

(4) If God did exist in reality, then He would be greater than He is. [from (1) and (2)]

(5) It is conceivable that there is a being greater than God is. [(3) and (4)]

(6) It is conceivable that there be a being greater than the being than which nothing greater can be conceived. [(5) by the definition of "God"]

But surely (6) is absurd and self-contradictory; how could we conceive of a being greater than the being than which none greater can be conceived? So we may conclude that

(7) It is false that God exists in the understanding but not in reality.

It follows that if God exists in the understanding, He also exists in reality; but clearly enough He *does* exist in the understanding, as even the fool will testify; therefore, He exists in reality as well.

Now when Anselm says that a being *exists in the understanding*, we may take him, I think, as saying that someone has *thought of* or thought about that being. When he says that something *exists in reality*, on the other hand, he means to say simply that the thing in question really does exist. And when he says that a certain state of affairs is *conceivable*, he means to say, I believe, that this state of affairs is possible in our broadly logical sense; there is a possible world in which it obtains. This means that step (3) above may be put more perspicuously as

(3′) It is possible that God exists

and step (6) as

(6′) It is possible that there be a being greater than the being than which it is not possible that there be a greater.

An interesting feature of this argument is that all of its premises are *necessarily* true if true at all. (1) is the assumption from which Anselm means to deduce a contradiction. (2) is a premise, and presumably necessarily true in Anselm's view; and (3) is the only remaining premise (the other items are consequences of preceding steps); it says of some *other* proposition (*God exists*) that it is possible. Propositions which thus ascribe a modality—possibility, necessity, contingency—to another proposition are themselves either necessarily true or necessarily false. So all the premises of the argument are, if true at all, necessarily true. And hence if the premises of this argument are true, then [provided that (6) is really inconsistent] a contradiction can be deduced from (1) together with necessary propositions; this means that (1) entails a contradiction and is, therefore, necessarily false.

GAUNILO'S OBJECTION

Gaunilo, a contemporary of Anselm's, wrote a reply which he entitled *On Behalf of the Fool*. . . .

Gaunilo was the first of many to try to discredit the ontological argument by showing that one can find similar arguments to prove the existence of all sorts of absurd things—a greatest possible island, a highest possible mountain, a greatest possible middle linebacker, a meanest possible man, and the like. But Anselm was not without a reply.

He points out, first, that Gaunilo misquotes him. What is under consideration is not a being that is *in fact* greater than any other, but one such that a greater *cannot be conceived*; a being than which it's *not possible* that there be a greater. Gaunilo seems to overlook this. And thus his famous lost island argument isn't strictly parallel to Anselm's argument; his conclusion should be only that there is an island such that no other island is greater than it—which, if there are any islands at all, is a fairly innocuous conclusion.

But obviously Gaunilo's argument can be revised. Instead of speaking, as he did, of an island that is more excellent than all others, let's speak instead of an island than which a greater or more excellent cannot be conceived—an island, that is, than which it's not possible that there be a greater. Couldn't we use an argument like Anselm's to "establish" the existence of such an island, and if we could, wouldn't that show that Anselm's argument is fallacious?

ANSELM'S REPLY

Not obviously. Anselm's proper reply, it seems to me, is that it's impossible that there be such an island. The idea of an island than which it's not possible that there be a greater is like the idea of a natural number than which it's not possible that there be a greater, or the idea of a line than which none more crooked is possible. There neither is nor could be a greatest possible natural number; indeed, there isn't a greatest *actual* number, let alone a greatest possible. And the same goes for islands. No matter how great an island is, . . . there could always be a greater. . . . The qualities that make for greatness in islands—number of palm trees, amount and quality of coconuts, for example—most of these qualities have no *intrinsic maximum*. That is, there is no degree of productivity or number of palm trees (or of dancing girls) such that it is impossible that an island display more of that quality. So the idea of a greatest possible island is an inconsistent or incoherent idea; it's not possible that there be such a thing. And hence the analogue of step (3) of Anselm's argument (it is possible that God exists) is not true for the perfect island argument; so that argument fails.

But doesn't Anselm's argument itself founder upon the same rock? If the idea of a greatest possible island is inconsistent, won't the same hold for the idea of a greatest possible being? Perhaps not. For what are the properties in virtue of which one being is greater, just as a being, than another? Anselm clearly has in mind such properties as wisdom, knowledge, power, and moral excellence or moral perfection. And certainly knowledge, for example, does have an intrinsic maximum: if for every proposition *p*, a being *B* knows whether or not *p* is true, then *B* has a degree of knowledge that is utterly unsurpassable. So a greatest possible being would have to have this kind of knowledge: it would have to be *omniscient*. Similarly for *power*; omnipotence is a degree of power that can't possibly be excelled. Moral perfection or moral excellence is perhaps not quite so clear; still a being could perhaps always do what is morally right, so that it would not be possible for it to be exceeded along those lines. . . .

The usual criticisms of Anselm's argument, then, leave much to be desired. Of course, this doesn't mean that the argument is successful, but it does mean that we shall have to take an independent look at it. What about Anselm's argument? Is it a good one? The first thing to recognize is that the ontological argument comes in an enormous variety of versions, some of which may be much more promising than others. Instead of speaking of *the* ontological argument, we must recognize that what we have here is a whole family of related arguments. (Having said this I shall violate my own directive and continue to speak of *the* ontological argument.)

THE ARGUMENT RESTATED

Let's look once again at our initial schematization of the argument. I think perhaps it is step (2)

(2) Existence in reality is greater than existence in the understanding alone

that is most puzzling here. Earlier we spoke of the properties in virtue of which one being is greater, just as a being, than another. Suppose we call them *great-making properties.* Apparently Anselm means to suggest that *existence* is a great-making property. He seems to suggest that a nonexistent being would be greater than in fact it is, if it did exist. But how can we make sense of that? How could there be a nonexistent being anyway? Does that so much as make sense?

Perhaps we can put this perspicuously in terms of possible worlds. An object may exist in some possible worlds and not others. There are possible worlds in which you and I do not exist; these worlds are impoverished, no doubt, but are not on that account impossible. Furthermore, an object can have different properties in different worlds. In the actual world Paul J. Zwier is not a good tennis player; but surely there are worlds in which he wins the Wimbledon Open. Now if a person can have different properties in different worlds, then he can have different degrees of greatness in different worlds. In the actual world Raquel Welch has impressive assets; but there is a world RW_f in which she is fifty pounds overweight and mousy. Indeed, there are worlds in which she does not so much as exist. What Anselm means to be suggesting, I think, is that Raquel Welch enjoys very little greatness in those worlds in which she does not exist. But of course this condition is not restricted to Miss Welch. What Anselm means to say, more generally, is that for any being x and worlds W and W', if x exists in W but not in W', then x's greatness in W exceeds x's greatness in W'. Or, more modestly, perhaps he means to say that if a being x does not exist in a world W (and there is a world in which x does exist), then *there is at least one world* in which the greatness of x exceeds the greatness of x in W. Suppose Raquel Welch does not exist in some world W. Anselm means to say that there is at least one possible world in which she has a degree of greatness that exceeds the degree of greatness she has in that world W. (It is plausible, indeed, to go much further and hold that she has *no greatness at all* in worlds in which she does not exist.)

But now perhaps we can restate the whole argument in a way that gives us more insight into its real structure. Once more, use the term "God" to abbreviate the phrase "the being than which it is not possible that there be a greater." Now suppose

(13) God does not exist in the actual world

Add the new version of premise (2):

(14) For any being x and world W, if x does not exist in W, then there is a world W' such that the greatness of x in W' exceeds the greatness of x in W.

Restate premise (3) in terms of possible worlds:

(15) There is a possible world in which God exists.

And continue on:

(16) If God does not exist in the actual world, then there is a world W' such that the greatness of God in W' exceeds the greatness of God in the actual world. [from (14)]

(17) So there is a world W' such that the greatness of God in W' exceeds the greatness of God in the actual world. [(13) and (16)]

(18) So there is a possible being x and a world W' such that the greatness of x in W' exceeds the greatness of God in actuality. [(17)]

(19) Hence it's possible that there be a being greater than God is. [(18)]

(20) So it's possible that there be a being greater than the being than which it's not possible that there be a greater. (19), replacing "God" by what it abbreviates

But surely

(21) It's not possible that there be a being greater than the being than which it's not possible that there be a greater.

So (13) [with the help of premises (14) and (15)] appears to imply (20), which, according to (21), is necessarily false. Accordingly, (13) is false. So the actual world contains a being than which it's not possible that there be a greater—that is, God exists.

Now where, if anywhere, can we fault this argument? Step (13) is the hypothesis for *reductio*, the assumption to be reduced to absurdity, and is thus entirely above reproach. Steps (16) through (20) certainly look as if they follow from the items they are said to follow from. So that leaves only (14), (15), and (20). Step (14) says only that it is possible that God exists. Step (15) also certainly seems plausible: if a being doesn't even *exist* in a given world, it can't have much by way of greatness in that world. At the very least it can't have its *maximum* degree of greatness—a degree of greatness that it does not excel in any other world—in a world where it doesn't exist. And consider (20): surely it has the ring of truth. How could there be a being greater than the being than which it's not possible that there be a greater? Initially, the argument seems pretty formidable.

ITS FATAL FLAW

But there is something puzzling about it. We can see this if we ask what sorts of things (14) is supposed to be *about*. It starts off boldly: "For any being x and world W, . . ." So (14) is talking about worlds and beings. It says something about each world-being pair. And (16) follows from it, because (16) asserts of *God* and *the actual world* something that according to (14) holds of every being and world. But then if (16) follows from (14), God must be a *being*. That is, (16) follows from (14) only with the help of the additional premise that God is a being. And doesn't this statement—that God is a being—imply that *there is* or *exists* a being than which it's not possible that there be a greater? But if so, the argument flagrantly begs the question; for then we can accept the inference from (14) to (16) only if we already know that the conclusion is true.

We can approach this same matter by a slightly different route. I asked earlier what sorts of things (14) was *about*; the answer was: beings and worlds. We can ask the same or nearly the same question by asking about the *range* of the *quantifiers*—"for any being," "for any world"—in (14). What do these quantifiers range over? If we reply that they range over possible worlds and beings—*actually existing* beings—then the inference to (16) requires the additional premise that God is an actually existing being, that there *really is* a being than which it is not possible that there be a greater. Since this is supposed to be our conclusion, we can't very gracefully add it as a *premise*. So perhaps the quantifiers don't range just over actually existing beings. But what else is there? Step (18) speaks of a *possible being*—a thing that may not in fact exist, but *could* exist. Or we could put it like this. A possible being is a thing that exists in some possible world or other; a thing x for which there is a world W, such that if W had been actual, x would have existed. So (18) is really about worlds and *possible beings*. And what it says is this: take any possible being x and any possible world W. If x does not exist in W, then there is a possible world W' where x has a degree of greatness that surpasses the greatness that it has in W. And hence to make the argument complete perhaps we should add the affirmation that God is a *possible being*.

But *are* there any possible beings—that is, *merely* possible beings, beings that don't in fact exist? If so, what sorts of things are they? Do they have properties? How are we to think of them? What is their status? And what reasons are there for supposing that there are any such peculiar items at all?

These are knotty problems. Must we settle them in order even to consider this argument? No. For instead of speaking of *possible beings* and the worlds in which they do or don't exist, we can speak of *properties* and the worlds in which they do or don't *have instances*, are or are not *instantiated* or *exemplified*. Instead of speaking of a possible being named by the phrase, "the being than which it's not possible that there be a greater," we may speak of the property *having an unsurpassable degree of greatness*—that is, *having a degree of greatness such that it's not possible that there exist a being having more*. And then we can ask whether this property is instantiated in this or other possible worlds. Later on I shall show how to restate the argument this way. For the moment please take my word for the fact that we can speak as freely as we wish about possible objects; for we can always translate ostensible talk about such things into talk about properties and the worlds in which they are or are not instantiated.

The argument speaks, therefore, of an unsurpassably great being—of a being whose greatness is not excelled by any being in any world. This being has a degree of greatness so impressive that no other being in any world has more. But here we hit the question crucial for this version of the argument. *Where* does this being have that degree of greatness? I said above that the same being may have different degrees of greatness in different worlds; in which world does the possible being in question have the degree of greatness in question? All we are really told, in being told that God is a possible being, is this: among the possible beings there is one that in some world or other has a degree of greatness that is nowhere excelled.

And this fact is fatal to this version of the argument. I said earlier that (21) has the ring of truth; a closer look (listen?) reveals that it's more of a dull thud. For it is ambiguous as between

(21′) It's not possible that there be a being whose greatness surpasses that enjoyed by the unsurpassably great being *in the worlds where its greatness is at a maximum*

and

(21″) It's not possible that there be a being whose greatness surpasses that enjoyed by the unsurpassably great being *in the actual world.*

There is an important difference between these two. The greatest possible being may have different degrees of greatness in different worlds. Step (21′) points to the worlds in which this being has its maximal greatness; and it says, quite properly, that the degree of greatness this being has in those worlds is nowhere excelled. Clearly this is so. The greatest possible being is a possible being who in some world or other has unsurpassable greatness. Unfortunately for the argument, however, (21′) does not contradict (20). Or to put it another way, what follows from (13) [together with (14) and (15)] is not the denial of (21′). If that *did* follow, then the *reductio* would be complete and the argument successful. But what (20) says is not that there is a possible being whose greatness exceeds that enjoyed by the greatest possible being *in a world where the latter's greatness is at a maximum*; it says only that there is a possible being whose greatness exceeds that enjoyed by the greatest possible being *in the actual world*—where, for all we know, its greatness is *not* at a maximum. So if we read (21) as (21′), the *reductio* argument falls apart.

Suppose instead we read it as (21″). Then what it says is that there couldn't be a being whose greatness surpasses that enjoyed by the greatest possible being in Kronos, the actual world. So read, (21) does contradict (20). Unfortunately, however, we have no reason, so far, for thinking that (21″) is true at all, let alone necessarily true. If, among the possible beings, there is one whose greatness *in some world or other* is absolutely maximal—such that no being in any world has a degree of greatness surpassing it—then indeed there couldn't be a being that was greater than *that*. But it doesn't follow that this being has that degree of greatness in the *actual* world. It has it *in some world or other* but not necessarily in Kronos, the actual world. And so the argument fails. If we take (21) as (21′), then it follows from the assertion that God is a possible being; but it is of no use to the argument. If we take it as (21″), on the other hand, then indeed it is useful in the argument, but we have no reason whatever to think it true. So this version of the argument fails.[1]

A MODAL VERSION OF THE ARGUMENT

But of course there are many other versions; one of the argument's chief features is its many-sided diversity. The fact that *this* version is unsatisfactory does not show that *every* version is or must be. Professors Charles Hartshorne[2] and Normal Malcolm[3] claim to detect two quite different versions of the argument in Anselm's work. In the first of these versions *existence* is held to be a perfection or a great-making property; in the second it is *necessary existence*. But what could *that* amount to? Perhaps something like this. Consider a pair of beings *A* and *B* that both do in fact exist. And suppose that *A* exists in every other possible world as well—that is, if any other possible world has been actual, *A* would have existed. On the other hand, *B* exists in only some possible worlds; there are worlds *W* such that had any of *them* been actual, *B* would not have existed. Now according to the doctrine under consideration, *A* is so far greater than *B*. Of course, *on balance* it may be that *A* is not greater than *B*; I believe that the number seven, unlike Spiro Agnew, exists in every possible world; yet I should be hesitant to affirm on that account that the number seven is greater than Agnew. Necessary existence is just one of several great-making properties, and no doubt Agnew has more of some of these others than does the number seven. Still, all this is compatible with saying that necessary existence is a great-making property. And given this notion, we can restate the argument as follows:

(22) It is possible that there is a greatest possible being.

(23) Therefore, there is a possible being that in some world *W′* or other has a maximum degree of greatness—a degree of greatness that is nowhere exceeded.

(24) A being *B* has the maximum degree of greatness in a given possible world *W* only if *B exists in every possible world*.

(22) and (24) are the premises of this argument; and what follows is that if *W′* had been actual, *B* would have existed in every possible world. That is,

if *W'* had been actual, *b*'s nonexistence would have been impossible. But logical possibilities and impossibilities do not vary from world to world. That is to say, if a given proposition or state of affairs is impossible in at least one possible world, then it is impossible in every possible world. There are no propositions that in fact are possible but could have been impossible; there are none that are in fact impossible but could have been possible.[4] Accordingly, *B*'s nonexistence is impossible in every possible world; hence it is impossible in *this* world; hence *B* exists and exists necessarily.

A FLAW IN THE OINTMENT

This is an interesting argument, but it suffers from at least one annoying defect. What it shows is that if it is possible that there be a greatest possible being (if the idea of a greatest possible being is coherent) and if that idea includes necessary existence, then in fact there is a being that exists in every world and in *some* world has a degree of greatness that is nowhere excelled. Unfortunately it doesn't follow that the being in question has the degree of greatness in question in Kronos, the actual world. For all the argument shows, this being might *exist* in the actual world but be pretty insignificant here. In some world or other it has maximal greatness; how does this show that it has such greatness in Kronos? . . .

In determining the greatness of a being *B* in a world *W*, what counts is not merely the qualities and properties possessed by *B* in *W*; what *B* is like in *other* worlds is also relevant. Most of us who believe in God think of Him as a being than whom it's not possible that there be a greater. But we don't think of Him as a being who, had things been different, would have been powerless or uninformed or of dubious moral character. God doesn't *just happen* to be a greatest possible being; He couldn't have been otherwise.

Perhaps we should make a distinction here between *greatness* and *excellence*. A being's excellence in a given world *W*, let us say, depends only upon the properties it has in *W*; its *greatness* in *W* depends upon these properties but also upon what it is like in other worlds. Those who are fond of the calculus might put it by saying that there is a function assigning to each being in each world a degree of excellence; and a being's *greatness* is to be computed (by someone unusually well informed) by integrating its excellence over all possible worlds. Then it is plausible to suppose that the maximal degree of greatness entails *maximum excellence in every world*. A being, then, has the maximal degree of *greatness* in a given world *W* only if it has *maximal excellence in every possible world*. But *maximal excellence* entails *omniscience, omnipotence,* and *moral perfection*. That is to say, a being *B* has maximal excellence in a world *W* only if *B* has omniscience, omnipotence, and moral perfection in *W*—only if *B* would have been omniscient, omnipotent, and morally perfect if *W* had been actual.

THE ARGUMENT RESTATED

Given these ideas, we can restate the present version of the argument in the following more explicit way.

(25) It is possible that there be a being that has maximal greatness.

(26) So there is a possible being that in some world *W* has maximal greatness.

(27) A being has maximal greatness in a given world only if it has maximal excellence in every world.

(28) A being has maximal excellence in a given world only if it has omniscience, omnipotence, and moral perfection in that world.

And now we no longer need the supposition that necessary existence is a perfection; for obviously a being can't be omnipotent (or for that matter omniscient or morally perfect) in a given world unless it *exists* in that world. From (25), (27), and (28) it follows that there actually exists a being that is omnipotent, omniscient, and morally perfect; this being, furthermore, exists and has these qualities in every other world as well. For (26), which follows from (25), tells us that there is a possible world *W′*, let's say, in which there exists a being with maximal greatness. That is, had *W′* been actual, there would have been a being with maximal greatness. But then according to (27) this being has maximal excellence in every world. What this means, according to (28), is that in *W′* this being has omniscience, omnipotence, and moral perfection *in every world*. That is to say, if *W′* had been actual, there would have existed a being who was omniscient and omnipotent and morally perfect and who would have had these properties in every possible world. So if *W′* had been actual, it would have been *impossible* that there be no omnipotent, omniscient, and morally perfect being. But . . . while *contingent* truths vary from world to world, what is logically impossible does not. Therefore, in every possible world *W* it is impossible that there be no such being; each possible world *W* is such that if it had been actual, it would have been impossible that there be no such being. And hence it is impossible in the *actual* world (which is one of the possible worlds) that there be no omniscient, omnipotent, and morally perfect being. Hence there really does exist a being who is omniscient, omnipotent, and morally perfect and who exists and has these properties in every possible world. Accordingly these premises, (25), (27), and (28), entail that God, so thought of, exists. Indeed, if we regard (27) and (28) as consequences of a *definition*—a definition of maximal greatness—then the only premise of the argument is (25).

But now for a last objection suggested earlier. What about (25)? It says that there is a *possible being* having such and such characteristics. But what *are* possible beings? We know what *actual* beings are—the Taj Mahal, Socrates, you and I, the Grand Teton—these are among the more impressive examples of actually existing beings. But what is a *possible* being? Is there a possible mountain just like Mt. Rainier two miles directly south of the Grand Teton? If so, it is located at the same place as the Middle Teton. Does that matter? Is there another such possible mountain three miles east of the Grand Teton, where Jenny Lake is? Are there possible mountains like this all over the world? Are there also possible oceans at all the places where there are possible mountains? For any place you mention, of course, it is *possible* that there be a mountain there; does it follow that in fact *there is* a possible mountain there?

These are some questions that arise when we ask ourselves whether there are merely possible beings that don't in fact exist. And the version of the ontological argument we've been considering seems to make sense only on the assumption that there are such things. The earlier versions also depended on that assumption; consider for example, this step of the first version we considered:

(18) So there is a possible being x and a world W' such that the greatness of x in W' exceeds the greatness of God in actuality.

This possible being, you recall, was God Himself, supposed not to exist in the actual world. We can make sense of (18), therefore, only if we are prepared to grant that there are possible beings who don't in fact exist. Such beings exist in other worlds, of course; had things been appropriately different, they would have existed. But in fact they don't exist, although nonetheless there *are* such things.

I am inclined to think the supposition that there are such things—things that are possible but don't in fact exist—is either unintelligible or necessarily false. But this doesn't mean that the present version of the ontological argument must be rejected. For we can restate the argument in a way that does not commit us to this questionable idea. Instead of speaking of *possible beings* that do or do not exist in various possible worlds, we may speak of *properties* and the worlds in which they are or are not *instantiated*. Instead of speaking of the possible fat man in the corner, noting that he doesn't exist, we may speak of the property *being a fat man in the corner*, noting that it isn't instantiated (although it could have been). Of course, the *property* in question, like the property *being a unicorn*, exists. It is a perfectly good property which exists with as much equanimity as the property of equininity, the property of being a horse. But it doesn't happen to apply to anything. That is, in *this* world it doesn't apply to anything; in other possible worlds it does.

THE ARGUMENT TRIUMPHANT

Using this idea we can restate this last version of the ontological argument in such a way that it no longer matters whether there are any merely possible beings that do not exist. Instead of speaking of the possible being that has, in some world or other, a maximal degree of greatness, we may speak of *the property of being maximally great* or *maximal greatness.* The premise corresponding to (25) then says simply that maximal greatness is possibly instantiated, i.e., that

(29) There is a possible world in which maximal greatness is instantiated.

And the analogues of (27) and (28) spell out what is involved in maximal greatness:

(30) Necessarily, a being is maximally great only if it has maximal excellence in every world

and

(31) Necessarily, a being has maximal excellence in every world only if it has omniscience, omnipotence, and moral perfection in every world.

Notice that (30) and (31) do not imply that there are possible but nonexistent beings—any more than does, for example,

(32) Necessarily, a thing is a unicorn only if it has one horn.

But if (29) is true, then there is a possible world *W* such that if it had been actual, then there would have existed a being that was omnipotent, omniscient, and morally perfect; this being, furthermore, would have had these qualities in every possible world. So it follows that if *W* had been actual, it would have been *impossible* that there be no such being. That is, if *W* had been actual,

(33) There is no omnipotent, omniscient, and morally perfect being

would have been an impossible proposition. But if a proposition is impossible in at least one possible world, then it is impossible in every possible world; what is impossible does not vary from world to world. Accordingly (33) is impossible in the *actual* world, i.e., impossible *simpliciter.* But if it is impossible that there be no such being, then there actually exists a being that is omnipotent, omniscient, and morally perfect; this being, furthermore, has these qualities essentially and exists in every possible world.

What shall we say of this argument? It is certainly valid; given its premise, the conclusion follows. The only question of interest, it seems to me, is whether its main premise—that maximal greatness *is* possibly instantiated—is *true.* It think it *is* true; hence I think this version of the ontological argument is sound.

But here we must be careful; we must ask whether this argument is a successful piece of natural theology, whether it *proves* the existence of God. And the answer must be, I think, that it does not. An argument for God's existence may be *sound*, after all, without in any useful sense proving God's existence.[5] Since I believe in God, I think the following argument is sound:

Either God exists or $7 + 5 = 14$
It is false that $7 + 5 = 14$
Therefore God exists.

But obviously this isn't a *proof*; no one who didn't already accept the conclusion, would accept the first premise. The ontological argument we've been examining isn't just like this one, of course, but it must be conceded that not everyone who understands and reflects on its central premise—that the existence of a maximally great being is *possible*—will accept it. Still, it is evident, I think, that there is nothing *contrary to reason* or *irrational* in accepting this premise.[6] What I claim for this argument, therefore, is that it establishes, not the *truth* of theism, but its rational acceptability. And hence it accomplishes at least one of the aims of the tradition of natural theology.

NOTES

1. This criticism of this version of the argument essentially follows David Lewis, "Anselm and Actuality," *Nous* 4 (1970): 175–188. See also Plantinga, *The Nature of Necessity*, pp. 202–205.
2. Charles Hartshorne, *Man's Vision of God* (New York: Harper and Row, 1941). Portions reprinted in Plantinga, *The Ontological Argument*, pp. 123–135.
3. Norman Malcolm, "Anselm's Ontological Arguments," *Philosophical Review* 69 (1960); reprinted in Plantinga, *The Ontological Argument*, pp. 136–139.
4. See Plantinga, "World and Essence," *Philosophical Review* 79 (October 1970): 475; and Plantinga, *The Nature of Necessity*, chap. 4, sec. 6.
5. See George Mavrodes, *Belief in God* (New York: Macmillan Co., 1970), pp. 22ff.
6. For more on this see Plantinga, *The Nature of Necessity*, chap. 10, sec. 8.

THOMAS AQUINAS

The Classical Cosmological Argument

In this selection, Thomas Aquinas (1224–1274) offers a version of the cosmological argument that is deductive in form. He states that we obviously witness things in motion in our world. Now, that which moves either is moved by another thing in motion or is itself unmoved (in which case an unmoved mover

From *Summa Contra Gentiles* I, trans. Anton Pegis. Notre Dame: University of Notre Dame, 1975.

exists). But the former option invokes an infinite regress of movers, which is impossible. Hence there must be an unmoved mover, which religious believers take to be God.

⌘

THE OPINION OF THOSE WHO SAY THAT THE EXISTENCE OF GOD CANNOT BE DEMONSTRATED BUT IS HELD BY FAITH ALONE

[1] There are others who hold a certain opinion, contrary to the position mentioned above, through which the efforts of those seeking to prove the existence of God would likewise be rendered futile. For they say that we cannot arrive at the existence of God through the reason; it is received by way of faith and revelation alone. . . .

[6] The falsity of this opinion is shown to us, first, from the art of demonstration which teaches us to arrive at causes from their effects. Then, it is shown to us from the order of the sciences. For, as it is said in the *Metaphysics,*[1] if there is no knowable substance higher than sensible substance, there will be no science higher than physics. It is shown, thirdly, from the pursuit of the philosophers, who have striven to demonstrate that God exists. Finally, it is shown to us by the truth in the words of the Apostle Paul: "For the invisible things of God . . . are clearly seen, being understood by the things that are made" (Rom. 1:20). . . .

[9] It is thereby likewise evident that, although God transcends all sensible things and the sense itself, His effects, on which the demonstration proving His existence is based, are nevertheless sensible things. And thus, the origin of our knowledge in the sense applies also to those things that transcend the sense.

ARGUMENTS IN PROOF OF THE EXISTENCE OF GOD

[1] We have now shown that the effort to demonstrate the existence of God is not a vain one. We shall therefore proceed to set forth the arguments by which both philosophers and Catholic teachers have proved that God exists. . . .

[3] Of these ways the first is as follows.[2] Everything that is moved is moved by another. That some things are in motion—for example, the sun—is evident from sense. Therefore, it is moved by something else that moves it. This mover is itself either moved or not moved. If it is not, we have reached our conclusion—namely, that we must posit some unmoved mover. This we call God. If it is moved, it is moved by another mover. We must, consequently, either proceed to infinity, or we must arrive at some unmoved

mover. Now, it is not possible to proceed to infinity. Hence, we must posit some prime unmoved mover.

[4] In this proof, there are two propositions that need to be proved, namely, that *everything that is moved is moved by another*, and that *in movers and things moved one cannot proceed to infinity*.

[5] The first of these propositions Aristotle proves in three ways. The *first* way is as follows. If something moves itself, it must have within itself the principle of its own motion; otherwise, it is clearly moved by another. Furthermore, it must be primarily moved. This means that it must be moved by reason of itself, and not by reason of a part of itself, as happens when an animal is moved by the motion of its foot. For, in this sense, a whole would not be moved by itself, but a part, and one part would be moved by another. It is also necessary that a self-moving being be divisible and have parts, since, as it is proved in the *Physics*,[3] whatever is moved is divisible.

[6] On the basis of these suppositions Aristotle argues as follows. That which is held to be moved by itself is primarily moved. For if, while one part was at rest, another part in it were moved, then the whole itself would not be primarily moved; it would be that part in it which is moved while another part is at rest. But nothing that is at rest because something else is at rest is moved by itself; for that being whose rest follows upon the rest of another must have its motion follow upon the motion of another. It is thus not moved by itself. Therefore, that which was posited as being moved by itself is not moved by itself. Consequently, everything that is moved must be moved by another. . . .

[8] In the *second* way, Aristotle proves the proposition by induction.[4] Whatever is moved by accident is not moved by itself, since it is moved upon the motion of another. So, too, as is evident, what is moved by violence is not moved by itself. Nor are those beings moved by themselves that are moved by their nature as being moved from within; such is the case with animals, which evidently are moved by the soul. Nor, again, is this true of those beings, such as heavy and light bodies, which are moved through nature. For such beings are moved by the generating cause and the cause removing impediments. Now, whatever is moved is moved through itself or by accident. If it is moved through itself, then it is moved either violently or by nature; if by nature, then either through itself, as the animal, or not through itself, as heavy and light bodies. Therefore, everything that is moved is moved by another.

[9] In the *third* way, Aristotle proves the proposition as follows.[5] The same thing cannot be at once in act and in potency with respect to the same thing. But everything that is moved is, as such, in potency. For motion is *the act of something that is in potency inasmuch as it is in potency*.[6] That which moves, however, is as such in act, for nothing acts except according as it is in act. Therefore, with respect to the same motion, nothing is both mover and moved. Thus, nothing moves itself. . . .

[11] The second proposition, namely, *that there is no procession to infinity among movers and things moved*, Aristotle proves in three ways.

[12] The *first* is as follows.[7] If among movers and things moved we

proceed to infinity, all these infinite beings must be bodies. For whatever is moved is divisible and a body, as is proved in the *Physics*.[8] But every body that moves some thing moved is itself moved while moving it. Therefore, all these infinites are moved together while one of them is moved. But one of them, being finite, is moved in a finite time. Therefore, all those infinites are moved in a finite time. This, however, is impossible. It is, therefore, impossible that among movers and things moved one can proceed to infinity.

[13] Furthermore, that it is impossible for the above-mentioned infinites to be moved in a finite time Aristotle proves as follows. The mover and the thing moved must exist simultaneously. This Aristotle proves by induction in the various species of motion. But bodies cannot be simultaneous except through continuity or contiguity. Now, since, as has been proved, all the aforementioned movers and things moved are bodies, they must constitute by continuity or contiguity a sort of single mobile. In this way, one infinite is moved in a finite time. This is impossible, as is proved in the *Physics*.[9]

[14] The *second* argument proving the same conclusion is the following.[10] In an ordered series of movers and things moved (this is a series in which one is moved by another according to an order), it is necessarily the fact that, when the first mover is removed or ceases to move, no other mover will move or be moved. For the first mover is the cause of motion for all the others. But, if there are movers and things moved following an order to infinity, there will be no first mover, but all would be as intermediate movers. Therefore, none of the others will be able to be moved, and thus nothing in the world will be moved.

[15] The *third* proof comes to the same conclusion, except that, by beginning with the superior, it has a reversed order. It is as follows. That which moves as an instrumental cause cannot move unless there be a principal moving cause. But, if we proceed to infinity among movers and things moved, all movers will be as instrumental causes, because they will be moved movers and there will be nothing as a principal mover. Therefore, nothing will be moved.

[16] Such, then, is the proof of both propositions assumed by Aristotle in the first demonstrative way by which he proved that a first unmoved mover exists.

NOTES

1. Aristotle, *Metaphysics*, IV, 3 (1005a 18).
2. Aristotle, *Physics*, VII, 1 (241b 24).
3. Aristotle, *Physics*, VI, 4 (234b 10).
4. Aristotle, *Physics*, VIII, 4 (254b 8).
5. Aristotle, *Physics*, VIII, 5 (257a 39).
6. Aristotle, *Physics*, III, 1 (201a 10).
7. Aristotle, *Physics*, VII, 1 (241b 24).

8. Aristotle, *Physics*, VI, 4 (234b 10).
9. Aristotle, *Physics*, VII, 1 (241b 12); VI, 7 (237b 23ff.).
10. Aristotle, *Physics*, VIII, 5 (256a 12).

RICHARD TAYLOR

A Contemporary Version of the Cosmological Argument

Richard Taylor (1919–) introduces the cosmological argument through the analogy of finding a ball while strolling in the woods. One would want to know how the ball came to be: why does it exist rather than not? The question invokes an appeal to the principle of sufficient reason, a principle he then applies to the world as a whole, suggesting that there must be a sufficient reason for its existence. This reason, according to Taylor, is found neither in other things in nature nor in the fact that it has existed for a long time, but rather in God as an uncaused or necessary being.

⌘

An active, living, and religious belief in the gods has probably never arisen and been maintained on purely metaphysical grounds. Such beliefs are found in every civilized land and time, and are often virtually universal in a particular culture, yet relatively few men have much of a conception of metaphysics. There are in fact entire cultures, such as ancient Israel, to whom metaphysics is quite foreign, though these cultures may nevertheless be religious. . . .

The sources of religious belief are doubtless [very] . . . complex . . . but they seem to lie in man's will rather than in his speculative intelligence, nevertheless. Men who possess such a belief seldom permit any metaphysical considerations to wrest it from them, while those who lack it are seldom turned toward it by other metaphysical considerations. Still, in every land in which philosophy has flourished, there have been profound thinkers who have sought to discover some metaphysical basis for a rational belief in the existence of some supreme being or beings. Even though religion may properly be a matter of faith rather than reason, still, a philosophical person can

Richard Taylor, *Metaphysics*, 4e, © 1992, pp. 99–108. Reprinted by permission of Prentice Hall, Englewood Cliffs, N.J.

hardly help wondering whether it might, at least in part, be also a matter of reason, and whether, in particular, the existence of God might be something that can be not merely believed but shown. It is this question that we want now to consider; that is, we want to see whether there are not strong metaphysical considerations from which the existence of some supreme and supranatural being might reasonably be inferred.

THE PRINCIPLE OF SUFFICIENT REASON

Suppose you were strolling in the woods and, in addition to the sticks, stones, and other accustomed litter of the forest floor, you one day came upon some quite unaccustomed object, something not quite like what you had ever seen before and would never expect to find in such a place. Suppose, for example, that it is a large ball, about your own height, perfectly smooth and translucent. You would deem this puzzling and mysterious, certainly, but if one considers the matter, it is no more inherently mysterious that such a thing should exist than that anything else should exist. If you were quite accustomed to finding such objects of various sizes around you most of the time, but had never seen an ordinary rock, then upon finding a large rock in the woods one day you would be just as puzzled and mystified. This illustrates the fact that something that is mysterious ceases to seem so simply by its accustomed presence. It is strange indeed, for example, that a world such as ours should exist; yet few men are very often struck by this strangeness, but simply take it for granted.

Suppose, then, that you have found this translucent ball and are mystified by it. Now whatever else you might wonder about it, there is one thing you would hardly question; namely, that it did not appear there all by itself, that it owes its existence to something. You might not have the remotest idea whence and how it came to be there, but you would hardly doubt that there was an explanation. The idea that it might have come from nothing at all, that it might exist without there being any explanation of its existence, is one that few people would consider worthy of entertaining.

This illustrates a metaphysical belief that seems to be almost a part of reason itself, even though few men ever think upon it; the belief, namely, that there is some explanation for the existence of anything whatever, some reason why it should exist rather than not. The sheer nonexistence of anything, which is not to be confused with the passing out of existence of something, never requires a reason; but existence does. That there should never have been any such ball in the forest does not require any explanation or reason, but that there should ever be such a ball does. If one were to look upon a barren plain and ask why there is not and never has been any large translucent ball there, the natural response would be to ask why there should be; but if one finds such a ball, and wonders why it is there, it is not quite so natural to ask why it should *not* be, as though existence should simply be taken for granted. That anything should not exist, then, and that, for instance, no such ball should exist in the forest, or that there should be no forest for it to occupy, or no continent containing a forest, or no earth, nor any world at all, do not seem to be things for which there needs to be any explanation or reason; but that such things should be, does seem to require a reason.

The principle involved here has been called the principle of sufficient reason. Actually, it is a very general principle, and is best expressed by saying that, in the case of any positive truth, there is some sufficient reason for it, something which, in this sense, makes it true–in short, that there is some sort of explanation, known or unknown, for everything.

Now some truths depend on something else, and are accordingly called *contingent,* while others depend only upon themselves, that is, are true by their very natures and are accordingly called *necessary*. There is, for example, a reason why the stone on my window sill is warm; namely, that the sun is shining upon it. This happens to be true, but not by its very nature. Hence, it is contingent, and depends upon something other than itself. It is also true that all the points of a circle are equidistant from the center, but this truth depends upon nothing but itself. No matter what happens, nothing can make it false. Similarly, it is a truth, and a necessary one, that if the stone on my window sill is a body, as it is, then it has a form, since this fact depends upon nothing but itself for its confirmation. Untruths are also, of course, either contingent or necessary, it being contingently false, for example, that the stone on my window sill is cold, and necessarily false that it is both a body and formless, since this is by its very nature impossible.

The principle of sufficient reason can be illustrated in various ways, as we have done, and if one thinks about it, he is apt to find that he presupposes it in his thinking about reality, but it cannot be proved. It does not appear to be itself a necessary truth, and at the same time it would be most odd to say it is contingent. If one were to try proving it, he would sooner or later have to appeal to considerations that are less plausible than the principle itself. Indeed, it is hard to see how one could even make an argument for it, without already assuming it. For this reason, it might properly be called a presupposition of reason itself. One can deny that it is true, without embarrassment or fear of refutation, but one is then apt to find that what he is denying is not really what the principle asserts. We shall, then, treat it here as a datum—not something that is provably true, but as something which all men, whether they ever reflect upon it or not, seem more or less to presuppose.

THE EXISTENCE OF A WORLD

It happens to be true that something exists, that there is, for example, a world, and while no one ever seriously supposes that this might not be so, that there might exist nothing at all, there still seems to be nothing the least necessary in this, considering it just by itself. That no world should ever exist at all is perfectly comprehensible and seems to express not the slightest absurdity. Considering any particular item in the world it seems not at all necessary in itself that it should ever have existed, nor does it appear any more necessary that the totality of these things, or any totality of things, should ever exist.

From the principle of sufficient reason it follows, of course, that there must be a reason, not only for the existence of everything in the world but for the world itself, meaning by "the world" simply everything that ever does exist, except God, in case there is a god. This principle does not imply that there must be some purpose or goal for everything, or for the totality of all things; for explanations need not, and in fact seldom are, teleological or purposeful. All the principle requires is that there be some sort of reason for everything. And it would certainly be odd to maintain that everything in the world owes its existence to something, that nothing in the world is either purely accidental, or such that it just bestows its own being upon itself, and then to deny this of the world itself. One can indeed *say* that the world is in some sense a pure accident, that there simply is no reason at all why this or any world should exist, and one can equally say that the world exists by its very nature, or is an inherently necessary being. But it is at least very odd and arbitrary to deny of this existing world the need for any sufficient reason, whether independent of itself or not, while presupposing that there is a reason for every other thing that ever exists.

Consider again the strange ball that we imagine has been found in the forest. Now we can hardly doubt that there must be an explanation for the existence of such a thing, though we may have no notion what that explanation is. It is not, moreover, the fact of its having been found in the forest rather than elsewhere that renders an explanation necessary. It matters not in the least where it happens to be, for our question is not how it happens to be *there* but how it happens to exist at all. If we in our imagination annihilate the forest, leaving only this ball in an open field, our conviction that it is a contingent thing and owes its existence to something other than itself is not reduced in the least. If we now imagine the field to be annihilated, and in fact everything else as well to vanish into nothingness, leaving only this ball to constitute the entire physical universe, then we cannot for a moment suppose that its existence has thereby been explained, or the need of any explanation eliminated, or that its existence is suddenly rendered self-explanatory. If we now carry this thought one step further and suppose that no other reality ever has existed or ever will exist, that this ball forever constitutes the entire physical universe, then we must still insist on there being some reason independent of itself why it should exist rather than not. If there must be a reason for the existence of any particular thing, then the necessity of such a reason is not eliminated by the mere supposition that certain other things do *not* exist. And again, it matters not at all what the thing in question is, whether it be large and complex, such as the world we actually find ourselves in, or whether it be something small, simple and insignificant, such as a ball, a bacterium, or the merest grain of sand. We do not avoid the necessity of a reason for the existence of something merely by describing it in this way or that. And it would, in any event, seem quite plainly absurd to say that if the world were comprised entirely of a single ball about six feet in diameter, or of a single grain of sand, then it would be contingent and there would have to be some explanation other than itself why such a thing exists, but that, since the actual world is vastly more complex than this, there is no need for an explanation of its existence, independent of itself.

BEGINNINGLESS EXISTENCE

It should now be noted that it is no answer to the question, why a thing exists, to state *how long* it has existed. A geologist does not suppose that he has explained why there should be rivers and mountains merely by pointing out that they are old. Similarly, if one were to ask, concerning the ball of which we have spoken, for some sufficient reason for its being, he would not receive any answer upon being told that it had been there since yesterday. Nor would it be any better answer to say that it had existed since before anyone could remember, or even that it had always existed; for the question was not one concerning its age but its existence. If, to be sure, one were to ask where a given thing came from, or how it came into being, then upon learning that it had always existed he would learn that it never really *came* into being at all; but he could still reasonably wonder why it should exist at all. If, accordingly, the world—that is, the totality of all things excepting God, in case there is a god—had really no beginning at all, but has always existed in some form or other, then there is clearly no answer to the question, where it came from and when; it did not, on this supposition, *come* from anything at all, at any time. But still, it can be asked why there is a world, why indeed there is a beginningless world, why there should have perhaps always been something rather than nothing. And, if the principle of sufficient reason is a good principle, there must be an answer to that question, an answer that is by no means supplied by giving the world an age, or even an infinite age.

CREATION

This brings out an important point with respect to the concept of creation that is often misunderstood, particularly by those whose thinking has been influenced by Christian ideas. People tend to think that creation—for example, the creation of the world by God—*means* creation *in time,* from which it of course logically follows that if the world had no beginning in time, then it cannot be the creation of God. This, however, is erroneous, for creation means essentially *dependence*, even in Christian theology. If one thing is the creation of another, then it depends for its existence on that other, and this is perfectly consistent with saying that both are eternal, that neither ever came into being, and hence, that neither was ever created at any point of time. Perhaps an analogy will help convey this point. Consider, then, a flame that is casting beams of light. Now there seems to be a clear sense in which the beams of light are dependent for their existence upon the flame, which is their source, while the flame, on the other hand, is not similarly dependent for its existence upon them. The beams of light arise from the flame, but the flame does not arise from them. In this sense, they are the creation of the flame; they derive their existence from it. And none of this has any reference to time; the relationship of dependence in such a case would not be altered in the slightest if we supposed that the flame, and with it the beams of light, had always existed, that neither had ever *come* into being.

Now if the world is the creation of God, its relationship to God should be thought of in this fashion; namely, that the world depends for its existence upon God, and could not exist independently of God. If God is eternal, as those who believe in God generally assume, then the world may (though it need not) be eternal too, without that altering in the least its dependence upon God for its existence, and hence without altering its being the creation of God. The supposition of God's eternality, on the other hand, does not by itself imply that the world is eternal too; for there is not the least reason why something of finite duration might not depend for its existence upon something of infinite duration—though the reverse is, of course, impossible.

GOD

If we think of God as "the creator of heaven and earth," and if we consider heaven and earth to include everything that exists except God, then we appear to have, in the foregoing considerations, fairly strong reasons for asserting that God, as so conceived, exists. Now of course most people have much more in mind than this when they think of God, for religions have ascribed to God ever so many attributes that are not at all implied by describing him merely as the creator of the world; but that is not relevant here. Most religious persons do, in any case, think of God as being at least the creator, as that being upon which everything ultimately depends, no matter what else they may say about him in addition. It is, in fact, the first item in the creeds of Christianity that God is the "creator of heaven and earth." And, it seems, there are good metaphysical reasons, as distinguished from the persuasions of faith, for thinking that such a creative being exists.

If, as seems clearly implied by the principle of sufficient reason, there must be a reason for the existence of heaven and earth—i.e., for the world—then that reason must be found either in the world itself, or outside it, in something that is literally supranatural, or outside heaven and earth. Now if we suppose that the world—i.e., the totality of all things except God—contains within itself the reason for its existence, we are supposing that it exists by its very nature, that is, that it is a necessary being. In that case there would, of course, be no reason for saying that it must depend upon God or anything else for its existence; for if it exists by its very nature, then it depends upon nothing but itself, much as the sun depends upon nothing but itself for its heat. This, however, is implausible, for we find nothing about the world or anything in it to suggest that it exists by its own nature, and we do find, on the contrary, ever so many things to suggest that it does not. For in the first place, anything which exists by its very nature must necessarily be eternal and indestructible. It would be a self-contradiction to say of anything that it exists by its own nature, or is a necessarily existing thing, and at the same time to say that it comes into being or passes away, or that it ever could come into being or pass away. Nothing about the world seems at all like this, for concerning anything in the world, we can perfectly easily think of it as being annihilated, or as never having existed in the first place, without there being the slightest hint of any absurdity in such a supposition. Some of the things in the universe are, to be sure, very old; the moon, for example, or the stars and the planets. It is even possible to imagine that they have always existed. Yet it seems quite impossible to suppose that they owe their existence to nothing but themselves, that they bestow existence upon themselves by their very natures, or that they are in themselves things of such nature that it would be impossible for them not to exist. Even if we suppose that something, such as the sun, for instance, has existed forever, and will never cease, still we cannot conclude just from this that it exists by its own nature. If, as is of course very doubtful, the sun has existed forever and will never cease, then it is possible that its heat and light have also existed forever and will never cease; but that would not show that the heat and light of the sun exist by their own natures. They are obviously contingent and depend on the sun for their existence, whether they are beginningless and everlasting or not.

There seems to be nothing in the world, then, concerning which it is at all plausible to suppose that it exists by its own nature, or contains within itself the reason for its existence. In fact, everything in the world appears to be quite plainly the opposite, namely, something that not only need not exist, but at some time or other, past or future or both, does not in fact exist. Everything in the world seems to have a finite duration, whether long or short. Most things, such as ourselves, exist only for a short while; they come into being, then soon cease. Other things, like the heavenly bodies, last longer, but they are still corruptible, and from all that we can gather about them, they too seem destined eventually to perish. We arrive at the conclusion, then, that while the world may contain some things which have always existed and are destined never to perish, it is nevertheless doubtful that it contains any such thing and, in any case, everything in the world is capable of perishing, and nothing in it, however long it may already have existed and however long it may yet remain, exists by its own nature, but depends instead upon something else.

While this might be true of everything in the world, is it necessarily true of the world itself? That is, if we grant, as we seem forced to, that nothing in the world exists by its own nature, that everything in the world is contingent and perishable, must we also say that the world itself, or the totality of all these perishable things, is also contingent and perishable? Logically, we are not forced to, for it is logically possible that the totality of all perishable things might itself be imperishable, and hence, that the world might exist by its own nature, even though it comprises exclusively things which are contingent. It is not logically necessary that a totality should share the defects of its members. For example, even though every man is mortal, it does not follow from this that the human race, or the totality of all men, is also mortal, for it is possible that there will always be human beings, even though there are no human beings which will always exist. Similarly, it is possible that the world is in itself a necessary thing, even though it comprises entirely things that are contingent.

This is logically possible, but it is not plausible. For we find nothing whatever about the world, any more than in its parts, to suggest that it exists by its own nature. Concerning anything in the world, we have not the slightest difficulty in supposing that it should perish, or even, that it should never have existed in the first place. We have almost as little difficulty in supposing this of the world itself. It might be somewhat hard to think of everything as utterly perishing and leaving no trace whatever of its ever having been, but there seems to be not the slightest difficulty in imagining that the world should never have existed in the first place. We can, for instance, perfectly easily suppose that nothing in the world had ever existed except, let us suppose, a single grain of sand, and we can thus suppose that this grain of sand has forever constituted the whole universe. Now if we consider just this grain of sand, it is quite impossible for us to suppose that it exists by its very nature, and could never have failed to exist. It clearly depends for its existence upon something other than itself, if it depends on anything at all. The same will be true if we consider the world to consist, not of one grain of sand, but of two, or of a million, or, as we in fact find, of a vast number of stars and planets and all their minuter parts.

It would seem, then, that the world, in case it happens to exist at all—and this is quite beyond doubt—is contingent and thus dependent upon something other than itself for its existence, if it depends upon anything at all. And it must depend upon something, for otherwise there could be no reason why it exists in the first place. Now that upon which the world depends must be something that either exists by its own nature or does not. If it does not exist by its own nature, then it, in turn, depends for its existence upon something else, and so on. Now then, we can say either of two things; namely, (1) that the world depends for its existence upon something else, which in turn depends on still another thing, this depending upon still another, *ad infinitum*; or (2) that the world derives its existence from something that exists by its own nature and which is accordingly eternal and imperishable, and is the creator of heaven and earth. The first of these alternatives, however, is impossible, for it does not render a sufficient reason why anything should exist in the first place. Instead of supplying a reason why any world should exist, it repeatedly begs off giving a reason. It explains what is dependent and perishable in terms of what is itself dependent and perishable, leaving us still without a reason why perishable things should exist at all, which is what we are seeking. Ultimately, then, it would seem that the world, or the totality of contingent or perishable things, in case it exists at all, must depend upon something that is necessary and imperishable, and which accordingly exists, not in dependence upon something else, but by its own nature.

"SELF-CAUSED"

What has been said thus far gives some intimation of what meaning should be attached to the concept of a self-caused being, a concept that is quite generally misunderstood, sometimes even by scholars. To say that something—God, for example—is self-caused, or is the cause of its own existence, does not mean that this being brings itself into existence, which is a perfectly absurd idea. Nothing can *bring* itself into existence. To say that something is self-caused (*causa sui*) means only that it exists, not contingently or in dependence upon something else, but by its own nature, which is only to say that it is a being which is such that it can neither come into being nor perish. Now whether such a being in fact exists or not, there is in any case no absurdity in the idea. We have found, in fact, that the principle of sufficient reason seems to point to the existence of such a being, as that upon which the world, with everything in it, must ultimately depend for its existence.

"NECESSARY BEING"

A being that depends for its existence upon nothing but itself, and is in this sense self-caused, can equally be described as a necessary being; that is to say, a being that is not contingent, and hence not perishable. For in the case of anything which exists by its own nature, and is dependent upon nothing else, it is impossible that it should not exist, which is equivalent to saying that it is necessary. Many persons have professed to find the gravest difficulties in this concept, too, but that is partly because it has been confused with other notions. If it makes sense to speak of anything as an *impossible* being, or something which by its very nature does not exist, then it is hard to see why the idea of a necessary being, or something which in its very nature exists, should not be just as comprehensible. And of course, we have not the slightest difficulty in speaking of something, such as a square circle or a formless body, as an impossible being. And if it makes sense to speak of something as being perishable, contingent, and dependent upon something other than itself for its existence, as it surely does, then there seems to be no difficulty in thinking of something as imperishable and dependent upon nothing other than itself for its existence.

J. P. MORELAND

The Kalam Cosmological Argument

According to the kalam cosmological argument, developed originally by medieval Arabic philosophers and more recently by William Craig, the universe had a beginning in time. James P. Moreland (1948–) argues that this can be established by four arguments, two from philosophy and two from physics. One philosophical argument shows that an actual infinite cannot exist, and the other that if it could exist one could not traverse it. The dual arguments from physics appeal to the big bang model of the origin of the universe and certain implications of the second law of thermodynamics. In the end, Moreland concludes that, since the universe had a beginning, it was caused, and the cause had to be personal.

⌘

One of the most important arguments for God's existence is the cosmological argument. It has had a tarnished yet sturdy history and, like the Bible, it has outlived most of its critics. The argument gets its name from the Greek word *kosmos*, which means "world" or "universe." The argument generally begins with the existence of the world or some part of it and seeks to establish the existence of a necessary Being who causes the existence of the world.

Actually, there are three very different forms of the cosmological argument. . . . The three forms of the cosmological argument are the Thomist argument, the Leibnizian argument, and the kalam argument. The main burden of this chapter is to state and defend the kalam cosmological argument. . . .

THE KALAM ARGUMENT

The kalam cosmological argument gets its name from the word *kalam*, which refers to Arabic philosophy or theology. The kalam argument was popular among Arabic philosophers in the late Middle Ages. Christian philosophers during that period did not generally accept the argument, perhaps due to the influence of Aquinas, who, following Aristotle, rejected it. A notable exception was Saint Bonaventure, a contemporary of Aquinas, who argued extensively for the soundness of the kalam argument.

In recent years, there has been a small but growing number of thinkers who have defended this line of reasoning. But without doubt, the most thorough and articulate advocate of the argument has been William Lane Craig.[1]

Statement of the Kalam Argument

Overview

Consider the following diagram offered by Craig[2]:

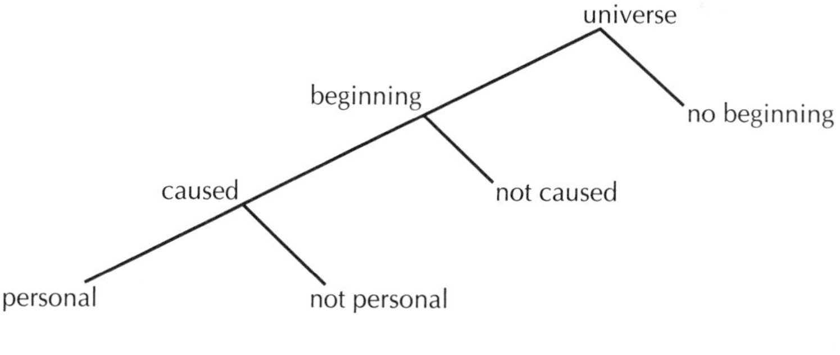

The kalam argument presents a number of dilemmas. First, the argument states that the universe either had a beginning or it did not. If it had a beginning, then this beginning was either caused or uncaused. If the beginning was caused, the cause was either personal or not personal. The burden of the argument is to establish one horn of each dilemma, and in so doing, to argue for the existence of a personal Creator. Thus, the argument attempts to show that there had to be a beginning to the universe which was caused by a personal Being.

In order to defend the argument, a premise must be established at each dilemma. Here are the major premises of the argument:

1. The universe had a beginning.
2. The beginning of the universe was caused.
3. The cause for the beginning of the universe was personal.

Actual and Potential Infinites

Before we attempt to establish these premises, it is important to distinguish between two kinds of infinity—a potential infinite and an actual infinite. The distinction goes back to Aristotle, but it has been made more precise in recent years by modern set theory. . . .

From the preceding discussion, several properties of actual infinities emerge. First, an actual infinite is a timeless totality which neither increases nor decreases in the number of members it contains. Second, a proper subset or part of an actual infinite can be put into one-to-one correspondence with (be made equal to) that actual infinite. . . . This contrasts with a finite set, which *cannot* be put into one-to-one correspondence with one of its proper subsets. In finite sets, the whole is always greater than any of its proper parts. . . .

A potential infinite has three important properties relevant to our discussion. First, a potential infinite increases its number through time by adding new members to the series. Second, a potential infinite is always finite. A potential infinite can increase forever and it will never become an actual infinite. Adding one more member to a finite set no matter how often this is done, will simply result in a larger finite set. Third, since a potential infinite is always finite, at no time will the finite set formed from the members of the series traversed at that moment be equal to one of its proper subsets. . . .

Defense of the Kalam Argument

Premise 1: The Universe Had a Beginning

The first premise we need to defend is the one stating that the universe had a beginning. Four general considerations can be raised which support this premise.[3] Two of these considerations are philosophical and two are scientific in nature.

The Nonexistence of an Actual Infinite

Puzzles with an Actual Infinite. The first argument is this: An actual infinite cannot exist. A beginningless temporal series of events is an actual infinite. Therefore, a beginningless temporal series of events cannot exist. It seems clear that if one claims that there was no beginning to the universe, then this is equivalent to saying that there have been an actual infinite number of past events in the history of the universe. If these events are collected into a set, . . . it would have an actual infinite number of members.

It does not seem possible for an actual infinite to exist in the real world. In order to prove this, we can assume that it *is* possible for an actual infinite to exist and try to show that this assumption implies unreasonable consequences. And since these consequences seem to be false, the assumption which led to them must be rejected.

Certain examples can be given which show that an actual infinite which exists in the real world leads to unacceptable consequences and that thus there is no such thing as a really existent actual infinite. Craig offers the following case.[4] Imagine a library with an actually infinite number of books. Suppose further that there is an infinite number of red books and an infinite number of black books in the library. Does it really make sense to say that there are as many black books in the library as there are red and black books together? Surely not. Furthermore, I could withdraw all the black books and not change the total holdings in the library. Let us also assume that each book has an actual infinite number of pages. There would be just as many pages in the first book in the library as there are in the entire, infinite collection. If someone read the first book, she would read just as many pages as someone who read every page of every book in the library!

Consider a second example offered by Russell.[5] The example is about a person, Tristam Shandy, who writes his autobiography so slowly that it takes him a whole year to write about just one day of his life. If he lives an actually infinite number of days, he will allegedly be able to complete his autobiography. This is because the set of all the days in his life can be put into one-to-one correspondence with the set of all his years. But does this really make sense? It would seem that the longer he lives the further behind he would get. . . .

These puzzles illustrate some unreasonable consequences which follow if actual infinites really exist. The properties of an actual infinite create the problems. After all, it does not seem reasonable to affirm that the number of points on a line a billionth of an inch long is equal to the number of points in an infinite space of $\aleph_0$ dimensions.

[*Two*] *Objections to the Puzzles.* In spite of the intuitive appeal of the puzzles, some philosophers have not been persuaded by them. Three major objections have been raised against this way of attacking the reality of an actual infinite. First, some have argued that the mere presence of infinite set theory in mathematics is enough to dispel these puzzles. The fact that there is such a thing as infinite set theory—and this theory includes the properties attacked by the puzzles listed—shows that the language and theory of infinite sets are coherent and we must adjust our view of the world accordingly.

This objection does not succeed. The mere presence of a generally accepted theory in mathematics says nothing, by itself, about anything in the real world of entities. For example, it is well known that there are at least three different and internally consistent geometries of space. Euclidean space is built on the axiom that through a given point not on a straight line, exactly one line can be drawn parallel to the straight one. Two other geometries of space can be formed if this axiom is replaced by one saying that either more than one line or no line could be drawn. These are called Lobachevskian and

Riemannian geometries respectively. But it does not follow from the mere presence of these three geometries of space that actual space in the real world fits all three.

One simply cannot move from the mathematical to the real without further argument. . . .

A second objection has been raised against the puzzles which criticize the actual infinite. Fraenkel states that the attitude of some philosophers about the existence of an actual infinite "may be explained by their adherence to the classical principle *totum parte maiuis* (the whole is greater than a part). This principle in its proper meaning is, however, limited to the domain of finite sets. . . . Its invalidity in the domain of infinity is just characteristic of the latter."[6]

Fraenkel's point is this. The puzzles raised against an actual infinite all turn on a problematic feature of infinite sets: a part of the set can be equal to the whole. In finite sets two principles apply. First, the whole is greater than any of its parts. Second, two sets are equal if there is a one-to-one correspondence between their members. But in infinite sets only the second principle applies. My puzzles fault infinite sets for violating the first principle. But this is simply faulting infinite sets for not being finite sets. In infinite sets a part can equal the whole and that is all there is to it. . . .

The defender of the kalam argument says that a whole is greater than any of its parts and thus the puzzles argue against the existence of an actual infinite. There do not seem to be sufficient, independent reasons for accepting an actual infinite with its unusual properties. As has been pointed out, the mere presence of the mathematics of infinity is insufficient, and I know of no other reason which sufficiently justifies acceptance of infinite sets. Further, the lack of justification becomes more troublesome when we realize that terms like "part," "add," or "subtract" are being used in such an odd way in connection with the actual infinite that this usage should be rejected because it lacks sufficient justification. How can something still be a part of a whole if it equals that whole? How can members be "added to" or "subtracted from" a set without increasing or decreasing its members?

It would seem, then, that this second objection fails to remove the force of the puzzles against the actual infinite. . . .

THE IMPOSSIBILITY OF TRAVERSING AN ACTUAL INFINITE

Statement and Support of the Argument. There is a second argument for the fact that the universe had a beginning. Let us assume that someone has not been persuaded by our first argument against the existence of an actual infinite. This second argument works even if an actual infinite is possible. It states that if there is an actual infinite, it must occur, as it were, all at once. It can be put as follows: It is impossible to traverse (cross) an actual infinite by successive addition. The temporal series of past events has been formed by successive addition. Therefore, it cannot be actually infinite. But since it is not infinite, it must be finite (i.e., it must have a first term). And this is what we mean by saying the universe had a beginning.

This second argument, therefore, can grant the existence of an actual infinite. But it does not grant that such an infinite could be traversed.

Several reasons can be offered for the contention that an actual infinite cannot be traversed by successive addition. The first is an argument from the nature of causal sequences. Consider any event: for instance, a helicopter passing overhead. This event is caused by another event which preceded it in time—the pilot got in the vehicle. In order for any event to take place, the entire chain of its causal antecedents must have already occurred and be actual. Otherwise, a necessary precondition for the last member in the chain (the event under consideration) would not have occurred and the rest of the chain would not have occurred either (since its existence depends upon this necessary precondition).

Now the present moment has as its ultimate chain of causal antecedents the entire history of the cosmos. If any past event has not already been actualized, then the present could not have occurred. This means that the past is actual and contains a specifiable, determinate number of events. This chain of events must have had a first member. Without a first member, there would be no second, third, or *n*th member in the chain where the *n*th member is the present event. A causal sequence leading up to an event must have a first member and a determinate number of members in the sequence, since the entire sequence is already actual. But an infinite succession of past events would not have a determinate number of members nor would it have a first member. So if the past is actually infinite, the present moment could not have been caused; that is, it could not have come to be.

Consider a second argument. It is impossible to count to infinity. For if one counts forever and ever, he will still be, at every moment, in a place where he can always specify the number he is currently counting. Furthermore, he can always add one more member to what he has counted and thereby increase the series by one. A series formed by successive addition is a potential infinite. Such a series can increase forever without limit, but it will *always* be finite. This means that the past must have been finite. For the present moment is the last member of the series of past events formed by successive addition. And since one cannot reach infinity one at a time, then if the past was actually infinite, the present moment could not have been reached. For to come to the present moment, an actual infinite would have to have been crossed.

Third, suppose a person were to think backward through the events in the past. In reality, time and the events within it move in the other direction. But mentally he can reverse that movement and count backward farther and farther into the past. Now he will either come to a beginning or he will not. If he comes to a beginning, then the universe obviously had a beginning. But if he never could, even in principle, reach a first moment, then this means that it would be impossible to start with the present and run backward through all of the events in the history of the cosmos. Remember, if he did run through all of them, he would reach a first member of the series, and the finiteness of the past would be established. In order to avoid this conclusion, one must hold that, starting with the present, it is *impossible* to go backward through all of the events in history.

But since events really move in the other direction, this is equivalent to admitting that if there was no beginning, the past could have never been exhaustively traversed to reach the present. Counting to infinity through the series 1, 2, 3, . . . involves the same number of steps as does counting down *from* infinity to zero through the series . . . , −5, −4, −3, −2, −1, 0. In fact this second series may be even more difficult to traverse than the first. Apart from the fact that both series have the same number of members to be traversed, the second series cannot even get started. This is because it has no first member!

A beginningless universe has no first member. Before any event in the history of the cosmos, there has already transpired an actual infinite number of events. So no matter how far back one goes in one's mind, one is no closer to traversing the past than before he began counting—even if he counts back through an infinite number of events (which is impossible). In light of such a beginningless infinite series, neither the present, nor tomorrow, nor *any* moment in the past could be reached. . . .

Objections to the Argument. These arguments present a strong case for the fact that the universe had a beginning. Nevertheless, some have tried to defend the possibility of traversing an actual infinite by criticizing the arguments presented. Four major criticisms have been raised. First, Wallace Matson has argued that one cannot traverse an actual infinite in finite time. But given an infinite amount of time one could accomplish this task.[7] But Matson's statement is inaccurate. The problems with traversing an actual infinite have nothing to do with how much time one has. The problems focus on the nature of an actual infinite itself. All Matson has done is to postulate one actual infinite to resolve problems with another actual infinite. He posits, as it were, a time above time. But this merely begs the question at issue. And it does not solve the problems with traversing an actual infinite. It merely shifts those problems from one actual infinite to another.

Second, William Wainwright and J. L. Mackie argue that the objections assume an infinitely distant beginning. But, they argue, there is *no* beginning, not even one infinitely far away. Thus, if a person goes back mentally through the cosmos, she will never reach a point that is infinitely far away. She will always be at a point which is a finite distance away from the present, and thus that distance will be traversable.[8]

This objection seems to me to be very weak. For one thing, the defender of the kalam argument does *not* assume an infinitely distant beginning to the universe to generate his puzzles against traversing an actual infinite. Rather, he—not Wainwright or Mackie—takes the actual infinite seriously. If the past is actually infinite, then there is no beginning at all. It is precisely this lack of a beginning that causes most of the problems. If there were no beginning, then reaching the present would be like counting to zero from negative infinity. As Craig points out, this is like trying to jump out of a bottomless pit. One could get no foothold in the series to even get started, for to get to any point, one *already* has to have crossed infinity.[9] Furthermore, I agree with Mackie that if one goes back in time one never reaches a point an infinite distance away. But this proves that the past was finite. For if the past had been infinite, he could never *in principle* traverse the past. This is equivalent to saying that all the events in an infinite past could not be crossed to reach the present, since the number of events traversed is not a function of the direction one takes in traversing them.

Third, some have argued that it may be impossible to count *to* infinity, but it is possible to count down *from* infinity. But this objection seems patently absurd. For one thing, the number of members in both series is the same. Why would one be easier to cross than the other? Second, assume that someone had been counting toward zero from negative infinity from eternity past. If a person goes back in time from the present moment, he will *never* reach a point when he is finishing his count or even engaging in the count itself. This is because at every point, he will have already had an infinity to conduct the count. As Zeno's paradox of the race course points out, the problem with such a situation is not merely that one cannot complete an infinite task; one cannot even start an infinite task from a beginningless situation. For one could never reach a determinate position in the infinite series which alone would allow the series to be traversed and ended at zero (the present moment). . . . [The fourth objection is omitted here.]

It seems, then, that it is impossible to traverse an actual infinite. And since a beginningless series of past events would be an actual infinite, then such a series—given that we have reached the present moment—must be impossible. The universe had a beginning. I now turn to two scientific arguments which establish that the universe had a beginning.

THE BIG BANG COSMOLOGY

In the late 1920s, astronomer Edwin Hubble discovered a phenomenon known as the red shift—light from distant galaxies is shifted toward the red end of the spectrum. This indicates that the universe is expanding. Galaxies are moving away from one another much like dots on the surface of an inflating balloon. This discovery has led to what is now known as the big bang theory of the origin of the universe.[10]

The big bang theory includes two important features. First, the universe as we know it began from a large explosion some fifteen billion years ago and has continued to expand ever since. Second, the original configuration of the big bang was a state of "infinite" density where all of the mass, energy, space, and time were contained in a single mathematical point with no dimensions. These two features jointly imply that the universe sprang into existence from nothing a finite time ago. As scientist Robert Jastrow puts it, "What is the ultimate solution to the origin of the Universe? The answers provided by the astronomers are disconcerting and remarkable. Most remarkable of all is the fact that in science, as in the Bible, the world begins with an act of creation."[11]

The major rival cosmology at present is called the oscillating universe model. This model holds that the universe has gone through an infinite number of expansions and contractions and will continue to do so into the future. The main debate between this model and the big bang model as I have represented it here is the question of whether or not there was just one initial expansion.

Several factors indicate that there was only one initial expansion and the explosion which caused it was an absolute beginning to the universe of mass/energy and space-time. First, there is no known mechanism to explain how all the mass of the universe could converge simultaneously, reconvene into a dimensionless mathematical point, and bounce back into a new expansion with 100 percent efficiency. The second law of thermodynamics states that there is no such thing as a 100 percent efficient perpetual-motion machine. Second, even if such a mechanism could be conceived, there could not have been an actual infinite number of past cycles because of the problems with an actual infinite. Third, if the universe is going to contract into another point, then the only thing that will draw the matter of the universe back together is gravity. The strength of the gravity in the universe is a function of the density of the mass in the universe. According to Craig, the universe would need to be at least twice as dense as scientists currently hold it to be for it to reach a point of expansion and then contract again.[12] The universe appears to be open; that is, there was one and only one explosion. The universe had a beginning.

One objection should be considered briefly. The objection goes back to Immanuel Kant and has been raised several times since.[13] The idea of an absolute beginning to time is inconceivable, for one can always ask what happened before the first moment. And to answer this, one must postulate a time before time, which is absurd. So the notion of a first moment in time is incoherent.

Most theists—at least those who hold that God is timeless—respond by saying that the first event was not the first moment *in* time, but the first moment *of* time. There was no time before the first moment. Whatever existed "prior" to the first moment was timeless and immutable. And when we use the word *prior* here, we do not mean temporally prior to time, but outside time altogether. God existed "prior" to the first moment in that he was—and is—timeless. This may be mysterious and inspiring, but it is not incoherent and contradictory.

Some have thought that the idea of God existing "prior" to the first moment is like saying something is north of the North Pole, which is absurd. But it should now be evident what is wrong with this comparison. If something exists north of the North Pole, it is still being treated as a thing existing at a spatial location. But when the theist says that God exists "prior" to the first moment, she is not treating God as a thing existing at a temporal location. So the analogy breaks down.

THE SECOND LAW OF THERMODYNAMICS

The Argument. Thermodynamics is an exact science which deals with energy. The second law of thermodynamics is one of the most fundamental, best-established laws in all of science. The second law involves a concept known as entropy (*S*). Entropy can be understood in terms of energy, disorder, or information. The second law states that the entropy of the universe (or any isolated system therein, where an isolated system is one which has neither mass nor energy flow in or out of the system) is increasing. Put differently, the amount of energy available to do work is decreasing and becoming uniformly distributed. The universe is moving irreversibly toward a state of maximum disorder and minimum energy.

An example may be helpful. Suppose someone enters a room and discovers a cup of coffee which is still warm. He would be able to tell that it had not been there forever; in fact, given the right information, he could even calculate how long it had been cooling off. The second law states that the cup will cool off and the temperature of the room will move toward a state of uniform temperature distribution. . . .

Applied to the universe as a whole, the second law tells us that the universe is wearing down irreversibly. It is heading toward a state of maximum disorder and uniform energy distribution. The sun will burn up and all other localized sources of energy will burn up as well. But since a state of maximum entropy has not yet been reached, the universe has not been here forever. If the universe had already undergone an infinite past, it would have reached such a state by now. As theoretical physicist Paul Davies puts it: "If the universe has a finite stock of order, and is changing irreversibly towards disorder—ultimately to thermodynamic equilibrium—two very deep inferences follow immediately. The first is that the universe will eventually die, wallowing, as it were, in its own entropy. This is known among physicists as the 'heat death' of the universe. The second is that the universe cannot have existed forever, otherwise it would have reached its equilibrium end state an infinite time ago. Conclusion: the universe did not always exist."[14]

It would seem, then, that the second law implies a beginning to the universe when the universe was, as it were, wound up and energy and order were put into it.

Two Objections. Two major objections have been raised against this kind of argument from the second law.[15] First, it has been argued that the universe is infinite and, therefore, the argument does not work. The universe could be infinite in two ways relevant to this objection: either it is infinite in extension and in the matter/energy already present in it, or it is finite but there is a constant creation of new energy from an infinite source of energy or from nothingness. This objection runs aground on the problems already raised with an actual infinite. Furthermore, the most widely accepted current understanding of the universe is one which views it as finite and not infinite. And there is no scientific evidence for continuous creation of matter or energy, even if such a notion could be squared with the highly rational principle that something cannot come from nothing without a cause.... [The second objection is omitted here.]

Premise 2: The Beginning of the Universe Was Caused

Since the universe began to exist, it would seem that the most reasonable view to take would be that the first event was caused. The principle that something does not come from nothing without a cause is a reasonable one. This is especially true with regard to events. Events have a definite beginning and end, and do not happen without something causing them. By contrast, God does not need a cause, since he is neither an event nor a contingent being. He is a necessary being and such a being does not need a cause. In fact, it is a category fallacy to ask for a cause for God since this is really asking for a cause for an uncaused being.

The first event, then, needs a cause, for unlike God, it was not a necessary being and it had a beginning and an end. Some have objected to this line of reasoning, however, and have maintained that it is not true to maintain that all events need a cause. Usually this objection makes an appeal to certain features of quantum mechanics. Quantum mechanics, according to this objection, shows that there is an ultimate indeterminacy in nature at the subatomic level. The law of cause and effect does not hold, events occur without a cause, and entities come into existence from nothing.

Two things can be said about this objection. First, not all philosophers and physicists are agreed as to how to interpret quantum mechanics. A number of thinkers, including those who adhere to the Copenhagen school of thought, argue that the laws and theoretical entities of quantum mechanics should be treated in nonrealist terms. This involves taking the statements of quantum mechanics as statements about our knowledge (or language) of reality, and not about a mind-independent reality itself. Thus, nature is not really indeterminate; we just do not know—perhaps cannot know—the underlying causes of quantum phenomena (if it makes sense in the Copenhagen view to even talk about a mind-independent realm of reality underlying the world we observe).

Second, even if one interprets quantum mechanics along realist lines (quantum theory states, at least approximately, the way the world is), it does not follow that events above the subatomic level do not have causes. Even if one grants that a photon of light can pop into existence from a "quantum ghost" (sheer nothingness which underlies every thing), it does not follow that the first event did not need a cause. Even if one can make statements like the one about quantum ghosts intelligible, and I personally doubt that this is possible, macroevents still have causes. When an apple falls something caused it. When an event as massive as the big bang occurred, something caused it. It is an unwarranted extrapolation to argue from the microlevel to the macrolevel.

It could be argued that the origin of the universe *was* a quantum phenomenon at the microlevel and, therefore, the first event could have occurred without a cause since it was not a macroevent. Two things can be said in response to this. First, I have already pointed out that there is no agreed-upon interpretation of quantum mechanics. In particular, most seem to take quantum mechanics in nonrealist terms. Our knowledge of reality at the quantum level may be probabilistic and not deterministic, but that does not mean no causes operate at that level. It means only that we have no ability to predict them with certainty.

Second, in the absence of a clear consensus on quantum interpretation, it seems reasonable to hold to the well-established law of cause and effect. Surely the burden of proof is on those who deny that law, and if quantum theory can be understood in a way which preserves the law of cause and effect, then that interpretation of quantum theory is preferable for that reason. . . .

One suspects that at bottom, the assertion that the universe came from nothing without a cause is a mere assertion without support; a sort of ungrounded logical possibility which provides the atheist with a last-ditch effort to avoid the existence of a first Cause. Atheist B. C. Johnson asserts that "if time might have been nonexistent [prior to the first event], then so might causality. The universe and time might have just popped into existence without a cause."[16] Such a view is a logical possibility, but one which is most likely metaphysically impossible, and in any case, one without sufficient reasons. There is no reason to deny what we experience as true every day. Events have causes. So did the first one.

Premise 3: The Cause for the Beginning of the Universe Was Personal

The first event was caused either by something personal or by something impersonal. Prior to the first event—where prior means "ontologically prior," not "temporally prior"—there was a state of affairs which can be described by the following: there was no time, space, or change of any kind.

It is hard to conceive of such a state of affairs in physicalist terms (i.e., in terms of matter and energy). But let us grant that such a state of affairs could exist.

In this state of affairs, either the necessary and sufficient conditions for the first event existed from all eternity in a state of immutability or they did not. If they did not, then the coming-to-be of those conditions was the first event. One can then ask about the necessary and sufficient conditions for *that* event. No matter how far back this regress goes, the coming-to-be of any set of necessary and sufficient conditions for a further event will itself be an event. And it will be an event which becomes a part of the series of past events which occurs *after* the first event—unless, of course, it is the first event itself.

It seems, then, that the only way a physicalist understanding of the beginning of the universe can avoid the first event being uncaused is to say that the necessary and sufficient conditions for the first event existed from all eternity in a timeless, changeless state. These conditions for some reason or other gave rise to the first event.

The problem with this scenario is this. In the physical universe, when *A* is the efficient cause of *B*, then given the presence of *A*, *B* obtains spontaneously. If the necessary and sufficient conditions for a match to light are present, the match lights spontaneously. There is no deliberation, no waiting. In such situations, when *A* is the efficient cause of *B*, spontaneous change or mutability is built into the situation itself.

The only way for the first event to arise spontaneously from a timeless, changeless, spaceless state of affairs, and at the same time to be caused, is this—the event resulted from the free act of a person or agent. In the world, persons or agents spontaneously act to bring about events. I myself raise my arm when it is done deliberately. There may be necessary conditions for me to do this (e.g., I have a normal arm, I am not tied down), but these are not sufficient. The event is realized only when I freely act. Similarly, the first event came about when an agent freely chose to bring it about, and this choice was not the result of other conditions which were sufficient for that event to come about.

In summary, it is most reasonable to believe that the universe had a beginning which was caused by a timeless, immutable agent. This is not a proof that such a being is the God of the Bible, but it is a strong statement that the world had its beginning by the act of a person. And this is at the very least a good reason to believe in some form of theism.

NOTES

1. I am deeply indebted to several of Craig's writings, among which are these: *The Cosmological Argument from Plato to Leibnitz*, Library of Philosophy and Religion series (New York: Barnes and Noble, 1980); *The Existence of God and the Beginning of the Universe* (San Bernadino, Calif.: Here's Life, 1979); *Apologetics: An Introduction* (Chicago: Moody, 1984); "Philosophical and Scientific Pointers to Creatio ex Nihilo," *Journal of the American Scientific Affiliation* 32 (March 1980): 5–13; "Professor Mackie and the Kalam Cosmological Argument," *Religious Studies* 20 (1985): 367–75.

2. Craig, "Philosophical and Scientific Pointers," p. 5.

3. See Craig, *Apologetics*, pp. 75–93.

4. Craig, "Philosophical and Scientific Pointers," pp. 6–7; see also G. J. Whitrow, "On the Impossibility of an Infinite Past," *British Journal for the Philosophy of Science* 29 (1978): 39–45.

5. Cited in Fraenkel, *Abstract Set Theory*, p. 6.

6. Fraenkel, *Abstract Set Theory*, p. 20. See also J. L. Mackie, *The Miracle of Theism* (Oxford: Clarendon Press, 1982), pp. 92–95.

7. William Lane Craig, "Wallace Matson and the Crude Cosmological Argument," *Australasian Journal of Philosophy* 57 (June 1979): 163–70.

8. William Wainwright, review of *The Kalam Cosmological Argument* by William Lane Craig, in *Nous* 16 (May 1982) 328–34; Mackie, *The Miracle of Theism*, p. 93.

9. See Craig, *Apologetics*, pp. 79–81.

10. For introductory treatments of the big bang theory, see John Polkinghorne, *The Way the World Is: The Christian Perspective of a Scientist* (Grand Rapids: Eerdmans, 1984), pp. 7–16; John Wiester, *The Genesis Connection* (Nashville: Nelson, 1983), pp. 17–45; Paul Davies, *God and the New Physics* (New York: Simon and Schuster, 1983), pp. 9–57.

11. Cited in Wiester, *The Genesis Connection*, p. 24.

12. Craig, *Apologetics*, p. 86.

13. See Ernan McMullin, "How Should Cosmology Relate to Theology?" in *The Sciences and Theology in the Twentieth Century*, ed. A. R. Peacocke (Notre Dame: University of Notre Dame Press, 1981), pp. 36–38.

14. Davies, *God and the New Physics*, p. 11.

15. *Encyclopedia of Philosophy*, s.v. "Entropy," G. J. Whitrow; Craig, *The Existence of God*, pp. 66–69; Robert E. D. Clark, *The Universe: Plan or Accident?* (Grand Rapids: Zondervan, 1949), pp. 26–42.

16. B. C. Johnson, *The Atheist Debater's Handbook*, Skeptics Bookshelf series (Buffalo: Prometheus, 1981), pp. 70–71.

J. L. MACKIE

Critique of the Cosmological Argument

J. L. Mackie (1917–1981) considers various versions of the cosmological argument. Versions that appeal to the principle of sufficient reason he rejects on the ground that there is no reason to think that this principle is true or that its denial commits one to the unintelligibility of things. He rejects versions of the argument (e.g., Aquinas's) that appeal to the impossibility of an infinite regress of causes on the grounds that they presuppose that contingent things must depend on something else for their existence. He argues to the contrary that there might simply be permanent matter whose existence is not dependent on anything else. He rejects the kalam argument on the ground that the alleged paradoxes found in infinite sets can be resolved by the careful application of two criteria for determining the size of groups in the series. Further, even if the universe were finite in time, there is no reason for holding that it could not have originated by itself. Indeed, for Mackie, the same problem of why something exists applies to God.

⌘

CONTINGENCY AND SUFFICIENT REASON

Leibniz gives what is essentially the same proof in slightly different forms in different works; we can sum up his line of thought as follows.[1] He assumes

From *The Miracle of Theism*.

the *principle of sufficient reason*, that nothing occurs without a sufficient reason why it is so and not otherwise. There must, then, be a sufficient reason for the world as a whole, a reason why something exists rather than nothing. Each thing in the world is contingent, being causally determined by other things: it would not occur if other things were otherwise. The world as a whole, being a collection of such things, is therefore itself contingent. The series of things and events, with their causes, with causes of those causes, and so on, may stretch back infinitely in time; but, if so, then however far back we go, or if we consider the series as a whole, what we have is still contingent and therefore requires a sufficient reason outside this series. That is, there must be a sufficient reason *for* the world which is *other than* the world. This will have to be a necessary being, which contains its own sufficient reason for existence. Briefly, things must have a sufficient reason for their existence, and this must be found ultimately in a necessary being. There must be something free from the disease of contingency, a disease which affects everything in the world and the world as a whole, even if it is infinite in past time.

This argument, however, is open to criticisms of two sorts, summed up in the questions 'How do we know that everything must have a sufficient reason?' and 'How can there be a necessary being, one that contains its own sufficient reason?' These challenges are related: if the second question cannot be answered satisfactorily, it will follow that things as a whole cannot have a sufficient reason, not merely that we do not know that they must have one. . . .

But perhaps we can still make something like Kant's point, even if we are relying only on a criticism of the second sort. Since it is always a further question whether a concept is instantiated or not, no matter how much it contains, the existence even of a being whose essence included existence would not be self-explanatory: there might have failed to be any such thing. This 'might' expresses at least a conceptual possibility; if it is alleged that this being nonetheless exists by a metaphysical necessity, we are still waiting for an explanation of this kind of necessity. The existence of this being is not logically necessary; it does not exist in all logically possible worlds; in what way, then, does it necessarily exist in this world and satisfy the demand for a sufficient reason?

It might be replied that we understand what it is for something to exist contingently, in that it would not have existed if something else had been otherwise: to exist necessarily is to exist but not contingently in this sense. But then the premise that the natural world as a whole is contingent is not available: though we have some ground for thinking that each part, or each finite temporal stretch, of the world is contingent in this sense upon something else, we have initially no ground for thinking that the world as a whole would not have existed if something else had been otherwise; inference from the contingency of every part to the contingency *in this sense* of the whole is invalid. Alternatively, we might say that something exists contingently if and only if it might not have existed, and by contrast that something exists necessarily if and only if it exists, but it is not the case that it might not have existed. In this sense we could infer the contingency of the whole from the contingency of every part. But once it is conceded, for reasons just given, that it is not logically impossible that the alleged necessary being might not have existed, we have no understanding of how it could be true of this being that it is not the case that it might not have existed. We have as yet no ground for believing that it is even possible that something should exist necessarily in the sense required.

This criticism is reinforced by the other objection, 'How do we know that everything must have a sufficient reason?' I see no plausibility in the claim that the principle of sufficient reason is known *a priori* to be true. Leibniz thought that reliance on this principle is implicit in our reasoning both about physics and about human behaviour. . . .

The principle of sufficient reason expresses a demand that things should be intelligible *through and through*. The simple reply to the argument which relies on it is that there is nothing that justifies this demand, and nothing that supports the belief that it is satisfiable even in principle. As we have seen in considering the other main objection to Leibniz's argument, it is difficult to see how there even could be anything that would satisfy it. If we reject this demand, we are not thereby committed to saying that things are utterly unintelligible. The sort of intelligibility that is achieved by successful causal inquiry and scientific explanation is not undermined by its inability to make things intelligible through and through. Any particular explanation starts with premises which state 'brute facts,' and although the brutally factual starting-points of one explanation may themselves be further explained by another, the latter in turn will have to start with something that it does not explain, *and so on however far we go*. But there is no need to see this as unsatisfactory. . . .

The principle of sufficient reason, then, is more far-reaching than the principle that every occurrence has a preceding sufficient cause: the latter, but not the former, would be satisfied by a series of things or events running back infinitely in time, each determined by earlier ones, but with no further explanation of the series as a whole. Such a series would give us only what Leibniz called 'physical' or 'hypothetical' necessity, whereas the demand for a sufficient reason for the whole body of contingent things and events and laws calls for something with 'absolute' or 'metaphysical' necessity. But even the weaker, deterministic, principle is not an *a priori* truth, and indeed it may not be a truth at all; much less can this be claimed for the principle of sufficient reason. Perhaps it just expresses an arbitrary demand; it may be intellectually satisfying to believe that there is, objectively, an explanation for everything together, even if we can only guess at what the explanation might be. But we have no right to assume that the universe will comply with our intellectual preferences. Alternatively, the supposed principle may be an unwarranted extension of the determinist one, which, in so far as it is supported, is supported only empirically, by our success in actually finding causes, and can at most be accepted provisionally, not as an *a priori* truth.

The form of the cosmological argument which relies on the principle of sufficient reason therefore fails completely as a demonstrative proof.

THE REGRESS OF CAUSES

There is a popular line of thought, which we may call the first cause argument, and which runs as follows: things must be caused, and their causes will be other things that must have causes, and so on; but this series of causes cannot go back indefinitely; it must terminate in a first cause, and this first cause will be God. This argument envisages a regress of causes in time, but says (as Leibniz, for one, did not) that this regress must stop somewhere. Though it has some initial plausibility, it also has obvious difficulties. Why must the regress terminate at all? Why, if it terminates, must it lead to a single termination, to one first cause, rather than to a number—perhaps an indefinitely large number—of distinct uncaused causes? And even if there is just one first cause, why should we identify this with God? I shall come back to this argument and to possible replies to these objections; but first I want to look at a more elaborate philosophical argument that has some, though not much, resemblance to it.

Of Aquinas's 'five ways,' the first three are recognizably variants of the cosmological proof, and all three involve some kind of terminated regress of causes.[2] But all of them are quite different from our first cause argument. The first way argues to a first mover, using the illustration of something's being moved by a stick only when the stick is moved by a hand; here the various movings are simultaneous, we do not have a regress of causes in time. Similarly the 'efficient causes' in the second way are contemporary agents. Both these arguments, as Kenny has shown, depend too much on antiquated physical theory to be of much interest now. The third way is much more significant. . . .

This argument is quite different from our first cause argument and also from Leibniz's argument from contingency. Although it uses the contrast between things which are able-not-to-be (and therefore contingent) and those which are necessary, it is not satisfied with the conclusion that there is something necessary; it allows that there may be many necessary things, and reaches God only at the end of the second stage, as what has its necessity 'through itself' (*per se*). Clearly 'necessary' does not mean the same for Aquinas as for Leibniz. What it does mean will become clearer as we examine the reasoning.

In the first stage, the premise 'what is able-not-to-be, at some time is not' seems dubious: why should not something which is *able* not to be nevertheless just happen to exist always? But perhaps Aquinas means by 'things that are able-not-to-be (*possibilia non esse*) something like 'impermanent things,' so that this premise is analytic. Even so, the statement that if everything were such, at some time there would have been nothing, does not follow: some impermanent things might have lasted through all past time, and be going to display their impermanence by perishing only at some time in the future. But we may be able to understand Aquinas's thought by seeing what is said more explicitly by Maimonides, by whom Aquinas appears to have been influenced here.[3] His corresponding proof seems to assume that past time has been finite—and reasonably so, for if past time has been finite there would seem to be an easier argument for a divine creator, such as we shall consider below. The suggestion is that it would not have been possible for impermanent things to have lasted throughout an infinite time, and hence they would have perished already.

However, another objection is that there might be a series of things, each of which was impermanent and perished after a finite period, but whose periods of existence overlapped so that there never was a time when there was nothing. It would be clear logical fallacy (of which some commentators have accused Aquinas) to infer 'at some time everything is not' from 'each thing at some time is not.' But we might defend Aquinas in either of two ways. First, if each thing were impermanent, it would be the most improbable good luck if the overlapping sequence kept up through infinite time. Secondly, even if this improbable luck holds, we might regard the series of overlapping things as itself a thing which had already lasted through infinite time, and so could not be impermanent. Indeed, if there were such a series which never failed, this might well indicate that there was some *permanent* stock of material of which the perishable things were composed and into which they disintegrated, thereby contributing to the composition of other things.

A third objection concerns the premise that 'what does not exist cannot begin to be except through something that is.' This is, of course, a form of the principle that nothing can come from nothing; the idea then is that if our series of impermanent things had broken off, it could never have started again after a gap. But is this an *a priori* truth? As Hume pointed out, we can certainly conceive an uncaused beginning-to-be of an object; if what we can thus conceive is nevertheless in some way impossible, this still requires to be shown.[4] Still, this principle has some plausibility, in that it is constantly confirmed in our experience (and also used, reasonably, in interpreting our experience).

Altogether, then, the first stage of Aquinas's argument falls short of watertight demonstration, but it gives some lower degree of support to the conclusion that there is at least one thing that is necessary in the sense, which has now become clear, that it is permanent, that *for some reason* it is not able-not-to-be.

The second stage takes this conclusion as its starting-point. One permanent thing, it allows, may be caused to be permanent, sustained always in existence, by another. But, it holds, there cannot be an infinite regress of such things. Why not? Aquinas refers us to his earlier proof about efficient causes, in the second way. This runs:

> It is not possible to go to infinity in a series of efficient causes. For in all ordered efficient causes the first item is the cause of the intermediate one and the intermediate is the cause of the last (whether there is only one intermediate or more than one); now if the cause is removed, so is the effect. Therefore if there has not been a first item among efficient causes there will not be a last or an intermediate. But if one goes to infinity in a series of efficient causes, there will not be a first efficient cause, and so there will not be a last effect or intermediate efficient causes.

Unfortunately this argument is unsound. Although in a *finite* ordered series of causes the intermediate (or the earliest intermediate) is caused by the first item, this would not be so if there were an infinite series. In an infinite series, every item is caused by an earlier item. The way in which the first item is 'removed' if we go from a finite to an infinite series does not entail the removal of the later items. In fact, Aquinas (both here and in the first way) has simply begged the question against an infinite regress of causes. But is this a sheer mistake, or is there some coherent thought behind it? Some examples (some of which would not themselves have been available to Aquinas, though analogues of them would have been) may suggest that there is. If we were told that there was a watch without a mainspring, we would hardly be reassured by the further information that it had, however, an infinite train of gear-wheels. Nor would we expect a railway train consisting of an infinite number of carriages, the last pulled along by the second last, the second last by the third last, and so on, to get along without an engine. Again, we see a chain, consisting of a series of links, hanging from a hook; we should be surprised to learn that there was a similar but infinite chain, with no hook, but links supported by links above them for ever. The point is that in these examples, and in the series of efficient causes or of necessary things, it is assumed that there is a relation of *dependence*—or, equivalently, one in the reverse direction of *support*—and, if the series were infinite, there would in the end be nothing for the effects to depend on, nothing to support them. And the same would be true if the regress were not infinite but circular.

There is here an implicit appeal to the following general principle: Where items are ordered by a relation of dependence, the regress must end somewhere; it cannot be either infinite or circular. Perhaps this principle was intended by al Farabi in the dictum that is translated 'But a series of contingent beings which would produce one another cannot proceed to infinity or move in a circle' (p. 83). As our examples show, this principle is at least highly plausible; the problem will be to decide when we have such a relation of dependence.

In the second stage of Aquinas's argument, therefore, the key notion is that any necessary—that is, permanent—thing either depends for its permanence on something else or is *per se necessarium* in a sense which can apply only to God. The actual text of the third way does not reveal Aquinas's thinking about this. But comparison of it with other passages in his writings and with Maimonides's proof suggests that the implicit assumption is that anything whose essence does not involve existence must, even if it is permanent, depend for its existence on something else.[5] This assumption would give the dependence which would call for an end to the regress and also ensure that nothing could end it but a being whose essence involved existence—which would explain the assertion that what is *per se necessarium* is what men all call God.

But the final objection to the argument is that we have no reason for accepting this implicit assumption. Why, for example, might there not be a permanent stock of matter whose essence did not involve existence but which did not derive its existence from anything else? . . .

But what about the popular first cause argument? Can we not now answer our earlier queries? Why must the regress of causes in time terminate? Because things, states of affairs, and occurrences *depend* on their antecedent causes. Why must the regress lead to one first cause rather than to many uncaused causes, and why must that one cause be God? Because anything other than God would need something else causally to depend upon. Moreover, the assumption needed for this argument is more plausible than that needed for Leibniz's proof, or for Aquinas's. The notion that everything must have a sufficient reason is a metaphysician's demand, as is the notion that anything permanent must depend for its permanence on something else unless its essence involves existence. But the notion that an effect *depends* on a temporally earlier cause is part of our ordinary understanding of causation: we all have some grasp of this asymmetry between cause and effect, however hard it may be to give an exact analysis of it.[6]

Nevertheless, this argument is not demonstratively cogent. Though we understand that where something has a temporally antecedent cause, it depends somehow upon it, it does not follow that everything (other than God) *needs* something else to depend on in this way. Also, what we can call al Farabi's principle, that where items are ordered by a relation of dependence, the regress must terminate somewhere, and cannot be either infinite or circular, though plausible, may not be really sound. But the greatest weakness of this otherwise attractive argument is that some reason is required for making God the one exception to the supposed need for something else to depend on: why should God, rather than anything else, be taken as the only satisfactory termination of the regress? If we do not simply accept this as a sheer mystery (which would be to abandon rational theology and take refuge in faith), we shall have to defend it in something like the ways that the metaphysicians have suggested. But then this popular argument takes on board the burdens that have sunk its more elaborate philosophical counterparts.

FINITE PAST TIME AND CREATION

There is, as Craig explains, a distinctive kind of cosmological argument which, unlike those of Aquinas, Leibniz, and many others, assumes or argues that the past history of the world is finite.[7] This, which Craig calls, by its Arabic name, the *kalam* type of argument, was favoured by Islamic thinkers who were suspicious of the subtleties of the philosophers and relied more on revelation than on reason. Nevertheless, they did propound this as a rational proof of God's existence, and some of them used mathematical paradoxes that are descended from Zeno's, or that anticipate Cantor's, to show that there cannot be an actual infinite—in particular, an infinite past time. For example, if time past were infinite, an infinite stretch would have actually to have been traversed in order to reach the present, and this is thought to be impossible. Then there is an ingenious argument suggested by al Ghazali: the planet Jupiter revolves in its orbit once every twelve years, Saturn once every thirty years; so Jupiter must have completed more than twice as many revolutions as Saturn; yet if past time were infinite they would each have completed the same (infinite) number; which is a contradiction. The first of these (which Kant also uses in the thesis of his First Antinomy) just expresses a prejudice against an actual infinity. It assumes that, even if past time were infinite, there would still have been a starting-point of time, but one infinitely remote, so that an actual infinity would have had to be traversed to reach the present from there. But to take the hypothesis of infinity seriously would be to suppose that there was no starting-point, not even an infinitely remote one, and that from any specific point in past time there is only a finite stretch that needs to be traversed to reach the present. Al Ghazali's argument uses an instance of one of Cantor's paradoxes, that in an infinite class a part can indeed be equal to the whole: for example, there are just as many even numbers (2, 4, 6, etc.) as there are whole numbers (1, 2, 3, etc.), since these classes can be matched one-one with each other. But is this not a contradiction? Is not the class of even numbers both equal to that of the integers (because of this one-one correlation) and smaller than it (because it is a proper part of it, the part that leaves out the odd numbers)? But what this brings out is that we ordinarily have and use a criterion for one group's being smaller than another—that it is, or can be correlated one-one with, a proper part of the other—and a criterion for two groups' being equal in number—that they can be correlated one-one with each other—which together ensure that *smaller than* and *equal to* exclude one another for all pairs of finite groups, but not for pairs of infinite groups. Once we understand the relation between the two criteria, we see that there is no real contradiction.

In short, it seems impossible to disprove, *a priori*, the possibility of an infinite past time. Nevertheless, many people have shared, and many still do share, these doubts about an actual infinite in the real world, even if they are willing to leave mathematicians free to play their Cantorian games—which, of course, not all mathematicians, or all philosophers of mathematics, want to play. Also the view that, whatever we say about *time*, the *universe* has a finite past history, has in recent years received strong empirical support from the cosmology that is a branch of astronomy. So let us consider what the prospects would be for a proof of the existence of a god if we were supplied, from whatever source, with the premise that the world has only a finite past history, and therefore a beginning in time, whether or not this is also the beginning of time. Here the crucial assumption is stated by al Ghazali: '[We] know by rational necessity that nothing which originates in time originates by itself, and that, therefore, it needs a creator' (p. 102). But *do* we know this by rational necessity? Surely the assumption required here is just the same as that which is used differently in the first cause argument, that anything other than a god needs a cause or a creator to depend on. But there is *a priori* no good reason why a sheer origination of things, not determined by anything, should be unacceptable, whereas the existence of a god with the power to create something out of nothing is acceptable.

When we look hard at the latter notion we find problems within it. Does God's existence have a sheer origination in time? But then this would be as great a puzzle as the sheer origination of a material world. Or has God existed for ever through an infinite time? But this would raise again the problem of the actual infinite. To avoid both of these, we should have to postulate that God's own existence is not in time at all; but this would be a complete mystery.

Alternatively, someone might not share al Ghazali's worries about the actual infinite, and might rely on an empirical argument—such as the modern cosmological evidence for the 'big bang'—to show that the material world had a beginning in time. For him, therefore, God's existence through an infinite time would be unproblematic. But he is still using the crucial assumptions that God's existence and creative power would be self-explanatory whereas the unexplained origination of a material world would be unintelligible and therefore unacceptable. But the first of these leads us back to the criticism stated [earlier]. The notion, embedded in the ontological argument, of a being whose existence is self-explanatory because it is not the case that it might not have existed, is *not* defensible; so we cannot borrow that notion to complete any form of the cosmological argument. The second assumption is equally questionable. We have no good ground for an *a priori* certainty that there could not have been a sheer unexplained beginning of things. But in so far as we find this improbable, it should cast doubt on the interpretation of the big bang as an absolute beginning of the material universe; rather, we should infer that it must have had *some* physical antecedents, even if the big bang has to be taken as a discontinuity so radical that we cannot explain it, because we can find no laws which we can extrapolate backwards through this discontinuity.

In short, the notion of creation seems more acceptable than any other way out of the cosmological maze only because we do not look hard either at it or at the human experiences of making things on which it is modelled. It is vaguely explanatory, apparently satisfying; but these appearances fade away when we try to formulate the suggestion precisely.

NOTES

1. The clearest account is in 'On the Ultimate Origination of Things,' printed, e.g., in G. W. Leibniz, *Philosophical Writings* (Dent, London, 1934), pp. 32–41.

2. A. Kenny, *The Five Ways* (Routledge & Kegan Paul, London, 1969).
3. William L. Craig, *The Cosmological Argument from Plato to Leibniz* (Macmillan, London, 1980), chap. 4.
4. *Treatise*, Book I, Part 3, Section 3; contrast Kenny, op. cit., p. 67.
5. Craig, op. cit., pp. 142–143, 146–148.
6. Cf. chapter 7 of *The Cement of the Universe* (see n. 2 to Chapter 1 above).
7. Craig, op. cit., Chapter 3.

L. STAFFORD BETTY
with BRUCE CORDELL

The Anthropic Teleological Argument

L. Stafford Betty (1942–) and Bruce Cordell (1949–) develop a cumulative argument that cites various features of the universe to establish the probability that God exists. They think that a universe described by a grand universal theory (GUT) or by a theory of superstrings is unlikely to have evolved this way merely by chance. Also, the Anthropic principle indicates that a large number of basic physical constants were needed for conscious life to arise; yet each individual constant, let alone all of them together, are a priori extraordinarily improbable. Thus our own unlikely situation—that we exist and are able to observe the universe—inductively suggests a universal, creative intelligence. Last, for Betty and Cordell, the existence of an intelligent creator explains the origin of life better than any neo-Darwinian account. Finally, they propose the law that the significantly greater cannot come from the significantly less, with the result that it is reasonable to hold that the supermind behind the universe is superior to us in every respect.

⌘

The Teleological Argument (*telos* in the Greek means "purpose," "end," or "design") presented here is akin to, yet somewhat different from the "wider teleological argument" of F. R. Tennant.[1] Tennant did not think that his arguments were conclusive; taken together they only *suggested* "an intelligent Designer."[2] The present argument, however, is largely based on mathematics and physics, and these yield probabilities. Quite a few neo-teleologists in the scientific community hold that the orthodox model of randomly evolving complexity and order in the universe is *overwhelmingly improbable*, for, they argue, the mathematics of the case makes it so. An intel-

From *International Philosophical Quarterly* 27, no. 4 (December 1987). Reprinted by permission.

ligent designer, they say, is, by a very wide margin, the best available explanation of the universe. . . .

This paper will present, under four headings, the most important evidences which, we believe, point to an intelligent designer as the best explanation of our orderly universe. These headings are the following: (a) intuitive factors, (b) cosmology, (c) the fossil record, and (d) biochemical complexity. [(a) and (c) are omitted.]

COSMOLOGY

[W]e will consider three arguments for the existence of a cosmic orderer. They are based on the Big Bang and the anthropic principle.

The Big Bang. The first of these, the argument based on the Big Bang, is in many ways the most impressive. But it does not lend itself to mathematical analysis, and hence to a probability calculus (with odds computed for or against the argument), as readily as the other two arguments. Thus, we will treat it first and regard it as the weakest, i.e., the most "intuitive" of the arguments.

Most scientists and philosophers stop well short of reasoning backward from the cosmos as it exists today to the necessary existence of an ultimate mind and will behind the primeval explosion. But at least one, Hannes Alfven, concluded that the Big Bang "necessarily presupposes a divine creation,"[3] while another, the British physicist Edmund Whitaker, maintained that there "is no ground for supposing that matter and energy existed before [the Big Bang] and was suddenly galvanized into action . . . It is simpler to postulate creation *ex nihilo*–Divine will constituting Nature from nothingness."[4] Whatever one's particular view of the ultimate cause of the Big Bang, it is certainly the case that a universe with a beginning in time—anywhere from thirteen to twenty billion years ago, according to latest estimates—is more likely to arouse speculation about a Creator than a steady-state, apparently beginningless universe of infinite duration.

This is reasonable because the Big Bang refers, according to latest refinements of the theory, to a time when matter-energy arose out of a condition which is mysterious to us, and will probably always be. Even if the Big Bang is the result of a "zero-point fluctuation," as some physicists have recently speculated, it would be necessary to ask what caused this fluctuation. At best this theory only moves back the unexplainable one step; the order, immensity, complexity, and beauty of our present universe remains anchored in an irresistible surd.

At this point we must ask ourselves what is easier to imagine and thus to believe: that the cosmos' entire history should have arisen from this self-creating and self-explaining surd; or that a pre-existing mind and power of vast magnitude should have created the ingredients of the universe and triggered it at the Big Bang? This second alternative seems to us somewhat more likely. It is certainly no more preposterous. . . .

Many scientists hold that it is impossible to extrapolate as far back into the past. The distinguished MIT physicist Victor Weisskopf is one of these. "It is very difficult," he says, "to know what happened at periods earlier than about 10^{-6} sec . . . but scientists like to speculate and to construct hypotheses."[5] And they do. One speculation that has enjoyed wide currency is called the grand unification theory (GUT), so called because it postulates a time when all forces of nature, apart from gravity, were reduced to a single force.

GUT yields a universe which not only boggles the imagination, but which is utterly spectacular in its elegantly simple unfolding. Could such a universe have unfurled by chance alone? Or was there a mind of indescribable magnitude behind the whole thing? Mike Corwin, a physicist who has studied and written about the universe's beginning according to the GUT scenario, is "filled with a sense of wonder and mystery" at "the natural miracle of our existence."[6] Corwin is, of course, speaking poetically, but that is exactly the point. A study of the universe's beginning leaves some people speechless or stammering; or inclined to write poetry; or, in a few cases, to believe.

Potentially more revolutionary than GUT—or supersymmetry, or the electroweak theory, or quantum chromodynamics (QCD), which are alternative attempts to reduce the universe to a sublime primeval simplicity—is superstrings. "Superstrings," writes Gary Taubes in *Discover*, "is a theory of the universe, a ten-dimensional one, in which the fundamental building blocks of matter and energy aren't infinitesimal points but infinitesimal strings."[7] So comprehensive is superstrings—it neatly and elegantly accommodates all four of the fundamental forces of the universe—that physicists are calling it the Theory of Everything (T.O.E.). Not even taken seriously by the huge majority of physicists until 1984, today it is considered to be the theory with the best chance of reducing the universe, including gravity, to a single fundamental force. "It's beautiful, wonderful, majestic—and strange, if you like,"[8] says mathematician Edward Witten of Princeton. It still remains to reduce superstrings' ivory-tower ten-dimensional universe to the common-sense four-dimensional one in which we live, but many physicists and mathematicians are confident that this will be done. If so, then "all matter and energy, all forces, all people, planets, stars, cats and dogs, quasars, atoms, automobiles and everything else, from the instant of the Big Bang to the end of time," will be shown to be the result of the twitchings, vibrations, and interactions of these infinitesimal strings.

Again the question arises: How likely is it that our spectacularly complex, orderly universe should have arisen from the *chance* twitchings and interactions of these strings? Is it not more likely that there is an ordering, creating intelligence attached (if you'll forgive us) to the strings? . . .

The Anthropic Principle. One scientist who did take Dirac's principle seriously was Robert H. Dicke of Princeton. Influenced by Dirac's reasoning,

Dicke in 1961 introduced the scientific world to the "anthropic principle." Like Dirac's large-number hypothesis, the anthropic principle derives its force from certain "coincidences" in the values of the basic physical constants. Dicke was specifically concerned to show that the Hubble constant, which governs the rate of expansion of the universe, could not have been much different from what it in fact is, or otherwise life could not have evolved. Cambridge University physicist Brandon Carter, whose name is more often associated with the anthropic principle, applied Dicke's reasoning to all of the initial conditions of the universe (temperature, chemical environment, etc.). According to Carter, if the initial conditions at the Big Bang had been any different from what they were, life as we know it could not have evolved. Paraphrasing Descartes, Carter writes, "*Cogito ergo mundus talis est*" (I think, therefore, the world is as it is).[9]

According to Dewey Schwartzenburg, the anthropic principle (*anthropos*, Greek for "man") boils down to this: ". . . if the universe were in fact different in any significant way from the way it is, we wouldn't be here to wonder why it is the way it is."[10] B. J. Carr and M. J. Rees, whose 1979 article in *Nature* is perhaps the most impressive scientific statement of the principle yet to appear, explain that the "possibility of life as we know it evolving in the Universe depends on the values of a few basic physical constants—and is in some respects remarkably sensitive to their numerical values."[11]

What are those constants? Physicists speak of "coupling constants," but these in turn depend on such basic constants as the charge of the proton, the mass of the proton, the speed of light, the gravitational constant G in Newton's law of universal gravitation, and Planck's constant, h, which allows us to determine a quantum of energy emitted by an electron radiating at a particular frequency. In mathematical notation, h is equal to 6.625×10^{-34} J. sec, and "Big G," the gravitational constant, is equal to 6.67×10^{-11} newton-m^2/kg^2.

What is remarkable—and it is this that forms the basis of the anthropic principle—is that if, for instance, Planck's constant had a different value, say 6.626×10^{-33} instead of 10^{-34}, the whole universe would be different from the way it is. More importantly, intelligent life could not have evolved in a substantially altered universe. For example, if gravity were significantly stronger than it is, stars would exhaust their hydrogen fuels much faster, and humanoid life (as we know it) could not appear in a universe where stars "died young." Or if the "strong force," which binds the nuclei of atoms together, were stronger, helium nuclei would dominate the universe, and no hydrogen would be left over; without hydrogen there would be no water, and without water there could not be life as we know it. This list of examples could go on indefinitely. The point is that, as far as we can tell, intelligent humanoid life could have evolved in only one narrowly select set of universes: the set including the universe we find ourselves in, a universe whose physical processes are governed by the precise basic constants that it possesses. Corwin states the case well:

> Life as we conceive it demands severe constraints on the initial conditions of the universe. Life and consciousness are not only the direct result of the initial conditions, but could only have resulted from a narrow range of initial conditions (i.e., the constants had to be precisely as they are). It is not that changes in the initial conditions would have changed the character of life, but rather that any significant change in the initial conditions would have ruled out the possibility of life evolving later . . . the universe would have evolved as a lifeless, unconscious entity.[12]

It is no wonder that today a few scientists who are aware of the anthropic principle are asking the question, "Does all this mean that cosmology has come to the point of having to postulate a 'Creator'?"[13] The answer would seem, at first glance, to be Yes. For how else can we explain all these "coincidences"? Let us use an analogy: Imagine nine jars, each containing ten slips of paper with one number from 0 to 9, one number to a slip, with each number represented, placed side by side. Suppose now that a mechanical device drew at random one slip from each jar, and that the numbers drawn in sequence happened to correspond *exactly* to your nine-numbered Social Security Number. What are the chances of a random drawing giving such a result? They are exactly one in a billion. Now suppose, unlike a legitimate, genuinely random lottery drawing, there was no special reason dictating that the drawing had to be random, even though the mechanical device *suggested* randomness. If your number were drawn, would it not be far more reasonable to assume that the drawing was *not* random, that it was instead being superintended by some intelligence behind the scenes who was in some way invisibly manipulating the mechanical device? Would it not, in other words, be reasonable to conclude that the drawing was fixed—fixed in your favor?

Don N. Page of the Institute for Advanced Study in Princeton, N.J., recently calculated the odds against the formation of our universe, and the figure was a good deal more than one in a billion.[14] His exact computation was in fact one in $10{,}000{,}000{,}000^{124}$, a number so large that to call it "astronomical" would be to engage in a wild understatement. But are the odds *against a Cosmic Designer* so high? If we must make a forced choice between an unintelligent random process and an invisible Intelligence behind the scenes, as it appears we must, and if, furthermore, the chance against a random process accounting for the precise values of the basic constants of physics is well in excess of a billion to one, then a designer may be considered highly probable. In other words, the anthropic principle looks as if it might succeed, after careful analysis, in making highly probable the existence of a universal designer-creator.

There are three reasons, however, to think that it might not. Though they may seem like quibbles to some, they have been thought by others to tip the balance back in the opposite direction, or if not in the opposite direction, then in a new direction leading to a destination that altogether baffles the human mind.

First, as Carr and Rees point out, the anthropic principle

> is based on what may be an unduly anthropocentric concept of an observer. The arguments invoked here assume that life requires elements heavier than hydrogen and helium, water, galaxies, and special types of stars and planets. It is conceivable [however] that some form of intelligence could exist without all of these features.[15]

In other words, intelligent life might have evolved out of a very different kind of universe, and not just the one we know, with its particular governing constants. Of course, this "life" would have almost nothing in common (at least physically) with the biological life forms to which our universe has given rise. But what, except our own narrow experience, is guiding us when we limit life to conditions such as our universe provides?

Second, it is possible that an infinite number of universes coexist alongside our own or have existed sequentially in the beginningless past prior to our own. University of Texas physicist John Archibald Wheeler, who helped develop the many-worlds theory of coexisting universes first proposed in 1957 by Princeton physicist Hugh Everett, championed the "Everett Hypothesis" as a way of explaining the anthropic coincidences. He reasoned that, given enough universes, it is not unlikely that one would come along which had the right ingredients for life; and our universe is it. As for the others, "nothing 'interesting' would ever happen—there would be universes without stars, and others without atoms, and still others without even matter."[16] Wheeler's view has found few supporters, largely for the reason that such universes have never been observed and, moreover, are in principle unobservable. Even Wheeler himself is now looking elsewhere for the clue to our universe's existence, namely, to the "magic central idea"[17] which will at last make intelligible quantum theory, and with it our seemingly improbable universe. In any case, there is nothing intrinsically absurd about this many-worlds hypothesis.

The third refutation is very much the brainchild of Wheeler. Though it might at first sound fantastic because incompatible with our commonsense realism, it is in fact consistent with quantum mechanics, which describes the activity of tiny particles (electrons, for example) on an atomic or molecular scale. Wheeler predicted that an experimenter would be able to observe either the particle's diffraction pattern (single slit) or its interference pattern (double slit), whichever one he chose, *even though the particle had already moved* and, as it were, "committed itself" to one, and *only* one, of these patterns. Wheeler writes: "After the quantum of energy has *already* gone through the doubly slit screen, a last-instant free choice on our part—we have found—gives at will a double-slit-interference record or a one-slit-beam count."[18] On the basis of this extraordinary prediction, scientists in France, West Germany, and at the University of Maryland recently set up "delayed choice" experiments to test the prediction. All of the findings seemed to support Wheeler: ". . . whether you make the choice before or after the event occurs, the effect of the choice [is] the same."[19] As Corwin puts it, "observership becomes the mechanism of genesis. . . . What we choose to measure, argues Wheeler, is really an inseparable part of a phenomenon that in earlier thinking one would have said has 'already happened.' "[20]

How is this way of thinking—"observership becomes the mechanism of genesis"—a threat to the thesis that our universe was created by a supermind ("God")? In this way: if we are capable of creating the experimental outcome that we desire, the next logical step is to suggest that scientists in some way create (imagine?) the basic constants of physics that our argument is based on. In that case there would be nothing special about the constants, and the only mind proven by them would be our own. One could not say of them that they were "true"; nor could one say that the "universe" they described really existed. A cosmic creator would become an unnecessary hypothesis.

What defense can we give against these three arguments? We admit that the theory of life's emergence from conditions greatly dissimilar to what we know on Earth, however unlikely this scenario may be, and the theory of an infinite number of universes, however farfetched it may seem, are at least not intrinsically absurd; but with this last hypothesis just sketched, although it is seemingly more plausible, there are grave philosophical difficulties. Indeed such a position can be regarded as self-refuting. Wheeler states that the experimenter would have ended up with a "different story for the doings of the electron if he had done different measurements in a different sequence."[21] In other words, there is not "a world sitting 'out there' "[22] for us to discover, measure, and describe. But if this is so, we would argue, then human observation is intrinsically suspect, and truth ceases to have any meaning. In such a solipsistic universe, or what Wheeler calls a "participatory universe,"[23] where we in some sense create what we set out to find, science is turned into a creative art; elegance and beauty, rather than correspondence to reality, might conceivably become the ultimate meaningful measures of "good science."

Philosophy aside, Wheeler's controversial views are rejected by physicists who call themselves realists, such as Fritz Rohrlich. Although the apparatus "plays a much more important role in measurements of the quantum world than in measurements of the classical world," as Rohrlich says, that does not mean "that reality is created by the observer. . . . The world of electrons, protons, and all the rest does exist out there even if we do not observe it."[24] Three physicists working in England—David Bohm, C. Dewdney, and B. H. Hiley—would agree. They recently published a paper in which they claim to give "a simple and intelligible account of a typical delayed-choice experiment."[25] If their account holds up, they will have succeeded to a degree in demystifying the quantum, and Wheeler's hypothesis that a quantum phenomenon does not exist until we observe it, will be discardable, and with it the threat to our present thesis.

To summarize, the anthropic principle presents us with a potentially powerful argument for the existence of a universal creating intelligence. Although three refutations can be brought forth, each has its problems. Nevertheless, there is nothing intrinsically implausible about the first two, and it is too early to dispose of the third. We must look elsewhere—to biology—for a more compelling argument. . . .

BIOCHEMICAL COMPLEXITY

So far we have concentrated on the fossil record and restricted our investigation to the last six hundred million years of Earth's 4.6 billion year history; we have said nothing about the evolution of life itself during the first billion or so years of Earth's history. What do we find when we try to account for the earliest, simplest life forms on Earth? How did the first protein, the first enzyme, the first DNA or RNA molecule come to be? Does the Neo-Darwinian Synthesis, with its dependence on exclusively random processes, give a plausible account of the appearance of these early biomolecules? Does it adequately account for the jump from nonlife to life? Or are we forced to look elsewhere for a more plausible explanation? These are the questions that this last section will address.

Charles-Eugene Guye, a Swiss physicist who died in 1942, was the first to apply the probability calculus to the question of life's origin. He calculated the mathematical odds against the random formation of a single protein molecule (protein is an essential ingredient in every organism) at $1{:}2.02 \times 10^{321}$. . . .

Thirty-four years later another book appeared. . . . This was Fred Hoyle's and N. C. Wickramasinghe's *Evolution from Space*.[26] Reasoning and calculating in much the same way as Guye, they tried to show that mathematical probability is stacked against Neo-Darwinism. Far more likely is it, they believe, that some kind of Super-Intelligence is behind the evolution of life on our planet.

Hoyle, one of the great astronomers of our century, and Wickramasinghe, currently (1987) Head of the Department of Applied Mathematics and Astronomy at University College in Cardiff, Wales, base their argument on the molecular structure of enzymes, which are complex macromolecules essential for the evolution of life. The two scientists hold that the "usual theory of mutation and natural selection cannot produce complex biomolecules from a random association of atoms,"[27] and, therefore, that the essential building blocks of even the most rudimentary forms of life could not have formed in the way in which Neo-Darwinists say they did.

Hoyle and Wickramasinghe are especially interested in refuting the "organic soup myth." This is the theory that the primeval stew of water (H_2O), ammonia (NH_3), methane (CH_4), and other simple compounds which made up our planet in its infancy, *randomly* generated, when subjected to lightning flashes or other energy sources, the enzymes so critical to life. After pointing out that there are "some ten to twenty distinct amino acids which determine the basic backbone of the enzyme" and that these "simply must be in the correct position in the polypeptide structure,"[28] Hoyle and Wickramasinghe calculate the chance of one enzyme forming anywhere on earth through the random ordering of amino acids at one in 10^{20}. The brunt of their argument follows:

> By itself, this small probability could be faced, because one must contemplate not just a single shot at obtaining the enzyme, but a very large number of trials such as are supposed to have occurred in an organic soup early in the history of the Earth. The trouble is that there are about two thousand enzymes, and the chance of obtaining them all in a random trial is only one part in $(10^{20})^{2000} = 10^{40,000}$, an outrageously small probability that could not be faced even if the whole universe consisted of organic soup.[29]

This immense figure is only the beginning. They continue:

> Nothing has been said of the origin of DNA itself, nothing of DNA transcription to RNA, nothing of the origin of the program whereby cells organize themselves, nothing of mitosis or meiosis. These issues are too complex to set numbers to.[30]

The two scientists go on to say that the chance of these biochemical systems being formed "through random shufflings of simple organic molecules is exceedingly minute, to a point where it is insensibly different from zero."[31]

Hoyle and Wickramasinghe are now poised for the strike. If Neo-Darwinism cannot account for the biochemical complexity necessary for the origin of life, what can? They answer:

> Any theory with a probability of being correct that is larger than one part in $10^{40,000}$ must be judged superior to random shuffling. The theory that life was assembled by an intelligence has, we believe, a probability vastly higher than one part in $10^{40,000}$ of being the correct explanation. . . . Indeed, such a theory is so obvious that one wonders why it is not widely accepted as being self-evident.[32] . . .

A trio of scientists headed by chemist Charles Thaxton, Director of Curriculum Research for the Foundation for Thought and Ethics in Dallas, provide another angle of vision on the problem of life's origin; and their conclusions are just as vexatious for traditional Neo-Darwinists as were the above. Their 1984 book *The Mystery of Life's Origin* is especially valuable for its summary of experiments—thousands of them—undertaken all over the world to show how life might have arisen on earth. All these experiments try to simulate earth's primitive geological condition ("the prebiotic soup") and atmosphere. In some experiments ultraviolet light is directed through the system, in others heat, in others special chemical reactants, and so forth. Many energy sources have been tried, and just as many varieties and conditions of "soup." Has anything like proteins, enzymes, RNA, or DNA ever turned up? Thaxton offers this summary: "The uniform failure in literally thousands of experimental attempts to synthesize protein or DNA under even questionable prebiotic conditions is a monument to [its] difficulty. . . ."[33] By "questionable" Thaxton and his colleagues mean "illegitimate." In their survey of the kinds of experiments being carried out, they show that most investigators, in an effort to achieve the hoped for results, more or less fudge; in other words, they create conditions that were not likely to have existed on the primitive earth. Thaxton and his colleagues find that the less fudging there is, the less satisfactory are the results.

The conclusion of their study is that chemical evolution along the lines of the Neo-Darwinian synthesis "is highly implausible."[34] It is noteworthy that the esteemed biologist Sidney W. Fox, one of the leading proponents and a veteran of early-earth simulation experiments, agrees. Fox views amino acids as "self-ordering," not at all the lucky result of random processes. He is convinced that "matter organizes itself"[35] and that "all evolutionary processes are highly nonrandom."[36] Many biologists, chemists, and philosophers of science agree with Fox. While declining to say what it is which might account for the self-ordering—or more precisely, what it is which might account for the fortuitous morphology of amino acids that results in "molecular selection"[37]—they nevertheless acknowledge that self-ordering, as opposed to random interaction, is a fact of pre-life.

Thaxton and his colleagues, however, do not decline to say what they think is behind the "self-ordering." Risking certain censure by fellow scientists, they conclude, in agreement with Hoyle and Wickramasinghe, that an ordering intelligence is the most plausible way of accounting for the evolution of proteins, RNA, and DNA on early earth. They do not regard this conclusion as "religious," but as solidly scientific:

> We have observational evidence in the present that intelligent investigators can (and do) build ways to bring about some complex chemical synthesis, even gene building. May not the principle of uniformity then be used in a broader frame of consideration to suggest that DNA had an intelligent cause at the beginning?[38]

All in all, the biochemical argument, with an assist from the probability calculus, is a most imposing argument for the existence of a universal creative intelligence. In conjunction with the arguments centering on the physical constants (see the second argument, considered earlier) and on the inadequacy of Neo-Darwinism's doctrine of gradualism (our third argument), this last acquires even stronger force; just as three sticks held together in a bunch are harder to break as a module than each by itself. We can liken the argument to the reasoning process of an archaeologist. He sees no designer, no maker, no orderer physically laid out alongside the chard that he uncovers. If he finds only one chard, dirty and worn, he might wonder if it is after all merely a strangely shaped rock, an anomaly. But if he finds two others alongside the first, he confidently infers a designer, though the designer is never seen. Why should we not do this with respect to the earth (and, by extension, the universe)?

We are struck by the way that the old notion of a "God of the gaps"—a God needed to explain a diminishing number of mysteries, until at some time in the future He Himself fades away when the last mystery is unfolded—has been stood on its head. The gaps are proving to be more and more resistant to conventional scientific theory. It is as if they are fighting back, resisting closure, frustrating every attempt to bridge them, and widening in the process. If anything, science nowadays is creating new gaps, not closing old ones. We find ourselves wondering if the term "God of the gaps" may someday be used not by atheists to make fun of theists but by theists to remind atheists of the facts. In the meantime, we have on our hands a formidable teleological argument for the existence of a creative supermind.

With that, we come to the last question that we must treat.

WHAT GOD MIGHT BE

If our argument is sound, if we are justified in concluding that a supermind exists, can we say anything about what He, She, or It might be? Might It be something so impersonal that, besides its consciousness and computational skills, there is nothing else at all to which we can relate? Or might She be a Cosmic Mother who loves her creatures, especially her more intelligent species, analogously to the way we love our children, and who is as perfect in goodness as She is immense and unfathomable in her intelligence? Or is He a Cosmic Scientist experimenting with life forms in his laboratory, which we call the universe—a God neither loving nor callous by nature, but exceedingly curious? Does this God pre-exist the universe and create it out of nothing, or coexist everlastingly alongside it? Does this God suffuse our beings, and can we experience Her within, as the mystics of all the great religions have proclaimed? Is this God essentially spiritual, and does He have a body, perhaps the universe itself, as the Hindu theologian Ramanuja supposed?[39] Or is God an all-comprehending Absolute that specifies Itself in conscious persons, only to draw them back into unity with It in some ineffable perfection, as the modern philosopher J. N. Findlay thinks?[40] Does our argument help us answer such questions as these?

Strictly speaking, it doesn't. All it can do is point to the existence of a supermind behind nature's orderly, evolving processes. But there is a certain logic that we have been using throughout which, if applied to the question now before us, allows us to say more, if at great risk. We have seen in our investigation of biomolecular processes that there is good reason to believe that the significantly greater does not *randomly* come forth out of the significantly less. Simple amino acids, to be sure, are randomly generated, not surprisingly, by inorganic compounds; but the *significantly* greater (because vastly more complex) enzymes have never revealed how they might be randomly generated by the amino acids. Indeed it seems there is no way they *could* have been generated without the help of intelligent orchestration.

In order to learn more about the *nature* of the proposed supermind, let's indulge in a little speculation and see where it takes us. We have just seen that there is good reason to think that the significantly greater cannot evolve unaided from the significantly less. Now let's postulate that it is a *universal law* that the significantly greater cannot be generated by the significantly less, and then apply it to the supermind, which is exponentially, perhaps even infinitely greater than we are. Would it not be a violation of this law if so much moral goodness as appears in this world were to exceed the goodness of the supermind? Consider for a moment the world we live in. We occasionally meet Mahatmas, more frequently little old ladies who unfailingly greet us with cheerful smiles in spite of severe arthritis. Not only is there much nobility and goodness in our own species; there is also a reverence for truth and a love of beauty. Beauty, truth, and goodness: those three fundamental values of the Greeks. Do large numbers of human beings significantly surpass the supermind in these "constants of the spirit?" This would have to be so if the supermind were merely a mind. We, its creations, would significantly surpass it in the area of values. It would have succeeded in creating a good that it knows nothing of, and the law that the significantly greater cannot come from the significantly less would have been violated.

This universal law—if it in fact is a law, as I tentatively propose—has enormously important implications for our discussion of the supermind's nature. If such a law holds, then it would follow that the supermind must be superior to us, not only with respect to intelligence (which seems obvious), but in every other important way as well. That mind must be characterized by knowledge, power, beauty, goodness, and love to a degree not known to us mortals. If so, it must in some sense be personal (perhaps "superpersonal" is a better way of putting it), for such traits as goodness and love would seem to adhere only in that which is at least analogous to persons. Whether or not the supermind has these perfections to an *infinite* degree—whatever that might involve—cannot be predicted by our argument. Nonetheless, it is clear that we are not too far away from a God whom we can at least admire. And if admiration should grow to love—a not unnatural progression—then the God of the great theistic religions is not far away. Religion and science will have joined hands.

NOTES

1. F. R. Tennant, *Philosophical Theology*, 2 vols. (Cambridge: Cambridge Univ. Press, 1969).
2. Ian G. Barbour, *Issues in Science and Religion* (New York: Harper and Row, 1966), p. 392.
3. Hannes Alfven in Wolfgang Yourgrau and Allen D. Breck, eds., *Cosmology, History, and Theology* (New York: Plenum Press, 1977), p. 7.
4. Robert Jastrow, *God and the Astronomers* (New York: W. W. Norton and Co., 1978), pp. 111–12.
5. Victor Weisskopf, "The Origin of the Universe," *American Scientist* (September–October 1983), 478, 479.
6. Mike Corwin, "From Chaos to Consciousness," *Astronomy* (February 1983), 22.

7. Gary Taubes, "Everything's Now Tied to Strings," *Discover* (November 1986), 34.

8. *Ibid.*

9. Quoted in Corwin, p. 20.

10. Dewey Schwartzenburg, "Does Cosmology Have a Future? *Astronomy* (July 1979), 37.

11. B. J. Carr and M. J. Rees, "The Anthropic Principle and the Structure of the Physical world," *Nature* 12 (April 1979), 612.

12. Corwin, p. 19.

13. Schwartzenburg, p. 37.

14. Dietrick E. Thomsen, "The Quantum Universe: A Zero-Point Fluctuation?" *Science News* 128 (August 3, 1985), 73.

15. Carr and Rees, p. 612.

16. Schwartzenburg, p. 38.

17. John Archibald Wheeler, "Hermann Weyl and the Unity of Knowledge," *American Scientist* (July–August 1986), 371.

18. John Archibald Wheeler, "The 'Past' and the 'Delayed-Choice' Double-slit Experiment," *Mathematical Foundations of Quantum Theory*, ed. A. R. Marlow (New York: Academic Press, 1978), p. 41.

19. Dietrick E. Thomsen, "Changing Your Mind in a Hurry," *Science News* (March 1, 1986), 137.

20. Corwin, p. 22.

21. Wheeler, "The 'Past,' " p. 42.

22. *Ibid.*, p. 41.

23. *Ibid.*

24. Fritz Rohrlich, "Facing Quantum Mechanical Reality," *Science* (23 September 1983), 1253, 1255.

25. D. J. Bohm, C. Dewdney and B. H. Hiley, "A Quantum Potential Approach to the Wheeler Delayed-Choice Experiment," *Nature* 315 (23 May 1985), 297.

26. Sir Fred Hoyle and N. C. Wickramasinghe, *Evolution from Space: A Theory of Cosmic Creationism* (New York: Simon and Schuster, 1981). An earlier work, *Mathematical Challenges to the Neo-Darwinian Interpretation of Evolution*, P. Moorhead and M. Kaplan (Philadelphia: Wiser Institute Press, 1967), showed the inadequacy of the "randomness postulate" but advanced no alternative hypothesis.

27. Hoyle and Wickramasinghe, p. 23.

28. *Ibid.*, p. 24.

29. *Ibid.*

30. *Ibid.*, p. 30.

31. *Ibid.*, p. 3.

32. *Ibid.*, p. 130.

33. Charles B. Thaxton, Walter L. Bradley, Roger L. Olsen, *The Mystery of Life's Origins: Reassessing Current Theories* (New York: Philosophical Library, 1984), p. 164.

34. *Ibid.*, p. 186.

35. Sidney W. Fox, "The Evolutionary Sequence: Origin and Emergences," *The American Biology Teacher* 43 (March 1986), 147.

36. *Ibid.*, p. 148.

37. *Ibid.*, p. 143.

38. Thaxton, p. 211.

39. See Ramanuja, *The Vedanta-Sutra with the Commentary of Ramanuja*, 2d ed. trans. George Thibaut (Delhi: Motilal Banarsidass, 1966).

40. See especially J. N. Findlay, *Ascent to the Absolute* (London: George Allen and Unwin, 1970), chapters 1–3.

PAUL DAVIES

A Naturalistic Account of the Universe

Paul Davies (1946–) proposes an inflationary model to explain the Big Bang, which was able to counteract the force of gravity. The initial state was empty space (a quantum vacuum) filled with immense energy, but with a negative pressure that resulted in a universe expanding extremely rapidly. Rejecting the view that the law of conservation of energy applies to the earliest stages of the universe, Davies maintains that the initial energy comes from the repulsive forces in the initial empty space. As repulsion occurs, the energy increases until the Big Bang can occur. Davies then goes on to show how the inflationary model accounts for the critical features of the universe necessary for life appealed to by the Anthropic principle. Finally, he argues that, contrary to the theistic arguments, in quantum physics it is not unreasonable to hold that something (the space-time vacuum) came out of nothing.

⌘

THE GENESIS PARADOX

Whenever I give a lecture on cosmology one question never fails to be asked: What caused the big bang? A few years ago I had no real answer. Today, I believe we know what caused the big bang.

The question is actually two rolled into one. We should like to know why the universe began with a bang, what triggered this explosive outburst in the first place. But behind this physical enigma lies a deeper metaphysical mystery. If the big bang represents the origin of physical existence, including that of space and time, in what sense can anything be said to have *caused* this event?

On a purely physical level, the abrupt appearance of the universe in a huge explosion is something of a paradox. Of the four forces of nature which control the world, only gravity acts systematically on a cosmic scale, and in all our experience gravity is attractive. It is a pulling force. But the explosion which marked the creation of the universe would seem to require a pushing force of unimaginable power to blast the cosmos asunder and set it on a path of expansion which continues to this day.

People are often puzzled in the belief that if the universe is dominated by the force of gravity it ought to be contracting, not expanding. As a pulling force, gravity causes objects to implode rather than explode. For example, a highly compact star will be unable to support its own weight, and may collapse to form a neutron star or a black hole. In the very early universe, the compression of material exceeded that of even the densest star, and this fact often prompts the question of why the primeval cosmos did not itself turn into a black hole at the outset.

The traditional response leaves something of a credibility gap. It is argued that the primeval explosion must simply be accepted as an initial condition. Certainly, under the influence of gravity, the rate of cosmic expansion has continually slowed since the first moment, but at the instant of its creation the universe was expanding infinitely rapidly. No force caused it to explode in this way, it simply started with an initial expansion. Had the explosive vigour been less extreme, then gravity would very soon have overwhelmed the dispersing material, reversing the expansion and engulfing the entire cosmos in a catastrophic implosion, producing something rather like a black hole. As it happened, the bang was big enough to enable the universe either to escape its own gravity and go on expanding for ever under the impetus of the initial explosion, or at least to survive for many thousands of millions of years before succumbing to implosion and annihilation.

The trouble with this traditional picture is that it is in no sense an explanation for the big bang. Once again, a fundamental feature of the universe is merely attributed to an *ad hoc* initial condition. The big bang 'just happened.' We are left uncomprehending as to why the force of the explosion had the strength that it did. Why did the universe not explode more violently still, in which case it would be expanding much faster today? Alternatively, why is it not expanding much slower, or even contracting by now? Of course, had the cosmos *failed* to explode with sufficient violence, and rapid collapse overtaken it, we should not be here to ask such questions; but that is hardly an explanation.

Closer investigation shows that the genesis paradox is actually deeper than this. Careful measurement puts the rate of expansion very close to a critical value at which the universe will just escape its own gravity and expand for ever. A little slower, and the cosmos would collapse, a little faster and the cosmic material would have long ago completely dispersed. It is interesting to ask precisely how delicately the rate of expansion has been 'fine-tuned' to fall on this narrow dividing line between two catastrophes. If at time 1 s (by which time the pattern of expansion was already firmly established) the expansion rate had differed from its actual value by more than 10^{-18}, it would have been sufficient to throw the delicate balance out. The explosive vigour of the universe is thus matched with almost unbelievable accuracy to its gravitating power. The big bang was not, evidently, any old bang, but an explosion of exquisitely arranged magnitude. In the traditional version of the big bang theory we are asked to accept not only that the explosion just happened, but that it happened in an exceedingly contrived fashion. The initial conditions had to be very special indeed.

The rate of expansion is only one of several apparent cosmic 'miracles.' Another concerns the pattern of expansion. As we observe it today, the universe is extraordinarily uniform on the large scale, in the way that matter and energy are distributed. From the viewpoint of a distant galaxy, the overall structure of the cosmos would appear almost identical to its aspect from Earth. The galaxies are scattered throughout space with a constant average density, and at every point the universe would look the same at all orientations. The primeval heat radiation which bathes the universe arrives at Earth with a uniform temperature in every direction accurate to one part in ten thousand. This radiation has travelled to us across thousands of millions of light years of space, and would carry the imprint of any departures from uniformity encountered on the way.

The large-scale uniformity of the universe continues to be preserved with time as the universe expands. It follows that the expansion itself must be uniform to a very high degree. Not only is the rate of expansion the same in all directions, it is the same from region to region within the cosmos. If the universe were to expand faster in one direction than the others, it would depress the temperature of the background heat radiation coming from that direction, and also distort the pattern of motion of the galaxies as viewed from Earth. So not only did the universe commence with a bang of a quite precise magnitude, it was a highly orchestrated explosion as well, a simultaneous outburst of exactly uniform vigour everywhere and in every direction.

The extreme improbability that such a coherent, synchronized eruption would occur spontaneously is exacerbated by the fact that, in the traditional big bang theory, the different regions of the primeval cosmos would have been causally isolated. The point here is that, on account of the theory of relativity, no physical influence can propagate faster than light. Consequently, different regions of the universe can come into causal contact only after a period of time has elapsed. For example, at 1 s after the initial explosion, light can have travelled at most one light-second which is 300 000 km. Regions of the universe separated by greater than this distance could not, at 1 s, have exercised any influence on each other. But at that time, the universe we observe today occupied a region of space at least 10^{14} km across. It must therefore have been made up of some 10^{27} causally separate regions, all of them nevertheless expanding at exactly the same rate. Even today, when we observe the cosmic heat radiation coming from opposite sides of the sky, we are receiving identical thumbprints from regions of the universe that are separated from each other by ninety times the distance that light could have travelled at the time the heat radiation was emitted towards us.

How is it possible to explain this remarkable degree of co-operation between different parts of the universe that apparently have never been in communication with each other? How have they come to behave so similarly? The traditional response is, yet again, to fall back on special initial conditions. The extreme uniformity of the primeval explosion is simply regarded as a brute fact: 'The universe began that way.'

The large-scale uniformity of the universe is all the more mysterious on account of the fact that, on a somewhat smaller scale, the universe is *not* uniform. The existence of galaxies and galactic clusters indicates a departure from exact uniformity, a departure which is, moreover, of the same magnitude and scale everywhere. Because gravity tends to amplify any initial clumping of material, the degree of non-uniformity required to produce galaxies was far less during the big bang than it is today. In spite of this, some small degree of irregularity must have been present in the primeval phase or galaxies would never have started to form. In the old big bang theory these early irregularities were also explained away as initial conditions. Thus, we were required to believe that the universe began in a peculiar state of extraordinary but not quite perfect order.

The explanation can be summarized as follows: with gravitational attraction the only cosmic force available, the big bang must simply be accepted as god-given, an event without a cause, an assumed initial condition. Furthermore, it was an event of quite astonishing fidelity, for the present highly structured cosmos could not have arisen unless the universe was set up in just the right way at the outset. This is the genesis paradox. . . .

INFLATION: THE BIG BANG EXPLAINED

If a cosmic repulsive force exists, it must be very weak and far too weak to have had any significant effect on the big bang. But this conclusion rests on the assumption that the strength of the repulsive force does not change with time. In Einstein's day everybody made this assumption because the force was put into the theory 'by hand.' No one considered the possibility that cosmic repulsion might be *generated* by other physical processes that could change as the universe expands. Had such a possibility been entertained, then the history of cosmology would have been very different, for one could then conceive of a scenario in which, under the extreme conditions of the early universe, cosmic repulsion momentarily dominated gravity causing the universe to explode, before fading into insignificance.

This general scenario is precisely what has come out of recent work on the behaviour of matter and forces in the very early universe. It is now clear that a huge cosmic repulsion is an inevitable by-product of the activities of the superforce. The 'antigravity' that Einstein threw out of the door has come back in through the window.

The key to understanding the re-discovered cosmic repulsion is the nature of the quantum vacuum. We have seen how such a repulsion can be produced by a bizarre invisible medium which looks identical to empty space but which possesses a negative pressure. Physicists now believe that this is exactly how a quantum vacuum would be. . . .

The vacuum must be regarded as a ferment of quantum activity, teeming with virtual particles and full of complex interactions. It is important to appreciate that, at the quantum level of description, the vacuum is the dominant structure. What we call particles are only minor disturbances bubbling up over this background sea of activity.

In the late 1970s it became apparent that the unification of the four forces required a drastic re-appraisal of the physical nature of the vacuum. The theory suggested that all this vacuum energy could arrange itself in more than one way. To put it simply, the vacuum could become excited and adopt a number of states of very different energy, in the same way that an atom can be excited to higher energy levels. These several vacuum states would look identical if we could view them, but they possess very different properties.

First of all, the energy involved leaps by huge amounts from one vacuum state to another. In the grand unified theories, to take an example, the gap between the least and greatest vacuum energy is almost incomprehensibly large. To get some feeling for the enormity of the numbers involved, consider the huge outpouring of energy from the sun, accumulated over its entire lifetime of about 5 thousand million years. Conceive of taking this colossal quantity of energy—the entire output of the sun during its whole history—and compressing it into a volume of space less than that occupied by the solar system. You then begin to approach the sort of energy density contained in a GUT vacuum state.

Alongside these staggering energy differences are equally enormous changes in the pressure of the vacuum states. But here comes the important twist: the pressures are all *negative*. The quantum vacuum behaves exactly like the previously hypothetical medium which produces cosmic repulsion, only this time the numbers are so big that the strength of the repulsive force is 10^{120} times greater than Einstein needed to prop up a static universe.

The way now lies open for an explanation of the big bang. Suppose that, in the beginning the universe found itself in an excited vacuum state (physicists call this a 'false' vacuum). In this state the universe would be subject to a cosmic repulsion force of such magnitude that it would cause headlong expansion at a huge rate. In fact, during this phase, the universe would resemble de Sitter's model mentioned in the previous section. The difference is that, whereas de Sitter envisaged a universe sedately expanding over an astronomical time-scale, the de Sitter phase driven by the false quantum vacuum is far from sedate. A typical region of space would double in size every 10^{-34} s or so!

The way in which this hyper-expansion proceeds is distinctive: distances increase in size exponentially fast. . . . This means that every 10^{-34} s every region of the universe doubles its size, and then goes on doubling again and again in a progression. This type of runaway expansion has been dubbed 'inflation' by Alan Guth of MIT, who invented the idea in 1980. Under the impact of the exceedingly rapid and accelerating expansion, the universe would soon have found itself swelling explosively fast. This was the big bang.

Somehow, the inflationary phase has to terminate. As with all excited quantum systems, the false vacuum is unstable and will tend to decay. When that happens, the repulsion force disappears. This would have put a stop to inflation, bringing the universe under the control of ordinary, attractive gravity. The universe would have continued to expand, of course, from the initial impetus imparted by the inflationary episode, but at a steadily falling rate. The only trace that now remains of the cosmic repulsion is this dwindling expansion.

According to the inflationary scenario, the universe started out in a vacuum state, devoid of matter or radiation. Even if matter and radiation were present initially, all traces would soon have been eradicated because the universe swelled by such an enormous factor during the inflationary phase. During this incredibly brief phase, the region of space which today forms the entire observable universe grew from one-thousand-millionth of the size of a proton to several centimetres. The density of any pre-existing material would have fallen essentially to zero.

At the end of inflation, then, the universe was empty and cold. As soon as inflation ceased, however, the universe was suddenly filled with intense heat. This flash of heat which illuminated the cosmos owed its origin to the huge reserves of energy locked up in the false vacuum. When the false vacuum decayed, its energy was dumped in the form of radiation, which instantly heated the universe to about 10^{27} K, hot enough for GUT processes to occur. From this point on the universe evolved according to the standard hot big bang theory. The heat energy created matter and antimatter, the universe began to cool, and in a succession of steps all the structure we observe today began to 'freeze' out.

The thorny problem of what caused the big bang is therefore solved by the inflationary theory: empty space itself exploded under the repulsive power of the quantum vacuum. But an enigma still remains. The colossal energy of the primeval explosion—the energy that went to generate all the matter and radiation we now see in the universe—surely had to come from somewhere? We will not have explained the existence of the universe until we have traced the source of the primeval energy.

THE COSMIC BOOTSTRAP

The universe came into existence amid a huge burst of energy. This energy survives in the background heat radiation and in the cosmic material—the atoms which make up the stars and planets—as 'mass' or locked-up energy. It also lives on in the outward rush of the galaxies and in the swirling activities of all the astronomical bodies. The primeval energy wound up the nascent universe and continues to drive it to this day.

Whence came this vital energy which triggered our universe into life? According to the inflationary theory the energy came out of empty space, out of the quantum vacuum. But is this a fully satisfactory answer? We can still ask how the vacuum acquired the energy in the first place.

When we ask where the energy came from we are making an important assumption about the nature of energy. One of the fundamental laws of physics is the law of *conservation* of energy, which says that although you can change energy from one form to another, the total quantity of energy stays fixed. It is easy to think of examples where this law can be tested. Suppose you have a motor and a supply of fuel, and the motor is used to drive an electric generator which in turn powers a heater. When the fuel is expended, its stored chemical energy will have been converted, via electrical energy, into heat energy. If the motor had been used instead to haul a weight to the top of a tower, and the weight were then released, on impact with the ground it would generate the same amount of heat energy as you would have obtained using the heater. The point is that however you move it about or change its form, energy apparently cannot be created or destroyed. It is a law used by engineers every day.

If energy cannot be created or destroyed, how did the primeval energy come to exist? Was it simply injected at the beginning of time, another *ad hoc* initial condition? If so, why does the universe contain the amount of energy that it does? There are about 10^{68} joules of energy in the observable universe; why not 10^{99} or $10^{10\,000}$ or any other number?

The inflation theory is one possible scientific (as opposed to metaphysical) answer to this mystery. According to the theory, the universe started out with essentially zero energy, and succeeded in conjuring up the lot during the first 10^{-32} s. The key to this miracle lies with a most remarkable fact about cosmology: the law of conservation of energy *fails* in its usual sense when applied to the expanding universe.

In fact, we have already encountered this point. The cosmological expansion causes the temperature of the universe to fall. The radiant heat energy that was so intense in the primeval phase had dwindled to a temperature close to absolute zero. Where has all that heat energy gone? The answer is, that in a sense it has depleted itself by helping the universe to expand, adding its pressure to the explosive violence of the big bang. When an ordinary fluid expands, its pressure pushes outwards and does work, so using up its energy. This means that if you expand an ordinary gas, its internal energy must fall to pay for the work done. In stark contrast to this conventional behaviour, the cosmic repulsion behaves like a fluid with *negative* pressure. When a negative-pressure fluid is expanded, its energy goes *up* rather than down. This is precisely what happened in the inflationary period, when the cosmic repulsion drove the universe into accelerated expansion. All the while the total energy of the vacuum kept on rising until, at the cessation of the inflationary era, it had accumulated to a huge amount. As soon as inflation stopped, this energy was released in a single great burst, generating all the heat and matter that eventually emerged from the big bang. From then on, the conventional positive-pressure expansion took over, and the energy began to decline again.

The creation of the primeval energy has an air of magic to it. The vacuum, with its weird negative pressure, seems to have a truly incredible capability: on the one hand it produces a powerful repulsive force, bringing about its own accelerating expansion; on the other hand, that very expansion goes on boosting the energy of the vacuum more and more. The vacuum essentially pays itself vast quantities of energy. It has an inbuilt instability to continue expanding and generating unlimited quantities of energy for free. Only the quantum decay of the false vacuum puts a stop to the bonanza.

The vacuum is nature's miraculous jar of energy. There is in principle no limit to how much energy can be self-generated by inflationary expansion. It is a revolutionary result at total variance with the centuries-old tradition that 'nothing can come out of nothing,' a belief that dates at least from the time of Paremenides in the fifth century B.C. The idea of creation from nothing has, until recently, belonged solely to the province of religion. Christians have long believed that God created the universe out of nothing, but the possibility that all the cosmic matter and energy might appear spontaneously as a result of purely physical processes would have been regarded as utterly untenable by scientists only a decade ago.

For those who feel uncomfortable with the whole concept of something for nothing, there is an alternative way of looking at the creation of energy by the expanding universe. Because gravitational forces are normally attractive, it is necessary to do work to pull matter apart against its own gravity. This means that the gravitational energy of a collection of bodies is negative; if more bodies are added to the system, energy is released and the gravitational energy becomes more negative to pay for it. In the context of the inflationary universe, the appearance of heat and matter could be viewed as exactly compensated by the negative gravitational energy of the newly created mass, in which case the total energy of the universe is zero, and no net energy has appeared after all! Attractive though this way of looking at the creation may be, it should not be taken too seriously because the whole concept of energy has dubious status as far as gravity is concerned.

The antics of the vacuum are reminiscent of the story, much beloved of physicists, about the boy who falls into a bog and escapes by pulling himself up by his own bootstraps. The self-creating universe is rather like this boy since it too pulls itself up 'by its own bootstraps': entirely from within its own physical nature, the universe infuses itself with all the energy necessary to create and animate matter, driving its own explosive origin. This is the cosmic bootstrap. We owe our existence to its astonishing power.

SUCCESSES OF INFLATION

Once the basic idea had been mooted by Guth that the universe underwent an early period of extremely rapid expansion, it became apparent that the scenario provides an elegant explanation for many of the previously *ad hoc* features of big bang cosmology.

In an earlier section we encountered several 'fine-tuning' paradoxes relating to the way that the primeval explosion was apparently highly orchestrated and precisely arranged. One of these remarkable 'coincidences' related to the way in which the strength of the explosion was exactly matched to the gravitational power of the cosmos such that the expansion rate today lies very close to the borderline between re-collapse and rapid dispersal. A crucial test of the inflationary scenario is whether it produces a big bang of this precisely matched magnitude. It turns out that because of the nature of exponential expansion—the characteristic feature of the inflationary phase—the explosive power is indeed automatically adjusted to yield exactly the right value corresponding to the universe just escaping its own gravity. Inflation can give no other expansion rate than the one that is observed.

A second major puzzle relates to the large-scale uniformity of the universe. This too is immediately explained by inflation. Any irregularities initially present in the universe would have been stretched to death by the enormous distension, rather like the wrinkles in a deflated balloon are smoothed out by inflation. With regions of space being expanded by factors of 10^{50}, any prior disorder would be diluted to insignificance. . . .

Though the inflationary scenario remains a partially developed and speculative theory, it has thrown up a set of ideas that promise to change forever the face of cosmology. Not only can we now contemplate an explanation for why there was a big bang, but we can begin to understand why it was as big as it was, and why it took the form that it did. We can start to see how it is that the large-scale uniformity of the universe has come about at the same time as the controlled smaller-scale irregularities such as galaxies. The primeval explosion that produced what we know as the universe need no longer be regarded as a mystery forever beyond the scope of physical science.

THE SELF-CREATING UNIVERSE

In spite of the great success of inflation in explaining the origin of the universe, a mystery remains. How did the universe arrive in the false vacuum state in the first place? What happened *before* inflation?

A completely satisfactory scientific account of the creation would have to explain how space (strictly spacetime) came to exist, in order that it might then undergo inflation. Some scientists are content to assume either that space always existed, or that its creation lies beyond the scope of science. A few are more ambitious, however, and believe that it is possible to discuss how space in general, and the false vacuum in particular, might have come out of literally nothing as a result of physical processes that are in principle amenable to study. . . .

Nevertheless, can we conceive of physical objects, or even the entire universe, coming into existence out of nothing? One place where such a bold possibility is taken seriously is on the east coast of the United States where there is a curious concentration of theoretical physicists and cosmologists who have been manipulating mathematics in an attempt to divine the truth about creation *ex nihilo*. Among this esoteric coterie is Alan Guth at MIT, Sidney Coleman of Harvard, Alex Vilenkin of Tufts University, and Ed Tryon and Heinz Pagels in New York. All of them believe that in one sense or another 'nothing is unstable' and that the physical universe blossomed forth spontaneously out of nothing, driven by the laws of physics. 'Such ideas are speculation squared,' concedes Guth, 'but on some level they are probably right. . . . It is sometimes said there is no such thing as a free lunch. The universe, however, is a free lunch.'

In all these conjectures it is the quantum factor that provides the key. The central feature of quantum physics is the disintegration of the cause-effect link. In the old classic physics, the science of mechanics exemplified the rigid control of causality. The activity of every particle, each twist and turn, was considered to be legislated in detail by the laws of motion. . . .

Quantum physics wrecked the orderly, yet sterile Laplacian scheme. Physicists learned that at the atomic level matter and motion are vague and unpredictable. Particles can behave erratically, rebelling against rigidly prescribed motions, turning up in unexpected places without discernible reason and even appearing or disappearing without warning.

Causality is not completely absent in the quantum realm, but it is faltering and ambiguous. If an atom, for example, is excited somehow by a collision with another atom, it will usually return quickly to its lowest energy state by emitting a photon. The coming-to-being of the photon is, naturally, a consequence of the atom's being excited in the first place. We can certainly say that the excitation caused the creation of the photon. In that sense cause and effect remain linked. Nevertheless, the actual moment of creation of the photon is unpredictable; the atom might decay at any instant. Physicists can compute the expected, or average, delay before the photon appears, but they can never know in any individual case when this event will happen. Perhaps it is better to describe such a state of affairs by saying that the excitation of the atom 'prompts' rather than causes the photon to come into being.

The quantum microworld is not, therefore, linked by a tight network of causal influences, but more by a pandemonium of loosely obeyed commands and suggestions. In the old Newtonian scheme a force would address a body with the unchallengable imperative 'You will move!' In quantum physics the communication is more of an invitation than an order.

Why do we find the idea of an object abruptly appearing from nothing so incredible? What is it about such an occurrence that suggests miracles and the supernatural? Perhaps the answer lies with familiarity. We never encounter the uncaused appearance of objects in daily life. When the conjurer pulls the rabbit out of a hat we know we have been duped.

Suppose that we actually lived in a world where objects did from time to time noticeably pop out of nowhere, for no reason, in a completely unpredictable way. Once we had grown accustomed to such events we would cease to marvel at them. Spontaneous creation would be accepted as a quirk of nature. Maybe in such a world it would no longer strain credulity to imagine the entire physical universe bursting into existence from nothing. . . .

The spontaneous appearance of matter out of empty space is often referred to as creation 'out of nothing,' and comes close to the spirit of the creation *ex nihilo* of Christian doctrine. For the physicist, however, empty space is a far cry from nothing: it is very much part of the physical universe. If we want to answer the ultimate question of how the universe came into existence it is not sufficient to assume that empty space was there at the outset. We have to explain where space itself came from. The idea of *space* being created might seem exotic, yet in a sense it is happening around us all the time. The expansion of the universe is nothing but a continual swelling of space. Every day the region of the universe accessible to our telescopes swells by 10^{18} cubic light-years. Where is all this space 'coming from'? A helpful analogy is with a piece of elastic. When an elastic string is stretched you get 'more of it.' Space is rather like super-elastic in that it can go on stretching for ever (as far as we know) without 'snapping.'

The stretching and warping of space also resembles elastic inasmuch as the 'motion' of space is subject to laws of mechanics in the same way as matter. These are the laws of gravity. Just as the quantum theory applies to the activities of matter, so it applies to space and time. In earlier chapters we have seen how quantum gravity is an indispensable part of the search for the superforce, which suggests a curious possibility: if quantum theory allows particles of matter to pop into existence out of nowhere, could it also, when applied to gravity, allow space to come into existence out of nothing? And if so, should the spontaneous appearance of the universe 18 000 million years ago occasion such surprise after all?

C. S. LEWIS

The Moral Argument

C. S. Lewis (1898–1963) argues that we all know the difference between right and wrong, and accordingly we acknowledge that there is an objective Moral Law, a Law of Human Nature. Looking within ourselves, we see that there is a Law of Human Nature that indicates that someone or something wants us to behave in a certain way. This somebody or something, which urges us to do right and makes us uncomfortable when we do wrong, is best understood in terms of a Power who directs the universe.

⌘

Every one has heard people quarrelling. Sometimes it sounds funny and sometimes it sounds merely unpleasant; but however it sounds, I believe we can learn something very important from listening to the kind of things they say. They say things like this: "How'd you like it if anyone did the same to you?"—"That's my seat, I was there first"—"Leave him alone, he isn't doing you any harm"—"Why should you shove in first?"—"Give me a bit of your orange, I gave you a bit of mine"—"Come on, you promised." People say things like that every day, educated people as well as uneducated and children as well as grown-ups.

Now what interests me about all these remarks is that the man who makes them is not merely saying that the other man's behaviour does not happen to please him. He is appealing to some kind of standard of behaviour which he expects the other man to know about. And the other man very seldom replies: "To hell with your standard." Nearly always he tries to make out that what he has been doing does not really go against the standard, or that if it does there is some special excuse. He pretends there is some special reason in this particular case why the person who took the seat first should not keep it, or that things were quite different when he was given the bit of orange, or that something has turned up which lets him off keeping his promise. It looks, in fact, very much as if both parties had in mind some kind of Law or Rule of fair play or decent behaviour or morality or whatever you like to call it, about which they really agreed. And they have. If they had not, they might, of course, fight like animals, but they could not *quarrel* in the human sense of the word. Quarrelling means trying to show that the other man is in the wrong. And there would be no sense in trying to do that unless you and he had some sort of agreement as to what Right and Wrong are; just as there would be no sense in saying that a footballer had committed a foul unless there was some agreement about the rules of football.

Now this Law or Rule about Right and Wrong used to be called the Law of Nature. Nowadays, when we talk of the "laws of nature" we usually mean things like gravitation, or heredity, or the laws of chemistry. But when the older thinkers called the Law of Right and Wrong "the Law of Nature," they really meant the Law of *Human* Nature. The idea was that, just as all bodies are governed by the law of gravitation and organisms by biological laws, so the creature called man also had *his* law—with this great difference, that a body could not choose whether it obeyed the law of gravitation or not, but a man could choose either to obey the Law of Human Nature or to disobey it.

We may put this another way. Each man is at every moment subjected to several different sets of law but there is only one of these which he is free to disobey. As a body, he is subjected to gravitation and cannot disobey it; if you leave him unsupported in mid-air, he has no more choice about falling than a stone has. As an organism, he is subjected to various biological laws which he cannot disobey any more than an animal can. That is, he cannot disobey those laws which he shares with other things; but the law which is peculiar to his human nature, the law he does not share with animals or vegetables or inorganic things, is the one he can disobey if he chooses.

This law was called the Law of Nature because people thought that every one knew it by nature and did not need to be taught it. They did not mean, of course, that you might not find an odd individual here and there who did not know it, just as you find a few people who are colour-blind or have no ear for a tune. But taking the race as a whole, they thought that the human idea of decent behaviour was obvious to every one. And I believe they were right. If they were not, then all things we said about the war were nonsense. What was the sense in saying the enemy were in the wrong unless Right is a real thing which the Nazis at bottom knew as well as we did and ought to have practised? If they had had no notion of what we mean by right, then, though we might still have had to fight them, we could no more have blamed them for that than for the colour of their hair.

I know that some people say the idea of a Law of Nature or decent behaviour known to all men is unsound, because different civilisations and different ages have had quite different moralities.

But this is not true. There have been differences between their moralities, but these have never amounted to anything like a total difference. If anyone will take the trouble to compare the moral teaching of, say, the ancient Egyptians, Babylonians, Hindus, Chinese, Greeks and Romans, what will really strike him will be how very like they are to each other and to our own. Some of the evidence for this I have put together in the appendix of another book called *The Abolition of Man*; but for our present purpose I need only ask the reader to think what a totally different morality would mean. Think of a country where people were admired for running away in battle, or where a man felt proud of double-crossing all the people who had been kindest to him. You might just as well try to imagine a country where two and two made five. Men have differed as regards what people you ought to be unselfish to—whether it was only your own family, or your fellow countrymen, or everyone. But they have always agreed that you ought not to put yourself first. Selfishness has never been admired. Men have differed as to whether you should have one wife or four. But they have always agreed that you must not simply have any woman you liked.

But the most remarkable thing is this. Whenever you find a man who says he does not believe in a real Right and Wrong, you will find the same man going back on this a moment later. He may break his promise to you, but if you try breaking one to him he will be complaining "It's not fair" before you can say Jack Robinson. A nation may say treaties do not matter; but then, next minute, they spoil their case by saying that the particular treaty they want to break was an unfair one. But if treaties do not matter, and if there is no such thing as Right and Wrong—in other words, if there is no Law of Nature—what is the difference between a fair treaty and an unfair one? Have they not let the cat out of the bag and shown that, whatever they say, they really know the Law of Nature just like anyone else?

It seems, then, we are forced to believe in a real Right and Wrong. People may be sometimes mistaken about them, just as people sometimes get their sums wrong; but they are not a matter of mere taste and opinion any more than the multiplication table. Now if we are agreed about that, I go on to my next point, which is this. None of us are really keeping the Law of Nature. If there are any exceptions among you, I apologise to them. They had much better read some other work, for nothing I am going to say concerns them. And now, turning to the ordinary human beings who are left. . . .

I do not succeed in keeping the Law of Nature very well, and the moment anyone tells me I am not keeping it, there starts up in my mind a string of excuses as long as your arm. The question at the moment is not whether they are good excuses. The point is that they are one more proof of how deeply, whether we like it or not, we believe in the Law of Nature. If we do not believe in decent behaviour, why should we be so anxious to make excuses for not having behaved decently? The truth is, we believe in decency so much—we feel the Rule or Law pressing on us so—that we cannot bear to face the fact that we are breaking it, and consequently we try to shift the responsibility. For you notice that it is only for our bad behaviour that we find all these explanations. It is only our bad temper that we put down to being tired or worried or hungry; we put our good temper down to ourselves.

These, then, are the two points I wanted to make. First, that human beings, all over the earth, have this curious idea that they ought to behave in a certain way, and cannot really get rid of it. Secondly, that they do not in fact behave in that way. They know the Law of Nature; they break it. These two facts are the foundation of all clear thinking about ourselves and the universe we live in. . . .

Let us sum up what we have reached so far. In the case of stones and trees and things of that sort, what we call the Laws of Nature may not be anything except a way of speaking. When you say that nature is governed by certain laws, this may only mean that nature does, in fact, behave in a certain way. The so-called laws may not be anything real—anything above and beyond the actual facts which we observe. But in the case of Man, we saw that this will not do. The Law of Human Nature, or of Right and Wrong, must be something above and beyond the actual facts of human behaviour. In this case, besides the actual facts, you have something else—a real law which we did not invent and which we know we ought to obey.

I now want to consider what this tells us about the universe we live in. Ever since men were able to think, they have been wondering what this universe really is and how it came to be there. And, very roughly, two views have been held. First, there is what is called the materialist view. People who take that view think that matter and space just happen to exist, and always have existed, nobody knows why; and that the matter, behaving in certain fixed ways, has just happened, by a sort of fluke, to produce creatures like ourselves who are able to think. By one chance in a thousand something hit our sun and made it produce the planets; and by another thousandth chance the chemicals necessary for life, and the right temperature, occurred on one of these planets, and so some of the matter on this earth came alive; and then, by a very long series of chances, the living creatures developed into things like us. The other view is the religious view. According to it, what is behind the universe is more like a mind than it is like anything else we know. That is to say, it is conscious, and has purposes, and prefers one thing to another. And on this view it made the universe, partly for purposes we do not know, but partly, at any rate, in order to produce creatures like itself—I mean, like itself to the extent of having minds. Please do not think that one of these views was held a long time ago and that the other has gradually taken its place. Wherever there have been thinking men both views turn up. And note this too. You cannot find out which view is the right one by science in the ordinary sense. Science works by experiments. It watches how things behave. Every scientific statement in the long run, however complicated it looks, really means something like, "I pointed the telescope to such and such a part of the sky at 2:20 A.M. on January 15th and saw so-and-so," or "I put some of this stuff in a pot and heated it to such-and-such a temperature and it did so-and-so." Do not think I am saying anything against science: I am only saying what its job is. And the more scientific a man is, the more (I believe) he would agree with me that this is the job of science—and a very useful and necessary job it is too. But why anything comes to be there at all, and whether there is anything behind the things science observes—something of a different kind—this is not a scientific question. If there is "Something Behind," then either it will have to remain altogether unknown to men or else make itself known in some different way. The statement that there is any such thing, and the statement that there is no such thing, are neither of them statements that science can make. And real scientists do not usually make them. It is usually the journalists and popular novelists who have picked up a few odds and ends of half-baked science from textbooks who go in for them. After all, it is really a matter of common sense. Supposing science ever became complete so that it knew every single thing in the whole universe. Is it not plain that the questions, "Why is there a universe?" "Why does it go on as it does?" "Has it any meaning?" would remain just as they were?

Now the position would be quite hopeless but for this. There is one thing, and only one, in the whole universe which we know more about than we could learn from external observation. That one thing is Man. We do not merely observe men, we *are* men. In this case we have, so to speak, inside information; we are in the know. And because of that, we know that men find themselves under a moral law, which they did not make, and cannot quite forget even when they try, and which they know they ought to obey. Notice the following point. Anyone studying Man from the outside as we study electricity or cabbages, not knowing our language and consequently not able to get any inside knowledge from us, but merely observing what we did, would never get the slightest evidence that we had this moral law. How could he? for his observations would only show what we did, and the moral law is about what we ought to do. In the same way, if there were anything above or behind the observed facts in the case of stones or the weather, we, by studying them from outside, could never hope to discover it.

The position of the question, then, is like this. We want to know whether the universe simply happens to be what it is for no reason or whether there is a power behind it that makes it what it is. Since that power, if it exists, would be not one of the observed facts but a reality which makes them, no mere observation of the facts can find it. There is only one case in which we can know whether there is anything more, namely our own case. And in that one case we find there is. Or put it the other way round. If there was a controlling power outside the universe, it could not show itself to us as one of the facts inside the universe—no more than the architect of a house could actually be a wall or staircase or fireplace in that house. The only way in which we could expect it to show itself would be inside ourselves as an influence or a command trying to get us to behave in a certain way. And that is just what we do find inside ourselves. Surely this ought to arouse our suspicions? In the only case where you can expect to get an answer, the answer turns out to be Yes; and in the other cases, where you do not get an answer, you see why you do not. Suppose someone asked me, when I see a man in a blue uniform going down the street leaving little paper packets at each house, why I suppose that they contain letters? I should reply, "Because whenever he leaves a similar little packet for me I find it does contain a letter." And if he then objected, "But you've never seen all these letters which you think the other people are getting," I should say, "Of course not, and I shouldn't expect to, because they're not addressed to me. I'm explaining the packets I'm not allowed to open by the ones I am allowed to open." It is the same about this question. The only packet I am allowed to open is Man. When I do, especially when I open that particular man called Myself, I find that I do not exist on my own, that I am under a law; that somebody or something wants me to behave in a certain way. I do not, of course, think that if I could get inside a stone or a tree I should find exactly the same thing, just as I do not think all the other people in the street get the same letters as I do. I should expect, for instance, to find that the stone had to obey the law of gravity—that whereas the sender of the letters merely tells me to obey the law of my human nature, He compels the stone to obey the laws of its stony nature. But I should expect to find that there was, so to speak, a sender of letters in both cases, a Power behind the facts, a Director, a Guide. . . .

[What] I have got to is a Something which is directing the universe, and which appears in me as a law urging me to do right and making me feel responsible and uncomfortable when I do wrong. I think we have to assume it is more like a mind than it is like anything else we know—

because after all the only other thing we know is matter and you can hardly imagine a bit of matter giving instructions.

SUGGESTED READING

Barrow, John D., and Frank J. Tipler. *The Anthropic Cosmological Principle.* Oxford: Clarendon Press, 1986.

Bertoli, F., and U. Curi. *The Conditions for the Existence of Mankind in the Universe.* Cambridge: Cambridge University Press, 1991.

Carter, Brandon. "Large Number Coincidences and the Anthropic Principle in Cosmology," in *Confrontation of Cosmological Theories with Observational Data.* Dordrecht: Reidel, 1974, pp. 291–298.

Craig, William L. *The Cosmological Argument from Plato to Leibniz.* New York: Barnes & Noble, 1980.

———. The Kalam Cosmological Argument. London: Macmillan, 1979.

——— and Quentin Smith. *Theism, Atheism, and Big Bang Cosmology.* New York: Oxford University Press, 1993.

Davis, Stephen T. "What Good are Theistic Proofs?" in Louis P. Pojman, ed., *Philosophy of Religion.* Belmont, Calif.: Wadsworth, 1987, pp. 80–88.

Dore, Clement. *Theism.* Dordrecht: D. Reidel, 1984.

Flew, Antony. *God and Philosophy.* London: Hutchinson, 1966, chaps. 3–5.

Gale, Richard. *On the Nature and Existence of God.* Cambridge: Cambridge University Press, 1991.

Hallberg, Fred W. "Barrow and Tipler's Anthropic Cosmological Principle." *Zygon* 23 (June 1988): 139–157.

Hartshorne, Charles. *A Natural Theology for Our Time.* LaSalle, Ill.: Open Court, 1967

Hick, John, and Arthur C. McGill, eds. *The Many Faced Argument.* New York: Macmillan, 1967.

Hume, David. *Dialogues Concerning Natural Religion.* Indianapolis, Ind.: Hackett, 1980.

Kelly, Charles. "Some Arguments Concerning the Principle of Sufficient Reason and Cosmological Proofs." *The Thomist* 40 (April 1976): 258–293.

Kenny, Anthony. *The Five Ways.* New York: Schocken Books, 1969.

Leslie, John. "The Anthropic Principle, World Ensemble, Design." *American Philosophical Quarterly* 19, no. 2 (April 1982): 141–151.

Lewis, C. S. *Mere Christianity.* New York: Macmillan, 1943.

Mackie, J. L. *The Miracle of Theism.* Oxford: Clarendon Press, 1982.

Martin, Michael. *Atheism: A Philosophical Justification.* Philadelphia: Temple University Press, 1990.

———. *The Case Against Christianity.* Temple University Press, 1991.

Meynell, Hugo. *The Intelligible Universe: A Cosmological Argument.* Totawa, N.Y.: Barnes & Noble, 1982.

Miethe, Terry L. "The Cosmological Argument: A Research Bibliography." *New Scholasticism* 52 (Spring 1978): 285–305.

Miller, Barry. *From Existence to God: A Contemporary Philosophical Argument.* London: Routledge, 1992.

Owen, H. P. *The Moral Argument for Christian Theism.* London: Allen & Unwin, 1965.

Paley, William. *Natural Theology.* Charlottesville, Va.: Ibis, 1986.

Plantinga, Alvin. *God, Freedom and Evil.* New York: Harper & Row, 1974, Part II.

———. *The Nature of Necessity*. Oxford: Clarendon Press, 1974, chap. 10.
———. *The Ontological Argument*. New York: Doubleday, 1965.
Polkinghorne, John. *Science and Creation*. London: SPCK, 1988.
Prevost, Robert. *Probability and Theistic Explanation*. Oxford: Clarendon Press, 1990.
Reichenbach, Bruce R. *The Cosmological Argument: A Reassessment*. Springfield, Ill.: Charles Thomas, 1972.
Robson, John M., ed. *Origin and Evolution of the Universe: Evidence for Design?* Kingston: McGill-Queen's University Press, 1987.
Rowe, William L. *The Cosmological Argument*. Princeton: Princeton University Press, 1975.
Swinburne, Richard. *The Existence of God*. Oxford: Clarendon Press, 1979.
Taylor, Richard. *Metaphysics*. Englewood Cliffs, N.J.: Prentice-Hall, 1983, chap. 7.
Tennant, F. R. *Philosophical Theology II*. Cambridge: Cambridge University Press, 1930.
Yandell, Keith. *Christianity and Philosophy*. Grand Rapids: Eerdmans, 1984, chap. 2.

PART FIVE THE PROBLEM OF EVIL

Pain, suffering, injustice, deformity, catastrophe, and many other negative features of our world perplex us and demand a response. Not surprisingly, every major world view offers its distinctive response to the presence of evil. Historically, the "problem of evil" has been a serious difficulty for thoughtful believers who want to square their lofty claims about God's perfect power, knowledge, and goodness with claims about evil in the world. Philosophers often make a helpful distinction between natural and moral evils before engaging the debate. Natural evils are caused by impersonal objects and forces. Moral evils are brought about by the wrongful actions of persons, and can be conceived broadly to include bad intentions and character traits.

The argument from evil has been given two quite different formulations: the logical version and the evidential version. The typical statement of the logical argument from evil contends that theism is irrational because it includes an inconsistent set of beliefs, beliefs that God is omnipotent, omniscient, and wholly good as well as the belief that evil exists in God's created world. Critics claim that these two theistic beliefs are inconsistent with one another and thus that both together cannot be rationally accepted. Philosophical theists have developed a defense against the logical argument that essentially seeks to show, not that theism is indeed true, but that it is not inconsistent in its beliefs about God and evil.

In the hands of the critics, the evidential argument from evil involves a different strategy from the previous one. It does not purport that theistic belief is inconsistent, but that it is improbable or implausible in light of what we know about evil. Here critics treat theism as a kind of global metaphysical and theological hypothesis that implies certain things about whether, and the extent to which, there should be evil in the world. Evaluating theism in this manner, critics say that the broad facts of human experience reveal that the world is not as we would expect it to be if theism were true. Thus, these "facts of evil" count as evidence against the truth of theism.

The long-standing theistic tradition of "theodicy" seeks to explain why God might allow evil, even in its great extent and variety. Many thinkers, past and present, have taken up the task of "theodicy." Numerous important theistic explanations for why an omnipotent, omniscient, and wholly good God would allow evil have been developed—ranging from building our character to educating us to preparing us for heaven. Process theists take a somewhat different tack, insisting that God's power is persuasive rather than coercive, and so he cannot ensure that human beings always choose the good.

In recent years, the most vigorously debated rendition of the evidential argument from evil might be called the "evidential argument from gratuitous evil." Critics who advance this objection say that some evil may indeed have some justifiable purpose, but that some evils are pointless or gratuitous. For them, this alarmingly large class of evils, which seem to serve no good purpose whatsoever, strongly counts against the rational credibility of theism. The challenge of gratuitous evil is calling forth new theistic rejoinders, some which question our ability to know that an apparently gratuitous evil is really gratuitous and others that admit that there are gratuitous evils but explain why they can occur in a theistic universe.

SAINT AUGUSTINE

Evil Is Privation of Good

Augustine (354–430) was one of the first Christian writers to attempt a comprehensive and systematic explanation of evil in an allegedly theistic universe. His complete explanation of evil—his "theodicy"—weaves together several key themes which can be seen in the selection to follow: that God, who alone is supremely and immutably good, creates all other things; that all created things are good in their nature; that evil is a privation or lack in created things but not a positive reality; that moral evil in humans results from a deficiency in the will; and that all things we call evil from our finite perspective are actually part of the higher order and harmony in God's economy. Augustine's theodicy represents his understanding of historic orthodox Christianity as well as his progress away from the dualistic Manichean view that good and evil in our experience can be traced to a conflict between supremely Good and supremely Evil cosmic powers.

⌘

ALL FINITELY GOOD THINGS ARE CORRUPTIBLE

And it was made clear to me that all things are good even if they are corrupted. They could not be corrupted if they were supremely good; but unless they were good they could not be corrupted. If they were supremely good, they would be incorruptible; if they were not good at all, there would be nothing in them to be corrupted. For corruption harms; but unless it could diminish goodness, it could not harm. Either, then, corruption does not harm—which cannot be—or, as is certain, all that is corrupted is thereby deprived of good. But if they are deprived of all good, they will cease to be. For if they are at all and cannot be at all corrupted, they will become better, because they will remain incorruptible. Now what can be more monstrous than to maintain that by losing all good they have become better? If, then, they are deprived of all good, they will cease to exist. So long as they are, therefore, they are good. Therefore, whatsoever is, is good. Evil, then, the origin of which I had been seeking, has no substance at all; for if it were a substance, it would be good. For either it would be an incorruptible substance and so a supreme good, or a corruptible substance, which could not be corrupted unless it were good. I understood, therefore, and it was made clear to me that thou madest all things good, nor is there any substance at

Reprinted from *Augustine: Confessions and Enchiridion*, trans. and ed. by Albert C. Outler (Philadelphia: Westminster Press, 1955). Used by permission of Westminster Press.

all not made by thee. And because all that thou madest is not equal, each by itself is good, and the sum of all of them is very good, for our God made all things very good.

EVIL AS PRIVATIVE

To thee there is no such thing as evil, and even in thy whole creation taken as a whole, there is not; because there is nothing from beyond it that can burst in and destroy the order which thou hast appointed for it. But in the parts of creation, some things, because they do not harmonize with others, are considered evil. Yet those same things harmonize with others and are good, and in themselves are good. And all these things which do not harmonize with each other still harmonize with the inferior part of creation which we call earth, having its own cloudy and windy sky of like nature with itself. Far be it from me, then, to say, "These things should not be." For if I could see nothing but these, I should indeed desire something better—but still I ought to praise thee, if only for these created things. For that thou art to be praised is shown from the fact that "earth, dragons, and all deeps; fire, and hail, snow and vapors, stormy winds fulfilling thy word; mountains, and all hills, fruitful trees, and all cedars; beasts and all cattle; creeping things, and flying fowl; things of the earth, and all people; princes, and all judges of the earth; both young men and maidens, old men and children," praise thy name! But seeing also that in heaven all thy angels praise thee, O God, praise thee in the heights," and all thy hosts, sun and moon, all stars and light, the heavens of heavens, and the waters that are above the heavens" praise thy name—seeing this, I say, I no longer desire a better world, because my thought ranged over all, with a sounder judgment I reflected that the things above were better than those below, yet that all creation together was better than the higher things alone. . . .

GOD, EVIL, AND THE SCHEME OF THE UNIVERSE

. . . For the Christian, it is enough to believe that the cause of all created things, whether in heaven or on earth, whether visible or invisible, is nothing other than the goodness of the Creator, who is the one and the true God. Further, the Christian believes that nothing exists save God himself and what comes from him; and he believes that God is triune, i.e., the Father, and the Son begotten of the Father, and the Holy Spirit proceeding from the same Father, but one and the same Spirit of the Father and the Son.

By this Trinity, supremely and equally and immutably good, were all things created. But they were not created supremely, equally, nor immutably good. Still, each single created thing is good, and taken as a whole they are very good, because together they constitute a universe of admirable beauty.

In this universe, even what is called evil, when it is rightly ordered and kept in its place, commends the good more eminently, since good things yield greater pleasure and praise when compared to the bad things. For the Omnipotent God, whom even the heathen acknowledge as the Supreme Power over all, would not allow any evil in his works, unless in his omnipotence and goodness, as the Supreme God, he is able to bring forth good out of evil. What, after all, is anything we call evil except the privation of good? In animal bodies, for instance, sickness and wounds are nothing but the privation of health. When a cure is effected, the evils which were present (i.e., the sickness and the wounds) do not retreat and go elsewhere. Rather, they simply do not exist any more. For such evil is not a substance; the wound or the disease is a defect of the bodily substance which, as a substance, is good. Evil, then, is an accident, i.e., a privation of that good which is called health. Thus, whatever defects there are in a soul are privations of a natural good. When a cure takes place, they are not transferred elsewhere but, since they are no longer present in the state of health, they no longer exist at all.

THE PROBLEM OF EVIL

All of nature, therefore, is good, since the Creator of all nature is supremely good. But nature is not supremely and immutably good as is the Creator of it. Thus the good in created things can be diminished and augmented. For good to be diminished is evil; still, however much it is diminished, something must remain of its original nature as long as it exists at all. For no matter what kind or however insignificant a thing may be, the good which is its "nature" cannot be destroyed without the thing itself being destroyed. There is good reason, therefore, to praise an uncorrupted thing, and if it were indeed an incorruptible thing which could not be destroyed, it would doubtless be all the more worthy of praise. When, however, a thing is corrupted, its corruption is an evil because it is, by just so much, a privation of the good. Where there is no privation of the good, there is no evil. Where there is evil, there is a corresponding diminution of the good. As long, then, as a thing is being corrupted, there is good in it of which it is being deprived; and in this process, if something of its being remains that cannot be further corrupted, this will then be an incorruptible entity [*natura incorruptibilis*], and to this great good it will have come through the process of corruption. But even if the corruption is not arrested, it still does not cease having some good of which it cannot be further deprived. If, however, the corruption comes to be total and entire, there is no good left either, because it is no longer an entity at all. Wherefore corruption cannot consume the good without also consuming the thing itself. Every actual entity [*natura*] is therefore good; a greater good if it cannot be corrupted, a lesser good if it can be. Yet only the foolish and unknowing can deny that it is still good even when corrupted. Whenever a thing is consumed by corruption, not even the corruption remains, for it is nothing in itself, having no subsistent being in which to exist.

From this it follows that there is nothing to be called evil if there is nothing good. A good that wholly lacks an evil aspect is entirely good. Where there is some evil in a thing, its good is defective or defectible. Thus there can be no evil where there is no good. This leads us to a surprising conclusion: that, since every being, in so far as it is a being, is good, if we then say that a defective thing is bad, it would seem to mean that we are saying that what is evil is good, that only what is good is ever evil and that there is no evil apart from something good. This is because every actual entity is good [*omnis natura bonum est*.] Nothing evil exists *in itself*, but only as an evil aspect of some actual entity. Therefore, there can be nothing evil except something good. Absurd as this sounds, nevertheless the logical connections of the argument compel us to it as inevitable. At the same time, we must take warning lest we incur the prophetic judgment which reads: "Woe to those who call evil good and good evil: who call darkness light and light darkness; who call the bitter sweet and the sweet bitter." Moreover the Lord himself saith: "An evil man brings forth evil out of the evil treasure of his heart." What, then, is an evil man but an evil entity [*natura mala*], since man is an entity? Now, if a man is something good because he is an entity, what, then, is a bad man except an evil good? When, however, we distinguish between these two concepts, we find that the bad man is not bad because he is a man, nor is he good because he is wicked. Rather, he is a good entity in so far as he is a man, evil in so far as he is wicked. Therefore, if anyone says that simply to be a man is evil, or that to be a wicked man is good, he rightly falls under the prophetic judgment: "Woe to him who calls evil good and good evil." For this amounts to finding fault with God's work, because man is an entity of God's creation. It also means that we are praising the defects in this particular man *because* he is a wicked person. Thus, every entity, even if it is a defective one, in so far as it is an entity, is good. In so far as it is defective, it is evil.

Actually, then, in these two contraries we call evil and good, the rule of the logicians fails to apply. No weather is both dark and bright at the same time; no food or drink is both sweet and sour at the same time; no body is, at the same time and place, both white and black, nor deformed and well-formed at the same time. This principle is found to apply in almost all disjunctions: two contraries cannot coexist in a single thing. Nevertheless, while no one maintains that good and evil are not contraries, they can not only coexist, but the evil cannot exist at all without the good, or in a thing that is not a good. On the other hand, the good can exist without evil. For a man or an angel could exist and yet not be wicked, whereas there cannot be wickedness except in a man or an angel. It is good to be a man, good to be an angel; but evil to be wicked. These two contraries are thus coexistent, so that if there were no good in what is evil, then the evil simply could not be, since it can have no mode in which to exist, nor any source from which corruption springs, unless it be something corruptible. Unless this something is good, it cannot be corrupted, because corruption is nothing more than the deprivation of the good. Evils, therefore, have their source in the good, and unless they are parasitic on something good, they are not anything at all. There is no other source whence an evil thing can come to be. If this is the case, then, in so far as a thing is an entity, it is unquestionably good. If it is an incorruptible entity, it is a great good. But even if it is a corruptible entity, it still has no mode of existence except as an aspect of something that is good. Only by corrupting something good can corruption inflict injury.

But when we say that evil has its source in the good, do not suppose that this denies our Lord's judgment: "A good tree cannot bear evil fruit." This cannot be, even as the Truth himself declareth: "Men do not gather grapes from thorns," since thorns cannot bear grapes. Nevertheless, from good soil we can see both vines and thorns spring up. Likewise, just as a bad tree does not grow good fruit, so also an evil will does not produce good deeds. From a human nature, which is good in itself, there can spring forth either a good or an evil will. There was no other place from whence evil could have arisen in the first place except from the nature—good in itself—of an angel or a man. This is what our Lord himself most clearly shows in the passage about the trees and the fruits, for he said: "Make the tree good and the fruits will be good, or make the tree bad and its fruits will be bad." This is warning enough that bad fruit cannot grow on a good tree nor good fruit on a bad one. Yet from that same earth to which he was referring, both sorts of trees can grow.

DAVID HUME

Evil Makes a Strong Case Against God's Existence

David Hume (1711–1776) constructs an impressive list of natural evils and then builds an argument against the existence of God. Careful exegesis of the text reveals two distinguishable arguments, each of which finds representation in contemporary scholarship. The first argument by this eloquent skeptic is clear enough: the claims "God exists" and "evil exists" are logically incompatible; and, since we can be sure that evil does exist, we know that God does not exist.

From *Dialogues Concerning Natural Religion,* Part X.

The second argument is somewhat less direct: even if "God exists" and "evil exists" are logically compatible claims, the truth of the latter provides strong, though not conclusive, grounds or evidence for rejecting the former.

⌘

It is my opinion, . . . replied Demea, that each man feels, in a manner, the truth of religion within his own breast, and, from a consciousness of his imbecility and misery rather than from any reasoning, is led to seek protection from that Being on whom he and all nature is dependent. So anxious or so tedious are even the best scenes of life that futurity is still the object of all our hopes and fears. We incessantly look forward and endeavour, by prayers, adoration, and sacrifice, to appease those unknown powers whom we find, by experience, so able to afflict and oppress us. Wretched creatures that we are! What resource for us amidst the innumerable ills of life did not religion suggest some methods of atonement, and appease those terrors with which we are incessantly agitated and tormented?

I am indeed persuaded, said Philo, that the best and indeed the only method of bringing everyone to a due sense of religion is by just representations of the misery and wickedness of men. And for that purpose a talent of eloquence and strong imagery is more requisite than that of reasoning and argument. For is it necessary to prove what everyone feels within himself? It is only necessary to make us feel it, if possible, more intimately and sensibly.

The people, indeed, replied Demea, are sufficiently convinced of this great and melancholy truth. The miseries of life, the unhappiness of man, the general corruptions of our nature, the unsatisfactory enjoyment of pleasures, riches, honours—these phrases have become almost proverbial in all languages. And who can doubt of what all men declare from their own immediate feeling and experience?

In this point, said Philo, the learned are perfectly agreed with the vulgar; and in all letters, *sacred* and *profane*, the topic of human misery has been insisted on with the most pathetic eloquence that sorrow and melancholy could inspire. The poets, who speak from sentiment, without a system, and whose testimony has therefore the more authority, abound in images of this nature. From Homer down to Dr. Young, the whole inspired tribe have ever been sensible that no other representation of things would suit the feeling and observation of each individual.

As to authorities, replied Demea, you need not seek them. Look round this library of Cleanthes. I shall venture to affirm that, except authors of particular sciences, such as chemistry or botany, who have no occasion to treat of human life, there is scarce one of those innumerable writers from whom the sense of human misery has not, in some passage or other, extorted a complaint and confession of it. At least, the chance is entirely on that side; and no one author has ever, so far as I can recollect, been so extravagant as to deny it.

There you must excuse me, said Philo: Leibniz has denied it, and is perhaps the first who ventured upon so bold and paradoxical an opinion; at least, the first who made it essential to his philosophical system.

And by being the first, replied Demea, might he not have been sensible of his error? For is this a subject in which philosophers can propose to make discoveries especially in so late an age? And can any man hope by a simple denial (for the subject scarcely admits of reasoning) to bear down the united testimony of mankind, founded on sense and consciousness?

And why should man, added he, pretend to an exemption from the lot of all other animals? The whole earth, believe me, Philo, is cursed and polluted. A perpetual war is kindled amongst all living creatures. Necessity, hunger, want stimulate the strong and courageous; fear, anxiety, terror agitate the weak and infirm. The first entrance into life gives anguish to the new-born infant and to its wretched parent; weakness, impotence, distress attend each stage of that life, and it is, at last, finished in agony and horror.

Observe, too, says Philo, the curious artifices of nature in order to embitter the life of every living being. The stronger prey upon the weaker and keep them in perpetual terror and anxiety. The weaker, too, in their turn, often prey upon the stronger, and vex and molest them without relaxation. Consider that innumerable race of insects, which either are bred on the body of each animal or, flying about, infix their stings in him. These insects have others still less than themselves which torment them. And thus on each hand, before and behind, above and below, every animal is surrounded with enemies which incessantly seek his misery and destruction.

Man alone, said Demea, seems to be, in part, an exception to this rule. For by combination in society he can easily master lions, tigers, and bears, whose greater strength and agility naturally enable them to prey upon him.

On the contrary, it is here chiefly, cried Philo, that the uniform and equal maxims of nature are most apparent. Man, it is true, can, by combination, surmount all his *real* enemies and become master of the whole animal creation; but does he not immediately raise up to himself *imaginary* enemies, the demons of his fancy, who haunt him with superstitious terrors and blast every enjoyment of life? His pleasure, as he imagines, becomes in their eyes a crime; his food and repose give them umbrage and offence; his very sleep and dreams furnish new materials to anxious fear; and even death, his refuge from every other ill, presents only the dread of endless and innumerable woes. Nor does the wolf molest more the timid flock than superstition does the anxious breast of wretched mortals.

Besides, consider, Demea: This very society by which we surmount those wild beasts, our natural enemies, what new enemies does it not raise to us? What woe and misery does it not occasion? Man is the greatest enemy of man. Oppression, injustice, contempt, contumely, violence, sedition, war, calumny, treachery, fraud—by these they mutually torment each other, and they would soon dissolve that society which they had formed were it not for the dread of still greater ills which must attend their separation.

But though these external insults, said Demea, from animals, from men, from all the elements, which assault us form a frightful catalogue of woes, they are nothing in comparison of those which arise within ourselves, from the distempered condition of our mind and body. How many lie under the lingering torment of diseases? Hear the pathetic enumeration of the great poet.

> Intestine stone and ulcer, colic-pangs,
> Demoniac frenzy, moping melancholy,
> And moon-struck madness, pining atrophy,
> Marasmus, and wide-wasting pestilence.
> Dire was the tossing, deep the groans: *Despair*
> Tended the sick, busiest from couch to couch.
> And over them triumphant *Death* his dart
> Shook: but delay'd to strike, though oft invok'd
> With vows, as their chief good and final hope.

The disorders of the mind, continued Demea, though more secret, are not perhaps less dismal and vexatious. Remorse, shame, anguish, rage, disappointment, anxiety, fear, dejection, despair—who has ever passed through life without cruel inroads from these tormentors? How many have scarcely ever felt any better sensations? Labour and poverty, so abhorred by everyone, are the certain lot of the far greater number; and those few privileged persons who enjoy ease and opulence never reach contentment or true felicity. All the goods of life united would not make a very happy man, but all the ills united would make a wretch indeed; and any one of them almost (and who can be free from every one?), nay, often the absence of one good (and who can possess all?) is sufficient to render life ineligible.

Were a stranger to drop on a sudden into this world, I would show him, as a specimen of its ills, an hospital full of diseases, a prison crowded with malefactors and debtors, a field of battle strewed with carcases, a fleet foundering in the ocean, a nation languishing under tyranny, famine, or pestilence. To turn the gay side of life to him and give him a notion of its pleasures—whether should I conduct him? To a ball, to an opera, to court? He might justly think that I was only showing him a diversity of distress and sorrow.

There is no evading such striking instances, said Philo, but by apologies which still further aggravate the charge. Why have all men, I ask, in all ages, complained incessantly of the miseries of life? . . . They have no reason, says one: these complaints proceed only from their discontented, repining, anxious disposition. . . . And can there possibly, I reply, be a more certain foundation of misery than such a wretched temper?

But if they were really as unhappy as they pretend, says my antagonist, why do they remain in life? . . .

Not satisfied with life, afraid of death—this is the secret chain, say I, that holds us. We are terrified, not bribed to the continuance of our existence.

It is only a false delicacy, he may insist, which a few refined spirits indulge, and which has spread these complaints among the whole race of mankind. . . . And what is this delicacy, I ask, which you blame? Is it anything but a greater sensibility to all the pleasures and pains of life? And if the man of a delicate, refined temper, by being so much more alive than the rest of the world, is only so much more unhappy, what judgment must we form in general of human life?

Let men remain at rest, says our adversary, and they will be easy. They are willing artificers of their own misery. . . . No! reply I: an anxious languor follows their repose; disappointment, vexation, trouble, their activity and ambition.

I can observe something like what you mention in some others, replied Cleanthes, but I confess I feel little or nothing of it in myself, and hope that it is not so common as you represent it.

If you feel not human misery yourself, cried Demea, I congratulate you on so happy a singularity. Others, seemingly the most prosperous, have not been ashamed to vent their complaints in the most melancholy strains. Let us attend to the great, the fortunate emperor, Charles V, when, tired with human grandeur, he resigned all his extensive dominions into the hands of his son. In the last harangue which he made on that memorable occasion, he publicly avowed *that the greatest prosperities which he had ever enjoyed had been mixed with so many adversities that he might truly say he had never enjoyed any satisfaction or contentment*. But did the retired life in which he sought for shelter afford him any greater happiness? If we may credit his son's account, his repentance commenced the very day of his resignation.

Cicero's fortune, from small beginnings, rose to the greatest lustre and renown; yet what pathetic complaints of the ills of life do his familiar letters, as well as philosophical discourses, contain? And suitably to his own experience, he introduces Cato, the great, the fortunate Cato protesting in his old age that had he a new life in his offer he would reject the present.

Ask yourself, ask any of your acquaintance, whether they would live over again the last ten or twenty years of life. No! but the next twenty, they say, will be better:

> And from the dreges of life, hope to receive
> What the first sprightly running could not give.

Thus, at last, they find (such is the greatness of human misery, it reconciles even contradictions) that they complain at once of the shortness of life and of its vanity and sorrow.

And is it possible, Cleanthes, said Philo, that after all these reflections, and infinitely more which might be suggested, you can still persevere in your anthropomorphism, and assert the moral attributes of the Deity, his justice, benevolence, mercy, and rectitude, to be of the same nature with these virtues in human creatures? His power, we allow, is infinite; whatever he wills is executed; but neither man nor any other animal is happy; therefore, he does not will their happiness. His wisdom is infinite; he is never mistaken in choosing the means to any end; but the course of nature tends not to human or animal felicity; therefore, it is not established for that purpose.

Through the whole compass of human knowledge there are no inferences more certain and infallible than these. In what respect, then, do his benevolence and mercy resemble the benevolence and mercy of men?

Epicurus' old questions are yet unanswered.

Is he willing to prevent evil, but not able? then is he impotent. Is he able, but not willing? then is he malevolent. Is he both able and willing? whence then is evil?

You ascribe, Cleanthes, (and I believe justly) a purpose and intention to nature. But what, I beseech you, is the object of that curious artifice and machinery which she has displayed in all animals—the preservation alone of individuals, and propagation of the species? It seems enough for her purpose, if such a rank be barely upheld in the universe, without any care or concern for the happiness of the members that compose it. No resource for this purpose: no machinery in order merely to give pleasure or ease; no fund of pure joy and contentment; no indulgence without some want or necessity accompanying it. At least, the few phenomena of this nature are overbalanced by opposite phenomena of still greater importance.

Our sense of music, harmony, and indeed beauty of all kinds, gives satisfaction, without being absolutely necessary to the preservation and propagation of the species. But what racking pains, on the other hand, arise from gouts, gravels, megrims, toothaches, rheumatisms, where the injury to the animal machinery is either small or incurable? Mirth, laughter, play, frolic seem gratuitous satisfactions which have no further tendency; spleen, melancholy, discontent, superstition are pains of the same nature. How then does the Divine benevolence display itself, in the sense of you anthropomorphites? None but we mystics, as you were pleased to call us, can account for this strange mixture of phenomena, by deriving it from attributes infinitely perfect but incomprehensible.

And have you, at last, said Cleanthes smiling, betrayed your intentions, Philo? Your long agreement with Demea did indeed a little surprise me, but I find you were all the while erecting a concealed battery against me. And I must confess that you have now fallen upon a subject worthy of your noble spirit of opposition and controversy. If you can make out the present point, and prove mankind to be unhappy or corrupted, there is an end at once of all religion. For to what purpose establish the natural attributes of the Deity, while the moral are still doubtful and uncertain?

You take umbrage very easily, replied Demea, at opinions the most innocent and the most generally received, even amongst the religious and devout themselves; and nothing can be more surprising than to find a topic like this—concerning the wickedness and misery of man—charged with no less than atheism and profaneness. Have not all pious divines and preachers who have indulged their rhetoric on so fertile a subject, have they not easily, I say, given a solution of any difficulties which may attend it? This world is but a point in comparison of the universe; this life but a moment in comparison of eternity. The present evil phenomena, therefore, are rectified in other regions, and in some future period of existence. And the eyes of men, being then opened to larger views of things, see the whole connection of general laws, and trace, with adoration, the benevolence and rectitude of the Deity through all the mazes and intricacies of his providence.

No! replied Cleanthes, no! These arbitrary suppositions can never be admitted, contrary to matter of fact, visible and uncontroverted. Whence can any cause be known but from its known effects? Whence can any hypothesis be proved but from the apparent phenomena? To establish one hypothesis upon another is building entirely in the air; and the utmost we ever attain by these conjectures and fictions is to ascertain the base possibility of our opinion, but never can we, upon such terms, establish its reality.

The only method of supporting Divine benevolence—and it is what I willingly embrace—is to deny absolutely the misery and wickedness of man. Your representations are exaggerated; your melancholy views mostly fictitious; your inferences contrary to fact and experience. Health is more common than sickness; pleasure than pain; happiness than misery. And for one vexation which we meet with, we attain, upon computation, a hundred enjoyments.

Admitting your position, replied Philo, which yet is extremely doubtful, you must at the same time allow that, if pain be less frequent than pleasure, it is infinitely more violent and durable. One hour of it is often able to outweigh a day, a week, a month of our common insipid enjoyments; and how many days, weeks, and months are passed by several in the most acute torments? Pleasure, scarcely in one instance, is ever able to reach ecstasy and rapture; and in no one instance can it continue for any time at its highest pitch and altitude. The spirits evaporate, the nerves relax, the fabric is disordered, and the enjoyment quickly degenerates into fatigue and uneasiness. But pain often, good God, how often! rises to torture and agony; and the longer it continues, it becomes still more genuine agony and torture. Patience is exhausted, courage languishes, melancholy seizes us, and nothing terminates our misery but the removal of its cause or another event which is the sole cure of all evil, but which, from our natural folly, we regard with still greater horror and consternation.

But not to insist upon these topics, continued Philo, though most obvious, certain, and important, I must use the freedom to admonish you, Cleanthes, that you have put the controversy upon a most dangerous issue, and are unawares introducing a total scepticism into the most essential articles of natural and revealed theology. What! no method of fixing a just foundation for religion unless we allow the happiness of human life, and maintain a continued existence even in this world, with all our present pains, infirmities, vexations, and follies, to be eligible and desirable! But this is contrary to everyone's feeling and experience; it is contrary to an authority so established as nothing can subvert. No decisive proofs can ever be produced against this authority; nor is it possible for you to compute, estimate, and compare all the pains and all the pleasures in the lives of all men and of all animals; and thus, by your resting the whole system of religion on a point which, from its very nature, must for ever be uncertain, you tacitly confess that that system is equally uncertain.

But allowing you what never will be believed, at least, what you never possibly can prove, that animal or, at least, human happiness in this life exceeds its misery, you have yet done nothing; for this is not, by any means, what we expect from infinite power, infinite wisdom, and infinite goodness. Why is there any misery at all in the world? Not by chance, surely. From some cause then. Is it from the intention of the Deity? But he is perfectly benevolent. Is it contrary to his intention? But he is almighty. Nothing can shake the solidity of this reasoning, so short, so clear, so decisive, except we assert that these subjects exceed all human capacity, and that our common measures of truth and falsehood are not applicable to them—a topic which I have all along insisted on, but which you have, from the beginning, rejected with scorn and indignation.

But I will be contented to retire still from this intrenchment, for I deny that you can ever force me in it. I will allow that pain or misery in man is *compatible* with infinite power and goodness in the Deity, even in your sense of these attributes: what are you advanced by all these concessions? A mere possible compatibility is not sufficient. You must *prove* these pure, unmixt, and uncontrollable attributes from the present mixed and confused phenomena, and from these alone. A hopeful undertaking! Were the phenomena ever so pure and unmixed, yet, being finite, they would be insufficient for that purpose. How much more, where they are also so jarring and discordant!

Here, Cleanthes, I find myself at ease in my argument. Here I triumph. Formerly, when we argued concerning the natural attributes of intelligence and design, I needed all my sceptical and metaphysical subtilty to elude your grasp. In many views of the universe and of its parts, particularly the latter, the beauty and fitness of final causes strike us with such irresistible force that all objections appear (what I believe they really are) mere cavils and sophisms; nor can we then imagine how it was ever possible for us to repose any weight on them. But there is no view of human life or of the condition of mankind from which, without the greatest violence, we can infer the moral attributes or learn that infinite benevolence, conjoined with infinite power and infinite wisdom, which we must discover by the eyes of faith alone. It is your turn now to tug the labouring oar, and to support your philosophical subtilties against the dictates of plain reason and experience.

J. L. MACKIE

Evil and Omnipotence

J. L. Mackie (1917–1981) offers a contemporary statement of what professional philosophers call the "logical problem of evil." Essentially, he argues that the theistic claim that God is omnipotent, omniscient, and wholly good is inconsistent with the theistic claim that there is evil in the world. He then goes on to examine weak theistic attempts to eliminate the inconsistency, concluding that any successful attempt will have to modify at least one key theistic concept (i.e., omnipotence) and thus will implicitly surrender the theistic position. According to Mackie, it is not possible both that God is omnipotent and that he was unable to create a universe containing moral good but no moral evil.

⌘

The traditional arguments for the existence of God have been fairly thoroughly criticised by philosophers. But the theologian can, if he wishes, accept this criticism. He can admit that no rational proof of God's existence is possible. And he can still retain all that is essential to his position, by holding that God's existence is known in some other, non-rational way. I think, however, that a more telling criticism can be made by way of traditional problem of evil. Here it can be shown, not that religious beliefs lack rational support, but that they are positively irrational, that the several parts of the essential theological doctrine are inconsistent with one another, so that the theologian can maintain his position as a whole only by a much more extreme rejection of reason than in the former case. He must now be prepared to believe, not merely what cannot be proved, but what can be *disproved* from other beliefs that he also holds.

The problem of evil, in the sense in which I shall be using the phrase, is a problem only for someone who believes that there is a God who is both omnipotent and wholly good. And it is a logical problem, the problem of clarifying and reconciling a number of beliefs: it is not a scientific problem that might be solved by further observations, or a practical problem that might be solved by a decision or an action. These points are obvious; I mention them only because they are sometimes ignored by theologians, who sometimes parry a statement of the problem with such remarks as "Well, can you solve the problem yourself?" or "This is a mystery which may be revealed to us later" or "Evil is something to be faced and overcome, not to be merely discussed."

In its simplest form the problem is this: God is omnipotent; God is wholly good; and yet evil exists. There seems to be some contradiction between these three propositions, so that if any two of them were true the third would be false. But at the same time all three are essential parts of most

From *Mind* 64 (1955), pp. 200–212. Reprinted by permission of Oxford University Press.

theological positions: the theologian, it seems, at once *must* adhere and *cannot consistently* adhere to all three. (The problem does not arise only for theists, but I shall discuss it in the form in which it presents itself for ordinary theism.)

However, the contradiction does not arise immediately; to show it we need some additional premises, or perhaps some quasi-logical rules connecting the terms 'good,' 'evil,' and 'omnipotent.' These additional principles are that good is opposed to evil, in such a way that a good thing always eliminates evil as far as it can, and that there are no limits to what an omnipotent thing can do. From these it follows that a good omnipotent thing eliminates evil completely, and then the propositions that a good omnipotent thing exists, and the evil exists, are incompatible.

ADEQUATE SOLUTIONS

Now once the problem is fully stated it is clear that it can be solved, in the sense that the problem will not arise if one gives up at least one of the propositions that constitute it. If you are prepared to say that God is not wholly good, or not quite omnipotent, or that evil does not exist, or that good is not opposed to the kind of evil that exists, or that there are limits to what an omnipotent thing can do, then the problem of evil will not arise for you.

There are, then, quite a number of adequate solutions of the problem of evil, and some of these have been adopted, or almost adopted, by various thinkers. For example, a few have been prepared to deny God's omnipotence, and rather more have been prepared to keep the term 'omnipotence' but severely to restrict its meaning, recording quite a number of things that an omnipotent being cannot do. Some have said that evil is an illusion, perhaps because they held that the whole world of temporal, changing things is an illusion, and that what we call evil belongs only to this world, or perhaps because they held that although temporal things *are* much as we see them, those that we call evil are not really evil. Some have said that what we call evil is merely the privation of good, that evil in a positive sense, evil that would really be opposed to good, does not exist. Many have agreed with Pope that disorder is harmony not understood, and that partial evil is universal good. Whether any of these views is *true* is, of course, another question. But each of them gives an adequate solution of the problem of evil in the sense that if you accept it this problem does not arise for you, though you may, of course, have *other* problems to face.

But often enough these adequate solutions are only *almost* adopted. The thinkers who restrict God's power, but keep the term 'omnipotence,' may reasonably be suspected of thinking, in other contexts, that his power is really unlimited. Those who say that evil is an illusion may also be thinking, inconsistently, that this illusion is itself an evil. Those who say that "evil" is merely privation of good may also be thinking, inconsistently, that privation of good is an evil. (The fallacy here is akin to some forms of the "naturalistic fallacy" in ethics, where some think, for example, that "good" is just what contributes to evolutionary progress, and that evolutionary progress is itself good.) If Pope meant what he said in the first line of his couplet, that "disorder" is only harmony not understood, the "partial evil" of the second line must, for consistency, mean "that which, taken in isolation, falsely appears to be evil," but it would more naturally mean "that which, in isolation, really is evil." The second line, in fact, hesitates between two views, that "partial evil" isn't really evil, since only the universal quality is real, and that "partial evil" is really an evil, but only a little one.

In addition, therefore, to adequate solutions, we must recognise unsatisfactory inconsistent solutions, in which there is only a half-hearted or temporary rejection of one of the propositions which together constitute the problem. In these, one of the constituent propositions is explicitly rejected, but it is covertly re-asserted or assumed elsewhere in the system.

FALLACIOUS SOLUTIONS

Besides these half-hearted solutions, which explicitly reject but implicitly assert one of the constituent propositions, there are definitely fallacious solutions which explicitly maintain all the constituent propositions, but implicitly reject at least one of them in the course of the argument that explains away the problem of evil.

There are, in fact, many so-called solutions which purport to remove the contradiction without abandoning any of its constituent propositions. These must be fallacious, as we can see from the very statement of the problem, but it is not so easy to see in each case precisely where the fallacy lies. I suggest that in all cases the fallacy has the general form suggested above: in order to solve the problem one (or perhaps more) of its constituent propositions is given up, but in such a way that it appears to have been retained, and can therefore be asserted without qualification in other contexts. Sometimes there is a further complication: the supposed solution moves to and fro between, say, two of the constituent propositions, at one point asserting the first of these but covertly abandoning the second, at another point asserting the second but covertly abandoning the first. These fallacious solutions often turn upon some equivocation with the words "good" and "evil," or upon some vagueness about the way in which good and evil are opposed to one another, or about how much is meant by "omnipotence." I propose to examine some of these so-called solutions, and to exhibit their fallacies in detail. Incidentally, I shall also be considering whether an adequate solution could be reached by a minor modification of one or more of the constituent propositions, which would, however, still satisfy all the essential requirements of ordinary theism.

1. "Good Cannot Exist Without Evil" or "Evil Is Necessary as a Counterpart to Good"

It is sometimes suggested that evil is necessary as a counterpart to good, that if there were no evil there could be no good either, and that this solves the problem of evil. It is true that it points to an answer to the question "Why should there be evil?" But it does so only by qualifying some of the propositions that constitute the problem.

First, it sets a limit to what God can do, saying that God *cannot* create good without simultaneously creating evil, and this means either that God is not omnipotent or that there are *some* limits to what an omnipotent thing can do. It may be replied that these limits are always presupposed, that omnipotence has never meant the power to do what is logically impossible, and on the present view the existence of good without evil would be a logical impossibility. This interpretation of omnipotence may, indeed, be accepted as a modification of our original account which does not reject anything that is essential to theism, and I shall in general assume it in the subsequent discussion. It is, perhaps, the most common theistic view, but I think that some theists at least have maintained that God can do what is logically impossible. Many theists, at any rate, have held that logic itself is created or laid down by God, that logic is the way in which God arbitrarily chooses to think. (This is, of course, parallel to the ethical view that morally right actions are those which God arbitrarily chooses to command, and the two views encounter similar difficulties.) And *this* account of logic is clearly inconsistent with the view that God is bound by logical necessities—unless it is possible for an omnipotent being to bind himself, an issue which we shall consider later, when we come to the Paradox of Omnipotence. This solution of the problem of evil cannot, therefore, be consistently adopted along with the view that logic is itself created by God.

But, secondly, this solution denies that evil is opposed to good in our original sense. If good and evil are counterparts, a good thing will not "eliminate evil as far as it can." Indeed, this view suggests that good and evil are not strictly qualities of things at all. Perhaps the suggestion is that good and evil are related in much the same way as great and small. Certainly, when the term "great" is used relatively as a condensation of "greater than so-and-so," and "small" is used correspondingly, greatness and smallness are counterparts and cannot exist without each other. But in this sense greatness is not a quality, not an intrinsic feature of anything; and it would be absurd to think of a movement in favour of greatness and against smallness in this sense. Such a movement would be self-defeating, since relative greatness can be promoted only by a simultaneous promotion of relative smallness. I feel sure that no theists would be content to regard God's goodness as analogous to this—as if what he supports were not the *good* but the *better*, and as if he had the paradoxical aim that all things should be better than other things.

This point is obscured by the fact that "great" and "small" seem to have an absolute as well as a relative sense. I cannot discuss here whether there is absolute magnitude or not, but if there is, there could be an absolute sense for "great," it could mean of at least a certain size, and it would make sense to speak of all things getting bigger, of a universe that was expanding all over, and therefore it would make sense to speak of promoting greatness. But in *this* sense great and small are not logically necessary counterparts: either quality could exist without the other. There would be no logical impossibility in everything's being small or in everything's being great.

Neither in the absolute nor in the relative sense, then, of "great" and "small" do these terms provide an analogy of the sort that would be needed to support this solution of the problem of evil. In neither case are greatness and smallness *both* necessary counterparts *and* mutually opposed forces or possible objects for support and attack.

It may be replied that good and evil are necessary counterparts in the same way as any quality and its logical opposite: redness can occur, it is suggested, only if non-redness also occurs. But unless evil is merely the privation of good, they are not logical opposites, and some further argument would be needed to show that they are counterparts in the same way as genuine logical opposites. Let us assume that this could be given. There is still doubt of the correctness of the metaphysical principle that a quality must have a real opposite: I suggest that it is not really impossible that everything should be, say, red, that the truth is merely that if everything were red we should not notice redness, and so we should have no word "red"; we observe and give names to qualities only if they have real opposites. If so, the principle that a term must have an opposite would belong only to our language or to our thought, and would not be an ontological principle, and, correspondingly, the rule that good cannot exist without evil would not state a logical necessity of a sort that God would just have to put up with. God might have made everything good, though *we* should not have noticed it if he had.

But, finally, even if we concede that this *is* an ontological principle, it will provide a solution for the problem of evil only if one is prepared to say, "Evil exists, but only just enough evil to serve as the counterpart of good." I doubt whether any theist will accept this. After all, the *ontological* requirement that non-redness should occur would be satisfied even if all the universe, except for a minute speck, were red, and, if there were a corresponding requirement for evil as a counterpart to good, a minute dose of evil would presumably do. But theists are not usually willing to say, in all contexts, that all the evil that occurs is a minute and necessary dose.

2. "Evil Is Necessary as a Means to Good"

It is sometimes suggested that evil is necessary for good not as a counterpart but as a means. In its simple form this has little plausibility as a solution of the problem of evil, since it obviously implies a severe restriction of God's power. It would be a *causal* law that you cannot have a certain end without a certain means, so that if God has to introduce evil as a means to good, he must be subject to at least some causal laws. This certainly conflicts with what a theist normally means by omnipotence. This view of God as limited by causal laws also conflicts with the view that causal laws are themselves made by God, which is more widely held than the corresponding view about the laws of logic. This conflict, would, indeed, be resolved if it were possible for an omnipotent being to bind himself, and this possibility has still to be considered. Unless a favourable answer can be given to this question, the suggestion that evil is necessary as a means to good solves the problem of evil only by denying one of its constituent propositions, either that God is omnipotent or that "omnipotent" means what it says.

3. "The Universe Is Better With Some Evil in It Than It Could Be if There Were No Evil"

Much more important is a solution which at first seems to be a mere variant of the previous one, that evil may contribute to the goodness of a whole in which it is found, so that the universe as a whole is better as it is, with some evil in it, than it would be if there were no evil. This solution may be developed in either of two ways. It may be supported by an aesthetic analogy, by the fact that contrasts heighten beauty, that in a musical work, for example, there may occur discords which somehow add to the beauty of the work as a whole. Alternatively, it may be worked out in connexion with the notion of progress, that the best possible organisation of the universe will not be static, but progressive, that the gradual overcoming of evil by good is really a finer thing than would be the eternal unchallenged supremacy of good.

In either case, this solution usually starts from the assumption that the evil whose existence gives rise to the problem of evil is primarily what is called physical evil, that is to say, pain. In Hume's rather half-hearted presentation of the problem of evil, the evils that he stresses are pain and disease, and those who reply to him argue that the existence of pain and disease makes possible the existence of sympathy, benevolence, heroism, and the gradually successful struggle of doctors and reformers to overcome these evils. In fact, theists often seize the opportunity to accuse those who stress the problem of evil of taking a low, materialistic view of good and evil, equating these with pleasure and pain, and of ignoring the more spiritual goods which can arise in the struggle against evils.

But let us see exactly what is being done here. Let us call pain and misery 'first order evil' or 'evil (1).' What contrasts with this, namely, pleasure and happiness, will be called 'first order good' or 'good (1).' Distinct from this is 'second order good' or 'good (2)' which somehow emerges in a complex situation in which evil (1) is a necessary component—logically, not merely causally, necessary. (Exactly *how* it emerges does not matter: in the crudest version of this solution good (2) is simply the heightening of happiness by the contrast with misery, in other versions it includes sympathy with suffering, heroism in facing danger, and the gradual decrease of first order evil and increase of first order good.) It is also being assumed that second order good is more important than first order good or evil, in particular that it more than outweighs the first order evil it involves.

Now that is a particularly subtle attempt to solve the problem of evil. It defends God's goodness and omnipotence on the ground that (on a sufficiently long view) this is the best of all logically possible worlds, because it includes the important second order goods, and yet it admits that real evils, namely first order evils, exist. But does it still hold that good and evil are opposed? Not, clearly, in the sense that we set out originally: good does not tend to eliminate evil in general. Instead, we have a modified, a more complex pattern. First order good (*e.g.* happiness) *contrasts with* first order evil (*e.g.* misery): these two are opposed in a fairly mechanical way; some second order goods (*e.g.* benevolence) try to maximize first order good and minimize first order evil; but God's goodness is not this, it is rather the will to maximize *second* order good. We might, therefore, call God's goodness an example of a third order goodness, or good (3). While this account is different from our original one, it might well be held to be an improvement on it, to give a more accurate description of the way in which good is opposed to evil, and to be consistent with the essential theist position.

There might, however, be several objections to this solution.

First, some might argue that such qualities as benevolence—and a *fortiori* the third order goodness which promotes benevolence—have a merely derivative value, that they are not higher sorts of good, but merely means to good (1), that is, to happiness, so that it would be absurd for God to keep misery in existence in order to make possible the virtues of benevolence, heroism, etc. The theist who adopts the present solution must, of course, deny this, but he can do so with some plausibility, so I should not press this objection.

Secondly, it follows from this solution that God is not in our sense benevolent or sympathetic: he is not concerned to minimise evil (1), but only to promote good (2); and this might be a disturbing conclusion for some theists.

But, thirdly, the fatal objection is this. Our analysis shows clearly the possibility of the existence of a *second* order evil, an evil (2) contrasting with good (2) as evil (1) contrasts with good (1). This would include malevolence, cruelty, callousness, cowardice, and states in which good (1) is decreasing an evil (1) increasing. And just as good (2) is held to be the important kind of good, the kind that God is concerned to promote, so evil (2) will, by analogy, be the important kind of evil, the kind which God, if he were wholly good and omnipotent, would eliminate. And yet evil (2) plainly exists, and indeed most theists (in other contexts) stress its existence more than that of evil (1). We should, therefore, state the problem of evil in terms of second order evil, and against this form of the problem the present solution is useless.

An attempt might be made to use this solution again, at a higher level, to explain the occurrence of evil (2): indeed the next main solution that we shall examine does just this, with the help of some new notions. Without any fresh notions, such a solution would have little plausibility: for example, we could hardly say that the really important good was a good (3), such as the increase of benevolence in proportion to cruelty, which logically required for its occurrence the occurrence of some second order evil. But even if evil (2) could be explained in this way, it is fairly clear that there would be third order evils contrasting with this third order good: and we should be well on the way to an infinite regress, where the solution of a problem of evil, stated in terms of evil (n), indicated the existence of an evil ($n + 1$), and a further problem to be solved.

4. "Evil Is Due to Human Freewill"

Perhaps the most important proposed solution of the problem of evil is that evil is not to be ascribed to God at all, but to the independent actions of human beings, supposed to have been endowed by God with freedom of the will. This solution may be combined with the preceding one: first order evil (*e.g.* pain) may be justified as a logically necessary component in second order good (*e.g.* sympathy) while second order evil (*e.g.* cruelty) is not *justified*, but is so ascribed to human beings that God cannot be held responsible for it. This combination evades my third criticism of the preceding solution.

The freewill solution also involves the preceding solution at a higher level. To explain why a wholly good God gave men freewill although it would lead to some important evils, it must be argued that it is better on the whole that men should act freely, and sometimes err, than that they should be innocent automata, acting rightly in a wholly determined way. Freedom, that is to say, is now treated as a third order good, and as being more valuable than second order goods (such as sympathy and heroism) would be if they were deterministically produced, and it is being assumed that second order evils, such as cruelty, are logically necessary accompaniments of freedom, just as pain is a logically necessary pre-condition of sympathy.

I think that this solution is unsatisfactory primarily because of the incoherence of the notion of freedom of the will: but I cannot discuss this topic adequately here, although some of my criticisms will touch upon it.

First I should query the assumption that second order evils are logically necessary accompaniments of freedom. I should ask this: if God has made men such that in their free choices they sometimes prefer what is good and sometimes what is evil, why could He not have made men such that they always freely choose the good? If there is no logical impossibility in a man's freely choosing the good on one, or on several, occasions, there cannot be a logical impossibility in his freely choosing the good on every occasion. God was not, then, faced with a choice between making innocent automata and making beings who, in acting freely, would sometimes go wrong: there was open to him the obviously better possibility of making beings who would act freely but always go right. Clearly, his failure to avail himself of this possibility is inconsistent with his being both omnipotent and wholly good.

If it is replied that this objection is absurd, that the making of some wrong choices is logically necessary for freedom, it would seem that 'freedom' must here mean complete randomness or indeterminacy, including randomness with regard to the alternatives good and evil, in other words that men's choices and consequent actions can be "free" only if they are not determined by their characters. Only on this assumption can God escape the responsibility for men's actions; for if he made them as they are, but did not determine their wrong choices, this can only be because the wrong choices are not determined by men as they are. But then if freedom is randomness, how can it be a characteristic of *will*? And, still more, how can it be the most important good? What value or merit would there be in free choices if these were random actions which were not determined by the nature of the agent?

I conclude that to make this solution plausible two different senses of 'freedom' must be confused, one sense which will justify the view that freedom is a third order good, more valuable than other goods would be without it, and another sense, sheer randomness, to prevent us from ascribing to God a decision to make men such that they sometimes go wrong when he might have made them such that they would always freely go right.

This criticism is sufficient to dispose of this solution. But besides this there is a fundamental difficulty in the notion of an omnipotent God creating men with free will, for if men's wills are really free this must mean that even God cannot control them, that is, that God is no longer omnipotent. It may be objected that God's gift of freedom to men does not mean that he *cannot* control their wills, but that he always *refrains* from controlling their wills. But why, we may ask, should God refrain from controlling evil wills? Why should he not leave men free to will rightly, but intervene when he sees them beginning to will wrongly? If God could do this, but does not, and if he is wholly good, the only explanation could be that even a wrong free act of will is not really evil, that its freedom is a value which outweighs its wrongness, so that there would be a loss of value if God took away the wrongness and the freedom together. But this is utterly opposed to what theists say about sin in other contexts. The present solution of the problem of evil, then, can be maintained only in the form that God has made men so free that he *cannot* control their wills.

This leads us to what I call the Paradox of Omnipotence: can an omnipotent being make things which he cannot subsequently control? Or, what is practically equivalent to this, can an omnipotent being make rules which then bind himself? (These are practically equivalent because any such rules could be regarded as setting certain things beyond his control, and *vice versa*.) The second of these formulations is relevant to the suggestions that we have already met, that an omnipotent God creates the rules of logic or causal laws, and is then bound by them.

It is clear that this is a paradox: the questions cannot be answered satisfactorily either in the affirmative or in the negative. If we answer "Yes," it follows that if God actually makes things which he cannot control, or makes rules which bind himself, he is not omnipotent once he has made them: there are *then* things which he cannot do. But if we answer "No," we are immediately asserting that there are things which he cannot do, that is to say that he is already not omnipotent.

It cannot be replied that the question which sets this paradox is not a proper question. It would make perfectly good sense to say that a human mechanic has made a machine which he cannot control: if there is any difficulty about the question it lies in the notion of omnipotence itself.

This, incidentally, shows that although we have approached this paradox from the free will theory, it is equally a problem for a theological determinist. No one thinks that machines have free will, yet they may well be beyond the control of their makers. The determinist might reply that anyone who makes anything determines its ways of acting, and so determines its subsequent behaviour: even the human mechanic does this by his *choice* of materials and structure for his machine, though he does not know all about either of these: the mechanic thus determines, though he may not foresee, his machine's actions. And since God is omniscient, and since his creation of things is total, he both determines and foresees the ways in which his creatures will act. We may grant this, but it is beside the point. The question is not whether God *originally* determined the future actions of his creatures, but whether he can *subsequently* control their actions, or whether he was able in his original creation to put things beyond his subsequent control. Even on determinist principles the answers "Yes" and "No" are equally irreconcilable with God's omnipotence.

Before suggesting a solution of this paradox, I would point out that there is a parallel Paradox of Sovereignty. Can a legal sovereign make a law restricting its own future legislative power? For example, could the British parliament make a law forbidding any future parliament to socialise banking, and also forbidding the future repeal of this law itself? Or could the British parliament, which was legally sovereign in Australia in, say, 1899, pass a valid law, or series of laws, which made it no longer sovereign in 1933? Again, neither the affirmative nor the negative answer is really satisfactory. If we were to answer "Yes," we should be admitting the validity of a law which, if it were actually made, would mean that parliament was no longer sovereign. If we were to answer "No," we should be admitting that there is a law, not logically absurd, which parliament cannot validly make, that is, that parliament is not now a legal sovereign. This paradox can be solved in the following way. We should distinguish between first order laws, that is laws governing the actions of individuals and bodies other than the legislature, and second order laws, that is laws about laws, laws governing the actions of the legislature itself. Correspondingly, we should distinguish two orders of sovereignty, first order sovereignty (sovereignty (1)) which is unlimited authority to make first order laws, and second order sovereignty (sovereignty (2)) which is unlimited authority to make second order laws. If we say that parliament is sovereign we might mean that any parliament at any time has sovereignty (1), or we might mean that parliament has both sovereignty (1) and sovereignty (2) at present, but we cannot without contradiction mean both that the present parliament has sovereignty (2) and that every parliament at every time has sovereignty (1), for if the present parliament has sovereignty (2) it may use it to take away the sovereignty (1) of later parliaments. What the paradox shows is that we cannot ascribe to any continuing institution legal sovereignty in an inclusive sense.

The analogy between omnipotence and sovereignty shows that the paradox of omnipotence can be solved in a similar way. We must distinguish between first order omnipotence (omnipotence (1)), that is unlimited power to act, and second order omnipotence (omnipotence (2)), that is unlimited power to determine what powers to act things shall have. Then we could consistently say that God all the time has omnipotence (1), but if so no beings at any time have powers to act independently of God. Or we could say that God at one time had omnipotence (2), and used it to assign independent powers to act to certain things, so that God thereafter did not have omnipotence (1). But what the paradox shows is that we cannot consistently ascribe to any continuing being omnipotence is an inclusive sense.

An alternative solution of this paradox would be simply to deny that God is a continuing being, that any times can be assigned to his actions at all. But on this assumption (which also has difficulties of its own) no meaning can be given to the assertion that God made men with wills so free that he could not control them. The paradox of omnipotence can be avoided by putting God outside time, but the freewill solution of the problem of evil cannot be saved in this way, and equally it remains impossible to hold that an omnipotent God *binds himself* by causal or logical laws.

CONCLUSION

Of the proposed solutions of the problem of evil which we have examined, none has stood up to criticism. There may be other solutions which require examination, but this study strongly suggests that there is no valid solution of the problem which does not modify at least one of the constituent propositions in a way which would seriously affect the essential core of the theistic position.

Quite apart from the problem of evil, the paradox of omnipotence has shown that God's omnipotence must in any case be restricted in one way or another, that unqualified omnipotence cannot be ascribed to any being that continues through time. And if God and his actions are not in time, can omnipotence, or power of any sort, be meaningfuly ascribed to him?

ALVIN PLANTINGA The Free Will Defense

Alvin Plantinga (1932–) seeks to refute J. L. Mackie's basic contention, that it is not possible both that God is omnipotent and that he was unable to create a universe containing moral good but no moral evil. He develops a "possible worlds" scenario of human freedom in relation to divine omnipotence, now known as the Free Will Defense. In his scenario, God actualizes a world that contains free creatures who sometimes choose good and sometimes evil. After carefully navigating through certain technical logical considerations, Plantinga claims to have shown—contrary to Mackie—that it is logically possible for God to exist and evil to exist.

⌘

In a widely discussed piece entitled "Evil and Omnipotence" John Mackie repeats this claim:

> I think, however, that a more telling criticism can be made by way of the traditional problem of evil. Here it can be shown, not that religious beliefs lack rational support, but that they are positively irrational, that the several parts of the essential theological doctrine are *inconsistent* with one another.[1]

Is Mackie right? Does the theist contradict himself? But we must ask a prior question: just what is being claimed here? That theistic belief contains an inconsistency or contradiction, of course. But what, exactly, is an inconsistency or contradiction? There are several kinds. An *explicit* contradiction is a *proposition* of a certain sort—a conjunctive proposition, one conjunct of which is the denial or negation of the other conjunct. For example:

> Paul is a good tennis player, and it's false that Paul is a good tennis player.

(People seldom assert explicit contradictions.) Is Mackie charging the theist with accepting such a contradiction? Presumably not; what he says is:

> In its simplest form the problem is this: God is omnipotent; God is wholly good; yet evil exists. There seems to be some contradiction between these three propositions, so that if any two of them were true the third would be false. But at the same time all three are essential parts of most theological positions; the theologian, it seems, at once *must* adhere and *cannot consistently* adhere to all three.[2]

According to Mackie, then, the theist accepts a group or set of three propositions; this set is inconsistent. Its members, of course are,

(1) God is omnipotent

(2) God is wholly good

and

(3) Evil exists.

Call this set A; the claim is that A is an inconsistent set. But what is it for a *set* to be inconsistent or contradictory? Following our definition of an explicit contradiction, we might say that a set of propositions is explicitly contradictory if one of the members is the denial or negation of another member. But then, of course, it is evident that the set we are discussing is not explicitly contradictory; the denials of (1), (2), and (3), respectively, are

(1′) God is not omnipotent (or it's false that God is omnipotent)

(2′) God is not wholly good

and

(3′) There is no evil

none of which is in set A.

Of course many sets are pretty clearly contradictory, in an important way, but not *explicitly* contradictory. For example, set B:

(4) If all men are mortal, then Socrates is mortal

(5) All men are mortal

(6) Socrates is not mortal.

This set is not explicitly contradictory; yet surely *some* significant sense of that term applies to it. What is important here is that by using only the rules of ordinary logic—the laws of propositional logic and quantification theory found in any introductory text on the subject—we can deduce an explicit contradiction from the set. Or to put it differently, we can use the laws of logic to deduce a proposition from the set, which proposition, when added to the set, yields a new set that is explicitly contradictory. For by using the law *modus ponens* (if *p*, then *q*; *p*; therefore *q*) we can deduce

(7) Socrates is mortal

from (4) and (5). The result of adding (7) to B is the set {(4), (5), (6), (7)}. This set, of course, is explicitly contradictory in that (6) is the denial of (7). We might say that any set which shares this characteristic with set B is *formally* contradictory. So a formally contradictory set is one from whose members an explicit contradiction can be deduced by the laws of logic. Is Mackie claiming that set A is formally contradictory?

If he is, he's wrong. No laws of logic permit us to deduce the denial of one of the propositions in A from the other members. Set A isn't formally contradictory either.

But there is still another way in which a set of propositions can be contradictory or inconsistent. Consider set C, whose members are

(8) George is older than Paul

(9) Paul is older than Nick

and

(10) George is not older than Nick.

This set is neither explicitly nor formally contradictory; we can't, just by using the laws of logic, deduce the denial of any of these propositions from the others. And yet there is a good sense in which it is consistent or contradictory. For clearly it is *not possible* that its three members all be true. It is *necessarily true* that

(11) If George is older than Paul, and Paul is older than Nick, then George is older than Nick.

And if we add (11) to set C, we get a set that is formally contradictory; (8), (9), and (11) yield, by the laws of ordinary logic, the denial of (10).

I say that (11) is *necessarily true*; but what does *that* mean? Of course we might say that a proposition is necessarily true if it is impossible that it be false, or if its negation is not possibly true. This would be to explain necessity in terms of possibility. Chances are, however, that anyone who does not know what necessity is will be equally at a loss about possibility; the explanation is not likely to be very successful. Perhaps all we can do by way of explanation is to give some examples and hope for the best. In the first place many propositions can be established by the laws of logic alone—for example,

(12) If all men are mortal and Socrates is a man, then Socrates is mortal.

Such propositions are truths of logic; and all of them are necessary in the sense of question. But truths of arithmetic and mathematics generally are also necessarily true. Still further, there is a host of propositions that are neither truths of logic nor truths of mathematics but are nonetheless necessarily true; (11) would be an example, as well as

(13) Nobody is taller than himself

(14) Red is a color

(15) No numbers are persons

(16) No prime number is a prime minister

and

(17) Bachelors are unmarried.

So here we have an important kind of necessity—let's call it "broadly logical necessity." Of course there is a correlative kind of *possibility*: a proposition *p* is possibly true (in the broadly logical sense) just in case its negation or denial is not necessarily true (in that same broadly logical sense). This sense of necessity and possibility must be distinguished from another that we may call *causal* or *natural* necessity and possibility. Consider

(18) Henry Kissinger has swum the Atlantic.

Although this proposition has an implausible ring, it is not necessarily false in the broadly logical sense (and its denial is not necessarily true in that sense). But there is a good sense in which it is impossible: it is *causally* or *naturally* impossible. Human beings, unlike dolphins, just don't have the physical equipment demanded for this feat. Unlike Superman, furthermore, the rest of us are incapable of leaping tall buildings at a single bound or (without auxiliary power of some kind) traveling faster than a speeding bullet. These things are *impossible* for us—but not *logically* impossible, even in the broad sense.

So there are several senses of necessity and possibility here. There are a number of propositions, furthermore, of which it's difficult to say whether they are or aren't possible in the broadly logical sense; some of these are subjects of philosophical controversy. Is it possible, for example, for a person never to be conscious during his entire existence? Is it possible for a (human) person to exist *disembodied*? If that's possible, is it possible that there be a person who *at no time at all* during his entire existence has a body? Is it possible to see without eyes? These are propositions about whose possibility in that broadly logical sense there is disagreement and dispute.

Now return to set C. What is characteristic of it is the fact that the conjunction of its members—the proposition expressed by the result of putting "and's" between (8), (9), and (10)—is necessarily false. Or we might put it like this: what characterizes set C is the fact that we can get a formally contradictory set by adding a necessarily true proposition—namely (11). Suppose we say that a set is *implicitly contradictory* if it resembles C in this respect. That is, a set *S* of propositions is implicitly contradictory if there is a necessary proposition *p* such that the result of adding *p* to *S* is a formally contradictory set. Another way to put it: *S* is implicitly contradictory if there is some necessarily true proposition *p* such that by using just the laws of ordinary logic, we can deduce an explicit contradiction from *p* together with the members of *S*. And when Mackie says that set A is contradictory, we may properly take him, I think, as holding that it is implicitly contradictory in the explained sense. As he puts it:

> However, the contradiction does not arise immediately; to show it we need some additional premises, or perhaps some quasi-logical rules connecting the terms "good" and "evil" and "omnipotent." These additional principles are

> that good is opposed to evil, in such a way that a good thing always eliminates evil as far as it can, and that there are no limits to what an omnipotent thing can do. From these it follows that a good omnipotent thing eliminates evil completely, and then the propositions that a good omnipotent thing exists, and that evil exists, are incompatible.[3]

Here Mackie refers to "additional premises"; he also calls them "additional principles" and "quasi-logical rules"; he says we need them to show the contradiction. What he means, I think, is that to get a formally contradictory set we must add some more propositions to set A; and if we aim to show that set A is implicitly contradictory, these propositions must be necessary truths—"quasi-logical rules" as Mackie calls them. The two additional principles he suggests are

(19) A good thing always eliminates evil as far as it can

and

(20) There are no limits to what an omnipotent being can do.

And, of course, if Mackie means to show that set A is implicitly contradictory, then he must hold that (19) and (20) are not merely *true* but *necessarily true.*

But, are they? What about (20) first? What does it mean to say that a being is omnipotent? That he is *all-powerful,* or *almighty,* presumably. But are there no limits *at all* to the power of such a being? Could he create square circles, for example, or married bachelors? Most theologians and theistic philosophers who hold that God is omnipotent, do not hold that He can create round squares or bring it about that He both exists and does not exist. These theologians and philosophers may hold that there are no *nonlogical* limits to what an omnipotent being can do, but they concede that not even an omnipotent being can bring about logically impossible states of affairs or cause necessarily false propositions to be true. Some theists, on the other hand—Martin Luther and Descartes, perhaps—have apparently thought that God's power is unlimited even by the laws of logic. For these theists the question whether set A is contradictory will not be of much interest. As theists they believe (1) and (2), and they also presumably, believe (3). But they remain undisturbed by the claim that (1), (2), and (3) are jointly inconsistent—because, as they say, God can do what is logically impossible. Hence He can bring it about that the members of set A are all true, even if that set is contradictory (concentrating very intensely upon this suggestion is likely to make you dizzy). So the theist who thinks that the power of God isn't limited *at all,* not even by the laws of logic, will be unimpressed by Mackie's argument and won't find any difficulty in the contradiction set A is alleged to contain. This view is not very popular, however, and for good reason; it is quite incoherent. What the theist typically means when he says that God is omnipotent is not that there are *no* limits to God's power, but at most that there are no nonlogical limits to what He can do; and given this qualification, it is perhaps initially plausible to suppose that (20) is necessarily true.

But what about (19), the proposition that every good thing eliminates every evil state of affairs that it can eliminate? Is that necessarily true? Is it true at all? Suppose, first of all, that your friend Paul unwisely goes for a drive on a wintry day and runs out of gas on a deserted road. The temperature dips to $-10°$, and a miserably cold wind comes up. You are sitting comfortably at home (twenty-five miles from Paul) roasting chestnuts in a roaring blaze. Your car is in the garage; in the trunk there is the full five-gallon can of gasoline you always keep for emergencies. Paul's discomfort and danger are certainly an evil, and one which you could eliminate. You don't do so. But presumably you don't thereby forfeit your claim to being a "good thing"—you simply didn't know of Paul's plight. And so (19) does not appear to be necessary. It says that every good thing has a certain property—the property of eliminating every evil that it can. And if the case I described is possible—a good person's failing through ignorance to eliminate a certain evil he can eliminate—then (19) is by no means necessarily true.

But perhaps Mackie could sensibly claim that if you *didn't know* about Paul's plight, then in fact you were *not*, at the time in question, able to eliminate the evil in question; and perhaps he'd be right. In any event he could revise (19) to take into account the kind of case I mentioned:

(19a) Every good thing always eliminates every evil that *it knows about* and can eliminate.

{(1), (2), (3), (20), (19a)}, you'll notice is not a formally contradictory set—to get a formal contradiction we must add a proposition specifying that God *knows about* every evil state of affairs. But most theists do believe that God is omniscient or all-knowing; so if this new set—the set that results when we add to set A the proposition that God is omniscient—is implicitly contradictory then Mackie should be satisfied and the theist confounded. (And, henceforth, set A will be the old set A together with the proposition that God is omniscient.)

But is (19a) necessary? Hardly. Suppose you know that Paul is marooned as in the previous example, and you also know another friend is similarly marooned fifty miles in the opposite direction. Suppose, furthermore, that while you can rescue one or the other, you simply can't rescue both. Then each of the two evils is such that it is within your power to eliminate it; and you know about them both. But you can't eliminate *both;* and you don't forfeit your claim to being a good person by eliminating only one—it wasn't within your power to do more. So the fact that you don't doesn't mean that you are not a good person. Therefore (19a) is false; it is not a necessary truth or even a truth that every good thing eliminates every evil it knows about and can eliminate.

We can see the same thing another way. You've been rock climbing. Still something of a novice, you've acquired a few cuts and bruises by inelegantly using your knees rather than your feet. One of these bruises is fairly painful. You mention it to a physician friend, who predicts the pain will leave of its own accord in a day or two. Meanwhile, he says, there's nothing he can do, short of amputating your leg above the knee, to remove the pain. Now the pain in your knee is an evil state of affairs. All else being equal, it would be better if you had no such pain. And it is within the power of your friend to eliminate this evil state of affairs. Does his failure to do so mean that he is not a good person? Of course not; for he could eliminate this evil state of affairs only by bringing about another, much worse evil. And so it is once again evident that (19a) is false. It is entirely possible that a good person can fail to eliminate an evil state of affairs that he knows about and can eliminate. This would take place, if, as in the present example, he couldn't eliminate the evil without bringing about a *greater* evil.

A slightly different kind of case shows the same thing. A really impressive good state of affairs G will *outweigh* a trivial *E*—that is, the conjunctive state of affairs *G and E* is itself a good state of affairs. And surely a good person would not be obligated to eliminate a given evil if he could do so only by eliminating a good that outweighed it. Therefore (19a) is not necessarily true; it can't be used to show that set A is implicitly contradictory.

These difficulties might suggest another revision of (19); we might try

(19b) A good being eliminates every evil *E* that it knows about and that it can eliminate without either bringing about a greater evil or eliminating a good state of affairs that outweighs *E*.

Is this necessarily true? It takes care of the second of the two difficulties afflicting (19a) but leaves the first untouched. We can see this as follows. First, suppose we say that a being *properly eliminates* an evil state of affairs if it eliminates that evil without either eliminating an outweighing good or bringing about a greater evil. It is then obviously possible that a person find himself in a situation where he could properly eliminate an evil *E* and could also properly eliminate another evil *E'*, but couldn't properly eliminate them *both*. You're rock climbing again, this time on the dreaded north face of the Grand Teton. You and your party come upon Curt and Bob, two mountaineers stranded 125 feet apart on the face. They untied to reach their cigarettes and then carelessly dropped the rope while lighting up. A violent, dangerous thunderstorm is approaching. You have time to rescue one of the stranded climbers and retreat before the storm hits; if you rescue both, however, you and your party and the two climbers will be caught on the face during the thunderstorm, which will very likely destroy your entire party. In this case you can eliminate one evil (Curt's being stranded on the face) without causing more evil or eliminating a greater good; and you are also able to properly eliminate the other evil (Bob's being thus stranded). But you can't properly eliminate them *both*. And so the fact that you don't rescue Curt, say, even though you could have, doesn't show that you aren't a good person. Here, then, each of the evils is such that you can properly eliminate it; but you can't properly eliminate them both, and hence can't be blamed for failing to eliminate one of them.

So neither (19a) nor (19b) is necessarily true. You may be tempted to reply that the sort of counterexamples offered—examples where someone is able to eliminate an evil A and also able to eliminate a different evil *B*, but unable to eliminate them both—are irrelevant to the case of a being who, like God, is both omnipotent and omniscient. That is, you may think that if an omnipotent and omniscient being is able to eliminate *each* of two evils, it follows that he can eliminate them *both*. Perhaps this is so; but it is not strictly to the point. The fact is the counterexamples show that (19a) and (19b) are not necessarily true and hence can't be used to show that set A is implicitly inconsistent. What the reply does suggest is that perhaps the atheologian will have more success if he works the properties of omniscience and omnipotence into (19). Perhaps he could say something like

(19c) An omnipotent and omniscient good being eliminates every evil that it can properly eliminate.

And suppose, for purposes of argument, we concede the necessary truth of (19c). Will it serve Mackie's purposes? Not obviously. For we don't get a set that is formally contradictory by adding (20) and (19c) to set A. This set (call it A′) contains the following six members:

(1) God is omnipotent

(2) God is wholly good

(2′) God is omniscient

(3) Evil exists

(19c) An omnipotent and omniscient good being eliminates every evil that it can properly eliminate

and

(20) There are no nonlogical limits to what an omnipotent being can do.

Now if A′ were formally contradictory, then from any five of its members we could deduce the denial of the sixth by the laws of ordinary logic. That is, any five would *formally entail* the denial of the sixth. So if A′ were formally inconsistent, the denial of (3) would be formally entailed by the remaining five. That is, (1), (2), (2′), (19c), and (20) would formally entail

(3′) There is no evil.

But they don't; what they formally entail is not that there is no evil *at all* but only that

(3″) There is no evil that God can properly eliminate.

So (19c) doesn't really help either—not because it is not necessarily true but because its addition [with (20)] to set A does not yield a formally contradictory set.

Obviously, what the atheologian must add to get a formally contradictory set is

(21) If God is omniscient and omnipotent, then he can properly eliminate every evil state of affairs.

Suppose we agree that the set consisting in A plus (19c), (20), and (21) is formally contradictory. So if (19c), (20), and (21) are all necessarily true, then set A is implicitly contradictory. We've already conceded that (19c) and (20) are indeed necessary. So we must take a look at (21). Is this proposition necessarily true?

No. To see this let us ask the following question. Under what conditions would an omnipotent being be unable to eliminate a certain evil *E* without eliminating an outweighing good? Well, suppose that *E* is *included in* some good state of affairs that outweighs it. That is, suppose there is some good state of affairs *G* so related to *E* that it is impossible that *G* obtain or be actual and *E* fail to obtain. (Another way to put this: a state of affairs *S* includes *S′* if the conjunctive state of affairs *S but not S′* is impossible, or if it is necessary that *S′* obtains if *S* does.) Now suppose that some good state of affairs *G* includes an evil state of affairs *E* that it outweighs. Then not even an omnipotent being could eliminate *E* without eliminating *G*. But *are* there any cases where a good state of affairs includes, in this sense, an evil that it outweighs?[4] Indeed there are such states of affairs. To take an artificial example, let's suppose that *E* is Paul's suffering from a minor abrasion and *G* is your being deliriously happy. The conjunctive state of affairs, *G and E*—the state of affairs that obtains if and only if both *G* and *E* obtain—is then a good state of affairs: it is better, all else being equal, that you be intensely happy and Paul suffer a mildly annoying abrasion than that this state of affairs not obtain. So *G and E* is a good state of affairs. And clearly *G and E* includes *E*: obviously it is necessarily true that if you are deliriously happy and Paul is suffering from an abrasion, then Paul is suffering from an abrasion.

But perhaps you think this example trivial, tricky, slippery, and irrelevant. If so, take heart; other examples abound. Certain kinds of values, certain familiar kinds of good states of affairs, can't exist apart from evil of some sort. For example, there are people who display a sort of creative moral heroism in the face of suffering and adversity—a heroism that inspires others and creates a good situation out of a bad one. In a situation like this the evil, of course, remains evil; but the total state of affairs—someone's bearing pain magnificently, for example—may be good. If it is, then the good present must outweigh the evil; otherwise the total situation would not be *good*. But, of course, it is not possible that such a good state of affairs obtain unless some evil also obtain. It is a necessary truth that if someone bears pain magnificently, then someone is in pain.

The conclusion to be drawn, therefore, is that (21) is not necessarily true. And our discussion thus far shows at the very least that it is no easy matter to find necessarily true propositions that yield a formally contradictory set when added to set A.[5] One wonders, therefore, why the many atheologians who confidently assert that this set is contradictory make no attempt whatever to *show* that it is. For the most part they are content just to *assert* that there is a contradiction here. Even Mackie, who sees that some "additional premises" or "quasi-logical rules" are needed, makes scarcely a beginning towards finding some additional premises that are necessarily true and that together with the members of set A formally entail an explicit contradiction.

CAN WE SHOW THAT THERE IS NO INCONSISTENCY HERE?

To summarize our conclusions so far: although many atheologians claim that the theist is involved in contradiction when he asserts the members of set A, this set, obviously, is neither *explicitly* nor *formally* contradictory; the claim, presumably, must be that it is *implicitly* contradictory. To make good this claim the atheologian must find some necessarily true proposition *p* (it could be a conjunction of several propositions) such that the addition of *p* to set A yields a set that is formally contradictory. No atheologian has produced even a plausible candidate for this role, and it certainly is not easy to see what such a proposition might be. Now we might think we should simply declare set A implicitly consistent on the principle that a proposition (or set) is to be presumed consistent or possible until proven otherwise. This course, however, leads to trouble. The same principle would impel us to declare the atheologian's claim—that set A is *in*consistent—possible or consistent. But the claim that a given set of propositions is implicitly contradictory is itself either necessarily true or necessarily false; so if such a claim is *possible*, it is not necessarily false and is, therefore, true (in fact, necessarily true). If we followed the suggested principle, therefore, we should be obliged to declare set A implicitly consistent (since it hasn't been shown to be otherwise), but we should have to say the same thing about the atheologian's claim, since we haven't shown *that* claim to be inconsistent or impossible. The atheologian's claim, furthermore, is necessarily true if it is possible. Accordingly, if we accept the above principle, we shall have to declare set A both implicitly consistent and implicitly inconsistent. So all we can say at this point is that set A has not been shown to be implicitly inconsistent.

Can we go any further? One way to go on would be to try to *show* that set A is implicitly consistent or possible in the broadly logical sense. But what is involved in showing such a thing? Although there are various ways to approach this matter, they all resemble one another in an important respect. They all amount to this: to show that a set *S* is consistent you think of a *possible state of affairs* (it needn't *actually obtain*) which is such that if it were actual, then all of the members of *S* would be true. This procedure is sometimes called *giving a model of S*. For example, you might construct an axiom set and then show that it is consistent by giving a model of it; this is how it was shown that the denial of Euclid's parallel postulate is formally consistent with the rest of his postulates.

There are various special cases of this procedure to fit special circumstances. Suppose, for example, you have a pair of propositions p and q and wish to show them consistent. And suppose we say that a proposition p_1 *entails* a proposition p_2 if it is impossible that p_1 be true and p_2 false—if the conjunctive proposition p_1 *and not* p_2 is necessarily false. Then one way to show that p is consistent with q is to find some proposition r whose conjunction with p is both possible, in the broadly logical sense, and entails q. A rude and unlettered behaviorist, for example, might hold that thinking is really nothing but movements of the larynx; he might go on to hold that

P Jones did not move his larynx after April 30

is inconsistent (in the broadly logical sense) with

Q Jones did some thinking during May.

By way of rebuttal, we might point out that *P* appears to be consistent with

R While convalescing from an April 30 laryngotomy, Jones whiled away the idle hours by writing (in May) a splendid paper on Kant's *Critique of Pure Reason*.

So the conjunction of *P* and *R* appears to be consistent; but obviously it also entails *Q* (you can't write even a passable paper on Kant's *Critique of Pure Reason* without doing some thinking); so *P* and *Q* are consistent.

We can see that this is a special case of the procedure I mentioned above as follows. This proposition *R* is consistent with *P*; so the proposition *P and R* is possible, describes a possible state of affairs. But *P and R* entails *Q*; hence if *P and R* were true, *Q* would also be true, and hence both *P* and *Q* would be true. So this is really a case of producing a possible state of affairs such that, if it were actual, all the members of the set in question (in this case the pair set of *P* and *Q*) would be true.

How does this apply to the case before us? As follows, let us conjoin propositions (1), (2), and (2′) and henceforth call the result (1):

(1) God is omniscient, omnipotent, and wholly good.

The problem, then, is to show that (1) and (3) (evil exists) are consistent. This could be done, as we've seen, by finding a proposition *r* that is consistent with (1) and such that (1) and (*r*) together entail (3). One proposition that might do the trick is

(22) God creates a world containing evil and has a good reason for doing so.

If (22) is consistent with (1), then it follows that (1) and (3) (and hence set A) are consistent. Accordingly, one thing some theists have tried is to show that (22) and (1) are consistent.

One can attempt this in at least two ways. On the one hand, we could try to apply the same method again. Conceive of a possible state of affairs such that, if it obtained, an omnipotent, omniscient, and wholly good God would have a good reason for permitting evil. On the other, someone might try to specify *what God's reason is* for permitting evil and try to show, if it is not obvious, that it is a good reason. St. Augustine, for example, one of the greatest and most influential philosopher-theologians of the Christian Church, writes as follows:

> . . . some people see with perfect truth that a creature is better if, while possessing free will, it remains always fixed upon God and never sins; then, reflecting on men's sins, they are grieved, not because they continue to sin, but because they were created. They say: He should have made us such that we never willed to sin, but always to enjoy the unchangeable truth.
>
> They should not lament or be angry. God has not compelled men to sin just because He created them and gave them the power to choose between sinning and not sinning. There are angels who have never sinned and never will sin.
>
> Such is the generosity of God's goodness that He has not refrained from creating even that creature which He foreknew would not only sin, but remain in the will to sin. As a runaway horse is better than a stone which does not run away because it lacks self-movement and sense perception, so the creature is more excellent which sins by free will than that which does not sin only because it has no free will.[6]

In broadest terms Augustine claims that God could create a better, more perfect universe by permitting evil than He could by refusing to do so:

> Neither the sins nor the misery are necessary to the perfection of the universe, but souls as such are necessary, which have the power to sin if they so will, and become miserable if they sin. If misery persisted after their sins had been abolished, or if there were misery before there were sins, then it might be right to say that the order and government of the universe were at fault. Again, if there were sins but no consequent misery, that order is equally dishonored by lack of equity.[7]

Augustine tries to tell us *what God's reason is* for permitting evil. At bottom, he says, it's that God can create a more perfect universe by permitting evil. A really top-notch universe requires the existence of free, rational, and moral agents; and some of the free creatures He created went wrong. But the universe with the free creatures it contains and the evil they commit is better than it would have been had it contained neither the free creatures nor this evil. Such an attempt to specify God's reason for permitting evil is what I earlier called a *theodicy;* in the words of John Milton it is an attempt to "justify the ways of God to man," to show that God is just in permitting evil. Augustine's kind of theodicy might be called a Free Will Theodicy, since the idea of rational creatures with free will plays such a prominent role in it.

A theodicist, then, attempts to tell us why God permits evil. Quite distinct from a Free Will Theodicy is what I shall call a Free Will Defense. Here the aim is not to say what God's reason *is*, but at most what God's reason *might possibly be*. We could put the difference like this. The Free Will Theodicist and Free Will Defender are both trying to show that (1) is consistent with (22), and of course if so, then set A is consistent. The Free Will Theodicist tries to do this by finding some proposition *r* which in conjunction with (1) entails (22); he claims, furthermore, that this proposition is *true*, not just consistent with (1). He tries to tell us what God's reason for permitting evil *really is*. The Free Will Defender, on the other hand, though he also tries to find a proposition *r* that is consistent with (1) and in conjunction with it entails (22), does *not* claim to know or even believe that *r* is true. And here, of course, he is perfectly within his rights. His aim is to show that (1) is consistent with (22); all he need do then is find an *r* that is consistent with (1) and such that (1) and (*r*) entail (22); whether *r* is *true* is quite beside the point.

So there is a significant difference between a Free Will Theodicy and a Free Will Defense. The latter is sufficient (if successful) to show that set A is consistent; in a way a Free Will Theodicy goes beyond what is required. On the other hand, a theodicy would be much more satisfying, if possible to achieve. No doubt the theist would rather know what God's reason *is* for permitting evil than simply that it's possible that He has a good one. But in the present context (that of investigating the consistency of set A), the latter is all that's needed. Neither a defense or a theodicy, of course, gives any hint to what God's reason for some *specific* evil—the death or suffering of someone close to you, for example—might be. And there is still another function—a sort of pastoral function[8]—in the neighborhood that neither serves. Confronted with evil in his own life or suddenly coming to realize more clearly than before the *extent* and *magnitude* of evil, a believer in God may undergo a crisis in faith. He may be tempted to follow the advice of Job's "friends"; he may be tempted to "curse God and die." Neither a Free Will Defense nor a Free Will Theodicy is designed to be of much help or comfort to one suffering from such a storm in the soul (although in a specific case, of course, one or the other could prove useful). Neither is to be thought of first of all as a means of pastoral counseling. Probably neither will enable someone to find peace with himself and with God in the face of the evil the world contains. But then, of course, neither is intended for that purpose.

THE FREE WILL DEFENSE

In what follows I shall focus attention upon the Free Will Defense. I shall examine it more closely, state it more exactly, and consider objections to it;

and I shall argue that in the end it is successful. Earlier we saw that among good states of affairs there are some that not even God can bring about without bringing about evil: those goods, namely, that *entail* or *include* evil states of affairs. The Free Will Defense can be looked upon as an effort to show that there may be a very different kind of good that God can't bring about without permitting evil. These are good states of affairs that don't include evil; they do not entail the existence of any evil whatever; nonetheless God Himself can't bring them about without permitting evil.

So how does the Free Will Defense work? And what does the Free Will Defender mean when he says that people are or may be free? What is relevant to the Free Will Defense is the idea of *being free with respect to an action.* If a person is free with respect to a given action, then he is free to perform that action and free to refrain from performing it; no antecedent conditions and/or causal laws determine that he will perform the action, or that he won't. It is within his power, at the time in question, to take or perform the action and within his power to refrain from it. Freedom so conceived is not to be confused with unpredictability. You might be able to predict what you will do in a given situation even if you are free, in that situation, to do something else. If I know you well, I may be able to predict what action you will take in response to a certain set of conditions; it does not follow that you are not free with respect to that action. Secondly, I shall say that an action is *morally significant,* for a given person, if it would be wrong for him to perform the action but right to refrain or *vice versa.* Keeping a promise, for example, would ordinarily be morally significant for a person, as would refusing induction into the army. On the other hand, having Cheerios for breakfast (instead of Wheaties) would not normally be morally significant. Further, suppose we say that a person is *significantly free,* on a given occasion, if he is then free with respect to a morally significant action. And finally we must distinguish between *moral evil* and *natural evil.* The former is evil that results from free human activity; natural evil is any other kind of evil.[9]

Given these definitions and distinctions, we can make a preliminary statement of the Free Will Defense as follows. A world containing creatures who are significantly free (and freely perform more good than evil actions) is more valuable, all else being equal, than a world containing no free creatures at all. Now God can create free creatures, but He can't *cause* or *determine* them to do only what is right. For if He does so, then they aren't significantly free after all; they do not do what is right *freely.* To create creatures capable of *moral good,* therefore, He must create creatures capable of moral evil; and He can't give these creatures the freedom to perform evil and at the same time prevent them from doing so. As it turned out, sadly enough, some of the free creatures God created went wrong in the exercise of their freedom; this is the source of moral evil. The fact that free creatures sometimes go wrong, however, counts neither against God's omnipotence nor against His goodness; for He could have forestalled the occurrence of moral evil only by removing the possibility of moral good.

I said earlier that the Free Will Defender tries to find a proposition that is consistent with

(1) God is omniscient, omnipotent, and wholly good

and together with (1) entails that there is evil. According to the Free Will Defense, we must find this proposition somewhere in the above story. The heart of the Free Will Defense is the claim that it is *possible* that God could not have created a universe containing moral good (or as much moral good as this world contains) without creating one that also contained moral evil. And if so, then it is possible that God has a good reason for creating a world containing evil.

Now this defense has met with several kinds of objections. For example, some philosophers say that *causal determinism* and *freedom*, contrary to what we might have thought, are not really incompatible.[10] But if so, then God could have created free creatures who were free, and free to do what is wrong, but nevertheless were causally determined to do only what is right. Thus He could have created creatures who were free to do what was wrong, while nevertheless preventing them from ever performing any wrong actions—simply by seeing to it that they were causally determined to do only what is right. Of course this contradicts the Free Will Defense, according to which there is inconsistency in supposing that God determines free creatures to do only what is right. But is it really possible that all of a person's actions are causally determined while some of them are free? How could that be so? According to one version of the doctrine in question, to say that George acts freely on a given occasion is to say only this: *if George had chosen to do otherwise, he would have done otherwise.* Now George's action A is causally determined if some event *E*—some event beyond his control—has already occurred, where the state of affairs consisting in *E*'s occurrence conjoined with George's *refraining* from performing A, is a causally impossible state of affairs. Then one can consistently hold both that all of a man's actions are causally determined and that some of them are free in the above sense. For suppose that all of a man's actions are causally determined and that he *couldn't*, on any occasion, have made any choice or performed any action different from the ones he did make and perform. It could still be true that if he *had* chosen to do otherwise, he would have done otherwise. Granted, he couldn't have chosen to do otherwise; but this is consistent with saying that *if* he had, things would have gone differently.

This objection to the Free Will Defense seems utterly implausible. One might as well claim that being in jail doesn't really limit one's freedom on the grounds that if one were *not* in jail, he'd be free to come and go as he pleased. So I shall say no more about this objection here.[11]

A second objection is more formidable. In essence it goes like this. Surely it is possible to do only what is right, even if one is free to do wrong. It is *possible*, in that broadly logical sense, that there would be a world containing free creatures who always do what is right. There is certainly no *contradiction* or *inconsistency* in this idea. But God is omnipotent; his power has no non-logical limitations. So if it's possible that there be a world containing creatures who are free to do what is wrong but never in fact do so, then it follows that an omnipotent God could create such a world. If so, however, the Free Will Defense must be mistaken in its insistence upon the possibility that God is omnipotent but unable to create a world containing moral good without permitting moral evil. J. L. Mackie . . . states this objection:

> If God has made men such that in their free choices they sometimes prefer what is good and sometimes what is evil, why could he not have made men such that they always freely choose the good? If there is no logical impossibility in a man's freely choosing the good on one, or on several occasions, there cannot be a logical impossibility in his freely choosing the good on every occasion. God was not, then, faced with a choice between making innocent automata and making beings who, in acting freely, would sometimes go wrong; there was open to him the obviously better possibility of making beings who would act freely but always go right. Clearly, his failure to avail himself of this possibility is inconsistent with his being both omnipotent and wholly good.[12]

Now what, exactly, is Mackie's point here? This. According to the Free Will Defense, it is possible both that God is omnipotent and that He was unable to create a world containing moral good without creating one containing moral evil. But, replies Mackie, this limitation on His power to create is inconsistent with God's omnipotence. For surely it's *possible* that there be a world containing perfectly virtuous persons—persons who are significantly free but always do what is right. Surely there are *possible worlds* that contain moral good but no moral evil. But God, if He is omnipotent, can create any possible world he chooses. So it is *not* possible, contrary to the Free Will Defense, both that God is omnipotent and that he could create a world containing moral good only by creating one containing moral evil. If He is omnipotent, the only limitations of His power are *logical* limitations; in which case there are no possible worlds He could not have created.

This is a subtle and important point. According to the great German philosopher G. W. Leibniz, *this* world, the actual world, must be the best of all possible worlds. His reasoning goes as follows. Before God created anything at all, He was confronted with an enormous range of choices; He could create or bring into actuality any of the myriads of different possible worlds. Being perfectly good, He must have chosen to create the best world He could; being omnipotent, He was able to create any possible world He pleased. He must, therefore, have chosen the best of all possible worlds; and hence *this* world, the one He did create, must be the best possible. Now Mackie, of course, agrees with Leibniz that God, if omnipotent, could have created any world He pleased and would have created the best world he could. But while Leibniz draws the conclusion that this world, despite appearances, must be the best possible, Mackie concludes instead that there is no omnipotent, wholly good God. For, he says, it is obvious enough that this present world is not the best of all possible worlds.

The Free Will Defender disagrees with both Leibniz and Mackie. In the first place, he might say, what is the reason for supposing that *there is* such a thing as the best of all possible worlds? No matter how marvelous a world is—containing no matter how many persons enjoying unalloyed bliss—isn't it possible that there be an even better world containing even more persons enjoying even more unalloyed bliss? But what is really characteristic and central to the Free Will Defense is the claim that God, though omnipotent, could not have actualized just any possible world He pleased.

WAS IT WITHIN GOD'S POWER TO CREATE ANY POSSIBLE WORLD HE PLEASED?

This is indeed the crucial question for the Free Will Defense. If we wish to discuss it with insight and authority, we shall have to look into the idea of *possible worlds*. And a sensible first question is this: what sort of thing is a possible world? The basic idea is that a possible world is a *way things could have been*; it is a *state of affairs* of some kind. Earlier we spoke of states of affairs, in particular of good and evil states of affairs. Suppose we look at this idea in more detail. What sort of thing is a state of affairs? The following would be examples:

Nixon's having won the 1972 election
7 + 5's being equal to 12
All men's being mortal

and

Gary, Indiana's, having a really nasty pollution problem.

These are *actual* states of affairs: states of affairs that do in fact *obtain*. And corresponding to each such actual state of affairs there is a true proposition—in the above cases, the corresponding propositions would be *Nixon won the 1972 presidential election*, 7 + 5 *is equal to* 12, *all men are mortal*, and *Gary, Indiana, has a really nasty pollution problem*. A proposition *p corresponds* to a state of affairs *s*, in this sense, if it is impossible that *p* be true and *s* fail to obtain and impossible that *s* obtain and *p* fail to be true.

But just as there are false propositions, so there are states of affairs that do *not* obtain or are *not* actual. *Kissinger's having swum the Atlantic* and *Hubert Horatio Humphrey's having run a mile in four minutes* would be examples. Some states of affairs that do not obtain are *impossible*: e.g., *Hubert's having drawn a square circle*, 7 + 5*'s being equal to* 75, and *Agnew's having a brother who was an only child*. The propositions corresponding to these states of affairs, of course, are necessarily false. So there are states of affairs that *obtain* or *are actual* and also states of affairs that don't obtain. Among the latter some are *impossible* and others are possible. And a possible world is a possible state of affairs. Of course not every possible state of affairs is a possible world; *Hubert's having run a mile in four miles* is a possible state of affairs but not a possible world. No doubt it is an *element* of many possible worlds, but it isn't itself inclusive enough to be one. To be a possible world, a state of affairs must be very large—so large as to be *complete* or *maximal.*

To get at this idea of completeness we need a couple of definitions. As we have already seen a state of affairs A *includes* a state of affairs B if it is not possible that A obtain B not obtain or if the conjunctive state of affairs *A but not B*—the state of affairs that obtains if and only if A obtains and B does not—is not possible. For example, *Jim Whittaker's being the first American to climb Mt. Everest* includes *Jim Whittaker's being an American.* It also includes *Mt. Everest's being climbed, something's being climbed, no American's having climbed Everest before Whittaker did,* and the like. *Inclusion* among states of affairs is like *entailment* among propositions; and where a state of affairs A includes a state of affairs B, the proposition corresponding to A entails the one corresponding to B. Accordingly, *Jim Whittaker is the first American to climb Everest* entails *Mt. Everest has been climbed, something has been climbed,* and *no American climbed Everest before Whittaker did.* Now suppose we say further that a state of affairs A *precludes* a state of affairs B if it is not possible that *both* obtain, or if the conjunctive state of affairs *A and B* is impossible. Thus *Whittaker's being the first American to climb Mt. Everest* precludes *Luther Jerstad's being the first American to climb Everest,* as well as *Whittaker's never having climbed any mountains.* If A precludes B, then A's corresponding proposition entails the denial of the one corresponding to B. Still further, let's say that the *complement* of a state of affairs is the state of affairs that obtains just in case A does not obtain. [Or we might say that the complement (call it $\overline{A}$) of A is the state of affairs corresponding to the *denial* or *negation* of the proposition corresponding to A.] Given these definitions, we can say what it is for a state of affairs to be *complete*: A is a complete state of affairs if and only if for every state of affairs B, either *A includes B* or *A precludes B.* (We could express the same thing by saying that if A is a complete state of affairs, then for every state of affairs B, either A includes B or A includes $\overline{B}$, the complement of B.) And now we are able to say what a possible world is: a possible world is any possible state of affairs that is complete. If A is a possible world, then it says something about everything; every state of affairs S is either included in or precluded by it.

Corresponding to each possible world W, furthermore, there is a set of propositions that I'll call *the book on* W. A proposition is in the book on W just in case the state of affairs to which it corresponds is included in W. Or we might express it like this. Suppose we say that a proposition *P is true in a world* W if and only if *P would have been true if W had been actual*—if and only if, that is, it is not possible that W be actual and P be false. Then the book on W is the set of propositions true in W. Like possible worlds, books are *complete*; if B is a book, then for any proposition P, either P or the denial of *P* will be a member of *B*. A book is a *maximal consistent set* of propositions; it is so large that the addition of another proposition to it always yields an explicitly inconsistent set.

Of course, for each possible world there is exactly one book corresponding to it (that is, for a given world *W* there is just one book *B* such that each member of *B* is true in *W*); and for each book there is just one world to which it corresponds. So every world has its book.

It should be obvious that exactly one possible world is actual. At *least* one must be, since the set of true propositions is a maximal consistent set and hence a book. But then it corresponds to a possible world, and the possible world corresponding to this set of propositions (since it's the set of *true* propositions) will be actual. On the other hand there is at *most* one actual world. For suppose there were two: *W* and *W*′. These worlds cannot include all the very same states of affairs; if they did, they would be the very same world. So there must be at least one state of affairs *S* such that *W* includes *S* and *W*′ does not. But a possible world is maximal; *W*′, therefore, includes the complement *S* of *S*. So if both *W* and *W*′ were actual, as we have supposed, then both *S* and $\overline{S}$ would be actual—which is impossible. So there can't be more than one possible world that is actual.

Leibniz pointed out that a proposition *p* is necessary if it is true in every possible world. We may add that *p* is possible if it is true in one world and impossible if true in none. Furthermore, *p entails q* if there is no possible world in which *p* is true and *q* is false, and *p is consistent with q* if there is at least one world in which both *p* and *q* are true.

A further feature of possible worlds is that people (and other things) *exist* in them. Each of us exists in the actual world, obviously; but a person also exists in many worlds distinct from the actual world. It would be a mistake, of course, to think of all these worlds as somehow "going on" at the same time, with the same person reduplicated through these worlds and actually existing in a lot of different ways. This is not what is meant by saying that the same person exists in different possible worlds. What is meant, instead, is this: a person Paul exists in each of those possible worlds *W* which is such that, if *W had been actual*, Paul would have existed—actually existed. Suppose Paul had been an inch taller than he is, or a better tennis player. Then the world that does in fact obtain would not have been actual; some other world—*W*′, let's say—would have obtained instead. If *W*′ had been actual, Paul would have existed; so Paul exists in *W*′. (Of course there are still other possible worlds in which Paul does not exist—worlds, for example, in which there are no people at all). Accordingly, when we say that Paul exists in a world *W*, what we mean is that Paul *would have* existed had *W* been actual. Or we could put it like this: Paul exists in each world W that includes the state of affairs consisting in Paul's existence. We can put this still more simply by saying that Paul exists in those worlds whose books contain the proposition *Paul exists.*

But isn't there a problem here? *Many* people are named "Paul": Paul the apostle, Paul J. Zwier, John Paul Jones, and many other famous Pauls.

So who goes with "Paul exists"? Which Paul? The answer has to do with the fact that books contain *propositions*—not sentences. They contain the sort of thing sentences are used to express and assert. And the same sentence—"Aristotle is wise," for example—can be used to express many different propositions. When Plato used it, he asserted a proposition predicating wisdom of his famous pupil; when Jackie Onassis uses it, she asserts a proposition predicating wisdom of her wealthy husband. These are distinct propositions (we might even think they differ in truth value); but they are expressed by the same sentence. Normally (but not always) we don't have much trouble determining which of the several propositions expressed by a given sentence is relevant in the context at hand. So in this case a given person, Paul, exists in a world *W* if and only if *W*'s book contains the proposition that says that *he*—that particular person—exists. The fact that the sentence we use to express this proposition can also be used to express *other* propositions is not relevant.

After this excursion into the nature of books and worlds we can return to our question. Could God have created just any world He chose? Before addressing the question, however, we must note that God does not, strictly speaking, *create* any possible worlds or states of affairs at all. What He creates are the heavens and the earth and all that they contain. But He has not created states of affairs. There are, for example, the state of affairs consisting in God's existence and the states of affairs consisting in His nonexistence. That is, there is such a thing as the state of affairs consisting in the existence of God, and there is also such a thing as the state of affairs consisting in the nonexistence of God, just as there are the two propositions *God exists* and *God does not exist.* The theist believes that the first state of affairs is actual and the first proposition true, the atheist believes that the second state of affairs is actual and the second proposition true. But, of course, both propositions *exist*, even though just one is true. Similarly, there are two states of affairs here, just one of which is actual. So both states of affairs *exist*, but only one *obtains.* And God has not created either one of them since there never was a time at which either did not exist. Nor has He created the state of affairs consisting in the earth's existence; there was a time when *the earth* did not exist, but none when the state of affairs consisting in the earth's existence didn't exist. Indeed, God did not bring into existence any states of affairs at all. What He did was to perform actions of a certain sort—creating the heavens and the earth, for example—which resulted in the *actuality* of certain states of affairs. God *actualizes* states of affairs. He actualizes the possible world that does in fact obtain; He does not create it. And while He has created Socrates, He did not create the state of affairs consisting in Socrates' existence.[13]

Bearing this in mind, let's finally return to our question. Is the atheologian right in holding that if God is omnipotent, then he could have actualized or created any possible world He pleased? Not obviously. First, we must ask ourselves whether God is a *necessary* or a *contingent* being. A *necessary* being is one that exists in every possible world—one that would have existed no matter which possible world had been actual; a contingent being exists only in some possible worlds. Now if God is not a necessary being (and many, perhaps most, theists think that He is not), then clearly enough there will be many possible worlds He could not have actualized—all those, for example, in which He does not exist. Clearly, God could not have created a world in which He doesn't even exist.

So, if God is a contingent being then there are many possible worlds beyond His power to create. But this is really irrelevant to our present concerns. For perhaps the atheologian can maintain his case if he revises his claim to avoid this difficulty; perhaps he will say something like this: if God is omnipotent, then He could have actualized any of those possible worlds *in which He exists.* So if He exists and is omnipotent, He could have actualized (contrary to the Free Will Defense) any of those possible worlds in which He exists and in which there exist free creatures who do no wrong. He could have actualized worlds containing moral good but no moral evil. Is this correct?

Let's begin with a trivial example. You and Paul have just returned from an Australian hunting expedition: your quarry was the elusive double-wattled cassowary. Paul captured an aardvark, mistaking it for a cassowary. The creature's disarming ways have won it a place in Paul's heart; he is deeply attached to it. Upon your return to the States you offer Paul $500 for his aardvark, only to be rudely turned down. Later you ask yourself, "What would he have done if I'd offered him $700?" Now what is it, exactly, that you are asking? What you're really asking in a way is whether, under a *specific set of conditions,* Paul would have sold it. These conditions include your having offered him $700 rather than $500 for the aardvark, everything else being as much as possible like the conditions that did in fact obtain. Let S' be this set of conditions or state of affairs. S' includes the state of affairs consisting in your offering Paul $700 (instead of the $500 you did offer him); of course it does not include his *accepting* your offer, and it does not include his *rejecting* it; for the rest, the conditions it includes are just like the ones that did obtain in the actual world. So, for example, S' includes Paul's being free to accept the offer and free to refrain; and if in fact the going rate for an aardvark was $650, then S' includes the state of affairs consisting in the going rate's being $650. So we might put your question by asking which of the following conditionals is true:

(23) If the state of affairs S' had obtained, Paul would have accepted the offer

(24) If the state of affairs S' had obtained, Paul would not have accepted the offer.

It seems clear that at least one of these conditionals is true, but naturally they can't both be; so exactly one is.

Now since S' includes neither Paul's accepting the offer nor his rejecting it, the antecedent of (23) and (24) does not entail the consequent of either. That is,

(25) S' obtains

does not entail either

(26) Paul accepts the offer

or

(27) Paul does not accept the offer.

So there are possible worlds in which both (25) and (26) are true, and other possible worlds in which both (25) and (27) are true.

We are now in a position to grasp an important fact. Either (23) or (24) is in fact true; and either way there are possible worlds God could not have actualized. Suppose, first of all, that (23) is true. Then it was beyond the power of God to create a world in which (1) Paul is free to sell his aardvark and free to refrain, and in which the other states of affairs included in S' obtain, and (2) Paul does not sell. That is, it was beyond His power to create a world in which (25) and (27) are both true. There is at least one possible world like this, but God, despite His omnipotence, could not have brought about its actuality. For let W be such a world. To actualize W, God must bring it about that Paul is free with respect to this action, and that the other states of affairs included in S' obtain. But (23), as we are supposing, is true; so if God had actualized S' and left Paul *free* with respect to this action, he would have sold: in which case W would not have been actual. If, on the other hand, God had *brought it about* that Paul didn't sell or had *caused him* to refrain from selling, then Paul would not have been free with respect to this action; then S' would not have been actual (since S' includes Paul's being free with respect to it), and W would not have been actual since W includes S'.

Of course if it is (24) rather than (23) that is true, then another class of worlds was beyond God's power to actualize—those, namely, in which S' obtains and Paul *sells* his aardvark. These are the worlds in which both (25) and (26) are true. But either (23) or (24) is true. Therefore, there are possible worlds God could not have actualized. If we consider whether or not God could have created a world in which, let's say, both (25) and (26) are true, we see that the answer depends upon a peculiar kind of fact; it depends upon what Paul would have freely chosen to do in a certain situation. So there are any number of possible worlds such that it is partly up to Paul whether God can create them.[14]

That was a past tense example. Perhaps it would be useful to consider a future tense case, since this might seem to correspond more closely to God's situation in choosing a possible world to actualize. At some time t in the near future Maurice will be free with respect to some insignificant action—having freeze-dried oatmeal for breakfast, let's say. That is, at time t Maurice will be free to have oatmeal but also free to take something else—shredded wheat, perhaps. Next, suppose we consider S', a state of affairs that is included in the actual world and includes Maurice's being free with respect to taking oatmeal at time t. That is, S' includes Maurice's being free at time t to take oatmeal and free to reject it. S' does not include Maurice's taking oatmeal, however; nor does it include his rejecting it. For the rest S' is as much as possible like the actual world. In particular there are many conditions that do in fact hold at time t and are *relevant* to his choice—such conditions, for example, as the fact that he hasn't had oatmeal lately, that his wife will be annoyed if he rejects it, and the like; and S' includes each of these conditions. Now God no doubt knows what Maurice will do at time t, if S obtains; He knows which action Maurice would freely perform if S were to be actual. That is, God knows that one of the following conditionals is true:

(28) If S' were to obtain, Maurice will freely take the oatmeal

or

(29) If S' were to obtain, Maurice will freely reject it.

We may not know which of these is true, and Maurice himself may not know; but presumably God does.

So either God knows that (28) is true, or else He knows that (29) is. Let's suppose it is (28). Then there is a possible world that God, though omnipotent, cannot create. For consider a possible world W' that shares S' with the actual world (which for ease of reference I'll name "Kronos") and in which Maurice does *not* take oatmeal. (We know there *is* such a world, since S' does not include Maurice's taking the oatmeal.) S' obtains in W' just as it does in Kronos. Indeed, everything in W' is just as it is in Kronos up to time t. But whereas in Kronos Maurice takes oatmeal at time t, in W' he does not. Now W' is a perfectly possible world; but it is not within God's power to create it or bring about its actuality. For to do so He must actualize S'. But (28) is in fact true. So if God actualizes S' (as He must to create W') and leaves Maurice free with respect to the action in question, then he will take the oatmeal; and then, of course, W' will not be actual. If, on the other hand, God causes Maurice to *refrain* from taking the oatmeal, then he is not *free* to take it. That means, once again, that W' is not actual; for in W' Maurice is free to take the oatmeal (even if he doesn't do so). So if (28) is true, then this world W' is one that God can't actualize, it is not within His power to actualize it even though He is omnipotent and it is a possible world.

Or course, if it is (29) that is true, we get a similar result; then too there are possible worlds that God can't actualize. These would be worlds which share S' with Kronos and in which Maurice *does* take oatmeal. But either (28) or (29) *is* true; so either way there is a possible world that God can't create. If we consider a world in which S' obtains and in which Maurice freely chooses oatmeal at time t, we see that whether or not it is within God's power to actualize it depends upon what Maurice would do if he were free in a certain situation. Accordingly, there are any number of possible worlds such that it is partly up to Maurice whether or not God can actualize them. It is, of course, up to God whether or not to create Maurice and also up to God whether or not to make him free with respect to the action of taking oatmeal at time *t*. (God could, if He chose, cause him to succumb to the dreaded *equine obsession*, a condition shared by some people and most horses, whose victims find it *psychologically impossible* to refuse oats or oat products.) But if He creates Maurice and creates him free with respect to this action, then whether or not he actually performs the action is up to Maurice—not God.[15]

Now we can return to the Free Will Defense and the problem of evil. The Free Will Defender, you recall, insists on the possibility that it is not within God's power to create a world containing moral good without creating one containing moral evil. His atheological opponent—Mackie, for example—agrees with Leibniz in insisting that *if* (as the theist holds) God is omnipotent, then it *follows* that He could have created any possible world He pleased. We now see that this contention—call it "Leibniz' Lapse"—is a mistake. The atheologian is right in holding that there are many possible worlds containing moral good but no moral evil; his mistake lies in endorsing Leibniz' Lapse. So one of his premises—that God, if omnipotent, could have actualized just any world He pleased—is false.

COULD GOD HAVE CREATED A WORLD CONTAINING MORAL GOOD BUT NO MORAL EVIL?

Now suppose we recapitulate the logic of the situation. The Free Will Defender claims that the following is possible:

> (30) God is omnipotent, and it was not within His power to create a world containing moral good but no moral evil.

By way of retort the atheologian insists that there are possible worlds containing moral good but no moral evil. He adds that an omnipotent being could have actualized any possible world he chose. So if God is omnipotent, it follows that He could have actualized a world containing moral good but no moral evil, hence (30), contrary to the Free Will Defender's claim, is not possible. What we have seen so far is that his second premise—Leibniz' Lapse—is false.

Of course, this does not settle the issue in the Free Will Defender's favor. Leibniz' Lapse (appropriately enough for a lapse) is false; but this doesn't show that (30) is possible. To show this latter we must demonstrate the possibility that among the worlds God could not have actualized are all the worlds containing moral good but no moral evil. How can we approach this question?

Instead of choosing oatmeal for breakfast or selling an aardvark, suppose we think about a morally significant action such as taking a bribe. Curley Smith, the mayor of Boston, is opposed to the proposed freeway route; it would require destruction of the Old North Church along with some other antiquated and structurally unsound buildings. L. B. Smedes, the director of highways, asks him whether he'd drop his opposition for $1 million. "Of course," he replies. "Would you do it for $2?" asks Smedes. "What do you take me for?" comes the indignant reply. "That's already established," smirks Smedes; "all that remains is to nail down your price." Smedes then offers him a bribe of $35,000; unwilling to break with the fine old traditions of Bay State politics, Curley accepts. Smedes then spends a sleepless night wondering whether he could have bought Curley for $20,000.

Now suppose we assume that Curley was free with respect to the action of taking the bribe—free to take it and free to refuse. And suppose, furthermore, that he would have taken it. That is, let us suppose that

(31) If Smedes had offered Curley a bribe of $20,000, he would have accepted it.

If (31) is true, then there is a state of affairs S' that (1) includes Curley's being offered a bribe of $20,000; (2) does not include either his accepting the bribe or his rejecting it; and (3) is otherwise as much as possible like the actual world. Just to make sure S' includes every relevant circumstance, let us suppose that it is a *maximal world segment*. That is, add to S' any state of affairs compatible with but not included in it, and the result will be an entire possible world. We could think of it roughly like this: S' is included in at least one world W in which Curley takes the bribe and in at least one world W' in which he rejects it. If S' is a maximal world segment, then S' is what remains of W when *Curley's taking the bribe* is deleted; it is also what remains of W' when *Curley's rejecting the bribe* is detected. More exactly, if S' is a maximal world segment, then every possible state of affairs that includes S', but isn't included by S', is a possible world. So if (31) is true, then there is a maximal world segment S' that (1) includes Curley's being offered a bribe of $20,000; (2) does not include either his accepting the bribe or his rejecting it; (3) is otherwise as much as possible like the actual world—in particular, it includes Curley's being free with respect to the bribe; and (4) is such that if it were actual then Curley would have taken the bribe. That is,

(32) if S' were actual, Curley would have accepted the bribe is true.

Now, of course, there is at least one possible world W' in which S' is actual and Curley does not take the bribe. But God could not have created W'; to do so, He would have been obliged to actualize S', leaving Curley free with respect to the action of taking the bribe. But under these conditions Curley, as (32) assures us, would have accepted the bribe, so that the world thus created would not have been S'.

Curley, as we see, is not above a bit of Watergating. But there may be worse to come. Of course, there are possible worlds in which he is significantly free (i.e., free with respect to a morally significant action) and never does what is wrong. But the sad truth about Curley may be this. Consider W', any of these worlds: in W' Curley is significantly free, so in W' there are some actions that are morally significant for him and with respect to which he is free. But at least one of these actions—call it *A*—has the following peculiar property. There is a maximal world segment *S′* that obtains in *W′* and is such that (1) *S′* includes Curley's being free *re A* but neither his performing *A* nor his refraining from *A*; (2) *S′* is otherwise as much as possible like *W′*; and (3) if *S′* had been actual, Curley would have gone wrong with respect to *A*.[16] (Notice that this third condition holds in fact, in the actual world; it does not hold in that world *W′*.)

This means, of course, that God could not have actualized *W′*. For to do so He'd have been obliged to bring it about that *S′* is actual; but then Curley would go wrong with respect to *A*. Since in *W′* he always does what is right, the world thus actualized would not be *W′*. On the other hand, if God *causes* Curley to go right with respect to *A* or *brings it about that* he does so, then Curley isn't free with respect to *A*; and so once more it isn't *W′* that is actual. Accordingly God cannot create *W′*. But *W′* was just any of the worlds in which Curley is significantly free but always does only what is right. It therefore follows that it was not within God's power to create a world in which Curley produces moral good but no moral evil. Every world God can actualize is such that if Curley is significantly free in it, he takes at least one wrong action.

Obviously Curley is in serious trouble. I shall call the malady from which he suffers *transworld depravity*. (I leave as homework the problem of comparing transworld depravity with what Calvinists call "total depravity.") By way of explicit definition:

(33) A person *P suffers from transworld depravity* if and only if the following holds: for every world *W* such that *P* is significantly free in *W* and *P* does only what is right in *W*, there is an action *A* and a maximal world segment *S′* such that

(1) *S′* includes *A*'s being morally significant for *P*

(2) *S′* includes *P*'s being free with respect to *A*

(3) *S′* is included in *W* and includes neither *P*'s performing *A* nor *P*'s refraining from performing *A*

and

(4) If *S′* were actual, *P* would go wrong with respect to *A*.

(In thinking about this definition, remember that (4) is to be true in fact, in the actual world—not in that world *W*.)

What is important about the idea of transworld depravity is that if a person suffers from it, then it wasn't within God's power to actualize any world in which that person is significantly free but does no wrong—that is, a world in which he produces moral good but no moral evil.

We have been here considering a crucial contention of the Free Will Defender: the contention, namely, that

(30) God is omnipotent, and it was not within His power to create a world containing moral good but no moral evil.

How is transworld depravity relevant to this? As follows. Obviously it is possible that there be persons who suffer from transworld depravity. More generally, it is possible that *everybody* suffers from it. And if this possibility were actual, then God, though omnipotent, could not have created any of the possible worlds containing just the persons who do in fact exist, and containing moral good but no moral evil. For to do so He'd have to create persons who were significantly free (otherwise there would be no moral good) but suffered from transworld depravity. Such persons go wrong with respect to at least one action in any world God could have actualized and in which they are free with respect to morally significant actions; so the price for creating a world in which they produce moral good is creating one in which they also produce moral evil.

NOTES

1. John Mackie, "Evil and Omnipotence," in *The Philosophy of Religion*, ed. Basil Mitchell (London: Oxford University Press, 1971), p. 92.

2. Ibid., pp. 92–93.

3. Ibid., p. 93.

4. More simply the question is really just whether any good state of affairs includes an evil; a little reflection reveals that no good state of affairs can include an evil that it does *not* outweigh.

5. In Plantinga, *God and Other Minds* (Ithaca, NY: Cornell University Press, 1967), chap. 5, I explore further the project of finding such propositions.

6. *The Problem of Free Choice*, vol. 22 of *Ancient Christian Writers* (Westminster, MD: Newman Press, 1955), bk. 2, pp. 14–15.

7. Ibid., bk. 3, p. 9.

8. I am indebted to Henry Schuurman (in conversation) for helpful discussion of the difference between this pastoral function and those served by a theodicy or a defense.

9. This distinction is not very precise (how, exactly, are we to construe "results from"?), but perhaps it will serve our present purposes.

10. See, for example, A. Flew, "Divine Omnipotence and Human Freedom," in *New Essays in Philosophical Theology*, eds. A. Flew and A. MacIntyre (London: SCM, 1955), pp. 150–153.

11. For further discussion of it see Plantinga, *God and Other Minds*, pp. 132–135.

12. Mackie, in *The Philosophy of Religion*, pp. 100–101.

13. Strict accuracy demands, therefore, that we speak of God as *actualizing* rather than creating possible worlds. I shall continue to use both locutions, thus sacrificing accuracy to familiarity. For more about possible worlds see my book *The Nature of Necessity* (Oxford: The Clarendon Press, 1974), chaps. 4–8.

14. For a fuller statement of this argument see Plantinga, *The Nature of Necessity*, chap. 9, secs. 4–6.

15. For a more complete and more exact statement of this argument see Plantinga, *The Nature of Necessity*, chap. 9, secs. 4–6.

16. A person goes wrong with respect to an action if he either wrongfully performs it or wrongfully fails to perform it.

JOHN HICK

Soul-Making Theodicy

In the following piece, John Hick (1922–) offers a theodicy—that is, a justification of the ways of God in light of evil in the world. In contrast to the Augustinian type of theodicy, which sees present evil as representing a fall from a pristine, original state of the world, Hick develops a theodicy following Irenaeus, a bishop of the ancient church. The major theme here is not one of causal genesis, but of progress and development. Rather than view the present condition of the world as fallen from a kind of perfection, Hick views the world as a necessary stage in the evolution of a relatively immature creation into a more mature state. God seeks to bring forth mature moral and spiritual beings who are capable of freely exercising faith in him and love toward their fellows. Hick discusses the main features of an environment that would be conducive to bringing about these results, such as the world's not making it clear whether God exists and our being mutually vulnerable to one another. Also, Hick believes that the divine program of soul-making will culminate in the afterlife, which Hick believes must involve "universal salvation."

⌘

Can a world in which sadistic cruelty often has its way, in which selfish lovelessness is so rife, in which there are debilitating diseases, crippling accidents, bodily and mental decay, insanity, and all manner of natural disasters be regarded as the expression of infinite creative goodness? Certainly all this could never by itself lead anyone to believe in the existence of a limitlessly powerful God. And yet even in a world which contains these things innumerable men and women have believed and do believe in the reality of an infinite creative goodness, which they call God. The theodicy project starts at this point, with an already operating belief in God, embodied in human living, and attempts to show that this belief is not rendered irrational by the fact of evil. It attempts to explain how it is that the universe, assumed to be created and ultimately ruled by a limitlessly good and limitlessly powerful Being, is as it is, including all the pain and suffering and all the wickedness and folly that we find around us and within us. The theodicy project is thus an exercise in metaphysical construction, in the sense that it consists in the formation and criticism of large-scale hypotheses concerning the nature and process of the universe.

Since a theodicy both starts from and tests belief in the reality of God, it naturally takes different forms in relation to different concepts of God. In this essay I shall be discussing the project of a specifically Christian theodicy;

I shall not be attempting the further and even more difficult work of comparative theodicy, leading in turn to the question of a global theodicy.

The two main demands upon a theodicy hypothesis are (1) that it be internally coherent, and (2) that it be consistent with the data both of the religious tradition on which it is based, and of the world, in respect both of the latter's general character as revealed by scientific enquiry and of the specific facts of moral and natural evil. These two criteria demand, respectively, possibility and plausibility.

Traditionally, Christian theology has centered upon the concept of God as both limitlessly powerful and limitlessly good and loving; and it is this concept of deity that gives rise to the problem of evil as a threat to theistic faith. The threat was definitively expressed in Stendhal's bombshell, "The only excuse for God is that he does not exist!" The theodicy project is the attempt to offer a different view of the universe which is both possible and plausible and which does not ignite Stendhal's bombshell.

Christian thought has always included a certain range of variety, and in the area of theodicy it offers two broad types of approach. The Augustinian approach, representing until fairly recently the majority report of the Christian mind, hinges upon the idea of the fall, which has in turn brought about the disharmony of nature. This type of theodicy is developed today as "the free will defense." The Irenaean approach, representing in the past a minority report, hinges upon the creation of humankind through the evolutionary process as an immature creature living in a challenging and therefore person-making world. I shall indicate very briefly why I do not find the first type of theodicy satisfactory, and then spend the remainder of this essay in exploring the second type.

In recent years the philosophical discussion of the problem of evil has been dominated by the free-will defense. A major effort has been made by Alvin Plantinga and a number of other Christian philosophers to show that it is logically possible that a limitlessly powerful and limitlessly good God is responsible for the existence of this world. For all evil may ultimately be due to misuses of creaturely freedom. But it may nevertheless be better for God to have created free than unfree beings; and it is logically possible that any and all free beings whom God might create would, as a matter of contingent fact, misuse their freedom by falling into sin. In that case it would be logically impossible for God to have created a world containing free beings and yet not containing sin and the suffering which sin brings with it. Thus it is logically possible, despite the fact of evil, that the existing universe is the work of a limitlessly good creator.

These writers are in effect arguing that the traditional Augustinian type of theodicy, based upon the fall from grace of free finite creatures—first angels and then human beings—and a consequent going wrong of the physical world, is not logically impossible. I am in fact doubtful whether their argument is sound, and will return to the question later. But even if it should be sound, I suggest that their argument wins only a Pyrrhic victory, since the logical possibility that it would establish is one which, for very many people today, is fatally lacking in plausibility. For most educated inhabitants of the modern world regard the biblical story of Adam and Eve, and their temptation by the devil, as myth rather than as history; and they believe that so far from having been created finitely perfect and then falling, humanity evolved out of lower forms of life, emerging in a morally, spiritually, and culturally primitive state. Further, they reject as incredible the idea that earthquake and flood, disease, decay, and death are consequences either of a human fall, or of a prior fall of angelic beings who are now exerting an evil influence upon the earth. They see all this as part of a pre-scientific world view, along with the stories of the world having been created in six days and of the sun standing still for twenty-four hours at Joshua's command. One cannot, strictly speaking, disprove any of these ancient biblical myths and sagas, or refute their confident elaboration in the medieval Christian picture of the universe. But those of us for whom the resulting theodicy, even if logically possible, is radically implausible, must look elsewhere for light on the problem of evil.

I believe that we find the light that we need in the main alternative strand of Christian thinking, which goes back to important constructive suggestions by the early Hellenistic Fathers of the Church, particularly St. Irenaeus (A.D. 120–202). Irenaeus himself did not develop a theodicy, but he did—together with other Greek-speaking Christian writers of that period, such as Clement of Alexandria—build a framework of thought within which a theodicy became possible which does not depend upon the idea of the fall, and which is consonant with modern knowledge concerning the origins of the human race. This theodicy cannot, as such, be attributed to Irenaeus. We should rather speak of a type of theodicy, presented in varying ways by different subsequent thinkers (the greatest of whom has been Friedrich Schleiermacher), of which Irenaeus can properly be regarded as the patron saint.

The central theme out of which this Irenaean type of theodicy has arisen is the two-stage conception of the creation of humankind, first in the "image" and then in the "likeness" of God. Re-expressing this in modern terms, the first stage was the gradual production of *homo sapiens*, through the long evolutionary process, as intelligent ethical and religious animals. The human being is an animal, one of the varied forms of earthly life and continuous as such with the whole realm of animal existence. But the human being is uniquely intelligent, having evolved a large and immensely complex brain. Further, the human being is ethical—that is, a gregarious as well as an intelligent animal, able to realize and respond to the complex demands of social life. And the human being is a religious animal, with an innate tendency to experience the world in terms of the presence and activity of supernatural beings and powers. This then is early *homo sapiens*, the intelligent social animal capable of awareness of the divine. But early *homo sapiens* is not the Adam and Eve of Augustinian theology, living in perfect harmony with self, with nature, and with God. On the contrary, the life of this being must have been a constant struggle against a hostile environment, and capable of savage violence against one's fellow human beings, particularly outside one's own immediate group; and this being's concepts of the divine were primitive and often bloodthirsty. Thus existence "in the image of God" was a potentiality for knowledge of and relationship with one's Maker rather than such knowledge and relationship as a fully realized state. In other words, people were created as spiritually and morally immature creatures, at the beginning of a long process of further growth and development, which constitutes the second stage of God's creative work. In this second stage, of which we are a part, the intelligent, ethical, and religious animal is being brought through one's own free responses into what Irenaeus called the divine "likeness." The human animal is being created into a child of God. Irenaeus' own terminology (*eikon, homoiosis; imago, similitudo*) has no particular merit, based as it is on a misunderstanding of the Hebrew parallelism in Genesis 1:26; but his conception of a two-stage creation of the human, with perfection lying in the future rather than in the past, is of fundamental importance. The notion of the fall was not basic to this picture, although it was to become basic to the great drama of salvation depicted by St. Augustine and accepted within western Christendom, including the churches stemming from the Reformation, until well into the nineteenth century. Irenaeus himself however could not, in the historical knowledge of his time, question the fact of the fall; though he treated it as a relatively minor lapse, a youthful error, rather than as the infinite crime and cosmic disaster which has ruined the whole creation. But today we can acknowledge that there is no evidence at all of a period in the distant past when humankind was in the ideal state of a fully realized "child of God." We can accept that, so far as actual events in time are concerned, there never was a fall from an original righteousness and grace. If we want to continue to use the term fall, because of its hallowed place in the Christian tradition, we must use it to refer to the immense gap between what we actually are and what in the divine intention is eventually to be. But we must not blur our awareness that the ideal state is not something already enjoyed and lost, but is a future and as yet unrealized goal. The reality is not a perfect creation which has gone tragically wrong, but a still continuing creative process whose completion lies in the eschaton.

Let us now try to formulate a contemporary version of the Irenaean type of theodicy, based on this suggestion of the initial creation of humankind, not as a finitely perfect, but as an immature creature at the beginning of a long process of further growth and development. We may begin by asking why one should have been created as an imperfect and developing creature rather than as the perfect being whom God is presumably intending to create? The answer, I think, consists in two considerations which converge in their practical implications, one concerned with the human's relationship to God and the other with the relationship to other human beings. As to the first, we could have the picture of God creating finite beings, whether angels or persons, directly in God's own presence, so that in being conscious of that which is other than one's self the creature is automatically conscious of God, the limitless divine reality and power, goodness and love, knowledge and wisdom, towering above one's self. In such a situation the disproportion between Creator and creatures would be so great that the latter would have no freedom in relation to God; they would indeed not exist as independent autonomous persons. For what freedom could finite beings have in an immediate consciousness of the presence of the one who has created them, who knows them through and through, who is limitlessly powerful as well as limitlessly loving and good, and who claims their total obedience? In order to be a person, exercising some measure of genuine freedom, the creature must be brought into existence, not in the immediate divine presence, but at a "distance" from God. This "distance" cannot of course be spatial; for God is omnipresent. It must be an epistemic distance, a distance in the cognitive dimension. And the Irenaean hypothesis is that this "distance" consists, in the case of humans, in their existence within and as part of a world which functions as an autonomous system and from within which God is not overwhelmingly evident. It is a world, in Bonhoeffer's phrase, *etsi deus non daretur,* as if there were no God. Or rather, it is religiously ambiguous, capable both of being seen as a purely natural phenomenon and of being seen as God's creation and experienced as mediating God's presence. In such a world one can exist as a person over against the Creator. One has space to exist as a finite being, a space created by the epistemic distance from God and protected by one's basic cognitive freedom, one's freedom to open or close oneself to the dawning awareness of God which is experienced naturally by a religious animal. This Irenaean picture corresponds, I suggest, to our actual human situation. Emerging within the evolutionary process as part of the continuum of animal life, in a universe which functions in accordance with its own laws and whose workings can be investigated and described without reference to a creator, the human being has a genuine, even awesome, freedom in relation to one's Maker. The human being is free to acknowledge and worship God; and is free—particularly since the emergence of human individuality and the beginnings of critical consciousness during the first millennium B.C.—to doubt the reality of God.

Within such a situation there is the possibility of the human being coming freely to know and love one's Maker. Indeed, if the end state which God is seeking to bring about is one in which finite persons have come in their own freedom to know and love God, this requires creating them initially in a state which is not that of their already knowing and loving God. For it is logically impossible to create beings already in a state of having come into that state by their own free choices.

The other consideration, which converges with this in pointing to something like the human situation as we experience it, concerns our human moral nature. We can approach it by asking why humans should not have been created at this epistemic distance from God, and yet at the same time as morally perfect beings? That persons could have been created morally perfect and yet free, so that they would always in fact choose rightly, has been argued by such critics of the free-will defense in theodicy as Antony Flew and J. L. Mackie, and argued against by Alvin Plantinga and other upholders of that form of theodicy. On the specific issue defined in the debate between them, it appears to me that the criticism of the free-will defense stands. It appears to me that a perfectly good being, although formally free to sin, would in fact never do so. If we imagine such a being in a morally frictionless environment, involving no stresses or temptation, then we must assume that one would exemplify the ethical equivalent of Newton's first law of motion, which states that a moving body will continue in uniform motion until interfered with by some outside force. By analogy, a perfectly good being would continue in the same moral course forever, there being nothing in the environment to throw one off it. But even if we suppose the morally perfect being to exist in an imperfect world, in which one is subject to temptations, it still follows that, in virtue of moral perfection, one will always overcome those temptations—as in the case, according to orthodox Christian belief, of Jesus Christ. It is, to be sure, logically possible, as Plantinga and others argue, that a free being, simply as such, may at any time contingently decide to sin. However, a responsible free being does not act randomly, but on the basis of moral nature. And a free being whose nature is wholly and unqualifiedly good will accordingly never in fact sin.

But if God could, without logical contradiction, have created humans as wholly good free beings, why did God not do so? Why was humanity not initially created in possession of all the virtues, instead of having to acquire them through the long hard struggle of life as we know it? The answer, I suggest, appeals to the principle that virtues which have been formed within the agent as a hard-won deposit of her own right decisions in situations of challenge and temptation, are intrinsically more valuable than virtues created within her ready made and without any effort on her own part. This principle expresses a basic value judgment, which cannot be established by argument but which one can only present, in the hope that it will be as morally plausible, and indeed compelling, to others as to oneself. It is, to repeat, the judgment that a moral goodness which exists as the agent's initial given nature, without ever having been chosen by her in the face of temptations to the contrary, is intrinsically less valuable than a moral goodness which has been built up through the agent's own responsible choices through time in the face of alternative possibilities.

If, then, God's purpose was to create finite persons embodying the most valuable kind of moral goodness, God would have to create them, not as already perfect beings but rather as imperfect creatures who can then attain to the more valuable kind of goodness through their own free choices as in the course of their personal and social history new responses prompt new insights, opening up new moral possibilities, and providing a milieu in which the most valuable kind of moral nature can be developed.

We have thus far, then, the hypothesis that one is created at an epistemic distance from God in order to come freely to know and love the Maker; and that one is at the same time created as a morally immature and imperfect being in order to attain through freedom the most valuable quality of goodness. The end sought, according to this hypothesis, is the full realization of the human potentialities in a unitary spiritual and moral perfection in the divine kingdom. And the question we have to ask is whether humans as we know them, and the world as we know it, are compatible with this hypothesis.

Clearly we cannot expect to be able to deduce our actual world in its concrete character, and our actual human nature as part of it, from the general concept of spiritually and morally immature creatures developing ethically in an appropriate environment. No doubt there is an immense range of possible worlds, any one of which, if actualized, would exemplify this concept. All that we can hope to do is to show that our actual world is one of these. And when we look at our human situation as part of the evolving life of this planet we can, I think, see that it fits this specification. As animal organisms, integral to the whole ecology of life, we are programmed for survival. In pursuit of survival, primitives not only killed other animals for food but fought other human beings when their vital interests conflicted. The life of prehistoric persons must indeed have been a constant struggle to stay alive, prolonging an existence which was, in Hobbes' phrase, "poor, nasty, brutish and short." And in his basic animal self-regardingness humankind was, and is, morally imperfect. In saying this I am assuming that the essence of moral evil is selfishness, the sacrificing of others to one's own interests. It consists, in Kantian terminology, in treating others, not as ends in themselves, but as means to one's own ends. This is what the survival instinct demands. And yet we are also capable of love, of self-giving in a common cause, of a conscience which responds to others in their needs and dangers. And with the development of civilization we see the growth of moral insight, the glimpsing and gradual assimilation of higher ideals, and tension between our animality and our ethical values. But that the human being has a lower as well as a higher nature, that one is an animal as well as a potential child of God, and that one's moral goodness is won from a struggle with one's own innate selfishness, is inevitable given one's continuity with the other forms of animal life. Further, the human animal is not responsible for having come into existence as an animal. The ultimate responsibility for humankind's existence, as a morally imperfect creature, can only rest with the Creator. The human does not, in one's own degree of freedom and responsibility, choose one's origin, but rather one's destiny.

This then, in brief outline, is the answer of the Irenaean type of theodicy to the question of the origin of moral evil: the general fact of humankind's basic self-regarding animality is an aspect of creation as part of the realm of organic life; and this basic self-regardingness has been expressed over the centuries both in sins of individual selfishness and in the much more massive sins of corporate selfishness, institutionalized in slavery and exploitation and all the many and complex forms of social injustice.

But nevertheless our sinful nature in a sinful world is the matrix within which God is gradually creating children of God out of human animals. For it is as men and women freely respond to the claim of God upon their lives, transmuting their animality into the structure of divine worship, that the creation of humanity is taking place. And in its concrete character this response consists in every form of moral goodness, from unselfish love in individual personal relationships to the dedicated and selfless striving to end exploitation and to create justice within and between societies.

But one cannot discuss moral evil without at the same time discussing the non-moral evil of pain and suffering. (I propose to mean by "pain" physical pain, including the pains of hunger and thirst; and by "suffering" the mental and emotional pain of loneliness, anxiety, remorse, lack of love, fear, grief, envy, etc.) For what constitutes moral evil as evil is the fact that it causes pain and suffering. It is impossible to conceive of an instance of moral evil, or sin, which is not productive of pain or suffering to anyone at any time. But in addition to moral evil there is another source of pain and suffering in the structure of the physical world, which produces storms, earthquakes, and floods and which afflicts the human body with diseases—cholera, epilepsy, cancer, malaria, arthritis, rickets, meningitis, etc.—as well as with broken bones and other outcomes of physical accident. It is true that a great deal both of pain and of suffering is humanly caused, not only by the 'inhumanity of man to man' but also by the stresses of our individual and corporate lifestyles, causing many disorders—not only lung cancer and cirrhosis of the liver but many cases of heart disease, stomach and other ulcers, strokes, etc.—as well as accidents. But there remain nevertheless, in the natural world itself, permanent causes of human pain and suffering. And we have to ask why an unlimitedly good and unlimitedly powerful God should have created so dangerous a world, both as regards its purely natural hazards of earthquake and flood, etc., and as regards the liability of the human body to so many ills, both psychosomatic and purely somatic.

The answer offered by the Irenaean type of theodicy follows from and is indeed integrally bound up with its account of the origin of moral evil. We have the hypothesis of humankind being brought into being within the evolutionary process as a spiritually and morally immature creature, and then growing and developing through the exercise of freedom in this religiously ambiguous world. We can now ask what sort of a world would constitute an appropriate environment for this second stage of creation? The development of human personality—moral, spiritual, and intellectual—is a product of challenge and response. It does not occur in a static situation demanding no exertion and no choices. So far as intellectual development is concerned, this is a well-established principle which underlies the whole modern educational process, from preschool nurseries designed to provide a rich and stimulating environment, to all forms of higher education designed to challenge the intellect. At a basic level the essential part played in learning by the learner's own active response to environment was strikingly demonstrated by the Held and Heim experiment with kittens.[1] Of two littermate kittens in the same artificial environment one was free to exercise its own freedom and intelligence in exploring the environment, while the other was suspended in a kind of "gondola" which moved whenever and wherever the free kitten moved. Thus the second kitten had a similar succession of visual experiences as the first, but did not exert itself or make any choices in obtaining them. And whereas the first kitten learned in the normal way to conduct itself safely within its environment, the second did not. With no interaction with a challenging environment there was no development in its behavioral patterns. And I think we can safely say that the intellectual development of humanity has been due to interaction with an objective environment functioning in accordance with its own laws, an environment which we have had actively to explore and to cooperate with in order to escape its perils and exploit its benefits. In a world devoid both of dangers to be avoided and rewards to be won we may assume that there would have been virtually no development of the human intellect and imagination, and hence of either the sciences or the arts, and hence of human civilization or culture.

The fact of an objective world within which one has to learn to live, on penalty of pain or death, is also basic to the development of one's moral nature. For it is because the world is one in which men and women can suffer harm—by violence, disease, accident, starvation, etc.—that our actions affecting one another have moral significance. A morally wrong act is, basically, one which harms some part of the human community; while a morally right action is, on the contrary, one which prevents or neutralizes harm or which preserves or increases human well being. Now we can imagine a paradise in which no one can ever come to any harm. It could be a world which, instead of having its own fixed structure, would be plastic to human wishes. Or it could be a world with a fixed structure, and hence the possibility of damage and pain, but whose structure is suspended or adjusted by special divine action whenever necessary to avoid human pain. Thus, for example, in such a miraculously pain-free world one who falls accidentally off a high building would presumably float unharmed to the ground; bullets would become insubstantial when fired at a human body; poisons would cease to poison; water to drown, and so on. We can at least begin to imagine such a world. And a good deal of the older discussion of the problem of evil—for example in Part xi of Hume's *Dialogues Concerning Natural Religion*—assumed that it must be the intention of a limitlessly good and powerful Creator to make for human creatures a pain-free environment; so that the very existence of pain is evidence against the existence of God. But such an assumption overlooks the fact that a world in which there can be no pain or suffering would also be one in which there can be no moral choices and hence no possibility of moral growth and development. For in a situation in which no one can ever suffer injury or be liable to pain or suffering there would be no distinction between right and wrong action. No action would be morally wrong, because no action could have harmful consequences; and likewise no action would be morally right in contrast to wrong. Whatever the values of such a world, it clearly could not serve a purpose of the development of its inhabitants from self-regarding animality to self-giving love.

Thus the hypothesis of a divine purpose in which finite persons are created at an epistemic distance from God, in order that they may gradually become children of God through their own moral and spiritual choices, requires that their environment, instead of being a pain-free and stress-free paradise, be broadly the kind of world of which we find ourselves to be a part. It requires that it be such as to provoke the theological problem of evil. For it requires that it be an environment which offers challenges to be met, problems to be solved, dangers to be faced, and which accordingly involves real possibilities of hardship, disaster, failure, defeat, and misery as well as of delight and happiness, success, triumph and achievement. For it is by grappling with the real problems of a real environment, in which a person is one form of life among many, and which is not designed to minister exclusively to one's well-being, that one can develop in intelligence and in such qualities as courage and determination. And it is in the relationships of human beings with one another, in the context of this struggle to survive and flourish, that they can develop the higher values of mutual love and care, of self-sacrifice for others, and of commitment to a common good.

To summarize thus far:

(1) The divine intention in relation to humankind, according to our hypothesis, is to create perfect finite personal beings in filial relationship with their Maker.

(2) It is logically impossible for humans to be created already in this perfect state, because in its spiritual aspect it involves coming freely to an uncoerced consciousness of God from a situation of epistemic distance, and in its moral aspect, freely choosing the good in preference to evil.

(3) Accordingly the human being was initially created through the evolutionary process, as a spiritually and morally immature creature, and as part of a world which is both religiously ambiguous and ethically demanding.

(4) Thus that one is morally imperfect (i.e., that there is moral evil), and that the world is a challenging and even dangerous environment (i.e., that there is natural evil), are necessary aspects of the present stage of the process through which God is gradually creating perfected finite persons.

In terms of this hypothesis, as we have developed it thus far, then, both the basic moral evil in the human heart and the natural evils of the world are compatible with the existence of a Creator who is unlimited in both goodness and power. But is the hypothesis plausible as well as possible? The principal threat to its plausibility comes, I think, from the sheer amount and intensity of both moral and natural evil. One can accept the principle that in order to arrive at a freely chosen goodness one must start out in a state of moral immaturity and imperfection. But is it necessary that there should be the depths of demonic malice and cruelty which each generation has experienced, and which we have seen above all in recent history in the Nazi attempt to exterminate the Jewish population of Europe? Can any future fulfillment be worth such horrors? This was Dostoyevski's haunting question: "Imagine that you are creating a fabric of human destiny with the object of making men happy in the end, giving them peace and rest at last, but that it was essential and inevitable to torture to death only one tiny creature—that baby beating its breast with its fist, for instance—and to found that edifice on its unavenged tears, would you consent to be the architect on those conditions?"[2] The theistic answer is one which may be true but which takes so large a view that it baffles the imagination. Intellectually one may be able to see, but emotionally one cannot be expected to feel, its truth; and in that sense it cannot satisfy us. For the theistic answer is that if we take with full seriousness the value of human freedom and responsibility, as essential to the eventual creation of perfected children of God, then we cannot consistently want God to revoke that freedom when its wrong exercise becomes intolerable to us. From our vantage point within the historical process we may indeed cry out to God to revoke his gift of freedom, or to overrule it by some secret or open intervention. Such a cry must have come from millions caught in the Jewish Holocaust, or in the yet more recent laying waste of Korea and Vietnam, or from the victims of racism in many parts of the world. And the thought that humankind's moral freedom is indivisible, and can lead eventually to a consummation of limitless value which could never be attained without that freedom, and which is worth any finite suffering in the course of its creation, can be of no comfort to those who are now in the midst of that suffering. But while fully acknowledging this, I nevertheless want to insist that this eschatological answer may well be true. Expressed in religious language it tells us to trust in God even in the midst of deep suffering, for in the end we shall participate in his glorious kingdom.

Again, we may grant that a world which is to be a person-making environment cannot be a pain-free paradise but must contain challenges and dangers, with real possibilities of many kinds of accident and disaster, and the pain and suffering which they bring. But need it contain the worst forms of disease and catastrophe? And need misfortune fall upon us with such heartbreaking indiscriminateness? Once again there are answers, which may well be true, and yet once again the truth in this area may offer little in the way of pastoral balm. Concerning the intensity of natural evil, the truth is probably that our judgments of intensity are relative. We might identify some form of natural evil as the worst that there is—say, the agony that can be caused by death from cancer—and claim that a loving God would not have allowed this to exist. But in a world in which there was no cancer, something else would then rank as the worst form of natural evil. If we then eliminate this, something else; and so on. And the process would continue until the world was free of all natural evil. For whatever form of evil for the time being remained would be intolerable to the inhabitants of that world. But in removing all occasions of pain and suffering, and hence all challenge and all need for mutual care, we should have converted the world from a person-making into a static environment, which could not elicit moral growth. In short, having accepted that a person-making world must have its dangers and therefore also its tragedies, we must accept that whatever form these take will be intolerable to the inhabitants of that world. There could not be a person-making world devoid of what we call evil; and evils are never tolerable—except for the sake of greater goods which may come out of them.

But accepting that a person-making environment must contain causes of pain and suffering, and that no pain or suffering is going to be acceptable, one of the most daunting and even terrifying features of the world is that calamity strikes indiscriminately. There is no justice in the incidence of disease, accident, disaster and tragedy. The righteous as well as the unrighteous are struck down by illness and afflicted by misfortune. There is no security in goodness, but the good are as likely as the wicked to suffer "the slings and arrows of outrageous fortune." From the time of Job this fact has set a glaring question mark against the goodness of God. But let us suppose that things were otherwise. Let us suppose that misfortune came upon humankind, not haphazardly and therefore unjustly, but justly and therefore not haphazardly. Let us suppose that instead of coming without regard to moral considerations, it was proportioned to desert, so that the sinner was punished and the virtuous rewarded. Would such a dispensation serve a person-making purpose? Surely not. For it would be evident that wrong deeds bring disaster upon the agent whilst good deeds bring health and prosperity; and in such a world truly moral action, action done because it is right, would be impossible. The fact that natural evil is not morally directed, but is a hazard which comes by chance, is thus an intrinsic feature of a person-making world.

In other words, the very mystery of natural evil, the very fact that disasters afflict human beings in contingent, undirected and haphazard ways, is itself a necessary feature of a world that calls forth mutual aid and builds up mutual caring and love. Thus on the one hand it would be completely wrong to say that God sends misfortune upon individuals, so that their death, maiming, starvation or ruin is God's will for them. But on the other hand God has set us in a world containing unpredictable contingencies and dangers, in which unexpected and undeserved calamities may occur to anyone; because only in such a world can mutual caring and love be elicited. As an abstract philosophical hypothesis this may offer little comfort. But translated into religious language it tells us that God's good purpose enfolds the entire process of this world, with all its good and bad contingencies, and that even amidst tragic calamity and suffering we are still within the sphere of God's love and are moving towards God's kingdom.

But there is one further all-important aspect of the Irenaean type of theodicy, without which all the foregoing would lose its plausibility. This is the eschatological aspect. Our hypothesis depicts persons as still in course of creation towards an end state of perfected personal community in the divine kingdom. This end state is conceived of as one in which individual egoity has been transcended in communal unity before God. And in the present phase of that creative process the naturally self-centered human animal has the opportunity freely to respond to God's non-coercive self-disclosures, through the work of prophets and saints, through the resulting religious traditions, and through the individual's religious experience. Such response always has an ethical aspect; for the growing awareness of God is at the same time a growing awareness of the moral claim which God's presence makes upon the way in which we live.

But it is very evident that this person-making process, leading eventually to perfect human community, is not completed on this earth. It is not completed in the life of the individual—or at best only in the few who have attained to sanctification, or moksha, or nirvana on this earth. Clearly the enormous majority of men and women die without having attained to this. As Eric Fromm has said, "The tragedy in the life of most of us is that we die before we are fully born."[3] And therefore if we are ever to reach the full realization of the potentialities of our human nature, this can only be in a continuation of our lives in another sphere of existence after bodily death. And it is equally evident that the perfect all-embracing human community, in which self-regarding concern has been transcended in mutual love, not only has not been realized in this world, but never can be, since hundreds of generations of human beings have already lived and died and accordingly could not be part of any ideal community established at some future moment of earthly history. Thus if the unity of humankind in God's presence is ever to be realized it will have to be in some sphere of existence other than our earth. In short, the fulfillment of the divine purpose, as it is postulated in the Irenaean type of theodicy, presupposes each person's survival, in some form, of bodily death, and further living and growing towards that end state. Without such an eschatological fulfillment, this theodicy would collapse.

A theodicy which presupposes and requires an eschatology will thereby be rendered implausible in the minds of many today. I nevertheless do not see how any coherent theodicy can avoid dependence upon an eschatology. Indeed I would go further and say that the belief in the reality of a limitlessly loving and powerful deity must incorporate some kind of eschatology according to which God holds in being the creatures whom God has made for fellowship with himself, beyond bodily death, and brings them into the eternal fellowship which God has intended for them. I have tried elsewhere to argue that such an eschatology is a necessary corollary of ethical monotheism; to argue for the realistic possibility of an afterlife or lives, despite the philosophical and empirical arguments against this; and even to spell out some of the general features which human life after death may possibly have.[4] Since all this is a very large task, which would far exceed the bounds of this essay, I shall not attempt to repeat it here but must refer the reader to my existing discussion of it. It is that extended discussion that constitutes my answer to the question whether an Irenaean theodicy, with its eschatology, may not be as implausible as an Augustinian theodicy, with its human or angelic fall. (If it is, then the latter is doubly implausible; for it also involves an eschatology!)

There is however one particular aspect of eschatology which must receive some treatment here, however brief and inadequate. This is the issue of "universal salvation" versus "heaven and hell" (or perhaps annihilation instead of hell). If the justification of evil within the creative process lies in the limitless and eternal good of the end state to which it leads, then the completeness of the justification must depend upon the completeness, or universality, of the salvation achieved. Only if it includes the entire human race can it justify the sins and sufferings of the entire human race throughout all history. But, having given human beings cognitive freedom, which in turn makes possible moral freedom, can the Creator bring it about that in the end all his human creatures freely turn to God in love and trust? The issue is a very difficult one; but I believe that it is in fact possible to reconcile a full affirmation of human freedom with a belief in the ultimate universal success of God's creative work. We have to accept that creaturely freedom always occurs within the limits of a basic nature that we did not ourselves choose; for this is entailed by the fact of having been created. If then a real though limited freedom does not preclude our being endowed with a certain nature, it does not preclude our being endowed with a basic Godward bias, so that, quoting from another side of St. Augustine's thought, "our hearts are restless until they find their rest in Thee."[5] If this is so, it can be predicted that sooner or later, in our own time and in our own way, we shall all freely come to God; and universal salvation can be affirmed, not as a logical necessity but as the contingent but predictable outcome of the process of the universe, interpreted theistically. Once again, I have tried to present this argument more fully elsewhere, and to consider various objections to it.[6]

On this view the human, endowed with a real though limited freedom, is basically formed for relationship with God and destined ultimately to find the fulfillment of his or her nature in that relationship. This does not seem to me excessively paradoxical. On the contrary, given the theistic postulate, it seems to me to offer a very probable account of our human situation. If so, it is a situation in which we can rejoice; for it gives meaning to our temporal existence as the long process through which we are being created, by our own free responses to life's mixture of good and evil, into "children of God" who "inherit eternal life."

NOTES

1. R. Held and A. Heim, "Movement-produced stimulation in the development of visually guided behaviour," *Journal of Comparative and Physiological Psychology* 56 (1963): 872–876.
2. Fyodor Dostoyevsky, *The Brothers Karamozov*, trans. Constance Garnett (New York: Modern Library, n.d.), Bk. V, chap. 4, p. 254.
3. Erich Fromm, "Values, Psychology, and Human Existence," in *New Knowledge of Human Values*, ed. A. Maslow (New York: Harper & Row, 1959), p. 156.
4. John Hick, *Death and Eternal Life* (New York: Harper & Row; and London: Collins, 1976; revised, London: Macmillan, 1987).
5. *The Confessions of St. Augustine*, trans. F. J. Sheed (New York: Sheed and Ward, 1942), Bk. 1, chap. 1, p. 3.
6. Hick, *Death and Eternal Life*, chap. 13.

WILLIAM ROWE

Evil and Theodicy

William Rowe (1931–) analyzes the general structure of the problem of evil as raised by the anti-theist. Rowe essentially argues that, since there are evils that apparently have no good justification, we are rationally warranted in concluding that God does not exist. He discusses what it would take for some belief or set of beliefs to overturn or "defeat" the tendency of apparently unjustified evil to support an atheistic conclusion to the argument from evil. In moving toward his conclusion, he considers three different kinds of responses to his argument: that his reasoning is faulty, that we have independent offsetting reasons to believe in the existence of God, and that we would not know what goods justify evils even if there were such goods. Last, he critiques John Hick's "soul-making" theodicy in light of his earlier points.

⌘

Many people feel that some of the human and animal suffering going on in our world makes it difficult to believe in the existence of an omnipotent, omniscient, wholly good being (hereafter referred to as 'O'). Why, for example, would such a being permit the awful suffering and near extermination of the Jews in Europe? Clearly, it is very difficult to understand why an omnipotent, omniscient, perfectly good being would permit this evil. But if our awareness of such evils does make it difficult to believe that O exists, what sort of difficulty is it? It might be a psychological difficulty. We might be so disposed that when we view films of the victims being herded into box cars, being forced into gas chambers, etc., we simply find ourselves inclined to doubt the existence of O, or inclined to abandon our belief in O. On the other hand, the difficulty may be epistemological. We may think that disbelief is somehow rationally justified by our awareness of these terrible evils. It is this latter topic that I want to discuss.

THE STRUCTURE OF THE PROBLEM

I will begin with two instances of evil that have been mentioned in the literature. The first is a case of animal suffering due to natural forces, what would be called a *natural evil.* The second is a case of human suffering and death due to the intentional action of a human agent, what would be called a *moral evil.* The first case, although I made it up, is surely a familiar sort of tragedy, played not infrequently on the stage of nature.

From *Philosophical Topics* 16, no. 2 (1988): 119–132. Reprinted by permission of the author.

> In some distant forest lightning strikes a dead tree, resulting in a forest fire. In the fire a fawn is trapped, horribly burned, and lies in terrible agony for several days before death relieves its suffering.

I turn now to a second case, an actual case reported in the *Detroit Free Press* of January 3, 1986. The case involves a little girl in Flint, Michigan who was severely beaten, raped and then strangled early on New Year's Day of 1986. Here is Bruce Russell's account of the case, which I take from his paper, "The Persistent Problem of Evil."[1]

> The girl's mother was living with her boyfriend, another man who was unemployed, her two children, and her 9-month-old infant fathered by the boyfriend. On New Year's Eve all three adults were drinking at a bar near the woman's home. The boyfriend had been taking drugs and drinking heavily. He was asked to leave the bar at 8:00 p.m. After several reappearances he finally stayed away for good at about 9:30 p.m. The woman and the unemployed man remained at the bar until 2:00 a.m. at which time the woman went home and the man to a party at a neighbor's home. Perhaps out of jealousy, the boyfriend attacked the woman when she walked into the house. Her brother was there and broke up the fight by hitting the boyfriend who was passed out and slumped over a table when the brother left. Later the boyfriend attacked the woman again, this time she knocked him unconscious. After checking the children, she went to bed. Later the woman's 5-year-old girl went downstairs to go to the bathroom. The unemployed man returned from the party at 3:45 a.m. and found the 5-year-old dead. She had been raped, severely beaten over most of her body and strangled to death by the boyfriend.

Let's refer to these two cases as E1 (for the fawn's case) and E2 (for the little girl's case). Now about E1 and E2, I want to make the following initial judgment.

> P. No good state of affairs we know of is such that an omnipotent, omniscient being's obtaining it would morally justify that being's permitting E1 or E2.

What am I implying in making this assertion? I am implying that we have *good reason* to believe that no good state of affairs we know of would justify an omnipotent, omniscient being in permitting either E1 or E2. I don't mean simply that we can't see how some good we know about (say, my enjoyment on smelling a good cigar) would justify an omnipotent being's permitting E1 or E2. I mean that we can see how such a good would *not* justify an omnipotent being's permitting E1 or E2. For we can see that an omnipotent being wouldn't have to permit E1 or E2 in order to obtain the good of my enjoyment on smelling a good cigar. And we can see that even were that not so, obtaining such a good wouldn't justify any being in permitting E1 or E2. Is there some other good state of affairs we know of that would justify an omnipotent being in permitting E1 or E2? I don't believe there is. The good states of affairs I know of, when I reflect on them, meet one or both of the following conditions: either an omnipotent being could obtain them without having to permit E1 or E2, or obtaining them wouldn't morally justify that being in permitting E1 or E2. And if this is so, I have reason to conclude that:

Q. No good state of affairs is such that an omnipotent, omniscient being's obtaining it would morally justify that being in permitting E1 or E2.

THREE RESPONSES

I propose now to describe three general ways of responding to the line of reasoning that moves from consideration of E1 and E2 to the conclusion Q.

A. One response would be to argue that the reasoning is in some way faulty. Either it makes some untenable or unsupported claim or engages in some faulty inference. For example, one might challenge the claim that among the goods we know about none is such that obtaining it would justify an omnipotent, omniscient being in permitting E1 or E2. Alternatively, one might argue that the reasoning is fallacious, engaging in an inference from 'we don't know of any such good' to the conclusion that there aren't any, or in an inference from 'no goods we know about would justify such a being in permitting E1 or E2' to the conclusion that no goods we don't know about would justify such a being in permitting E1 or E2.

B. A second response might acknowledge that the considerations I've mentioned do tend to support Q. But it might be argued that we have good reasons to believe that O exists. And surely, if O exists then there is some good state that O brings about that justifies O in permitting E1, and some good state O brings about that justifies O in permitting E2.[2] So, since if O exists Q is false, it might be contended that our reasons to believe that O exists *outweigh* the tendency of the considerations mentioned to support Q. In brief, this response contends that although the considerations mentioned do support Q, when we take into account our reasons for thinking that O exists we see that on balance we have more reason to think Q false than to think it true.

C. A third response, like the second, may acknowledge that the considerations mentioned support Q. Again, like the second this response contends that there is something we know or have good reason to believe that, when conjoined with the considerations mentioned, gives us something that on balance does not support Q. Unlike the second response, however, the thing we know or have good reason to believe is neutral with respect to Q. For example, one might have good reason to believe that if there are good states of affairs the obtaining of which would justify an omnipotent, omniscient being in permitting E1 or E2, all would be goods we know nothing about. Now this information by itself does not make Q unlikely, but when we conjoin this information with our initial judgment P (no good we know of is such that obtaining it would justify an omnipotent, omniscient being's permitting E1 or E2), the conjunction does not support Q. So here, instead of saying that the tendency of these considerations to support Q is outweighed, we shall say that it is *defeated*.

My chief interest here is to discuss the first and third of these responses. To evaluate the strength of the second response would require an evaluation of our reasons for believing that O exists, a topic far too large to take up here.

According to the first response, the attempt we have made to reason from the existence of certain evils, such as E1 and E2, to the nonexistence of O is flawed in one of two ways, if not both. First, it may be flawed in its implicit claim to have good reason to make the initial judgment P (no good we know of is such that obtaining it would justify an omnipotent, omniscient being in permitting E1 or E2). Second, it may be flawed in concluding from this initial judgment that Q (no good is such that obtaining it would justify an omnipotent, omniscient being in permitting E1 or E2). Let's now consider whether this first sort of response is successful.

To simplify our discussion, I will use the letter 'J' to stand for the property a good has just in case obtaining that good would justify an omnipotent, omniscient being in permitting E1 or E2. If a good is such that obtaining it would justify an omnipotent, omniscient being in permitting E1 or E2, then that good has J; and if not, the good lacks J. The first question, then, that this response raises is whether we are really able to judge with any assurance that P: all the goods we know of lack J. And the second question this response raises is whether from our initial judgment, P, we can reasonably infer that Q: all goods (including those we don't know of) lack J?

Before turning to these questions, however, it's worth noting that both questions imply that the class of goods can be divided into those we know of and those we don't know of. What is it to know of an intrinsically good state of affairs?[3] Well, as a start, I'm sure we would all be able to list some states that are intrinsically good, some that are intrinsically bad, and some that are neutral, neither intrinsically good nor bad. On our good list we would have: pleasure, happiness, love, the exercise of virtue, good intentions, etc. On our bad list we would have pain, unhappiness, hatred, the exercise of vice, bad intentions, etc. Other states, the existence of a stone, say, we would judge to be neither intrinsically good nor intrinsically bad. Now if we could imagine the list of intrinsic goods as *completed*, I think the completed list would include some states of affairs we would recognize as intrinsically good, even though they did not come to mind when we first started composing the list. We might, for example, find *knowledge* on the list, and respond with the recognition that it too is intrinsically good. But the *complete* list might well include states that are enormously complex, so complex as to tax our powers of comprehension. Determining that such a state is intrinsically good may be as difficult for us as it would be for a child of three to determine whether Bayes' theorem is true. Goods of this sort are what I have in mind when I speak of goods we don't know of.[4]

Among the goods we know of, is any such that it has J? It is obvious that many of these goods lack J. For when we contemplate them we see that their value is not high enough (e.g., my enjoyment on smelling a good cigar) to offset the evils in question. Other goods we know of may have a great deal of intrinsic value, perhaps even more value than E1 or E2 have disvalue. But here we readily see that an omnipotent, omniscient being could obtain them without permitting E1 or E2.[5] Reflections of this sort justify us, I believe, in making our initial judgment, P, that the goods we know about lack J.

Suppose we accept P. What about the inference to Q? Are we justified in believing that no goods (including those we don't know of) have J on the basis of our justified premise that no goods we know of have J? Perhaps any such inference commits some fallacy. After all, if we don't know of these goods, how can we be justified in concluding either that they do or do not have J? My answer is that we are justified in making this inference in the same way we are justified in making the many inferences we constantly make from the known to the unknown. All of us are constantly inferring from the A's we know of to the A's we don't know of. It we observe many A's and all of them are B's we are justified in believing that the A's we haven't observed are also B's. If I encounter a fair number of pit bulls and all of them are vicious, I have reason to believe that all pit bulls are vicious. Of course, there are all sorts of considerations that may defeat this inference. I may discover that all the pit bulls I've encountered have been trained for dog-fighting, a training that engenders viciousness. I may also come to know that there are many pit bulls that are not so trained. If so, then this additional information, along with my initial information, may *not justify* me in believing that the pit bulls I haven't encountered are also vicious. So, too, with my inference from P to Q. But considerations of this sort (defeaters) properly belong to the third response, not the first. The first response, I believe, is not successful.[6]

The third response holds greater hope for discrediting the argument from evil here being considered. Before seeing how it proceeds, we should look a bit more carefully at the notion of *defeat*. Let's do this with an example. Suppose it is true that

1. The wall appears red.

From (1) we infer that

2. The wall is not white.

The inference is undoubtedly justified. If (1) were all we knew relative to the truth of (2), we would be justified in believing (2). How might the tendency of (1) to support (2) be defeated? Well, suppose we know the following proposition:

3. If the wall were white, the wall would appear red anyway.

Clearly, although (1) tends to support (2), this tendency would be defeated if (3) were added to our knowledge. That is, the *conjunction* of (1) and (3) does *not support* (2). [Note that (3) by itself does not support the denial of (2). So this is not a case in which our new knowledge *outweighs* the support we have for (2).] How might we come to know or rationally believe (3)? Well, suppose we learn that

4. There are red lights shining on the wall and when red lights shine on a white wall the wall will appear red.

(4) gives us a good reason for accepting (3), and, as we've seen, when we conjoin (3) with (1) we no longer are justified in believing (2)—the tendency of (1) to support (2) is *defeated.*

Although it is risky to generalize from a single example, let's note the following pattern. From A we infer B. Instead of having evidence against B itself, as in attempting to *outweigh* A's tendency to support B, we have reason to believe that *if not-B, A would be (or would likely be) true anyway.* When we conjoin this hypothetical with A, we have a conjunction that does not support B. With this pattern in mind, let's return to our original inference to Q (no goods have J) from P (no goods we know of have J). To defeat P's tendency to support Q we need some good reason to believe that if not-Q (some good has J), P would be (or likely be) true anyway. Do we have any good reason to believe that if not-Q, P would be true anyway?

In considering our question it is important to note that our hypothetical refers to omniscience and omnipotence, as opposed to something akin to human knowledge and power. If a human being permits some great evil to occur, we would have some reason to think that if the obtaining of some good does justify the permission, we would likely know of the good; for another human being's knowledge and power resembles quite closely our own. For this reason we generally would have reason to reject the hypothetical that if the obtaining of some good would justify this person in permitting the evil, it would still be true that it is a good we do not know. But omniscience would view all goods, including the ones we don't know of. So, unlike the hypothetical referring to human knowledge and power, we have no similar reason to think that if some good is such that obtaining it would justify an omnipotent, omniscient being in permitting E1 or E2, it would likely be one we know of.

But all that we have seen, thus far, is that when we replace omniscience by human knowledge and power we have good reason to think that the hypothetical that would correspond to If not-Q, P anyway (i.e., the hypothetical concerning human knowledge and power), is *false.* The question before us, however, is whether we have some reason to think the original hypothetical [if not-Q, P anyway] is *true.* And I must confess that I cannot think of any special reason to think that this hypothetical is true. Given the high degree of intrinsic badness of E1 and E2, we do know that the justifying goods would be very significant goods. But this, by itself, is no good reason to think that the goods would be ones we don't know of. For we do know of very significant goods. Consider, for example, the state consisting of a vast number of conscious beings deeply enjoying the admirable qualities exhibited by one another. This is a very significant good we know of. So the mere fact that the goods must be significant is not, of itself, good reason to think that the goods that might justify an omnipotent, omniscient being in permitting E1 or E2 would be goods we do not know. Perhaps there is some fact such that if we knew it we would have a good reason to think that the hypothetical is true. We certainly cannot rule out there being such a fact. But until we learn of it we have no good reason to think that if Q were false, P would be true anyway. And lacking such a reason, we are unable to defeat P's tendency to support Q.[7]

Let's look back, briefly, at the path along which we have come. Our original question was whether certain facts about evil provide rational support for the view that O does not exist. In considering this question, we noted two particular instances of evil, E1 and E2, and noted that P [no good we know of would justify an omnipotent, omniscient being in permitting E1 or E2]. From P we inferred Q [no good at all would justify an omnipotent, omniscient being in permitting E1 or E2]. Suppose we are justified in believing Q on the basis of our belief that P. If so, then, since we see that Q would be false if O existed, we are justified in believing that O does not exist. In response to this line of argument, I suggested that there are three responses worthy of consideration, only two of which (the first and third responses) I would take up in this paper. Against the first response, I argued that we are justified in believing P and in inferring Q from P. Against the third response, I argued that although having a good reason for believing the hypothetical [If not-Q, P anyway] would *defeat* our acceptance of Q on the basis of P, we do not in fact have a good reason to accept this hypothetical. In short, unless we have good reasons to think that O exists (or some other reason to reject Q), we are justified in believing that O does not exist.

THEODICY AND THE PROBLEM OF EVIL

Thus far we've taken no account of the various theodicies that have been mounted to reconcile our belief in theism with the difficulty raised by some of the human and animal suffering that goes on in our world. What I propose to do in this section is to look briefly at one of the more promising theodicies to determine just where it impinges on the difficulty, as we have developed it. In addition, we will need to consider the extent to which the theodicy reduces the difficulty.

The theodicy I have in mind is the one developed and defended by John Hick, and referred to as a theodicy of "soul-making."[8] Before giving a synopsis of this theodicy, it will be helpful to reflect on the general bearing of theodicies on the difficulty we have developed. Just what does a theodicy endeavor to do? Does it propose to tell us in some detail just what good state it is that justifies O, if O exists, in permitting E1 and E2? No. Such an account would presume a knowledge of O's specific purposes, a knowledge that it would be unreasonable to expect we would have without some detailed revelation to us from O. What a theodicy does endeavor to do is to fasten on some good state of affairs and argue that it would justify O in permitting evils like E1 and E2. Whether obtaining the good in question is O's actual reason for permitting evils like E1 and E2 is not really part of what a theodicy tries to establish. It only hopes to show that *if* obtaining the good in question were O's aim in permitting evils like E1 and E2, then (given what we know) O would be justified in permitting such evils. In addition, it is important to the success of the theodicy that the good in question not be a good we have reason to believe does not obtain. It would not be helpful, for example, to argue that the good in question is every human being turning to Christ before that person experiences bodily death. For we have very good reason to think that such a good does not obtain. The theodicist doesn't have to establish that the good in question does obtain, but she must at least argue that we do not have any really strong reasons to think that it doesn't obtain. In terms of our presentation of the difficulty, then, we should see the theodicist as denying P. What the theodicist claims, so it seems to me, is that *some good we know of* is such that obtaining it would justify O in permitting E1 and E2. Need a theist be a theodicist? I don't think so. A theist *must* reject Q. But she need not reject P. Someone could hold that her reasons for thinking O exists *outweigh* P's support of Q, so that it is rational on balance for the theist to believe that Q is false. Such a theist might hold that the good that would justify O in permitting E1 and E2 is a good that is totally beyond our ken in this life. Such a position is not inconsistent with theism, although it does abandon the project of providing a theodicy.[9]

Some theodicies depend on having very strong reasons for believing that O exists. Leibniz' theodicy, as I read it, is a case in point. Having established to his satisfaction that O exists, Leibniz claimed to deduce that the good in question is this being the best of all possible worlds. Now if this is the best of all possible worlds then clearly such a good would justify an omnipotent, omniscient being in permitting E1, E2 and all the other evils our world contains.[10] Other theodicies need not depend for their success on proving the existence of O. Hick's theodicy, as I read it, does not depend on such a proof. With these preliminary remarks out of the way, we can now consider the basic structure of Hick's "soul-making" theodicy.

There are two good states that figure in Hick's theodicy. The first is the state in which all human beings develop themselves through their free choices into moral and spiritual beings. The second good state is that in which all such beings enter into an eternal life of bliss and joy in fellowship with O. The second of these good states (and probably the first) obtains only if O exists. But, as I've suggested, in order to be successful a theodicy need not *establish* that the good in question obtains. Let's begin our synopsis by considering the first of these states, the state in which all human beings develop themselves through their free choices into moral and spiritual beings. How might the obtaining of such a good justify an omnipotent, omniscient being in permitting evils like E1 or E2?

Since E1 and E2 are instances of natural and moral evil, different answers may be required. Let's begin with horrendous moral evils like E2. Hick's first step is to argue that if moral and spiritual development through free choices is the good in question then an environment in which there is no significant suffering, no occasion for significant moral choices, would not be one in which moral and spiritual growth would be possible. In particular, a world in which no one can harm another, in which no pain or suffering results from any action, would not be a world in which such moral and spiritual growth could occur.

I think we can concede to Hick that a pain-free paradise, a world in which no one could be injured and no one could do harm, would be a world devoid of significant moral and spiritual development. But what are we to make of the fact that the world we live in is so often inimical to such moral and spiritual development? For clearly, as Hick is careful to note, much of the pain and suffering in our world frustrates such development.

> The overall situation is thus that, so far as we can tell, suffering occurs haphazardly, uselessly, and therefore unjustly. It appears to be only randomly related either to past desert or to future soul-making. Instead of serving a constructive purpose, pain and misery seem to fall upon men patternlessly and meaninglessly, with the result that suffering is often undeserved and often occurs in amounts exceeding anything that could have been morally planned.[11]

Hick's response to this point is to ask us what would happen were our world one in which suffering occurred "... not haphazardly and therefore unjustly, but on the contrary justly and therefore non-haphazardly."[12] In such a world, Hick, following Kant, reasons that people would avoid wrongdoing out of fear rather than from a sense of duty. Moreover, once we saw that suffering was always for the good of the sufferer, human misery would no longer "... evoke deep personal sympathy or call forth organized relief and sacrificial help and service. For it is presupposed in those compassionate reactions both that the suffering is not deserved and that it is *bad* for the sufferer."[13] Hick then concludes:

> It seems, then, that in a world that is to be the scene of compassionate love and self-giving for others, suffering must fall upon mankind with something of the haphazardness and inequity that we now experience. It must be apparently unmerited, pointless, and incapable of being morally rationalized. For it is precisely this feature of our common human lot that creates sympathy between man and man and evokes the unselfishness, kindness and goodwill which are among the highest values of personal life.[14]

Let's assume with Hick that an environment fit for human beings to develop the highest qualities of moral and spiritual life must be one that includes real suffering, hardships, disappointments, failure and defeat. For moral and spiritual growth presuppose these. Let's also assume that such an environment must operate, at least for the most part, according to general and dependable laws, for only on the basis of such general laws can a person engage in the purposeful decision-making essential to rational and moral life.[15] And given these two assumptions it is, I think, understandable how an omniscient, omnipotent being may be morally justified in permitting the occurrence of evils, both moral and natural.

Our excursion into John Hick's theodicy has shown us, perhaps, how a theodicy may succeed in justifying O's permission of both natural and moral evil. But so far we haven't been given any justification for O's permission of E1 or E2. In the case of E1 we can say that *given* the existence of the animals in our world and the operation of the world according to natural laws, it is unavoidable that instances of intense and prolonged animal suffering would occur. In the case of E2 we can say that on their way toward moral and spiritual development it is perhaps unavoidable that human beings will sometimes seriously harm others through a bad use of freedom. But neither of these points will morally justify an omnipotent, omniscient being in permitting E1 and E2. In the case of E2, it is simply unreasonable to believe that if the boyfriend acted freely in brutally beating and raping the little girl, his moral and spiritual development would have been permanently frustrated had he been prevented from doing what he did. And it is also unreasonable to believe that permitting such an act is morally justified even if preventing it would somehow diminish the boyfriend's moral and spiritual odyssey.[16] And in the case of E1, it is simply unreasonable to believe that preventing the fawn's being severely burned, or mercifully ending its life so that it does not suffer intensely for several days, would so shake our confidence in the orderliness of nature that we would forsake our moral and spiritual development. I think Hick is not unaware of this limitation to his theodicy, at least with respect to natural evils. With respect to human pain due to sources independent of the human will, he remarks:

> In response to it, theodicy, if it is wisely conducted, follows a negative path. It is not possible to show positively that each item of human pain serves God's purpose of good; on the other hand, it does seem possible to show that the divine purpose, [. . .] could not be forwarded in a world that was designed as a permanent hedonistic paradise.[17]

What Hick says here is, I believe, right, with one minor modification. The minor modification is this. In Hick's theodicy some evils themselves are necessary to the attainment of the good of moral and spiritual development. But many evils, particularly those resulting from the operation of the laws of nature, will not themselves serve moral and spiritual development. They may even hinder it. Nevertheless, as the by-product of the general operation of the laws of nature, something that is essential to rational decision-making and moral living, an omnipotent, omniscient being would have reason to permit even these evils, at least to the extent that further intervention on its part would diminish our expectation that the world operates on general laws.

What we've seen is that Hick's theodicy fails if it is intended to provide a good that would justify an omnipotent, omniscient being in permitting E1 or E2. The best that Hick can do is to argue that a world *utterly devoid* of natural or moral evil would preclude the realization of the goods he postulates as justifying an omnipotent, omniscient being in permitting evil. However, since the prevention of E1 or E2 would not leave our world utterly devoid of natural or moral evil, his all-or-nothing argument provides no answer to our question. Nor will it do to say that if an omnipotent, omniscient being were to be morally obligated to prevent E1 or E2 it would thereby be obligated to prevent all such evils. For were it to do so it may well be that we would cease to engage in very significant soul-making. The problem Hick's theodicy leaves us is that it is altogether reasonable to believe that some of the evils that occur (E1 and E2, for example) could have been prevented without either diminishing our moral and spiritual development or undermining our confidence that the world operates according to natural laws. Hick's theodicy, therefore, does not succeed in showing that we have no good reason to accept P. Nor does his theodicy show that we aren't justified in inferring Q from P. In short, Hick's theodicy does little to diminish the claim that the existence of certain evils provides rational grounds for atheism.

Some may feel that I have criticized Hick's theodicy for failing to do what it was never meant to do: to show us the good the obtaining of which would justify an omnipotent, omniscient being in permitting E1 or E2. Theodicies, one might argue, are not intended to provide a justification for *particular evils.* I acknowledge the merit of this criticism. There are, I think, four different things a theodicy might aim at doing, each more difficult than its predecessor. First, a theodicy might seek to explain why O would permit *any evil* at all. Second, a theodicy might endeavor to explain why there are instances of the various *kinds* of evil we find in our world—animal pain, human suffering, wickedness, etc. Third, a theodicy might endeavor to explain why there is the *amount* of evil (of these kinds) that we find in our world. And, finally, a theodicy might endeavor to explain certain *particular evils* that obtain. I think Hick's theodicy may be successful on the first level, and perhaps the second. In so far, therefore, as we argue against the existence of O solely by appealing to the fact that our world contains evil, or to the fact that our world contains certain kinds of evil, Hick's theodicy may show that the relevant P-like premise can be reasonably rejected. But arguments based on the third and fourth levels, so far as I can see, remain undiminished by Hick's theodicy. If his theodicy is not intended to diminish the strength of these arguments—by giving grounds for rejecting their P-like premises—then it is a mistake to charge that the theodicy fails to accomplish *its end.* But the point will remain that the theodicy does little or nothing to diminish the force of the strongest arguments from evil.

NOTES

1. Bruce Russell's paper is forthcoming in *Faith and Philosophy.*

2. For the sake of simplicity, I shall ignore the possibility that O permits E1 or E2 in order to prevent some equal or worse state from obtaining. I shall also ignore the possibility that there are two evils equally bad

such that either could be prevented without loss of the justifying good, but one or the other must be permitted to obtain the good.

3. Roughly, to know of a good state of affairs is to (a) conceive of that state of affairs, and (b) recognize that it is intrinsically good.

4. In addition, there may be simple properties we have never thought of, properties whose presence in a state of affairs might render that state a great intrinsic good.

5. Of course, the *conjunction* of one of these great goods, G, with E1, say, will be unattainable by omnipotence without permitting E1. But since we have reason to think that G can be obtained by omnipotence without permitting E1, obtaining the conjunction of G and E1 won't justify this being in permitting E1. The conjunction of G and E1, like G itself, will lack J.

6. The first response in effect claims that if P were all we knew relative to the truth or falsity of Q, we would not be rationally justified in believing Q. It is this claim that I am rejecting as false.

7. Stephen Wykstra has pointed out to me that it may suffice to defeat P's support of Q to show that if not-Q, P would be no less likely than not-P. We should, therefore, distinguish a stronger and more modest defeater. To give a reason for believing *if not-Q P would be true anyway* is to provide a strong defeater. To give a reason for believing *if not-Q P would be no less likely than not-P* is to provide a modest defeater. In the text I discuss only the strong defeater. A more comprehensive discussion would need to consider the more modest defeater as well.

8. See *Evil and the God of Love* (New York: Harper and Row, 1966), particularly Ch. XVII of the revised edition, published in 1978, *God and the Universe of Faiths* (New York: St. Martin's Press, 1973), and Chapter Four of *Philosophy of Religion*, 3rd edition (Englewood Cliffs, New Jersey: Prentice-Hall, 1983).

9. The account I've given of the aim of a theodicy takes it to be providing a plausible justification for O's permitting *particular evils*. Perhaps this is too ambitious. Perhaps the aim of a theodicy is only to provide a plausible justification for O's permitting *some instances of various types of evil*. One might succeed at the latter and yet fail at the former. If we do take the second account, we need to revise my judgment of Hick's theodicy. One might then conclude that although Hick's theodicy is successful, it is largely irrelevant to the question of whether the existence of particular evils provides rational grounds for atheism. (See the final paragraph of this essay.)

10. Is *this being the best of all possible worlds* a good we know of? I'm not sure of the proper answer to this question. If it isn't, then my suggestion that theodicies are committed to denying P needs to be qualified. But apart from good reasons to believe that O exists, I would argue that we have reason to think that this is not the best of all possible worlds.

11. *God and the Universe of Faiths*, p. 58.

12. *Ibid.*

13. *Ibid.*, p. 60.

14. *Ibid.*

15. This point is forcefully argued by William Hasker in "Suffering, Soul-Making and Salvation," *International Philosophical Quarterly*, vol. 28, No. 1 (March 1988), pp. 3–19.

16. See Bruce Russell's paper for further argument on this point.

17. *Philosophy of Religion*, p. 46.

SUGGESTED READING

Griffin, David Ray. *God, Power, and Evil: A Process Theodicy*. Philadelphia: Westminster, 1976.

Hick, John. *Evil and the God of Love*. San Francisco: Harper and Row, rev. ed. 1978; 1968 rpt.

Mackie, J. L. *The Miracle of Theism*. Oxford: Clarendon Press, 1982, chap. 9.

Madden, Edward, and Peter Hare. *Evil and the Concept of God*. Springfield, Ill.: Charles C. Thomas, 1968.

Peterson, Michael. *Evil and the Christian God*. Grand Rapids: Baker Book House, 1982.

———. *The Problem of Evil: Selected Readings*. Notre Dame: University of Notre Dame Press, 1992.

Plantinga, Alvin. *God, Freedom, and Evil*. Grand Rapids: Eerdmans, 1977; rpt. 1974.

———. *The Nature of Necessity*. Oxford: Oxford University Press, 1974, chap. 9.

Reichenbach, Bruce. *Evil and A Good God*. New York: Fordham University Press, 1982.

PART SIX

KNOWING GOD WITHOUT ARGUMENTS

The selections in the previous two parts of this anthology illustrate an assumption that has been made by most non-fideistic philosophers of religion. The assumption, which may be termed *evidentialism,* is that whether or not it is reasonable to believe in God depends on one's *evidence*—that is, on the other things one knows or reasonably believes to be true. If the evidence one possesses provides the basis for strong arguments in favor of God's existence, and one has little evidence (or at any rate, less evidence) against it, then one rationally ought to believe in God. But if the evidence is weak, and if arguments for atheism (such as the problem of evil) are strong, then belief is rationally inappropriate.

One of the most striking recent developments in the philosophy of religion has been the emergence of an approach to religious knowledge that sharply rejects evidentialism. Yet this approach is not fideistic, since it agrees that it is appropriate to assess the rational acceptability of religious beliefs. What proponents of this new approach point out is that we may not have to accept the standard evidentialist manner of performing this assessment (i.e., weighing evidence for and against the beliefs in question). They go on to point out that we all do in fact believe implicitly in the reality of the physical objects we encounter in everyday life, and we do this without paying any serious attention to arguments for and against the existence of the "external world." They suggest that belief in God be approached in much the same way. They raise important questions in this regard: Why can't the *experience of God,* which many believers say they have, furnish the basis for our belief in God, just as our experiences of the physical world furnishes the basis for our belief in physical objects? Why can't belief in God be a *basic* belief, one that it is perfectly reasonable to accept *without* trying to find a basis for it in *other* things one believes to be true?

An important expression of this thinking is known as "Reformed epistemology" because of certain associations with the Reformed, or Calvinistic, branch of Christianity. (Note, however, that one need not be a Calvinist, or even a Christian, to be a Reformed epistemologist.) Leading proponents of this approach include Alvin Plantinga, Nicholas Wolterstorff, and William Alston. One aim of the Reformed epistemologists is to critique traditional "natural theology" and to contrast their view with it. (The part of this anthology on the theistic arguments would be to provide a good representation of natural theology, which has been popular for centuries in some branches of the Christian church.)

Reformed epistemology has come under fire from a number of directions. Some critics accuse it of unfairly and inaccurately caricaturing natural theology. Another group of critics accuse Reformed epistemology of surrendering the fairly standard view of knowledge that must be accepted by any rational person. In light of this, these critics ask whether there is really any point in claiming to *know*—as opposed to deeply and sincerely *believe*—that God exists. What additional point is made by the claim to knowledge? Other critics point out the problems raised for Reformed epistemology when we encounter the sincerely held but conflicting beliefs of adherents of other religions. Religious diversity would seem to make it unavoidable that we must evaluate the various religious options according to their distinctive and different explanations of the available evidence.

ALVIN PLANTINGA

The Reformed Objection to Natural Theology

In this essay Alvin Plantinga (1932–) sets out the essentials of an approach to religious knowledge that has come to be known as "Reformed epistemology." Plantinga notes that the tradition of "natural theology," which seeks to prove God's existence on the basis of premises that are obvious to any thinking person, has often met with resistance in the Reformed (or Calvinistic) branch of Christianity. Not only has it been felt that the arguments are insufficient as a basis for religious belief, but it is also thought that the whole idea of basing belief on arguments is misguided. This is not to say, however, that belief in God is irrational. On the contrary, Reformed Christians typically have held that belief in God is a *properly basic* belief, one that is not held on the basis of any other beliefs, and does not need to be justified in terms of other beliefs one holds. In the following piece, Plantinga develops briefly the epistemological position that seeks to make sense of these claims.

⌘

Suppose we think of natural theology as the attempt to prove or demonstrate the existence of God. This enterprise has a long and impressive history—a history stretching back to the dawn of Christendom and boasting among its adherents many of the truly great thinkers of the Western world. Chief among these is Thomas Aquinas, whose work, I think, is the natural starting point for Christian philosophical reflection, Protestant as well as Catholic. Here we Protestants must be, in Ralph McInerny's immortal phrase, Peeping Thomists. Recently—since the time of Kant, perhaps—the tradition of natural theology has not been as overwhelming as it once was: yet it continues to have able defenders both within and without officially Catholic philosophy.[1]

Many Christians, however, have been less than totally impressed. In particular Reformed or Calvinist theologians have for the most part taken a dim view of this enterprise. A few Reformed thinkers—B. B. Warfield,[2] for example,—endorse the theistic proofs; but for the most part the Reformed attitude has ranged from indifference, through suspicion and hostility, to outright accusations of blasphemy. And this stance is initially puzzling. It looks a little like the attitude some Christians adopt towards faith healing: it can't be done, but even if it could, it shouldn't be. What exactly, or even

From *Christian Scholar's Review* 11, no. 3 (1982): 187–198. Reprinted by permission of *American Catholic Philosophical Quarterly* (formerly *The New Scholasticism*).

approximately, do these sons and daughters of the Reformation have against proving the existence of God? What *could* they have against it? What could be less objectionable to any but the most obdurate atheist?

PROOF AND BELIEF IN GOD

Let's begin with the nineteenth century Dutch theologian Herman Bavinck:

> Scripture urges us to behold heaven and earth, birds and flowers and lilies, in order that we may see and recognize God in them. "Lift up your eyes on high, and see who hath created these." Is. 40:26. Scripture does not reason in the abstract. It does not make God the conclusion of a syllogism, leaving it to us whether we think the argument holds or not. But it speaks with authority. Both theologically and religiously it proceeds from God as the starting point.[3]

> We receive the impression that belief in the existence of God is based entirely upon these proofs. But indeed that would be "a wretched faith, which, before it invokes God, must first prove his existence." The contrary, however, is the truth. . . . Of the existence of self, of the world round about us, of logical and moral laws, etc., we are so deeply convinced because of the indelible impressions which all these things make upon our consciousness that we need no arguments or demonstration. Spontaneously, altogether involuntarily: without any constraint or coercion, we accept that existence. Now the same is true in regard to the existence of God. The so-called proofs are by no means the final grounds of our most certain conviction that God exists: This certainly is established only by faith; i.e., by the spontaneous testimony which forces itself upon us from every side.[4]

According to Bavinck, then, a Christian's belief in the existence of God is not based upon proofs or arguments. By 'argument' here, I think he means arguments in the style of natural theology—the sort given by Aquinas and Scotus and later by Descartes, Leibniz, Clarke and others. And what he means to say, I think, is that Christians don't *need* such arguments. Don't need them for what?

Here I think Bavinck means to hold two things. First, arguments or proofs are not, in general, the source of the believer's confidence in God. Typically, the believer does not believe in God on the basis of arguments; nor does he believe such truths as, for example, that God has created the world on the basis of arguments. Secondly, argument is not needed for *rational justification*; the believer is entirely within his epistemic right in believing that God has created the world, even if he has no argument at all for that conclusion. The believer doesn't need natural theology in order to achieve rationality or epistemic propriety in believing; his belief in God can be perfectly rational even if he knows of no cogent argument, deductive or inductive, for the existence of God—indeed, even if there *isn't* any such argument.

Bavinck has three further points. First he means to add, I think, that we *cannot* come to knowledge of God on the basis of argument; the arguments of natural theology just don't work. (And he follows this passage with a more or less traditional attempt to refute the theistic proofs, including an endorsement of some of Kant's fashionable confusions about the ontological argument.) Secondly, Scripture "proceeds from God as the starting point," and so should the believer. There is nothing by way of proofs or arguments for God's existence in the Bible; that is simply presupposed. The same should be true of the Christian believer then, he should *start* from belief in God, rather than from the premises of some argument whose conclusion is that God exists. What is it that makes those premises a better starting point anyway? And third, Bavinck points out that belief in God relevantly resembles belief in the existence of the self and of the external world—and, we might add, belief in other minds and the past. In none of these areas do we typically *have* proof or arguments, or *need* proofs or arguments.

According to John Calvin, who is as good a Calvinist as any, God has implanted in us all an innate tendency, or nisus, or disposition to believe in him:

> 'There is within the human mind, and indeed by natural instinct, an awareness of divinity.' This we take to be beyond controversy. To prevent anyone from taking refuge in the pretense of ignorance, God himself has implanted in all men a certain understanding of his divine majesty. Ever renewing its memory, he repeatedly sheds fresh drops. Since, therefore, men one and all perceive that there is a God and that he is their Maker, they are condemned by their own testimony because they have failed to honor him and to consecrate their lives to his will. If ignorance of God is to be looked for anywhere, surely one is most likely to find an example of it among the more backward folk and those more remote from civilization. Yet there is, as the eminent pagan says, no nation so barbarous, no people so savage, that they have not a deep-seated conviction that there is a God. So deeply does the common conception occupy the minds of all, so tenaciously does it inhere in the hearts of all! Therefore, since from the beginning of the world there has been no region, no city, in short, no household, that could do without religion, there lies in this a tacit confession of a sense of deity inscribed in the hearts of all.[5]

> Indeed, the perversity of the impious, who though they struggle furiously are unable to extricate themselves from the fear of God, is abundant testimony that this conviction, namely, that there is some God, is naturally inborn in all, and is fixed deep within, as it were in the very marrow. . . . From this we conclude that it is not a doctrine that must first be learned in school, but one of which each of us is master from his mother's womb and which nature itself permits no one to forget.[6]

Calvin's claim, then, is that God has created us in such a way that we have a strong propensity or inclination towards belief in him. This tendency has been in part overlaid or suppressed by sin. Were it not for the existence of sin in the world, human beings would believe in God to the same degree and with the same natural spontaneity that we believe in the existence of other persons, an external world, or the past. This is the natural human condition; it is because of our presently unnatural sinful condition that many of us find belief in God difficult or absurd. The fact is, Calvin thinks, one who doesn't believe in God is in an epistemically substandard position—rather like a man who doesn't believe that his wife exists, or thinks she is like a cleverly constructed robot and has no thoughts, feelings, or consciousness.

Although this disposition to believe in God is partially suppressed, it is nonetheless universally present. And it is triggered or actuated by widely realized conditions:

> Lest anyone, then, be excluded from access to happiness, he not only sowed in men's minds that seed of religion of which we have spoken, but revealed himself and daily discloses himself in the whole workmanship of the universe. As a consequence, men cannot open their eyes without being compelled to see him.[7]

Like Kant, Calvin is especially impressed in this connection, by the marvelous compages of the starry heavens above:

> Even the common folk and the most untutored, who have been taught only by the aid of the eyes, cannot be unaware of the excellence of divine art, for it reveals itself in this innumerable and yet distinct and well-ordered variety of the heavenly host.[8]

And Calvin's claim is that one who accedes to this tendency and in these circumstances accepts the belief that God has created the world—perhaps upon beholding the starry heavens, or the splendid majesty of the mountains, or the intricate, articulate beauty of a tiny flower—is entirely within his epistemic rights in so doing. It isn't that such a person is justified or rational in so believing by virtue of having an implicit argument—some version of the teleological argument, say. No; he doesn't need any argument for justification or rationality. His belief need not be based on any other propositions at all; under these conditions he is perfectly rational in accepting belief in God in the utter absence of any argument, deductive or inductive. Indeed, a person in these conditions, says Calvin, *knows* that God exists, has knowledge of God's existence, apart from any argument at all.

Elsewhere Calvin speaks of "arguments from reason" or rational arguments:

> The prophets and apostles do not boast either of their keenness or of anything that obtains credit for them as they speak; nor do they dwell upon rational proofs. Rather, they bring forward God's holy name, that by it the whole world may be brought into obedience to him. Now we ought to see how apparent it is not only by plausible opinion but by clear truth that they do not call upon God's name heedlessly or falsely. If we desire to provide in the best way for our consciences—that they may not be perpetually beset by the instability of doubt or vacillation, and that they may not also boggle at the smallest quibbles—we ought to seek our conviction in a higher place than human reasons, judgments, or conjectures, that is, in the secret testimony of the Spirit.[9]

Here the subject for discussion is not belief in the existence of God, but belief that God is the author of the Scriptures; I think it is clear, however, that Calvin would say the same thing about belief in God's existence. The Christian doesn't *need* natural theology, either as the source of his confidence or to justify his belief. Furthermore, the Christian *ought* not to believe on the basis of argument; if he does, his faith is likely to be unstable and wavering. From Calvin's point of view, believing in the existence of God on the basis of rational argument is like believing in the existence of your spouse on the basis of the analogical argument for other minds—whimsical at best and not at all likely to delight the person concerned.

FOUNDATIONALISM

We could look further into the precise forms taken by the Reformed objection to Natural Theology; time is short, however; what I shall do instead is tell you what I think underlies these objections, inchoate and unfocused as they are. The reformers mean to say, fundamentally, that belief in God can properly be taken as *basic*. That is, a person is entirely within his epistemic rights, entirely rational, in believing in God, even if he has no argument for this belief and does not believe it on the basis of any other beliefs he holds. And in taking belief in God as properly basic, the reformers were implicitly rejecting a whole picture or way of looking at knowledge and rational belief; call it *classical foundationalism*. This picture has been enormously popular ever since the days of Plato and Aristotle; it remains the dominant way of thinking about knowledge, justification, belief, faith, and allied topics. Although it has been thus dominant, Reformed theologians and thinkers have, I believe, meant to reject it. What they say here tends to be inchoate and not well-articulated; nevertheless the fact is they meant to reject classical foundationalism. But how shall we characterize the view rejected? The first thing to see is that foundationalism is a *normative* view. It aims to lay down conditions that must be met by anyone whose system of beliefs is *rational*; and here "rational" is to be understood normatively. According to the foundationalist, there is a right way and a wrong way with respect to belief. People have responsibilities, duties and obligations with respect to their believings just as with respect to their (other) actions. Perhaps this sort of obligation is really a special case of a more general moral obligation; or perhaps, on the other hand, it is *sui generis*. In any event there are such obligations: to conform to them is to be rational and to go against them is to be irrational. To be rational, then, is to exercise one's epistemic powers *properly*—to exercise them in such a way as to go contrary to none of the norms for such exercise.

Foundationalism, therefore, is in part a normative thesis. I think we can understand this thesis more fully if we introduce the idea of a *noetic structure*. A person's noetic structure is the set of propositions he believes together with certain epistemic relations that hold among him and these propositions. Thus some of his beliefs may be *based on* other things he believes; it may be that there are a pair of propositions *A* and *B* such that he believes *A on the basis of B*. Although this relation isn't easy to characterize in a revealing and non-trivial fashion, it is nonetheless familiar. I believe that the word 'umbrageous' is spelled u-m-b-r-a-g-e-o-u-s: this belief is based on another belief of mine, the belief that that's how the dictionary says it's spelled. It believe that $72 \times 71 = 5112$. This belief is based upon several other beliefs I hold—such beliefs as that $1 \times 72 = 72$; $7 \times 2 = 14$; $7 \times 7 = 49$; $49 + 1 = 50$; and others. Some of my beliefs, however, I accept but don't accept on the basis of any other beliefs. I believe that $2 + 1 = 3$, for example, and don't believe it on the basis of other propositions. I also believe that I am seated at my desk, and that there is a mild pain in my right knee. These too are basic for me; I don't believe them on the basis of any other propositions.

An account of a person's noetic structure, then, would include a specification of which of his beliefs are basic and which are non-basic. Of course it is abstractly possible that *none* of his beliefs is basic; perhaps he holds just three beliefs, A, B, and C, and believes each of them on the basis of the other two. We might think this improper or irrational, but that is not to say it couldn't be done. And it is also possible that *all* of his beliefs are basic; perhaps he believes a lot of propositions, but doesn't believe any of them on the basis of any others. In the typical case, however, a noetic structure will include both basic and non-basic beliefs.

Secondly, an account of a noetic structure will include what we might call an index of degree of belief. I hold some of my beliefs much more firmly than others. I believe both that $2 + 1 = 3$ and that London, England, is north of Saskatoon, Saskatchewan; but I believe the former more resolutely than the latter. Here we might make use of the personalist[10] interpretation of probability theory; think of an index of degree of belief as a function Ps(*A*) from the set of propositions a person *S* believes or disbelieves into the real numbers between 0 and 1. Ps(*A*) = n, then, records something like the degree to which *S* believes *A*, or the strength of his belief that *A*. Ps(*A*) = 1 proclaims *S*'s utter and abandoned commitment to *A*; Ps(*A*) = 0 records a similar commitment to not-*A*; Ps(*A*) = .5 means that *S*, like Buridan's ass, is suspended in equilibrium between *A* and not-*A*. We could then go on to consider whether the personalist is right in holding that a rational noetic structure conforms to the Calculus of Probability.[11]

Thirdly, a somewhat vaguer notion; an account of *S*'s noetic structure would include something like an index of *depth of ingression*. Some of my beliefs are, we might say, on the periphery of my noetic structure. I accept them, and may even accept them quite firmly; but if I were to give them up, not much else in my noetic structure would have to change. I believe there are some large boulders on the top of the Grand Teton. If I come to give up this belief, however (say by climbing it and not finding any), that change wouldn't have extensive reverberations throughout the rest of my noetic structure; it could be accommodated with minimal alteration elsewhere. So its depth of ingression into my noetic structure isn't great. On the other hand, if I were to come to believe that there simply is no such thing as the Grand Teton, or no mountains at all, or no such thing as the state of Wyoming, that would have much greater reverberations. And if, *per impossible,* I were to come to think there hadn't been much of a past (that the world was created just five minutes ago, complete with all its apparent memories and traces of the past), or that there weren't any other persons, that would have even greater reverberations; these beliefs of mine have great depth of ingression into my noetic structure.

Now classical foundationalism is best construed, I think, as a thesis about *rational* noetic structures. A noetic structure is rational if it could be the noetic structure of a person who was completely rational. To be completely rational, as I am here using the term, is not to believe only what is true, or to believe all the logical consequences of what one believes, or to believe all necessary truths with equal firmness, or to be uninfluenced by emotion; it is, instead, to do the right thing with respect to one's believings. As we have seen, the foundationalist holds that there are responsibilities and duties that pertain to believings as well as to actions, or other actions; these responsibilities accrue to us just by virtue of our having the sorts of noetic capabilities we do have. There are norms or standards for beliefs. To criticize a person as irrational, then, is to criticize her for failing to fulfill these duties or responsibilities, or for failing to conform to the relevant norms or standards. From this point of view, a rational person is one whose believings meet the appropriate standards. To draw the ethical analogy, the irrational is the impermissible; the rational is the permissible.

A rational noetic structure, then, is one that could be the noetic structure of a perfectly rational person. And classical foundationalism is, in part, a thesis about such noetic structures. The foundationalist notes, first of all, that some of our beliefs are based upon others. He immediately adds that a belief can't properly be accepted on the basis of just *any* other belief; in a rational noetic structure, *A* will be accepted on the basis of *B* only if *B supports A,* or is a member of a set of beliefs that together support *A*. It isn't clear just what this supports relation is; different foundationalists propose different candidates. One candidate, for example, is *entailment*; *A* supports *B* only if *B* is entailed by *A*, or perhaps is self-evidently entailed by *A*, or perhaps follows from *A* by an argument where each step is a self-evident entailment. Another and more permissive candidate is probability; perhaps *A* supports *B* if *B* is likely or probable with respect to *A*. And of course there are other candidates.

More important for present purposes, however, is the following claim: in a rational noetic structure, there will be some beliefs that are not based upon others: call these its *foundations.* If every belief in a rational noetic structure were based upon other beliefs, the structure in question would contain infinitely many beliefs. However things may stand for more powerful intellects—angelic intellects, perhaps—human beings aren't capable of believing infinitely many propositions. Among other things, one presumably doesn't believe a proposition one has never heard of, and no one has had time, these busy days, to have heard of infinitely many propositions. So every rational noetic structure has a foundation.

Suppose we say that *weak* foundationalism is the view that (1) every rational noetic structure has a foundation, and (2) in a rational noetic structure, non-basic belief is proportional in strength to support from the foundations. When I say Reformed thinkers have meant to reject foundationalism, I do not mean to say that they intended to reject weak foundationalism. On the contrary; the thought of many of them tends to support or endorse weak foundationalism. What then do they mean to reject? Here we meet a further and fundamental feature of classic varieties of foundationalism: they all lay down certain conditions of proper or rational basicality. From the foundationalist point of view, not just any kind of belief can be found in the foundations of a rational noetic structure; a belief, to be properly basic (i.e., basic in a rational noetic structure) must meet certain conditions. It is plausible to see Thomas Aquinas, for example, as holding that a proposition is properly basic for a person only if it is self-evident to him (such that his understanding or grasping it is sufficient for his seeing it to be true) or "evident to the senses," as he puts it. By this latter term I think he means to refer to propositions whose truth or falsehood we can determine by looking or listening or employing some other sense—such propositions as

(1) There is a tree before me

(2) I am wearing shoes

and

(3) That tree's leaves are yellow.

Many foundationalists have insisted that propositions basic in a rational noetic structure must be *certain* in some important sense. Thus it is plausible to see Descartes as holding that the foundations of a rational noetic structure don't include such propositions as (1) – (3) but more cautious claims—claims about one's own mental life, for example:

(4) It seems to me that I see a tree

(5) I seem to see something green

or, as Professor Chisholm puts it,

(6) I am appeared greenly to.

Propositions of this latter sort seem to enjoy a kind of immunity from error not enjoyed by those of the former. I could be mistaken in thinking I see a pink rat; perhaps I am hallucinating or the victim of an illusion. But it is at the least very much harder to see that I could be mistaken in believing that I *seem* to see a pink rat, in believing that I am appeared pinkly (or pink ratly) to. Suppose we say that a proposition with respect to which I enjoy this sort of immunity from error is *incorrigible* for me; then perhaps Descartes means to hold that a proposition is properly basic for *S* only if it is either self-evident or incorrigible for *S*.

Aquinas and Descartes, we might say, are *strong* foundationalists; they accept weak foundationalism and add some conditions for proper basicality. Ancient and medieval foundationalists tended to hold that a proposition is properly basic for a person only if it is either self-evident or evident to the senses; modern foundationalists—Descartes, Locke, Leibniz and the like—tended to hold that a proposition is properly basic for *S* only if either self-evident or incorrigible for *S*. Of course this is a historical generalization and is thus subject to contradiction by scholars, such being the penalty for historical generalization; but perhaps it is worth the risk. And now suppose we say that *classical foundationalism* is the disjunction of ancient and medieval with modern foundationalism.

THE REFORMED REJECTION OF CLASSICAL FOUNDATIONALISM

These Reformed thinkers, I believe, are best understood as rejecting classical foundationalism.[12] They were inclined to accept weak foundationalism, I think; but they were completely at odds with the idea that the foundations of a rational noetic structure can at most include propositions that are self-evident or evident to the senses or incorrigible. In particular, they were prepared to insist that a rational noetic structure can include belief in God as basic. As Bavinck put it "Scripture . . . does not make God the conclusion of a syllogism, leaving it to us whether we think the argument holds or not. But it speaks with authority." Both theologically and religiously it proceeds from God as the starting point (above, n. 3). And of course Bavinck means to say that we must emulate Scripture here.

In the passages I quoted earlier on, Calvin claims the believer doesn't need argument—doesn't need it, among other things, for epistemic respectability. We may understand him as holding, I think, that a rational noetic structure may perfectly well contain belief in God among its foundations. Indeed, he means to go further, and in two separate directions. In the first place, he thinks a Christian *ought* not believe in God on the basis of other propositions; a proper and well formed Christian noetic structure will *in fact* have belief in God among its foundations. And in the second place Calvin claims that one who takes belief in God as basic can nonetheless *know* that God exists. Calvin holds that one can *rationally accept* belief in God as basic; he also claims that one can *know* that God exists even if he has no argument, even if he does not believe on the basis of other propositions. A weak foundationalist is likely to hold that some properly basic beliefs are such that anyone who accepts them, *knows* them. More exactly, he is likely to hold that among the beliefs properly basic for a person *S*, some are such that if *S* accepts them *S* knows them. A weak foundationalist could go on to say that *other* properly basic beliefs can't be known, if taken as basic, but only rationally believed; and he might think of the existence of God as a case in point. Calvin will have none of this; as he sees it, one needs no arguments to know that God exists.

Among the central contentions of these Reformed thinkers, therefore, are the claims that belief in God is properly basic, and the view that one who takes belief in God as basic can also *know* that God exists.

THE GREAT PUMPKIN OBJECTION

Now I enthusiastically concur in these contentions of Reformed epistemology, and by way of conclusion I want to defend them against a popular objection. It is tempting to raise the following sort of question. If belief in God is properly basic, why can't just any belief be properly basic? Couldn't we say the same for any bizarre aberration we can think of? What about voodoo or astrology? What about the belief that the Great Pumpkin returns every Halloween? Could I properly take *that* as basic? And if I can't, why can I properly take belief in God as basic? Suppose I believe that if I flap my arms with sufficient vigor, I can take off and fly about the room; could I defend myself against the charge of irrationality by claiming this belief is basic? If we say that belief in God is properly basic, won't we be committed to holding that just anything, or nearly anything, can properly be taken as basic, thus throwing wide the gates to irrationalism and superstition?

Certainly not. What might lead one to think the Reformed epistemologist is in this kind of trouble? The fact that he rejects the criteria for proper basicality purveyed by the classical foundationalist? But why should *that* be thought to commit him to such tolerance of irrationality? Consider an analogy. In the palmy days of positivism, the positivists went about confidently wielding their verifiability criterion and declaring meaningless much that was obviously meaningful. Now suppose someone rejected a formulation of that criterion—the one to be found in the second edition of A. J. Ayer's *Language, Truth and Logic*, for example. Would that mean she was committed to holding that

(7) 'T was brillig; and the slithy toves did gyre and gymble in the wabe,

contrary to appearances, makes good sense? Of course not. But then the same goes for the Reformed epistemologist; the fact that he rejects the criteria of Classical Foundationalism does not mean that he is committed to supposing just anything is properly basic.

But what then is the problem? Is it that the Reformed epistemologist not only rejects those criteria for proper basicality, but seems in no hurry to produce what he takes to be a better substitute? If he has no such criterion, how can he fairly reject belief in the Great Pumpkin as properly basic?

This objection betrays an important misconception. How *do* we rightly arrive at or develop criteria for meaningfulness, or justified belief, or proper basicality? Where do they come from? Must one have such a criterion before one can sensibly make any judgments—positive or negative—about proper basicality? Surely not. Suppose I don't know of a satisfactory substitute for the criteria proposed by classical foundationalism; I am nevertheless entirely within my rights in holding that certain propositions are not properly basic in certain conditions. Some propositions seem self-evident when in fact they are not; that is the lesson of some of the Russell Paradoxes.[13] Nevertheless it would be irrational to take as basic the denial of a proposition that seems self-evident to you. Similarly, suppose it seems to you that you see a tree; you would then be irrational in taking as basic the proposition that you don't see a tree, or that there aren't any trees. In the same way, even if I don't know of some illuminating criterion of meaning, I can quite properly declare (7) meaningless, even if I don't have a successful substitute for the positivist's verifiability criterion.

And this raises an important question—one Roderick Chisholm has taught us to ask.[14] What is the status of criteria for meaningfulness, or proper basicality, or justified belief? These are typically universal statements. The modern foundationalist's criterion for proper basicality, for example, is doubly universal:

(8) For any proposition *A* and person *S*, *A* is properly basic for *S* if and only if *A* is incorrigible for *S* or self-evident to *S*.

But how does one know a thing like that? Where does it come from? (8) certainly isn't self-evident or just obviously true. But if it isn't, how does one arrive at it? What sorts of arguments would be appropriate? Of course a philosopher might find (8) so appealing that he simply takes it to be true, neither offering argument for it, nor accepting it on the basis of other things he believes. If he does so, however, his noetic structure will be self-referentially incoherent. (8) itself is neither self-evident nor incorrigible; hence in accepting (8) as basic, the classical foundationalist violates the condition of proper basicality he himself lays down in accepting it. On the other hand, perhaps the philosopher has some argument for it from premises that are self-evident; it is exceeding hard to see, however, what such arguments might be like. And until he has produced such arguments, what shall the rest of us do—we who do not find (8) at all obvious or compelling? How could he use (8) to show us that belief in God, for example, is not properly basic? Why should we believe (8), or pay it any attention?

The fact is, I think, that neither (8) nor any other revealing necessary and sufficient condition for proper basicality follows from obviously self-evident premises by obviously acceptable arguments. And hence the proper way to arrive at such a criterion is, broadly speaking, *inductive*. We must assemble examples of beliefs and conditions such that the former are obviously properly basic in the latter, and examples of beliefs and conditions such that the former are obviously not properly basic in the latter. We must then frame hypotheses as to the necessary and sufficient conditions of proper basicality and test these hypotheses by reference to those examples. Under the right conditions, for example, it is clearly rational to believe that you see a human person before you: a being who has thoughts and feelings, who knows and believes things, who makes decisions and acts. It is clear, furthermore, that you are under no obligation to reason to this belief from others you hold; under those conditions that belief is properly basic for you. But then (8) must be mistaken; the belief in question, under those circumstances, is properly basic, though neither self-evident not incorrigible for you. Similarly, you may seem to remember that you had breakfast this morning, and perhaps you know of no reason to suppose your memory is playing you tricks. If so, you are entirely justified in taking that belief as basic. Of course it isn't properly basic on the criteria offered by classical foundationalists; but that fact counts not against you but against those criteria.

Accordingly, criteria for proper basicality must be reached from below rather than above; they should not be presented as *obiter dicta,* but argued to and tested by a relevant set of examples. But there is no reason to assume, in advance, that everyone will agree on the examples. The Christian will of course suppose that belief in God is entirely proper and rational; if he doesn't accept this belief on the basis of other propositions, he will conclude that it is basic for him and quite properly so. Followers of Bertrand Russell and Madalyn Murray O'Hair may disagree; but how is that relevant? Must my criteria, or those of the Christian community, conform to their examples? Surely not. The Christian community is responsible to *its* set of examples, not to theirs.

Accordingly, the Reformed epistemologist can properly hold that belief in the Great Pumpkin is not properly basic, even though he holds that belief in God is properly basic and even if he has no full fledged criterion of proper basicality. Of course he is committed to supposing that there is a relevant *difference* between belief in God and belief in the Great Pumpkin, if he holds that the former but not the latter is properly basic. But this should be no great embarrassment; there are plenty of candidates. Thus the Reformed epistemologist may concur with Calvin in holding that God has implanted in us a natural tendency to see his hand in the world around us; the same cannot be said for the Great Pumpkin, there being no Great Pumpkin and no natural tendency to accept beliefs about the Great Pumpkin.

By way of conclusion then, the Reformed objection to natural theology, unformed and inchoate as it is, may best be seen as a rejection of classical foundationalism. As the Reformed thinker sees things, being self-evident, or incorrigible, or evident to the senses is not a necessary condition of proper basicality. He goes on to add that belief in God is properly basic. He is not thereby committed, even in the absence of a general criterion of proper basicality, to suppose that just any or nearly any belief—belief in the Great Pumpkin, for example—is properly basic. Like everyone should, he begins with examples; and he may take belief in the Great Pumpkin as a paradigm of irrational basic belief.

NOTES

1. See, for example, James Ross, *Philosophical Theology* (Indianapolis: Bobbs-Merrill, 1969), and Richard Swinburne, *The Existence of God* (Oxford: Clarendon Press, 1979).

2. "God," in *Studies in Theology* (New York: Oxford University Press, 1932), pp. 110–11.

3. *The Doctrine of God*, trans. William Hendriksen (Grand Rapids: Eerdmans, 1951). This is a translation of vol. 2 of Bavinck's *Gereformeerde Dogmatiek* (Kampen: Kok, 1918), p. 76.

4. *Ibid.*, p. 78.

5. *Institutes of the Christian Religion*, ed. J. T. McNeill and trans. Ford Lewis Battles (Philadelphia: Westminster Press, 1960), Book 1, Chap. iii, sec. 1.

6. *Institutes*, 1, iii, 3.

7. *Institutes*, V, v, 1.

8. *Institutes*, V, v, 2.

9. *Institutes*, I, vii, 4.

10. See, for example, Richard Jeffrey's *The Logic of Decision* (New York: McGraw-Hill, 1965).

11. See my paper "The Probabilistic Argument from Evil," *Philosophical Studies* 30 (1979): 21.

12. Here I think they were entirely correct; both ancient and modern foundationalism are self-referentially incoherent. See my paper "Is Belief in God Rational?" (*Rationality and Religious Belief*, ed. C. Delany (South Bend: University of Notre Dame Press, 1979), p. 26.

13. "Is Belief in God Rational?" p. 22.

14. *The Problem of the Criterion* (Milwaukee: Marquette University Press, 1973).

JAY M. VAN HOOK

Knowledge, Belief, and Reformed Epistemology

Jay Van Hook (1939–) raises questions about the "Reformed epistemology" developed by such thinkers as Alvin Plantinga and Nicholas Wolterstorff. He notes that, in the recent past, "foundationalist" epistemologies have generally reserved the term "knowledge" for beliefs so firmly based that (it was thought) any rational person would be forced to agree with them. However, in this "post-foundationalist" era, it is recognized that there are rather few beliefs of this kind; all the most important questions are "up for grabs," and no methods are available that can be counted upon to produce general agreement. In view of this, Van Hook asks: What precisely is "knowledge" on a post-foundationalist or Reformed model and how, if at all, does it differ from mere "belief," or even from "rational" belief? Do Reformed epistemologists gain anything of substance

From *The Reformed Journal*, July 1981, pp. 12–17. Reprinted by permission of *Perspectives* (formerly *The Reformed Journal*).

by claiming that they *know* that God exists, as opposed merely to *believing* in God?

⌘

Philosophers have long been perplexed by the problem of which, and under what conditions, human beliefs may properly lay claim to being not merely beliefs, but also "knowledge." Christian thinkers, too, have labored over this issue, and not only in general, but also with reference to religious beliefs. May any of our beliefs about God, for example, ever properly be considered *knowledge*? If so, which and when? If not, why not?

The claim to know is ordinarily construed by philosophers and laymen alike as stronger than the claim to believe. Beliefs may turn out to be mistaken. We find nothing unusual about a friend's confession that one of his beliefs has turned out to be false. But we would consider it peculiar if someone admitted that some of her knowledge had proven to be false. Knowledge, unlike belief, is supposed to be immune to falsity. And in a case where a knowledge claim does turn out to be false, the conclusion to be drawn is that the person did not know what he thought he knew rather than that his knowledge itself is false.

The dominant theories of knowledge in Western philosophy have been one or another version of what is often termed "foundationalism." According to this view, a statement of belief may be taken as knowledge if and only if it is either a "foundational" (or "basic") proposition or one which is derived from foundational propositions in some appropriate way. Foundational propositions are alleged to be self-evident and incorrigible; they are grasped immediately and with certitude. While there is little agreement as to which propositions are properly foundational, Descartes's well-known "I think, therefore I am" and the reports of immediate sensations such as "I am in pain" are frequently advanced as candidates. Both deduction and induction (or probabilism) have been advocated as appropriate methods for building additional knowledge upon the foundational certitudes. Thus for some foundationalists, propositions which can be deduced from foundational propositions meet the requirement for inclusion in the house of knowledge, while for others propositions justified probabilistically in terms of basic propositions will so qualify.

Of late, considerable discussion has taken place among Reformed philosophers about the relation of religious beliefs to the foundation of knowledge. This discussion has been occasioned, I think, by at least two factors: first, the foundationalist theory just outlined has itself fallen upon hard times; and second, Reformed Christians have felt a continuing need to address a persistent legacy of logical positivism according to which statements of religious belief are at best emotive utterances which fall completely outside the scope of knowledge.

In what follows, I want to take up the issue of religious belief and knowledge as it has been dealt with by philosophers Nicholas Wolterstorff, whose critique of foundationalism is familiar to many professionals both within and beyond the Reformed community, and Alvin Plantinga, whose work in the philosophy of religion has received international attention (and earned him the designation from *Time* magazine as "orthodox Christianity's leading philosopher of God"). I shall be especially concerned here with what Plantinga has recently called "Reformed epistemology." Along the way, I shall detour in order to consider Princeton University philosopher Richard Rorty's notion of knowledge as "what our peers will let us get away with saying." My aim is more to raise some questions in the hope of provoking further discussion than it is to try to defend or refute some particular theory of knowledge.

The basic question I shall pose is this: What precisely *is* "knowledge" on a post-foundationalist or Reformed model and how, if at all, does it differ from mere "belief," or even from "rational" belief?

First, a further look at foundationalism and Wolterstorff's criticism of it.

As noted above, foundationalism attempts to set down the conditions upon which beliefs may properly be taken as knowledge. Its aim is to separate the prejudice and conjecture associated with opinion from objectively certain knowledge. To achieve this aim, it attempts to construct the superstructure of knowledge on a firm foundation of certitude using the method either of deduction or of induction. Wolterstorff contends, however, that both of these methods face insurmountable difficulties.

The appeal of deduction, of course, is not hard to discern. Every elementary logic student learns the simple deductive syllogism: "All men are mortal; Socrates is a man; therefore, Socrates is mortal." The advantage of deduction is that if the premises are true and the argument form valid, the conclusion follows with inexorable necessity. So propositions deduced from indubitable foundational propositions would seem also to have the prized characteristic of indubitability. But the problem for the deductive approach lies in the fact that little of what we know proves deducible from foundational certitudes. Thus Wolterstorff observes that while deduction promises certainty, "most universal propositions about physical objects would not be warranted."[1] "All swans have wings," for example, cannot be deduced from my knowledge (even if that knowledge were certain) that the specific swans I have encountered (however great the number) all have wings. But neither is "All swans have wings" a foundational proposition. There is nothing immediately self-evident about it.

Since deductivism has not worked very well, many foundationalists have turned instead to an inductive or probabilistic approach to adding propositions to the stock of foundational certitudes. The inductive method proceeds from the foundational certitudes to propositions which are seen as having more or less probability with respect to that foundation. But Wolterstorff correctly notes that the shift to probabilism already involves "a radical lowering of standards" as to what constitutes knowledge, one which would be rejected by deductivists who "would have refused to regard conjectures—no matter how probable—as knowledge at all."[2] Thus, even if successful, the probabilistic route involves weakening the original goal of certainty and incorrigibility. And beyond all this, Wolterstorff argues that theorists have so far failed to provide a convincing justification for induction itself.

Another way of looking at the same matter is this: the foundationalist is confronted with the difficulty of finding an adequate supply of foundational propositions to support the superstructure of knowledge; for these must be both true and "known noninferentially and with certitude to be true."[3] It turns out that basic propositions are not easy to come by. If one wishes to take the reports of immediate perception as basic, one must then face the problem that our reports of these perceptions are by no means infallible. I may be wrong about what I think I see, though perhaps I can't be wrong that I *seem* to see what I think I see. Thus even such an elementary report of sense perception as "I see a cat on the roof" seems to dissolve, after a hard-nosed search for the incorrigible, into the much more cautious claim that "I am appeared to cat-on-roofishly." Statements attempting to discuss real objects turn out to be statements about our own states of consciousness. And as Wolterstorff puts it, "It seems unlikely that from our introspective knowledge of propositions about our own states of consciousness we could erect the whole structure of objective science."[4] We apparently do not have enough basic propositions on which to build the house of knowledge.

These considerations provide the background for Wolterstorff's verdict that foundationalism is mortally ill and must be given up. He is careful to stress, however, that his rejection of foundationalism involves neither skepticism (the view that nothing can be known) nor epistemological permissiveness ("anything goes"). It is not entirely clear, though, just how skepticism is to be avoided. Given the demise of foundationalism, it seems to me that essentially two routes are open. One may either adhere to the foundationalist criterion and simply concede that we do not have any knowledge (or at least not much), or adopt a weaker criterion which makes knowledge possible (just as, by analogy, one can always give a passing grade to all of one's students if the standards are lowered sufficiently). It is not clear to me, moreover, that either of these approaches is intrinsically superior to the other. Wolterstorff, I believe, opts for a weakened criterion, though he has not yet published a formulation of such a criterion. If this indeed is what he wishes to do, then we need to recognize that the standards for what counts as knowledge have in fact been lowered.

My point, quite simply, is this. The basic aim of the whole enterprise of epistemology from Plato to our own day has been to provide what can be called a "common ground" on the basis of which knowledge claims can be made, criticized, justified, and settled. Now it may well be the case, as many philosophers and others have begun to suspect, that no such common ground exists or can be identified. But to say that we can have knowledge anyway, without a common ground, is surely to propose a radical alteration in the very idea of knowledge. Even so, there may be nothing amiss; perhaps the idea of knowledge needs to be altered. But one may legitimately ask, I think, what the criterion for knowledge is now going to be. But to this question Wolterstorff has not as yet provided an answer. Perhaps the new "Reformed epistemology" will furnish the needed criterion.

Before taking up Reformed epistemology, however, I wish to focus my concern by considering Richard Rorty's suggestion that knowledge is basically "what our peers will let us get away with saying." I do so not because I expect Reformed thinkers to find this suggestion congenial, but because it is not clear to me that even a Reformed epistemology can get very far beyond such a view.

Like Wolterstorff, Rorty believes that foundationalism is untenable. He also thinks that we need not trouble ourselves about trying to replace current theories of knowledge with a new and better epistemology. He suggests instead that we learn to do without epistemology altogether, and that we substitute "edifying conversation" for the scholastic argumentation (that is, abstruse logical arguments comprehensible only to other logicians) which constitutes the bulk of contemporary philosophizing. These are refreshing recommendations, the more so because they come from a recent president of the American Philosophical Association. But they cannot be pursued here. I shall consider, however, Rorty's admittedly pragmatic view of knowledge.

At first glance, to be sure, the notion of knowledge as "what our peers let us get away with saying" seems a rather slim and disappointing result of 2500 years of earnest philosophical reflection. But there is some plausibility about the idea, and it may well contain more truth than most of us would happily admit to. Consider the following examples (which are not Rorty's). . . .

Among the things I claim to know is that George Washington was the first president of the United States. Now on what basis can I be so audacious as to claim to know this? I never saw Washington at all, and certainly not functioning presidentially. My teachers told me? But surely my teachers are not infallible. I read it in books? But I can't rely on everything I read. Government documents? Perhaps a part of government myth-making. And on we could go. Is it all that farfetched to say that a claim to know holds in this case precisely because no one challenges the claim? In those cases where I believe just what everyone else also believes, I am very likely to be able to "get away with saying" that I *know*.

A person's claims to know will also ordinarily go unchallenged in cases where he is thought to have privileged access (for example, his own pains or mental states), where he is regarded as an expert, or where the claim simply doesn't arouse enough interest to make it worth challenging. I say "ordinarily" because there may be exceptional cases where even a person's knowledge of his own pain would be challenged (consider the skeptical reaction to Roberto Duran's alleged stomach cramps during his fight with Sugar Ray Leonard . . .) and in all of these cases one's status in the opinion of his peers will have much to do with whether or not the claim to know is challenged. Some people have the good fortune to have their every pronouncement taken as almost oracular (such people, I believe, are likely to feel little inclination to skepticism); but others try in vain to have their words taken seriously.

The claims to know in the examples above are rather trivial. But now suppose that I claim to know that God exists and created the world. This is a controversial claim, and not all of my peers will let it pass. My fellow church members and Christian colleagues may well accept the claim; a typical gathering of American philosophers probably would not. So it appears that I can properly be said to know things about God in some groups of peers, but not in others. Thus Rorty's view seems to have the unsatisfying result that one both knows and does not know the truth of certain controversial propositions, or at least the consequence that the more narrowly one construes her peers the more she will be able to know (a consequence which explains, as sociologists of religion have long understood, why many religious groups discourage contact with the outside world). Knowledge is peer-group relative.

As unhappy as we may be with such a relativistic theory of knowledge, we need to recognize that it stems from the failure to locate a common ground which could serve as a neutral basis for human knowledge. Although Rorty does not construe the idea of a common ground in a specifically theological way, his claim that there appears to be no common ground seems not all that far removed from what some Reformed theologians (notably followers of Cornelius Van Til) have also claimed. My purpose here, however, is not to engage in a critique of Rorty but to ask whether "Reformed epistemology" will serve us better. For this we turn to Alvin Plantinga.

Plantinga, too, concurs in the judgment that the usual versions of foundationalism (what he calls "strong" or "classical" foundationalism) are untenable and even incoherent. But Plantinga is inclined to accept what he calls "weak" foundationalism. Indeed, he argues that belief in God may be placed in the foundation of knowledge; or, to put it another way, belief in God is "properly basic." What this means is that Plantinga will not attempt to deduce God's existence from some other self-evident propositions (as does a traditional deductivist like Descartes), nor will he try to reach God's existence inductively from some indubitable givens of sensation (like, say, Aquinas). Instead he begins by boldly placing God's existence in the foundation of knowledge. As attractive as this move will surely appear to many Reformed Christians, the question I suppose is whether it will wash outside of Grand Rapids (or some similar place).

Now as I understand Plantinga's work in the philosophy of religion, its main thrust is to refute the charge that belief in God is irrational. Through powerful and often complicated arguments, Plantinga has repeatedly demolished the claims of anti-theists that belief in God is unjustified, irrational, and perhaps even immoral. One of his tactics has been to show that belief in God is in the same boat, epistemically, with beliefs which the anti-theists (and virtually everyone else) *do* hold, but which can no more easily be demonstrated than can the existence of God. Such beliefs include the belief in the existence of other minds and in the existence of a physical world which has existed for more than five minutes. But if it is not irrational to believe in the existence of minds other than our own (even though such existence can't be proved), Plantinga asks, why is it irrational to believe in God? The anti-theist has not demonstrated that such belief *is* irrational. Hence the theist violates no epistemological principles by believing in God.

Plantinga's work in this area has been a major achievement. Its primary beneficiaries, I think, are those theists who feel rather defensive and even apologetic about holding beliefs which "rational" people consider irrational. Armed with Plantinga, the theist need not allow herself to be bamboozled by the slurs of secularists.

I have no objection to Plantinga's contention that belief in God is rational even if, for some people, it is basic. It is not clear, however, why we can move from this to the claim of *knowledge*. Further, some of the theist's peers will undoubtedly protest that if belief in God can be properly basic, then just any belief can be claimed to be basic. But Plantinga anticipates and replies to this objection:

> If belief in God is properly basic, why can't *just any* belief be properly basic? Couldn't we say the same for any bizarre aberration we can think of? What about voodoo or astrology? What about the belief that the Great Pumpkin returns every Halloween? . . . If we say that belief in God is properly basic, won't we be committed to holding that just anything, or nearly anything, can properly be taken as basic, thus throwing wide the gates to irrationalism and superstition?
>
> Certainly not. What might lead one to think the Reformed epistemologist is in this kind of trouble? The fact that he rejects the criteria for proper basicality purveyed by classical foundationalism? But why should *that* be thought to commit him to such tolerance of irrationality?[5]

Now it seems to me that Plantinga takes this objection too lightly. Surely, as he says, the Reformed epistemologist is not *herself* committed to taking belief in the Great Pumpkin as properly basic! But that isn't the point. The question is whether the Reformed epistemologist could show a serious Great Pumpkin advocate (let's call him a "Pumpkinite") that *his* belief is *not* properly basic. And if she cannot show this, aren't we back to Rorty's relativistic peer groups? Couldn't a disinterested observer judge that the main difference between the theist and the Pumpkinite claims to proper basicality is that one has a much larger supporting community than the other? But how is that relevant? Even if we concede Plantinga's point that not anything goes and agree to throw out seemingly absurd candidates for basicality, it is difficult to see why, at the very lest, the adherents of the world's major religions and anti-religions could not claim that their beliefs are properly placed in the foundation of knowledge.

One of the problems here, I think is that the standard of "rationality" is too permissive and relativistic to serve as a criterion for knowledge. As Plantinga construes rationality, whether or not a person is rational has to do with the relations among her various beliefs, or with what he calls a person's "noetic structure." A person whose beliefs are mutually consistent or who has good reasons for some particular beliefs, for example, may be considered rational even though many of his beliefs are false. If all of the weather reports call for a major snow storm, a person's belief that it will snow and that he should take his boots to work would be considered rational. But the storm may pass over. One can hold a belief rationally which turns out to be false. Rationality is not truth-guaranteeing.

Consider one of Plantinga's examples:

> What about a fourteen-year-old theist brought up to believe in God in a community where everyone believes? This fourteen-year-old theist, we may suppose, doesn't believe on the basis of evidence. . . . Instead, he simply believes what he is taught. Is he violating an all-things-considered intellectual duty? Surely not.[6]

The fourteen-year-old theist, I take it, may be considered "rational" in this case. He violates no epistemological principles. But, of course, the very same thing can be said for *any* fourteen year old who believes what he is taught (perhaps even a fourteen-year-old Pumpkinite raised in an isolated rural Pumpkinite community). So rationality will not help us make the transition from belief to knowledge; or so it seems to me. And this is made quite clear, I think, in Plantinga's reply to one of his questioners at the Wheaton Conference:

> I think it's not appropriate to take as basic the proposition that God doesn't exist. But it doesn't follow from that that I either do or ought to think that I could prove to somebody who thinks it is appropriate to take that proposition as basic that he's wrong. Maybe I can't. Maybe when he and I sit down together to work out our criteria for proper basicality, maybe we don't start from enough of the same examples, maybe we just won't arrive at the same criteria. So I can't prove it to him. But nonetheless, I've got my views and he's got his. He thinks I'm starting in the wrong place. I think he's starting in the wrong place.

Can either of the parties in the unresolvable dispute above claim to know? I rather doubt it. Both parties may be rational in the sense that they think consistently relative to what they take to be properly basic. But rationality, as we have seen, does not guarantee truth; so rational belief, while surely preferable to irrational belief, does not seem to add up to knowledge.

I do not dispute Plantinga's claim that belief in God is rational as he construes the term "rationality." But the question remains: Can we *know* anything about God? Can we advance beyond the choice between skepticism and peer-group relativism? At one point Plantinga seems close to opting for peer-group relativism. He says:

> . . . perhaps a religious belief (as opposed to a memory belief, or a sense belief) is properly basic only if it is *shared by a community*; perhaps a merely private religion is irrational.[7]

But here again he is talking about rationality, not about knowledge. And even if the rationality of religious belief depends on community sharing, the questions of truth and knowledge are still unanswered. Contradictory sets of beliefs can be rational relative to their adherents.

While further developments in Reformed epistemology may serve to clarify some of the issues I have raised, it appears so far to have failed to supply a criterion for knowledge to replace that of the classical foundationalism which it rejects. Lacking a criterion for what may legitimately count as knowledge (and specifically for what sorts of propositions may be taken as foundational or basic), one may wonder whether Reformed epistemology can avoid a relativism like that of Rorty. Or perhaps knowledge as a sort of universal currency negotiable among all peoples is simply not available to mortals. But then one may also wonder whether the choice between Reformed epistemology and a fideistic skepticism (one, say, which believes in God but doesn't claim to know) involves much more than mere linguistic preference about how to use the admittedly useful word "knowledge." For as the noted historian of skepticism Richard Popkin has observed, skepticism about the merits of knowledge claims is by no means necessarily incompatible with religious belief. One can heartily believe in "God the father, almighty, maker of heaven and earth, and in Jesus Christ his only son, our Lord" without claiming to *know* these things. Does a claim to know here *add* anything to the heartfelt belief, and inner certainty? Does it mean *more* than that the belief is without doubt, unshakeable, and at the very core of one's being? If so, what more?

NOTES

1. Nicholas Wolterstorff, *Reason within the Bounds of Religion* (Grand Rapids: Eerdmans, 1976), p. 33.
2. Wolterstorff, *Reason*, p. 34.
3. Wolterstorff, *Reason*, p. 42.
4. Wolterstorff, *Reason*, p. 50.
5. Plantinga, "Reformed Objection." Also, Lecture III presented at Wheaton Annual Philosophy Conference, 1980.
6. Plantinga, Wheaton Lecture, I.
7. Plantinga, "Reformed Objection."

ALVIN PLANTINGA

On Reformed Epistemology

Here Alvin Plantinga (1932–) replies to Van Hook. He agrees with Van Hook that he does not have any philosophical method that will result in agreement among all rational people concerning the existence of God or other important religious matters. Nevertheless, he is not willing to give up the claim to knowledge—and he emphatically rejects the relativistic suggestion that knowledge is "what our peers will let us get away with saying." He concludes by suggesting a "picture" of what knowledge in this situation means. He argues that "a belief constitutes *knowledge*, if it is true, and if it arises as a result of the right use and proper functioning of our epistemic capacities."

⌘

In his interesting essay "Knowledge, belief, and Reformed epistemology" Jay Van Hook notes that several Reformed philosophers have recently been arguing that classical foundationalism ought to be rejected. Van Hook raises two questions about this. If we reject classical foundationalism, won't we find ourselves committed to a relativistic view of knowledge? And if the answer to this first question is No, how *shall* we think of knowledge? What picture of knowledge can we put in place of the picture purveyed by classical foundationalists?

Before trying to answer these questions, let me explain them a bit. Classical foundationalism takes many forms. For our purposes, however, we can understand it as follows. A classical foundationalist holds that there is a *foundation* for knowledge shared by all persons, or perhaps all *sane* persons, or perhaps all *rational* persons—the exact details don't matter here. Of course, there is some disagreement about what goes into this foundational or basic level of knowledge, but one proposal has been by far the most popular ever since the beginnings of modern philosophy. According to this proposal, two sorts of propositions or beliefs are to be found in the foundations of knowledge.

In the first place, there are such *self-evident* propositions as *all black dogs are black* and $2 + 1 = 3$. These propositions have the unusual property that you can't so much as understand them without believing them to be true. The second sort of proposition includes those about one's own mental life—one's beliefs, experiences, feelings, and the like. Perhaps it seems to me that I see something yellow before me; that is, perhaps it looks to me as if there is something yellow here. To use Roderick Chisholm's charming terminology, perhaps I am "appeared to yellowly." Now I might be mistaken as to

From *The Reformed Journal*, January 1982, pp. 13–17. Reprinted by permission of *Perspectives* (formerly *The Reformed Journal*).

whether there really *is* something yellow before me (perhaps I'm suffering from yellow jaundice, so that everything looks yellow to me no matter what its real color), but I can hardly be mistaken in thinking that things *look* yellow to me. Since I can't be mistaken about propositions of this sort, we might say that they are *incorrigible.* Clearly, incorrigible propositions are good candidates for the foundational layer of knowledge.

On this version of classical foundationalism, then, the propositions that form the basic or foundational level of knowledge are either self-evident or incorrigible. What I know in this foundational fashion isn't based on any other knowledge; I don't infer it from other propositions or believe it on the basis of other things I know. To put it another way, I know these things immediately, so that they form the basic level of knowledge.

Of course I know more than just what is self-evident and incorrigible. But anything else I know, on this way of looking at things, must be provable from what is in the foundational level of knowledge, that is, from what is self-evident or incorrigible. There may be things I believe but can't prove; but anything I *know* is something I can prove from the foundations of knowledge. So the classical foundationalist can distinguish knowledge from mere belief as follows: a person knows a certain proposition—say, that Vitamin C cures colds—only if he can prove it from beliefs in the foundations of knowledge, only if he can trace it back to the foundations by way of arguments that are themselves in the foundations.

Classical foundationalism thus makes it plausible to look at knowledge as that which can be proved from common ground—ground common at least to all rational persons of good will. It is then plausible to suppose that if you and I disagree about something—you think it's true and I think it's false—even after we've thought it over and discussed it at some length, then neither of us *knows* what he claims. For if either of us *did* know, he could show the other that his claim follows from foundational propositions, in which case there would no longer be any room for disagreement. On the classical foundationalist picture of knowledge, then, persistent disagreement is a sure sign of lack of knowledge on the parts of both disputants.

There is a powerful tradition in Reformed thought (though actually it goes back much further and can be seen perhaps inchoately in Augustine) which utterly *rejects* this picture of knowledge. According to Calvin, Kuyper, Bavinck, Dooyeweerd, and many others, this classical foundationalist way of looking at knowledge is completely mistaken. A person can perfectly well know something even if he can't demonstrate it in this fashion to everyone else. You and I might for example know that there is such a person as God, that he loves and cares for us, and that he was in Christ, reconciling the world to himself, even if we can't prove this to Bertrand Russell or the philosophers at Harvard. Furthermore, according to this Reformed tradition, we may perfectly well know these things even if they aren't either self-evident or incorrigible, and even if they cannot be proved from propositions that *are* self-evident or incorrigible.

Indeed, on the Reformed tradition in question, the proposition that there is such a person as God belongs itself in the foundational level of knowledge. It is a proposition that believers (many of them, at any rate) know *immediately*. According to this tradition, the most appropriate way to believe in God is not to believe on the basis of evidence or argument from other propositions, but to take this belief—that there is such a person as God—as basic. One who does so, furthermore, typically *knows* that there is such a person as God, even if she can't show and doesn't even try to show that it can be proved by reference to what is self-evident and incorrigible.

This way of looking at the matter is part of what we may call "Reformed epistemology." Other tenets of Reformed epistemology are that sin has had an important effect on our intellectual or noetic condition, that Scripture is (as Calvin says) "self-authenticating," and that science and intellectual inquiry are not in general religiously neutral. A central point at which the Reformed epistemologist differs from the classical foundationalist, then, is this: according to the former but not the latter, belief in God belongs in the foundations of knowledge, even if there are many people who don't believe in God at all. Reformed epistemology thus rejects the idea that knowledge is what can be proved from propositions accepted by all rational persons.

Here, as I see it, is where Van Hook enters the discussion. He is inclined to think that if we give up this idea of knowledge as what can be proved from common ground, then we really give up the idea of knowledge altogether. "The basic question I shall pose," he says, "is this: what, precisely, is knowledge on a post-foundationalist or Reformed model, and how, if at all, does it differ from mere belief or even from rational belief?" He suspects there isn't an answer:

> The basic aim of the whole enterprise of epistemology from Plato to our own day has been to provide what can be called a "common ground" on the basis of which knowledge claims can be made, criticized, justified, and settled. Now it may well be the case, as many philosophers and others have begun to suspect, that no such common ground exists or can be identified. But to say that we can have knowledge anyway, without a common ground, is surely to propose a radical alteration in the very idea of knowledge.

According to Van Hook, the Reformed epistemologist is in danger of losing the whole idea of knowledge. He *speaks* of knowledge, but he has really put something else in its place. Indeed, Van Hook is inclined to think that the Reformed epistemologist may be committed to a thoroughly *relativistic* view of knowledge. Speaking of Princeton philosopher Richard Rorty's view that knowledge is only "what our peers will let us get away with saying," he says "it is not clear to me that even a Reformed epistemology can get very far beyond such a view."

So Van Hook thinks that Reformed epistemology, insofar as it rejects classical foundationalism, is giving up the whole idea of knowledge and is likely to find itself embracing Rortian relativism. Now if the Reformed epistemologist *were* committed to Rorty's relativism, she would indeed be in hot water. To be sure, there is a minor lapse in Van Hook's piece here: in the quotation with which Van Hook begins his piece, Rorty speaks not of *knowledge* but of *truth* as what our peers will let us get away with saying. Of course there is a close connection between truth and knowledge; and no doubt Rorty would say something similar about knowledge. In any event, Rorty's suggestion is extremely unpromising.

In England, that home of lost causes, there is a Flat Earth Society, dedicated to the defense and promulgation of the claim that the earth is flat. Suppose the flat-earthers mount an enormously high-powered campaign on behalf of their views. They assimilate the latest techniques of mass communication and belief manipulation and direct mail campaigning; television is filled with endorsements of their views by Brooke Shields and other influential molders of public opinion. This goes on for years; and we oldsters begin to notice, to our dismay, that the younger generation is nearly united in believing that the earth is flat. After a few more years, the older, skeptical generation dies out; everyone believes that the earth is flat—and, of course, everyone's peers let him get away with saying that indeed the earth *is* flat. Would it then be true that the earth *is* flat? Of course not. But then truth can't just be what our peers will let us get away with saying.

Furthermore, neither my peers not Rorty's will let either him or me get away with saying that truth is what our peers will let us get away with saying. So if Rorty's suggestion were true, it would also be false, and hence both true and false. But even in these days of technological marvels, no proposition can manage that. So Rorty's suggestion is false.

This suggestion, then, has little enough to recommend it; and if the Reformed epistemologist were committed to it, she'd surely be in trouble. But what leads Van Hook to think that she probably is? Fundamentally, I think, it's because Van Hook is inclined to hold (in accordance with the classical foundationalist picture of knowledge) that if you can't demonstrate what you believe to other people, then you may be within your rights in believing it, but you don't *know* it. If you can't convince the other interested parties to the dispute that you are right, then even if you *are* right, you don't *know* what you claim. A necessary condition of knowing that God created the world is being able to convince *others—all* others, or at any rate all honest and reasonable others. Knowing that something is the case is believing it and being able to prove it from beliefs common to all reasonable persons.

There are several passages in Van Hook's essay which suggest that this is what he thinks; I shall cite just one. Following Calvin and others, I had claimed (in the Freemantle Lectures at Oxford in May 1980 and at the Wheaton College philosophy conference later than year) that belief in God is properly basic—i.e., such that it is entirely rational and reasonable to accept it *immediately,* without believing it on the basis of evidence or argument from other propositions. I then went on to consider "The Great Pumpkin Objection"; if the Reformed epistemologist holds that belief in God is properly basic, won't she be committed to holding that just *any* belief—the belief, say, that the Great Pumpkin returns every Hallowe'en to the most sincere pumpkin patch—is properly basic? I argued that she *won't*; and Van Hook comments as follows:

> Now it seems to me that Plantinga takes this objection too lightly. Surely, as he says, the Reformed epistemologist is not *herself* committed to taking belief in the Great Pumpkin as properly basic! But that isn't the point. The question is whether the Reformed epistemologist could show a serious Great Pumpkin advocate . . . that *his* belief is *not* properly basic. And if she cannot show this, aren't we back to Rorty's relativistic peer groups?

But why is *that* the question? Suppose the theist can't show the Great Pumpkinite (or the secular humanist) that he is mistaken in rejecting belief in God. How would that show that the theist doesn't know that, for example, God created the world? Why should we suppose that if the theist can't prove his contentions to the satisfaction of the skeptic, he doesn't know what he claims to know? Suppose St. Paul, on his visit to Athens, had been unable to prove to an early Bertrand Russell type—call him Callicles—that there really was such a person as God and that he created the world. Would it follow that St. Paul didn't *know* these things? Surely not. Notice: the question isn't whether St. Paul *did* know that God created the world. (Of course I think he did, but that's neither here nor there.) The question is rather whether his being unable to prove it to Callicles is enough to *show* that he didn't know. And surely it isn't. Surely it could be the case (in fact it *is* the case) that many Christians know that God created the world even if they cannot convince the Bertrand Russells of this world.

Let me elaborate a bit. It certainly seems possible that St. Paul should know that God created the world, even if he couldn't convince Callicles. Perhaps the denial of this claim had been drummed into Callicles since early childhood; or maybe his peers wouldn't let him get away with saying it and would ridicule and ostracize him if he did. Perhaps Callicles finds Paul's claim threatening: were he to accept it, he would have to change his life in some way, or give up thinking of himself as entirely free and totally autonomous, beholden to nothing and no one. For whatever reason, he may believe and continue to believe the denial of St. Paul's claim despite the latter's best efforts. But would this show that St. Paul doesn't know that God created the world? Not in the least. St. Paul may perfectly well know it, even if there is some factor at work that makes it impossible for him to prove it to Callicles.

On the Christian view of the matter, or course, there is such a factor—*sin*. It is the existence of sin in the world that, for many, interferes with belief in God. Were it not for the existence of sin, we should all believe in God with the same natural and wholehearted spontaneity with which we believe in other persons, the past, and the external world. It is only because of sin in the world that some of us human beings find belief in God difficult or absurd. (It doesn't follow that if belief in God is difficult for a given person, then that person is in some special way a sinner. Disease is also a result of sin, but the diseased person need not be more sinful than those of us in glowing health.)

If there were no sin in the world, then perhaps there wouldn't be any irresolvable disputes or fundamental disagreements or deeply different ways of looking at the world (no doubt everyone would believe just what I do!). If there were no sin in the world, the classical foundationalist picture of knowledge as what can be proved from common ground—ground common to all human beings—might very well be correct. It is certainly natural to think that in the absence of sin I *would* be able to prove whatever I know to anyone else. From this perspective, then, the classical foundationalist way of looking at knowledge is considerably out of date—not merely antediluvian but positively prelapsarian! This picture is appropriate to an unfallen world; sadly enough, however, it is not appropriate to ours.

So the picture of knowledge as what you can prove to all or nearly all normal rational human beings must be given up. It is perfectly possible that theists, or supply-side economists, or for that matter classical foundationalists should know something even if they can't prove it to the rest of us. The Reformed epistemologist rejects the classical foundational view of knowledge; but that doesn't in the least mean that she is committed to some sort of Rortian relativism, either about truth or about knowledge. What's true is true, regardless of what my peers will let me get away with saying; and this is so even if there isn't sufficient common ground between believer and unbeliever so that the former can demonstrate to the latter the error of his ways. . . .

Perhaps Van Hook is prepared to concede all this. But that still leaves his other question: if the Reformed epistemologist gives up this classical picture of knowledge, what picture will she put in its place? Granted the classical foundationalist picture must be rejected: how than *shall* we think of knowledge? This is a fair question, and a *hard* question. As Van Hook observes, it is a question that hasn't yet received the attention it deserves from Reformed epistemologists. Working out a complete and satisfying answer to it should be high on their agenda.

But the general *picture* of knowledge, I think, should go as follows. According to John Calvin—the *fons et origo* of all things Reformed and thus of Reformed epistemology—God has created us with a tendency or disposition to see his hand in nature, and to recognize that he is both the creator of the world and the person to whom we owe ultimate allegiance. This disposition to form these beliefs is activated or triggered by widely realized conditions:

> Lest anyone, then, be excluded from access to happiness, [God] not only sowed in men's minds that seed of religion of which we have spoken, but revealed himself and daily discloses himself in the whole workmanship of the universe. As a consequence, men cannot open their eyes without being compelled to see him (*Inst.*, I. v. 1).

Like Kant, Calvin is especially impressed in this connection by the marvelous starry heavens above:

> Even the common folk and the most untutored, who have been taught only by the aid of the eyes, cannot be unaware of the excellence of divine art, for it

reveals itself in this innumerable and yet distinct and well-ordered variety of the heavenly host.

What Calvin means, I think, is that God has created us in such a way that under the right conditions we naturally form such beliefs as that he has created us and that we owe him allegiance. The disposition to form these beliefs, then, is really a capacity for grasping certain truths about God. This capacity is part of our native intellectual endowment. It has been distorted and partially suppressed by sin, but it is present nevertheless; it is among the epistemic powers and capacities with which God has created us. Of course, in creating us he has also given us other capacities for grasping truth: perception, memory, and the capacity to apprehend certain truths as self-evident.

As a result of sin these capacities and powers sometimes malfunction. Sometimes they fail to work as God intended them to. Furthermore (also as a result of sin), human beings sometimes don't employ these capacities as God intended them to be employed. The result is error, confusion, fundamental wrong-headedness, and all the other epistemic ills to which humanity is heir. But when our epistemic powers *are* employed the way God meant them to be, and when, furthermore, they work in the way God intended them to work, the result is knowledge.

The correct picture of knowledge, then, goes as allows: a belief constitutes *knowledge,* if it is true, and if it arises as a result of the right use and proper functioning of our epistemic capacities. Of course this is only a *picture,* not a full-fledged account of knowledge. Of course there are many hard questions to be asked and answered about it. But I do think it is the *right* picture.

DAVID BASINGER

Reformed Epistemology and Hick's Religious Pluralism

In this piece, David Basinger (1947–) juxtaposes the Reformed epistemology advocated by Alvin Plantinga and the religious pluralism espoused by John Hick, and suggests a way to mediate the difference between them. On the one hand, he thinks that the Reformed epistemologists are right in saying that it is

From *Faith and Philosophy* 5 (1988): pp. 421–432. Reprinted by permission.

possible to be rational in one's religious beliefs without attempting to prove them on the basis of other things one believes. But the situation changes, he thinks, once we seriously confront the sincerely held but conflicting beliefs of adherents of other religions, as Hick would have us do. In this situation, argues Basinger, we must look at the many internally consistent hypotheses that *could* rationally be affirmed and try to decide which hypothesis best explains the phenomena.

⌘

No one denies that the basic tenets of many religious perspectives are, if taken literally, quite incompatible. The salvific claims of some forms of Judeo-Christian thought, for example, condemn the proponents of all other perspectives to hell, while the incompatible salvific claims of some forms of Islamic thought do the same.

Such incompatibility is normally explained in one of three basic ways. The non-theist argues that all religious claims are false, the product perhaps of wish fulfillment. The religious pluralist argues that the basic claims of at least all of the major world religions are more or less accurate descriptions of the same reality. Finally, the religious exclusivist argues that the tenets of only one religion (or some limited number of religions) are to any significant degree accurate descriptions of reality.[1]

The purpose of this discussion is to analyze comparatively the influential argument for religious pluralism offered by John Hick and the argument for religious exclusivism which can be (and perhaps has been) generated by proponents of what has come to be labeled 'Reformed Epistemology.' I shall argue that while Hick and the Reformed epistemologist appear to be giving us incompatible responses to the same question about the true nature of 'religious' reality, they are actually responding to related, but distinct questions, each of which must be considered by those desiring to give a religious explanation for the phenomenon of religious diversity. Moreover, I shall conclude that the insights offered by both Hick and the Reformed epistemologist are of value and, accordingly, that those of neither ought to be emphasized at the expense of the other.

JOHN HICK'S THEOLOGICAL PLURALISM

Hick's contention is not that different religions make no conflicting truth claims. In fact, he believes that "the differences of belief between (and within) the traditions are legion," and has often in great detail discussed them.[2] His basic claim, rather, is that such differences are best seen as "different ways of conceiving and experiencing the one ultimate divine Reality."[3]

However, if the various religions are really "responses to a single ultimate transcendent Reality," how then do we account for such significant differences?[4] The best explanation, we are told, is the assumption that "the limitless divine reality has been thought and experienced by different human mentalities forming and formed by different intellectual frameworks and devotional techniques."[5] Or, as Hick has stated the point elsewhere, the best explanation is the assumption that the correspondingly different ways of responding to divine reality "owe their differences to the modes of thinking, perceiving and feeling which have developed within the different patterns of human existence embodied in the various cultures of the earth." Each "constitutes a valid context of salvation/liberation; but none constitutes the one and only such context."[6]

But why accept such a pluralistic explanation? Why not hold, rather, that there is no higher Reality beyond us and thus that all religious claims are false—i.e., why not opt for naturalism? Or why not adopt the exclusivistic contention that the religious claims of only one perspective are true?

Hick does not reject naturalism because he sees it to be an untenable position. It is certainly *possible,* he tells us, that the "entire realm of [religious] experience is delusory or hallucinatory, simply a human projection, and not in any way or degree a result of the presence of a greater divine reality."[7] In fact, since the "universe of which we are part is religiously ambiguous," it is not even *unreasonable or implausible* "to interpret any aspect of it, including our religious experience, in non-religious as well as religious ways."[8]

However, he is quick to add, "it is perfectly reasonable and sane for us to trust our experience"—including our religious experience—"as generally cognitive of reality except when we have some reason to doubt it."[9] Moreover, "the mere theoretical possibility that any or all [religious experience] may be illusory does not count as a reason to doubt it." Nor is religious experience overturned by the fact that the great religious figures of the past, including Jesus, held a number of beliefs which we today reject as arising from the now outmoded science of their day, or by the fact that some people find "it impossible to accept that the profound dimension of pain and suffering is the measure of the cost of creation through creaturely freedom."[10]

He acknowledges that those who have "no positive ground for religious belief within their own experience" often do see such factors as "insuperable barriers" to religious belief.[11] But given the ambiguous nature of the evidence, he argues, it cannot be demonstrated that all rational people must see it this way. That is, belief in a supernatural realm can't be shown to be any less plausible than disbelief. Accordingly, he concludes, "those who actually participate in this field of religious experience are fully entitled, as sane and rational persons, to take the risk of trusting their own experience together with that of their tradition, and of proceeding to live and to believe on the basis of it, rather than taking the alternative risk of distrusting it and so—for the time being at least—turning their backs on God."[12]

But why choose pluralism as the best religious hypothesis? Why does Hick believe we ought not be exclusivists? It is not because he sees exclusivism as incoherent. It is certainly possible, he grants, that "one particular 'Ptolomaic' religious vision does correspond uniquely with how things are."[13] Nor does Hick claim to have some privileged "cosmic vantage point from which [he can] observe both the divine reality in itself and the different partial human awarenesses of that reality."[14] But when we individually consider the evidence in the case, he argues, the result is less ambiguous. When "we start from the phenomenological fact of the various forms of religious experience, and we seek an hypothesis which will make sense of this realm of phenomena" from a religious point of view, "the theory that most naturally suggests itself postulates a divine Reality which is itself limitless, exceeding the scope of human conceptuality and language, but which is humanly thought and experienced in various conditioned and limited ways."[15]

What is this evidence which makes the pluralistic hypothesis so "considerably more probable" than exclusivism? For one thing, Hick informs us, a credible religious hypothesis must account for the fact, "evident to ordinary people (even though not always taken into account by theologians) that in the great majority of cases—say 98 to 99 percent—the religion in which a person believes and to which he adheres depends upon where he was born."[16] Moreover, a credible hypothesis must account for the fact that within all of the major religious traditions, "basically the same salvific process is taking place, namely the transformation of human existence from self-centeredness to Reality-centeredness."[17] And while pluralism "illuminates" these otherwise baffling facts, the strict exclusivist's view "has come to seem increasingly implausible and unrealistic."[18]

But even more importantly, he maintains, a credible religious hypothesis must account for the fact, of which "we have become irreversibly aware in the present century, as the result of anthropological, sociological and psychological studies and the work of philosophy of language, that there is no one universal and invariable" pattern for interpreting human experience, but rather a range of significantly different patterns or conceptual schemes "which have developed within the major cultural streams." And when considered in light of this, Hick concludes, a "pluralistic theory becomes inevitable."[19]

THE REFORMED OBJECTION

There are two basic ways in which Hick's pluralistic position can be critiqued. One "appropriate critical response," according to Hick himself, "would be to offer a better [religious] hypothesis."[20] That is, one way to challenge Hick is to claim that the evidence he cites is better explained by some form of exclusivism.

But there is another, potentially more powerful type of objection, one which finds its roots in the currently popular 'Reformed Epistemology' being championed by philosophers such as Alvin Plantinga. I will first briefly outline Plantinga's latest version of this epistemological approach and then discuss its impact on Hick's position.

According to Plantinga, it has been widely held since the Enlightenment that if theistic beliefs—e.g., religious hypotheses—are to be considered rational, they must be based on propositional evidence. It is not enough for the theist just to refute objections to any such belief. The theist "must also have something like an argument for the belief, or some positive reason to think that the belief is true."[21] But this is incorrect, Plantinga maintains. There are beliefs which acquire their warrant propositionally—i.e., have warrant conferred on them by an evidential line of reasoning from other beliefs. And for such beliefs, it may well be true that proponents need something like an argument for their veridicality.

However, there are also, he tells us, *basic* beliefs which are not based on propositional evidence and, thus, do not require propositional warrant. In fact, *if* such beliefs can be affirmed "without either violating an epistemic duty or displaying some kind of noetic defect," they can be considered *properly basic*.[22] And, according to Plantinga, many theistic beliefs can be properly basic: "Under widely realized conditions it is perfectly rational, reasonable, intellectually respectable and acceptable to believe [certain theistic tenets] without believing [them] on the basis of [propositional] evidence."[23]

But what are such conditions? Under what conditions can a belief have positive epistemic status if it is not conferred by other propositions whose epistemic status is not in question? The answer, Plantinga informs us, lies in an analysis of belief formation.

> [We have] cognitive faculties designed to enable us to achieve true beliefs with respect to a wide variety of propositions—propositions about our immediate environment, about our interior lives, about the thoughts and experiences of other persons, about our universe at large, about right and wrong, about the whole realm of *abstracta*—numbers, properties, propositions, states of affairs, possible worlds and their like, about modality—what is necessary and possible—and about [ourselves]. These faculties work in such a way that under the appropriate circumstances we form the appropriate belief. More exactly, the appropriate belief is *formed in us*; in the typical case we do not *decide* to hold or form the belief in question, but simply find ourselves with it. Upon considering an instance of *modus ponens*, I find myself believing its corresponding conditional; upon being appeared to in the familiar way, I find myself holding the belief that there is a large tree before me; upon being asked what I had for breakfast, I reflect for a moment and find myself with the belief that what I had was eggs on toast. In these and other cases I do not *decide* what to believe; I don't total up the evidence (I'm being appeared to redly; on most occasions when thus appeared to I am in the presence of something red, so most probably in this case I am) and make a decision as to what seems best supported; I simply find myself believing.[24]

And from a theistic point of view, Plantinga continues, the same is true in the religious realm. Just as it is true that when our senses or memory are functioning properly, "appropriate belief is formed in us," so it is that God has created us with faculties which will, "when they are working the way they were designed to work by the being who designed and created us and them," produce true theistic beliefs.[25] Moreover, if these faculties are functioning properly, a basic belief thus formed has "positive epistemic status to the degree [the individual in question finds herself] inclined to accept it."[26]

What, though, of the alleged counter-evidence to such theistic beliefs? What, for example, of all the arguments the conclusion of which is that God does not exist? Can they all be dismissed as irrelevant? Not immediately, answers Plantinga. We must seriously consider potential defeaters of our basic beliefs. With respect to the belief that God exists, for example, we must seriously consider the claim that religious belief is mere wish fulfillment and the claim that God's existence is incompatible with (or at least improbable given) the amount of evil in the world.

But to undercut such defeaters, he continues, we need not engage in positive apologetics: produce propositional evidence for our beliefs. We need only engage in *negative* apologetics: refute such arguments.[27] Moreover, it is Plantinga's conviction that such defeaters do normally exist. "The non-propositional warrant enjoyed by [a person's] belief in God, for example, [seems] itself sufficient to turn back the challenge offered by some alleged defeaters"—e.g., the claim that theistic belief is mere wish fulfillment. And other defeaters such as the "problem of evil," he tells us, can be undercut by identifying validity or soundness problems or even by appealing to the fact that "experts think it unsound or that the experts are evenly divided as to its soundness."[28]

Do Plantinga or other proponents of this Reformed epistemology maintain that their exclusivistic religious hypotheses are properly basic and can thus be 'defended' in the manner just outlined? I an not *certain* that they do. However, when Plantinga, for example, claims that "God exists" is for most adult theists properly basic, he appears to have in mind a classical Christian conception of the divine—i.e., a being who is the triune, omnipotent, omniscient, perfectly good, *ex nihilo* creator of the universe. In fact, given his recent claim that "the internal testimony of the Holy Spirit . . . is a source of reliable and perfectly acceptable beliefs about what is communicated [by God] in Scripture," and the manner in which most who make such a claim view the truth claims of the other world religions, it would appear that Plantinga's 'basic' conception of God is quite exclusive.[29]

However, even if no Reformed epistemologist actually does affirm an exclusivistic hypothesis she claims is properly basic, it is obvious that the Reformed analysis of belief justification can be used to critique Hick's line of reasoning. Hick claims that an objective inductive assessment of the relevant evidence makes his pluralistic thesis a more plausible religious explanation than any of the competing exclusivistic hypotheses. But a Reformed exclusivist could easily argue that this approach to the issue is misguided. My affirmation of an exclusivistic Christian perspective, such an argument might begin, is not evidential in nature. It is, rather, simply a belief I have found formed in me, much like the belief that I am seeing a tree in front of me or the belief that killing innocent children is wrong.

Now, of course, I must seriously consider the allegedly formidable defeaters with which pluralists such as Hick have presented me. I must consider the fact, for example, that the exclusive beliefs simply formed in most people are not similar to mine, but rather tend to mirror those beliefs found in the cultures in which such people have been raised. But I do not agree with Hick that this fact is best explained by a pluralistic hypothesis. I attribute this phenomenon to other factors such as the epistemic blindness with which must of humanity has been plagued since the fall.[30]

Moreover, to defend my position—to maintain justifiably (rationally) that I am right and Hick is wrong—I need not, as Hick seems to suggest, produce objective 'proof' that his hypothesis is weaker than mine. That is, I need not produce 'evidence' that would lead most rational people to agree with me. That would be to involve myself in Classical Foundationalism, which is increasingly being recognized as a bankrupt epistemological methodology. All I need do is undercut Hick's defeaters—i.e., show that his challenge does not require me to abandon my exclusivity thesis. And this I can easily do. For Hick has not demonstrated that my thesis is self-contradictory. And it is extremely doubtful that there exists any other nonquestion-begging criterion for plausibility by which he could even attempt to demonstrate that my thesis is less plausible (less probable) than his.

Hick, of course, believes firmly that his hypothesis makes the most sense. But why should this bother me? By his own admission, many individuals firmly believe that, given the amount of seemingly gratuitous evil in the world, God's nonexistence is by far most plausible. Yet this does not keep him from affirming theism. He simply reserves the right to see things differently and continues to believe. And there is no reason why I cannot do the same.

Moreover, even if what others believed were relevant, by Hick's own admission, the majority of theists doubt that his thesis is true.[31] Or, at the very least, I could rightly maintain that "the experts are evenly divided as to its soundness." Thus, given the criteria for defeater assessment which we Reformed exclusivists affirm, Hick's defeaters are clearly undercut. And, accordingly, I remain perfectly justified in continuing to hold that my exclusivity thesis is correct and, therefore, that all incompatible competing hypotheses are false.

A MIDDLE GROUND

It is tempting to see Hick and the Reformed exclusivist as espousing incompatible approaches to the question of religious diversity. If Hick is correct—if the issue is primarily evidential in nature—then the Reformed exclusivist is misguided and vice versa. But this, I believe, is an inaccurate assessment of the situation. There are two equally important, but distinct, questions which arise in this context, and Hick and the Reformed exclusivist, it seems to me, each *primarily* address only one.

The Reformed exclusivist is primarily interested in the following question:

> Q1: Under what conditions is an individual within her epistemic rights (is she rational) in affirming one of the many mutually exclusive religious diversity hypotheses?

In response, as we have seen, the Reformed exclusivist argues (or at least could argue) that a person need not grant that her religious hypothesis (belief) requires propositional (evidential) warrant. She is within her epistemic rights in maintaining that it is a *basic* belief. And if she does so, then to preserve rationality, she is not required to 'prove' in some objective manner that her hypothesis is most plausible. She is fulfilling all epistemic requirements solely by defending her hypothesis against claims that it is less plausible than competitors.

It seems to me that the Reformed exclusivist is basically right on this point. I do believe, for reasons mentioned later in this essay, that attempts by any knowledgeable exclusivist to define her hypothesis will ultimately require her to enter the realm of positive apologetics—i.e., will require her to engage in a comparative analysis of her exclusivistic beliefs. But I wholeheartedly agree with the Reformed exclusivist's contention that to preserve rationality, she need not actually demonstrate that her hypothesis is most plausible. She need ultimately only defend herself against the claim that a thoughtful assessment of the matter makes the affirmation of some incompatible perspective—i.e., pluralism or some incompatible exclusivistic perspective—the only rational option. And this, I believe, she can clearly do.

What this means, of course, is that if Hick is actually arguing that pluralism is the only rational option, then I think he is wrong. And his claim that pluralism "is considerably more probable" than exclusivism does, it must be granted, make it appear as if he believes pluralism to be the only hypothesis a knowledgeable theist can justifiably affirm.

But Hick never actually calls his opponents irrational in this context. That is, while Hick clearly believes that sincere, knowledgeable exclusivists are *wrong*, he has never to my knowledge claimed that they are guilty of violating the basic epistemic rules governing rational belief. Accordingly, it seems best to assume that Q1—a concern with what can be rationally affirmed—is not Hick's primary interest in this context.

But what then is it with which Hick is concerned? As we have seen, Q1 is defensive in nature. It asks for identification of conditions under which we can justifiably continue to affirm a belief we *already* hold. But *why* hold the specific religious beliefs we desire to defend? Why, specifically, choose to defend religious pluralism rather than exclusivism or vice versa? Or, to state this question of 'belief origin' more formally:

> Q2: Given that an individual can be within her epistemic rights (can be rational) in affirming either exclusivism or pluralism, upon what basis should her actual choice be made?

This is the type of question in which I believe Hick is primarily interested.

Now, it might be tempting for a Reformed exclusivist to contend that she is exempt from the consideration of Q2. As I see it, she might begin, this question is based on the assumption that individuals consciously choose their religious belief systems. But the exclusivistic hypothesis which I affirm was not the result of a conscious attempt to choose the most plausible option. I have simply discovered this exclusivistic hypothesis formed in me in much the same fashion I find my visual and moral beliefs just formed in me. And thus Hick's question is simply irrelevant to my position.

But such a response will not do. There is no reason to deny that Reformed exclusivists do have, let's say, a Calvinistic religious hypothesis just formed in them. However, although almost everyone in every culture does in the appropriate context have similar 'tree-beliefs' just formed in them, there is no such unanimity within the religious realm. As Hick rightly points out, the religious belief that the overwhelming majority of people in any given culture find just formed in them is the dominant hypothesis of that culture or subculture. Moreover, the dominant religious hypotheses in most of these cultures are exclusivistic—i.e., incompatible with one another.

Accordingly, it seems to me that Hick can rightly be interpreted as offering the following challenge to the knowledgeable Reformed exclusivist (the exclusivist aware of pervasive religious diversity): I will grant that your exclusivistic beliefs were not originally the product of conscious deliberation. But given that most sincere theists initially go through a type of religious belief-forming process similar to yours and yet usually find formed in themselves the dominant exclusivistic hypotheses of their own culture, upon what basis can you justifiably continue to claim that the hypothesis you affirm has some special status just because you found it formed in you? Or, to state the question somewhat differently, Hick's analysis of religious diversity challenges knowledgeable Reformed exclusivists to ask themselves why they now believe that their religious belief-forming mechanisms are functioning properly while the analogous mechanisms in all others are faulty.

Some Reformed exclusivists, as we have seen, have a ready response. Because of 'the fall,' they maintain, most individuals suffer from religious epistemic blindness—i.e., do not possess properly functioning religious belief-forming mechanisms. Only our mechanisms are trustworthy. However, every exclusivistic religious tradition can—and many do—make such claims. Hence, an analogous Hickian question again faces knowledgeable Reformed exclusivists: Why do you believe that only those religious belief-forming mechanisms which produce exclusivistic beliefs compatible with yours do not suffer from epistemic blindness?

Reformed exclusivists cannot at this point argue that they have found this belief just formed in them for it is *now* the reliability of the belief-forming mechanism, itself, which is being questioned. Nor, since they are anti-foundationalists, can Reformed exclusivists argue that the evidence demonstrates conclusively that their position is correct. So upon what then can they base their crucial belief that their religious belief-forming mechanisms *alone* produce true beliefs?

They must, it seems to me, ultimately fall back on the contention that their belief-forming mechanisms can alone be trusted because that set of beliefs thus generated appears to them to form the most plausible religious explanatory hypothesis available. But to respond in this fashion brings them into basic methodological agreement with Hick's position on Q2. That is, it appears that knowledgeable Reformed exclusivists must ultimately maintain with Hick that when attempting to discover which of the many self-consistent hypotheses that *can* rationally be affirmed is the one that *ought* to be affirmed, a person must finally decide which hypothesis she believes best explains the phenomena. Or, to state this important point differently yet, what Hick's analysis of religious diversity demonstrates, I believe, is that even for those knowledgeable Reformed exclusivists who claim to find their religious perspectives just formed in them, a conscious choice among competing religious hypotheses is ultimately called for.

This is not to say, it must again be emphasized, that such Reformed exclusivists must attempt to 'prove' their choice is best. But, given the culturally relative nature of religious belief-forming mechanisms, a simple appeal to such a mechanism seems inadequate as a basis for such exclusivists to continue to affirm their perspective. It seems rather that knowledgeable exclusivists must ultimately make a conscious decision whether to retain the religious hypothesis that has been formed in them or choose another. And it further appears that they should feel some prima facie obligation to consider the available options—consciously consider the nature of the various religious hypotheses formed in people—before doing so.

Now, of course, to agree that such a comparative analysis should be undertaken is not to say that Hick's pluralistic hypothesis is, in fact, the most plausible alternative. I agree with the Reformed exclusivist that 'plausibility' is a very subjective concept. Thus, I doubt that the serious consideration of the competing explanatory hypotheses for religious phenomena, even by knowledgeable, open-minded individuals, will produce consensus.

However, I do not see this as in any sense diminishing the importance of engaging in the type of comparative analysis suggested. For even if such comparative assessment will not lead to consensus, it will produce two significant benefits. First, only by such assessment, I feel, can a person acquire 'ownership' of her religious hypothesis. That is, only by such an assessment can she insure herself that her belief is not solely the product of environmental conditioning. Second, such an assessment should lead all concerned to be more tolerant of those with whom they ultimately disagree. And in an age where radical religious exclusivism again threatens world peace, I believe such tolerance to be of inestimable value.

This does not mean, let me again emphasize in closing, that the consideration of Q1—the consideration of the conditions under which a religious hypothesis can be rationally affirmed—is unimportant or even less important than the consideration of Q2. It is crucial that we recognize who must actually shoulder the 'burden of proof' in this context. And we need to thank Reformed exclusivists for helping us think more clearly about this matter. But I fear that a preoccupation with Q1 can keep us from seeing the importance of Q2—the consideration of the basis upon which we choose the hypothesis to be defended—and the comparative assessments of hypotheses to which such consideration leads us. And we need to thank pluralists such as Hick for drawing our attention to this fact.

NOTES

1. This terminology basically comes from John Hick, "On Conflicting Religious Truth-Claims," *Religious Studies* 19 (1983): 487.
2. *Ibid.*, p. 491.
3. John Hick, "The Philosophy of World Religions," *Scottish Journal of Theology* 37:229.
4. *Ibid.*
5. John Hick, "The Theology of Religious Pluralism," *Theology* (1983): 335.
6. Hick, *Scottish Journal of Theology*, pp. 229, 231.
7. John Hick, *Why Believe in God?* (London: SCM Press, Ltd., 1983), p. 43–44.
8. *Ibid.*, p. 67.
9. *Ibid.*, p. 34.
10. *Ibid.*, pp. 64, 100.
11. *Ibid.*, p. 100.
12. *Ibid.*, 67.
13. Hick, *Theology*, p. 338.
14. *Ibid.*, p. 336.
15. Hick, *Scottish Journal of Theology*, p. 231.
16. John Hick, *God Has Many Names* (London: The Macmillan Press, Ltd., 1980), p. 44.
17. Hick, *Scottish Journal of Theology*, p. 231.
18. Hick, *God Has Many Names*, p. 49.
19. Hick, *Scottish Journal of Theology*, p. 232.
20. Hick, *Theology*, p. 336.
21. Alvin Plantinga, "The Foundations of Theism: A Reply," *Faith and Philosophy* 3 (July 1986): 307.
22. *Ibid.*, p. 300.
23. Alvin Plantinga, "On Taking Belief in God as Basic," Wheaton College Philosophy Conference (October 23–25, 1986), Lecture I handout, p. 1.
24. Alvin Plantinga, "Justification and Theism," *Faith and Philosophy* 4 (October 1987): 405–406.
25. *Ibid.*, p. 411.
26. *Ibid.*, p. 410.
27. Plantinga, "The Foundations of Theism," p. 313, n. 11.
28. *Ibid.*, p. 312.
29. Alvin Plantinga, "Sheehan's Shenanigans," *The Reformed Journal* (April 1987): 25.
30. Mark Talbot, "On Christian Philosophy," *The Reformed Journal* (September 1984).
31. John Hick, *Scottish Journal of Theology*, p. 236.

SUGGESTED READING

Alston, William P. "Christian Experience and Christian Belief," in *Faith and Rationality: Reason and Belief in God*, ed. Alvin Plantinga and Nicholas Wolterstorff. Notre Dame, Ind.: University of Notre Dame Press, 1983, pp. 103–134.

———. "Perceiving God." *Journal of Philosophy* 83 (1986), pp. 655–665.

———. "Religious Diversity and Perceptual Knowledge of God." *Faith and Philosophy* 5 (1988), pp. 433–448.

Boyle, Joseph, J. Hubbard, and Thomas Sullivan. "The Reformed Objection to Natural Theology: A Catholic Perspective." *Christian Scholar's Review* 11 (1982), pp. 199–211.

Gutting, Gary, *Religious Belief and Religious Skepticism*. Notre Dame, Ind.: University of Notre Dame Press, 1982.

———. "The Catholic and the Calvinist: A Dialogue on Faith and Reason." *Faith and Philosophy* 2 (1985): 236–256.

Hasker, William. "On Justifying the Christian Practice." *The New Scholasticism* 60 (Spring 1986): 129–144.

Marcus Hester, ed. *Faith, Reason, and Skepticism*. Philadelphia: Temple University Press, 1991.

Plantinga, Alvin. "Is Belief in God Rational?" in *Rationality and Religious Belief*, ed. C. F. Delaney. Notre Dame, Ind.: University of Notre Dame Press, 1979, pp. 7–27.

———. "Reason and Belief in God." *Faith and Rationality*, pp. 16–93.

———. "Replies," in Alvin Plantinga, ed. James E. Tomberlin and Peter Van Inwagen, Profiles Volume 5. Dordrecht: D. Riedel, 1985, pp. 390–393.

———. "The Foundations of Theism: A Reply." *Faith and Philosophy* 3 (1986): 298–313.

———. "Coherentism and the Evidentialist Objection to Belief in God," in *Rationality, Religious Belief, and Moral Commitment*, ed. Robert Audi and William J. Wainwright. Ithaca: Cornell University Press, 1986, pp. 109–138.

Quinn, Philip. "On Finding the Foundations of Theism." *Faith and Philosophy* 2 (1985): 469–486.

Wolterstorff, Nicholas. "Can Belief in God Be Rational If It Has No Foundations?" in *Faith and Rationality*, pp. 135–186.

Wykstra, Stephen. "Toward a Sensible Evidentialism: On the Notion of 'Needing Evidence'," in *Philosophy of Religion: Selected Readings*, 2d ed., ed. William L. Rowe and William J. Wainwright. New York: Harcourt Brace Jovanovich, 1989, pp. 426–437.

Zagzebski, Linda. *Rational Faith: Catholic Responses to Reformed Epistemology*. Notre Dame, Ind.: University of Notre Dame Press, 1993.

PART SEVEN

RELIGIOUS LANGUAGE

Philosophers have always had an intense interest in language, and particularly in problems of reference and meaning. Over the years, philosophers of language have focused attention on a variety of important stretches of human language—including language employed to speak of mental phenomena, of ethics and character, and of theological entities. Of course, the theological entity at the heart of the controversy is God. One of the key issues for philosophers of religious language is how we can speak meaningfully of God. Obviously, all we have at our disposal is human language, but we are attempting to speak of something that is drastically different from the ordinary realities we humans encounter. That creates the problem.

The heyday of widespread philosophical debate over the nature of religious language has passed, but it is possible to survey some of the important viewpoints that have been expressed. One classic medieval view is the theory of analogy formulated by Aquinas, who held that terms used theologically have meaning analogous to their meaning when applied to creatures.

Many challenges have arisen to confront any traditional view of the meaningfulness of religious discourse. One frontal assault was waged early in this century by logical positivists, who found that religious language failed to meet either their verifiability criterion or falsifiability criterion of meaning. Another challenge came in the middle portion of the twentieth century from those philosophers who took themselves to be following the later Wittgenstein's approach to language. These philosophers developed theories revolving around the function or use of key aspects of religious language. For these thinkers, the meaning of terms is donated by their role in a whole "language-game," so that the meaning of religious terms is connected to their functioning within a given religious community.

In the last portion of this century, we have seen a number of theories based on the conviction that the meaning of religious language is essentially non-literal, some claiming that it has "symbolic meaning" and others claiming it has "irreducibly metaphorical meaning." In other quarters, theories have been advanced asserting that religious language has only a kind of existential meaning as we relate ourselves obediently to God.

Only in recent years has there been much discussion in professional philosophical circles of whether the long-standing assumption that religious language is non-literal is warranted.

SAINT THOMAS AQUINAS

The Doctrine of Analogy

The theory of analogy, deriving ultimately from Aristotle, plays an important role in the philosophy of Thomas Aquinas (1224–1274). Misunderstood by some critics as an analogical strategy for arguing that God exists, this scholastic doctrine really pertains to how it is possible to say anything meaningful about God in human language. More precisely, it is general theory about the way in which we actually extend meaningful discourse from familiar circumstances to circumstances in which normal experience no longer applies. Here it is a theory about how ordinary predicates (e.g. "good" and "wise") apply to God. Aquinas steers a middle course between saying that such predicates have *univocal* meaning when applied to God (i.e., exactly the same meaning when applied to creatures) and that they have *equivocal* meaning (i.e., completely different meaning when applied to creatures). The Angelic Doctor's middle course was to give an explication of how ordinary terms have *analogical* meaning, replete with a number of technical rules. A confident realist, Aquinas was trying to account for the fact that discourse about God has already been taking place in human affairs in spite of various considerations that might seem to rule its possibility out of court.

⌘

It is impossible that anything should be predicated of both creatures and God univocally. Any effect that falls short of the power of its cause resembles its cause inadequately because it differs from it. Thus, what is found diversely and in various ways in the effect exists simply and in a single way in the cause; so, the sun by a single power produces many different kinds of lower things. In just that way, . . . all the perfections which are found among creatures in diverse and various ways preexist in God as united in one.

When we predicate of creatures some term which indicates a perfection, that term signifies the perfection as something distinct by its definition from every other perfection; for instance, when we predicate the term "wise" of some man, we signify some perfection which is distinct from the essence of the man, and also from his powers and from his existence. But when we predicate such a term of God, we do not intend to signify something which is distinct from His essence, power and existence. Also, when we predicate the term "wise" of some man, it circumscribes and isolates what is signified;

From *Summa Theologica*, 1.13.5 and *Disputed Questions: On Truth*, 2.11, trans. by James Ross. Used by permission of James Ross.

but this is not so then the term "wise" is predicated of God because the reality signified by the term remains unisolated and exceeds the signification (the linguistic intention) of the term. Therefore, it is obvious that the term "wise" does not have exactly the same meaning when predicated of God and of some creature. And the same reasoning holds for all the other terms which indicate perfection. So no term is predicated of God and creatures univocally.

But the terms are not used purely equivocally either, as some have claimed. For, if that were so, nothing would be knowable or demonstrable concerning God from our knowledge of creatures; our reasoning would always commit the fallacy of equivocation. Such a view would be as discordant with the philosophers who demonstrate a number of things about God, as it would be with the Apostle Paul who said: "The invisible things of God are made known by the things that are made."

We have to say, then, that terms are used of creatures and God analogously, that is, according to an ordering between them. We can distinguish two ways in which analogy based upon the order among things can be found among terms: First, one word may be used of two things because each of them has some order or relation to a third thing. Thus we use the term "healthy" of both medicine and urine because both things have a relation to another thing, namely the health of the animal, of which the latter is the sign and the former the cause. Secondly, one word may be used of two things because of the relation the one thing has to the other; thus "healthy" is used of both the medicine and the animal because the medicine is the cause of the health in the man. In this way some terms are used of creatures and God, neither univocally nor purely equivocally, but analogously.

We are unable to speak of God except in the language we use of creatures. . . . And so, whatever is said of both creatures and God is said on the basis of the order or relation which holds between the creature and God, namely, that God is the source and cause in which all the perfections of things preexist eminently.

This kind of community is a middle-ground between pure equivocation and simply univocity. For among those terms which are used analogously, there is not a common or single concept, as there is among univocal terms; but neither are the concepts wholly diverse, as is the case among equivocal terms. Rather, the term which is predicated in different ways signifies different relations to some one thing; thus "healthy" when predicated of urine means "is a sign of the health of the animal," whereas when predicated of the medicine it means "is a cause of the health of the animal."

Nothing can be predicated of a creature and of God univocally. For when a term is used univocally or more than one thing, what the term signifies is common to each of the things of which it is univocally predicated. So far as the signification of the term is concerned, the things of which it is univocally predicated are undifferentiated, even though they may precede one another in being; for instance, all numbers are equally numbers although one is prior to another. But no matter how much a creature may resemble God, a point cannot be reached at which something belongs to it and to God for the same reason. For things which are in different subjects and have the same formal definition are common to the subjects in substance and quiddity but are distinct in *esse*. Whatever is in God, however, is His own *esse*; for just as His essence is the same as His *esse*, so His knowledge is the same as His knowing. Since the *esse* which is proper to one thing cannot be communicated to another, it cannot happen that a creature should ever attain to having something for the same reason that God has it because it is impossible that the creature should come into possession of the same *esse* as is God's. The same is true for us; if 'man' and 'to *be* as a man' did not differ in Peter and Paul it would not be possible for the term "man" to be predicated univocally of Peter and of Paul whose *esse* is distinct.

Still, it cannot be maintained that whatever is predicated of God and a creature is predicated purely equivocally because if there were not some real resemblance between the creature and God, His essence would not be a likeness of creatures, and thus He could not understand creatures by understanding His essence. Similarly, we would not be able to come to know God from created things either; nor would it be that from among the terms which apply to creatures, one rather than another, ought to be predicated of God; for with equivocal terms it makes no difference which is applied since the term does not imply any real agreement among the things to which it applies.

So we have to say that the term "acknowledge" is predicated of God's knowledge and of ours neither wholly univocally nor purely equivocally. Instead it is predicated analogously, which is the same as proportionally.

Resemblance on account of a proportion (relation) can be of two kinds, and so two kinds of analogous community can be distinguished. There is a community between things of which one is related to another in virtue of their having a fixed distance or other determinate relationship to each other, as the number 2 to the number 1, in that the former is the double of the latter. Sometimes there is a community (or resemblance) between two things, not accounted for because the one is a function of the other but rather, because of a likeness of two relations; for instance, 6 resembles 4 in that as 6 is the double of 3, so is 4 the double of 2. The first kind of resemblance is one of proportion; the second is one of parity of proportion or proportionality.

We find something said analogically of two things in virtue of the first type of resemblance when one of them has a direct and determinate relationship to the other, as, for instance, "being" is predicated of accident and of substance because of the relationship which accident has to substance; and "healthy" is predicated of urine and of an animal because urine has some relation to the health of the animal. Sometimes something is predicated analogically in virtue of the second type of resemblance, as when the term insight is predicated of bodily sight and of understanding, because sight is to the eye what understanding is to the mind.

There must be some determinate (definite) relationship between things to which something is common by analogy of the first sort; consequently, it cannot be that anything is predicated of God and creatures by this type of analogy because no creature has such a determinate relationship to God. But the other type of analogy requires no determinate type of relationship between the things in which something is common by analogy; and so nothing excludes some term's being predicated analogously of God and creatures in this manner.

This can happen in two ways: sometimes the term implies that something, which cannot be common to God and a creature even in a proportionality, belongs to what it primarily designated. This is so of everything which is predicated metaphorically of God as when He is said to be a lion, the sun, and so forth, because the definitions include matter which cannot be attributed to God. In other cases, a term which is used of God and creatures has no implications in its primary uses which preclude a resemblance of the kind described between God and creatures. To this class belong all those predicates which do not imply a defect (limitation) and which do not depend upon matter for their *esse*; for instance, "being," "good," and so forth.

ANTONY FLEW

The Falsification Challenge

The following piece is part of the famous "University Discussion" among several British analytic philosophers. Opening the discussion, Antony Flew (1923–) applies to religious language the criteria of meaningfulness taught by logical positivism. He argues that religious statements, like scientific and other factually meaningful statements, must be empirically falsifiable in order to be cognitively meaningful. Yet, he goes on to argue, believers refuse to specify falsification conditions for their claims. According to Flew, we should therefore reject religious claims, not because they have proved to be in fact false but because their lack of falsifiability makes them cognitively meaningless. In other words, they say nothing about the way the world is.

⌘

Let us begin with a parable. It is a parable developed from a tale told by John Wisdom in his haunting and revelatory article 'Gods.'[1] Once upon a time two explorers came upon a clearing in the jungle. In the clearing were growing many flowers and many weeds. One explorer says, 'Some gardener must tend this plot.' The other disagrees, 'There is no gardener.' So they pitch their tents and set a watch. No gardener is ever seen. 'But perhaps he is an invisible gardener.' So they set up a barbed-wire fence. They electrify it. They patrol with bloodhounds. (For they remember how H. G. Wells's *The Invisible Man* could be both smelt and touched though he could not be seen.) But no shrieks ever suggest that some intruder has received a shock. No movements of the wire ever betray an invisible climber. The bloodhounds never give cry. Yet still the Believer is not convinced. 'But there is a gardener, invisible, intangible, insensible to electric shocks, a gardener who has no scent and makes no sound, a gardener who comes secretly to look after the garden which he loves.' At last the Sceptic despairs, 'But what remains of your original assertion? Just how does what you call an invisible, intangible, eternally elusive gardener differ from an imaginary gardener or even from no gardener at all?'

In this parable we can see how what starts as an assertion, that something exists or that there is some analogy between certain complexes of phenomena, may be reduced step by step to an altogether different status, to an expression perhaps of a 'picture preference.'[2] The Sceptic says there is no gardener. The Believer says there is a gardener (but invisible, etc.). One man talks about sexual behaviour. Another man prefers to talk of Aphrodite (but knows that there is not really a superhuman person additional to, and somehow responsible for, all sexual phenomena).[3] The process of qualification may be checked at any point before the original assertion is completely withdrawn and something of that first assertion will remain (Tautology). Mr. Wells's invisible man could not, admittedly, be seen, but in all other respects he was a man like the rest of us. But though the process of qualification may be, and of course usually is, checked in time, it is not always judiciously so halted. Someone may dissipate his assertion completely without noticing that he has done so. A fine brash hypothesis may thus be killed by inches, the death by a thousand qualifications.

And in this, it seems to me, lies the peculiar danger, the endemic evil, of theological utterance. Take such utterances as 'God has a plan,' 'God created the world,' 'God loves us as a father loves his children.' They look at first sight very much like assertions, vast cosmological assertions. Of course, this is no sure sign that they either are, or are intended to be, assertions. But let us confine ourselves to the cases where those who utter such sentences intend them to express assertions. (Merely remarking parenthetically that those who intend or interpret such utterances as crypto-commands, expressions of wishes, disguised ejaculations, concealed ethics, or as anything else but assertions, are unlikely to succeed in making them either properly orthodox or practically effective.)

Now to assert that such and such is the case is necessarily equivalent to denying that such and such is not the case.[4] Suppose then that we are in doubt as to what someone who gives vent to an utterance is asserting, or suppose that, more radically, we are sceptical as to whether he is really asserting anything at all, one way of trying to understand (or perhaps it will be to expose) his utterance is to attempt to find what he would regard as counting against, or as being incompatible with, its truth. For if the utterance is indeed an assertion, it will necessarily be equivalent to a denial of the negation of that assertion. And anything which would count against the assertion, or which would induce the speaker to withdraw it and to admit that it had been mistaken, must be part of (or the whole of) the meaning of the negation of that assertion. And to know the meaning of the negation of an assertion, is as near as makes no matter, to know the meaning of that assertion.[5] And if there is nothing which a putative assertion denies then there is nothing which it asserts either: and so it is not really an assertion. When the Sceptic in the parable asked the Believer, 'Just how does what you call an invisible, intangible, eternally elusive gardener differ from an imaginary gardener or even from no gardener at all?' he was suggesting that the Believer's earlier statement had been so eroded by qualification that it was no longer an assertion at all.

Now it often seems to people who are not religious as if there was no conceivable event or series of events the occurrence of which would be admitted by sophisticated religious people to be a sufficient reason for conceding 'There wasn't a God after all' or 'God does not really love us then.' Someone tells us that God loves us as a father loves his children. We are reassured. But then we see a child dying of inoperable cancer of the throat. His earthly father is driven frantic in his efforts to help, but his Heavenly Father reveals no obvious sign of concern. Some qualification is made—God's love is 'not a merely human love' or it is 'an inscrutable love,' perhaps—and we realize that such sufferings are quite compatible with the truth of the assertion that 'God loves us as a father (but, of course, . . .).' We are reassured again. But then perhaps we ask: what is this assurance of God's (appropriately qualified) love worth, what is this apparent guarantee really a guarantee against? Just what would have to happen not merely (morally and wrongly) to tempt but also (logically and rightly) to entitle us to say 'God does not love us' or even 'God does not exist?' I therefore put to the succeeding symposiasts the simple central questions, 'What would have to occur or to have occurred to constitute for you a disproof of the love of, or the existence of, God?'

NOTES

1. *P.A.S.*, 1944–5, reprinted as Ch. X of *Logic and Language*, Vol I (Blackwell, 1951), and in his *Philosophy and Psychoanalysis* (Blackwell, 1953).
2. Cf. J. Wisdom, "Other Minds," *Mind*, 1940; reprinted in his *Other Minds* (Blackwell, 1952).

3. Cf. Lucretius, *De Rerum Natura,* II, 655–60:

   Hic siquis mare Neptunum Cereremque vocare
   Constituet fruges et Bacchi nomine abuti
   Mavolat quam laticis proprium proferre vocamen
   Consedamus ut hic terrarum dictitet orbem
   Esse deum matrem dum vera re tamen ipse
   Religione animum turpi contingere parcat.

4. For those who prefer symbolism: $p \equiv \sim\sim p$.
5. For by simply negating $\sim p$ we get p: $\sim\sim p \equiv p$.

PAUL TILLICH

Religious Language as Symbolic

Paul Tillich (1886–1965) develops the view that religious language cannot be understood literally but must be understood symbolically. Tillich argues that there are levels of reality besides that which can be known empirically. Religious symbols, then, "open up" a level of divine reality to us. Tillich's affirmation that God is not an individual being but is "Being Itself" gives specific shape to his analysis of the status and function of religious symbols. The piece here analyzes several aspects of the role of symbols in general and religious symbols in particular.

⌘

The fact that there is so much discussion about the meaning of symbols going on in this country as well as in Europe is a symptom of something deeper, something both negative and positive in its import. It is a symptom of the fact that we are in a confusion of language in theology and philosophy and related subjects which has hardly been surpassed at any time in history. Words do not communicate to us any more what they originally did and what they were invented to communicate. This has something to do with the fact that our present culture has no clearing house such as medieval scholasticism was, Protestant scholasticism in the seventeenth century at least tried to be, and philosophers like Kant tried to renew. We have no such clearing house, and this is the one point at which we might be in sympathy with the present day so-called logical positivists or symbolic logicians or logicians generally. They at least try to produce a clearing house. The only criticism is that this clearing house is a very small room, perhaps only a

From "The Nature of Religious Language," *The Christian Scholar* 38, no. 3 (September 1955).

corner of a house, and not a real house. It excludes most of life. But it could become useful if it increased in reach and acceptance of realities beyond the mere logical calculus.

The positive point is that we are in a process in which a very important thing is being rediscovered: namely, that there are levels of reality of great difference, and that these different levels demand different approaches and different languages; not everything in reality can be grasped by the language which is most adequate for mathematical sciences. The insight into this situation is the most positive side of the fact that the problem of symbols is again taken seriously.

Let us proceed with the intention of clearing concepts as much as we are able, and let us take five steps, the first of which is the discussion of "symbols and signs." Symbols are similar to signs in one decisive respect: both symbols and signs point beyond themselves to something else. The typical sign, for instance the red light at the corner of the street, does not point to itself but it points to the necessity of cars stopping. And every symbol points beyond itself to a reality for which it stands. In this, symbols and signs have an essential identity—they point beyond themselves. And this is the reason that the confusion of language mentioned above has also conquered the discussion about symbols for centuries and has produced confusion between signs and symbols. The first step in any clearing up of the meaning of symbols is to distinguish it from the meaning of signs.

The difference, which is a fundamental difference between them is that signs do not participate in any way in the reality and power of that to which they point. Symbols, although they are not the same as that which they symbolize, participate in its meaning and power. The difference between symbol and sign is the participation in the symbolized reality which characterizes the symbols, and the nonparticipation in the "pointed-to" reality which characterizes a sign. For example, letters of the alphabet as they are written, an "A" or an "R" do not participate in the sound to which they point; on the other hand, the flag participates in the power of the king or the nation for which it stands and which it symbolizes. There has, therefore, been a fight since the days of William Tell as to how to behave in the presence of the flag. This would be meaningless if the flag did not participate as a symbol in the power of that which it symbolizes. The whole monarchic idea is itself entirely incomprehensible, if you do not understand that the king always is both: on the one hand, a symbol of the power of the group of which he is the king and on the other hand, he who exercises partly (never fully, of course) this power.

But something has happened which is very dangerous for all our attempts to find a clearing house for the concepts of symbols and signs. The mathematician has usurped the term "symbol" for mathematical "sign," and this makes a disentanglement of the confusion almost impossible. The only thing we can do is to distinguish different groups, signs which are called symbols, and genuine symbols. The mathematical signs are signs which are wrongly called symbols.

Language is a very good example of the difference between signs and symbols. Words in a language are signs for a meaning which they express. The word "desk" is a sign which points to something quite different—namely, the thing on which a paper is lying and at which we might be looking. This has nothing to do with the word "desk," with these four letters. But there are words in every language which are more than this, and in the moment in which they get connotations which go beyond something to which they point as signs, then they can become symbols; and this is a very important distinction for any speaker. He can speak almost completely in signs, reducing the meaning of his words almost to mathematical signs, and this is the absolute ideal of the logical positivist. The other pole of this is liturgical or poetic language where words have a power through centuries, or more than centuries. They have connotations in situations in which they appear so that they cannot be replaced. They have become not only signs pointing to a meaning which is defined, but also symbols standing for a reality in the power of which they participate.

Now we come to a second consideration dealing with the functions of symbols. This first function is implied in what has already been said—namely, the representative function. The symbol represents something which is not itself, for which it stands and in the power and meaning of which it participates. This is a basic function of every symbol, and therefore, if that word had not been used in so many other ways, one could perhaps even translate '"symbolic" as "representative," but for some reason that is not possible. If the symbols stand for something which they are not, then the question is, "Why do we not have that for which they stand directly? Why do we need symbols at all?" And now we come to something which is perhaps the main function of the symbol—namely, the opening up of levels of reality which otherwise are hidden and cannot be grasped in any other way.

Every symbol opens up a level of reality for which nonsymbolic speaking is inadequate. Let us interpret this, or explain this, in terms of artistic symbols. The more we try to enter into the meaning of symbols, the more we become aware that it is a function of art to open up levels of reality; in poetry, in visual art, and in music, levels of reality are opened up which can be opened up in no other way. Now if this is the function of art, then certainly artistic creations have symbolic character. You can take that which a landscape of Rubens, for instance, mediates to you. You cannot have this experience in any other way than through this painting made by Rubens. This landscape has some heroic character; it has character of balance, of colors, of weights, of values, and so on. All this is very external. What this mediates to you cannot be expressed in any other way than through the painting itself. The same is true also in the relationship of poetry and philosophy. The temptation may often be to confuse the issue by bringing too many philosophical concepts into a poem. Now this is really the problem; one cannot do this. If one uses philosophical language or scientific language, it does not mediate the same thing which is mediated in the use of really poetic language without a mixture of any other language.

This example may show what is meant by the phrase "opening up of levels of reality." But in order to do this, something else must be opened up—namely, levels of the soul, levels of our interior reality. And they must correspond to the levels in exterior reality which are opened up by a symbol. So every symbol is two-edged. It opens up reality and it opens up the soul. There are, of course, people who are not opened up by music or who are not opened up by poetry, or more of them (especially in Protestant America) who are not opened up at all by visual arts. The "opening up" is a two-sided function—namely, reality in deeper levels and the human soul in special levels.

If this is the function of symbols then it is obvious that symbols cannot be replaced by other symbols. Every symbol has a special function which is just *it* and cannot be replaced by more or less adequate symbols. This is different from signs, for signs can always be replaced. If one finds that a green light is not so expedient as perhaps a blue light (this is not true, but could be true), then we simply put on a blue light, and nothing is changed. But a symbolic word (such as the word "God") cannot be replaced. No symbol can be replaced when used in its special function. So one asks rightly, "How do symbols arise, and how do they come to an end?" As different from signs, symbols are born and die. Signs are consciously invented and removed. This is a fundamental difference.

"Out of what womb are symbols born?" Out of the womb which is usually called today the "group unconscious" or "collective unconscious," or whatever you want to call it—out of a group which acknowledges, in this thing, this word, this flag, or whatever it may be, its own being. It is not invented intentionally; even if somebody would try to invent a symbol, as sometimes happens, then it becomes a symbol only if the unconscious of a group says "yes" to it. It means that something is opened up by it in the sense which I have just described. Now this implies further that in the moment in which this inner situation of the human group to a symbol has ceased to exist, then the symbol dies. The symbol does not "say" anything any more. In this way, all of the polytheistic gods have died; the situation in which they were born, has changed or does not exist any more, and so the symbols died. But these are events which cannot be described in terms of intention and invention.

Now we come to a third consideration—namely, the nature of religious symbols. Religious symbols do exactly the same thing as all symbols do—namely, they open up a level of reality, which otherwise is not opened at all, which is hidden. We can call this the depth dimension of reality itself, the dimension of reality which is the ground of every other dimension and every other depth, and which therefore, is not one level beside the others but is the fundamental level, the level below all other levels, the level of being itself, or the ultimate power of being. Religious symbols open up the experience of the dimension of this depth in the human soul. If a religious symbol has ceased to have this function, then it dies. And if new symbols are born, they are born out of a changed relationship to the ultimate ground of being, i.e., to the Holy.

The dimension of ultimate reality is the dimension of the Holy. And so we can also say, religious symbols are symbols of the Holy. As such they participate in the holiness of the Holy according to our basic definition of a symbol. But participation is not identity; they are not themselves *the* Holy. The wholly transcendent transcends every symbol of the Holy. Religious symbols are taken from the infinity of material which the experienced reality gives us. Everything in time and space has become at some time in the history of religion a symbol for the Holy. And this is naturally so, because everything that is in the world we encounter rests on the ultimate ground of being. This is the key to the otherwise extremely confusing history of religion. Those of you who have looked into this seeming chaos of the history of religion in all periods of history from the earliest primitives to the latest developments, will be extremely confused about the chaotic character of this development. The key which makes order out of this chaos is comparatively simple. It is that everything in reality can impress itself as a symbol for a special relationship of the human mind to its own ultimate ground and meaning. So in order to open up the seemingly closed door to this chaos of religious symbols, one simply has to ask, "What is the relationship to the ultimate which is symbolized in these symbols?" And then they cease to be meaningless; and they become, on the contrary, the most revealing creations of the human mind, the most genuine ones, the most powerful ones, those who control the human consciousness, and perhaps even more the unconsciousness, and have therefore this tremendous tenacity which is characteristic of all religious symbols in the history of religion.

Religion, as everything in life, stands under the law of ambiguity, "ambiguity" meaning that it is creative and destructive at the same time. Religion has its holiness and its unholiness, and the reason for this is obvious from what has been said about religious symbolism. Religious symbols point symbolically to that which transcends all of them. But since, as symbols, they participate in that to which they point, they always have the tendency (in the human mind, of course) to replace that to which they are supposed to point, and to become ultimate in themselves. And in the moment in which they do this, they become idols. All idolatry is nothing else than the absolutizing of symbols of the Holy, and making them identical with the Holy itself. In this way, for instance, holy persons can become a god. Ritual acts can take on unconditional validity, although they are only expressions of a special situation. In all sacramental activities of religion, in all holy objects, holy books, holy doctrines, holy rites, you find this danger which we call "demonization." They become demonic at the moment in which they become elevated to the unconditional and ultimate character of the Holy itself.

Now we turn to a fourth consideration—namely, the levels of religious symbols. There are two fundamental levels in all religious symbols: the transcendent level, the level which goes *beyond* the empirical reality we encounter, and the immanent level, the level which we find *within* the encounter with reality. Let us look at the first level, the transcendent level. The basic symbol on the transcendent level would be God himself. But we cannot simply say that God is a symbol. We must always say two things about him: we must say that there is a non-symbolic element in our image of God—namely, that he is ultimate reality, being itself, ground of being, power of being; and the other, that he is the highest being in which everything that we have does exist in the most perfect way. If we say this we have in our mind the image of a highest being, a being with the characteristics of highest perfection. That means, we have a symbol for that which is not symbolic in the idea of God—namely, "Being Itself."

It is important to distinguish these two elements in the idea of God. Thus all of these discussions going on about God being a person or not a person, God being similar to other things or not similar, these discussions which have a great impact on the destruction of the religious experience through false interpretations of it, could be overcome if we would say, "Certainly the awareness of something unconditional is in itself what it is, is not symbolic." We can call it *"Being Itself," esse qua esse, esse ipsum*, as the scholastics did. But in our relationship to this ultimate we symbolize and must symbolize. We could not be in communication with God if he were only "ultimate being." But in our relationship to him we encounter him with the highest of what we ourselves are, *person*. And so in the symbolic form of speaking about him, we have both that which transcends infinitely our experience of ourselves as persons, and that which is so adequate to our being persons that we can say, "Thou" to God, and can pray to him. And these two elements must be preserved. If we preserve only the element of the unconditional, then no relationship to God is possible. If we preserve only the element of the ego-thou relationship, as it is called today, we lose the element of the divine—namely, the unconditional which transcends subject and object and all other polarities. This is the first point on the transcendent level.

The second is the qualities, the attributes of God, whatever you say about him: that he is love, that he is mercy, that he is power, that he is omniscient, that he is omnipresent, that he is almighty. These attributes of God are taken from experienced qualities we have ourselves. They cannot be applied to God in the literal sense. If this is done, it leads to an infinite amount of absurdities. This again is one of the reasons for the destruction of religion through wrong communicative interpretation of it. And again the symbolic character of these qualities must be maintained consistently. Otherwise, every speaking about the divine becomes absurd.

A third element on the transcendent level is the acts of God, for example, when we say, "He has created the world," "He has sent his son," "He will fulfill the world." In all these temporal, causal, and other expressions we speak symbolically of God. As an example, look at the one small sentence: *"God has sent his son."* Here we have in the word "has" temporality. But God is beyond *our* temporality, though not beyond every temporality. Here is space; "sending somebody" means moving him from one place to another place. This certainly is speaking symbolically, although spatiality is in God as an element in his creative ground. We say that he "has sent"—that means that he has caused something. In this way God is subject to the category of causality. And when we speak of him and his Son, we have two different substances and apply the category of substance to him. Now all this, if taken literally, is absurd. If it is taken symbolically, it is a profound expression, the ultimate Christian expression, of the relationship between God and man in the Christian experience. But to distinguish these two kinds of speech, the non-symbolic and the symbolic, in such a point is so important that if we are not able to make understandable to our contemporaries that we speak symbolically when we use such language, they will rightly turn away from us, as from people who still live in absurdities and superstitions.

Now consider the immanent level, the level of the appearances of the divine in time and space. Here we have first of all the incarnations of the divine, different beings in time and space, divine beings transmuted into animals or men or any kinds of other beings as they appear in time and space. This is often forgotten by those within Christianity who like to use in every second theological proposition the word "incarnation." They forget that this is not an especially Christian characteristic, because incarnation is something which happens in paganism all the time. The divine beings always incarnate in different forms. That is very easy in paganism. This is not the real distinction between Christianity and other religions.

Here we must say something about the relationships of the transcendent to the immanent level just in connection with the incarnation idea. Historically, one must say that preceding both of them was the situation in which the transcendent and immanent were not distinguished. In the Indonesian doctrine of "Mana," that divine mystical power which permeates all reality, we have some divine presence which is both immanent in everything as a hidden power, and at the same time transcendent, something which can be grasped only through very difficult ritual activities known to the priest.

Out of this identity of the immanent and the transcendent, the gods of the great mythologies have developed in Greece and in the Semitic nations and in India. There we find incarnations as the immanent element of the divine. The more transcendent the gods become, the more incarnations of personal or sacramental character are needed in order to overcome the remoteness of the divine which develops with the strengthening of the transcendent element.

And from this follows the second element in the immanent religious symbolism, namely, the sacramental. The sacramental is nothing else than some reality becoming the bearer of the Holy in a special way and under special circumstances. In this sense, the Lord's Supper, or better the materials in the Lord's Supper, are symbolic. Now you will ask perhaps, "only symbolic?" That sounds as if there were something more than symbolic, namely, "literal." But the literal is not more but less than symbolic. If we speak of those dimensions of reality which we cannot approach in any other way than by symbols, then symbols are not used in terms of "only" but in terms of that which is necessary, of that which we *must* apply. Sometimes, because of nothing more than the confusion of signs with symbols, the phrase "only a symbol" means "only a sign." And then the question is justified. "Only a sign?" "No." The sacrament is not only a sign. In the famous discussion between Luther and Zwingli, in Marburg in 1529, it was just this point on which the discussion was held. Luther wanted to maintain the genuinely symbolic character of the elements, but Zwingli said that the sacramental materials, bread and wine, are "only symbolic." Thus, Zwingli meant that they are only signs pointing to a story of the past. Even in that period there was semantic confusion. And let us not be misled by this. In the real sense of symbol, the sacramental materials are symbols. But if the symbol is used as *only* symbol (i.e., only signs), then of course the sacramental materials are more than this.

Then there is the third element on the immanent level. Many things—like special parts of the church building, like the candles, like the water at the entrance of the Roman Church, like the cross in all churches, especially Protestant churches—were originally only signs, but in use became symbols; call them sign-symbols, signs which have become symbols.

And now a last consideration—namely, the truth of religious symbols. Here we must distinguish a negative, a positive, and an absolute statement. First the negative statement. Symbols are independent of any empirical criticism. You cannot kill a symbol by criticism in terms of natural sciences or in terms of historical research. As was said, symbols can only die if the situation in which they have been created has passed. They are not on a level on which empirical criticism can dismiss them. Here are two examples, both connected with Mary, the mother of Jesus, as Holy Virgin. First of all you have here a symbol which has died in Protestantism by the changed situation of the relation to God. The special, direct, immediate relationship to God, makes any mediating power impossible. Another reason which has made this symbol disappear is the negation of the ascetic element which is implied in the glorification of virginity. And as long as the Protestant religious situation lasts it cannot be reestablished. It has not died because Protestant scholars have said, "Now there is no empirical reason for saying all this about the Holy Virgin." There certainly is not, but this the Roman Church also knows. But the Roman Church sticks to it on the basis of its tremendous symbolic power which step by step brings her nearer to Trinity itself, especially in the development of the last decade. If this should ever be completed as is now discussed in groups of the Roman Church, Mary would become co-Saviour with Jesus. Then, whether this is admitted or not, she is actually taken into the divinity itself.

Another example is the story of the virginal birth of Jesus. This is from the point of view of historical research a most obviously legendary story, unknown to Paul and to John. It is a late creation, trying to make understandable the full possession of the divine Spirit of Jesus of Nazareth. But again its legendary character is not the reason why this symbol will die or has died in many groups of people, in even quite conservative groups within the Protestant churches. The reason is different. The reason is that it is theologically quasiheretical. It takes away one of the fundamental doctrines of Chalcedon, viz., the classical Christian doctrine that the full humanity of Jesus must be maintained beside his whole divinity. A human being who has no human father has no full humanity. This story then has to be criticized on inner-symbolic grounds, but not on historical grounds. This is the negative statement about the truth of religious symbols. Their truth is their adequacy to the religious situation in which they are created, and their inadequacy to another situation is their untruth. In the last sentence both the positive and the negative statement about symbols are contained.

Religion is ambiguous and every religious symbol may become idolatrous, may be demonized, may elevate itself to ultimate validity although nothing is ultimate but the ultimate itself; no religious doctrine and no religious ritual may be. If Christianity claims to have a truth superior to any other truth in its symbolism, then it is the symbol of the cross in which this is expressed, the cross of the Christ. He who himself embodies the fullness of the divine's presence sacrifices himself in order not to become an idol, another god beside God, a god into whom the disciples wanted to make him. And therefore the decisive story is the story in which he accepts the title "Christ" when Peter offers it to him. He accepts it under the one condition that he has to go to Jerusalem to suffer and to die, which means to deny the idolatrous tendency even with respect to himself. This is at the same time the criterion of all other symbols, and it is the criterion to which every Christian church should subject itself.

WILLIAM P. ALSTON

Speaking Literally of God

William P. Alston (1921–) brings his widely recognized expertise in the philosophy of language to bear upon issues related to religious language. In the following essay, he explores the question of whether we can speak literally of God. He recognizes the widespread professional opinion that our talk of God must be non-literal (e.g., symbolic, metaphorical, figurative). However, Alston frames the question as one of whether we can form subject-predicate sentences that can possibly be asserted truly of God conceived as an incorporeal being. In pursuing this question, Alston restricts his study to "P-predicates" (predicates that distinctively apply to personal agents) and concludes that there is no obstacle in the concept of God's incorporeality to applying P-predicates to God. He recognizes that much more work remains to be done to form a comprehensive argument that we can speak literally of God. This further work would include an analysis of timelessness, immutability, and other classical divine attributes to see if they constitute a bar to speaking literally of God.

⌘

LITERAL PREDICATION AND THEOLOGY

In this essay we shall be concerned with only one stretch of talk about God, but a particularly central stretch—subject-predicate statements in which the subject-term is used to refer to God. I mean this to be limited to *statements* in a strict sense, utterances that are put forward with a "truth claim." This is a crucial stretch of the territory, because any other talk that involves reference to God presupposes the truth of one or more *statements* about God. For example, if I ask God to give me courage, I am presupposing that God is the sort of being to whom requests can be sensibly addressed. Thus our more specific topic concerns whether terms can be literally predicated of God.

According to contemporary Protestant theologians of a liberal cast, it is almost an article of faith that this is impossible. Let us be somewhat more explicit than people like that generally are, as to just what is being denied. When someone says that we cannot speak literally of God, that person does not mean to deny us the capacity to form a subject-predicate sentence that contains a subject-term used to refer to God, making a literal use of the predicate term and uttering the sentence with the claim that the predicate is true of the subject. I could easily refute that denial here and now—"God has commanded us to love one another." I have just done it. But presumably it is not that sort of ability that is in question. It is rather a question as to whether any such truth claim can succeed. What is being denied is that any predicate term, used literally, can be *truly applied* to God, or as we might say, that any predicate is *literally true* of God.

But even this is stronger than a charitable interpretation would require. Presumably, no one who thinks it possible to refer to God would deny that some negative predicates are literally true of God—for instance, incorporeal, immutable, or not-identical-with-Richard-Nixon. Nor would all extrinsic predicates be ruled out; it would be difficult to deny that 'thought of now by me' could be literally true of God. Now it is notoriously difficult to draw an exact line between positive and negative predicates; and the class of predicates I am calling "extrinsic" is hardly easier to demarcate. It is either very difficult or impossible to give a precise characterization of the class of predicates to which the deniers of literal talk should be addressing themselves. Here I shall confine myself to the following brief statement. The reason various predicates are obvious examples of "negative" or "extrinsic" predicates is that they do not "tell us anything" about the subject—about the nature or operations of the subject. Let us call predicates that do "tell us something" about such matters "intrinsic" predicates. We may then take it that an opponent of literal theological talk is denying that any *intrinsic* predicate can be literally true of God. It will be noted that "intrinsic" predicates include various *relational* predicates, such as "made the heavens and the earth" and "spoke to Moses."

Various reasons have been given for the impossibility of literal predication in theology. Among the most prominent have been the following.

1. Since God is an absolutely undifferentiated unity, and since all positive predications impute complexity to their subject, no such predications can be true of God. This line of thought is most characteristic of the mystical tradition, but something like it can be found in other theologies as well.
2. God is so "transcendent," so "wholly other," that no concepts we can form would apply to him.
3. The attempt to apply predicates literally to God inevitably leads to paradoxes.

It is the second reason that bulks largest in twentieth-century Protestant theology. It has taken several forms, one of the more fashionable being the position of Paul Tillich that (a) God is not *a* being but Being-Itself, since anything that is *a* being would not be an appropriate object of "ultimate concern"; and (b) only what is *a* being can be literally characterized.

In my opinion, all these arguments are radically insufficient to support the sweeping denial that *any* intrinsic predicate can be literally true of God. But this is not the place to go into that. Nor will I take up the cudgel for the other side on this issue and argue that it must be possible for *some* intrinsic predicates or other to be literally true of God. Instead I will focus on a particularly important class of predicates—those I shall call "personalistic" (or, following Strawson, 'P-predicates')—and consider the more specific question, whether any P-predicates can be literally true of God. Or rather, as I shall make explicit shortly, I will consider one small part of this very large question. By "personalistic" predicates, I mean those that, as a group, apply to a being only if that being is a "personal agent"—an agent that carries out intentions, plans, or purposes in its actions, that acts in the light of knowledge or belief; a being whose actions express attitudes and are guided by standards and principles; a being capable of communicating with other such agents and entering into other forms of personal relations with them. The conception of God as a personal agent is deeply embedded in Christianity and in other theistic religions. Communication between God and man, verbal and otherwise, is at the heart of the Judaeo-Christian tradition. Equally fundamental is the thought of God as a being who lays down commands, injunctions, rules, and regulations, and who monitors compliance or non-compliance; who created the world and directs it to the attainment of certain ends; who enters into covenants; who rewards and punishes; who loves and forgives; who acts in history and in the lives of men to carry out His purposes. The last few sentences indicate some of the kinds of P-predicates that have traditionally been applied to God.

WHAT DOES IT MEAN TO SPEAK LITERALLY?

Before coming to grips with this problem, we must provide some clarification of the central term 'literal.' To begin on a negative note, despite the frequent occurrence of phrases such as 'literal *meaning*' and 'literal *sense*,' I believe that such phrases constitute a confused or at least a loose way of thinking about the subject. To get straight about the matter, we need to keep a firm hold on the distinction between *language* and *speech*. A (natural) language is an abstract system, a system of sound types or, in principle, types of other sorts of perceptible items. The systematicity involved is both "internal" and "external." The phonology, morphology, and syntax of a language reveal its internal system—the ways its elements can be combined to form larger units. The external system is revealed by the semantics of the language—the way units of language have the function of "representing" things in the world and features of the world.[1] A language serves as a means of communication; in fact, it is plausible to look on the entire complex structure as "being there" in order to make a language an effective device for communication. Speech, on the other hand, is the *use* of language in communication (using 'speech' in an extended sense, to cover written as well as oral communication). It is what we *do* in the course of exploiting a linguistic system for purposes of communication.

Now the fact that a given word or phrase has the meaning(s) or sense(s) that it has is a fact about the language; it is part of the semantic constitution of the language.[2] Thus it is a semantic fact about English that 'player' has among its meanings:

1. an idler;
2. one who plays some (specified) game;
3. a gambler;
4. an actor.[3]

It is partly the fact that a word *has* a certain meaning in a language that gives the word its usability for communication; this fact constitutes one of the linguistic resources we draw upon in saying what we have to say.

The term 'literal,' on the other hand, stands for a certain way of *using* words, phrases, and so on; it stands for a mode of *speech* rather than for a type of meaning or any other feature of *language*. As such, it stands in contrast with a family of *figurative* uses of terms—"figures of speech," as they are appropriately termed in the tradition—the most familiar of which is metaphor. Let us make explicit the difference between literal and metaphorical uses, restricting ourselves to uses of predicates in subject-predicate statements.

We may think of each meaning of a predicate term as "correlating" the term with some, possibly very complex, property.[4] Different theories of meaning provide differing accounts of the nature of this correlation. Thus the "ideational" theory of meaning, found for example in Locke's *Essay*, holds that a meaning of a predicate term correlates it with a certain property—P—*iff* the term functions as a sign of the *idea* of P in communication. Other theories provide other accounts. It will be convenient to speak of the predicate term as "signifying" or "standing for" the correlated property.

Now when I make a *literal* use of a predicate term (in one of its meanings) in a subject-predicate statement, I utter the sentence with the claim that the property signified by the predicate term is possessed by the subject (i.e., the referent of the subject-term), or holds between the subjects, if the predicate is a relational one. Thus, if I make a literal use of 'player' in saying "He's one of the players," I am claiming, let us say, that the person referred to has the property specified in the fourth definition listed above. And if my statement is true, if the person referred to really does have that property, we may say that 'player' is *literally true* of him in that sense—does *literally apply* to him in that sense.

But suppose I say, as Shakespeare has Macbeth say, "Life's . . . a poor player that struts and frets his hour upon the stage and then is heard no more." It is clear that life is not really an actor; nor, if we surveyed the other established meanings of 'player,' would we find any properties signified that are exemplified by life. Hence in uttering Macbeth's sentence, I will, if I am sensible, be using the term 'player' metaphorically rather than literally. Since figurative uses appear in this paper only as a foil for literal uses, I will not be able to embark on the complex task of characterizing the figures of speech. Suffice it to say that when I use a term metaphorically, I exploit some meaning the term has in the language, but not in the straightforward way that is involved in literal usage. Rather than claiming that the property signified by the predicate does apply to the subject(s), I do something more complex, more indirect. I first, so to speak, "present" the hearer with the sort of thing to which the term literally applies (call it an exemplar) and then suggest that the exemplar can be taken as a "model" of the subject(s); I suggest that by considering the exemplar, one will thereby be put in mind of certain features of the subject(s). In the example just given, the exemplar is an (insignificant) actor who plays his part in a stage production and then disappears from the view of the audience; the suggestion is that a human life is like that in some significant respect(s).[5]

The term 'literal' has picked up a number of adventitious associations in recent times. I think particularly of 'precise,' 'univocal,' 'specific,' 'empirical,' and 'ordinary.' However common the conflation, it is simply a confusion to suppose that 'literal,' in the historically distinctive sense just set out, implies any of the features just mentioned. Meanings that words have in a language can be more or less vague, open-textured, unspecific, and otherwise indeterminate. Hence I can be using words literally and still be speaking vaguely, ambiguously, or unspecifically. Again, I can be using my words just as literally when asking questions, cursing fate, or expressing rage, as when I am soberly asserting that the cat is on the mat. The conflation of 'literal' with 'empirical,' however, is more than a vulgar error; it reflects a conviction as to the conditions under which a word can acquire a meaning in the language. If this requires contact with "experience" in one or another of the ways spelled out in empiricist theories of meaning, then only terms with empirical meanings can be used literally, for only such terms *have* established senses. But that does not follow merely from the meaning of 'literal'; it also requires an empiricist theory of meaning, and it is by no means clear that any such theory is acceptable.

It might be thought that after the term 'literal' has been stripped of all these interesting connotations, the question as to whether we can speak literally of God has lost its importance. Not so. To demonstrate its importance, we merely need appeal to some highly plausible principles which connect meanings and concepts. It seems clear that I can attach a certain meaning to a predicate term only if I have a concept of the property signified by the term when used with that meaning; otherwise, how can I "get at" the property so as to signify it by that term? And on the other hand, if I do have a concept of that property, it could not be impossible for me to use a term to signify that property. And if a sufficient number of members of my linguistic community share that concept, it could not be, in principle, impossible for a term to signify that property in the language. Thus it is possible for a term in a certain language to signify a certain property *iff* speakers of that language have or can have a concept of that property. Hence our language can contain terms that stand for intrinsic properties of God *iff* we can form concepts of intrinsic properties of God. And since we can make true literal predications of God *iff* our language contains terms that stand for properties exemplified by God, we may say, finally, that we can speak literally of God (in the relevant sense of true literal predication) *iff* we can form concepts of intrinsic divine properties.[6] And whether this last is true is *obviously* an important issue—one that has been at the very center of metatheology from the beginning.

The question whether certain terms can be literally applied to God is often identified with the question whether those terms are literally true of God in senses they bear outside theology. Thus with respect to P-predicates, it is often supposed that God can be spoken of as literally having knowledge and intentions, as creating, commanding, and forgiving, only if those terms are literally true of God in the same senses as those in which they are literally true of human beings. The reason usually given for this supposition is that we first come to attach meaning to these terms by learning what it is for human beings to command, forgive, and so on, and that there is no other way we can proceed. We cannot begin by learning what it is for God to know, command, or forgive. I do not want to contest this claim about the necessary order of language learning, though there is much to be said on both sides. I will confine myself to pointing out that even if this claim is granted, it does *not* follow that terms can be literally applied to God only in senses in which they also are true of human beings and other creatures. For the fact that we must begin with creatures is quite compatible with the supposition that at some later stage terms take on special technical senses in theology. After all, that is what happens in science. There, too, it can be plausibly argued that we can learn theoretical terms in science only if we have already learned commonsense meanings of these and other terms—senses in which the terms are true of ordinary middle-sized objects. But even if that is true, it does not prevent such terms as 'force' and 'energy' from taking on new technical senses in the development of sophisticated theories. Why should not the same be true of theology?

Many will claim that the same cannot be true of theology, because the conditions that permit technical senses to emerge in science do not obtain in theology. For example, it may be claimed that theological systems do not have the kind of explanatory efficacy possessed by scientific theories. These are important questions, but I can sidestep them for now, because I will restrict myself here to whether (some) P-predicates can be true of God in (some of) the senses in which they are true of human beings. The only qualification I make on that is that I shall consider a simple transformation of certain human action predicates—"simple," in that the change does not involve any radical conceptual innovation. The revised action predicates are fundamentally of the same sort as human action predicates, though different in some details.

Whether certain predicates are literally true of God depends on both parties to the transaction; it depends both on what God is like and on the content of the predicates. To carry out a proper discussion of the present issue, I would need to (a) present and defend an account of the nature of God, and (b) present and defend an analysis of such P-predicates as will be considered. That would put us in a position to make some well-grounded judgments as to whether such predicates could be literally true of God. Needless to say, I will not have time for all that; I would not have had time, even if I had cut the preliminary cackle and buckled down to the job straight away. Hence I must scale down my aspirations. Instead of trying to "tell it like it is" with God, I shall simply pick one commonly recognized attribute of God—incorporeality—which has been widely thought to rule out personal agency, and I shall consider whether it does so. My main reasons for focusing on incorporeality, rather than on simplicity, infinity, timelessness, or immutability, are that it, much more than the others, is widely accepted today as a divine attribute and that it has bulked large in some recent arguments against the literal applicability of P-predicates. On the side of the predicates, I shall consider those types of analyses that are, in my judgment, the strongest contenders and ask what each of them implies as to literal applicability to an incorporeal being.[7]

This investigation is only a fragment of the total job. It is radically incomplete from both sides, and especially from the side of the divine nature. Even if we satisfy ourselves that personalistic terms can be literally true of an incorporeal being, that will by no means suffice to show that they are literally true of God. God is not just any old incorporeal being. There may well be other divine attributes that inhibit us from thinking literally of God as a personal agent—simplicity, infinity, immutability, and timelessness. But sufficient unto the day is the problem thereof.

MENTAL PREDICATES AND GOD

P-predicates may be conveniently divided into mental or psychological predicates (M-predicates) and action predicates (A-predicates). M-predicates have to do with cognitions, feelings, emotions, attitudes, wants, thoughts, fantasies, and other internal psychological states, events, and processes. A-predicates have to do with what, in a broad sense, an agent *does*. For reasons that will emerge in the course of the discussion, it will be best to begin with theories of M-predicates. I shall oscillate freely between speaking of the *meanings* of predicates and the *concepts* those predicates express by virtue of having those meanings.

The main divide in theories of M-predicates concerns whether they are properly defined in terms of their behavioral manifestations.[8] On the negative side of that issue is the view that was dominant from the seventeenth through the nineteenth century—what we may call the Private Paradigm (PP) view. According to this position, the meaning of an M-predicate—for example, 'feels depressed'—is given, for each person, by certain paradigms of feelings of depression within his own experience. By 'feels depressed' I mean a state such as X, Y, Z, . . . , where these are clear cases of feeling depressed that I can remember having experienced. We might say that on this model an M-predicate acquires meaning through "inner ostension"; I attach meaning to the term by "associating" it with samples of the state it signifies. On the PP view, an M-predicate is not properly defined in terms of its invariable, normal, or typical behavioral manifestations. Even if feelings of depression are typically manifested by droopy appearance, slowness of response, and lack of vigor, it is no part of the *meaning* of the term that these are the typical manifestations. Our *concept* of feeling depressed is such that it makes sense to think of a world in which feelings of depression typically manifest themselves in alert posture and vigorous reactions. Since the term simply designates certain feeling qualities, it is just a matter of fact that feelings of depression manifest themselves in the way they do.[9]

There are solid reasons for the PP view, especially for feeling and sensation terms. (1) If I have never felt depressed, then in an important sense, I do not understand the term, for I do not know *what it is like* to feel depressed; I simply do not have the concept of that sort of feeling. (2) My knowledge of my own feelings is quite independent of my knowledge of my behavior or demeanor; I do not have to watch myself in a mirror to know how I feel. Hence it seems that what I know when I know how I feel cannot consist in any behavioral manifestations or tendencies thereto. (3) It does seem an *intelligible* supposition that the kind of feeling we call a feeling of depression should be manifested in ways that are radically different from those that do in fact obtain. And the PP account allows for this.

However, the PP account has been under attack throughout this century. There are four main motives for dissatisfaction. (1) If feeling depressed is not, by definition, typically manifested in certain ways, then how can I tell what other people are feeling, on the basis of their behavior and demeanor? For I can discover a correlation between a certain kind of feeling and certain kinds of behavior only in my own case; and how can I generalize from one case? Thus the PP view has been felt to rule out knowledge of the mental states of others. (2) How can you and I have any reason to suppose that we attach the same meaning to any M-predicate, if each of us learns the meaning from nonshareable paradigms? How can I tell whether my paradigms of feeling depressed are like your paradigms? Thus the PP view has been thought to sap our conviction that we share a public language for talking about the mind. (3) On the widely influential Verifiability Theory of Meaning, the meaning of a term is given by specifying the ways in which we can tell that it applies. Since we can tell whether M-predicates apply to others by observing their demeanor and behavior, the latter must enter into the meaning of the term. (4) Wittgenstein mounted a very influential attack on the possibility of attaching meaning to terms by private ostension.[10]

These arguments against PP support the idea that mental states are identified in terms of their typical manifestations in overt behavior and demeanor. We may use the term Logical Connectionism (LC) as a general term for views of this sort, on the ground that these views hold that there is a logical (conceptual) connection between a mental state and its manifestations.

The general concept of LC allows plenty of room for variation. The simplest form that is not wildly implausible is Logical Behaviorism (LB). LB may be formulated as the view that an M-predicate signifies a set of behavioral dispositions—dispositions to behave a certain way, given certain conditions.[11] Thus a logical behaviorist would explain "S feels depressed" in some such way as this: If someone makes a suggestion to S, S will respond slowly and without enthusiasm; if S is presented with something S usually likes, S will not smile as S normally does in such situations, and so on.[12] LB is not nearly as prominent now as a decade or so ago, and in my opinion, there are excellent reasons for this decline. The fatal difficulty is this. The response tendencies associated with a particular case of a mental state will depend upon the total psychological field of the moment—that is, the other mental states present at the time. For example, whether a person who feels depressed will react in a characteristically depressed way depends upon whether he is sufficiently motivated to conceal his condition. If he is, the typical manifestation may well not be forthcoming. Thus any particular behavioral reaction emerges from the total contemporary psychological field and is not wholly determined by any one component thereof. This consideration should inhibit us from attempting to identify any particular M-concept with the concept of any particular set of behavioral dispositions.

Under the impact of these considerations, more subtle forms of LC have developed, for which we may use the generic term, 'Functionalism.' The general idea of Functionalism is that each M-concept is a concept of a certain functional role in the operation of the psyche. A major emphasis in this position has been the functional character of M-concepts. In attributing a certain belief, attitude, or feeling to S, we are committing ourselves to the position that a certain function is being carried out in S's psyche, or at least that S is prepared to carry it out if the need arises. We are not committing ourselves on the physical (or spiritual) structure or composition of whatever is performing this function; our concept is neutral as to that. M-concepts, on this position, are functional in essentially the same way as the concept of a mousetrap. A mousetrap, by definition, is a device for catching mice; the definition is neutral as to the composition and structure of devices that perform this function. That is why it is possible to build a better mousetrap.[13]

To exploit this initial insight, the functionalist will have to find a way of specifying functional roles in the psyche. It is now generally assumed by functionalists that the basic function of the psyche as a whole is the production of overt behavior. That is why Functionalism counts as a form of LC. To understand the concept of belief is, at least in part, to understand the role of beliefs in the production of behavior. But "at least in part" is crucial; it is what enables Functionalism to escape the above objections to LB. Functionalism is thoroughly systemic. The vicissitudes of LB have taught it to avoid the supposition that each distinguishable mental state is related separately to overt behavior. It has thoroughly internalized the point that a given belief, attitude, or feeling gives rise to a certain distinctive mode of behavior only in conjunction with the rest of the contemporary psychological field. Therefore in specifying the function of an enthusiasm for Mozart, for example, in the production of behavior, we must specify the way that enthusiasm combines with each of various other combinations of factors to affect behavioral output. It also recognizes that intrapsychic functions enter into M-concepts. Our concept of the *belief that it is raining now* includes (a) the way this belief will combine with others to inferentially generate other beliefs, and (b) the way it will combine with an aversion to rainy weather, to produce dismay, as well as (c) the way it will combine with an aversion to getting wet, to produce the behavior of getting out one's umbrella. Clearly, a full functionalist specification of an M-concept would be an enormously complicated affair.[14]

With an eye to putting some flesh on this skeleton, consider this attempt by R. B. Brandt and Jaegwon Kim to formulate a functionalist analysis of the ordinary concept of *want*, conceived in a broad sense as any state in which the object of the "want" has what Lewin called positive valence for the subject.[15]

"*X* wants *p*" has the meaning it does for us because we believe roughly the following statements.

1. If, given that *x* had not been expecting *p* but now suddenly judged that *p* would be the case, *x* would feel joy, then *x* wants *p*.
2. If, given that *x* had been expecting *p* but then suddenly judged that *p* would not be the case, *x* would feel disappointment, then *x* wants *p*.
3. If daydreaming about *p* is pleasant to *x*, then *x* wants *p*.
4. If *x* wants *p*, then, under favorable conditions, if *x* judges that doing *A* will probably lead to *p* and that not doing *A* will probably lead to not *p*, *x* will feel some impulse to do *A*.
5. If *x* wants *p*, then, under favorable conditions, if *x* thinks some means *M* is a way of bringing *p* about, *x* will be more likely to notice an *M* than he would otherwise have been.
6. If *x* wants *p*, then, under favorable conditions, if *p* occurs, without the simultaneous occurrence of events *x* does not want, *x* will be pleased.[16]

In terms of our general characterization of Functionalism, we can think of each of these lawlike generalizations as specifying a *function* performed by wants. Thus a "want" is the sort of state that (a) together with unexpected fulfillment, gives rise to feelings of joy; (b) renders daydreaming about its object pleasant, and so on. (c) is the crucial connection with behavior, though in this formulation it is quite indirect, coming through a connection with an "impulse" to perform a certain action.[17] This is in contrast to PP, which would view a want for *p* as a certain kind of introspectable state, event, or process with a distinctive "feel"—for instance, a sense of the attractiveness of *p*, or a felt urge to realize *p*.[18]

Now let us turn to the way these views bear upon the applicability of M-predicates to an incorporeal being. I believe it would be generally supposed that our two views have opposite consequences: that on a PP view, M-predicates could be applied to an incorporeal being, but not on an LC view. However, I will contest this received position to the extent of arguing that neither position presents any conceptual bar to the literal application of M-predicates.

First, a brief word about the bearing of the PP view before turning to the debate over LC, which is my main concern in this section. Presumably, an incorporeal subject could have states of consciousness with distinctive phenomenological qualities, just as well as we could. Hence terms that signify such states of consciousness would not be inapplicable in principle to such a being. But though I believe this is correct, I do not feel that it is of much significance for theology, and this for two reasons.

First, the PP account is most plausible with respect to feelings, sensations, and other M-states which clearly have a distinctive "feel." It is much less plausible with respect to "colorless" mental states such as beliefs, attitudes, thoughts, and intentions. We cannot hold an intention or a belief "before the mind" as we can a feeling of dismay, and thereby form a conception of "what it is like." But it is M-predicates of the colorless sort that are of most interest to theology. In thinking of God as a personal agent, we think of God as possessing (and using) knowledge, purpose, intention, and the like. Feelings and sensations either are not applicable to God at all, or they are of secondary importance. Theology quite properly avoids trying to figure out what it *feels* like to be God.

Second, suppose that one defends the applicability of M-predicates on a PP basis because he considers them inapplicable on an LC construal. This latter conviction would presumably be based on an argument similar to the one to be given shortly, to the effect that M-predicates, as analyzed in LC, are inapplicable to God because, as an incorporeal being, God is incapable of overt behavior. In that case, even if our theorist succeeds in showing that PP predicates can apply, he has won, at most a Pyrrhic victory. To secure application of M-predicates at the price of abandoning the idea that God acts in the world is to doom the enterprise to irrelevance. Whatever may be the case with the gods of Aristotle and the Epicureans, the God of the Judaeo-Christian tradition is preeminently a God who *acts*, in history and in the lives of individuals, not to mention His creation and preservation of the world. Hence even if, on the PP view, M-predicates are applicable to an incorporeal being incapable of overt action, that does nothing to show that M-predicates are applicable to the Judaeo-Christian God.

Turning now to LC, let us look at a typical statement by one who is arguing from an LC position.

> What would it be like for an x to be just loving without doing anything or being capable of doing anything? . . . Surely 'to do something,' 'to behave in a certain way,' is to make—though this is not all that it is—certain bodily movement. . . . For it to make sense to speak of x's acting or failing to act, x must have a body. Thus if 'love' is to continue to mean anything at all near to what it normally means, it is meaningless to say that God loves mankind. Similar considerations apply to the other psychological predicates tied to the concept of God.[19]

It will help us in evaluating this argument to set it out more carefully.

1. On LC, an M-concept is, at least in part, a concept of dispositions to overt behavior (perhaps through the mediation of other mental states).[20]

2. Overt behavior requires bodily movements of the agent.
3. An incorporeal being, lacking a body, cannot move its body.

∴4. An incorporeal being cannot engage in overt behavior.

5. A being that is, in principle, incapable of overt behavior cannot have dispositions to overt behavior.

∴6. M-concepts are, in principle, inapplicable to an incorporeal being.

This argument is certainly on sound ground in claiming that, on LC, an M-predicate is applicable to S only if A-predicates are so applicable. Its Achilles' heel, I will claim, is 2, the thesis that overt behavior requires bodily movements of the agent. My attack on that thesis will occupy the next section. Let us take the upshot of this section to be that, on the most plausible account of the M-predicates that are of most interest to theology, God can literally know, purpose, and will, only if God can literally perform overt actions. This result nicely mirrors the fundamental place of divine agency in Judaeo-Christian theology.

Before embarking on the discussion of A-predicates, I want to make two points.

First, there are forms of LC that do rule out the application of M-predicates to an incorporeal being. I am thinking of those views that put certain kinds of restrictions on the input, or output, of the psyche. Some forms of LB, for example, require that the behavioral output be specified in terms of bodily movements of the agent, and the input in terms of stimulations of the agent's sense receptors. Functionalist theories may also be so restricted. Clearly, M-predicates analyzed in this way are applicable only to beings capable of such inputs and outputs. But our concern in this paper is to determine whether any version of LC would allow the application of M-predicates to an incorporeal being.

Second, we should not suppose that the question of the applicability of A-predicates to an incorporeal being is prejudged by the fact that all cases of overt action with which we are most familiar involve bodily movements of the agent. A feature that is common to the familiar *denotata* of a term may not be reflected in the meaning of that term, even if this class of *denotata* is the one from which we learn the meaning of the term, and even if it contains the only *denotata* with which we are acquainted. It is doing small honor to human powers of conception to suppose that one must form one's concept of P in such a way as to be limited to the class of Ps from which the concept was learned. Surely we can think more abstractly and generically than that. Even though our concept of *animal* was formed solely from experience of land creatures, that concept might still be such that it contains only features that are equally applicable to fish. And even if that were not the case—even if the capacity to walk on legs is part of our concept of an animal—it may be that it can be easily extended to fish, merely by dropping out the feature just mentioned. The moral of the story is obvious. We cannot assume in advance that our concept of making, commanding, or forgiving includes the concept of bodily movements of the maker, commander, or forgiver. And even if it does, this may be a relatively peripheral component which can be sheared off, leaving intact a distinctive conceptual core.

ACTION PREDICATES AND GOD

Let us consider, then, whether it is conceptually possible for an incorporeal being to perform overt actions. Our entrée to that discussion will be a consideration of the vulnerable premise in the argument, the thesis that overt behavior requires bodily movements.

To understand the grounds for this thesis, we must introduce the notion of a *basic action*. Roughly speaking, a basic action is one that is performed *not* by or in (simultaneously) performing some other action. Thus if I sign my name, *that* is done by moving my hand in a certain way, so the action is not basic; but if moving my hand is *not* done *by* doing something else, it will count as a basic action. Just where to locate basic human actions is philosophically controversial. If contracting muscles in my hand is something I *do* (in the intended sense of 'do'), then it seems that I move my hand *by* contracting my muscles, and moving my hand will not count as a basic action. Again, if sending neural impulses to the muscles is something I *do*, then it seems that I contract the muscles *by* sending neural impulses to them, and so the contraction of muscles will not count as a basic action. Since I do not have time to go into this issue, I shall simply follow a widespread practice and assume that all overt human basic actions consist in the movements of certain parts of the body which ordinarily would be thought to be under "voluntary control," such as the hand.

It follows from our explanation of the term 'basic action' that every nonbasic action is done *by* performing a basic action. If we are further correct in ruling that every human basic action consists in moving some part of one's body, then it follows that every human nonbasic action is built on, or presupposes, some bodily movement of the agent. The relationship differs in different cases: Sometimes the nonbasic action involves an effect of some bodily movement(s), as in the action of knocking over a vase; sometimes it involves the bodily movement's falling under a rule or convention of some kind, as in signaling a turn. But whatever the details, it follows from what has been laid down thus far that a human being cannot do anything overt without moving some part of the body. Either the action is basic, in which case it merely *consists* in moving some part of one's body; or it is not, in which case it is done *by* moving some part of one's body.

But granted that this is the way it is with human action, what does this have to do with A-*concepts*? As noted earlier, our concept of a ϕ never includes all the characteristics that are in fact common to ϕs we have experienced. So why should we suppose that our concepts of various human actions—making or commanding, for example—contain any reference to bodily movement?

Again it will be most useful to divide this question in accordance with the basic-nonbasic distinction. Our concepts of particular types of human basic actions certainly do involve specifications of bodily movements. This is because that is what such actions *are*. Their whole content is a certain kind of movement of a certain part of the body. That is what distinguishes one type of human basic action from another. Hence we cannot say what kind of basic action we are talking about without mentioning some bodily movement—stretching, kicking, raising the arm, or whatever. Clearly, A-predicates such as these are not literally applicable to an incorporeal being. But this will be no loss to theology. I take it that none of us is tempted to think that it could be literally true that God stretches out His arm or activates His vocal organs.

The more relevant question concerns the status of such human nonbasic A-predicates as 'makes,' 'speaks,' 'commands,' 'forgives,' 'comforts,' and 'guides.' In saying of S that he commanded me to love my neighbor, am I thereby committing myself to the proposition that S moved some part of his body? Is bodily movement of the agent part of what is *meant* by commanding?

One point at least is clear. Nonbasic human A-concepts do not, in general, carry any reference to particular types of bodily movements. There is indeed wide variation in this regard. At the specific end of the continuum, we have a predicate such as 'kicks open the door,' which clearly requires a certain kind of motion of a leg. But 'make a soufflé' and 'command' are more typical, in that the concept is clearly not tied to any particular *kind* of underlying bodily movement. I can issue a command orally or in writing. Indeed, in view of the fact that no limit can be placed on what can be used as a system of communication, any bodily movements whatever could, with the appropriate background, subserve the issuing of a command. In like manner, although there are normal or typical ways of moving the body for making a soufflé, we cannot suppose that these exhaust the possibilities. In this age of electronic marvels, one could presumably make a soufflé by pushing some buttons on a machine with one's toes.

Thus, if any reference to bodily movement is included in such A-concepts as making and commanding, it will have to be quite unspecific. The most we could have would be along these lines:

> Making a soufflé—causing a soufflé to come into being by some movements of one's body.
> Commanding—producing a command by some movements of one's body.[21]

But can we have even this much? Is it any part of the meaning of these terms, in the sense in which they are applied to human beings, that the external effects in question are produced by movements of the agent's body? No doubt it is completely obvious to all of us that human beings cannot bring about such consequences except by moving their bodies. But to repeat the point once more, it does not follow that this fact is built into human A-concepts. Perhaps our *concept* of making a soufflé is simply that of *bringing a soufflé into existence,* the concept being neutral as to how this is done.

What we have here is one of the numerous difficulties in distinguishing between what we mean by a term and what we firmly believe to be true of the things to which the term applies—in other words, distinguishing between analytic and synthetic truths. These persistent difficulties have been among the factors leading to widespread skepticism about the viability of such distinctions. But for our purpose we need not decide the issue. Let us yield to our opponent. If we can make our case even on the position most favorable to our opponent, we can ignore the outcome of this skirmish.

Let us suppose, then, that all human A-concepts do contain a bodily movement requirement. It clearly follows that no *human* A-concepts are applicable to an incorporeal being. But that by no means shows that *no* A-concepts are applicable. Why should we suppose that the A-concepts we apply to human beings exhaust the field? We must at least explore the possibility that we can form A-concepts that are (a) distinctively and recognizably *action* concepts and (b) do not require any bodily movements of the agent.

In order to do this we must bring out the distinctive features of A-concepts that make them concepts of *actions.* Thus far in discussing human A-concepts, we have gone only as far as the thesis that every human A-concept involves some reference to bodily movement. But that by no means suffices to make them concepts of *actions.* The concept of a heart beat or of a facial tic involves reference to bodily movements, but it is not a concept of an action. What else is required?

I will continue to use human A-concepts as my point of departure for the exploration of the general field, since that is where we get our general concept of action. And I will continue to concentrate on concepts of *basic* actions; since they are relatively simple, the crucial features of A-concepts stand out more clearly there.[22] To focus the discussion further, I shall restrict attention to *intentional* actions—those the agent "meant" to perform.[23]

Now, as intimated above, although every human basic action consists in moving some part of the body, not just any bodily movement constitutes a basic *action.* It is possible for my arm to move without my having *moved* it, as in automatic twitches and jerks. In order for it to be the case that I performed the basic action of raising my arm, some further condition must hold, over and above the fact that my arm rose. Thus we can pose the crucial question about the constitution of human basic actions in the classic Wittgensteinian form: "What is left over if I subtract the fact that my arm goes up from the fact that I raise my arm?"[24] Or, putting it the other way round, what must be added to the fact that my arm goes up, to make it the case that I raise my arm?

The recent literature contains many attempts to answer this question, and I shall not have time for a survey. Leaving aside views that, in my opinion, do not survive critical scrutiny (such as the "ascriptive" view, according to which it is an action because we hold the agent responsible for it[25] and the view that "it all depends on context,"[26] we have two serious contenders.

1. *Psychological causation (explanation) view.* What distinguishes the action from the "mere" movement is the psychological background of the movement, what gives rise to it, or issues in it.[27]
2. *Agent causation view.* A bodily movement is an action *iff* it is caused in a certain special way—not by some other event or state, but by the agent itself.[28]

The psychological causation view exists in many forms, depending on just what psychological factors are specified and just what relation to the bodily movement is required. As for the former, popular candidates have been the will, volitions, intentions, and wants-and-beliefs. On the second score, it is generally required that the movement occur "because of" the psychological factor in question, but there has been considerable controversy over whether to regard the relation as "causal." So as to have a simple form of the view to work with, let us focus on the position that what makes a case of my arm's rising into a case of my raising my arm, is that my arm rose because it was in accordance with my dominant *intentions* at the moment that it should rise.

So the model of a basic action that we get from the human case is:

1. bodily movement
2. caused by ——

To construct an analogous model for incorporeal action that will be an unmistakable model for *action,* we must (a) find a suitable replacement for bodily movements and (b) show that incorporeality is no bar to the satisfaction of a causal condition that will make the whole package into an *action.* It will prove best to begin with the second task, since that poses the more complex and difficult, as well as more controversial, issues. It shall proceed as I did with M-concepts—by considering, with respect to each of our contenders, whether that condition could be satisfied by an incorporeal being.

As for the agent causation view, the concept of agent causation may well be obscure, and it certainly runs violently counter to some deeply rooted contemporary prejudices, but at least it is clear that it does not carry a restriction to *corporeal* substances. The theory avoids, on principle, any specification of the internal machinery by which an agent exercises its causal efficacy—"on principle," since the whole thrust of the position is that when I bring about a bodily movement in performing a basic action, I am not bringing about that movement by initiating certain other events which, in turn, bring about the movement by "event causation." Rather, I directly bring about the bodily movement simply by exploiting my basic capacity to do so. Hence the agent causality interpretation is not restricted to substances possessing one kind of internal structure or equipment rather than another.

On the psychological explanation view, things are a bit more complicated. Let us recall that the "causal condition" on this view is that the bodily movement results from an intention, or the like. So our question divides into two parts. (1) Can an incorporeal being have intentions, or whatever kind of psychological cause is required by the particular version of the theory under discussion? (2) Can an intention cause whatever substitutes for bodily movement in incorporeal basic action? As for (2), it is difficult to discuss this without deciding what does play the role of bodily movement in incorporeal basic actions. Hence we will postpone this question until we specify that substitute.

That leaves us with the question as to whether an incorporeal being can have intentions and the like. And now we find ourselves in a curious position. For that is exactly the question we were asking in the previous section on M-concepts. The conclusion we reached there, on an LC position, was that these concepts are applicable to a subject only if A-concepts are applicable. And now we see that, on the psychological explanation view, A-concepts are applicable to S only if M-concepts are applicable. Where does that leave us? We obviously are in some kind of circle. But is it the vicious circle of chasing our own tail, or a virtuous circle of the sort in which the heavenly bodies were once deemed to move?

Here it is crucial to remember the task we set out to accomplish. If we were trying to *prove* that M- and A-concepts *are* applicable to an incorporeal being, we would have reached an impasse. For since each application depends on the other as a necessary condition, we would not have established either, unless we had some independent argument for the applicability of one or the other. But in fact, we set ourselves a more modest goal—to determine whether the incorporeality of a being is sufficient ground for *denying* the applicability of such concepts. We are considering whether incorporeality renders their applicability impossible. And from that standpoint, the circle is virtuous. The reciprocity we have uncovered provides no reason for *denying* the applicability of either sort of concept. Psychological concepts are applicable only if action concepts are applicable, and vice versa. As far as that consideration goes, it is quite possible that both kinds are applicable. This circle leaves standing the *possibility* that an incorporeal being is such that actions and intentions fit smoothly into the economy of its operations.

Let us now return to the first condition of human basic action concepts, to the problem of finding something that could play the same role for incorporeal basic actions that bodily movements play for corporeal basic actions. I believe that the entrée to this question is an appreciation of the difference between the general concept of a basic action and specific concepts of particular human basic actions. Although concepts of the latter sort contain concepts of particular types of bodily movements, this is not because it is required by the general concept of a basic action. That general concept, as we set it out initially, is simply the concept of an action that is not performed *by* or *in* (simultaneously) performing some other action. This general concept is quite neutral as to what kinds of actions have that status for one or another type of agent. It is just a fact about human beings (*not* a general constraint on action or basic action) that only movements of certain parts of their bodies are under their direct voluntary control and that anything else they bring off, they must accomplish *by* moving their bodies in certain ways. If *I* am to knock over a vase or make a soufflé or communicate with someone, I must do so by moving my hands, legs, vocal organs, or whatever. But that is only because of my limitations. We can conceive of agents, corporeal or otherwise, such that things other than their bodies (if any) are under their direct voluntary control. Some agents might be such that they could knock over a vase or bring a soufflé into being without doing something else in order to do so.[29]

What these considerations suggest is that it is conceptually possible for any change whatsoever to be the core of a basic action. Movements of an agent's body are only what we happen to be restricted to in the human case. Just what changes are within the basic action repertoire of a given incorporeal agent would depend upon the nature of that agent. But the main point is that since such changes are not necessarily restricted to bodily movements of the agent, a subject's bodilessness is no conceptual bar to the performance of basic actions by that subject.

I believe that the case in which we are particularly interested, divine action, can be thought of along the lines of the preceding discussion. Of course, one can think of God as creating light by saying to himself, "Let there be light,"or as parting the sea of reeds by saying to himself, "Let the sea of reeds be parted." In that case the basic actions would be mental actions. But what the above discussion indicates is that we are not conceptually required to postulate this mental machinery. We could think just as well of the coming into being of light or of the parting of the sea of reeds as directly under God's voluntary control.

This further suggests that all God's actions might be basic actions. If any change whatsoever could conceivably be the core of a basic action, and if God is omnipotent, then clearly, God *could* exercise direct voluntary control over every change in the world which he influences by his activity. However, I do not claim to have done more than exhibit this as a possibility. It is equally possible that God chooses to influence some situations *indirectly*. He might choose to lead or inspire Cyrus to free the Israelites, thus using Cyrus as an instrument to bring about that result. In that case, freeing the Israelites would be a nonbasic action. I am quite willing to leave the decision on this one up to God.[30]

Now let us just glance at the question I postponed—whether it is possible for intentions, and the like, to give rise directly to changes outside the agent's body (if any). I do not have much to say about this—it obviously is something outside our ordinary experience. But I can see nothing in our present understanding of the psyche and of causality that would show it to be impossible in principle. So, pending further insights into those matters, I am inclined to take a quasi-Humean line and say that what can cause what is "up for grabs." And of course, if it is an omnipotent deity that is in question, I suppose He could ordain that intentions can directly cause a parting of waters, provided this is a logical possibility.

Let me sum up these last two sections. Action concepts applicable to an incorporeal being can be constructed that would differ from human action concepts (on the most plausible accounts of the latter) only by the substitution of other changes for bodily movements of the agent in basic action concepts. Hence there is no conceptual bar to the performance of *overt* actions by incorporeal agents and hence no conceptual bar, even on an LC position, to the application of M-predicates to incorporeal beings.

As indicated earlier, this paper constitutes but a fragment of a thoroughgoing discussion of the title question. Other fragments would go into the question as to whether timelessness, immutability, and other traditional attributes constitute a bar to the literal predication of one or another kind of predicate. And of course we would have to discuss whether God *is* timeless, immutable, and so on. Moreover, we would have to scrutinize the classical arguments for the denial that *any* intrinsic predicates can be literally predicated of God. But perhaps even this fragment has sufficed to show that the prospects for speaking literally about God are not as dim as is often supposed by contemporary thinkers.[31]

NOTES

1. This is a crude characterization of semantics, but it will have to do for now. There is no general agreement on what an adequate semantics would look like.

2. We shall not distinguish between *meaning* and *sense.*

3. *Webster's New Collegiate Dictionary* (Springfield, Mass.: Merriam, 1959). I am far from claiming that this is the most adequate way to specify these meanings. Indeed, it is far from clear what that way would be. But it is clear that 'player' has the meanings thus specified, however lamely and haltingly, and that its having these meanings is (a small) part of what makes the English language what it is at this stage of its history.

4. I want this supposition to be compatible with the fact that most or all predicate terms have meanings that are vague, exhibit "open texture," or suffer from indeterminacy in other ways. This implies that an adequate formulation would be more complicated than the one given here.

5. Metaphor is a topic of unlimited subtlety and complexity, and the above formulation barely scratches the surface. For a bit more detail, see my "Irreducible Metaphors in Theology," reprinted in my *Divine Nature and Human Language* (Ithaca and London: Cornell University Press, 1989), pp. 17–38.

6. This argument is developed more fully in "Irreducible Metaphors in Theology."

7. The question as to whether P-predicates could be applied to an incorporeal being presupposes that we can form a coherent notion of an incorporeal substance or other concrete subject of attributes. This has often been denied on the grounds that it is, in principle, impossible to identify, reidentify, or individuate such a being. See Antony Flew, *God and Philosophy* (London: Hutchinson, 1966), chap. 2; Terence Penelhum, *Survival and Disembodied Existence* (New York: Humanities Press, 1970), chap. 6; Sydney Shoemaker, *Self-Knowledge and Self-Identity* (Ithaca: Cornell University Press, 1963), chaps. 4 and 5. If arguments like this were successful, as I believe they are not, our problem would not arise.

8. Note that the issue here concerns the content (character, correct analysis) of psychological *predicates* or *concepts,* not the *nature* of the human psyche or the *nature* of human thought, intention, etc. Obviously the divine psyche, if there be such, is radically different in nature from the human psyche. The only question is as to whether there are any psychological *concepts* that apply to both. Hence our specific interest is in what we are *saying* about a human being when we say of that person that s/he is thinking, as a certain attitude,

or whatever. Thus the classification to follow is not a classification of theories of the nature of human mind—dualism, materialism, epiphenomenalism, etc.

9. The PP view was espoused or presupposed by the great seventeenth- and eighteenth-century philosophers: Descartes, Spinoza, Locke, Leibniz, Berkeley, Hume, and Reid. It surfaces as an explicit dogma in Book II of Locke's *Essay Concerning Human Understanding,* throughout Hume's *Treatise of Human Nature,* and in Essay I of Reid's *Essays on the Intellectual Powers of Man.*

10. Ludwig Wittgenstein, *Philosophical Investigations,* trans. G. E. M. Anscombe (Oxford: Basil Blackwell, 1953), nos. 258–70. In briefly indicating the main arguments for and against the PP view, I am merely trying to convey some sense of why various positions have seemed plausible. No endorsement of any particular argument is intended.

11. For an important statement of LB, see Rudolf Carnap, "Psychologie in physikalischer Sprache," *Erkenntnis,* Vol. 3 (1932). English translation, "Psychology in Physical Language," by George Schick in *Logical Positivism,* ed. A. J. Ayer (New York: The Free Press, 1959). Gilbert Ryle's *The Concept of Mind* (London: Hutchinson, 1949) is an influential work that is often regarded as a form of LB.

12. In this quick survey I am ignoring many complexities. For example, the most plausible LB account of feeling depressed would involve some categorical overt manifestations, such as "looking droopy," as well as response tendencies like those cited in the text. I am also forced to omit any consideration of the relation of LB to behaviorism in psychology.

13. I am indebted to Jerry Fodor, *Psychological Explanation* (New York: Random House, 1968), pp. 15–16, for this felicitous analogy.

14. The functionalist is not committed to holding that all functional relations in which a given mental state stands will enter into our ordinary concept of that state. Picking out those that do is admittedly a tricky job; but that difficulty is by no means restricted to Functionalism.

15. I follow Brandt and Kim in taking Functionalism, as well as the other views canvassed, to be an account of the ordinary meanings of M-predicates. Some theorists present it as a proposal for developing psychological concepts for scientific purposes, or as an account of the *nature* of mental states.

16. R. B. Brandt and Jaegwon Kim, "Wants as Explanations of Actions," *Journal of Philosophy,* 60 (1963), 427.

17. Different forms of Functionalism display special features not mentioned in this brief survey. Cybernetic analogies are prominent in many versions, with psychological functions thought of on the model of the machine table of a computer. Some, like the Brandt and Kim account, find a useful model in the way in which theoretical terms in science get their meaning from the ways in which they figure in the theory.

18. It may be doubted that 'want' is a serious candidate for theological predication. It would not be if the term were being used in a narrow sense that implies felt craving or lack of need. But I, along with many philosophers, mean to be using it in the broad sense just indicated. To indicate how the term might be applied to God in this sense, Aquinas uses the term 'appetition' more or less in the way Brandt and Kim explain 'want'; *will* for Aquinas is "intellectual appetition," and he applies 'will' to God.

19. Kai Nielsen, *Contemporary Critiques of Religion* (London: Macmillan, 1971), p. 117. See also Paul Edwards, "Difficulties in the Idea of God," in *The Idea of God,* ed. E. H. Madden, R. Handy, and M. Farber (Springfield, Ill.: Charles Thomas, 1968), pp. 45 ff.

20. Let us define "overt" behavior as action that essentially involves some occurrence outside the present consciousness of the agent. This will exclude, e.g., "mental" actions such as focusing one's attention on something or resolving to get out of bed. The kinds of actions that are crucial to the Judaeo-Christian concept of God—creating the world, issuing commands, and guiding and comforting individual—count as overt on this definition.

21. These formulations raise questions that are not directly relevant to our concerns in this paper, e.g., how to think of a "command" in such a way that it might be "produced" by an agent. I should note, however, that the causation involved is not restricted to direct causation; intermediaries are allowed.

22. There is another reason for this procedure. Since nonbasic actions presuppose basic actions, and not vice versa, there could conceivably be only basic actions, but it is not possible that there should be only nonbasic actions. We shall see that it is a live possibility that all God's actions are basic.

23. Again, the basic (but not as obvious) point is that intentional actions are conceptually more basic. It seems that the analysis of action concepts is best set out by beginning with intentional actions and then defining unintentional actions as a certain derivation from that, rather than beginning by analyzing a neutral concept and then explaining *intentional* and *unintentional* as different modifications of that. On the former approach it turns out that all basic actions are intentional. See Alvin I. Goldman, *A Theory of Human Action* (Englewood Cliffs: N.J.: Prentice-Hall, 1970), chap. 3

24. Wittgenstein, *Philosophical Investigations,* no. 621.

25. H. L. A. Hart, "The Ascription of Responsibility and Rights," *Proceedings of the Aristotelian Society,* 69 (1949), 171–94.

26. A. I. Melden, *Free Action* (New York: Humanities Press, 1961).

27. Goldman, *Theory*, chaps. 1–3; Charles Taylor, *The Explanation of Behavior* (New York: Humanities Press, 1964), chaps. 2 and 3; W. P. Alston, "Conceptual Prolegomena to a Psychological Theory of Intentional Action," in *Philosophy of Psychology*, ed. S. C. Brown (London: Macmillan, 1974), pt. 2.

28. Roderick M. Chisholm, "The Descriptive Element in the Concept of 'Action'," *Journal of Philosophy*, 61 (1964), 613–24; Richard Taylor, *Action and Purpose* (Englewood Cliffs, N.J.: Prentice-Hall, 1966), chaps. 1–9.

29. Be careful to envisage this situation just as I have described it. The agent knocks over the vase not by doing anything else—even anything mental. Telekinesis is often thought of as an agent saying to himself something like "Let the vase be knocked over," and *this* causes the vase to fall over. But that does not make knocking over the vase a basic action. It is still a matter of knocking over the vase *by* doing something else, albeit something mental. In order for knocking over a vase to be a basic action, it would have to be just as immediate as is my raising my arm in the normal case, where I do this not by saying to myself "Let the arm rise," whereupon it rises; but where I just raise the arm intentionally.

30. It might be contended that if the physical universe, or any part thereof, is under God's direct voluntary control, this implies that the world is the body of God, which in turn implies that God is not an incorporeal being; that would mean that our case for *incorporeal* basic action fails. That is, the contention would be that in order to ascribe basic actions to S we have to pay the price of construing the changes in question as movements of S's body. This claim could be supported by the thesis that a sufficient condition for something to be part of my body is that it be under my direct voluntary control. So if the physical universe is under God's direct voluntary control, it is His body. Against this, I would argue that we have many different ways of picking out the body of a human being. In addition to the one just mentioned, my body is distinctive in that it is the perspective from which I perceive the world; it provides the immediate causal conditions of my consciousness; and it constitutes the phenomenological locus of my "bodily sensations." With multiple criteria there is room for maneuver. Holding the other criteria constant, we can envisage a state of affairs in which *something other than my body*, e.g., my wristwatch, is under my direct voluntary control. Thus I deny that my position requires God to have a body.

31. This paper grew out of material presented in my NEH Summer Seminars on Theological Language, given in 1978 and 1979, and more directly out of a lecture delivered at the 1978 Wheaton College Philosophy Conference. I am grateful to the participants in my summer seminars and at the Wheaton Conference for many valuable reactions.

SUGGESTED READING

Alston, William P. *Divine Nature and Human Language*. Ithaca: Cornell University Press, 1989.

Ayer, A. J. *Language, Truth, and Logic*. New York: Dover, 1952.

Ferré, Frederick. *Language, Logic and God*. New York: Harper and Row, 1969.

Gilkey, Langdon. *Naming the Whirlwind*. Indianapolis, Ind.: Bobbs-Merrill, 1969.

Gilson, Etienne. *Linguistics and Philosophy*. Notre Dame, Ind.: University of Notre Dame Press, 1988.

High, Dallas, ed. *New Essays in Religious Language*. New York: Oxford University Press, 1969.

Mascall, E. L. *Existence and Analogy*. New York: Longmans, Green, & Co., Ltd., 1949.

Mitchell, Basil. *Faith and Logic*. London: Allen & Unwin, 1957.

McFague, Sallie. *Metaphorical Theology*. Philadelphia: Fortress Press, 1982.

Ramsey, Ian. *Religious Language*. London: SCM Press, 1957.

———, ed. *Words about God: The Philosophy of Religion*. New York: Harper and Row, 1971.

PART EIGHT MIRACLES

Does God at times *miraculously* intervene in earthly affairs? This is, do some events occur because God has entered our space-time continuum and directly modified or circumvented the relevant natural laws? Behind this question, of course, is the initial definition of a miracle as a violation of a natural law. Few philosophers today deny that miracles so defined are *possible*, but debate continues over whether we could ever justifiably maintain that such intervention has actually taken place.

Sometimes this debate centers around the question of whether we must grant that allegedly miraculous events—for example, healings—have actually occurred. As some philosophers see it, the evidence supporting the occurrence of such miraculous events is the personal testimony of only a few individuals who are possibly biased, while the basis for doubt is the massive amount of objective research upon which the relevant law is based. This is essentially the line taken by David Hume. Thus, he would argue, we are always rationally warranted in concluding that a report of a miracle is erroneous. Other philosophers argue, however, that the presence of some forms of evidence—for instance, independent confirmation from reputable sources—could, in some cases, make it reasonable to maintain that even the most unusual, unexpected events have actually occurred.

At other times, the debate over miracles focuses on the question of whether we could ever rationally conclude that an event could not have been produced by nature alone. Some thinkers have argued that we will never be in a position to identify all the phenomena that nature can produce, and thus that it will always be most reasonable to continue to look for a natural law explanation to any putative miracle. Others have argued to the contrary that natural science could never accommodate some conceivable occurrences. And still others see the question itself as misguided, since what is relevant in the case of any alleged miracle, they content, is not whether nature *could* in principle have produced the event but whether nature *was* in fact the sole causal agent in the case in question.

Finally, many philosophical discussions revolve around the question of whether the undisputed occurrence of certain unusual events could require all honest, thoughtful individuals to acknowledge that God has supernaturally intervened in earthly affairs. Some maintain that certain kinds of events (e.g., astonishing healings or resurrections) would force all to acknowledge divine intervention. Other philosophers argue that although belief in direct divine intervention may at times be acceptable for those who already believe that God exists, no single event or series of events could ever compel all rational people to assent to the existence of a perfectly good supernatural causal agent. For example, the tremendous amount of horrific evil in the world is taken by many people to offset or counterbalance whatever degree of evidential force the appeal to miracle might have. They would claim that, given all we experience (astonishing miracles as well as appalling evils), no single event or series of events could ever compel all thoughtful individuals to acknowledge the existence of a perfectly good supernatural causal agent.

DAVID HUME

The Evidence for Miracles Is Weak

This selection contains a classic and influential argument against belief in miracles crafted by David Hume (1711–1776). The wise person, Hume informs us, will always proportion his or her belief to the evidence. He goes on to say that our belief in the relevant laws of nature are based on uniform, public, past experience, which provides a great amount of objective evidence, while the evidence supporting alleged violations of these laws consists solely of personal testimonies that cannot be substantiated by independent testing. Hume then concludes that it is always most reasonable to assume that alleged miracles did not occur as reported.

⌘

A miracle is a violation of the laws of nature; and as a firm and unalterable experience has established these laws, the proof against a miracle, from the very nature of the fact, is as entire as any argument from experience can possibly be imagined. Why is it more than probable, that all men must die; that lead cannot, of itself, remain suspended in the air; that fire consumes wood, and is extinguished by water; unless it be, that these events are found agreeable to the laws of nature, and there is required a violation of these laws, or in other words, a miracle to prevent them? Nothing is esteemed a miracle, if it ever happen in the common course of nature. It is no miracle, if it ever happen in the common course of nature. It is no miracle that a man, seemingly in good health, should die of a sudden, because such a kind of death, though more unusual than any other, has yet been frequently observed to happen. But it is a miracle, that a dead man should come to life; because that has never been observed in any age or country. There must, therefore, be a uniform experience against every miraculous event, otherwise the event would not merit that appellation. And as a uniform experience amounts to a proof, there is here a direct and full *proof*, from the nature of the fact, against the existence of any miracle; nor can such a proof be destroyed, or the miracle rendered credible, but by an opposite proof, which is superior.

The plain consequence is (and it is a general maxim worthy of our attention), "That no testimony is sufficient to establish a miracle, unless the testimony be of such a kind, that its falsehood would be more miraculous, than the fact, which it endeavors to establish; and even in that case there is a mutual destruction of arguments, and the superior only gives as an assurance suitable to that degree of force, which remains, after deducting the

From "Of Miracles," in *An Inquiry Concerning Human Understanding*.

inferior." When anyone tells me, that he saw a dead man restored to life, I immediately consider with myself, whether it be more probable, that this person should either deceive or be deceived, or that the fact, which he relates, should really have happened. I weigh the one miracle against the other; and according to the superiority, which I discover, I pronounce my decision, and always reject the greater miracle. If the falsehood of his testimony would be more miraculous, than the event which he relates; then, and not till then, can he pretend to command my belief or opinion.

In the foregoing reasoning we have supposed, that the testimony, upon which a miracle is founded, may possibly amount to an entire proof, and that the falsehood of that testimony would be a real prodigy: But it is easy to show, that we have been a great deal too liberal in our concession, and that there never was a miraculous event established on so full an evidence.

For *first*, there is not to be found, in all history, any miracle attested by a sufficient number of men, of such unquestioned good sense, education, and learning, as to secure us against all delusion in themselves; of such undoubted integrity, as to place them beyond all suspicion of any design to deceive others; of such credit and reputation in the eyes of mankind, as to have a great deal to lose in case of their being detected in any falsehood; and at the same time, attesting facts performed in such a public manner and in so celebrated a part of the world, as to render the detection unavoidable: All which circumstances are requisite to give us a full assurance in the testimony of men.

Secondly. We may observe in human nature a principle which, if strictly examined, will be found to diminish extremely the assurance, which we might, from human testimony, have, in any kind of prodigy. The maxim, by which we commonly conduct ourselves in our reasonings, is, that the objects, of which we have no experience, resemble those, of which we have; that what we have found to be most usual is always most probable; and that where there is an opposition of arguments, we ought to give the preference to such as are founded on the greatest number of past observations. But though, in proceeding by this rule, we readily reject any fact which is unusual and incredible in an ordinary degree; yet in advancing farther, the mind observes not always the same rule; but when anything is affirmed utterly absurd and miraculous, it rather the more readily admits of such a fact, upon account of that very circumstance, which ought to destroy all its authority. the passion of *surprise* and *wonder*, arising from miracles, being an agreeable emotion, gives a sensible tendency towards the belief of those events, from which it is derived. And this goes so far, that even those who cannot enjoy this pleasure immediately, nor can believe those miraculous events, of which they are informed, yet love to partake of the satisfaction at second-hand or by rebound, and place a pride and delight in exciting the admiration of others.

With what greediness are the miraculous accounts of travelers received, their descriptions of sea and land monsters, their relations of wonderful adventures, strange men, and uncouth manners? But if the spirit of religion join itself to the love of wonder, there is an end of common sense; and human testimony, in these circumstances, loses all pretensions to authority. A religionist may be an enthusiast, and imagine he sees what has no reality: he may know his narrative to be false, and yet persevere in it, with the best intentions in the world, for the sake of promoting so holy a cause: or even where this delusion has not place, vanity, excited by so strong a temptation, operates on him more powerfully than on the rest of mankind in any other circumstances; and self-interest with equal force. His auditors may not have, and commonly have not, sufficient judgment to canvass his evidence: what judgment they have, they renounce by principle, in these sublime and mysterious subjects: or if they were ever so willing to employ it, passion and a heated imagination disturb the regularity of its operations. Their credulity increases his impudence: and his impudence overpowers their credulity.

Eloquence, when at its highest pitch, leaves little room for reason or reflection; but addressing itself entirely to the fancy or the affections, captivates the willing hearers, and subdues their understanding. Happily, this pitch it seldom attains. But what a Tully or a Demosthenes could scarcely effect over a Roman or Athenian audience, every *Capuchin*, every itinerant or stationary teacher can perform over the generality of mankind, and in a higher degree, by touching such gross and vulgar passions.

The many instances of forged miracles, and prophecies, and supernatural events, which, in all ages, have either been detected by contrary evidence, or which detect themselves by their absurdity, prove sufficiently the strong propensity of mankind to the extraordinary and the marvelous, and ought reasonably to beget a suspicion against all relations of this kind. This is our natural way of thinking, even with regard to the most common and most credible events. For instance: There is no kind of report which rises so easily, and spreads so quickly, especially in country places and provincial towns, as those concerning marriages; insomuch that two young persons of equal condition never see each other twice, but the whole neighborhood immediately join them together. The pleasure of telling a piece of news so interesting, of propagating it, and of being the first reporters of it, spreads the intelligence. And this is so well known, that no man of sense gives attention to these reports, till he find them confirmed by some greater evidence. Do not the same passions, and others still stronger, incline the generality of mankind to believe and report, with the greatest vehemence and assurance, all religious miracles?

Thirdly. It forms a strong presumption against all supernatural and miraculous relations, that they are observed chiefly to abound among ignorant and barbarous nations; or if a civilized people has ever given admission to any of them, that people will be found to have received them from ignorant and barbarous ancestors, who transmitted them with that inviolable sanction and authority, which always attend received opinions. When we peruse the first histories of all nations, we are apt to imagine ourselves transported into some new world; where the whole frame of nature is disjointed, and every element performs its operations in a different manner, from what it does at present. Battles, revolutions, pestilence, famine and death, are never the effect of those natural causes, which we experience. Prodigies, omens, oracles, judgments, quite obscure the few natural events, that are intermingled with them. But as the former grow thinner every page, in proportion as we advance nearer the enlightened ages, we soon learn, that there is nothing mysterious or supernatural in the case, but that all proceeds from the usual propensity of mankind towards the marvelous, and that, though this inclination may at intervals receive a check from sense and learning, it can never be thoroughly extirpated from human nature.

It is strange, a judicious reader is apt to say, upon the perusal of these wonderful historians, *that such prodigious events never happen in our days*. But it is nothing strange, I hope, that men should lie in all ages. You must surely have seen instances enough of that frailty. You have yourself heard many such marvelous relations started, which, being treated with scorn by all the wise and judicious, have at last been abandoned even by the vulgar. Be assured, that those renowned lies, which have spread and flourished to such a monstrous height, arose from like beginnings; but being sown in a more proper soil, shot up at last into prodigies almost equal to those which they relate.

It was a wise policy in that false prophet, Alexander, who though now forgotten, was once so famous, to lay the first scene of his impostures in Paphlagonia, where, as Lucian tells us, the people were extremely ignorant and stupid, and ready to swallow even the grossest delusion. People at a distance, who are weak enough to think the matter at all worth enquiry, have no opportunity of receiving better information. The stories come magnified to them by a hundred circumstances. Fools are industrious in propagating the imposture; while the wise and learned are contented, in general, to deride its absurdity, without informing themselves of the particular facts, by which it may be distinctly refuted. And thus the impostor above mentioned was enabled to proceed, from his ignorant Paphlagonians, to the enlisting of votaries, even among the Grecian philosophers, and men of the most eminent rank and distinction in Rome: nay, could engage the attention of that sage emperor Marcus Aurelius; so far as to make him trust the success of a military expedition to his delusive prophecies.

The advantages are so great, of starting an imposture among an ignorant people, that, even though the delusion should be too gross to impose on the generality of them (*which, though seldom, is sometimes the case*) it has a much better chance for succeeding in remote countries, than if the first scene had been laid in a city renowned for arts and knowledge. The most ignorant and barbarous of these barbarians carry the report abroad. None of their countrymen have a large correspondence, or sufficient credit and authority to contradict and beat down the delusion. Men's inclination to the marvelous has full opportunity to display itself. And thus a story, which is universally exploded in the place where it was first started, shall pass for certain at a thousand miles distance. But had Alexander fixed his residence at Athens, the philosophers of that renowned mart of learning had immediately spread, throughout the whole Roman empire, their sense of the matter; which, being supported by so great authority, and displayed by all the force of reason and eloquence, had entirely opened the eyes of mankind. It is true; Lucian, passing by chance through Paphlagonia, had an opportunity of performing this good office. But, though much to be wished, it does not always happen, that every Alexander meets with Lucian, ready to expose and detect his impostures.

I may add as a *fourth* reason, which diminishes the authority of prodigies, that there is no testimony for any, even those which have not been expressly detected, that is not opposed by an infinite number of witnesses; so that not only the miracle destroys the credit of testimony, but the testimony destroys itself. To make this the better understood, let us consider, that, in matters of religion, whatever is different is contrary; and that it is impossible the religions of ancient Rome, of Turkey, of Siam, and of China should, all of them, be established on any solid foundation. Every miracle, therefore, pretended to have been wrought in any of these religions (and all of them abound in miracles), as its direct scope is to establish the particular system to which it is attributed; so has it the same force, though more indirectly, to overthrow every other system. In destroying a rival system, it likewise destroys the credit of those miracles, on which that system was established; so that all the prodigies of different religions are to be regarded as contrary facts; and the evidences of these prodigies, whether weak or strong, as opposite to each other. According to this method of reasoning, when we believe any miracle of Mahomet or his successors, we have for our warrant the testimony of a few barbarous Arabians: And on the other hand, we are to regard the authority of Titus Livius, Plutarch, Tacitus, and, in short, of all the authors and witnesses, Grecian, Chinese, and Roman Catholic, who have related any miracle in their particular religion; I say, we are to regard their testimony in the same light as if they had mentioned that Mahometan miracle, and had in express terms contradicted it, with the same certainty as they have for the miracle they relate. This argument may appear over subtile and refined; but is not in reality different from the reasoning of a judge, who supposes, that the credit of two witnesses, maintaining a crime against any one, is destroyed by the testimony of two others, who affirm him to have been two hundred leagues distant, at the same instant when the crime is said to have been committed.

One of the best attested miracles in all profane history, is that which Tacitus reports of Vespasian, who cured a blind man in Alexandria, by means of his spittle, and a lame man by the mere touch of his foot; in obedience to a vision of the god Serapis, who had enjoined them to have recourse to the Emperor, for these miraculous cures. The story may be seen in that fine historian[1]; where every circumstance seems to add weight to the testimony, and might be displayed at large with all the force of argument and eloquence, if any one were now concerned to enforce the evidence of that exploded and idolatrous superstition. The gravity, solidity, age, and probity of so great an emperor, who, through the whole course of his life, conversed in a familiar manner with his friends and courtiers, and never affected those extraordinary airs of divinity assumed by Alexander and Demetrius. The historian, a contemporary writer, noted for candor and veracity, and withal, the greatest and most penetrating genius, perhaps, of all antiquity; and so free from any tendency to credulity, that he even lies under the contrary imputation, of atheism and profaneness: The persons, from whose authority he related the miracle, of established character for judgment and veracity, as we may well presume; eye-witnesses of the fact, and confirming their testimony, after the Flavian family was despoiled of the empire, and could no longer give any reward, as the price of a lie. *Utrumque, qui interfuere, nunc quoque memorant, postquam nullum mendacio pretium.* To which if we add the public nature of the facts, as related, it will appear, that no evidence can well be supposed stronger for so gross and so palpable a falsehood.

There is also a memorable story related by Cardinal de Retz, which may well deserve our consideration. When that intriguing politician fled into Spain, to avoid the persecution of his enemies, he passed through Saragossa, the capital of Arragon, where he was shown, in the cathedral, a man, who had served seven years as a doorkeeper, and was well known to everybody in town, that had ever paid his devotions at that church. He had been seen, for so long a time, wanting a leg; but recovered that limb by the rubbing of holy oil upon the stump; and the cardinal assures us that he saw him with two legs. This miracle was vouched by all the canons of the church; and the whole company in town were appealed to for a confirmation of the fact: whom the cardinal found, by their zealous devotion, to be thorough believers of the miracle. Here the relater was also contemporary to the supposed prodigy, of an incredulous and libertine character, as well as of great genius; the miracle of so *singular* a nature as could scarcely admit of a counterfeit, and the witnesses very numerous, and all of them, in a manner, spectators of the fact, to which they gave their testimony. And what adds mightily to the force of the evidence, and may double our surprise on this occasion, is, that the cardinal himself, who relates the story, seems not to give any credit to it, and consequently cannot be suspected of any concurrence in the holy fraud. He considered justly, that it was not requisite, in order to reject a fact of this nature, to be able accurately to disprove the testimony, and to trace its falsehood, through all the circumstances of knavery and credulity which produced it. He knew, that, as this was commonly altogether impossible at any small distance of time and place; so was it extremely difficult, even where one was immediately present, by reason of the bigotry, ignorance, cunning, and roguery of a great part of mankind. He therefore concluded, like a just reasoner, that such an evidence carried falsehood upon the very face of it, and that a miracle, supported by any human testimony, was more properly a subject of derision than of argument.

There surely never was a greater number of miracles ascribed to one person, than those, which were lately said to have been wrought in France upon the tomb of Abbé Paris, the famous Jansenist, with whose sanctity the people were so long deluded. The curing of the sick, giving hearing to the deaf, and sight to the blind, were every where talked of as the usual effects of that holy sepulchre. But what is more extraordinary; many of the miracles were immediately proved upon the spot, before judges of unquestioned integrity, attested by witnesses of credit and distinction, in a learned age, and on the most eminent theatre that is now in the world. Nor is this all: a relation of them was published and dispersed everywhere; nor were the *Jesuits,* though a learned body, supported by the civil magistrate, and determined enemies to those opinions, in whose favor the miracles were said to have been wrought, ever able distinctly to refute or detect them. Where shall we find such a number of circumstances, agreeing to the corroboration of one fact? And what have we to oppose to such a cloud of witnesses, but the absolute impossibility or miraculous nature of the events, which they relate? And this surely, in the eyes of all reasonable people, will alone be regarded as a sufficient refutation.

Is the consequence just, because some human testimony has the utmost force and authority in some cases, when it relates the battle of Philippi or Pharsalia for instance; that therefore all kinds of testimony must, in all cases, have equal force and authority? Suppose that the Casarean and Pompeian factions had, each of them, claimed the victory in these battles, and that the historians of each party had uniformly ascribed the advantage to their own side; how could mankind at this distance, have been able to determine between them? The contrariety is equally strong between the miracles related by Herodotus or Plutarch, and those delivered by Mariana, Bede, or any monkish historian.

The wise lend a very academic faith to every report which favors the passion of the reporter; whether it magnifies his country, his family, or himself, or in any other way strikes in with his natural inclinations and propensities. But what greater temptation than to appear a missionary, a prophet, an ambassador from heaven? Who would not encounter many dangers and difficulties, in order to attain so sublime a character? Or if, by the help of vanity and a heated imagination, a man has first made a convert of himself, and entered seriously into the delusion; who ever scruples to make use of pious frauds, in support of so holy and meritorious a cause?

The smallest spark may here kindle into the greatest flame; because the materials are always prepared for it. The *avidum genus auricularum,*[2] the gazing populace, receive greedily, without examination, whatever soothes superstition, and promotes wonder.

How many stories of this nature have, in all ages, been detected and exploded in their infancy? How many more have been celebrated for a time, and have afterwards sunk into neglect and oblivion? Where such reports, therefore, fly about, the solution of the phenomenon is obvious; and we judge in conformity to regular experience and observation, when we account for it by the known and natural principles of credulity and delusion. And shall we, rather than have a recourse to so natural a solution, allow of a miraculous violation of the most established laws of nature?

I need not mention the difficulty of detecting a falsehood in any private or even public history, at the place, where it is said to happen; much more when the scene is removed to ever so small a distance. Even a court of judicature, with all the authority, accuracy, and judgment, which they can employ, find themselves often at a loss to distinguish between truth and falsehood in the most recent actions. But the matter never comes to any issue, if trusted to the common method of altercations and debate and flying rumors; especially when men's passions have taken part on either side.

In the infancy of new religions, the wise and learned commonly esteem the matter too inconsiderable to deserve their attention or regard. And when afterwards they would willingly detect the cheat, in order to undeceive the deluded multitude, the season is now past, and the records and witnesses, which might clear up the matter, have perished beyond recovery.

No means of detection remain, but those which must be drawn from the very testimony itself of the reporters: and these, though always sufficient with the judicious and knowing, are commonly too find to fall under the comprehension of the vulgar.

Upon the whole, then, it appears, that no testimony for any kind of miracle has ever amounted to a probability, much less to a proof; and that, even supposing it amounted to a proof, it would be opposed by another proof; derived from the very nature of the fact, which it would endeavor to establish. It is experience only, which gives authority to human testimony; and it is the same experience, which assures us of the laws of nature. When, therefore, these two kinds of experience are contrary, we have nothing to do but subtract the one from the other, and embrace an opinion, either on one side or the other, with that assurance which arises from the remainder. But according to the principle here explained, this subtraction, with regard to all popular religions, amounts to an entire annihilation; and therefore we may establish it as a maxim, that no human testimony can have such force as to prove a miracle, and make it a just foundation for any such system of religion.

I beg the limitations here made may be remarked, when I say, that a miracle can never be proved, so as to be the foundation of a system of religion. For I own, that otherwise, there may possibly be miracles, or violations of the usual course of nature, of such a kind as to admit of proof from human testimony, though, perhaps, it will be impossible to find any such in all the records of history. Thus, suppose, all authors, in all languages, agree, that, from the first of January 1600, there was a total darkness over the whole earth for eight days: suppose that the tradition of this extraordinary event is still strong and lively among the people: that all travelers, who return from foreign countries, bring us accounts of the same tradition, without the least variation or contradiction: it is evident, that our present philosophers, instead of doubting the fact, ought to receive it as certain, and ought to search for the causes whence it might be derived. The decay, corruption, and dissolution of nature, is an event rendered probable by so many analogies, that any phenomenon, which seems to have a tendency towards that catastrophe, comes within the reach of human testimony, if that testimony be very extensive and uniform.

But suppose, that all the historians who treat of England, should agree, that, on the first of January 1600, Queen Elizabeth died; that both before and after her death she was seen by her physicians and the whole court, as is usual with persons of her rank; that her successor was acknowledged and proclaimed by the Parliament; and that, after been interred a month, she again appeared, resumed the throne, and governed England for three years: I must confess that I should be surprised at the concurrence of so many odd circumstances, but should not have the least inclination to believe so miraculous an event. I should not doubt of her pretended death, and of those other public circumstances that followed it: I should only assert it to have been pretended, and that it neither was, nor possibly could be real. You would in vain object to me the difficulty, and almost impossibility of deceiving the world in an affair of such consequence; the wisdom and solid judgment of that renowned queen; with the little or no advantage which she could reap from so poor an artifice: All this might astonish me; but I would still reply, that the knavery and folly of men are such common phenomena, that I should rather believe the most extraordinary events to arise from their concurrence, than admit of so signal a violation of the laws of nature.

But should this miracle be ascribed to any new system of religion; men, in all ages, have been so much imposed on by ridiculous stories of that kind, that this very circumstance would be a full proof of a cheat, and sufficient, with all men of sense, not only to make them reject the fact, but even reject it without farther examination. Though the Being to whom the miracle is ascribed, be, in this case, Almighty, it does not, upon that account, become a whit more probable; since it is impossible for us to know the attributes or actions of such a Being, otherwise than from the experience which we have of his productions, in the usual course of nature. This still reduces us to past observation, and obliges us to compare the instances of the violation of truth in the testimony of men, with those of the violation of the laws of nature by miracles, in order to judge which of them is most likely and probable. As the violations of truth are more common in the testimony concerning religious miracles, than in that concerning any other matter of fact; this must diminish very much the authority of the former testimony, and make us form a general resolution, never to lend any attention to it, with whatever specious pretence it may be covered.

Lord Bacon seems to have embraced the same principles of reasoning. "We ought," says he, "to make a collection or particular history of all monsters and prodigious births or productions, and in a word of every thing new, rare, and extraordinary in nature. But this must be done with the most severe scrutiny, lest we depart from truth. Above all, every relation must be considered as suspicious, which depends in any degree upon religion, as the prodigies of Livy: And no less so, every thing that is to be found in the writers of natural magic or alchemy, or such authors, who seem, all of them, to have an unconquerable appetite for falsehood and fable.[3]

I am the better pleased with the method of reasoning here delivered, as I think it may serve to confound those dangerous friends or disguised enemies to the *Christian Religion*, who have undertaken to defend it by the principles of human reason. Our most holy religion is founded on *Faith*, not on reason; and it is a sure method of exposing it to put it to such a trial as it is, by no means, fitted to endure. To make this more evident, let us examine those miracles, related in scripture; and not to lose ourselves in too wide a field, let us confine ourselves to such as we find in the *Pentateuch*, which we shall examine, according to the principles of these pretended Christians, not as the word or testimony of God himself, but as the production of a mere human writer and historian. Here then we are first to consider a book, presented to us by a barbarous and ignorant people, written in an age when they were still more barbarous, and in all probability long after the facts which it relates, corroborated by no concurring testimony, and resembling those fabulous accounts, which every nation gives of its origin. Upon reading this book, we find it full of prodigies and miracles. It gives an account of a state of the world and of human nature entirely different from the present: Of our fall from that state: Of the age of man, extended to near a thousand years: Of the destruction of the world by a deluge: Of the arbitrary choice of one people, as the favorites of heaven; and that people the countrymen of the author: Of their deliverance from bondage by prodigies the most astonishing imaginable: I desire any one to lay his hand upon his heart, and after a serious consideration declare, whether he thinks that the falsehood of such a book, supported by such a testimony, would be more extraordinary and miraculous than all the miracles it relates; which is, however, necessary to make it be received, according to the measures of probability above established.

NOTES

1. Hist. Lib. V. Cap. 8. Suetonius gives nearly the same account in *vita* Vesp.
2. Lucret.
3. Nov. Org. Lib. ii. aph. 29.

RICHARD SWINBURNE

Miracles and Historical Evidence

Hume argues that the minimal, subjective evidence supporting the report of an allegedly miraculous event can never outweigh the widespread, objective evidence supporting the contention that it did not occur as reported. In the selection here, Richard Swinburne (1934–) challenges this argument, claiming that the objective evidence for such an event is not insignificant. Such evidence can be furnished by our own apparent memories, the testimony of others, the relevant physical traces, or some combination of these factors, and could in some cases outweigh the familiar and seemingly uncontrovertible counterevidence.

⌘

[I have claimed] that we could have good reason to suppose that event *E*, if it occurred, was a violation of a law of nature *L*. But could one have good evidence that such an event *E* occurred? At this point we must face the force of Hume's own argument. This, it will be remembered, runs as follows. The evidence, which *ex hypothesi* is good evidence, that *L* is a law of nature is evidence that *E* did not occur. We have certain other evidence that *E* did occur. In such circumstances, writes Hume, the wise man "weighs the opposite experiments. He considers which side is supported by the greater number of experiments." Since he supposes that the evidence that *E* occurred would be that of testimony, Hume concludes "that no testimony is sufficient to establish a miracle, unless the testimony be of such a kind, that its falsehood would be more miraculous, than the fact which it endeavors to establish."

We have four kinds of evidence about what happened at some past instant—our own apparent memories of our past experiences, the testimony of others about their past experiences, physical traces and our contemporary understanding of what things are physically impossible or improbable. (The fourth is only a corrective to the other three, not an independent source of detailed information.) A piece of evidence gives grounds for believing that some past event occurred, except in so far as it conflicts with other pieces of evidence. In so far as pieces of evidence conflict, they have to be weighed against each other. . . .

The fundamental idea involved in . . . weighing evidence seems to be to obtain as coherent a picture as possible of the past as consistent as possible with the evidence. We can express this idea in the form of one basic principle for assessing evidence and several subsidiary principles limiting its operation. The most basic principle is to accept as many pieces of evidence as possible. If one witness says one thing, and five witnesses say a different thing, then, in the absence of further evidence (e.g., about their unreliability) take the testimony of the latter. If one method of dating an artifact gives one result, and five methods give a different result, then, in the absence of further information accept the latter result.

The first subsidiary principle is—apart from any empirical evidence about their relative reliability—that evidence of different kinds ought to be given different weights. How this is to be done can only be illustrated by examples. Thus one's own apparent memory ought as such to count for more than the testimony of another witness (unless and until evidence of its relative unreliability is forthcoming). If I appear to remember having seen Jones yesterday in Hull, but Brown says that he had Jones under observation all day yesterday and that he went nowhere near to Hull, then—*ceteris paribus*—I ought to stand by my apparent memory. This is because when someone else gives testimony it always makes sense to suppose that he is lying; whereas, when I report to myself what I appear to remember, I cannot be lying. For the liar is someone who says what he believes to be false. But if I report what I appear to remember (and I can *know* for certain what I appear to remember), I cannot be lying. Secondly, if I feel highly confident that I remember some event, my apparent memory ought to count for more than if I am only moderately confident. My apparent memory has a built-in weight, apart from empirical evidence which may be forthcoming about its reliability in different circumstances (e.g., that it is not reliable when I am drunk). In these and other ways for non-empirical reasons different pieces of evidence ought to be given different weights in assessing the balance of evidence.

The second subsidiary principle is that different pieces of evidence ought to be given different weights in accordance with any empirical evidence which may be available about their different reliability, obtained by a procedure which I may term narrowing the evidence class. In general we necessarily assume or have reason to believe that apparent memory, testimony and states of particular types are reliable evidence about past states and events. But clash of evidence casts doubt on this. So we test the reliability of a piece of evidence by classifying it as a member of a narrow class, and investigating the reliability of other members of that class which . . . would have to be classes whose members were described by projectible predicates. If the testimony of Jones conflicts with the testimony of Smith, then we must investigate not the worth of testimony in general, but the worth of Jones' testimony and of Smith's testimony. We do this by seeing if on all other occasions when we can ascertain what happened Jones or Smith correctly described what happened. In so far as each did, his testimony is reliable. Now this procedure will only work in so far as we can at some stage ascertain with sufficient certainty what happened without bringing in empirical evidence about the reliability of the evidence about what happened. Unless we could establish with sufficient certainty by mere balance of evidence what happened on a certain past occasion, without testing the worth of each piece of evidence by considering the worth of evidence of a narrow class to which it belongs, we could never establish anything at all. For the testing of evidence of one class can only be performed if we presuppose the reliability in general of other evidence. Thus, to test Jones' testimony we have to find out—by the testimony of others and traces—what happened on a number of occasions and then see whether Jones correctly reported this. But to do this we have to be able to ascertain what did happen on those occasions, and we will have various pieces of evidence as well as that of Jones about this. Unless the agreement of evidence apart from the testimony of Jones suffices to do this, we could never show Jones to be a reliable or unreliable witness. We may have empirical evidence about the reliability of such other evidence, but as such evidence will consist of more empirical evidence, we have to stop somewhere, with evidence which we can take to be reliable without empirical evidence thereof.

Similar tests to these tests of the reliability of testimony can be made of the reliability of traces, e.g., of methods of dating ancient documents.

For a given number of pieces of evidence in the class, the narrower the evidence class chosen for the assessment of the worth of a particular piece of evidence, the more reliable the assessment yielded by it. If we examine the worth of a particular piece of testimony given by a certain Soviet diplomat, Stamkovsky, to an official of M.I.5 by examining the worth of n pieces of testimony given by Soviet diplomats, then we have some knowledge of its worth, better than our knowledge of the worth of testimony in general. But we have a better assessment of its worth if we examine the worth of n pieces of testimony given by Stamkovsky and an even better estimate if we consider the worth of n pieces of testimony given by Stamkovsky to British counter-intelligence officers. But this raises a well-known difficulty about evidence classes—that the narrower the evidence class we choose, the fewer pieces of evidence we will have on which to base our assessment. We will have plenty of pieces of evidence by Soviet diplomats the reliability of which we can check, but few pieces of evidence given by Stamkovsky to British counter-intelligence agents the reliability of which we can check. The narrower the evidence class the better, but so long only as we have sufficient evidence to put in it to reach a well-substantiated conclusion.

The third subsidiary principle is not to reject coincident evidence (unless the evidence of its falsity is extremely strong) unless an explanation can be given of the coincidence; and the better substantiated is that explanation, the more justified the rejection of the coincident evidence. If five witnesses all say the same thing and we wish to reject their evidence, we are in general not justified in doing so unless we can explain why they all said the same thing. Such explanations could be that they were subject to common illusions, or all plotted together to give false testimony. The better substantiated is such an explanation the better justified is our rejection of the evidence. Substantiation of the theory of a common plot would be provided by evidence that the witnesses were all seen together before the event, that they stood to gain from giving false testimony etc. But ultimately the evidence rests on evidence about particular past events and would itself need to be substantiated in ways earlier described.

These subsidiary principles, and perhaps others which I have not described, then qualify the basic principle of accepting the majority of the evidence. They are the standards of investigation adopted, I would claim, by and large by all historical investigators. . . .

Bearing in mind these considerations about conflicting evidence and these principles for assessing different ways of weighing evidence, what are we to say when there is a conflict between evidence of the first three kinds that an event *E* occurred and evidence of the fourth kind that an event of the type of *E* is physically impossible? Hume's official answer . . . was that exceedingly strong evidence of other kinds, in particular testimony, would be needed for evidence about physical impossibility to be outweighed. A more extreme answer is given by Antony Flew in a passage in his *Hume's Philosophy of Belief.*

> The justification for giving the "scientific" this ultimate precedence here over the "historical" lies in the nature of the propositions concerned and in the evidence which can be displayed to sustain them . . . the candidate historical proposition will be particular, often singular, and in the past tense. . . . But just by reason of this very pastness and particularity it is no longer possible for anyone to examine the subject directly for himself . . . the law of nature will, unlike the candidate historical proposition, be a general nomological. It can thus in theory, though obviously not always in practice, be tested at any time by any person.

Flew seems here to be taking the view that evidence of the fourth kind ("scientific" evidence) could never be outweighed by evidence of the first three kinds ("historical" evidence), an answer suggested also by Hume's detailed discussions of three purported miracles. Flew's justification for this view is that while a historical proposition concerns a past event of which we have only the present remains (viz. evidence of the first three kinds), the scientific proposition, being a general statement (viz. about all entities of some kind at all times and places), can go on and on being tested by any person who wishes to test it. Flew's suggestion seems to be that the historical proposition cannot go on and on being tested by any person at any time.

If this is Flew's contrast, it is mistaken. Particular experiments on particular occasions only give a certain and far from conclusive support to claims that a purported scientific law is true. Any person can test for the truth of a purported scientific law, but a positive result to one test will give only limited support to the claim. Exactly the same holds for purported historical truths. Anyone can examine the evidence, but a particular piece of evidence gives only limited support to the claim that the historical proposition is true. But in the historical as in the scientific case, there is no limit to the testing which we can do. We can go on and on testing for the truth of historical as of scientific propositions. True, the actual traces, apparent memories and testimony, which I may term the direct evidence, available to an inquirer are unlikely to increase in number, at any rate after a certain time. Only so many witnesses will have seen the event in question and once their testimony has been obtained no more will be available. Further, it is an unfortunate physical fact, as we have noted, that many traces dissipate. But although the number of pieces of direct evidence about what happened may not increase, more and more evidence can be obtained about the reliability of the evidence which we have. One could show the evidence yielded by traces of certain types, or testimony given by witnesses of such-and-such character in such-and-such circumstances was always correct. This indirect evidence could mount up in just the way in which the evidence of the physical impossibility of an event could mount up. Hence by his examining the reliability of the direct evidence, the truth of the "historical" proposition like the "scientific" can also "be tested at any time by any person."

But if Flew's justification of his principle is mistaken, what can we say positively for or against the principle itself? Now I would urge that it is an unreasonable principle since claims that some formula L is a law of nature, and claims that apparent memory, testimony or traces of certain types are to be relied on are claims established ultimately in a similar kind of way . . . and will be strong or weak for the same reasons, and so neither ought to take automatic preference over the other. To make the supposition that they are to be treated differently is to introduce a complicating *ad hoc* procedure for assessing evidence. As we have seen, formulae about how events succeed each other are shown to be laws of nature by the fact that they provide the most simple and coherent account of a large number of observed data. Likewise testimony given by certain kinds of people or traces of certain kinds are established as reliable by well-established correlations between present and past phenomena. (The reliability of apparent memory could also be assessed in the same way but we will ignore this for the moment, as important only for the few who claim to have observed miracles.) The reliability of C_{14} dating is established by showing that the postulated correlation between the proportion of C_{14} in artifacts and their age since manufacture clearly established by other methods holds of the large number of cases studied without exception and is the simplest correlation that does. That testimony given by Jones on oath is to be relied on is to be established by showing that whatever Jones said on oath is often by other methods shown to be true and never shown to be false, and there is no other simple account of the matter coherent with the data than that Jones tells the truth on oath (e.g., the account that in each of these cases he told the truth because he knew that a lie could be detected).

So then a claim that a formula L is a law of nature and a claim that testimony or trace of a certain type is reliable are established in basically the same way—by showing that certain formulae connect observed data in a simple coherent way. This being so, whether we take the evidence of an established law of nature that E did not occur or the evidence of trace or testimony that it did would seem to be a matter of the firmness with which the law, if reliable, forbids and the firmness with which the trace or testimony, if reliable, establishes the occurrence of E, and of the reliability of each. If the law is universal, it will firmly rule out an exception; if it is statistical, it will merely show an exception to be highly improbable. . . . Likewise traces or testimony may, in virtue of the correlation used, either show to be certain or show to be highly probable the event in question.

If the correlation between (e.g.) testimony of a certain kind of witness and the past event testified to is statistical (e.g. "witnesses of such and such a type are reliable in 99% cases") then it shows that the event in question (what the witness reported) having happened is highly probable. If the correlation is universal ("witnesses of such and such a type are invariably reliable") then it makes certain the occurrence of the event in question (viz. given the truth of the correlation, it is then certain that the event happened). So whether the evidence on balance supports or opposes the occurrence of *E* is firstly a matter of whether the law or correlation in question is universal or statistical in form. It is secondly a matter of how well established the law or correlation is: a statistical law may have very strong evidence in its favor. The basic laws of quantum theory are statistical in form but the evidence in their favor is enormously strong. On the other hand, some universal laws are, though established, not very strongly established. Such are, for example, many of the generalizations of biology or anthropology. If *L* is a law, universal or statistical, to which the occurrence of *E* would be an exception, and *T* is a trace or piece of testimony of the occurrence of *E*, shown to be such by an established correlation *C*, whether the evidence on balance supports or opposes the occurrence of *E* is a matter of whether *L* and *C* are universal or statistical, and how well established respectively are *L* and *C*.

If *C* is universal and better established than *L*, then, surely, whether *L* is universal or statistical, the evidence on balance supports the occurrence of *E*; whereas if *L* is universal and is better established than *C*, then, whether *C* is universal or merely statistical, the evidence is against the occurrence of *E*. If *C* and *L* are both statistical, and *C* is no less well established than *L*, and *C* renders the occurrence of *E* more probable than *L* renders it improbable, then the evidence on balance supports the occurrence of *E*. If *C* and *L* are both statistical, and *L* is no less well established than *C*, and *L* renders the occurrence of *E* more improbable than *C* renders it probable, then the evidence on balance is against the occurrence of *E*. What we are to say in other cases depends on whether we can measure quantitatively how well established are *C* and *L* and compare these figures with the probability and the improbability which they respectively ascribe to *E*. How well established or confirmed are *L* or *C* is a matter of how well they (or the scientific theory of which they are part) integrate a large number of data into a simple and coherent pattern. Whether one can measure and how to measure quantitatively this degree of confirmation of scientific laws and of generalizations are disputed issues. They are the subject of a branch of philosophy of science known as confirmation theory which has not yet yielded any results of the kind which we could apply to our concern.

In so far as we have several traces or pieces of testimony that E occurred, to that extent the evidence provided by traces and testimony will be very much the weightier. Suppose for example that we have traces or pieces of testimony T_1 and T_2 that E occurred, and that E if it occurred would be an exception to a universal law of nature L. T_1 is evidence that E occurred in virtue of a universal correlation C_1, and T_2 is evidence that E occurred in virtue of a universal correlation C_2. If L is true with no exceptions at all then E did not occur, but (given the existence of T_1 and T_2) if *either* C_1 or C_2 is true, then E did occur. It will be more likely that one of C_1 and C_2 is true than that C_1 is true or that C_2 is true. Hence T_1 and T_2 together produce more evidence in favor of E having occurred than does just one of them. It is clearly in virtue of such considerations that the principle of coincident evidence, which I cited earlier, holds. This is the principle that we should not reject coincident evidence that an event E occurred unless the evidence that E did not occur is extremely strong or an explanation can be given of the coincidence. Evidence that E did not occur would be extremely strong if L was very well supported and far better supported than any of the very few correlations $C_1 \ldots C_n$ adduced as evidence of the reliability of traces of testimony $T_1 \ldots T_n$ to occurrence of E. Evidence that the coincident evidence is susceptible of another explanation is evidence of further traces and testimony backed by other correlations $C_{n+1} \ldots C_p$ that exceptional circumstances hold under which $T_1 \ldots T_n$ are not evidence that E occurred. But in general we assume (because $T_1 \ldots T_n$ being traces, it is highly likely) or have evidence that those circumstances do not hold.

It is not always easy to compare the strength of support for various proposed laws or correlations, let alone measure such strength quantitatively. But, as we have seen, laws and correlations are supported in a similar kind of way by instances. Hence it seems reasonable to suppose that in principle the degree of support for any correlation C or disjunction of correlations could exceed the degree of support for any law and hence render it more probable than not that the cited event E occurred. Flew's principle can only be saved if we suppose that support for the C's and support for L are to be treated differently just because of the different role which the C's and L play in supporting or opposing the occurrence of E. But this seems to be to make a complicating, *ad hoc* supposition. Flew's principle advocates treating evidence for generalizations in a different way from the way in which we ordinarily treat it, and is therefore for this reason to be rejected.

It must however be admitted that in general any one correlation C will be less well established than L, and since L will usually be a universal law, its evidence will in general be preferred to that of C. However, the more pieces of evidence there are that E occurred (e.g., the testimony of many independent witnesses), the more such evidence by its cumulative effect will tend to outweigh the counter-evidence of L. This accounts for our previous third subsidiary principle.

Although we do not yet have any exact laws about the reliability of testimony of different kinds, we have considerable empirical information which is not yet precisely formulated. We know that witnesses with axes to grind are less to be relied on than witnesses with no stake in that to which they testify; that primitive people whose upbringing conditions them to expect unusual events are more likely to report the occurrence of unusual events which do not occur than are modern atheists (perhaps too that modern atheists are more likely to deny the occurrence of unusual events which in fact occur in their environment than are primitive people); and so on.

I venture to suggest that generalizations of this kind about the reliability of testimony, although statistical in character, are extremely well established, perhaps better established than many laws of nature. However it must be added that while we can construct wide and narrow generalizations about the reliability of contemporary witnesses which are well confirmed, generalizations about the reliability of past witnesses will be more shaky, for we have less information about them and it is in practice often difficult to obtain more.

Now, although we are in no position yet (if ever we will be) to work out numerically the degree or balance of support for a violation *E* of a law of nature *L* having taken place, since *a priori* objections have been overruled, we can surely cite examples where the combined testimony of many witnesses to such an event is in the light of the above considerations to be accepted.

One interesting such example is given by Hume himself:

> Thus, suppose, all authors in all languages agree, that, from the first of January 1600, there was a total darkness over the whole earth for eight days: suppose that the tradition of this extraordinary event is still strong and lively among the people: that all travellers, who return from foreign countries, bring us accounts of the same tradition, without the least variation or contradiction: it is evidence, that our present philosophers, instead of doubting the fact, ought to receive it as certain, and ought to search for the causes whence it might be derived.

Hume unfortunately spoils this example by going on to suggest that such an event, although extraordinary, is not physically impossible, since

> The decay, corruption, and dissolution of nature, is an event rendered probable by so many analogies, that any phenomenon, which seems to have a tendency towards that catastrophe, comes within the reach of human testimony, if that testimony be very extensive and uniform.

We with our knowledge of natural laws, in particular the laws of meteorology and the Earth's motion, would not judge the matter in this way, but would surely judge the event to be physically impossible. Indeed Hume originally introduced it as an example of "violations of the usual course of nature, of such a kind to admit proof from human testimony." (He allowed in theory, it will be remembered, that there could be such, "though, perhaps, it will be impossible to find any such in all the records of history.") The example is similar to many which might be artificially constructed in which the amount, diversity and detail of testimony to the occurrence of E surely suffices to overwhelm any information provided by science that E is physically impossible.

So I conclude that although standards for weighing evidence are not always clear, apparent memory, testimony and traces could sometimes outweigh the evidence of physical impossibility. It is just a question of how much evidence of the former kind we have and how reliable we can show it to have been. Hume's general point must be admitted, that we should accept the historical evidence, viz. a man's apparent memory, the testimony of others and traces, only if the falsity of the latter would be 'more miraculous,' i.e., more improbable 'than the event *which* he relates.' However, my whole discussion in this chapter has ignored "background evidence." In so far as there is substantial other evidence in favor of the existence of God, less would be required in the way of historical evidence in favor of the occurrence of a miracle than this chapter has supposed hitherto. If we have already good grounds for believing that there is a gorilla loose in snowy mountains, we require less by way of evidence of footprints to show that he has visited a particular place. Conversely, if there is substantial evidence against the existence of God, more is required in the way of historical evidence in favor of the occurrence of a miracle than this chapter has supposed—for we have then substantial evidence for supposing that nothing apart from laws of nature determines what happens.

J. L. MACKIE

Miracles and Testimony

In this selection, J. L. Mackie (1917–1981) presents an updated version of Hume's argument against miracles. Those who want to claim that a miracle has occurred, he argues, have a double burden: to establish that the event has occurred and that it has violated a natural law. He emphasizes that the attempt to establish both points simultaneously is quite problematic, since the stronger the evidence for believing that an event has actually violated a *natural law* the weaker the evidence for believing that this event actually occurred as reported.

⌘

What Hume [expounds in *Of Miracles*] are the principles for the rational acceptance of testimony, the rules that ought to govern our believing or not believing what we are told. But the rules that govern people's actual acceptance of testimony are very different. We are fairly good at detecting dishonesty, insincerity, and lack of conviction, and we readily reject what we are told by someone who betrays these defects. But we are strongly inclined simply to accept, without question, statements that are obviously assured and sincere. As Hume would say, a firm association of ideas links someone else's saying, with honest conviction, that *p*, and its being the case that *p*, and we pass automatically from the perception of the one to belief in the other. Or, as he might also have said, there is an intellectual sympathy by which we tend automatically to share what we find to be someone else's belief, analogous to sympathy in the original sense, the tendency to share what we see to be someone else's feelings. And in general this is a useful tendency. People's beliefs about ordinary matters are right, or nearly right, more often than they are wildly wrong, so that intellectual sympathy enables fairly correct information to be passed on more smoothly than it could be if we were habitually cautious and constantly checked testimony against the principles for its rational acceptance. But what is thus generally useful can sometimes be misleading, and miracle reports are a special case where we need to restrain our instinctive acceptance of honest statements, and go back to the basic rational principles which determine whether a statement is really reliable or not. Even where we are cautious, and hesitate to accept what we are told—for example by a witness in a legal case—we often do not go beyond the question "How intrinsically reliable is this witness?" or, in detail, "Does he seem to be honest? Does he have a motive for misleading us? Is he the sort of person who might tell plausible lies? Or is he the sort of person who, in the circumstances, might have made a mistake?" If we are satisfied on all these scores, we are inclined to believe what the witness says, without weighing very seriously the question "How intrinsically improbable is what he has told us?" But, as Hume insists, this further question is highly relevant. His general approach to the problem of when to accept testimony is certainly sound.

Hume's case against miracles is an epistemological argument: it does not try to show that miracles never do happen or never could happen, but only that we never have good reasons for believing that they have happened. It must be clearly distinguished from the suggestion that the very concept of a miracle is incoherent. That suggestion might be spelled out as follows. A miracle is, by definition, a violation of a law of nature, and a law of nature is, by definition, a regularity—or the statement of a regularity—about what happens, about the way the world works; consequently, if some event actually occurs, no regularity which its occurrence infringes (or, no regularity-statement which it falsifies) can really be a law of nature; so this event, however unusual or surprising, cannot after all be a miracle. The two definitions together entail that whatever happens is not a miracle, that is, that miracles never happen. This, be it noted, is not Hume's argument. If it were correct, it would make Hume's argument unnecessary. Before we discuss Hume's case, then, we should consider whether there is a coherent concept of a miracle which would not thus rule out the occurrence of miracles *a priori*.

If miracles are to serve their traditional function of giving spectacular support to religious claims—whether general theistic claims, or the authority of some specific religion or some particular sect or individual teacher—the concept must not be so weakened that anything at all unusual or remarkable counts as a miracle. We must keep in the definition the notion of a violation of natural law. But then, if it is to be even possible that a miracle should occur, we must modify the definition given above of a law of nature. What we want to do is to contrast the order of nature with a possible divine or supernatural intervention. The laws of nature, we must say, describe the ways in which the world—including, of course, human beings—works when left to itself, when not interfered with. A miracle occurs when the world is not left to itself, when something distinct from the natural order as a whole intrudes into it.

This notion of ways in which the world works is coherent and by no means obscure. We know how to discover causal laws, relying on a principle of the uniformity of the course of nature—essentially the assumption that there are some laws to be found—in conjunction with suitable observations and experiments, typically varieties of controlled experiment whose underlying logic is that of Mill's "method of difference." Within the laws so established, we can further mark off basic laws of working from derived laws which hold only in a particular context or contingently upon the way in which something is put together. It will be a derived law that a particular clock, or clocks of a particular sort, run at such a speed, and this will hold only in certain conditions of temperature, and so on; but this law will be derived from more basic ones which describe the regular behavior of certain kinds of material, in view of the way in which the clock is put together, and these more basic laws of materials may in turn be derived from yet more basic laws about sub-atomic particles, in view of the ways in which those materials are made up of such particles. In so far as we advance towards a knowledge of such a system of basic and derived laws, we are acquiring an understanding of ways in which the world works. As well as what we should ordinarily call causal laws, which typically concern interactions, there are similar laws with regard to the ways in which certain kinds of things simply persist through time, and certain sorts of continuous process just go on. These too, and in particular the more basic laws of these sorts, help to constitute the ways in which the world works. Thus there are several kinds of basic "laws of working."[1] For our present purpose, however, it is not essential that we should even be approaching an understanding of how the world works; it is enough that we have the concept of such basic laws of working, that we know in principle what it would be to discover them. Once we have this concept, we have moved beyond the definition of laws of nature merely as (statements of) what always happens. We can see how, using this concept and using the assumption that there are some such basic laws of working to be found, we can hope to determine what the actual laws of working are by reference to a restricted range of experiments and observations. This opens up the possibility that we might determine that something *is* a basic law of working of natural objects, and yet also, independently, find that it was occasionally violated. An occasional violation does not in itself necessarily overthrow the independently established conclusion that this *is* a law of working.

Equally, there is no obscurity in the notion of intervention. Even in the natural world we have a clear understanding of how there can be for a time a closed system, in which everything that happens results from factors within that system in accordance with its laws of working, but how then something may intrude from outside it, bringing about changes that the system would not have produced of its own accord, so that things go on after this intrusion differently from how they would have gone on if the system had remained closed. All we need do, then, is to regard the whole natural world as being, for most of the time, such a closed system; we can then think of a supernatural intervention as something that intrudes into that system from outside the natural world as a whole.

If the laws by which the natural world works are deterministic, then the notion of a violation of them is quite clear-cut: such a violation would be an event which, given that the world was a closed system working in accordance with these laws, and given some actual earlier complete state of the world, simply could not have happened at all. Its occurrence would then be clear proof that either the supposed laws were not the real laws of working, or the earlier state was not as it was supposed to have been, or else the system was not closed after all. But if the basic laws of working are statistical or probabilistic, the notion of a violation of them is less precise. If something happens which, given those statistical laws and some earlier complete state of the world, is extremely improbable—in the sense of physical probability: that is, something such that there is a strong propensity or tendency for it *not* to happen—we still cannot say firmly that the laws have been violated: laws of this sort explicitly allow that what is extremely improbable may occasionally come about. Indeed it is highly probable (both physically and epistemically) that some events, each of which is very improbable, will occur at rare intervals.[2] If tosses of a coin were governed by a statistical law that gave a 50 per cent propensity to heads at each toss, a continuous run of ten heads would be a highly improbable occurrence; but it would be highly probable that there would be some such runs in a sequence of a million tosses. Nevertheless, we can still use the contrast between the way of working of the natural world as a whole, considered as a normally closed system, and an intervention or intrusion into it. This contrast does not disappear or become unintelligible merely because we lack decisive tests for its application. We can still define a miracle as an event which would not have happened in the course of nature, and which came about only through a supernatural intrusion. The difficulty is merely that we cannot now say with certainty, simply by reference to the relevant laws and some antecedent situation, that a certain event would not have happened in the course of nature, and therefore must be such an intrusion. But we may still be able to say that it is very probable—and this is now an epistemic probability—that it would not have happened naturally, and so is likely to be such an intrusion. For if the laws made it physically improbable that it would come about, this tends to make it epistemically improbable that it did come about through those laws, if there is any other way in which it could have come about and which is not equally improbable or more improbable. In practice the difficulty mentioned is not much of an extra difficulty. For even where we believe there to be deterministic laws and an earlier situation which together would have made an occurrence actually impossible in the course of nature, it is from our point of view at best epistemically very probable, not certain, that those are the laws and that that was the relevant antecedent situation.

Consequently, whether the laws of nature are deterministic or statistical, we can give a coherent definition of a miracle as a supernatural intrusion into the normally closed system that works in accordance with those laws, and in either case we can identify conceivable occurrences, and alleged occurrences, which if they were to occur, or have occurred, could be believed with high probability, though not known with certainty, to satisfy that definition.

However, the full concept of a miracle requires that the intrusion should be purposive, that it should fulfil the intention of a god or other supernatural being. This connection cannot be sustained by any ordinary causal theory; it presupposes a power to fulfil intentions directly, without physical means, which . . . is highly dubious; so this requirement for a miracle will be particularly hard to confirm. On the other hand it is worth noting that successful prophecy could be regarded as a form of miracle for which there could in principle be good evidence. If someone is reliably recorded as having prophesied at t_1 an event at t_2 which could not be predicted at t_1 on any natural grounds, and the event occurs at t_2, then at any later time t_3 we can assess the evidence for the claims both that the prophecy was made at t_1 and that its accuracy cannot be explained either causally (for example, on the ground that it brought about its own fulfilment) or as accidental, and hence that it was probably miraculous.

There is, then, a coherent concept of miracles. Their possibility is not ruled out *a priori*, by definition. So we must consider whether Hume's argument shows that we never have good reason for believing that any have occurred.

Hume's general principle for the evaluation of testimony, that we have to weigh the unlikelihood of the event reported against the unlikelihood that the witness is mistaken or dishonest, is substantially correct. It is a corollary of the still more general principle of accepting whatever hypothesis gives the best overall explanation of all the available and relevant evidence. But some riders are necessary. First, the likelihood or unlikelihood, the epistemic probability or improbability, is always relative to some body of information, and may change if additional information comes in. Consequently, any specific decision in accordance with Hume's principle must be provisional. Secondly, it is one thing to decide which of the rival hypotheses in the field at any time should be provisionally accepted in the light of the evidence then available; but it is quite another to estimate the weight of this evidence, to say how well supported this favored hypothesis is, and whether it is likely that its claims will be undermined either by additional information or by the suggesting of further alternative hypotheses. What is clearly the best-supported view of some matter at the moment may still be very insecure, and quite likely to be overthrown by some further considerations. For example, if a public opinion poll is the only evidence we have about the result of a coming election, this evidence may point, perhaps decisively, to one result rather than another; yet if the poll has reached only a small sample of the electorate, or if it was taken some time before the voting day, it will not be very reliable. There is a dimension of reliability over and above that of epistemic probability relative to the available evidence. Thirdly, Hume's description of what gives support to a prediction, or in general to a judgment about an unobserved case that would fall under some generalization, is very unsatisfactory. He seems to say that if *all* so far observed *A*s have been *B*s, then this amounts to a "proof" that some unobserved *A* will be (or is, or was), a *B*, whereas if some observed *A*s have been *B*s, but some have not, there is only a "probability" that an unobserved *A* will be a *B*.[3] This mises up the reasoning *to* a generalization with the reasoning *from* a generalization to a particular case. It is true that the premises "All *A*s are *B*s" and "This is an *A*" constitute a proof of the conclusion "This is a *B*," whereas the premises "*x* percent of *A*s are *B*s" and "This is an *A*" yield—if there is no other relevant information—a probability of *x* percent that this is a *B*: they *probabilify* the conclusion to this degree, or, as we can say, the probability of the conclusion "This is a *B*" relative to that evidence is *x* percent. But the inductive argument from the observation "All so far observed *A*s have been *B*s" to the generalization "All *A*s are *B*s" is far from secure, and it would be most misleading to call this a proof, and therefore misleading also to describe as a proof the whole line of inference from "All so far observed *A*s have been *B*s" to the conclusion "This as yet unobserved *A* is a *B*." Similarly, the inductive argument from "*x* percent of observed *A*s have been *B*s" to the statistical generalization "*x* percent of *A*s are *B*s" is far from secure, so that we cannot say that "*x* percent of observed *A*s have been *B*s" even probabilifies to the degree *x* percent the conclusion "This as yet unobserved *A* is a *B*." A good deal of other information and background knowledge is needed, in either case, before the generalization, whether universal or statistical, is at all well supported, and hence before the stage is properly set for either proof or probabilification about an as yet unobserved *A*. It is harder than Hume allows here to arrive at well-supported generalizations of either sort about how the world works.

These various qualifications together entail that what has been widely and reasonably thought to be a law of nature may not be one, perhaps in ways that are highly relevant to some supposed miracles. Our present understanding of psychosomatic illness, for example, shows that it is not contrary to the laws of nature that someone who for years has seemed, to himself as well as to others, to be paralyzed should rapidly regain the use of his limbs. On the other hand, we can still be pretty confident that it is contrary to the laws of nature that a human being whose heart has stopped beating for forty-eight hours in ordinary circumstances—that is, without any special life-support systems—should come back to life, or that what is literally water should without addition or replacement turn into what is literally good-quality wine.

However, any problems there may be about establishing laws of nature are neutral between the parties to the present debate, Hume's followers and those who believe in miracles; for both these parties need the notion of a well-established law of nature. The miracle advocate needs it in order to be able to say that the alleged occurrence is a miracle, a violation of natural law by supernatural intervention, no less than Hume needs it for his argument against believing that this event has actually taken place.

It is therefore not enough for the defender of a miracle to cast doubt (as he well might) on the certainty of our knowledge of the law of nature that seems to have been violated. For he must himself say that this *is* a law of nature: otherwise the reported event will not be miraculous. That is, he must in effort *concede* to Hume that the antecedent improbability of this event is as high as it could be, hence that, apart from the testimony, we have the strongest possible grounds for believing that the alleged event did not occur. This event must, by the miracle advocate's own admission, be contrary to a genuine, not merely a supposed, law of nature, and therefore maximally improbable. It is this maximal improbability that the weight of the testimony would have to overcome.

One further improvement is needed in Hume's theory of testimony. It is well known that the agreement of two (or more) *independent* witnesses constitutes very powerful evidence. Two independent witnesses are more than twice as good as each of them on his own. The reason for this is plain. If just one witness says that *p*, one explanation of this would be that it was the case that *p* and that he has observed this, remembered it, and is now making an honest report; but there are many alternative explanations, for example that he observed something else which he mistook for its being that *p*, or is misremembering what he observed, or is telling a lie. But if two witnesses who can be shown to be quite independent of one another both say that *p*, while again one explanation is that each of them has observed this and remembered it and is reporting honestly, the alternative explanations are not now so easy. They face the question "How has there come about this *agreement* in their reports, if it was not the case that *p*? How have the witnesses managed to misobserve to the same effect, or to misremember in the same way, or to hit upon the same lie?" It is difficult for even a single liar to keep on telling a *consistent* false story; it is much harder for two or more liars to do so. Of course if there is any collusion between the witnesses, or if either has been influenced, directly or indirectly, by the other, or if both stories have a common source, this question is easily answered. That is why the independence of the witnesses is so important. This principle of the improbability of coincident error has two vital bearings upon the problem of miracles. On the one hand, it means that a certain sort of testimony can be more powerful evidence than Hume's discussion would suggest. On the other, it means that where we seem to have a plurality of reports, it is essential to check carefully whether they really are independent of one another; the difficulty of meeting this requirement would be an important supplement to the points made in Part II of Hume's essay. Not only in remote and barbarous times, but also in recent ones, we are usually justified in suspecting that what look like distinct reports of a remarkable occurrence arise from different strands of a single tradition between which there has already been communication.

We can now put together the various parts of our argument. Where there is some plausible testimony about the occurrence of what would appear to be a miracle, those who accept this as a miracle have the double burden of showing both that the event took place and that it violated the laws of nature. But it will be very hard to sustain this double burden. For whatever tends to show that it would have been a violation of natural law tends for that very reason to make it most unlikely that it actually happened. Correspondingly, those who deny the occurrence of a miracle have two alternative lines of defense. One is to say that the event may have occurred, but in accordance with the laws of nature. Perhaps there were unknown circumstances that made it possible; or perhaps what were thought to be the relevant laws of nature are not strictly laws; there may be as yet unknown kinds of natural causation through which this event might have come about. The other is to say that this event would indeed have violated natural law, but that for this very reason there is a very strong presumption against its having happened, which it is most unlikely that any testimony will be able to outweigh. Usually one of these defenses will be stronger than the other. For many supposedly miraculous cures, the former will be quite a likely sort of explanation, but for such feats as the bringing back to life of those who are really dead the latter will be more likely. But the *fork*, the disjunction of these two sorts of explanation, is as a whole a very powerful reply to any claim that a miracle has been performed.

However, we should distinguish two different contexts in which an alleged miracle might be discussed. One possible context would be where the parties in debate already both accept some general theistic doctrines, and the point at issue is whether a miracle has occurred which would enhance the authority of a specific sect or teacher. In this context supernatural intervention, though *prima facie* unlikely on any particular occasion, is, generally speaking, on the cards: it is not altogether outside the range of reasonable expectation for these parties. Since they agree that there is an omnipotent deity, or at any rate one or more powerful supernatural beings, they cannot find it absurd to suppose that such a being will occasionally interfere with the course of nature, and this *may* be one of these occasions. For example, if one were already a theist and a Christian, it would not be unreasonable to weigh seriously the evidence of alleged miracles as some indication whether the Jansenists or the Jesuits enjoyed more of the favor of the Almighty. But it is a very different matter if the context is that of fundamental debate about the truth of theism itself. Here one party to the debate is initially at least agnostic, and does not yet concede that there is a supernatural power at all. From this point of view the intrinsic improbability of a genuine miracle, as defined above, is very great, and one or other of the alternative explanations in our fork will always be much more likely—that is, either that the alleged event is not miraculous, or that it did not occur, that the testimony is faulty in some way.

This entails that it is pretty well impossible that reported miracles should provide a worthwhile argument for theism addressed to those who are initially inclined to atheism or even to agnosticism. Such reports can form no significant part of what, following Aquinas, we might call a *Summa contra Gentiles*, or what, following Descartes, we could describe as being addressed to infidels. Not only are such reports unable to carry any rational conviction on their own, but also they are unable even to contribute independently to the kind of accumulation or battery of arguments referred to in the Introduction. To this extent Hume is right, despite the inaccuracies we have found in his statement of the case.

One further point may be worth making. Occurrences are sometimes claimed to be literally, and not merely metaphorically, miracles, that is, to be genuine supernatural interventions into the natural order, which are not even *prima facie* violations of natural law, but at most rather unusual and unexpected, but very welcome. Thus the combination of weather conditions which facilitated the escape of the British Army from Dunkirk in 1940, making the Luftwaffe less than usually effective but making it easy for ships of all sizes to cross the Channel, is sometimes called a miracle. However, even if we accepted theism, and could plausibly assume that a benevolent deity would have favored the British rather than the Germans in 1940, this explanation would still be far less probable than that which treats it as a mere meteorological coincidence: such weather conditions can occur in the ordinary course of events. Here, even in the context of a debate among those who already accept theistic doctrines, the interpretation of the event as a miracle is much weaker than the rival natural explanation. *A fortiori*, instances of this sort are utterly without force in the context of fundamental debate about theism itself.

There is, however, a possibility which Hume's argument seems to ignore—though, as we shall see, he did not completely ignore it. The argument has been directed against the acceptance of miracles on testimony; but what, it may be objected, if one is not reduced to reliance on testimony, but has observed a miracle for oneself? Surprisingly, perhaps, this possibility does not make very much difference. The first of the above-mentioned lines of defense is still available: maybe the unexpected event that one has oneself observed did indeed occur, but in accordance with the laws of nature. Either the relevant circumstances or the operative laws were not what one had supposed them to be. But at least a part of the other line of defense is also available. Though one is not now relying literally on another witness or other witnesses, we speak not inappropriately of the evidence of our senses, and what one takes to be an observation of one's own is open to questions of the same sort as is the report of some other person. I may have misobserved what took place, as anyone knows who has ever been fooled by a conjurer or "magician," and, though this is somewhat less likely, I may be misremembering or deceiving myself after an interval of time. And of course, the corroboration of one or more independent witnesses would bring in again the testimony of others which it was the point of this objection to do without. Nevertheless, anyone who is fortunate enough to have carefully observed and carefully recorded, for himself, an apparently miraculous occurrence is no doubt rationally justified in taking it very seriously; but even here it will be in order to entertain the possibility of an alternative natural explanation.

As I said, Hume does not completely ignore this possibility. The Christian religion, he says, cannot at this day be believed by any reasonable person without a miracle. "Mere reason is insufficient to convince us of its veracity: And whoever is moved by *Faith* to assent to it, is conscious of a continued miracle in his own person, which subverts all the principles of his understanding."[4] But of course this is only a joke. What the believer is conscious of in his own person, though it may be a mode of thinking that goes against "custom and experience," and so is contrary to the ordinary rational principles of the understanding, is not, as an occurrence, a violation of natural law. Rather it is all too easy to explain immediately by the automatic communication of beliefs between persons and the familiar psychological processes of wish fulfilment, and ultimately by what Hume himself was later to call "the natural history of religion."

NOTES

1. The notion of basic laws of working is fully discussed in chaps. 8 and 9 of my *The Cement of the Universe: A Study of Causation* (Oxford: Oxford University Press, 1974 and 1980).

2. The distinction between physical and epistemic probability has been drawn in my Introduction; the exact form of statistical laws is discussed in chap. 9 of *The Cement of the Universe.*

3. David Hume, "Of Miracles," reprinted in *Miracles* (New York: Macmillan Publishing House, 1989), pp. 24–26.

4. Hume, "Of Miracles," p. 40.

SUGGESTED READING

Flew, Antony. "Parapsychology Revisited: Laws, Miracles and Repeatability, *The Humanist* 36 (May/June 1976): 28–30.

———. "Miracles," *Encyclopedia of Philosophy*, ed. Paul Edwards, vol. 5. New York: Macmillan, 1967.

Holland, R. F. "The Miraculous," *American Philosophical Quarterly* 2 (1965): 43–51.

McKinnon, Alistair, " 'Miracle' and 'Paradox,' " *American Philosophical Quarterly* 4 (October 1976).

Basinger, David, and Randall Basinger. *Philosophy and Miracle: The Contemporary Debate.* Lewiston, N.Y.: Edwin Mellen Press, 1986.

Brown, Colin. *Miracles and the Critical Mind* (Grand Rapids, Mich.: Eerdmans, 1983).

Lewis, C. S. *Miracles*, rev. ed. London: Collins, Fontana Books, 1960.

Odegard, Douglas. "Miracles and Good Evidence," *Religious Studies* 18 (1982): 37–46.

Walker, Ian. "Miracles and Violations," *International Journal for Philosophy of Religion* 13 (1982): 103–108.

Nowell-Smith, Patrick. "Miracles—The Philosophical Approach," *The Hibbert Journal* 48 (1950): 354–360.

Williams, T. C. *The Idea of the Miraculous: The Challenge of Science and Religion.* New York: St. Martin's Press, 1991.

PART NINE

LIFE AFTER DEATH

It has been said that belief in life after death is so important to us that, if God does not exist, we would have to invent God to satisfy this longing. Philosophers of religion too are interested in the question whether there is any reason to think that people can live subsequent to their death. The topic involves several questions.

First, given the fact of universal human mortality and bodily corruption, is life after death possible? The classical response is that life after death is possible because humans possess or are in essence a soul that can be immortal. The soul, the locus of one's personal identity and characterized by mental functions like memory, allows the individual person to survive bodily corruption, remember its past life, and possibly even perceive its own unique world through such abilities as mental telepathy.

Some, like Richard Swinburne, think that the soul can exist apart from the physical but are dubious that the soul could function disembodied. However, this presents no insurmountable difficulties for belief in life after death, for it is possible that after death God could create for a person another body that would allow the soul to function. Should death and the installment of the soul in a body occur many times, we would have the doctrine of reincarnation, a belief found in many nonwestern religions.

Serious difficulties surround the view that humans have a soul. To the traditional problem of how the spiritual soul interacts with the physical body might be added questions about how one reconciles this view with the evolution of human beings. Further, the fact that the genetic plays such an important role in determining mental abilities suggests that the body is necessary, if not sufficient, for the very structure of the mind. The mind is what the brain does.

Though traditionally those who denied the existence of a human soul denied immortality, John Hick recently has argued that it is possible for God to create a being with the same properties as the deceased, a being that would be identical with the deceased. That is, our existence is gap inclusive, so that sometime after our death we take up living where we left off when we died.

This position faces the problem that the recreated person might be a mere replica of, and not identical with, the deceased. This can be seen by noting that God could make multiple replicas of the person, so that we could not distinguish which was the real person (the deceased) and which was merely like that person. Of course, this objection hinges on the contention that there cannot be two beings continuous with a prior being, which is not true, for example, of amebas.

The second major question concerns whether there is any evidence that people live subsequent to their death. Philosophers traditionally have presented a priori arguments, sometimes drawn from considerations of the nature of the human soul (Plato), human desires (Thomas Aquinas), or the need to have an adequate grounding for the moral law (Immanuel Kant). Contemporary arguments focus on alleged paranormal and near-death experiences. For considerations of space, these arguments have not been included in this anthology, but can be found summarized in our companion volume, *Reason and Religious Belief.*

Lack of direct experience of life after death should not curtail the search for whether beliefs about such are justified. Here, as elsewhere, reason can only proceed so far. The believer will want to appeal to something more, namely, revelation, whereas the skeptic, with a differing noetic structure, will take a different path.

H. H. PRICE

The Soul Survives and Functions after Death

H. H. Price (1899–1984) attempts to give meaning to the idea of a next world inhabited by disembodied persons. In this world, disembodied beings entertain mental images, which would be real to those who have them and give the impression of perceiving physical objects. In such a world, imaging, centered around a fundamental body image, replaces sense-perception, while encounters with other disembodied persons occurs by telepathy. Price goes on to consider where this other world is, whether and in what sense it is real, in what sense it could be public as the joint product of many telepathically interacting minds, and finally the role of desires and memories in creating this world.

⌘

I am here only concerned with the conception of Survival; with the *meaning* of the Survival Hypothesis, and not with its truth or falsity. When we consider the Survival Hypothesis, whether we believe it or disbelieve it, what is it that we have in mind? Can we form any idea, even a rough and provisional one, of what a disembodied human life might be like? Supposing we cannot, it will follow that what is called the Survival Hypothesis is a mere set of words and not a hypothesis at all. The evidence adduced in favour of it might still be evidence for something, and perhaps for something important, but we should no longer have the right to claim that it is evidence for Survival. There cannot be evidence for something which is completely unintelligible to us.

Now let us consider the situation in which we find ourselves after seventy years of psychical research. A very great deal of work has been done on the problem of Survival. . . . Yet there are the widest differences of opinion about the result. A number of intelligent persons would maintain that we now have a very large mass of evidence in favour of Survival; that some of it is of very good quality indeed, and cannot be explained away unless we suppose that the supernormal cognitive powers of some embodied human minds are vastly more extensive and more accurate than we can easily believe them to be; in short, that on the evidence available the Survival Hypothesis is more probable than not. Some people—and not all of them are silly or credulous—would even maintain that the Survival Hypothesis is proved, or as near to being so as any empirical hypothesis can be. On the other hand, there are also many intelligent persons who entirely reject these conclusions. Some of them, no doubt, have not taken the trouble to examine the evidence. But others of them have; they may even have given years of

From *Immortality,* ed. Terence Penelhum. Reprinted by permission of Wadsworth Publishing Co.

study to it. They would agree that the evidence is evidence of *something*, and very likely of something important. But, they would say, it cannot be evidence of Survival; there *must* be some alternative explanation of it, however difficult it may be to find out. Why do they take this line? I think it is because they find the very conception of Survival unintelligible. The very idea of a 'discarnate human personality' seems to them a muddled or absurd one; indeed not an idea at all, but just a phrase—an emotionally exciting one, no doubt—to which no clear meaning can be given. . . .

Now why should it be thought that the very idea of life after death is unintelligible? Surely it is easy enough to conceive (whether or not it is true) that experiences might occur after Jones's death which are linked with experiences which he had before his death, in such a way that his personal identity is preserved? But, it will be said, the idea of after-death *experiences* is just the difficulty. What kind of experiences could they conceivably be? In a disembodied state, the supply of sensory stimuli is perforce cut off, because the supposed experient has no sense organs and no nervous system. There can therefore be no sense-perception. One has no means of being aware of material objects any longer; and if one has not, it is hard to see how one could have any emotions or wishes either. For all the emotions and wishes we have in this present life are concerned directly or indirectly with material objects, including of course our own organisms and other organisms, especially other human ones. In short, one could only be said to have experiences at all, if one is aware of some sort of a *world*. In this way, the idea of Survival is bound up with the idea of 'another world' or a 'next world.' Anyone who maintains that the idea of Survival is after all intelligible must also be claiming that we can form some conception, however rough and provisional, of what 'the next world' or 'the other world' might be like. . . .

The Next World, I think, might be conceived as a kind of dream-world. When we are asleep, sensory stimuli are cut off, or at any rate are prevented from having their normal effects upon our brain-centres. But we still manage to have experiences. It is true that sense-perception no longer occurs, but something sufficiently like it does. In sleep, our image-producing powers, which are more or less inhibited in waking life by a continuous bombardment of sensory stimuli, are released from this inhibition. And then we are provided with a multitude of objects of awareness, about which we employ our thoughts and towards which we have desires and emotions. Those objects which we are aware of behave in a way which seems very queer to us when we wake up. The laws of their behaviour are not the laws of physics. But however queer their behaviour is, it does not at all disconcert us at the time, and our personal identity is not broken.

In other words, my suggestion is that the Next World, if there is one, might be a world of mental images. Nor need such a world be so 'thin and unsubstantial' as you might think. Paradoxical as it may sound, there is nothing imaginary about a mental image. It is an actual entity, as real as anything can be. The seeming paradox arises from the ambiguity of the verb 'to imagine.' It does sometimes mean 'to have mental images.' But more usually it means 'to entertain propositions without believing them'; and very often they are false propositions, and moreover we *dis*believe them in the act of entertaining them. This is what happens, for example, when we read Shakespeare's play *The Tempest*, and that is why we say that Prospero and Ariel are 'imaginary characters.' Mental images are not in this sense imaginary at all. We do actually experience them, and they are no more imaginary than sensations. To avoid the paradox, though at the cost of some pedantry, it would be well to distinguish between *imagining* and *imaging*, and to have two different adjectives 'imaginary' and 'imagy.' In this terminology, it is imaging, and not imagining, that I wish to talk about; and the Next World, as I am trying to conceive of it, is an *imagy* world, but not on that account an imaginary one.

Indeed, to those who experience it an image-world would be just as 'real' as this present world is; and perhaps so like it, that they would have considerable difficulty in realising that they were dead. We are, of course, sometimes told in mediumistic communications that quite a lot of people do find it difficult to realise that they are dead; and this is just what we should expect if the Next World is an image-world. . . . So far as I can see, there might be a set of visual images related to each other perspectively, with front views and side views and back views all fitting neatly together in the way that ordinary visual appearances do now. Such a group of images might contain tactual images too. Similarly it might contain auditory images and smell images. Such a family of inter-related images would make a pretty good object. It would be quite a satisfactory substitute for the material objects which we perceive in this present life. And a whole world composed of such families of mental images would make a perfectly good world.

It is possible, however, and indeed likely, that some of those images would be what Francis Galton called *generic* images. An image representing a dog or a tree need not necessarily be an exact replica of some individual dog or tree one has perceived. It might rather be a representation of a *typical* dog or tree. Our memories are more specific on some subjects than on others. How specific they are, depends probably on the degree of interest we had in the individual objects or events at the time when we perceived them. . . . Left to our own resources, as we should be in the Other World, with nothing but our memories to depend on, we should probably be able to form only generic images of such objects. In this respect, an image-world would not be an exact replica of this one, not even of those parts of this one which we have actually perceived. To some extent it would be, so to speak, a generalised picture, rather than a detailed reproduction.

Let us now put our question in another way, and ask what kind of experience a disembodied human mind might be supposed to have. We can then answer that it might be an experience in which *imaging* replaces sense-perception; 'replaces' it, in the sense that imaging would perform much the same function as sense-perception performs now, by providing us with objects about which we could have thoughts, emotions and wishes. There is no reason why we should not be 'as much alive,' or at any rate *feel* as much alive, in an image-world as we do now in this present material world, which we perceive by means of our sense-organs and nervous systems. And so the use of the word 'survival' ('life after death') would be perfectly justifiable.

It will be objected, perhaps, that one cannot be said to be alive unless one has a body. But what is meant here by 'alive'? It is surely conceivable (whether or not it is true) that *experiences* should occur which are not causally connected with a physical organism. If they did, should we or should we not say that 'life' was occurring? I do not think it matters much whether we answer Yes or No. It is purely a question of definition. If you define 'life' in terms of certain very complicated physico-chemical processes, as some people would, then of course life after death is by definition impossible, because there is no longer anything to be alive. In that case, the problem of survival (*life* after bodily death) is misnamed. Instead, it ought to be called the problem of after-death *experiences.* And this is in fact the problem with which all investigators of the subject have been concerned. After all, what people want to know, when they ask whether we survive death, is simply whether experiences occur after death, or what likelihood, if any, there is that they do; and whether such experiences, if they do occur, are linked with each other and with *ante mortem* ones in such a way that personal identity is preserved. It is not physico-chemical processes which interest us, when we ask such questions. But there is another sense of the words 'life' and 'alive' which may be called the psychological sense; and in this sense 'being alive' just *means* 'having experiences of certain sorts.' In this psychological sense of the word 'life,' it is perfectly intelligible to ask whether there is life after death, even though life in the physiological sense does *ex hypothesi* come to an end when someone dies. Or, if you like, the question is whether one could *feel* alive after bodily death, even though (by hypothesis) one would not *be* alive at that time. It will be just enough to satisfy most of us if the *feeling* of being alive continues after death. It will not make a halfpennyworth of difference that one will not then *be* alive in the physiological or biochemical sense of the word.

It may be said, however, that 'feeling alive' (life in the psychological sense) cannot just be equated with having experiences in general. Feeling alive, surely, consists in having experiences of a special sort, namely *organic sensations*—bodily feelings of various sorts. In our present experience, these bodily feelings are not as a rule separately attended to unless they are unusually intense or unusually painful. They are a kind of undifferentiated mass in the background of consciousness. All the same, it would be said, they constitute our feeling of being alive; and if they were absent (as surely they must be when the body is dead) the feeling of being alive could not be there.

I am not at all sure that this argument is as strong as it looks. I think we should still feel alive—or alive enough—provided we experienced emotions and wishes, even if no organic sensations accompanied these experiences, as they do now. But in case I am wrong here, I would suggest that *images* of organic sensations could perfectly well provide what is needed. We can quite well image to ourselves what it feels like to be in a warm bath, even when we are not actually in one; and a person who has been crippled can image what it felt like to climb a mountain. Moreover, I would ask whether we do not feel alive when we are dreaming. It seems to me that we obviously do—or at any rate quite alive enough to go on.

This is not all. In an image-world, a dream-like world such as I am trying to describe, there is no reason at all why there should not be *visual* images resembling the body which one had in this present world. In this present life (for all who are not blind) visual percepts of one's own body form as it were the constant centre of one's perceptual world. It is perfectly possible that visual images of one's own body might perform the same function in the next. They might form the continuing centre or nucleus of one's image world, remaining more or less constant while other images altered. If this were so, we should have an additional reason for expecting that recently dead people would find it difficult to realise that they were dead, that is, disembodied. To all appearances they *would* have bodies just as they had before, and pretty much the same ones. But, of course, they might discover in time that these image-bodies were subject to rather peculiar causal laws. For example, it might be found that in an image-world our wishes tend *ipso facto* to fulfil themselves in a way they do not now. A wish to go to Oxford might be immediately followed by the occurrence of a vivid and detailed set of Oxford-like images; even though, at the moment before, one's images had resembled Piccadilly Circus or the palace of the Dalai Lama in Tibet. In that case, one would realise that 'going somewhere'—transferring one's body from one place to another—was a rather different process from what it had been in the physical world. Reflecting on such experiences, one might come to the conclusion that one's body was not after all the same as the physical body one had before death. One might conclude perhaps that it must be a 'spiritual' or 'psychical' body, closely resembling the old body in appearance, but possessed of rather different causal properties. It has been said, of course, that phrases like 'spiritual body' or 'psychical body' are utterly unintelligible, and that no conceivable empirical meaning could be given to such expressions. But I would suggest that they might be a way (rather a misleading way perhaps) of referring to a set of body-like images. . . .

I think, then, that there is no difficulty in conceiving that the experience of feeling alive could occur in the absence of a physical organism; or, if you prefer to put it so, a disembodied personality could *be* alive in the psychological sense, even though by definition it would not be alive in the physiological or biochemical sense.

Moreover, I do not see why disembodiment need involve the destruction of personal identity. It is, of course, sometimes supposed that personal identity depends on the continuance of a background of organic sensation—the 'mass of bodily feeling' mentioned before. (This may be called the Somato-centric Analysis of personal identity.) We must notice, however, that this background of organic sensation is not literally the same from one period of time to another. The very most that can happen is that the organic sensations which form the background of my experience now should be *exactly similar* to those which were the background of my experience a minute ago. And as a matter of fact the present ones need not *all* be exactly similar to the previous ones. I might have a twinge of toothache now which I did not have then. I may even have an overall feeling of lassitude now which I did not have a minute ago, so that the whole mass of bodily feeling, and not merely one part of it, is rather different; and this would not interrupt my personal identity at all. The most that is required is only that the majority (not all) of my organic sensations should be closely (not exactly) similar to those I previously had. And even this is only needed if the two occasions are close together in my private time series; the organic sensations I have now might well be very unlike those I used to have when I was one year old. I say 'in my private time series.' For when I wake up after eight hours of dreamless sleep my personal identity is not broken, though in the physical or public time series there has been a long interval between the last organic sensations I experienced before falling asleep, and the first ones I experience when I wake up. But if similarity, and not literal sameness, is all that is required of this 'continuing organic background,' it seems to me that the continuity of it could be perfectly well preserved if there were organic *images* after death very like the organic *sensations* which occurred before death.

As a matter of fact, this whole 'somato-centric' analysis of personal identity appears to me highly disputable. I should have thought that Locke was much nearer the truth when he said that personal identity depends on memory. But I have tried to show that even if the 'somato-centric' theory of personal identity is right, there is no reason why personal identity need be broken by bodily death, provided there are images after death which sufficiently resemble the organic sensations one had before; and this is very like what happens when one falls asleep and begins dreaming.

There is, however, another argument against the conceivability of a disembodied person, to which some present-day Linguistic Philosophers would attach great weight. It is neatly expressed by Mr. A.G.N. Flew when he says, 'People are what you meet.'. . .

As a matter of fact, however, we can quite easily conceive that 'meeting' of a kind might still be possible between discarnate experients. And therefore, even if we do make it part of the definition of 'a person,' that he is capable of being met by others, it will still make sense to speak of 'discarnate persons,' provided we allow that telepathy is possible between them. It is true that a special sort of telepathy would be needed; the sort which in this life produces *telepathic apparitions*. It would not be sufficient that A's thoughts or emotions should be telepathically affected by B's. If such telepathy were sufficiently prolonged and continuous, and especially if it were reciprocal, it would indeed have some of the characteristics of social intercourse; but I do not think we should call it 'meeting,' at any rate in Mr. Flew's sense of the word. It would be necessary, in addition, that A should be aware of something which could be called 'B's body,' or should have an experience not too unlike the experience of *seeing* another person in this life. This additional condition would be satisfied if A experienced a telepathic apparition of B. It would be necessary, further, that the telepathic apparition by means of which B 'announces himself' (if one may put it so) should be recognisably similar on different occasions. And if it were a case of meeting some person *again* whom one had previously known in this world, the telepathic apparition would have to be recognisably similar to the physical body which that person had when he was still alive.

There is no reason why an image-world should not contain a number of images which are telepathic apparitions; and if it did, one could quite intelligently speak of 'meeting other persons' in such a world. All the experiences I have when I meet another person in this present life could still occur, with only this difference, that percepts would be replaced by images. It would also be possible for another person to 'meet' me in the same manner, if I, as telepathic agent, could cause him to experience a suitable telepathic apparition, sufficiently resembling the body I used to have when he formerly 'met' me in this life.

I now turn to another problem which may have troubled some of you. If there be a next world, *where* is it? . . . Surely the next world, if it exists, must be somewhere; and yet, it seems, there is nowhere for it to be.

The answer to this difficulty is easy if we conceive of the Next World in the way I have suggested, as a dream-like world of mental images. Mental images, including dream images, are in a space of their own. They do have spatial properties. Visual images, for instance, have extension and shape, and they have spatial relations to one another. But they have no spatial relation to objects in the physical world. If I dream of a tiger, my tiger-image has extension and shape. The dark stripes have spatial relations to the yellow parts, and to each other; the nose has a spatial relation to the tail. Again, the tiger image as a whole may have spatial relations to another image in my dream, for example to an image resembling a palm tree. But suppose we have to ask how far it is from the foot of my bed, whether it is three inches long, or longer, or shorter; is it not obvious that these questions are absurd ones? We cannot answer them, not because we lack the necessary information or find it impracticable to make the necessary measurements, but because the questions themselves have no meaning. In the space of the physical world these images are nowhere at all. But in relation to other images of mine, each of them is somewhere. Each of them is extended, and its parts are in spatial relations to one another. There is no *a priori* reason why all extended entities must be in physical space.

If we now apply these considerations to the Next World, as I am conceiving of it, we see that the question 'where is it?' simply does not arise. An image-world would have a space of its own. We could not find it anywhere in the space of the physical world, but this would not in the least prevent it from being a spatial world all the same. If you like, it would be its own 'where.'. . .

It follows that when we speak of 'passing' from this world to the next, this passage is not to be thought of as any sort of movement in space. It should rather be thought of as a change of consciousness, analogous to the change which occurs when we 'pass' from waking experience to dreaming. It would be a change from the perceptual type of consciousness to another type of consciousness in which perception ceases and imaging replaces it, but unlike the change from waking consciousness to dreaming in being irreversible. . . .

I now turn to another difficulty. It may be felt that an image-world is somehow a deception and a sham, not a *real* world at all. I have said that it would be a kind of dream-world. Now when one has a dream in this life, surely the things one is aware of in the dream are not *real* things. No doubt the dreamer really does have various mental images. These images do actually occur. But this is not all that happens. As a result of having these images, the dreamer believes, or takes for granted, that various material objects exist and various physical events occur; and these beliefs are mistaken. For example, he believes that there is a wall in front of him and that by a mere effort of will he succeeds in flying over the top of it. But the wall did not really exist, and he did not really fly over the top of it. He was in a state of delusion. Because of the images which he did really have, there *seemed* to him to be various objects and events which did not really exist at all. Similarly, you may argue, it may *seem* to discarnate minds (if indeed there are such) that there is a world in which they live, and a world not unlike this one. If they have mental images of the appropriate sort, it may even *seem* to them that they have bodies not unlike the ones they had in this life. But surely they will be mistaken. . . .

I would suggest, however, that this argument about the 'delusiveness' or 'unreality' of an image-world is based on a confusion.

One may doubt whether there is any clear meaning in using the words 'real' and 'unreal' *tout court*, in this perfectly general and unspecified way. One may properly say, 'this is real silver, and that is not,' 'this is a real pearl and that is not,' or again 'this is a real pool of water, and that is only a mirage.' The point here is that something X is mistakenly believed to be something else Y, because it does resemble Y in some respects. It makes perfectly good sense, then, to say that X is not really Y. This piece of plated brass is not real silver, true enough. It only looks like silver. But for all that, it cannot be called 'unreal' in the unqualified sense, in the sense of not existing at all. Even the mirage is something, though it is not the pool of water you took it to be. It is a perfectly good set of visual appearances, though it is not related to other appearances in the way you thought it was; for example, it does not have the relations to tactual appearances, or to visual appearances from other places, which you expected it to have. You may properly say that the mirage is not a real pool of water, or even that it is not a real physical object, and that anyone who thinks it is must be in a state of delusion. But there is no clear meaning in saying that it is just 'unreal' *tout court*, without any further specification or explanation. In short, when the word 'unreal' is applied to something, one means that it is different from something else, with which it might be mistakenly identified; what that something else is may not be explicitly stated, but it can be gathered from the context.

What, then, could people mean by saying that a next world such as I have described would be 'unreal?' If they are saying anything intelligible, they must mean that it is different from something else, something else which it does resemble in some respects, and might therefore be confused with. And what is that something else? It is this present physical world in which we now live. An image-world, then, is only 'unreal' in the sense that it is not really physical, though it might be mistakenly thought to be physical by some of those who experience it. But this only amounts to saying that the world I am describing would be an *other* world, other than this present physical world, which is just what it ought to be; other than this present physical world, and yet sufficiently like it to be possibly confused with it, because images do resemble percepts. And what would this otherness consist in? First, in the fact that it is in a *space* which is other than physical space; secondly, and still more important, in the fact that the *causal laws* of an image-world would be different from the laws of physics. And this is also our ground for saying that the events we experience in dreams are 'unreal,' that is, not really physical, though mistakenly believed by the dreamer to be so. They do in some ways closely resemble physical events, and that is why the mistake is possible. But the causal laws of their occurrence are quite different, as we recognise when we wake up; and just occasionally we recognise it even while we are still asleep. . . .

Let us now try to explore the conception of a world of mental images a little more fully. Would it not be a '*subjective*' world? And surely there would be many *different* next worlds, not just one; and each of them would be private. Indeed, would there not be as many next worlds as there are discarnate minds, and each of them wholly private to the mind which experiences it? In short, it may seem that each of us, when dead, would have his own dream world, and there would be no common or public Next World at all.

'Subjective,' perhaps, is rather a slippery word. Certainly, an image world would have to be subjective in the sense of being mind-dependent, dependent for its existence upon mental processes of one sort or another; images, after all, are mental entities. But I do not think that such a world need be completely private, if telepathy occurs in the next life. . . . It is reasonable to suppose that in a disembodied state telepathy would occur more frequently than it does now. It seems likely that in this present life our telepathic powers are constantly being inhibited by our need to adjust ourselves to our physical environment. It even seems likely that many telepathic 'impressions' which we receive at the unconscious level are shut out from consciousness by a kind of biologically-motivated censorship. Once the pressure of biological needs is removed, we might expect that telepathy would occur continually, and manifest itself in consciousness by modifying and adding to the images which one experiences. (Even in this life, after all, some dreams are telepathic.)

If this is right, an image-world such as I am describing would not be the product of one single mind only, nor would it be purely private. It would be the joint-product of a group of telepathically-interacting minds and public to all of them. Nevertheless, one would not expect it to have unrestricted publicity. It is likely that there would still be *many* next worlds, a different one for each group of like-minded personalities. I admit I am not quite sure what might be meant by 'like-minded' and 'unlike-minded' in this connection. Perhaps we could say that two personalities are like-minded if their memories or their characters are sufficiently similar. It might be that Nero and Marcus Aurelius do not have a world in common, but Socrates and Marcus Aurelius do.

So far, we have a picture of many 'semi-public' next worlds, if one may put it so; each of them composed of mental images, and yet not wholly private for all that, but public to a limited group of telepathically-interacting minds. Or, if you like, after death everyone does have his own dream, but there is still some overlap between one person's dream and another's, because of telepathy.

I have said that such a world would be mind-dependent, even though dependent on a group of minds rather than a single mind. In what way would it be mind-dependent? Presumably in the same way as dreams are now. It would be dependent on the *memories* and the *desires* of the persons who experienced it. Their memories and their desires would determine what sort of images they had. If I may put it so, the 'stuff' or 'material' of such a world would come in the end from one's memories, and the 'form' of it from one's desires. To use another analogy, memory would provide the pigments, and desire would paint the picture. One might expect, I think, that desires which had been unsatisfied in one's earthly life would play a specially important part in the process. That may seem an agreeable prospect. But there is another which is less agreeable. Desires which had been *repressed* in one's earthly life, because it was too painful or too disgraceful to admit that one had them, might also play a part, and perhaps an important part, in determining what images one would have in the next. And the same might be true of repressed memories. It may be suggested that what Freud (in one stage of his thought) called 'the censor'—the force or barrier or mechanism which keeps some of our desires and memories out of consciousness, or only lets them in when they disguise themselves in symbolic and distorted forms—operates only in this present life and not in the next. However we conceive of 'the censor,' it does seem to be a device for enabling us to adapt ourselves to our environment. And when we no longer have an environment, one would expect that the barrier would come down.

We can now see that an after-death world of mental images can also be quite reasonably described in the terminology of the Hindu thinkers as 'a world of desire' (*Kama Loka*). Indeed, this is just what we should expect if we assume that dreams, in this present life, are the best available clue to what the next life might be like. Such a world could also be described as 'a world of memories'; because imaging, in the end, is a function of memory, one of the ways in which our memory-dispositions manifest themselves. But this description would be less apt, even though correct as far as it goes. To use the same rather inadequate language as before, the 'materials' out of which an image-world is composed would have to come from the memories of the mind or group of minds whose world it is. But it would be their desires (including those repressed in earthly life) which determined the ways in which these memories were used, the precise kind of dream which was built up out of them or on the basis of them.

It will, of course, be objected that memories cannot exist in the absence of a physical brain, nor yet desires, nor images either. But this proposition, however plausible, is after all just an empirical hypothesis, not a necessary truth. Certainly there is empirical evidence in favour of it. But there is also empirical evidence against it. Broadly speaking one might say, perhaps, that the 'normal' evidence tends to support this Materialistic or Epiphenomenalist theory of memories, images and desires, whereas the 'supernormal' evidence on the whole tends to weaken the Materialist or Epiphenomenalist theory of human personality (of which this hypothesis about the brain-dependent character of memories, images and desires is a part). Moreover, any evidence which directly supports the Survival Hypothesis (and there is quite a lot of evidence which does, provided we are prepared to admit that the Survival Hypothesis is intelligible at all) is *pro tanto* evidence against the Materialistic conception of human personality.

In this lecture, I am not of course trying to argue in favour of the Survival Hypothesis. I am only concerned with the more modest task of trying to make it intelligible. All I want to maintain, then, is that there is nothing self-contradictory or logically absurd in the hypothesis that memories, desires and images can exist in the absence of a physical brain. The hypothesis may, of course, be false. My point is only that it is not absurd; or, if you like, that it is at any rate intelligible, whether true or not.

RICHARD SWINBURNE

The Soul Needs a Brain to Continue to Function

According to Richard Swinburne (1934–) the function but not the existence of a soul depends on a functioning physical brain. Thus, the soul can continue to exist but cannot function after death. Many philosophers now agree that it is unlikely that the soul continues to exist after death, arguments from psychical research and philosophers like Plato notwithstanding. However, since there is no natural law requiring the connection of souls with brains, the way is open for a metaphysical theory like theism to claim that it is possible that God could create the requisite conditions under which the soul could live and function after death. For example, God might create a different body.

⌘

A man's having a mental life must be understood as a non-bodily part of the man, his soul, having a mental life. . . .

THE EXISTENCE OF THE SOUL

What I have argued so far is that without a functioning brain, the soul will not function (i.e. have conscious episodes)—not that it will not exist. But what does it mean to suppose that the soul exists at some time without functioning? The distinction between existence and functioning is clear enough in the case of a material substance, which has some sort of life (e.g. a plant) or some sort of working (e.g. a machine). The substance continues to exist so long as the matter of which it is made continues to exist in roughly the same shape (with the possibility perhaps of gradual replacement of parts). But it functions only so long as normal life-processes or machine-use continue. The clock exists, when it no longer tells the time, so long as the parts remain joined in roughly the normal way; and a dead tree is still a tree, although it no longer takes in water through its roots and sunlight through its leaves.

The distinction is not, however, at all clear in the case of the soul, an immaterial substance. The soul functions while it is the subject of conscious episodes—while it has sensations or thoughts or purposes. But is it still there when the man is asleep, having no conscious episodes? This calls for a decision of what (if anything) we are to mean by saying of some soul that it exists but is not functioning.

We suppose that persons continue to exist while asleep, having no conscious life. In saying that some such person still exists, we mean, I suggest, that the sleeping body will again by normal processes give rise to a conscious life, or can be caused to give rise to a conscious life (e.g. by shaking it), a conscious life which will be the life of the person existing before sleep. Now, we could describe this latter fact by saying that, although persons only exist while they are conscious, the bodies which they previously owned continue to exist during the periods of unconsciousness and become thereafter the bodies of persons again (indeed the same persons who previously owned those bodies). However, that would be a very unnatural way to talk, largely because it has the consequence that certain substances (persons) are continually popping in and out of existence. Although there seems to me nothing contradictory in allowing to a substance many beginnings of existence, it seems a less cumbersome way to describe the cited fact to say that persons exist while not conscious, and mean by this that normal bodily processes or available artificial techniques can make those persons conscious. This will have the consequence that persons normally have only one beginning of existence during their life on Earth.

Our grounds for saying that persons exist while not conscious are similar to the grounds for saying that persons have desires and beliefs when they are not aware of them, i.e. that they can easily be made aware of them and that those desires and beliefs will influence their actions when they are put in appropriate circumstances.

Conscious persons consist of body and soul. We could say that souls exist only while conscious; while a person is asleep, his soul ceases to exist but it is made to exist again when he is woken up. But this would be a cumbersome way of talking. It is better to understand by a soul existing when not functioning that normal bodily processes on their own will, or available artificial techniques can, make that soul function. In saying this I am laying down rules for the use of a technical term, 'soul.' With this usage, a soul exists while its owner exists; and a soul will normally have only one beginning of existence during a man's life on Earth. . . .

Four thousand million years of evolution produced man, a body and soul in continuing interaction. A human soul is more dependent for its development on its own states than is an animal soul, for it has complex beliefs and desires kept in place and changing in accord with other beliefs and desires. Other animals having only much simpler beliefs and desires are much more dependent for their continuing beliefs and desires directly on their bodily states. Can this complex evolved human soul survive on its own apart from the body which sustains it? I have argued so far that the functioning of the human soul (i.e. its having conscious episodes) is guaranteed by the functioning of the brain currently connected with it (connected, in that the soul's acquisition of beliefs about its surroundings and action upon those surroundings is mediated by that brain). I have considered what it is for a man or his soul to exist unconscious, and I have argued that that was a matter which required to be settled by definition. The definition which I suggested was that a soul exists if normal bodily processes or available artificial techniques can bring the man to be conscious, i.e. his soul to function again.

When the body dies and the brain ceases to function, the evidence suggests that the soul will cease to function also. For that evidence suggests that the soul functions only when the brain has rhythms of certain kinds, and at death the brain ceases to function altogether. If the soul does not function before there is a functioning brain, or during deep sleep, when the brain is not functioning at a certain level, surely it will not function after there ceases to be a functioning brain. However, there are arguments and evidence of less usual kinds which purport to show that things are different after death from what they are before birth.

Before we face the question of whether the soul can function without the functioning of the brain currently connected with it, we must consider the question of whether, after death, the brain which ceases to function at death can be made to function again and whether thereby the soul can be revived.

CAN THE BRAIN BE REACTIVATED?

A crucial problem is that we do not know how much of the brain that was yours has to be reassembled and within what time interval in order that we may have *your* brain and so your soul function again. We saw this earlier in the split brain cases. If both half-brains are transplanted into empty skulls and the transplants take, both subsequent persons will satisfy to some extent the criterion of apparent memory (as well as the brain criterion) for being the original person. One subsequent person might satisfy the criterion better than the other, and that would be evidence that he was the original person; but the evidence could be misleading. The situation is equally unclear with possible developments at death.

Suppose you die of a brain haemorrhage which today's doctors cannot cure, but your relatives take your corpse and put it straight into a very deep freeze in California. Fifty years later your descendants take it out of the freeze; medical technology has improved and the doctors are able quickly to mend your brain, and your body is then warmed up. The body becomes what is clearly the body of a living person, and one with your apparent memory and character. Is it you? Although we might be mistaken, the satisfaction of the criterion of apparent memory (together with the—at any rate partial—satisfaction of the criterion of brain continuity) would suggest that we ought to say 'Yes.' So long as the same brain is revived, the same functioning soul would be connected with it—whatever the time interval. But what if the brain is cut up into a million pieces and then frozen? Does the same hold? Why should there be any difference? Suppose that the brain is reduced to its component atoms; and then these are reassembled either by chance or because they have been labelled radioactively. Again, if the subsequent person makes your memory claims, surely we ought to say that it is you. But how many of the original atoms do we need in the original locations? That we do not know. So long as the subsequent person had many similar atoms in similar locations in his brain, he would claim to have been you. So, the criterion of apparent memory will be satisfied. Total non-satisfaction of the brain criterion would defeat the claims of apparent memory (in the absence of any general failure of coincidence in results between these criteria). But it remains unclear and indeed insoluble exactly how much of the original brain is needed to provide satisfaction of the brain criterion.

This problem of how much of the original body is physically necessary when other matter is added to it so as to make a fully functioning body, in order that the original soul may be present and function, is a problem which concerned the thinkers of the early Christian centuries and of the Middle Ages. They considered the imaginary case of the cannibal who eats nothing but human flesh. Given that both the cannibal and his victims are to be brought to life in the General Resurrection, to whom will the flesh of the cannibal belong? Aquinas[1] begins his answer by saying that 'if something was materially present in many men, it will rise in him to whose perfection it belonged,' i.e. that that part of the body which is necessary for a man being the person he is will belong to him in the General Resurrection. But what part is that, and what guarantee is there that the matter of that part cannot come to form the essential part of a different man who cannot therefore be reconstituted at the same time as the original man (given the operation of normal processes)? Aquinas goes on to produce an argument that the 'radical seed' (i.e. the sperm, which according to Aristotle formed the original matter of the embryo) forms the minimum essential bodily core around which a man could be rebuilt. But we know now, as Aquinas did not, that the sperm does not remain as a unit within the organism, and there seems to me no reason why all the atoms which originally formed it should not be lost from the body, and indeed come to form parts of original cells of many subsequent men. The atoms of the original cell are not therefore the most plausible candidate for being the part of the body physically necessary for human personal identity. Aquinas's problem remains without modern solution.

Nevertheless, although neurophysiology cannot tell us which part of his brain is physically necessary for the embodiment of a given man, it does tell us, as I argued earlier, that some of the brain is thus necessary. For the functioning of a given human soul, there has to be a man whose brain contains certain of the matter of his original brain (but which matter we do not know), similarly arranged. A certain amount of the original brain matter has to be reassembled in a similar arrangement and reactivated by being joined to other brain matter and a body if the soul is to function again. And how likely is it that physical processes will bring about such a reassembly? As the time since death increases, and brain cells and then brain molecules are broken up, burnt by fire, or eaten by worms—it becomes very, very unlikely indeed that chance will reassemble them; or even that human agents can do so for they will not be able to re-identify the atoms involved. . . . I conclude that it is very, very unlikely (and with increasing time virtually impossible) that after death souls will again have reassembled the brain basis which we know makes them function.

Is there any good reason to suppose that the soul continues to function without the brain functioning? Arguments to show that the soul continues to function without the brain functioning may be divided into three groups, involving different amounts of theoretical structure, to reach their conclusions. First, we may consider arguments which purport to show that certain men have survived death, in the sense that their souls have functioned without their brains functioning, directly—i.e. without needing first to establish anything about the nature of the soul or any more systematic metaphysical structure. Arguments of this kind may be called parapsychological arguments.

ARGUMENTS FROM PARAPSYCHOLOGY

First, there is the alleged evidence of reincarnation, that souls function in new bodies with new brains on Earth. There are Indian children who claim to remember having lived a certain past life, and whose memory claims coincide with the events of some real past life about which—allegedly—they could not have learnt by what they were told or had read.[2] Now, it is of course open to serious question whether perhaps those Indian children had read or were told or learnt in some other perfectly normal way the details of those past lives. But even if for a few Indian children there was this coincidence between their memory claims and the events of a certain past person's life, without there being any normal cause of the accuracy of their memory claims that would not be enough evidence to show their identity with those persons. For, given the general coincidence of sameness of memory with continuity of brain, we must take continuity of brain as a criterion of identity; and the nonsatisfaction of that in the case of the few Indian children (who do not have the same brain matter as the cited past persons), must remain substantial evidence against the supposition that they are those persons.

Next, there is the alleged evidence of spiritualism, that souls function without bodies or with new bodies and brains in another world. Mediums purport to have telepathic communication with dead persons. The evidence that they do is allegedly provided by the knowledge of the details of the dead person's life on Earth (not obtainable by the medium by normal means) which the medium's reports of the telepathic communications reveal. In the reincarnation case there is no doubt that there exists in the present a living conscious person; the debatable question concerns his identity with the past person. In the spiritualism case the crucial issue concerns whether there is a conscious person with whom the medium is in communication.

A serious issue in medium cases, like the similar issue in the supposed reincarnation cases, concerns the source of the mysterious knowledge. Perhaps the medium gets her knowledge from some spy who has done research on the dead person's life. But even if investigation showed clearly that the mediums had gained their knowledge of the past lives of dead persons by no normal route, the evidence would still, I suggest, not support the hypothesis of telepathic communication with the dead. For also compatible with the evidence would be the hypothesis that the mediums have clairvoyance—they see directly into the past and acquire their knowledge thus.

(Adopting the latter hypothesis would involve supposing either that the mediums were deceiving us about the kind of experiences they were having (apparent two-way traffic with a living person), or that they were deceiving themselves, or that their experiences were illusory.) On the choice between the two hypotheses there seem to me to be two important reasons for preferring the clairvoyance hypothesis. First, there are no cross-checks between mediums about the alleged present experiences of the dead in the afterlife. Mediums never give independently verifiable reports on this. Secondly, their reports about the present alleged experiences of the dead are themselves very banal. Yet one would expect because of the total lack of dependence of the dead on their past bodies, that they would live in a very different world, and that this would emerge in their reports on that world.[3]

Finally, there is the interesting and recently published alleged evidence that souls function while their bodies are out of action. There has been careful analysis of the experiences of those who clinically were as good as dead and then recovered. Such experiences are often called 'near-death experiences.'[4] Fifteen per cent of subjects resuscitated after being in such a condition report strange experiences of one of two kinds. Many of them report the following 'transcendental experiences':

> an initial period of distress followed by profound calm and joy; out-of-the-body experiences with the sense of watching resuscitation events from a distance; the sensation of moving rapidly down a tunnel or along a road, accompanied by a loud buzzing or ringing noise or hearing beautiful music; recognising friends and relatives who have died previously; a rapid review of pleasant incidents from throughout the life as a panoramic playback (in perhaps twelve per cent of cases); a sense of approaching a border or frontier and being sent back; and being annoyed or disappointed at having to return from such a pleasant experience—"I tried not to come back," in one patient's words. Some describe frank transcendent experiences and many state that they will never fear death again. Similar stories have been reported from the victims of accidents, falls, drowning, anaphylaxis, and cardiac or respiratory arrest.[5]

Resuscitated patients other than those who had transcendental experiences have undergone 'a wide variety of vivid dreams, hallucinations, nightmares and delusions,' but some of those who had transcendental experiences also experienced these and sharply distinguished between the two kinds of experience. The 'dreams' were regarded as dreams, and were quickly forgotten; the 'supposed glimpses of a future life' were regarded as real and permanently remembered. These glimpses were reported as having occurred at moments when 'breathing had ceased, the heart had stopped beating, and the patients showed no visible signs of life.' The principle of credulity might suggest that we ought to take such apparent memories seriously, especially in view of the considerable coincidences between them, as evidence that what subjects thought they experienced, they really did. But although the subjects referred these experiences to moments at which the heart had stopped beating, etc., I do not know of any evidence that at these moments their brains had ceased to function. And if the brain was still functioning then, what the evidence would show is not that the soul may function when the brain does not, but only that its perceptual experiences (i.e. sensations and acquisitions of belief about far away places) are not dependent on normal sensory input.

The same conclusion will follow with respect to the considerable but not overwhelming evidence of those resuscitated patients who had experiences of the other strange kind, 'out-of-body-experiences,' i.e. being able to view their own bodies and events in the operating theatre from a distance, obtaining thereby information which they would not have been able to obtain by normal means (e.g. having visual experiences of events which they would not have got from use of their eyes, such as views of parts of the theatre hidden from their eyes).[6] This again suggests that the subject's acquisition of information is dependent on some factor quite other than normal sensory input to the brain. But again I know of no evidence that these experiences occurred while the brain was not functioning; and so the available evidence does not support the suggestion that the soul can function without the brain functioning.

My conclusion on parapsychology is that it provides no good evidence that the soul continues to function without the brain to which it is currently connected, functioning.

ARGUMENTS FOR NATURAL SURVIVAL

The second class of arguments purporting to show that the soul survives death purport to show from a consideration of what the soul is like when it functions normally that its nature is such that the failure of the brain to function would make no difference to the operation of the soul. Such arguments verge from very general arguments of what the soul must be like to be conscious at all to arguments which appeal to particular empirical data.

Dualist philosophers of the past have usually affirmed the natural immortality of the soul—that the soul has such a nature, or the laws of nature are such, that (barring suspension of natural laws) it will continue to function forever. There have been a variety of general arguments for the natural immortality of the soul. Each argument has, in my view, its own fallacies; and the fallacies being fairly evident today, there is no need for any extensive discussion of such arguments. (Expositions of the arguments do, incidentally, usually suffer from confusing the existence of the soul with its functioning; wrongly supposing that when it exists, necessarily it will function.)

To illustrate the fallacies of such arguments, I take just one famous argument, put forward by Plato.[7] Plato argues that the soul being an immaterial thing is unextended, and so does not have parts; but the destruction of a thing consists in separating from each other its parts; whence it follows that souls cannot be destroyed and must continue to exist forever.

Now certainly the normal way by which most material objects cease to exist is that they are broken up into parts. The normal end of a table is to be broken up; likewise for chairs, houses, and pens. But this need not be the way in which a material object ceases to exist. Things cease to exist when they lose their essential properties. The essential properties of a table include being solid. If a table was suddenly liquified, then, even if its constituent molecules remained arranged in the shape of a table by being contained in a table-shaped mould, the table would have ceased to exist. So if even material objects can cease to exist without being broken up into parts, souls surely can cease to exist by some other route than by being broken up into parts. . . .

IS THE SOUL NATURALLY EMBODIED?

If it cannot be shown that the soul has a nature so as to survive death without its connected brain functioning, can it be shown that the soul has a nature such that its functioning is dependent on that of the brain with which it is connected? Can we show that there is a natural law which (i) connects consciousness of a soul with the functioning of some material system, and (ii) connects the consciousness of each soul with the functioning of a particular material system; so that of natural necessity a soul can only function if the brain or other complex system with which it is at some time connected continues to function?

The answer given [previously] is that this cannot be shown. It has not been shown and probably never can be shown that there is any naturally necessary connection of these kinds between soul and body. All we are ever likely to get is correlations—between this kind of brain-event and that kind of mental event. And in the absence of a theory which explains why a material system of this kind is needed to produce a soul, how this sort of physical change will produce this kind of mental state, how just so much of the brain and no more is needed for the continuity of a certain soul (as opposed to the mere functioning of a soul with similar apparent memories), we have no grounds for saying that souls *cannot* survive the death of their brains. We do not know and are not likely to find out what if any natural necessity governs the functioning of souls.

The situation is simply that the fairly direct kinds of evidence considered so far give no grounds for supposing that anyone has survived death, but we know of no reason to suppose that it is not possible for anyone to survive death. The situation is thus similar to that in many areas of enquiry when no one has yet found a so-and-so but no one has shown that so-and-sos do not exist. Maybe there are living persons on other planets, naturally occurring elements with atomic numbers of over 1,000, or magnetic monopoles; but as yet no one has found them. Someone may argue that failure to find something when you have looked for it is evidence that it does not exist. But that is so only if you would recognize the object when you found it, and if there is a limited region within which the object can exist and you have explored quite a lot of the region. Failure to find oil in the English Channel after you have drilled in most parts of it, or to find the Abominable Snowman if you have explored most of the Himalayas, is indeed evidence that the thing does not exist. But that is hardly the case with souls whose brains have ceased to function. Maybe they are reincarnate in new bodies and brains on Earth but, as they have lost their memories, the evidence of their identity has gone. Or maybe they are where we cannot at present look. They may still function without being embodied . . . and so there be no place which they occupy. Or if they are re-embodied in another body with another brain, they may be anywhere in this universe or some other. Failure to find souls who have survived death shows no more than that if they do exist, they are not in the very few places where we have looked for them or that if they are, the marks of their identity (e.g. apparent memories of past lives) have been removed. In the absence of any further evidence as to whether souls do survive death we can only remain agnostic and wait until further evidence does turn up.

EVIDENCE OF SURVIVAL VIA METAPHYSICAL THEORY

There is however a third kind of evidence about whether men survive death which we have not yet considered. This is evidence of a wide ranging character which is most simply explained by a very general metaphysical theory of the world, which has as its consequence that human souls survive death as a result of their nature or as a result of the predictable action of some agent who has the power to bring them to life.

One such theory is the Hindu-Buddhist metaphysic of karma, a deep law of retribution in nature whereby an agent who lives a life thereafter lives another in which he gets the deserts (reward or punishment) for the previous life. (The establishment of such a system would have the consequence that, despite the lack of evidence for this on which I commented [previously], souls exist before birth; in order to be reborn they must then normally lose much of the character which, I have argued, comes to characterize the soul by the time of death.)

Another such theory is of course Christian theism. The theist has first to argue for the existence of God, a person (in a wide sense) of infinite power, wisdom, goodness, and freedom. He may argue that the existence of God provides the simplest explanation of the existence of the universe, the virtual total regularity of its behaviour in its conformity to natural laws, and various more particular phenomena within the universe. It would then follow that God, being omnipotent, would have the power to give to souls life after death (and if there is no natural law which ties the functioning of a soul to the operation of a brain, God would not need to suspend natural laws in order to do this). The Christian theist will need further to show that God intends to bring souls to function after death. He could show this either by showing that it was an obligation on an omnipotent being to do such a thing, and so that, being good, God would do it; or by showing that God had announced his intention of doing this (e.g. by doing something which God alone could do such as suspending a law of nature, in connection with the work of a prophet as a sign that the prophet who had said that God so intended was to be trusted).

It will be evident that any argument via metaphysical theory to the survival of death by human souls will have a lengthy and complicated structure. But of course those who produce such arguments are equally concerned about most of the other things which need to be proved on the way. Few people are interested in the existence of God solely for its value in proving life after death. And if I am right in my claim that we cannot show that the soul has a nature such that it survives 'under its own steam,' and that we cannot show that it has a nature such that it cannot survive without its sustaining brain, the only kind of argument that can be given is an argument which goes beyond nature, i.e. that shows there is something beyond the natural order embodied in laws of nature, and that the operation of that something is to some extent predictable.

If God did give to souls life after death in a new body or without a body, he would not in any way be violating natural laws—for, if I am right, there are no natural laws which dictate what will happen to the soul after death. The soul doesn't have a nature which has consequences for what will happen to it subsequent to the dissolution of its links to the body.

In the last chapter I argued that the human soul at death had a structure, a system of beliefs and desires which might be expected to be there to some degree in the soul if that soul were to be revived. If a man does survive death, he will take his most central desires and beliefs with him, which is the kind of survival for which, I suspect, most men hope. In hoping to survive death, a man hopes not only that subsequent to his death, he will have experiences and perform actions. He hopes also to take with him a certain attitude to the world. That attitude certainly does not always include all aspects of a man's present character. Much, no doubt, many a man would be happy to dispense with. But it does include some of his character, and that part just because it is the part which he desires should continue, is the most central part.

Note that if there does occur a general resurrection of souls with new bodies in some other world, yet with apparent memories of their past lives (or a general reincarnation on Earth with such memories), they would have grounds for reidentifying each other correctly. For then the general failure of the results of the criterion of bodily continuity to coincide with those of apparent memory would by arguments [I have offered elsewhere] justifiably lead us to abandon the former criterion and rely entirely on the latter. Not merely is a general resurrection logically possible but it would be known by the subjects to have occurred.

CONCLUSION

The view of the evolved human soul which I have been advocating may be elucidated by the following analogy. The soul is like a light bulb and the brain is like an electric light socket. If you plug the bulb into the socket and turn the current on, the light will shine. If the socket is damaged or the current turned off, the light will not shine. So, too, the soul will function (have a mental life) if it is plugged into a functioning brain. Destroy the brain or cut off the nutriment supplied by the blood, and the soul will cease to function, remaining inert. But it can be revived and made to function again by repairing or reassembling the brain—just as the light can be made to shine again by repairing the socket or turning on the current. But now, my analogy breaks down slightly (as all analogies do—else they would not be analogies). Humans can repair light sockets. But there is a practical limit to the ability of humans to repair brains; the bits get lost. Humans can move light bulbs and put them into entirely different sockets. But no human knows how to move a soul from one body and plug it into another; nor does any known natural force do this. Yet the task is one involving no contradiction and an omnipotent God could achieve it; or maybe there are other processes which will do so. And just as light bulbs do not have to be plugged into sockets in order to shine (loose wires can be attached to them), maybe there are other ways of getting souls to function than by plugging them into brains. But investigation into the nature of the soul does not reveal those ways. And humans cannot discover what else is needed to get souls to function again, unless they can discover the ultimate force behind nature itself.

NOTES

1. *Summa Contra Gentiles*, 4. 81. 12 and 13. (Book IV, translated under the title *On the Truth of the Catholic Faith*, Book IV, by C. J. O'Neill, Image Books, New York, 1957.)

2. For references to the literature, see John Hick, *Death and Eternal Life* (London: Collins, 1976), pp. 373–78.

3. On the alleged evidence of spiritualism, see John Hick, op. cit., ch. 7.

4. There is a brief and well-balanced survey of this evidence in Paul and Linda Badham, *Immortality or Extinction?* (London: Macmillan, 1982), ch. 5. My summary of the evidence is based on this chapter, but I also make use of a very careful and balanced account of a new programme of investigations by Michael B. Sabom, *Recollections of Death* (New York: Harper and Row, 1982).

5. Lancet, 24 June 1978, quoted in Badham, op. cit.

6. On this, see Sabom, op. cit., chs. 3, 6, 7, and 8.

7. *Phaedo* 78b–80c.

LINDA BADHAM

Problems with Accounts of Life after Death

Linda Badham (1950–) raises objections to various conceptions of life after death. She argues that people who believe that we will be resurrected with the same body we now have encounter two problems: that we share atoms with other persons over a lifetime and that such a resurrected body would again have to face its mortality. Badham explains that the claim that the new body is a reconstituted one fails to distinguish the same person from its replica. She says that the case for immortality of the soul fails to understand a person's intrinsic connection with his or her body and encounters the problem of deciding which beings have or do not have souls given the evolution of the species. Finally, Badham observes that near-death experiences do not require a theistic interpretation; indeed, they invoke all the problems facing a dualist. She concludes that there is no good reason to believe that life after death or immortality is possible.

⌘

It is a popularly held view that science and religion are antithetical. And this view is supported by the sociological fact that leading scholars and scientists are significantly less likely to be Christian than other groups in society.[1] Yet even so, there are a number of very eminent scientists, and particularly physicists, who claim that there is no real conflict between their scientific and religious beliefs.[2] And many Christian apologists have drawn comfort from such claims in an age where the tide of secularism threatens to engulf the ancient citadel of Christian belief.[3] However, I have my doubts as to whether or not Christianity is secure from attack by science in general on some of its most crucial tenets. And, in particular, what I want to argue in this chapter is that the implications of modern science are far more damaging to doctrines of life after death than many Christian writers have supposed.

RESURRECTION OF THE BODY (THIS FLESH)

Although many might think that belief in the resurrection of this flesh at the end of time is now unthinkable, it has to be recognized that this is the form

From *Death and Immortality in the Religions of the World*, ed. Paul Badham and Linda Badham. Reprinted by permission of Paragon Press.

that orthodox Christian belief took from at least the second century onwards. Thus the Apostles' Creed affirms belief in the resurrection of the flesh[4]; the Nicene Creed looks for the "upstanding of the dead bodies"[5]; and the Christian Fathers were utterly explicit that the resurrection was definitely a physical reconstitution.[6] Moreover, such belief is still Catholic orthodoxy: a recent *Catholic Catechism for Adults* declares that each one of us will rise one day "the same person he was, in the same flesh made living by the same spirit."[7]. . . Hence it seems reasonable to suppose that this form of resurrection belief is still held among Christians. Yet a minimal knowledge of modern science seems sufficient to undermine it completely.

First, there is the problem that 'this flesh' is only temporarily mine. I am not like a machine or artifact, which keeps its atoms and molecules intact throughout its existence, save for those lost by damage or replaced during repair. Rather, I am a biological system in dynamic equilibrium (more or less) with my environment, in that I exchange matter with that environment continually. As J. D. Bernal writes, "It is probable that none of us have more than a few atoms with which we started life, and that even as adults we probably change most of the material of our bodies in a matter of a few months."[8] Thus it might prove an extremely difficult business to resurrect 'this' flesh at the end of time, for the atoms that will constitute me at the moment of death will return to the environment and will doubtless become part of innumerable other individuals. Augustine discussed the case of cannibals having to restore the flesh they had "borrowed" as an exception.[9] But in the light of our current knowledge, shared atoms would seem the rule rather than the exception.

Moreover, there is the further problem that even if the exact atoms that constituted me at death could all be reassembled without leaving some other people bereft of vital parts, then the reconstituted body would promptly expire again. For whatever caused the systems' failure in my body, which led to my death originally, would presumably still obtain if the body exactly as it was prior to death were remade. But perhaps we can overcome this problem with a fairly simple proviso: the resurrection body should be identical to the body that died, malfunctions apart. After all, it might be said, we have no difficulty in accepting our television set returned in good working order from the repair shop after a breakdown as one and the same television set that we took to be repaired, even though some or even several of its components have been replaced. But people are not television sets. What counts as malfunction? Increasing age usually brings some diminution in physical and mental powers. Are all these to be mended too? How much change can a body take and still be the same person? Nor is it possible to suggest that the resurrection environment might be such as to reverse the effects of aging and disease. For this move implies such a great change in the properties of the matter that is 'this flesh' as to make it dubious whether 'this' flesh really had been resurrected. The more one actually fills out the vague notion of the resurrection of the same flesh that perished, the more problems arise.

And even if the problem of reconstituting each one of us to the same (healthy) flesh he was (or might have been) could be overcome, there would remain the question of where we could all be resurrected. There is a space problem. If the countless millions of human beings who have ever lived and may live in the future were all to be resurrected on this earth, then the overcrowding would be acute. Now there are at least two theological maneuvers that we could make to circumvent this embarrassment. If we want to retain resurrection on this earth, then we might say that only the chosen will be resurrected and thereby limit the numbers. But that solution raises insuperable problems about the morality of a God who would behave in such a way.[10] Alternatively, it might be argued that the resurrection will be to a new life in heaven and not to eternal life on earth. But in that case it has to be noted that resurrected bodies would need a biological environment markedly similar to the one we now live in. This leads to the implication that heaven would have to be a planet, or series of planets, all suitable for human life. The further one pushes this picture, the more bizarre and religiously unsatisfying it becomes.[11]

In sum, then, a little knowledge of the biochemistry of living organisms together with a brief consideration of the physicochemical conditions that such organisms require if they are to live, ought to have rendered the traditional notion of literal bodily resurrection unthinkable.

RESURRECTION OF THE BODY (TRANSFORMED)

It might be argued, as John Polkinghorne claims, that all this is irrelevant: "We know that there is nothing significant about the material which at any one time constitutes our body. . . . It is the pattern they [the atoms] form which persists and evolves. We are liberated, therefore, from the quaint medieval picture of the reassembly of the body from its scattered components. In very general terms it is not difficult to imagine the pattern recreated (the body resurrected) in some other world."[12]

At this point we should note that the doctrine being proposed here has shifted in a very significant way. The old doctrine of resurrection of the flesh guaranteed personal survival because the resurrected body was physically identical with the one laid in the grave. Physical continuity supplied the link between the person who died and the one who was resurrected. But Polkinghorne's version of the resurrection envisages recreation of a *pattern* in some other world. This is open to a host of philosophical problems about the sense in which the recreation of a replica can count as the survival of the person who died.[13]

What would we say, for example, if the replica were created *before* my death? Would I then die happily knowing that someone was around to carry on, as it were, in my place? Would I think to myself that the replica really was me? Consider the possibility of cloning. Let us imagine that science reaches a stage where a whole adult human individual can be regenerated from a few cells of a person in such a way that the original—Jones I—and the copy—Jones II—are genetically identical, and that the clone knows everything that Jones I knows. We may imagine that the purpose of doing this is to give a healthy body to house the thoughts of the physically ailing, but brilliant, Jones I. Now does Jones I die secure in the knowledge that he will live again? I would suggest that he might feel relieved to know that his life's work would carry on, and that his project would be entrusted to one incomparably suited to continue with it. He might also feel exceptionally close to Jones II and be deeply concerned for his welfare. But the other would not *be* him. In the end, Jones I would be dead and the other, Jones II, would carry on in his place. As far as Jones I was concerned, he himself would not live again, even though most other people would treat Jones II as if he were Jones I rejuvenated.[14]

If these intuitions are correct, then they suggest that whatever it is that we count as essential for being one and the same person, it is not a "pattern." And I would suggest that all theories of resurrection that speak of our rising with new and transformed bodies fall foul of what I term the replica problem. For without some principle of continuity between the person who died and the one who was resurrected, then what was resurrected would only be something very similar to the one who died, a replica, and not a continuation of the dead person.

THE SOUL

Such considerations have led theologians at least from Aquinas onwards to argue that any tenable resurrection belief hinges on a concept of the soul. For even if we hold to a belief in the resurrection of some "new and glorious body," then we need the soul to avoid the replica problem. There has to be a principle of continuity between this world and the next if what is raised to new life really is one and the same person as the one who died. Moreover, this principle of continuity must encapsulate enough of the real 'me' for both "old" and "new" versions to count as the same person. Might this requirement be fulfilled if we were to espouse a dualist concept of the person and say, with Descartes, that my essential personhood is to be identified with my mind, that is, with the subject of conscious experiencing.[15] However, I want to argue that not even this move is sufficient to rescue the Christian claim.

First, there are the practical problems of which contemporary dualists are very much aware.[16] Our personal experience and emotions are intimately linked to our body chemistry. Indeed, the limits to what we are able to think at all are set by our genetic endowment; so that one man's physicochemical equipment enables him to be a brilliant mathematician, while another's lack condemns him to lifelong imbecility. If our diet is imbalanced and inadequate, or if certain of our organs are malfunctioning, then our bodies may be starved of essential nutrients or poisoned by the excessive production of some hormone. In such cases, the whole personality may be adversely affected. The "subject of my conscious experiences" would seem to be very much at the mercy of my physicochemical constitution.

A second difficulty lies in deciding which organisms count as having souls and which do not. And if God is to give eternal life to the former class and not to the latter, then even He has to be able to draw a line somewhere, and that nonarbitrarily.[17] The problem occurs both in considering the evolution of the species Homo sapiens and the individual development of human beings. Even if we ignore the problem of nonhuman animals and restrict the possibility of possessing a soul to humans, there are still insuperable difficulties.[18]

Consider first the evolutionary pathway that led from the early mammals to man. Somewhere along that line we would be fairly secure in denying that such and such a creature had any awareness of self. And it is also true to say that most normal adult humans possess such an awareness. But between these extremes lies a gray area. To have a nonarbitrary dividing line, it has to be possible for us to decide (at least in principle) where a sharp division can be drawn between the last generation of anthropoid apes and the first generation of true Homo sapiens. Are we to suppose that in one generation there were anthropoid apes who gave birth to the next generation of true Homo sapiens, and that the changes between one generation and the next were so great that the children counted in God's eyes as the bearers of immortality while their parents were "mere animals"? Yet unless dualists are prepared to fly in the face of evolutionary biology, how can they avoid this unpalatable conclusion? . . .

There are, in addition, some further objections of a more purely philosophical nature, which I think need mentioning at this point. The subject of my conscious experiencing is singularly unconvincing as a principle of continuity that guarantees persistence of the "same" person through change. Moreover, defining the "real" me in this way actually misses a lot of what most of us would want to say is a part of the "real" me. I shall begin by discussing the question of a principle of continuity.

One great problem with my awareness of self is its lack of persistence, its transitoriness. My stream of consciousness is far from being a constant or even ever-present (though varying) flow. When I am unconscious, in a dreamless sleep, or even in a vacant mood, it just is not there. Yet *I* do not cease to exist whenever my conscious mind is, as it were, switched off temporarily. Secondly, we have to face the problem that this awareness of self is ever-changing. What I was as a child is very different from what I, as I am in myself, am today; and if I live to be an old lady, doubtless the subject of my conscious experiences will look back with a mixture of wry amusement and nostalgia at that other her of forty years ago. Now it might be thought that this problem of continual change is no greater a problem for the notion of same 'self' than it is for the notion of same 'body' since the body is also in a continual state of flux. But I would suggest that what supplies continuity through change is matter. It may be that all my constituent atoms will have changed in the next few months, but they will not have all changed simultaneously. Moreover, the physically-based blueprints from the chemistry that keeps my body going are passed on from one generation of cells to another in a direct physical line of succession. Thus, I would argue that what keeps the subject of my conscious experiencing belonging to one and the same person is this physical continuity.

The essential requirement of physical continuity can be illustrated if we return to the clone example. Let us modify the thought experiment a little, and make Jones II a copy of a perfectly healthy Jones I. And let us also stipulate that the two Jones emerge from the cloning laboratory not knowing who is the original and who the copy. In other words, Jones I and II are, seemingly, wholly similar. Neither they nor we can tell which is which, unless we trace the histories of the two bodies to ascertain which grew from a fertilized ovum and which developed as the result of cloning. Now if we apply the implications of this to the question of what might live again after death, we see that being "the subject of my conscious experiences" is not sufficient to guarantee that I am one and the same person as the one who died. For what the clone example shows is that both Jones I and Jones II may believe (or doubt) equally that he really is the same person as Jones I while he relies solely on his personal experience of himself as Jones. Only when he traces the path of physical continuity can he know whether he truly is Jones I or not. (Of course, we might want to say that where there had been one person, Jones, there were now two distinct individuals, both of whom were physically continuous with the original. But in that case the possibility of defining 'same person' in terms of 'same stream of consciousness' does not even arise.)[19]

Thus I contend, a dualist definition of what I really am fails because it cannot provide adequate criteria for recognizing the 'same' person through change. I can think of no other case where we would even be tempted to accept something as transitory and ever-changing as 'consciousness of self' to be the essential criterion for defining what it is that an entity has to retain if it is to count as remaining the same individual through change.

I move on now to the problems that arise from the restrictedness of defining me as the subject of my conscious experiences. A great deal of what I am does not involve my conscious thoughts at all, even when I am fully awake. Take the familiar example of driving a car. When I was learning to drive, I certainly employed a great amount of conscious effort. But nowadays my conscious thoughts are fairly free to attend to other matters when I am driving, even though, of course, intense conscious attention instantly returns if danger threatens. I certainly do not want to say 'my body' drove here. *I* drove here, even though most of the time the subject of my conscious experiences was not much involved.

Moreover, we cannot ignore the possibility that the conscious subject might actually fail to recognize a significant part of all that I really am. To exemplify the point: imagine someone who believes himself to be a great wit, when most of his colleagues find him a crashing bore. If he were to arrive in the resurrection world without his familiar characteristics—clumsiness of speech, repetitiveness, triviality, self-centeredness—would he really be the person who had died? Yet could he bring these characteristics with him if the subject of his conscious experiences, the 'real' him, was wholly unaware of having been like this?

In sum, what I have been arguing against dualism is that this concept of the soul cannot bear the weight put on it. Yet it has to bear this weight if it is to be the sine qua non of my surviving bodily death. Considerations from the natural sciences and philosophy, and even religious implications, combine to render it far from convincing. But, it might be countered, no amount of argument on the basis of current scientific theory, philosophy, or religious sentiments can count against hard empirical fact. So what about the reports that exist of near-death experiences, which seem to show that some people really do have experiences apart from their bodies?

NEAR-DEATH EXPERIENCES

Let me begin by stating quite clearly that I shall not be concerned to discuss the merits or otherwise of individual cases. I am going to suppose, for the purposes of discussion, that there is strong, bonafide evidence that some people come back from the brink of death fully convinced that they had left their bodies and had had apparently veridical experiences as if from a vantage point different from that of the body. The question then is, how do we interpret these "travelers tales."

I have three main points to make here. The first is that a present absence of satisfactory normal explanations for these cases does not imply that there are no such explanations ever to be found. We should not be hurried into a supernaturalist account merely because we can find no other, as if the God-of-the-gaps lesson had yet to be learned. . . .

My second point is that even if we take near-death experiences as supplying empirical proof of the existence, nay persistence, of the human soul or mind, that would not smooth out all the difficulties. All the problems that I have discussed earlier would still be there, awaiting some kind of resolution. And there would arise yet further problems. Take, for example, the question of how the soul actually "sees" physical objects while it supposedly hovers below the ceiling. William Rushton puts the point thus: "What is this out-of-the-body eye that can encode the visual scene exactly as does the real eye, with its hundred million photoreceptors and its million signaling optic nerves? Can you imagine anything but [that] a replica of a real eye could manage to do this? But if this floating replica is to see, it must catch light, and hence cannot be transparent, and so must be visible to people in the vicinity. In fact floating eyes are not observed, nor would this be expected, for they exist only in fantasy."[20] And if it be countered that the soul perceives without using the normal physicochemical mechanisms, then we might ask why on earth did such a complicated organ as the eye ever evolve (or remain unatrophied) if human beings possess souls that can "see" without normal eyes. Moreover, one might expect that blind people, deprived of normal visual stimuli, would use this psychic ability, if it really existed. These, and kindred problems concerned with modes of perception, would need answers if we were to take seriously supernatural interpretations of OBEs.

Finally, I suggest that to accept the existence of some nonmaterial soul in man would be to embrace a notion fundamentally at variance with other well-founded convictions about the nature of reality. For we would then have to allow for events happening in the world that rest on no underlying physicochemical mechanisms. Now I am very well aware that scientists are continually changing their theories to accommodate new data, and that from time to time some wholesale replacement of outmoded ideas has been necessary.[21] So, it might be asked, can we not envisage some new scientific outlook that embraces both the normal data and the paranormal? Just so. A new scientific outlook, which could encompass both normal and paranormal data, would clearly be more satisfactory than one which could in no way account for the paranormal. But it must be remembered that the whole scientific enterprise presupposes the existence of underlying mechanisms whose discovery enables us to understand the "how" of an event.[22] So it is hard to see how any unified scientific theory could embrace both the notion that most events in the world depend on underlying physicochemical mechanisms, and also that there are some events that do not utilize any such mechanisms at all. And if paranormal data are taken as support for the belief in the existence of nonmaterial entities (like souls) then these data fly in the face of normal science. Thus I concur with C. D. Broad that "It is certainly right to demand a much higher standard of evidence for events which are alleged to be paranormal than those which would be normal. . . . For in dealing with evidence we have always to take into account the antecedent probability or improbability of the alleged event, i.e. its probability or improbability relative to all the rest of our knowledge and well-founded belief other than the special evidence adduced in its favour."[23]

In sum then, it seems that at present paranormal data cannot be accommodated within naturalist science. But to move from that to claiming that we have empirical evidence for the existence of immaterial souls seems unwarranted, not least because to explicate the paranormal in terms of the activities of immaterial souls may appear to solve one explanatory difficulty, but only at the expense of raising a host of other problems.

CONCLUSION

When Christianity was originally formulated, man's entire world view was very different from our current beliefs. It was plausible to think in terms of a three-decker universe in which the center of God's interest was this Earth and its human population. The idea that God would raise man from the dead to an eternal life of bliss fitted neatly into this schema. However, the erosion of this picture, beginning from at least the time of Copernicus and Galileo, has cut the traditional Christian hope adrift from the framework of ideas in which it was originally formulated. What I have tried to show in this chapter is that various attempts, which have been made to try to accommodate some form of resurrection/immortality belief within our current world view, are inadequate and fail. I conclude, then, that a due consideration of man's place in nature leads us to the view that he belongs there and nowhere else.

NOTES

1. A sociological survey quoted by Daniel C. Batson and W. Larry Ventis in *The Religious Experience: A Social-Psychological Perspective* (Oxford: Oxford University Press, 1982), p. 225.

2. See, for example, John Polkinghorne, *The Way the World Is* (London: SPCK, 1983); and Russel Stannard, *Science and the Renewal of Belief* (London: SCM, 1982).

3. See, for example, Richard and Anthony Hanson, *Reasonable Belief* (Oxford: Oxford University Press, 1980), pp. 13ff.

4. It is to Cranmer's credit that he made the recitation of this creed easier for the English-speaking world by his deliberate mistranslation of "resurrectio carnis" as "resurrection of the body."

5. In more idiomatic English we usually say "resurrection of the dead."

6. Paul Badham, *Christian Beliefs about Life after Death* (London: SPCK, 1978), pp. 47ff.

7. R. Lawler, D. W. Whuerl and T. C. Lawler, *The Teaching of Christ: A Catholic Catechism for Adults* (Dublin: Veritas, 1976), p. 544.

8. J. D. Bernal, *Science in History*, vol. 3, (Harmondsworth: Penguin, 1969), p. 902.

9. Augustine, *City of God*, bk. 22, chap. 20.

10. Cf. Paul and Linda Badham, *Immortality or Extinction* (London: SPCK, 1984), pp. 58ff.

11. Cf. Paul Badham, *Christian Beliefs about Life after Death*, chap. 4.

12. John Polkinghorne, *The Way the World Is*, p. 93.

13. Cf. Bernard Williams, *Problems of the Self* (Cambridge: Cambridge University Press, 1978).

14. I imagine that a very close relative like a wife or mother would find the situation emotionally very fraught!

15. Cf. René Descartes, *Discourse 4*. This is the view Paul Badham expresses both in his earlier work and in our joint book. At the time the latter was written, I was in close agreement with his position. But since then I have come to think otherwise.

16. Cf. Paul and Linda Badham, *Immortality or Extinction*, chap. 3.

17. Paul and I are still in agreement that the survival of every living organism that ever existed makes no kind of sense, religious or any other.

18. I think the problem of animals is a very real one. Cf. Paul and Linda Badham, *Immortality or Extinction*, pp. 48ff.

19. Cf. Bishop Joseph Butler's point that "though we are thus certain, that we are the same agents . . . which

we were as far back as our remembrance reaches; yet it is asked, whether we may not possibly be deceived in it?" *Dissertation 1* "Of Personal Identity," paragraph 11.

20. Rushton is quoted in Susan Blackmore, *Beyond the Body* (London: Heinemann, 198?), pp. 227–228.

21. I devote Chapter 4 of my doctoral thesis *Emergence* (Ph.D. thesis, University of Wales) to this topic of change in science.

22. I exclude the "bottom line" on mechanistic explanations. It may be that there are some fundamental particles whose behavior is not further analyzable.

23. C. D. Broad, *Lectures on Psychical Research* (London: Routledge and Kegan Paul, 1962), p. 14.

JOHN HICK

Resurrection of the Person

John Hick (1922–   ) explores an understanding of life after death that invokes a view of the person as a psychophysical unity (having no soul). Hick develops three scenarios where one person disappears or dies and subsequently a "replica" exists elsewhere. He suggests that the most reasonable explanation in each case is that the *same* person again exists in a different place at a subsequent time. He goes on to respond to three objections to his view—one objection having to do with identity between unconnected places, another one regarding how to understand time according to his theory, and a last one pertaining to the possibility of multiple replication.

⌘

THE IDEA OF RESURRECTION

'I believe,' says the Apostles' Creed, 'in the resurrection of the body and the life everlasting.' The resurrection of the body, or of the flesh, has been given a variety of meanings in different ages and different theological circles; but we are not at present concerned with the history of the concept. We are concerned with the meaning that can be given to it today in terms of our contemporary scientific and philosophical understanding.

The prevailing view of man among both contemporary scientists and western philosophers is that he is an indissoluble psycho-physical unity. The only self of which we know is the empirical self, the walking, talking, acting, sleeping individual who lives, it may be, for some sixty to eighty years and then dies. Mental events and mental characteristics are analysed into the modes of behaviour and behavioural dispositions of this empirical self. The human being is described as an organism capable of acting in the high-level ways which we characterize as intelligent, resentful, humorous, calculating and the like. The concept of mind or soul is thus not that of a 'ghost in the machine' but of the more flexible and sophisticated ways in which human beings behave and have it in them to behave. On this view there is no room for the notion of soul in distinction from body; and if there is no soul in distinction from body there can be no question of the soul surviving the death of the body. Against this background of thought the specifically christian and jewish belief in the resurrection of the body, in contrast to the hellenic idea of the survival of a disembodied soul, might be expected to have attracted more attention than it has. For it is consonant with the conception of man as an indissoluble psycho-physical unity and yet it also offers the possibility of an empirical meaning for the idea of life after death.

St Paul is the chief biblical expositor of the idea of the resurrection of the body. His basic conception, as I understand it, is this. When someone has died he is, apart from any special divine action, extinct. A human being is by nature mortal and subject to annihilation at death. But in fact God, by an act of sovereign power, either sometimes or always resurrects or reconstitutes or recreates him—not however as the identical physical organism that he was before death, but as a *soma pneumatikon* ('spiritual body') embodying the dispositional characteristics and memory traces of the deceased physical organism, and inhabiting an environment with which the *soma pneumatikon* is continuous as our present bodies are continuous with our present world. We are not concerned here with the difficult exegetical question of how precisely Paul thought of the resurrection body but with the conceptual question as to how, if at all, we can intelligibly think of it today.

THE 'REPLICA' THEORY

I wish to suggest that we can think of it as the divine creation in another space of an exact psycho-physical 'replica' of the deceased person.

The first point requiring clarification is the idea of spaces in the plural.[1] In this context the possibility of two spaces is the possibility of two sets of extended objects such that each member of each set is spatially related to each other member of the same set but not spatially related to any member of the other set. Thus everything in the space in which I am is at a certain distance and in a certain direction from me, and vice versa; but if there is a second space, nothing in it is at any distance or in any direction from where I now am. In other words, from my point of view the other space is nowhere and therefore does not exist. But if there *is* a second space, unobservable by me, the objects in it are entirely real to an observer within that space, and our own world is to him nowhere—not at any distance nor in any direction—so that from his point of view it does not exist. Now it is logically possible for there to be any number of worlds, each in its own space, these worlds being all observed by the universal consciousness of God but only one of them being observed by an embodied being who is part of one of these worlds. And the idea of bodily resurrection requires (or probably requires) that there be at least two such worlds, and that when an individual dies in our present world in space number one he is either immediately or after a lapse of time re-created in a world in space number two.

In order to develop this idea more fully I shall present a series of three cases, which I claim to be logically possible of fulfilment.

We begin with the idea of someone suddenly ceasing to exist at a certain place in this world and the next instant coming into existence at another place which is not contiguous with the first. He has not moved from A to B by making a path through the intervening space but has disappeared at A and reappeared at B. For example, at some learned gathering in London one of the company suddenly and inexplicably disappears and the next moment an exact 'replica' of him suddenly and inexplicably appears at some comparable meeting in New York. The person who appears in New York is exactly similar, as to both bodily and mental characteristics, to the person who disappears in London. There is continuity of memory, complete similarity of bodily features, including fingerprints, hair and eye coloration and stomach contents, and also of beliefs, habits, and mental propensities. In fact there is everything that would lead us to identify the one who appeared with the one who disappeared, except continuous occupancy of space.

It is I think clear that this is a logically possible sequence of events. It is of course factually impossible: that is to say, so long as matter functions in accordance with the 'laws' which it has exhibited hitherto, such things will not happen. But nevertheless we can imagine changes in the behaviour of matter which would allow it to happen, and we can ask what effect this would have upon our concept of personal identity. Would we say that the one who appears in New York is the same person as the one who disappeared in London? This would presumably be a matter for decision, and perhaps indeed for a legal decision affecting such matters as marriage, property, debts, and other social rights and obligations. I believe that the only reasonable and generally acceptable decision would be to acknowledge identify. The man himself would be conscious of being the same person, and I suggest that his fellow human beings would feel obliged to recognize him as being the one whom he claims to be. We may suppose, for example, that a deputation of the colleagues of the man who disappeared fly to New York to interview the 'replica' of him which is reported there, and find that he is in all respects but one exactly as though he had travelled from London to New York by conventional means. The only difference is that he describes how, as he was listening to Dr Z reading a paper, on blinking his eyes he suddenly found himself sitting in a different room listening to a different paper by an american scholar. He asks his colleagues how the meeting had gone after he had ceased to be there, and what they had made of his disappearance, and so on. He clearly thinks of himself as the one who was present with them at their meeting in London. He is presently reunited with his wife, who is quite certain that he is her husband; and with his children, who are quite certain that he is their father. And so on. I suggest that faced with all these circumstances those who know him would soon, if not immediately, find themselves thinking of him and treating him as the individual who had so inexplicably disappeared from the meeting in London; and that society would accord legal recognition of his identity. We should be extending our normal use of 'same person' in a way which the postulated facts would both demand and justify if we said that the person who appears in New York is the same person as the one who disappeared in London. The factors inclining us to identify them would, I suggest, far outweigh the factors disinclining us to do so. The personal, social, and conceptual cost of refusing to make this extension would so greatly exceed the cost of making it that we should have no reasonable alternative but to extend our concept of 'the same person' to cover this strange new case.

This imaginary case, bizarre though it is, establishes an important conceptual bridgehead for the further claim that a post-mortem 'replica' of Mr X in another space would likewise count as the same person as the this-world Mr X before his death. However, let me strengthen this bridgehead at two points before venturing upon it.

The cyberneticist, Norbert Wiener, has graphically emphasized the non-dependence of human bodily identity through time upon the identity of the physical matter momentarily composing the body. He points out that the living human body is not a static entity but a pattern of change: 'The individuality of the body is that of a flame rather than that of a stone, of a form rather than of a bit of substance.'[2] The pattern of the body can be regarded as a message that is in principle capable of being coded, transmitted, and then translated back into its original form, as sight and sound patterns may be transmitted by radio and translated back into sound and picture. Hence 'there is no absolute distinction between the types of transmission which we can use for sending a telegram from country to country and the types of transmission which at least are theoretically possible for transmitting a living organism such as a human being.'[3] Strictly, one should not speak, as Wiener does here, of a living organism or body being transmitted; for it would not be the body itself but its coded form that is transmitted. At other times, however, Wiener is more precise. It is, he says, possible to contemplate transmitting 'the whole pattern of the human body, of the human brain with its memories and cross connections, so that a hypothetical receiving instrument could re-embody these messages in appropriate matter, capable of continuing the processes already in the body and the mind, and of maintaining the integrity needed for this continuation by a process of homeostasis.'[4] Accordingly Wiener concludes that the telegraphing of the pattern of a man from one place to another is theoretically possible even though it remains at the present time technically impossible.[5] And it does indeed seem natural in discussing this theoretical possibility to speak of the bodily individual who is constituted at the end of the process as being the same person as the one who was 'encoded' at the beginning. He is not composed of numerically the same parcel of matter; and yet it is more appropriate to describe him as the same person than as a different person because the matter of which he is composed embodies exactly the same 'information.' Similarly, the rendering of Beethoven's ninth symphony which reaches my ears from the radio loudspeaker does not consist of numerically the same vibrations that reached the microphone in the concert hall; those vibrations have not travelled on through another three hundred miles to me. And yet it is more appropriate to say that I am hearing this rendering of the ninth symphony than that I am hearing something else. . . .

Wiener's contribution to the present argument is his insistence that psycho-physical individuality does not depend upon the numerical identity of the ultimate physical constituents of the body but upon the pattern of 'code' which is exemplified. So long as the same 'code' operates, different parcels of matter can be used, and those parcels can be in different places.[6]

The second strengthening of the bridgehead concerns the term 'replica' which, it will be observed, I have used in quotes. The quotes are intended to mark a difference between the normal concept of a replica and the more specialized concept in use here. The paradigm sense of 'replica' is that in which there is an original object, such as a statue, of which a more or less exact copy is then made. It is logically possible (though not of course necessary) for the original and the replica to exist simultaneously; and also for there to be any number of replicas of the same original. In contrast to this, in the case of the disappearance in London and re-appearance in New York it is not logically possible for the original and the 'replica' to exist simultaneously or for there to be more than one 'replica' of the same original. If a putative 'replica' did exist simultaneously with its original it would not be a 'replica' but a replica; and if there were more than one they would not be 'replicas' but replicas. For 'replica' is the name that I am proposing for the second entity in the following case. A living person ceases to exist at a certain location, and a being exactly similar to him in all respects subsequently comes into existence at another location. And I have argued so far that it would be a correct decision, causing far less linguistic and conceptual disruption than the contrary one, to regard the 'replica' as the same person as the original.

Let us now move on to a second imaginary case, a step nearer to the idea of resurrection. Let us suppose that the event in London is not a sudden and inexplicable disappearance, and indeed not a disappearance at all, but a sudden death. Only, at the moment when the individual dies a 'replica' of him as he was at the moment before his death, and complete with memory up to that instant, comes into existence in New York. Even with the corpse on our hands it would still, I suggest, be an extension of 'same person' required and warranted by the postulated facts to say that the one who died has been miraculously re-created in New York. The case would, to be sure, be even odder than the previous one because of the existence of the dead body in London contemporaneously with the living person in New York. And yet, striking though the oddness undoubtedly is, it does not amount to a logical impossibility. . . . Once again the factors inclining us to say that the one who died and the one who appeared are the same person would far outweigh the factors inclining us to say that they are different people. Once again we should have to extend our usage of 'same person' to cover the new case.

However, rather than pause longer over this second picture let us proceed to the idea of 'replication' in another space, which I suggest can give content to the notion of resurrection. For at this point the problem of personal identity shifts its focus from second- and third-person criteria to first-person criteria. It is no longer a question of how we in this world could know that the 'replica' Mr X is the same person as the now deceased Mr X, but of how the 'replica' Mr X himself could know this. And since this raises new problems it will be well to move directly to this case and the issues which it involves.

The picture that we have to consider is one in which Mr X dies and his 'replica,' complete with memory, etc., appears, not in America, but as a resurrection 'replica' in a different world altogether, a resurrection world inhabited by resurrected 'replicas'—this world occupying its own space distinct from the space with which we are familiar. It is, I think, manifestly an intelligible hypothesis that after my death I shall continue to exist as a consciousness and shall remember both having died and some at least of my states of consciousness both before and after death. Suppose then that I exist, not as a disembodied consciousness but as a psycho-physical being, a psycho-physical being exactly like the being that I was before death, though existing now in a different space. I have the experience of waking up from unconsciousness, as I have on other occasions woken up from sleep; and I am no more inclined in the one case than in the others to doubt my own identity as an individual persisting through time. I realize, either immediately or presently, that I have died, both because I can remember being on my death-bed and because my environment is now different and is populated by people some of whom I know to have died. Evidences of this kind could mount up to the point at which they are quite as strong as the evidence which, in the previous two pictures, convinces the individual in question that he has been miraculously translated to New York. Resurrected persons would be individually no more in doubt about their own identity than we are now, and would presumably be able to identify one another in the same kinds of ways and with a like degree of assurance as we do now.

IDENTITY FROM WORLD TO WORLD

I suggest that if we knew it to be a 'law of nature' that re-creation or 'replication' occurs in another space, we should be obliged to modify our concept of 'same person' to permit us to say that the 'replica' Mr X in space two is the same person as the former Mr X in space one. For such an extension of use involves far less arbitrariness and paradox than would be generated by saying either that they are not the same person or that it is uncertain whether they are the same person. They have everything in common that they could possibly have, given that they exist successively in different spaces. They are physically alike in every particular; psychologically alike in every particular; and the Mr X stream of consciousness, memory, emotion and volition continues in 'replica' Mr X where it left off at the death of earthly Mr X. In these circumstances it would, I submit, be wantonly paradoxical to rule that they are not the same person and that the space-two 'replica' ought not to think of himself as the person whose past he remembers and whom he is conscious of being.

Terence Penelhum has discussed this concept of resurrection and suggests that although the identification of resurrection-world Mr X with the former earthly Mr X is permissible it is not mandatory. He argues that in my cases number two and number three (and probably number one also) it would be a matter for decision as to whether or not to make the identification. The general principle on which he is working is that there can only be an automatic and unquestionable identification when there is bodily continuity. As soon as this is lost, identity becomes a matter for decision, with arguments arising both for and against. He concludes that although 'the identification of the former and the later persons in each of the three pictures is not absurd,' yet 'in situations like these it is a matter of decision whether to say that physical tests of identity reveal personal identity or very close similarity. We can, reasonably, decide for identity, but we do not have to. And this seems to leave the description of the future life in a state of chronic ambiguity.'[7] In response to this I would agree, and have indeed already acknowledged, that these are cases for decision. Indeed, I would say that *all* cases other than ordinary straightforward everyday identity require a decision. Even physical identity, as such, is no guarantee against the need for decisions, as is shown by such imaginary cases as that of the prince whose consciousness, memory, and personality is transferred into the body of a cobbler, and vice versa.[8] Thus all cases outside the ordinary require linguistic legislation. My contention is not that the identification of resurrection-world Mr X with the former this-world Mr X is entirely unproblematic, but that the decision to identify is much more reasonable, and is liable to create far fewer problems, than would be the decision to regard them as different people.

TIMES AND SPACES

But if the notion of spaces in the plural, and of resurrection as psychophysical re-creation after death in another space, is accepted as meaningful, how can we understand the time relationship between the two spaces? Is not time so closely linked with space that the this-world series of events would have to be temporally as well as spatially unrelated to the resurrection-world series of events? And in that case how could someone be said to appear in the resurrection world *after* he had died in this world? . . .

Why should there not be a single time sequence in which events can occur simultaneously in different spaces, even though within each space the measurement of time must be in relation to physical movements peculiar to that space? Presumably the divine mind, conscious of all spaces and of the elapse of singular time, would be aware of the temporal relationship between events in different spaces. But the inhabitants of a given space could only be aware of the continuity of time through spaces as an inference from their own memories of life in another space. It could then be the case that 'replica' Mr X in space two comes into existence subsequently to the death of Mr X in space one, although the only direct evidence of this available to him is his own memory. Reversing Olding's conclusion: he remembers dying, and therefore his dying must have been a past event.

MULTIPLE REPLICATION?[9]

A further difficulty has been raised, based upon the logical spectre of the existence of two or more identical resurrection Mr X's.[10] If it makes sense to suppose that God might create a second-space reproduction of Mr X, then it makes sense to suppose that he might create two or more such second-space reproductions, namely X^2, X^3, etc. However, since X^2 and X^3 would then each be the same person as X^1, they would both be the same person; which is absurd. Thus the existence of X^3 would prohibit us from identifying X^2 as being the same person as X^1. Further, it has been argued by J. J. Clarke that the bare logical possibility of X^3 has the same effect. Speaking of several Hicks, H_1, H_2 and H_3, he says, 'It is not even necessary to suppose that God has *actually* created H_3, for the mere *possibility* of his doing so is as much a threat to H_2's identity as is H_3's actual existence. If the actual *existence* of H_3 alongside H_2 obliges us to refrain from identifying H_2 as Hick, then the mere *possibility* of H_3 ought similarly to restrain us from conferring identity. This is pinpointed by the fact that if H_3 became reconstituted some while after H_2, one would have to say that for a while H_2 *could* conceivably have been H_1, but then on H_3's arrival in the resurrection world this identification ceased to be possible. This is incoherent.'[11] That is to say, so long as it is true that it could turn out, through the arrival of H_3, that H_2 was not after all identical with H_1, that identification is not permissible. Accordingly, since there cannot be two or more re-created X's, there cannot be one re-created X. Applying his argument, appropriately, to myself, Mr Clarke concludes: 'Since multiples of re-embodied Hick cannot enter the resurrection world, then neither can one.'[12]

It might perhaps be thought that this difficulty has been avoided by so defining 'replica' that there cannot at any given time be more than one 'replica' of the same individual. As was said above, if there were two or more they would not be 'replicas' but replicas. But whilst this is, I believe, the correct conception of the entity whose existence would constitute the resurrected existence of a deceased individual, it does not obviate the 'if not two, then not one' argument. For if there were two (or more) identical post-mortem persons, none of them could be 'replica' Mr X, and thus their existence would render 'replication' impossible.

We are asked, then, to contemplate the idea of God re-creating Mr X, not as a 'one off' act but as the re-creation of a plurality of 'Mr X's,' each starting life in the world to come as a re-creation of the earthly Mr X, complete with his memories, etc. I think it must be granted that if this were to happen our present system of concepts would be unable to deal with it. We should simply not know how to identify the multiple 'Mr X's.' Our concept of 'the same person' has not been developed to cope with such a situation. It can tolerate a great deal of change in an individual—the changes, for example, that occur as between the baby, the young man, the middle-aged man and the very old man. And I have argued that it could if necessary tolerate gaps in occupancy of space (an instantaneous quantum jump from one point in space to another, or divine de-creation at one place and re-creation at another), or even in occupancy of time (a person ceasing to exist at t^1 and existing again after a, preferably short, time lapse at t^2). But one thing that it will not tolerate is multiplicity. A person is by definition unique. There cannot be two people who are exactly the same in every respect, including their consciousness and memories. That is to say, if there were a situation satisfying this description, our present concept of 'person' would utterly break down under the strain.

The question, then, is whether we can properly move from the premise that there cannot be two beings in the world to come each of whom is the same person as Mr X in this world, to the conclusion that there cannot be *one* being in the world to come who is the same person as Mr X in this world. And it seems clear to me that we cannot validly reach any such conclusion. Suppose that last week I was in New York and now I am in London. It would be absurd for someone to argue that since there cannot now be *two* JH's in London who are the same person as JH in New York last week, therefore there cannot be *one* JH in London now who is the same person as JH in New York last week! I freely grant that if there were two resurrection 'Mr X's' neither of them could be identified as the same person as the earthly Mr X, and that therefore, so far from there being two, there would not even be one. But I deny that the unrealized logical possibility of their being two resurrection 'Mr X's' makes it logically impossible for there to be one. It is a conceptual truth that if there were one resurrected 'Mr X' there could not be another; but this truth does not prohibit there being one and only one. The fact that if there were two or more 'Mr X's,' none of them would be Mr X, does not prevent there being the only kind of resurrected 'Mr X' that could exist, namely a single one.

In other words, it is impossible for the universe in which we are to have incompatible characteristics. If we are in a universe in which an individual can die and be re-created elsewhere, then we are not in a universe in which an individual can die and be multiply re-created elsewhere. But this fact does not show, or even tend to show, that we cannot be in the first kind of universe. . . .

It is in fact possible to conceive of a great number of situations and worlds in which our present understanding of personal identity would fail to apply and in which we should simply not know what to say. But these do not properly tell against the claim that our ordinary concept of 'the same person' can be applied, extended but not disrupted, to the resurrection situation which I have described. It is not an acceptable form of argument that because all manner of other conceivable situations would be unintelligible, or would undermine some of our basic concepts, therefore the possibility that I have outlined is to be rejected as either unintelligible or impossible. It has to be considered on its own merits. And I hope that this discussion has in fact established the conceivability of resurrection as the divine re-creation of the individual after his earthly death as a total psycho-physical 'replica' in another space. This can however, in relation to our present knowledge, be no more than a logical possibility; and if in due course we each discover that this possibility is realized we shall undoubtedly also discover that our present bare outline of it is filled out in ways which we do not foresee. That the basic notion of psycho-physical re-creation can only be the beginning of a full picture becomes evident when we remember that an exact 'replica' of a dying man at his last moment of life would be a dying man at his last moment of life! In other words, the first thing that the resurrection body would do is to expire. For we have thus far supposed that the body being replicated is one whose heart is failing, or whose breathing is being fatally obstructed, or which is in the terminal stage of cancer—or whatever other condition is the immediate cause of death. If, then, life is to continue in the post-mortem world we must suppose a change in the condition of the resurrection body. But what might be the nature of such a change? Could we, for example, suppose that the resurrection body, instead of being identical in form with the earthly body at the moment of death, is a 'replica' of it at some earlier point of life, when it was in full health and vigour?[13] No doubt we can conceive of this; but the cost would be high. For if we envisage the resurrection body as 'replicating' the individual in the physical prime of his life at, let us say, around the age of thirty or perhaps twenty-five, he will presumably lose in the resurrection all the memories and all the development of character that had accrued to him on earth since that age. It would seem, then, that we must think of the resurrection body as being created in the condition of the earthly body, not necessarily precisely at the last moment of physical life (which can be defined in several different ways), but perhaps at the last moment of conscious personal life. And then, instead of its immediately or soon dying, we must suppose that in its new environment it is subjected to processes of healing and repair which bring it into a state of health and activity. In the case of old people—and most people die in relatively old age—we might even conceive of a process of growing physically younger to an optimum age.

The reason for postulating full initial bodily similarity between the resurrected person and the pre-resurrection person is to preserve a personal identity which we are supposing to be wholly bound up with the body. If the person is an indissoluble psycho-physical unity, it would seem that he must begin his resurrection life as identically the person who has just died, even though he may then proceed to undergo changes which are not possible in our present world.

This, at least, represents the simplest model for a resurrection world. But this model is only the most accessible of a range of possibilities. It is conceivable that in the resurrection world we shall have bodies which are the outward reflection of our inner nature but which reflect it in ways quite different from that in which our present bodies reflect our personality. In supposing this we have already begun a process of speculation which we cannot profitably pursue. The consideration of logically coherent extrapolations can take us as far as the bare idea of divine reconstitution in another world which is not spatially related to our present world; but beyond this only creative imagination can paint pictures of the possible conditions of such a world and of human life within it.

NOTES

1. The conceivability of plural spaces is argued by Anthony Quinton in an important article to which I should like to draw the reader's attention: 'Spaces and Times,' in *Philosophy*, April 1962.

2. Norbert Wiener, *The Human Use of Human Beings*, p. 91.

3. Ibid.

4. Ibid., p. 86.

5. Ibid., p. 92.

6. For a discussion of Norbert Wiener's ideas in this connection, see David L. Mouton, 'Physicalism and Immortality,' in *Religious Studies*, March 1972.

7. *Survival and Disembodied Existence*, pp. 100–101.

8. Locke's *Essay concerning Human Understanding*, book II, ch. 27, para. 15.

9. Much of this section repeats, with the editor's permission, material in 'Mr Clarke's Resurrection Also,' in *Sophia*, October 1972.

10. This spectre was first raised in a different context by Bernard Williams in 'Personal Identity and Individuation,' in *Proc. Aristot. Soc.*, 1956–7, reprinted in *Problems of the Self*, particularly pp. 8–11. Williams's article provoked a valuable discussion in *Analysis*, with articles by C. B. Martin (March 1958), G. C. Nerlich (June 1958 and October 1960), R. C. Coburn (April 1960), Bernard Williams (December 1960), and J. M. Shorter (March 1962). See also: Robert Young, 'The Resurrection of the Body,' in *Sophia*, July 1970.

11. J. J. Clarke, 'John Hick's Resurrection,' in *Sophia*, October 1971, p. 20.

12. Ibid., p. 22.

13. In some medieval christian books about death it was stated that the blessed 'would be in the full vigour

of their age, for at the Resurrection of the Dead they would have the same age as that of Christ at his death, thirty-two years and three months, regardless of the age at which they died' (T. S. R. Boase, *Death in the Middle Ages*, pp. 19–21). Cf. Aquinas, *Summa Theologica, III* a (Suppl.), Q81, art. 1.

SUGGESTED READING

Badham, Paul. *Christian Beliefs about Immortality.* London: Macmillan, 1976.

Badham, Paul, and Linda Badham. *Immortality or Extinction?* London: Macmillan, 1982.

———. *Death and Immortality in the Religions of the World.* New York: Paragon, 1987.

Blackmore, Susan. *Dying to Live: Near-Death Experiences.* Buffalo: Prometheus Press, 1993.

Cooper, John. *Body, Soul, and Life Everlasting.* Grand Rapids, Mich.: William B. Eerdmans, 1989.

Davis, Stephen T., ed. *Death and Afterlife.* London: Macmillan, 1989.

Edwards, Paul, ed. *Immortality.* New York: Macmillan, 1992.

Hick, John. *Death and Eternal Life.* New York: Harper and Row, 1976.

Lamont, Corliss. *The Illusion of Immortality.* New York: Philosophical Library, 1959.

Lewis, H. D. *Persons and Life After Death.* London: Macmillan, 1978.

———. *The Self and Immortality.* New York: Seabury, 1973.

Lorimer, David. *Survival?* London: Routledge & Kegan Paul, 1984.

Moody, Raymond. *The Light Beyond.* New York: Bantam Books, 1989.

Penelhum, Terence. *Immorality.* Belmont, Calif.: Wadsworth, 1973.

———. *Survival and Disembodied Existence.* London: Routledge & Kegan Paul, 1970.

Perry, John. *Personal Identity and Immortality.* Indianapolis: Hackett, 1979.

Phillips, D. Z. *Death and Immortality.* New York: Macmillan, 1970.

Reichenbach, Bruce R. *Is Man the Phoenix? A Study of Immortality.* Grand Rapids: William B. Eerdmans, 1978.

———. *The Law of Karma: A Philosophical Study.* London: Macmillan, 1990.

Shoemaker, Sidney, and Richard Swinburne. *Personal Identity.* Oxford: Blackwell, 1984.

Swinburne, Richard. *The Evolution of the Soul.* Oxford: Oxford University Press, 1986.

PART TEN

RELIGION AND SCIENCE

Through the centuries, perhaps no two human activities have had a more problematic relationship than religion and science. The apparent conflicts between what religion has asserted, on the one hand, and what the science of the day teaches, on the other, have gained acute attention. History is frought with apparent conflict between religious and scientific establishments—from the Catholic Church's condemnation of the writings of Copernicus and Galileo to the Protestant fundamentalists' battle against evolutionary theory. What the multitude of controversies reveals, however, is that we need a general conception of the relation of religion and science as important human enterprises.

Some philosophers have found it helpful to understand religion and science in terms of their respective objects, aims, and methods. What are the objects about which religion and theology speak? Is there any overlap with the objects that science addresses? And what is the aim (or explanatory mission) of the theological enterprise compared to the aim of the scientific enterprise? What about their respective methods, how they go about their tasks, how they arrive at knowledge?

Those who envisage the objects or the aims or the methods of religion and science as being very much the same thereby open the door for potential conflict between the two enterprises. Religious fundamentalists who seek to refute scientific claims on theological grounds fall into this category, but so do scientific naturalists who think that natural science discredits the main tenets of religion.

If their objects, aims, and methods are seen as being utterly different, then the result is a total compartmentalization of religion and science. Several contemporary movements incline toward this kind of conclusion: neo-orthodox theology, existentialist philosophy, positivism, and ordinary language philosophy.

Finally, those who believe that religion and science can sometimes address the same object but do so for different purposes and with different explanatory methods are prone to view the two enterprises as being complementary. According to this view, religion and science are asking and seeking to answer different sorts of questions about the same things, but with their own unique methods. In their own ways, Alfred North Whitehead, Donald MacKay, and Holmes Rolston III espouse this position.

HOLMES ROLSTON III

Scientific and Religious Logic

Holmes Rolston III (1932–) is Professor of Philosophy at Colorado State University. In this piece, he argues that science and religion both assume that there is order in the world and therefore provide explanations relying on that order. Science and religion, however, operate under two very different "paradigms"—two totally distinct ways of looking at how the world is ordered. Science looks for *causes* and religion looks for *meanings*. This difference plays out in the distinctive logic of their respective types of explanation.

⌘

CAUSES AND MEANINGS

Science and religion share the conviction that the world is intelligible, susceptible to being logically understood, but they delineate this under different paradigms. In the cleanest cases we can say that science operates with the presumption that there are causes to things, religion with the presumption that there are meanings to things. Meanings and causes have in common a concept of order, but the type of order differs. "Cause" has proved a difficult notion to explicate. Some scientists have tried to reduce it to, or to substitute for it, bare functions between variables. But most scientists find it difficult to escape the conviction that the variables are efficaciously connected. In a stretched sense, or in loose everyday use, cause refers to any contributing factor in an explanation (as with Aristotle's four causes), and it may include deliberations, reasons, and even meanings. But in science cause is restricted to outward, empirically observable constant conjunctions, attended by an elusive notion of necessary production of consequent results by the preceding spatiotemporal events. Where causes are known, prediction is possible, and an effect is commonly thought explained if its causes are known, especially if it is subsumed under a covering law (as with gravitation, thermodynamics, or natural selection), that law giving a certain logic to the process. It does little explanatory work to refer x to the class X, and to notice that x produces y because all x's regularly produce y's, when we do not understand those other productions either; we have only gotten used to them. So law alone, although it permits deductive prediction, provides only the beginning of illumination, which further requires some intelligibility past regularity in the relationship between cause and effect.

"Meaning" is the perceived inner significance of something, again a

From "Scientific and Religious Logic," in *Science and Religion: A Critical Survey* (New York: Random House, 1987). Used by permission of the publisher.

murky but crucial notion. Occasional apprehension of meanings does not constitute a religion, any more than occasional recognition of causes constitutes a science. But where meanings are methodically detected out of a covering model, which is thought to represent an ultimate structure in reality, one has some sort of religion or one of its metaphysical cousins in philosophy. Science holds that causality runs deep in the nature of things; religion holds that what is highest in value runs deepest in the nature of things. It may be objected that one can search for meanings without being religious. This has not often been true historically in any broad sense, for, until the twentieth century, cultures, so far as they were systems of meaning, have been everywhere interwoven with religion.

More recently, under the impact of science some humanists and existentialists have held that meaning is merely a human construct, nonreligiously selected, since the world itself neither offers nor bears any meaning structures. It remains to be seen, in view of the contemporary problem of meaninglessness, how viable these latter accounts are and whether any culture can be sustained on them; but here perhaps one has the anomaly of systematic nonreligious meaning. However, if meaning is thought to be given in the world structure, or to be had in dialectical relationship with the natural order, or to evolve as a sacred cultural emergent, then one has a religion, though perhaps a new immanentist or naturalistic one rather than a classical supernaturalistic or transcendentalist one. Relative to the distinction between cause and meaning, it may be said that science answers how questions and religion answers why questions; but these words, while suggestive, are not reliable indicators of syntax and the kind of explanation sought.

Social scientists and psychologists are disagreed as to whether their sciences are ever sciences of meanings, and the puzzle as to how far human subjects can be causally understood has left the human sciences unsettled. Rigorous behaviorists insist that psychology is entirely a causal science, while humanistic psychologists seek to understand personality as a function of meaning. Social scientists find that causes operate in human affairs; there are causes of inflation, war, revolution, depression, suicide, birth and death rates, environmental crises, etc., and these causes operate comprehensively, including overriding or negating what the members of a society may mean and intend. At the same time no society is entirely understood without appreciating its meaning structures as these interlock with the causal factors that constrain it. Meaning structures too can be understood in terms of a governing model out of which conduct follows. Given a certain meaning model (M), a certain pattern of conduct (O) will be observed (if M, then O), and thus meaning models, no less than causal law, can be embraced under the sort of logical inquiry we have here been tracing. They too have their regular operations and predictable dynamics. We have already maintained that creeds and theologies can be studied in this way.

Although social scientists or psychologists may inquire what meanings other persons have and how these function in their lives, they do not use—

the majority will insist—their sciences to discover meanings for themselves. These sciences may describe the meanings that others have, but they do not prescribe what meanings scientists themselves ought to have. The scientist may find meanings in his subjects and make these his object of study, but he does not, with his science, find meanings in the world structure or cultural structure and make these life-orienting. Whenever one undertakes this latter task, one has passed over into the province of religion and its cognate fields—ethics, comparative religion, the humanities, philosophy. Thus, in the human sciences we find an overlap between science and religion, but so far as there is disputed ground this is because we know what the master paradigms in the two fields are—that science is a study of causes and religion is an inquiry into meanings.

NEGOTIABILITY AND COMPATIBILITY OF CAUSES AND MEANINGS

Each master paradigm is virtually nonnegotiable, a dogma within that discipline. These paradigms arise out of experience, for the scientist has found many causal connections, while the saint has discovered much of significance. Such realized causality and meaningfulness are universalized into the beliefs that everything is causally sequential and that all events are meaningfully interpretable, and with this they become presumptions brought to experience as well as derivations from it. In modern science this yields a universe of precise law, which persons can successfully study and profitably manipulate. In modern religion this yields a universe that has cumulative meaningfulness, coming to focus in God, the Absolute, or a divinity of the natural whole.

These dispositions to interpret things causally and also meaningfully are built into the deep structures of the mind, and we have to some degree an innate psychological drive to find things intelligible. But neither the causality found by science nor the significance found by religion is to be dismissed as merely psychological, for these also are present as logical structures in the mind. The mind has evolved as a natural fit in response to the environment in which life occurs. What an individual mind brings innately to the world recapitulates the edited genetic experience of this species.

There is some temptation to say here that causal relations are "really there," discovered, objective, but that meanings are invented, subjective, only "in us." A truth in this is that causal relations, after we have recognized how they are subject to our mental structures and constructions, may be outwardly reviewed for their constant conjunctions, while meanings appear as the subject is experientially related to her world. But, again subject to value structures provided by the mind, it would be anomalous if humans had evolved their enormous innate thirst for meaning in life in a world where life is a natural event but where all these investings of life's relations with meaning in the world (for example, those of love and hate, fear and joy, birth and death, of beauty and fruitfulness, of work and parenting) were inappropriate and superficial. In this case all those appearances of language as it seems to lodge meanings in things and relationships would in fact be deceiving and refer in a hidden way only to the psychic state of the user of such language, a state that was disjoined from his biological origins. This might be so, but any argument strong enough to prove it is likely also to carry the implication, with Immanuel Kant, that causes as well as meanings are nothing but compositions of the mind. Until such argument prevails, it is simpler to hold that causes are experienced in the world and that meanings, however self-involving, are sometimes given, often relational, even if on occasion created *ex nihilo* in the mind.

It is perhaps true that disciplined science can abstract out bare causes, devoid of any meaning; but this is a very sophisticated, high-level analysis, only recently accomplished in the intellectual life of humankind. The real world of nature and culture in which we live is one in which we meet facts, values, disvalues in fusion; they come at us together. It seems natural to say that we meet and find both causes and meanings there. The gut nature of living on, surviving, makes the world a field of values and disvalues, never neutral to the pursuit of life; and at this point it becomes artificial to leave by analysis the causes objectively there and wrench the meanings out of it as a subjective appearance or fabrication. What is given, what is protocol, is not naked sense data, not bare constant conjunctions, but a milieu of events, with causes and meanings in-mixed, sought and found, made and coming at us, opportunities, a world we have to move through and to evaluate.

Can either discipline tolerate anomalies? Yes, but both will so minimize the exceptions that their respective gestalts still govern. A pathologist may search without success across decades for the causes of a baffling disease, but she will not conclude that the disease is uncaused; a psychiatrist is likewise likely to insist that every mental disease has in fact some cause. A monotheist may admit frankly that he finds some events meaningless, although he also may believe that even these have some divine purpose, which he cannot now find. Quantum mechanics has come to permit the possibility that there is some genuine indeterminacy in subatomic nature. So far as evil prevents the assignment of meanings, its presence has always troubled theism.

Randomness on the one hand and absurdity on the other do challenge these paradigms but are allowed only when effectively overridden by a statistical causality or a net meaningfulness that does not interrupt a larger intelligibility. By some accounts this reduces these paradigms to regulative maxims. The scientist proceeds in the effort to find all the causes she can; the theological will pursue meanings as far as he can. Neither must then claim that her or his procedure will in every case be successful. But both are still prone to think of their procedures as appropriate because the world is constructed so as amply, if not universally, to bear relations of causality and of meaningfulness.

The warfare between science and theology is often a struggle to clarify to what extent causal explanations are compatible with or antagonistic to meaning explanations. Particular disputes may result in adjusted claims about the territory occupied by each account. While no one denies that each field commands some territory of its own and that there is partial complementarity, are they always commensurable? Some kinds of causal accounts, for example, the competitive survival of the fittest, do seem to inhibit some kinds of meaning accounts, such as that every species was divinely designed at an initial, sudden creation. Some causal explanations show some meaning explanations to be inaccurate, inadequate, or irrelevant. But if these are really different tracks of explanation, how can they compete as they sometimes do? Science, by redescribing nature, places constraints on what concepts of God are credible, even though science by this redescription prescribes nothing about God's existence. It sets limits within which meaning accounts can work.

Does the presence of sacred meanings in the world require any tearing in the weft of causes and effects, any perforation of the natural by a supernatural order? Does the meaning account sometimes constrain the causal, as when the experience of autonomy and moral responsibility seems to demand that persons be something more than effects predetermined by antecedent causes and stimuli? If there is randomness that proves causally baffling, inexplicable by science, does this imperfection correlate with the absurd in religion? Or can an account be reached whereby such causal looseness provides just that novelty and unfinished openness to nature and to life that religion can enjoy? Experience that is counted puzzling under the one paradigm may prove intelligible under the other.

DIFFERING KINDS OF LOGIC

The causal paradigm favors a computational logic, whether inductive or deductive (at least for routine science, though perhaps not for revolutionary science), while the meaning paradigm involves an intelligibility that is more holistic. Causes go into linear networks, which often permit a quantifying theoretical overlay measuring with numbers such things as wavelengths and stimulus-response correlations, although we should not forget that those numbers, which look so accurate and objective, even with their margins of error, are in the case of scientific measurement always the product of a theoretical overlay on nature and never purely natural computations at all. The validity of such quantifying depends on the quality of the overlay.

Even nonmetric science is prone to taxonomic serial catalogs and phylogenetic chains, the steps of which can be isolated for analysis. This brings a particular occurrence or individual under a covering law or type. Such repeatability and parallelism are not always found or verified by either induction or deduction, and just what counts as patterns similar enough to warrant their inclusion under the same law is always a matter of some discretion. But the causal character presumed here sometimes permits to science a level of rationality and thus of testability different from that in religion, a step-by-step checking that can be summed up into near-compulsory argument.

Religious meanings are not integrative in this scalar way. When set in their gestalt, the particulars give rise to meaning. In detecting more sophisticated patterns, as when, despite her aging, we recognize the face of a friend whom we have not seen for decades, there is a subtle interplay of textural features by which the whole is constituted. This sort of logic is present in science when a geologist recognizes the facies of rock strata, or when a dendrologist notices the differences between the bark of spruce and that of fir. But it looms much larger as one approaches the perception of meaning in a novel, such as *Gone with the Wind*, or in a historical career, as of Abraham Lincoln. One must join earlier and later significances in ways more qualitative than quantitative, more dramatic than linear. The sense of scenic scope is more crucial than that of incremental detail, hence the nonmetric character of religion.

Pattern statements differ from detail statements, alike in science and religion, but in some science it is easier to go from detail statements to pattern statements, owing to the metric-causal character. The holographic character of meaning models is not merely sequential with the chronology of life but requires more cross-play and interweaving, a logical network sometimes said to be more characteristic of the right than of the left cerebral hemisphere, more characteristic of the brain in general than of a computer. But this remains in the if-then mode, for even in the analysis of gestalts one says such things, to recall the reversible drawing, as "If that is a young woman, then this is a necklace and that an ear. But if it is a hag, then this is a mouth and that an eye."

The finding of meanings is not as simple as is identifying unvarying conjunctions. Those unique, nonrepeatable factors present in each occasion can often be integrated into its meaningfulness, while in subsuming an event under causal law these are irrelevant. The *Victory of Samothrace* instances certain universal forms of grace, strength, and flair, found also in other great sculptures. However, its aesthetic value is not constituted in abstracting these but rather just as these are indissolubly particularized in the individual integrity of one historical statue. There are recurrent religious meanings, as when persons rediscover the significance of forgiveness or of sacrificial love, but each occasion instantiating this will be cherished not only for its generality but also for its particularity.

There are various modes of interest of the human mind, not all of them either scientific or religious. Science and religion share a theoretical mode of

interest. Both want to operate out of a model or theory, a plot or a pattern, that gives a universal intelligibility to what is observed in particular episodes. But science has little interest in particulars for their particularity after they have been included as instances of a universal type. It has little interest, for instance, in proper names as essential to its content. But religion retains its interest in particulars both for their constitutive power in enriching the universal model and as loci of value. It is thus full of proper names, no less than of creedal models.

Because of this inclusion of particulars in the composition of meanings, religion can tolerate the presence of surprise more than can science. The history of science is beset with surprises, of course. But real surprises are quite upsetting to prevailing theory, for scientific models must be specifically extensible in advance to all forthcoming phenomena, and any incapacity to predict is unnerving. Religion is less inclined to predict, less insistent on similarity of cases; rather, it waits to see, after the fact, whether its paradigm can extend to cover these surprises, whether if the theory is true then a novel observation can be seen by retrodiction to follow from it. Neither the causal flow nor the meaning flow is reversible in fact. Yet causal accounts are projectable in thought symmetrically forward and backward (remembering, however, the logically troublesome status of induction). The admission of the singular existent implies that a meaning account cannot always, on the basis of recalled experience, limit its expectations as to what will and will not be absorbable into its creeds. In this sense a religious theory has an openness beside which a scientific theory is closed.

One does not always have to say in advance exactly what would refute one's theory, for that requires too much prophetic power; but one must be willing to examine each new bit of evidence as it comes along with widening ranges of human experience. A Christian judges Jesus, the Christ, to be the key to meaningful life in the world by perceiving in him the normative expression of a life style of agape. The claim follows that the agape life will always be found meaningful, but one is not able to say, in prospect, just what will count as a context for agape. Such contexts are too idiographic, although one can say, in retrospect, whether those meanings launched in Jesus have been continued as embodied in the historical particularity of each disciple's life. Here one has to judge the cumulative effect of severally inconclusive and partial verifications, which are woven not to prove but to corroborate a creed.

One can deduce only in a looser logic of weak connections. One can know out of his theory something of the possibilities that the future may hold, but he cannot make the watertight predictions that a positivist will insist that the hypothetico-deductive model requires. But to know, out of one's theory, something of the possibilities is already to know something, just as to know probabilities is already to know much, although it is not to know everything. Neither science nor religion arrives at certainties. They at best predict probabilities, but religion is looser here than is science and often can predict only a range of possibilities. Still, there is a logic to it, a model out of which one can derive the oncoming particulars and a symbolic system that functions as a regulatory model, albeit a noncausal one, into which the events of life are fitted (composing and recomposing this creed) and out of which they are interpreted.

Thus, the hypothetico-deductive method in religion does not employ the narrower sense of "deduce" that science sometimes uses. Although a new event cannot be entirely foreseen from the theory, that even, when it does occur, does follow and unfold from the theory, while some other events may not. From the first half of a play we cannot predict just how the second half will proceed, although as it proceeds we have a gathering sense of how the several events fit into an overall plot. We reason back down from the general to the particular, more broadly deriving from the paradigmatic plot what episodes may be allowed to constitute it. Thus, the dramatic plot is testable against unfolding experience. But this testability is not a stringent one. There is no single logically necessary deduction from what has gone before, although certain events can, and others cannot, be significantly emplaced in the scheme. Even in science this may occur, as in evolutionary theory, where later specific developments in their novelty cannot be unequivocably forecast, although after they occur they may be examined as to whether they are consistent with the theory.

Given that science remains causal, leaving off any assignment of meanings, it is a value-free enterprise, while religion is a valuational one. This is not a simple matter, however, because there is a spectrum of meanings attached to value and to neutrality. Science, as we have noticed, shares certain pervasive values with religion, such as those of truth and critical inquiry. In science one makes judgments about good instruments or research. One operates on the presumption that science itself is good, either instrumentally or intrinsically or both. But where science is confined to causal accounts, it never prescribes life values, for these lie in the realm of meanings.

Science is not, as is sometimes thought, merely instrumental to value, for intrinsic science does redescribe the world for us. The descriptions here cannot be ignored, for such discoveries as the age and extent of the universe, the evolution of life and its biochemical nature, the human neurophysiological structures, or the electronic character of matter have forced theology to reform earlier accounts of meanings. Persons always shape their values in some correspondence with what they believe the world to be actually like. But these descriptions never constitute prescriptions, however much they may force a reconstituting of them. In this sense religion is fully operational, completely functional in joining theory with practice, as science is not, for religion has its own value setup, which permits the translation of principles into conduct, while any scientific system is parasitic on some value system before it can become operational in life. Religion, however, is not so operational that it can ignore what science reveals about the character of the world and of life.

An older form of this claim is that science seeks knowledge, but the spiritual quest is for wisdom.[1] Knowledge and wisdom are neither coextensive nor mutually exclusive, but they overlap. In part, but only in part, a person remains naïve and unwise until she has integrated the best available knowledge from the current sciences into her world view. Still, such knowledge is not sufficient for wisdom, for no accumulation of causal explanations can ever produce the significance of a thing. The latter comes at another level of insight. In this sense, science explains but religion reveals; science informs, but religion reforms.

It is often said that science operates in an I-It mode, that of experience, while religion proceeds in dialogical encounter, the I-Thou mode. This distinction is founded on the biting difference, noticed daily, between dealing with persons and things.[2] This dichotomy recognizes the outward objectivity of science, where an "I" describes "things" in their causal relations and manipulates them as a result. In religion this "operational I" is replaced by a "relational I" that answers to the world and constitutes meanings in exchange with it. Demands flow to the "I" as well as proceed from it, for the existential "I" is called forth by that which is known. The subject has gone out to its object, which is no longer bare object, but is itself a subject, that is, a source of prescription to me. Wisdom appears in this intersubjective encounter, while the objective mode can provide only descriptive knowledge. So the notion of subjectivity loses some of its unwanted flavor, and the word "operational," often favorably linked with objectivity, becomes annoying so far as it is manipulative. The unilateral operator is ill fitted to hear the address of another or to respond to its worth.

Monotheism, moreover, detects the divine as a depth presence, an "Eternal Thou" in, with, and beyond the sacramental, superficial objectivity of the phenomenal world. This detection is comprehensively extended from the way in which we detect other minds in the behavior of human bodies. That sense of divine address is more elusively present in Eastern religions, but what is present is a depth engagement of the sacred so gripping as to draw forth the entire person, a meeting of the world at its inciting ground such that the whole self is called to respond, nearer like my relation with a "Thou" than with an "It." Further, though, theism and monism aside, meanings may arise where we attach no "Thou-hood" to this gripping other, as in encounters with nature or in aesthetics.

Some accounts find religion to be less linguistic and thus less logical than science. This may be taken by critics as a vice, but it also may be taken by proponents as a virtue, that religion plunges to deeper levels than the conventional ones of science. This latter position is not without merit, for the religious object, God, if it exists, is incomparably greater than any routine scientific object, such as rocks, fish, or atoms. Logic and language may have evolved, and be evolving, best to fit the mundane, phenomenal world, and they may ill fit the transmundane, noumenal world. Sometimes in the West and often in the East, mystics cultivate noncognitive states supposed to transcend all logic and language.

We do not need entirely to dismiss such claims to recognize that nevertheless logic and language enter steadily and decisively into religion, just as fully as they do into science. Interpersonal Thou relationships are hardly less linguistic than experiences of an It; if anything, they are more so. The discovery of meanings, which humanizes us, requires language no less than the discovery of causes. If meanings are more resistant to language than are causes, if they have nonverbal dimensions, that may indicate that the intelligibility that religion seeks requires a richer logic than the scientific sort. If all created things derive an intelligibility from their Creator, then the phenomenal world is a product of the noumenal Logos and sacramentally points to it. The prescription of values takes more, not less, thinking than does the description of events. Possibly our religion outruns our rational capacities further than does science, but, whatever consequently is the place occupied by mystical moments, these do not constitute the whole of religion; nor can they stand alone. All the classical faiths have their speechless moments, but they all have their supporting scriptures, creeds, arguments, and education.

The immediate experience of God, Brahman, or *nirvāṇa* always proves on examination to be quite as theory-laden as are any of the protocol data of the sciences. This does not disparage the intensity or firsthand directness of such experience; it only insists that there is a logic that leads up to and unfolds out of it. In this sense "God," "Brahman," and "*nirāṇa*" are postulates, inferential theoretical entities used to explain what underlies the world and certain marvelous encounters had within it. The personalness in religion does not prevent its being logical.

It is logically and empirically possible that religious knowledge would come by occasional interruption of an otherwise regular world order, by fluke and visitation, unprecedented, unrepeatable, not amenable to methodological study of even the theological sort, much less the scientific sort, proposed here. This could be not only in the context of discovery, which could well be nonpredictable, charismatic, mutational, revelational, but even in the context of verification. Revelation, miracles, oracles once confirmed could never again be reconfirmed, but would ever after have to be taken on sheer faith. But this would be an odd sort of knowledge, one that had no carry-forward features, with no way it could be shown to be true, reasonable, probable, repeatable in experience. Such knowledge would be just true, inserted once for all into historical time. Whatever elements of this kind one can find in the classical religions, those faiths have also claimed that their truths could, in some measure, be verified in life, tested out in each new generation, seen to work again and again, despite the once-for-all character of the launching visitation.

SELF-IMPLICATING MEANINGS

Meanings are always self-implicating. Values are by definition those things that make a difference. This might be thought to bias a person's capacities for logic in religion. One cannot think clearly about what one is wrapped up in. But the other side of this is that one will not think at all about that for which one does not care, or rightly think about that for which one does not rightly care. This caring becomes more self-reforming as the inquiry passes from the scientific to the humanistic to the religious. The task of religion is to examine that self in its relationships with the world, unmasking illusions and false cares, reforming it from self-centeredness, centering it on that which is of ultimate worth. This is worship, produced out of and returning to reflection. This worship, conceived as the self's disengagement from private concerns and engagement with the absolute, is precisely that universal intent that makes logic possible. Only such enthusiasm, or divine inspiriting, can get the self off-centered enough to reason aright.

The religious judgment is that the self must be reformed in order to eliminate its tendency toward rationalizing, and it is just this positive combination of worship and reflection that makes possible an unbiased rationality. Religion shares with science then a concern for objective rationality, only it knows far better than science that the path to true objectivity lies through subject reformation. This passion makes for genius. Religion is the science of the spirit, where a rationality suited for objects is inadequate. Here the reflective scientist will not say that he comes to nature without assumptions, despising the theologian as being overcome with them. But he will see that, so far as his selection employs empirical causation as his fishing net, he has a different set of assumptions; and he may even wonder whether just these assumptions might prevent him from receiving the data of religion in an undistorted form.

Perhaps some will complain that the account here has dealt too much with religion as a means of *copying* reality, with correspondence in truth, and too little with religion as a means of *coping* with reality, with its instrumental functions in life. So we readily grant that religion is a means of coping. But that is just as true of science, which is driven by the need to cope with reality not less than to copy it. Like different sorts of maps, both help us to get around in the world (supply a "method") because each in its own way represents that world ("follows after it") more or less faithfully.

NOTES

1. Augustine, *The Trinity*, 12–13.
2. Following Martin Buber, *I and Thou*, trans. Walter Kaufmann (New York: Charles Scribner's Sons, 1970).

A. DAVID KLINE

Theories and Facts in the Creation-Evolution Controversy

A. David Kline (1944–   ) writes here to clarify our understanding of "theory" and "fact" as it pertains to the overall creation-evolution debate. He shows, for example, that the creationists typically use the term "theory" to mean a purely speculative proposition or set of propositions that are not empirically established, but use the term "fact" to mean a proposition or set of propositions that are well established. But Kline points out that it is commonplace in science to use the term "theory" to mean a set of rather abstract propositions that are proposed and tested in a scientific context. Such theories are considered to be facts when appropriately confirmed. Contrary to caricatures, it is this second usage of the word "theory" that is fairer to the theory of evolution. He also considers how scientific theories are confirmed and other related issues.

⌘

To understand the basic issues in the creation-evolution debate, it is helpful to distinguish those arguments that are mainly empirical in nature from those that are philosophical or conceptual. On the empirical side, creationists have challenged a number of tenets of the evolutionists—for example, the thermodynamical possibility of the spontaneous origin of life or the accuracy and consistency of widely used techniques for dating geological strata. On the philosophical side, the areas of contention range beyond the theory of evolution to the nature of science itself. This chapter discusses four of these philosophical issues: (1) the relationship between theories and facts, (2) evidence for laws, (3) the relevance of "falsifiability" to evolutionary theory, and (4) the alleged place of God in scientific explanations. The discussion indicates why creationist arguments present an inconsistent and inaccurate view of the nature of scientific knowledge.

THEORIES OR FACTS

There is considerable and vitriolic disagreement over whether evolution is a theory or a fact. At Iowa State University, for example, such an interchange

From *Did the Devil Make Darwin Do It?: Modern Perspectives on the Creation-Evolution Controversy*, ed. David B. Wilson with Warren D. Dolphin. Ames, Iowa: The Iowa State University Press, 1983. Reprinted by permission.

between a biology professor and his student made the campus newspaper. The student apparently pointed out with some delight that the theory of evolution was only a theory; the professor with some impatience insisted that it wasn't a theory but a fact. Speaking to an evangelical group in Dallas, Texas, President Ronald Reagan gave this opinion: "Well, it is a theory. It is a scientific theory only, and it has in recent years been challenged in the world of science—that is, not believed in the scientific community to be as infallible as it once was."[1]

The disagreement is not restricted to contrary students and professors or admitted anti-intellectuals. Among vocal "authorities," the issue has been kept alive by Stephen Jay Gould's recent paper "Evolution as Fact and Theory"[2] and Duane Gish's creationist response.[3]

At the quick of the issue is an equivocation on the meaning of the term *theory*. A tip-off to this is that the theory-fact distinction is alien to scientific discourse. The distinction comes from ordinary or prescientific discourse, in which facts refer to statements that are known for certain, or that are indubitable or obviously true, whereas theories refer to statements that are speculative and not well established. That Jack Ruby shot Lee Harvey Oswald is a fact. Many, actually millions, saw the shooting on television. The event engendered many theories as to Ruby's motivations. Was he part of a larger plot to silence Oswald? Was he simply a man intent on avenging John Kennedy's death? Or what?

Let us label the ordinary sense of *theory*, theory_o. Now, as has been pointed out, if something is theory_o, then it is not well established.

In the scientific context, however, the contrast is between theories and data. We know, for example, that human memory appears to have a practically limitless capacity for storing information. But how (by means of what mechanism) do we retrieve information from memory? Some especially elegant experiments by Saul Sternberg hint at the answer.[4] His work also provides a clear illustration of the theory-data distinction.

Sternberg gave his subjects a short list of digits to memorize—called the "positive set." Then he gave them an additional digit—the "test stimulus." The subject's task was to determine quickly and accurately whether the test stimulus was in the positive set or not.

Figure 1 is an idealized visual representation of Sternberg's data. The actual data are a set of results of the form: subject 1 had a reaction time of t on positive set p of size s, where t, p, and s are particular values.

Sternberg proposed a theory to explain the data. He suggested that, at least in simple cases like the described task, memory retrieval proceeds by a *serial* and *exhaustive* search. That is, the subject internally represents the set and the test stimulus, then compares the test stimulus against the first item in the positive set for a match. He then proceeds to the next item and so on until the test stimulus has been compared with every item in the positive set. The subject goes through the entire procedure whether a match is found or not.

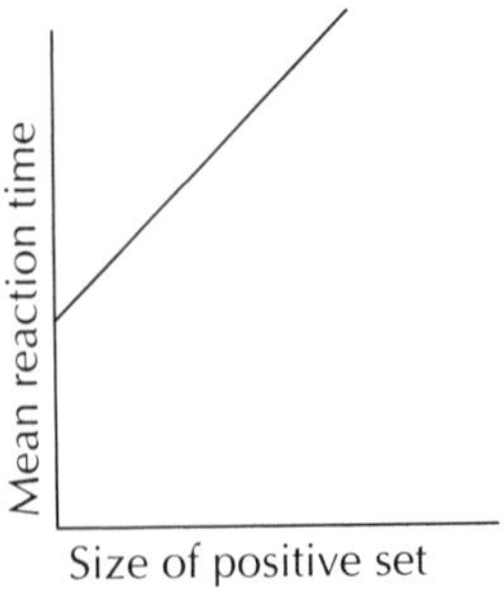

Figure 1 Graph of Sternberg's data.

Notice that the theory is not what we would normally expect—that is, that the search would be terminated as soon as a match occurred. Rather, the data support the theory that an *exhaustive* search occurs, since reaction times increase as the size of the positive set increases,[5] and since whether the test stimulus is actually in the positive set or not has no effect on the mean reaction time. Only the size of the positive set is relevant.

Several general points on the theory-data distinction are in order. First, data are typically used to support or justify a theory. Exactly how the data must be related to a theory in order to provide support is a complicated issue in inductive logic and, fortunately, one with which we need not be concerned here. Second, since it would be pointless to use *a* to justify *b* if *a* were less well established than *b*, typically the data are better established than the theories they support. Third, nevertheless, data are not certain or indubitable. The data are often discovered to be mistaken. The source of the error can be faulty instruments, false auxiliary assumptions, poor experimental design, and so on.[6] The point is that for data to be used in a justifying role requires that the data be correct, not that they be certain or indubitable.[7] If the data are correct and if they are related to the theory in the proper way, they provide some justification for the theory. Finally, justification is a historical as well as logical process. Although initially data are supposed to be much better established than the theory they support, they need not remain so. As the theory becomes supported by numerous data and explains more and more, our confidence in it rises. It can rise to such an extent that there is little difference between our confidence in the data and our confidence in the theory. Theories can come to be well established, indeed, very well established. Special relativity and transmission genetics are examples of such theories.

This last point is the important one for understanding the spat over whether evolution is a theory or fact. Let us label the scientific sense of *theory*, theory$_s$. The crucial conceptual truth is that to claim that a theory$_s$ is well established, even beyond a reasonable doubt, is not a contradiction.

Then how shall we speak of evolution? All should agree with the creationists that it is a theory, in that evolution is a systematically related set of regularities that allegedly explain numerous and diverse phenomena.[8] But the creationist concludes straightaway that evolution is not well established, a move made plausible only by an equivocation on the meaning of *theory*. The creationist's conclusion follows only on the supposition that evolution is a theory$_o$. But when biologists call evolution a theory, they mean that it is a theory$_s$. And on that reading the creationist conclusion does not follow. One cannot reason that since the theory of evolution is a *theory*, it is not well established.

The creationist may admit that the evolutionary account is a theory$_s$, yet not a well-established one. This point could be true, of course; but if so, it becomes an *empirical*, not a *philosophical*, point. The claim that evolution is not well established thus requires empirical justification.

REPEATABILITY OF EVENTS

Creationists charge that evolutionary theory has a special difficulty in conforming to one of the canons of scientific method. As Duane Gish notes: "Another criterion that must apply to a scientific theory is the ability to repeatedly observe the events, processes or properties used to support the theory. There were obviously no human witnesses to the origin of the universe, the origin of life, or in fact to the origin of a single living thing."[9] Gish's point, which is widely echoed in the popular creationist literature, seems to come down to this. Consider some scientific regularity—for example, that arsenic poisons or that copper conducts electricity. To have confidence in the truth of such a regularity or law, the creationists argue, one must be able to repeatedly observe instances of it. In the case of the regularities that make up the theory of evolution, it is in principle impossible to observe instances of them, since evolutionary history consists of a unique series of events.

This argument has two flaws.[10] First, the canons of scientific method do not require that one be able to observe the instances of the regularities or the particular event in order to justify one's belief in them. It is acceptable and standard practice to justify belief in a regularity by deducing certain observable consequences from it and certain auxiliary assumptions. The same procedure holds for establishing the occurrence of particular events. To insist that instances of the laws be observed would eliminate not only much of the theory of evolution but nearly the whole of modern physics. The kind of reasoning illustrated by the Sternberg experiments is standard fare in scientific inquiry. Sternberg did not observe the serial exhaustive search said to take place in the brain but observed consequences of it, namely, reaction times. Similarly, one does not observe the interaction of elementary particles but, rather, certain consequences or effects of those hypothesized interactions.

Second, even when instances of a regularity are observable—for example, Snell's Law ($\sin i/\sin r$ = constant)[11] or the gas law ($PV = NrT$)[12]—one cannot repeatedly observe the *same* events being instances of the regularity simply because every event is unique. No event occurs twice. So if we adhere rigorously to Gish's demand, no law can be confirmed.

Of course, given some notion of relevant similarity, relevantly similar events can occur an indefinitely large number of times. It is by observing such event *types* that scientists confirm observational laws. But there is no reason that the evolutionist cannot meet this demand. He claims that the same regularities hold now as in the past. Of course, he cannot observe past instances of the regularities. That is a trivial truth. Neither can he observe past instances of Newton's laws. But he can confirm Newton's laws in the laboratory and in nature. The same situation holds for the evolutionary regularities that have observable instances.[13]

In summary, Gish's supposed canon of method is far too strong. If confirmation requires the observation of instances of regularities, most of science will not meet the requirement. Even if we restrict the requirement to observational regularities, it is still too strict since events do not recur. If we weaken the requirement to event-types then there is no a priori reason that evolutionary regularities cannot meet the condition.

FALSIFIABILITY

The creationists' main criticism of evolutionary theory is the bold challenge that the theory is not scientific. This claim has had a powerful rhetorical effect among creationists. Scientists, they argue, have painted themselves as hard-nosed, no-nonsense fellows who claim that the weak-willed creationists have failed to properly limit religion and hence have tainted the truth. So the claim that evolutionary theory is a metaphysical system or, worse yet, an alternative religion is the ultimate criticism.

The creationist charge is based entirely on the work of the philosopher of science Karl Popper.[14] Over a half century ago Popper was impressed by the contrast between the "scientific" status of Marx's theory of history, Freud's psychoanalysis, and Alfred Adler's individual psychology on the one hand and Einstein's theory of gravitation on the other. He set for himself the problem of "demarcation," or the problem of defining when a theory should be regarded as scientific. Popper's answer is that the mark of a scientific theory is falsifiability.[15] In other words, theories are scientific if they prohibit some occurrences. There must be some observable events such that if they were to occur the theory would be false. Sternberg's theory, for example, could be falsified if subsequent data gave a different graph from that shown in Figure 1. As a matter of historical record, Popper believes that the theories of Marx, Freud, and Adler failed to meet the criterion, whereas

Einstein's theory did. He also stated that "Darwinism" was not falsifiable and therefore not scientific.

The creationist argument against the scientific status of evolutionary theory can be reduced to a simple syllogism: *premise one,* falsifiability is the criterion for scientific status; *premise two,* the theory of evolution is not falsifiable; *conclusion,* the theory of evolution is not a scientific theory. To evaluate this argument, three points must be considered:

1. Creationists defend the premises by nothing more than an appeal to Popper's authority. Popper *said* that falsifiability is the mark of a scientific theory. Popper *said* that the theory of evolution is not falsifiable. Nowhere in the creationist literature do we find a defense of falsificationism or Popper's evaluation of evolutionary theory. We do not even find a clear statement of Popper's ideas. What Popper actually says about "evolutionary theory" is that "Darwinism is not a testable scientific theory, but a metaphysical *research programme*—a possible framework for testable scientific theories."[16] Nowhere do creationists demonstrate that what Popper means by "Darwinism" is what contemporary biologists mean by "the theory of evolution." Perhaps the current theory is one of those testable theories that fall within the Darwinian framework.

The creationists' crude appeal to Popper's authority can perhaps be understood, though not justified, when it is noticed that many anticreationists also accept Popper with no questions asked. Popperianism appears to be gospel among many scientists. Efforts by scientists to counter the nonscientific components of our culture, such as astrology and extrasensory perception, have typically been fought under the banner of falsificationism. Here, too, the banner has simply been borrowed, not examined.[17]

2. If one's arguments rest merely on appeals to authority and the authority happens to change his mind, then one is left, as they say, holding the bag. Unfortunately for creationists, that is precisely the present situation. Popper's recent comments clearly indicate that he believes that the contemporary theory of evolution is testable.[18] Of course, he may be wrong. But what we need is an argument to that effect.

3. For the purposes of argument, let us suppose that falsifiability is the mark of a scientific theory. Present in this supposition are two embarrassing points that the creationists have overlooked. First, the bulk of the creationists' objections to evolutionary theory are straightforward empirical objections. For example, creationists claim that evolutionary theory is incompatible with our knowledge of thermodynamics and that evolutionary theory is incompatible with the fossil and sediment-layer records. It is by means of such objections that creationists attempt to establish their scientific expertise and to refute the theory of evolution.

Whether these critical claims are correct is not the present issue. The present point is that if creationists claim that observable evidence actually refutes a theory, then they must think that it is falsifiable. Therefore, the creationists cannot claim to have given evidence that the theory of evolution *is false* and also that it *is not falsifiable.* Second, is creationism itself a scientific theory? Despite some disagreement among creationists on this issue, most would say that it is. The following remarks are addressed to those who believe creationism is a scientific theory and that falsifiability is the mark of such a theory.

The obvious question is whether creationism is falsifiable. I shall be suggesting that in a sense it is not. My remarks could be understood as encouraging creationists to state what those observable occurrences are, which, if they were to happen, would constitute counterevidence to their theory.

To determine whether creationism is falsifiable, let us consider first a possible theory called 'originism,'' which is amazingly similar to creationism in that it denies almost every claim of evolutionary theory. According to originism, for example, the universe is about 10,000 years old, plants and animals appear in the universe as distinct kinds, the earth's history contains a massive catastrophic flood, and so on. Suppose that originism is just like creationism except that it is ''naturalized.'' Everywhere that creationism talks about such and such being supernaturally created, originism talks about such and such appearing or occurring. Originism, then, is just like creationism except that it has been purged of nonnatural creative activities and, of course, creators.

It is obvious that originism is falsifiable. There are possible fossil records, or sedimentary records, or carbon-dating results that would refute originism. Since originism is ''contained'' in creationism, creationism will also, at least in principle, be falsifiable. That is, the same results as just stated could falsify creationism.

But given that originism is a simpler view than creationism, on standard methodological grounds it should be preferred unless creationism has additional observational consequences—consequences in addition to those of originism. I suspect there are none. For those who disagree, it will be instructive to have the observational consequences clearly stated. The next section formulates a dilemma for anyone who takes up this challenge.

GOD AND SCIENTIFIC EXPLANATION

Is it possible, in principle, for concepts like God, creator, and creative process to play a role in scientific explanations? As we have seen in the previous discussion, the answer depends on what you mean by ''God,'' ''creator,'' and ''creative process.'' In particular, are these concepts understood in such a way that they play a role in a theory having observational consequences that the theory would not have without them?

This very general response is correct, but it makes it appear that the answer to the question is more open than it really is. It is not up to a specific speaker of a language to create for words whatever meanings he wants.

Lewis Carroll put the point humorously in *Alice in Wonderland*: "That's a great deal to make one word mean," Alice said in a thoughtful tone. "When I make a word do a lot of work like that," said Humpty Dumpty, "I always pay it extra."

Consider the concept of God. Within the standard Judeo-Christian tradition, one that scientific creationists accept and want to be identified with, God is a supernatural being that is all good, all knowing, and all powerful. The essential question, therefore, is whether this specific God can play a role in scientific explanations. There appear to be logical reasons why it cannot.

God's nature, being supernatural, is unlike natural entities such as electrons, genes, apples, and societies. Entities in the natural order interact with one another through efficient causal relations. Very generally in efficient causal relations the entities are spatially and temporally contiguous and undergo a transfer of energy from one to the other—for example, a hammer striking a nail causes the nail to move into the wood. The heart of scientific explanation is providing the efficient causes of events or phenomena.

Now is should be clear that there is a severe logical tension in the claim that God could play a role in scientific explanations. The most plausible reason for allowing God as a scientific entity is that God enters into efficient causal relations. But if an entity enters into efficient causal relations, it can be understood as natural, not supernatural. God can acquire a scientific status only by abandoning his supernatural status. For those within the standard Judeo-Christian tradition, that price must be judged too high.

The philosophical arguments used by creationists to refute the theory of evolution—that it is merely a theory, that it is about nonrepeatable phenomena, that it is unfalsifiable—are woefully inadequate. The dust raised by these arguments was agitated by various confused or uncritically held views about the nature of science.

NOTES

1. S. J. Gould, "Evolution as Fact and Theory," *Discovery* (May 1981): 34.

2. *Ibid.*, 34–37.

3. D. Gish, "Evolution as Fact and Theory," *Discovery* (July 1981): 6.

4. S. Sternberg, "Two Operations in Character Recognition: Some Evidence from Reaction-Time Measurements," *Perception and Psychophysics* 2 (1967): 45—53.

5. More precisely, the mean reaction time and the size of the positive set are linearly correlated.

6. Theories are tested by checking the predicted observational consequences of the theory. Typically, the predicted consequences do not follow merely from the theory being tested. The theory must be supplemented with auxiliary assumptions, such as assumptions about background conditions or the apparatus used in the experiment. If, for example, one's theory predicts that a microorganism will increase in size when placed in a certain solution, the test of this view will involve the auxiliary assumption that microscopes faithfully reveal at least the relative size of certain microorganisms. If the predicted consequences fail to occur, it is logically possible that the auxiliary assumptions are false and not the theory proper.

7. Being certain is a logically stronger notion than being correct. If the data are correct, they are true. If the data were certain, they would not merely be true. It would be *impossible* for the data to be false.

8. Typically phenomena are explained by being shown to be an instance of causal regularities or laws of

nature. For the details of scientific explanation and theories, see Part II of Klemke, Hollinger, and Kline and also see Suppe.

9. Gish, "Evolution as Fact and Theory," p. 6.

10. I do not wish to deny that there are interesting differences between the regularities of evolutionary theory and other theories. But those differences do not seem to be at issue in the creationists' criticism. See D. Hull, *Philosophy of Biological Science* (Englewood Cliffs, N.J.: Prentice-Hall, 1974), pp. 70–100.

11. Whenever any ray of light is incident at the surface that separates two media, it is bent in such a way that the ratio of the sine of the angle of incidence to the sine of the angle of refraction is always a constant quantity for those two media.

12. Very roughly, the product of the pressure and volume is proportional to the temperature.

13. For example, any characteristic will become more prevalent in the population if the individual possessing it produces a larger progeny that survives to adulthood than individuals not having the trait. See Chapter 7 of David Wilson, ed., *Did the Devil Make Darwin Do It?: Modern Perspective on the Creation-Evolution Controversy* (Ames: The Iowa State University Press, 1983).

14. See, for example, Gish, "Evolution as Fact and Theory," p. 6.

15. K. Popper, "Science: Conjectures and Refutations," reprinted in *Introductory Readings in the Philosophy of Science*, E. Klemke, R. Hollinger, and A. D. Kline, eds. (Buffalo, N.Y.: Prometheus Books, 1980), pp. 19–34.

16. K. Popper, "Autobiography of Karl Popper," in *The Philosophy of Karl Popper*, Book 1, P. Schilpp, ad., (La Salle, Ill.: Open Coun, 1974), p. 134.

17. There are serious problems with falsificationism. See P. Thagard, "Why Astrology is a Pseudoscience," and P. Feyerabend, "How to Defend Society against Science," both in *Introductory Readings in the Philosophy of Science*, E. Klemke, R. Hollinger, and A. D. Kline, eds. (Buffalo, N.Y.: Prometheus Books, 1980).

18. K. Popper, "Evolution," *New Scientist* (August 1980): 611.

ERNEST NAGEL

Science Must Not Be Subordinated to Metaphysics and Theology

Ernest Nagel (1901–) here argues against metaphysical and theological perspectives that attempt to limit the scope of scientific method. Contrary to those who claim a kind of knowledge superior to and more inclusive than scientific knowledge, Nagel argues that there is a legitimate sense in which science investigates the "why" of things. He further argues that the postulation of an "absolute cause" or God by metaphysicians and theologians to explain why the world exists is a rationally confused strategy, since the question then arises as to why this absolute cause exists arises. Nagel points out that reference to an absolute cause of all things provides no specific explanation of why we have the particular arrangements of objects and events in our world that we do. Last, he argues that appeals to special ways of knowing the secrets of the universe must inevitably face adjudication by science.

From "Malicious Philosophies of Science," in *Sovereign Reason* (New York: Free Press, 1954).

⌘

[Some views limit] the scope of scientific methods on the basis of considerations that are at least nominally scientific in character. [However,] the criticisms of science to which [I next direct your] attention . . . do not even pretend to adduce scientific grounds for their claims, and are frankly based upon explicit theological and metaphysical commitments for which no experimental evidence is invoked. The chief burden of their complaints is that science offers no "ultimate explanation" for the facts of existence; and their chief recommendation is the cultivation of "ontological wisdom" as the sole method for making "ultimately intelligible" both the order of the cosmos and the nature of the good life.

Some citations . . . will exhibit more clearly than would a paraphrase the unique mixture of pontifical dogmatism, oracular wisdom, and condescending obscurantism which seems to be the indispensable intellectual apparatus of this school of criticism. Professor Gilson characterizes the plight of science as follows:

> This world of ours is a world of change; physics, chemistry, biology can teach us the laws according to which change actually happens to it; what these sciences cannot teach us is why this world, taken together with its laws, its order, and its intelligibility is, or exists. . . . Scientists never ask themselves *why* things happen, but *how* they happen. Now as soon as you substitute the positivist's notion of relation for the metaphysical notion of cause, you at once lose all right to wonder *why* things are, and why they are what they are. . . . Why anything at all is, or exists, science knows not, precisely because it cannot even ask the question. To this supreme question the only answer is that each and every particular existential energy, and each and every particular existing thing depends for its existence upon a pure Act of existence. In order to be the ultimate answer to all existential problems, this supreme cause has to be absolute existence. Being absolute, such a cause is self-sufficient; if it creates, its creative act must be free. Since it creates not only being but order, it must be something which at least eminently contains the only principle of order known to us in experience, namely, thought.[1]

And Professor Maritain, building on the alleged subordination of science to metaphysics, indicates some of the immediate consequences of this hierarchial arrangement:

> Science . . . is distinguished from wisdom in this, that science aims at the detail of some special field of knowing and deals with the secondary, proximate or apparent causes, while wisdom aims at some universal knowing and deals with prime and deepest causes, with the highest sources of being. . . . Wisdom is not only distinct from but also superior to science, in the sense that its object is more universal and more deeply immersed in the mystery of things, and in the sense that the function of defending the first principles of knowledge and of discovering the fundamental structure and organization thereof belongs to wisdom, not to science. . . . Science puts means in man's hands, and teaches men how to apply these means for the happiest outcome, not for him who acts, but

> for the work to be done. Wisdom deals with ends in man's heart, and teaches man how to use means and apply science for the real goodness and happiness of him who acts, of the person himself. . . . Science is like art in this, that though both are good in themselves man can put them to bad uses and bad purposes: while in so far as man uses wisdom . . . he can only use it for good purposes.
>
> The paleontologist does not step out of his sphere when he establishes the hypothesis of evolution and applies it to the origin of the human being. But the philosopher must warn him that he is out of his field when he tries to deny for that reason that the human soul is a spiritual soul which cannot emanate from matter, so that if once upon a time the human organism was produced by a mutation of an animal organism, it was because of the infusion of a soul created by God.[2]

Although criticism of a position is futile when those who hold it make a virtue of its mysteries and when they regard themselves as superior to the usual canons of scientific intelligibility, those who are not so fortunately placed may find the following observations not irrelevant. In the first place, there is a perfectly clear sense in which science does supply answers as to "why" things happen and are what they are. Thus, if we ask why the moon becomes eclipsed at certain times, the answer is that at those times the moon moves into the earth's shadow; if we ask why the moon behaves in this way, the answer is given in part by the theory of gravitation; if we ask why bodies behave in the manner predicated by this theory, the answer is supplied by the general theory of relativity. On the other hand, if we repeat this question concerning relativity theory, no further answer is at present forthcoming, so that for the present at least this theory is an "ultimate" or "brute" fact. Furthermore, if some day relativity theory should become absorbed into a unified field-theory embracing both macroscopic and microscopic phenomena, the unified field-theory would explain why the equations of relativity theory hold, but at the same time it would become the (perhaps only temporary) "ultimate" structural fact. In science the answer to the question "why" is therefore always a theory, from which the specific fact at issue may be deduced when suitable initial conditions are introduced. The point of these familiar remarks is that no matter how far the question "why" is pressed—and it may be pressed indefinitely—it must terminate in a theory which is itself not logically demonstrable. For no theory which explains why things happen as they do and not otherwise can be a logically necessary truth. It follows that those who seek to discern the laws of nature to be necessary, as well as those who "hope to see that it is necessary that there should be an order of nature," are violating an elementary canon of discursive thought.

In the second place, it is obvious that anyone who invokes an "absolute cause" (or God) to explain "why" the world exists, merely postpones settling his accounts with the logic of his question: for the Being who has been postulated as the Creator of the world is simply one more being into the reasons of whose existence it is possible to inquire. If those who invoke such a Being declare that such questions about His existence are not legitimate, they surmount a difficulty only by dogmatically cutting short a discussion when the intellectual current runs against them. If, on the other hand, the question is answered with the assertion that God is his own cause, the question is resolved only by falling back upon another mystery; and at best, such a "reason" is simply an unclear statement of the grounds upon which scientists regard as unintelligible the *initial* "why" as to the world's existence. But a mystery is no answer if the question to which it is a reply has a definite meaning; and in the end, nothing is gained in the way of intellectual illumination when the discussion terminates in such a manner.

In the third place, the postulation of an "absolute cause" or an "ultimate reason" for the world and its structure provides no answer to any *specific* question which may be asked concerning any particular objects or events in the world. On the contrary, no matter what the world were like, no matter what the course of events might be, the same Ultimate Cause is offered as an "explanation." This is admitted in so many words by Professor Gilson: "The existence or non-existence of God . . . is a proposition whose negation or affirmation determines no change whatever in the structure of our scientific explanation of the world and is wholly independent of the contents of science as such. Supposing, for instance, there be design in the world, the existence of God cannot be posited as a *scientific* explanation for the presence of design in the world; it is a *metaphysical* one."[3]

But just what does an "explanation" explain when it explains nothing in particular? What understanding of our world does a metaphysics provide which is compatible both with a design in the processes of nature as well as with its absence, with the existence of specific goods as well as with their nonexistence, with one pervasive pattern of causal interactions as well as with another? A high price in unintelligibility must be paid when the canons of scientific discourse and inquiry are abandoned.

And finally, the assumption that there is a superior and more direct way of grasping the secrets of the universe than the painfully slow road of science has been so repeatedly shown to be a romantic illusion, that only those who are unable to profit from the history of the human intellect can seriously maintain it. Certainly, whatever enlightenment we possess about ourselves and the world has been achieved only after the illusion of a "metaphysical wisdom" superior to "mere science" had been abandoned. The methods of science do not guarantee that its conclusions are final and incorrigible by further inquiry; but it is by dropping the pretense of a spurious finality and recognizing the fallibility of its self-corrective procedures that science has won its victories. It may be a comfort to some to learn that in so far as man uses "wisdom" he can aim only at the good; since the most diverse kinds of action—kindly as well as brutal, beneficent as well as costly in human life—are undertaken in the name of wisdom, such a testimonial will doubtless enable everyone engaged in such an undertaking to redouble his zeal without counting the costs. But it is not wisdom but a mark of immaturity to recommend that we simply examine our hearts if we wish to discover the good life; for it is just because men rely on completely and unreflectively on recommend that we simply examine our hearts if we wish to discover the good life; for it is just because men rely so completely and unreflectively on their intuitive insights and passionate impulses that needless sufferings and conflicts occur among them. The point is clear: claims as to what is required by wisdom need to be adjudicated if such claims are to be warranted; and accordingly, objective methods must be instituted, on the basis of which the conditions, the consequences, and the mutual compatibility of different courses of action may be established. But if such methods are introduced, we leave the miasmal swamps of supra-scientific wisdom, and are brought back again to the firm soil of scientific knowledge.

NOTES

1. Etienne Gilson, *God and Philosophy*, pp. 72, 140. Although Whitehead's manner of arriving at his speculative cosmology is radically different from that cultivated by neo-Thomists, his evaluations of the limitations of natural science are frequently not dissimilar. He comments as follows on "the grand doctrine of Nature as a self-sufficient, meaningless complex of facts": "Newton left for empirical investigation the determination of the particular stresses now existing. In this determination he made a magnificent beginning by isolating the stresses indicated by his law of gravitation. But he left no hint, *why in the nature of things there should be any stresses at all*. The arbitrary motion of the bodies were thus explained by the arbitrary stresses between material bodies, conjoined with their spatiality, their mass, and their initial states of motion. By introducing stresses—in particular the law of gravitation—instead of the welter of detailed transformations of motion, he greatly increased the systematic aspect of nature. But he left all the factors of the system—more particularly, mass and stress—in the position of detached facts *devoid of reason* for their compresence. He thus illuminated a great philosophic truth, that a dead nature can give no reasons. All the ultimate reasons are in terms of aim at value. A dead nature aims at nothing." A. N. Whitehead, *Modes of Thought*, pp. 183–84, italics not in the text.

2. The first paragraph is taken from the essay "Science and Wisdom," contained in *Science and Man*, pp. 66–67, 72, 94. The second paragraph is from the essay "Science, Philosophy and Faith," contained in the volume *Science, Philosophy and Religion*, the proceedings of the First Conference on Science, Philosophy and Religion, p. 181.

3. Gilson, *God and Philosophy*, p. 141.

SUGGESTED READING

Barbour, Ian G., ed. *Science and Religion: New Perspectives on the Dialogue*. New York: Harper and Row, 1968.
Davies, Paul. *God and the New Physics*. New York: Simon and Schuster, 1983.
Dillenberger, John. *Protestant Thought and Natural Science*. New York: Doubleday, 1960.
Hawking, Steven. *A Brief History of Time*. (New York: Bantam, 1990).
Hempel, Carl. *Philosophy of Natural Science*. Englewood Cliffs, N.J.: Prentice-Hall, 1966.
Hull, David. *Philosophy of Biological Science*. Englewood Cliffs, N.J.: Prentice-Hall, 1974.
Klemke, Elmer, Robert Hollinger, and A. David Kline, eds. *Introductory Readings in the Philosophy of Science*. Buffalo: Prometheus Books, 1980.
Nebelsick, Harold. *Theology and Science in Mutual Modification*. New York: Oxford University Press, 1981.

Mascall, E. L. *Christian Theology and Natural Science*. London: Oxford University Press, 1979.
Polkinghorne, John. *One World*. Princeton: Princeton University Press, 1987.
———. *The Way the World Is*. xxx: Tringle, 1983.
Popper, Karl. *Conjectures and Refutations*. New York: Harper and Row, 1963.
Ratzsch, Del. *Philosophy of Science: The Natural Sciences in Humans Perspective*. Downers Grove, Ill.: InterVarsity Press, 1986.
Schlesinger, George. *Religion and Scientific Method*. Dordrecht: D. Reidel, 1977.
Suppe, Frederick, ed. *The Structure of Scientific Theories*. Urbana: University of Illinois Press, 1974.

PART ELEVEN

RELIGIOUS DIVERSITY

Diversity stands as a hallmark of contemporary culture, and it is no less significant in religion than elsewhere. Since different religions make sometimes compatible and other times incompatible claims, what are we to make both of the individual claims and of each religion as a whole?

Exclusivists like James Borland argue that though there are truths in other religions, basic claims about the nature of God and salvation/liberation are so different in different religions that they cannot possibly all be true. Consequently, one set of claims (and hence the religion that incorporates that set) is exclusively true; it alone describes the way of salvation or liberation.

Inclusivists like Karl Rahner agree with exclusivists that the absolute provision for salvation is revealed in one religion. God has acted in a particular way that makes salvation available for all. At the same time, God might reveal himself or act graciously in various ways in a variety of places and times; hence, people can encounter God and receive God's grace in diverse religions. That is, adherents of other religions can be saved/liberated because of persons or events specified by the true religion, without knowing anything about the religion that embodies the objective provision for salvation.

Pluralists like John Hick disagree with exclusivists and inclusivists: there is no one true religion. Rather, there are many paths to salvation/liberation. Each religion specifies its own unique way that, for adherents, can bring them release from the human predicament and contact with the Real. Of course, there must be checks and balances to religious claims, but they are provided for when the religious tradition has produced through the centuries profound scriptures, impressive intellectual systems, new visions of human existence, and saintly lives.

Critics of pluralism wonder how such diverse religious conceptions of God or Reality can all be true. Some pluralists respond that religion does not make truth claims at all, and hence there is no problem with diverse claims. Its sole concern is making life meaningful. Other pluralists hold that religious concepts express, not the Real itself, but our attempt to understand the Real. They express how the Real appears to us and hence should not be taken as literally descriptive of it. But if we have no clear concept of God, what distinguishes religious belief from atheism? What do we mean when we speak about God or the Real, and what would it mean to claim that such exists?

If religions make truth claims, a final issue concerns how one might assess religious systems. The criteria employed must be carefully chosen so that they do not bias the evaluation in favor of one religion. Keith Yandell [*Christianity and Philosophy*] suggests some cross-cultural criteria that might be employed in such an assessment.

Whatever position one takes on the matter of religious diversity, one must clearly distinguish understanding from matters of truth. Before one can get to the place of raising questions of truth, one must understand and appreciate the religious claims made. It is also important to distinguish making judgments about the truth of religious claims from the question of religious tolerance. To engage in the evaluation of claims should never interfere with the acceptance of others as valuable persons.

JAMES BORLAND

Religious Exclusivism

James Borland (1949–) contends that there are marked contrasts between Christianity and the other world religions. These contrasts are based on the very different concepts of God, the nature of humanity, the function and role of Jesus Christ, and the way of salvation. Indeed, other religions, he claims, are in total antithesis to Christianity on many of these points, so that all cannot be true in their entirety. He then marshals passages from the Christian New Testament which declare that salvation comes only through Jesus Christ, so that those who do not know of him or acknowledge him as Lord cannot reach heaven. For Borland, non-Christians can be saved only through hearing and believing the Christian Gospel.

⌘

So many religious systems vie for our trust. Can we sort out truth from error? Is it possible to differentiate among human claims, religious lore, and what might be absolute truth? If so, how would one go about the task? . . .

THE GOSPEL AND WORLD RELIGIONS CONTRASTED

As a Christian theologian let me sort out some of the questions related to the gospel and world religions and place them in theological categories. First, the Christian gospel makes several statements. The gospel speaks of Christology, for it was Jesus Christ our Lord who died, was buried and rose again the third day (1 Cor 15:3–4). The gospel also speaks of anthropology and hamartiology, because Christ died for sinful mankind—that is, "for our sins" (15:3), "while we were yet sinners" (Rom 5:8). Soteriology is also addressed in terms of substitution, vicariousness, justification, redemption, reconciliation, propitiation, forgiveness, union with Christ, aspects of election, sufficiency and security, and in the matter of the uniqueness and exclusivity of this message.

In addition God's attributes of wisdom, holiness and love come up for consideration. Indeed the gospel is not in a nutshell but is a bombshell with supernatural implications. Paul declares that the gospel of Christ "is the power of God unto salvation for everyone who believes" regardless of race, culture, sex, or any other differences (Rom 1:16; 1 Cor 1:18; Gal 3:28).

Let me now proceed to examine these theological categories, draw out

From *Journal of the Evangelical Theological Society* 33, no. 1 (March 1990): 3–11. Reprinted by permission.

some of their implications, and compare the Christian gospel with the message of the most prominent world religions. First, in the matter of God's attributes Christianity teaches that the triune God is all-wise and that his plan of salvation was in place from eternity (Eph 1:4). God's holiness demands righteousness of his creatures, whom he wisely allowed to fall into sin in accordance with his eternal redemptive plan. Man's predicament is that he cannot in any way save himself. God's love, however, balances the equation with a provision of imparted righteousness given freely to all whom he can wisely persuade to repent and believe.

But none of this theology has a familiar ring to the ear of a Muslim, Hindu or Buddhist. Islam's God is far different from the Christian's. No Trinity exists, and God's gracious redemptive provisions are overshadowed by Allah's power, justice and inscrutable determinism.[1] The Hindu and Buddhist primarily do not see sin in terms of relationship to a personal and moral God.[2] For the Hindu, salvation is primarily a "separation of the eternal soul from the phenomenal world."[3] It is not something God does for you but something you do for yourself. The Buddhist in turn seeks nirvana, the loss of all individual consciousness and existence by absorption into the impersonal all.[4]

The second theological area deals with the nature of man. Christianity teaches that man was created a perfect finite creature, a mixture of material and immaterial. By choice he is now fallen but is still redeemable. He has but one life on earth and will be resurrected bodily (Heb 9:27). He will either spend eternity with God and the redeemed, or else he will exist in conscious everlasting torment with the fallen angels and the rest of unredeemed mankind. Since man has offended God, man must bear the penalty of death. But here the love of God and his exacting holiness come together. As Anselm notes in *Cur Deus Homo*, Christ had to become man for that very reason. Man must suffer the deserved retribution of God, but only God himself could bear such a penalty.

Again, Islam somewhat approaches the Christian doctrine of the nature of man, but not in the part God plays in man's atonement. The Hindu and Buddhist doctrines of continuous reincarnation differ fundamentally from the Christian view of bodily resurrection, judgment, and the conscious eternal state.

That brings us to the third category: Christology. Christianity teaches that Jesus was no ordinary man. He was the eternal God, the Creator, in human form (Phil 2:6–7), expressing all the fulness of the Godhead bodily (Col 2:9), the exact image of God's person (Heb 1:3). There can be no doubt about Christ's virginal conception (Matt 1:22–23; Luke 1:35), which though not necessary to affirm for salvation cannot be consciously denied.

His sinless life (Heb 4:15; 7:26) was also a prerequisite to providing a sacrificial atonement for a fallen race. His historical death, burial and resurrection are constantly affirmed in the gospels, epistles and the apostolic preaching recorded in Acts. His resurrection is totally unique in the annals of all time. In addition Jesus, in view of his finished work of salvation, has ascended into glory, from whence we look for his imminent appearance to usher in the next stage of his divine plan.

In stark contrast to this "the Qur'an depicts him [Jesus] as expressly disclaiming deity and seems to deny that he ever died on the cross."[5] While Jesus is accepted in Islam as a former prophet, he is beneath Muhammad and has no supreme part to play in the future. Although the Hindu religion is eclectic and syncretistic, it takes only the ethics and ideals of Christianity while discarding the merit of the person and work of Christ.[6] Mahatma Gandhi, for example, "expressed great admiration for the ideal Christ, [but] he had no interest in the incarnation, atonement and resurrection of the historical Christ. To him the cross was an eternal event symbolizing self-sacrifice."[7] For the Buddhist, the life and death of Jesus Christ are irrelevant to what he must attain, and the teachings of Christianity are diametrically opposed to the key concepts of karma, impermanence and nirvana as taught in Buddhism.[8]

Fourth, the encompassing category of soteriology looms before us. Christianity teaches that man's salvation was provided entirely by God. No amount of good deeds, large or small, can fit into the equation of man's salvation. Christ's death on the cross was a complete substitution for man. His sacrificial death was the propitiation that secured forgiveness and reconciliation to God for everyone who casts the destiny of his soul upon Christ's finished work.

No other condition is imposed but faith. Convicted by God's Holy Spirit, the helpless sinner, who sees his need and the full provision made by Christ, does an about-face. He realizes that Christ is no mere man but Almighty God, and he trusts Christ Jesus completely to redeem him from the awful consequences of sin.

Christianity also teaches that the believing sinner is spiritually transformed immediately upon placing his faith in Christ. Jesus called this the new birth (John 3:3). Paul termed it a new creation (2 Cor 5:17). New spiritual life is imparted (2 Pet 1:4) as one is united to Christ spiritually, thus partaking of all that Christ accomplished for him through his shed blood, physical resurrection and bodily ascension. That union is eternal, immutable, vital, spiritual and personal. Christ did the saving, and he will not undo it. Nor can the believer ever break the new spiritual bond through any contemplated or actual lapse into sin.

Though following different models Islam, Hinduism and Buddhism teach that salvation is found in man's working to keep certain precepts rather than in God's imparting new life on the basis of Christ's finished work for us. Initiation into the Muslim faith is fairly simple, the majority of Muslims holding that "a mere recital of the creed [There is no God but God, and Muhammad is the Prophet of God] is enough to enroll a new convert."[9] But a plethora of rules follows for the faithful to keep.

Hinduism teaches that salvation comes from "self-purification and self-realization."[10] To accomplish this a process of many reincarnations is maintained, aided by yoga used to produce a detachment from the physical arena and a oneness with divine mind. For example, Buddha, who began as a Hindu, thought it had taken him 550 separate reincarnations to achieve what he finally did. At three score and ten for every imperfect reincarnation that would occupy nearly forty millennia, and it is assumed that most might take a bit longer than did Buddha himself.

Similarly, Buddhism's four truths and its eightfold path of right views, right aspirations, right speech, right conduct, right mode of livelihood, right effort, right awareness, and right concentration base salvation totally on human effort. The goal of nirvana is somewhere between annihilation and continued existence. Nicholls suggests: "If this goal seems unattractive, it should be remembered that to the Buddhist the curse from which he longs to escape is life itself, which is inextricably tainted with suffering."[11]

The world religions are in total antithesis to the Christian doctrine of salvation. How different from this simple dictum: "But to him who does not work but believes on him who justifies the ungodly, his faith is accounted for righteousness" (Rom 4:5)! Hear it again in Titus 3:5a: "Not by works of righteousness which we have done, but according to his mercy he saved us." Again, the one who has entered into God's rest, like a Sabbath, "has himself also ceased from his works as God did from his" (Heb 4:10).

EVERYONE MUST HEAR AND BELIEVE THE GOSPEL TO BE SAVED

Is it possible to be saved apart from believing the gospel of Christ? Can Christ save a good Hindu through his Hinduism? Are there "ascended masters" from all religions in heaven today? Can other religions be termed "saving structures" because they in some way direct people to the "cosmic Christ," as Raymond Panikkar teaches?[12] Is Cantwell Smith wrong to claim that the non-Christian religions are "channels through which God Himself comes into touch with these His children"[13] and that "both within and without the Church, so far as we can see, God does somehow enter into men's hearts?"[14]. . .

God's Word continuously presents many disclaimers. Jesus was fairly emphatic about the absolute impossibility of reaching heaven apart from himself. The English translation of John 14:6 preserves the precise original word order with its usual emphases: "I am the way, the truth, and the life. No one comes to the Father except through me."

The apostles of Christ are not evasive in this regard either. The apostle Peter, said to be filled with the Holy Spirit, boldly stated: "There is no salvation by anyone else, for no one else in all the wide world has been appointed among men as our only medium by which to be saved" (Acts 4:12).

The apostle Paul declared: "For no other foundation can anyone lay than that which is laid, which is Jesus Christ" (1 Cor 3:11). Again he stated: "For there is one God and one Mediator between God and men, the Man Christ Jesus" (1 Tim 2:5).

The apostle John plainly said, "This life is in his Son. He who has the Son has life; he who does not have the Son of God does not have life" (1 John 5:11b–12). John's gospel contains equally plain and strong statements as seen below.

Christ and the apostles taught that in order for one to appropriate the provision of Christ personal faith or belief was a necessity. Furthermore faith cannot be nebulous but must have an object—a correct object if one aspires to a certain goal. The ultimate provision for salvation has always been the death of Jesus Christ. The means of securing salvation has always been faith. But the actual content of faith—that is, what must be believed—has changed with the progressive nature of God's revelation.

Abel's faith, for example, was exhibited in that he "offered *the God appointed sacrifice.*"[15] The content of Abraham's justifying faith, as stated in Gen 15:6, was that God would fulfill his promise of many descendants.

Since Calvary, the unchanging required content of one's faith is the gospel. Nothing else saves, while all else damns. No substitutions, additions or imitations are permitted. Any other gospel is not another that can save. It only brings with it an anathema (Gal 1:6–9).

I take issue with Anderson's idea that it is "through the basic fact of God's general revelation, vouchsafed in nature and in all that is true (including, of course, the truth there is in other religions), and the equally fundamental facts of our common humanity, that the Spirit of God, or the 'cosmic Christ,' brings home to men and women something of their need."[16] Anderson's suggestion is that this conviction may be enough enlightenment to result in salvation apart from ever naming the name of Christ.

Is this possible? If it were, then it seems strange for Paul, who understood so much about general revelation in Romans 1–2, to insist several chapters later that men cannot "call on him in whom they have not believed. . . . And how shall they believe in him of whom they have not heard? And how shall they hear without a preacher? And how shall they preach unless they are sent?" (10:14–15a). Indeed Paul declared: "So then, faith comes by hearing, and hearing by the word of God" (10:17).

Christianity's founder and writing apostles unanimously state the absolute dictum that faith during this dispensation must be placed in none other than Jesus Christ and his finished work on Calvary.

Several examples of cross-cultural conversion in our dispensation are recorded in the NT. Each demonstrates hearing the special revelation of the gospel and placing faith in Christ, not a nebulous repentance and faith based on general revelation.

Philip traveled to Samaria, "preached Christ unto them" (Acts 8:5), and "when they believed the things concerning . . . the name of Jesus Christ, they were baptized" (8:12). If they could have been saved without hearing the gospel, why was Philip so concerned to go there? Later an educated court official from Ethiopia was reading Isaiah, perhaps in Hebrew or Aramaic.

An angel directed Philip to Gaza. Once he arrived there, the Holy Spirit had him join the inquiring Ethiopian. Philip "preached unto him Jesus" (8:35). This man's conviction and desire to know prompted God to send a prepared messenger to announce the gospel content necessary for salvation.

Cornelius' story in Acts 10 is similar. A Roman centurion, he was a devout and just man who feared God and even prayed to God. The text also makes it clear that he was lost. Yet God would not save him apart from his hearing and believing the gospel. In a vision an angel instructed Cornelius to send for Peter "to hear words" (v. 22), and Cornelius later recalled: "When he comes, he will speak to you" (v. 32). Peter in Acts 11:13–14 recounts concerning Cornelius: "And he told us how he had seen an angel standing in his house, who said to him, 'Send men to Joppa, and call for Simon whose surname is Peter, who will tell you words by which you and all your household will be saved.' "

What were Peter's words? After proclaiming the gospel he exhorted "that, through his name, whoever believes in him will receive remission of sins. While Peter was still speaking these words, the Holy Spirit fell upon all those who heard the word" (10:43b–44).

Every heathen who has ever gotten saved has had to believe that same gospel. The eunuch was saved that way. Cornelius was saved that way. The jailer at Philippi was saved that way. I was saved that way, and so were you if you name the name of Christ. And I do not believe we have any warrant to claim that God is doing things differently today, no matter how frequently it may be surmised.

The NT makes it abundantly clear that saving faith must be focused on the person and work of Jesus Christ. Ponder some of Jesus' own words in John's gospel: "Whoever believes in him should not perish but have eternal life" (3:15). "Whoever drinks the water that I shall give him will never thirst" (4:14). "You are not willing to come to me that you may have life" (5:40). "This is the work of God, that you believe in him whom he sent" (6:29). "I am the bread of life. He who comes to me shall never hunger, and he who believes in me shall never thirst" (6:35). "Everyone who sees the Son and believes in him may have everlasting life" (6:40). "He who believes in me has everlasting life" (6:47). "Unless you eat the flesh of the Son of Man and drink his blood, you have no life in you" (6:53). "He who believes in me" (7:38). "I am the light of the world. He who follows me shall not walk in darkness but have the light of life" (8:12).

"If you do not believe that I am he, you will die in your sins" (8:24). "I am the door. If anyone enters by me, he will be saved" (10:9). "I am the resurrection and the life. He who believes in me, though he may die, he shall live. And whoever lives and believes in me shall never die" (11:25–26). "I am the way, the truth, and the life. No one comes to the Father except through me" (14:6). "And when he has come, he will convict the world of sin, and of righteousness, and of judgment: of sin, because they do not believe in me" (15:8–9).

Jesus' final words on the necessity of faith being directed in him are in his high-priestly prayer: "I do not pray for these alone, but also for those who will believe in me through their word; that they all may be one, as you, Father, are in me, and I in you; that they also may be one in us, that the world may believe that you sent me" (17:20–21). Notice carefully how Jesus looks down across the centuries with the same plan of salvation in view. No changes are contemplated.

The apostles never moved away from the precept that saving faith can only be in Christ. Paul again and again proclaimed faith in Christ as the only way of salvation. In Galatians, one of Paul's earliest writings, he said, "Knowing that a man is not justified by the works of the law but by faith in Jesus Christ, even we have believed in Christ Jesus, that we might be justified by faith in Christ" (Gal 2:16).[17] John, who penned the last books of the NT, said, "But these are written that you may believe that Jesus is the Christ, the Son of God, and that believing you may have life in his name" (John 20:31). "He who has the Son has life; he who does not have the Son of God does not have life" (1 John 5:12). "He who believes in him is not condemned; but he who does not believe is condemned already, because he has not believed in the name of the only begotten Son of God" (John 3:18).

Were the apostles a bit too idealistic to hold that all are condemned who do not personally name Jesus on their lips and believe his gospel? Not at all. They were simply following orders, Jesus' marching orders for the Church as found in the great commission. It was Jesus who said, "Make disciples of all the nations" (Matt 28:19). It was Jesus who said, "Go into all the world and preach the gospel to every creature. He who believes and is baptized will be saved; but he who does not believe will be condemned" (Mark 16:15–16). It was Jesus who said, "It was necessary for the Christ to suffer and to rise from the dead the third day, and that repentance and remission of sins should be preached in his name to all nations, beginning at Jerusalem" (Luke 24:46–47).

CONCLUSION

If it was necessary to go then, why not now? If preaching the gospel is required to reach those who are near at hand, why should it not be required to reach those in far-flung lands? Let me pose the question in reverse: If God can save people in faraway places without their hearing and believing the gospel, why can he not accomplish the same everywhere? If taking the gospel to every creature was a concern of Christ's two thousand years ago, why should his *modus operandi* be abandoned now, especially without a word from him to that effect?

Are we more enlightened than our Master? Do we know something that Jesus failed to understand? Our methods can be improved, but our message never. Our methods can change, but our mission is unchanging. To hold out the possibility of any other way of salvation does not add to God's greatness but depreciates his Word and the work of the Church through the ages. To teach any other way of salvation for the heathen diminishes missionary zeal and leaves the helpless hopeless.

NOTES

1. N. Anderson, "Islam," in *The World's Religions* (4th ed., ed. N. Anderson, Grand Rapids, Eerdmans, 1976), 115.
2. B. J. Nicholls, "Hinduism," in *The World's Religions* (ed. N. Anderson), 145.
3. Ibid.
4. D. Bentley-Taylor and C. B. Offner, "Buddhism," in *The World's Religions* (ed., N. Anderson), 176.
5. Anderson, "Islam," 100–101.
6. Nicholls, "Hinduism," 137.
7. Ibid., 164.
8. Bentley-Taylor and Offner, "Buddhism," 174–177.
9. Anderson, "Islam," 118.
10. Nicholls, "Hinduism," 164.
11. Bentley-Taylor and Offner, "Buddhism," 176.
12. R. Panikkar, *The Unknown Christ of Hinduism* (New York: Humanities, 1968), 54.
13. W. C. Smith, *The Faith of Other Men* (New York: Harper, 1972), 136.
14. Ibid., 140.
15. A. Saphir, *The Epistle to the Hebrews* (7th ed., Loizeaux, 1943), 738.
16. Anderson, *The World's Religions*, 236.
17. See also Gal 2:20; 3:22, 26; Phil 1:29; Rom 10:9–13.

KARL RAHNER

Religious Inclusivism

Karl Rahner (1904–1984) maintains that Christianity is the true religion, which portrays God's grace as coming in his self-revelation in Jesus Christ. He argues that, before Christianity historically introduced the obligation to believe in Christ, there were other lawful religions that admittedly embodied an imperfect knowledge of God and yet contained some supernatural elements of grace. This grace, says Rahner, was effective for the salvation of many righteous but non-Christian persons who practiced those religions. He considers religions today to be similar to those which preceded the coming of Jesus in that their adherents likewise have no meaningful historical encounter with Christianity. He is confident that these religions, too, can be lawful because God, desiring that all be saved, gives people his grace through these religions. Adherents of these religions must be regarded as "anonymous Christians" until the Gospel brings them to an explicit knowledge of God's self-revelation in Jesus.

⌘

'Open Catholicism' involves two things. It signifies the fact that the Catholic Church is opposed by historical forces which she herself cannot disregard as if they were purely 'worldly' forces and a matter of indifference to her but which, on the contrary, although they do not stand in a positive relationship of peace and mutual recognition to the Church, do have a significance for her. 'Open Catholicism' means also the task of becoming related to these forces in order to understand their existence (since this cannot be simply acknowledged), in order to bear with and overcome the annoyance of their opposition and in order to form the Church in such a way that she will be able to overcome as much of this pluralism as should not exist, by understanding herself as the higher unity of this opposition. 'Open Catholicism' means therefore a certain attitude towards the present-day pluralism of powers with different outlooks on the world. We do not, of course, refer to pluralism merely as a fact which one simply acknowledges without explaining it. Pluralism is meant here as a fact which ought to be thought about and one which, without denying that—in part at least—it should not exist at all, should be incorporated once more from a more elevated viewpoint into the totality and unity of the Christian understanding of human existence. For Christianity, one of the gravest elements of this pluralism in which we live and with which we must come to terms, and indeed the element most difficult to incorporate, is the pluralism of religions. . . .

This pluralism is a greater threat and a reason for greater unrest for Christianity than for any other religion. For no other religion—not even Islam—maintains so absolutely that it is *the* religion, the one and only valid revelation of the one living God, as does the Christian religion.

The fact of the pluralism of religions, which endures and still from time to time becomes virulent anew even after a history of two thousand years, must therefore be the greatest scandal and the greatest vexation for Christianity. And the threat of this vexation is also greater for the individual Christian today than ever before. For in the past, the other religion was in practice the religion of a completely different cultural environment. It belonged to a history with which the individual only communicated very much on the periphery of his own history; it was the religion of those who were even in every other respect alien to oneself. It is not surprising, therefore, that people did not wonder at the fact that these 'others' and 'strangers' had also a different religion. No wonder that in general people could not seriously consider these other religions as a challenge posed to themselves or even as a possibility for themselves. Today things have changed. The West is no longer shut up in itself; it can no longer regard itself simply as the centre of the history of this world and as the centre of culture, with a religion which even from this point of view (i.e from a point of view which has really nothing to do with a decision of faith but which simply carries the weight of something quite self-evident) could appear as the obvious and indeed sole way of honouring God to be thought of for a European. Today everybody is the next-door neighbour and spiritual neighbour of everyone else in the world. And so everybody today is determined by the inter-communication of all those situations of life which affect the whole world. Every religion which exists in the world is—just like all cultural possibilities and actualities of other people—a question posed, and a possibility offered, to every person. . . . Hence, the question about the understanding of and the continuing existence of religious pluralism as a factor of our immediate Christian existence is an urgent one and part of the question as to how we are to deal with today's pluralism.

This problem could be tackled from different angles. In the present context we simply wish to try to describe a few of those basic traits of a Catholic dogmatic interpretation of the non-Christian religions which may help us to come closer to a solution of the question about the Christian position in regard to the religious pluralism in the world of today. . . .

1st Thesis: We must begin with the thesis . . . that Christianity understands itself as the absolute religion, intended for all men, which cannot recognize any other religion beside itself as of equal right. This proposition is self-evident and basic for Christianity's understanding of itself. There is no need here to prove it or to develop its meaning. After all, Christianity does not take valid and lawful religion to mean primarily that relationship of man to God which man himself institutes on his own authority. Valid and lawful religion does not mean man's own interpretation of human existence. . . .

Valid and lawful religion for Christianity is rather God's action on men, God's free self-revelation by communicating himself to man. It is God's relationship to men, freely instituted by God himself and revealed by God in this institution. *This* relationship of God to man is basically the same for all men, because it rests on the Incarnation, death and resurrection of the one Word of God become flesh. Christianity is God's own interpretation in his Word of this relationship of God to man founded in Christ by God himself. And so Christianity can recognize itself as the true and lawful religion for all men only where and when it enters with existential power and demanding force into the realm of another religion and—judging it by itself—puts it in question. Since the time of Christ's coming—ever since he came in the flesh as the Word of God in absoluteness and reconciled, i.e. united the world with God by his death and resurrection, not merely theoretically but really—Christ and his continuing historical presence in the world (which we call 'Church') is *the* religion which binds man to God.

Already we must, however, make one point clear as regards this first thesis. . . . It is true that the Christian religion itself has its own pre-history which traces this religion back to the beginning of the history of humanity—even though it does this by many basic steps. It is also true that this fact of having a pre-history is of much greater importance, according to the evidence of the New Testament, for the theoretical and practical proof of the claim to absolute truth made by the Christian religion than our current fundamental theology is aware of. Nevertheless, the Christian religion as such has a beginning in history; it did not always exist but began at some point in time. It has not always and everywhere been *the* way of salvation for men—at least not in its historically tangible ecclesio-sociological constitution and in the reflex fruition of God's saving activity in, and in view of, Christ. As a historical quantity Christianity has, therefore, a temporal and spatial starting point in Jesus of Nazareth and in the saving event of the unique Cross and the empty tomb in Jerusalem. It follows from this, however, that this absolute religion—even when it begins to be this for practically all men—must come in a historical way to men, facing them as the only legitimate and demanding religion for them. It is therefore a question of whether this moment, when the existentially real demand is made by the absolute religion in its historically tangible form, takes place really at the same chronological moment for all people, or whether the occurrence of this moment has itself a history and thus is not chronologically simultaneous for all people, cultures and spaces of history. . . . Normally the beginning of the objective obligation of the Christian message for all men—in other words, the abolition of the validity of the Mosaic religion *and* of all other religions which (as we will see later) may also have a period of validity and of being-willed-by-God—is thought to occur in the apostolic age. Normally, therefore, one regards the time between this beginning and the actual acceptance of the personally guilty refusal of Christianity in a non-Jewish world and history as the span between the already given promulgation of the law and the moment when the one to whom the law refers takes cognizance of it.

It is not just an idle academic question to ask whether such a conception is correct or whether, as we maintain, there could be a different opinion in this matter, i.e. whether one could hold that the beginning of Christianity for actual periods of history, for cultures and religions, could be postponed to those moments in time when Christianity became a real historical factor in an individual history and culture—a real historical moment in a particular culture. For instance, one concludes from the first, usual answer that *everywhere* in the world, since the first Pentecost, baptism of children dying before reaching the use of reason is necessary for their supernatural salvation, although this was not necessary before that time. . . . We cannot really answer this question here, but it may at least be pointed out as an open question; in practice, the correctness of the second theory may be presupposed since it alone corresponds to the real historicity of Christianity and salvation-history.

From this there follows a delicately differentiated understanding of our first thesis: we maintain positively only that, as regards destination, Christianity is the absolute and hence the only religion for all men. We leave it, however, an open question (at least in principle) at what exact point in time the absolute obligation of the Christian religion has in fact come into effect for every man and culture, even in the sense of the *objective* obligation of such a demand. Nevertheless—and this leaves the thesis formulated still sufficiently exciting—wherever in practice Christianity reaches man in the real urgency and rigour of his actual existence, Christianity—once understood—presents itself as the only still valid religion for this man, a necessary means for his salvation and not merely an obligation with the necessity of a precept. It should be noted that this is a question of the necessity of a *social* form for salvation. Even though this is Christianity and not some other religion, it may surely still be said without hesitation that this thesis contains implicitly another thesis which states that in concrete human existence as such, the nature of religion itself must include a social constitution—which means that religion can exist only in a social form. This means, therefore, that man, who is commanded to have a religion, is also commanded to seek and accept a social form of religion. It will soon become clear what this reflection implies for the estimation of non-Christian religions.

Finally, we may mention one further point in this connection. What is vital in the *notion* of *paganism* and hence also of the non-Christian pagan religions (taking 'pagan' here as a theological concept without any disparaging intent) is not the actual refusal to accept the Christian religion but the absence of any sufficient historical encounter with Christianity which would have enough historical power to render the Christian religion really present in this pagan society and in the history of the people concerned. If this is so, then paganism ceases to exist in this sense by reason of what is happening today. For the Western world is opening out into a universal world history in which every people and every cultural sector becomes an inner factor of every other people and every other cultural sector. Or rather, paganism is slowly entering a new phase: there is *one* history of the world, and in this *one* history both the Christians and the non-Christians (i.e. the old and new pagans together) live in one and the same situation and face each other in dialogue, and thus the question of the theological meaning of the other religions arises once more and with even greater urgency.

2nd Thesis: Until the moment when the Gospel really enters into the historical situation of an individual, a non-Christian religion (even outside the Mosaic religion) does not merely contain elements of a natural knowledge of God, elements, moreover, mixed up with human depravity which is the result of original sin and later aberrations. It contains also supernatural elements arising out of the grace which is given to men as a gratuitous gift on account of Christ. For this reason a non-Christian religion can be recognized as a *lawful* religion (although only in different degrees) without thereby denying the error and depravity contained in it. This thesis requires a more extensive explanation.

We must first of all note the point up to which this evaluation of the non-Christian religions is valid. This is the point in time when the Christian religion becomes a historically real factor for those who are of this religion. . . .

The thesis itself is divided into two parts. It means first of all that it is *a priori* quite possible to suppose that there are supernatural, grace-filled elements in non-Christian religions. Let us first of all deal with this statement. It does not mean, of course, that all the elements of a polytheistic conception of the divine, and all the other religious, ethical and metaphysical abberations contained in the non-Christian religions, are to be or may be treated as harmless either in theory or in practice. There have been constant protests against such elements throughout the history of Christianity and throughout the history of the Christian interpretation of the non-Christian religions, starting with the Epistle to the Romans and following on the Old Testament polemics against the religion of the 'heathens.' Every one of these protests is still valid in what was really meant and expressed by them. Every such protest remains a part of the message which Christianity and the Church has to give to the peoples who profess such religions. Furthermore, we are not concerned here with an *a posteriori* history of religions. Consequently, we also cannot describe empirically what should not exist and what is opposed to God's will in these non-Christian religions, nor can we represent these things in their many forms and degrees. We are here concerned with dogmatic theology and so can merely repeat the universal and unqualified verdict as to the unlawfulness of the non-Christian religions right from the moment when they came into real and historically powerful contact with Christianity (and at first only thus!). It is clear, however, that this condemnation does not mean to deny the very basic differences within the non-Christian religions especially since the pious, God-pleasing pagan was already a theme of the Old Testament, and especially since this God-pleasing pagan cannot simply be thought of as living absolutely outside the concrete socially constituted religion and constructing his own religion on his native foundations—just as St Paul in his speech on the Areopagus did not simply exclude a positive and basic view of the pagan religion.

The decisive reason for the first part of our thesis is basically a theological consideration. This consideration (prescinding from certain more precise qualifications) rests ultimately on the fact that, if we wish to be Christians, we must profess belief in the universal and serious salvific purpose of God towards all men which is true even within the post-paradisean phase of salvation dominated by original sin. We know, to be sure, that this proposition of faith does not say anything certain about the *individual* salvation of man understood as something which has in fact been reached. But God desires the salvation of everyone. And this salvation willed by God is the salvation won by Christ, the salvation of supernatural grace which divinizes man, the salvation of the beatific vision. It is a salvation really intended for all those millions upon millions of people who lived perhaps a million years before Christ—and also for those who have lived after Christ—in nations, cultures and epochs of a very wide range which were still completely shut off from the viewpoint of those living in the light of the New Testament. If, on the one hand, we conceive salvation as something specifically *Christian,* if there is no salvation apart from Christ, if according to Catholic teaching the supernatural divinization of mankind can never be replaced merely by goodwill on the part of man but is necessary as something itself given in this earthly life; and if, on the other hand, God has really, truly and seriously intended this salvation for all men—then these two aspects cannot be reconciled in any other way than by stating that every human being is really and truly exposed to the influence of divine, supernatural grace which offers an interior union with God and by means of which God communicates himself whether the individual takes up an attitude of acceptance or of refusal towards this grace. It is senseless to suppose cruelly—and without any hope of acceptance by the man of today, in view of the enormous extent of the extra-Christian history of salvation and damnation—that nearly all men living outside the official and public Christianity are so evil and stubborn that the offer of supernatural grace ought not even to be made in fact in most cases, since these individuals have already rendered themselves unworthy of such an offer by previous, subjectively grave offences against the natural moral law.

If one gives more exact theological thought to this matter, then one cannot regard nature and grace as two phases in the life of the individual which follow each other in time. It is furthermore impossible to think that this offer of supernatural, divinizing grace made to all men on account of the universal salvific purpose of God, should in general (prescinding from the relatively few exceptions) remain ineffective in most cases on account of the personal guilt of the individual. For, as far as the Gospel is concerned, we have no really conclusive reason for thinking so pessimistically of men. On the other hand, and contrary to every merely human experience, we do have every reason for thinking optimistically of God and his salvific will which is more powerful than the extremely limited stupidity and evil-mindedness of men. However little we can say with certitude about the final lot of an individual inside or outside the officially constituted Christian religion, we have every reason to think optimistically—i.e. truly hopefully and confidently in a Christian sense—of God who has certainly the last word and who has revealed to us that he has spoken his powerful word of reconciliation and forgiveness into the world. . . .

Once we take all this into consideration, we will not hold it to be impossible that grace is at work, and is even being accepted, in the spiritual, personal life of the individual, no matter how primitive, unenlightened, apathetic and earth-bound such a life may at first sight appear to be. We can say quite simply that, wherever, and in so far as, the individual makes a moral decision in his life, . . . this moral decision can also be thought to measure up to the character of a supernaturally elevated, believing and thus saving act, and hence to be more in actual fact than merely 'natural morality.' Hence, if one believes seriously in the universal salvific purpose of God towards all men in Christ, it need not and cannot really be doubted that gratuitous influences of properly Christian supernatural grace are conceivable in the life of all men (provided they are first of all regarded as individuals) and that these influences can be presumed to be accepted in spite of the sinful state of men and in spite of their apparent estrangement from God.

Our second thesis goes even further than this, however, and states in its second part that, from what has been said, the actual religions of 'pre-Christian' humanity too must not be regarded as simply illegitimate from the very start, but must be seen as quite capable of having a positive significance. This statement must naturally be taken in a very different sense which we cannot examine here for the various particular religions. This means that the different religions will be able to lay claim to being lawful religions only in very different senses and to very different degrees. But precisely this variability is not at all excluded by the notion of a 'lawful religion,' as we will have to show in a moment. A lawful religion means here an institutional religion whose 'use' by man at a certain period can be regarded on the whole as a positive means of gaining the right relationship to God and thus for the attaining of salvation, a means which is therefore positively included in God's plan of salvation.

That such a notion and the reality to which it refers can exist even where such a religion shows many theoretical and practical errors in its concrete form becomes clear in a theological analysis of the structure of the Old Covenant. We must first of all remember in this connection that only in the New Testament—in the Church of Christ understood as something which is eschatologically final and *hence* (and only for this reason) 'indefectible' and infallible—is there realized the notion of a Church which, because it is instituted by God in some way or other, already contains the permanent norm of differentiation between what is right (i.e. willed by God) and what is wrong in the religious sphere, and contains it both as a permanent institution and as an intrinsic element of this religion. There was nothing like this in the Old Testament, although it must undoubtedly be recognized as a lawful religion. . . .

Hence it cannot be a part of the notion of a lawful religion in the above sense that it should be free from corruption, error and objective moral wrong in the concrete form of its appearance, or that it should contain a clear objective and permanent final court of appeal for the conscience of the individual to enable the individual to differentiate clearly and with certainty between the elements willed and instituted by God and those which are merely human and corrupt.

We must therefore rid ourselves of the prejudice that we can face a non-Christian religion with the dilemma that it must either come from God in everything it contains and thus correspond to God's will and positive providence, or be simply a purely human construction. If man is under God's grace even in these religions—and to deny this is certainly absolutely wrong—then the possession of this supernatural grace cannot but show itself, and cannot but become a formative factor of life in the concrete, even where (though not only where) this life turns the relationship to the absolute into an explicit theme, viz. in religion. . . .

Furthermore, it must be borne in mind that the individual ought to and must have the possibility in his life of partaking in a genuine saving relationship to God, and at all times and in all situations of the history of the human race. Otherwise there could be no question of a serious and also actually effective salvific design of God for all men, in all ages and places. In view of the social nature of man and the previously even more radical social solidarity of men, however, it is quite unthinkable that man, being what he is, could actually achieve this relationship to God—which he must have and which if he is to be saved, is and must be made possible for him by God—in an absolutely private interior reality and this outside of the actual religious bodies which offer themselves to him in the environment in which he lives. If man had to be and could always and everywhere be a *homo religiosus* in order to be able to save himself as such, then he was this *homo religiosus* in the concrete religion in which 'people' lived and had to live at that time. He could not escape this religion, however much he may have and did take up a critical and selective attitude towards this religion on individual matters, and however much he may have and did put different stresses in practice on certain things which were at variance with the official theory of this religion. If, however, man can always have a positive, saving relationship to God, and if he always had to have it, then he has always had it within *that* religion which in practice was at his disposal by being a factor in his sphere of existence. As already stated above, the inherence of the individual exercise of religion in a social religious order is one of the essential traits of true religion as it exists in practice. Hence, if one were to expect from someone who lives outside the Christian religion that he should have exercised his genuine, saving relationship to God absolutely outside the religion which society offered him, then such a conception would turn religion into something intangibly interior, into something which is always and everywhere performed only indirectly, a merely transcendental religion without anything which could become tangible in categories. Such a conception would annul the above-mentioned principle regarding the necessarily social nature of all religion in the concrete, so that even the Christian Church would then no longer have the necessary presupposition of general human and natural law as proof of her necessity. And since it does not at all belong to the notion of a lawful religion intended by God for man as something positively salvific that it should be pure and positively willed by God in all its elements, such a religion can be called an absolutely legitimate religion for the person concerned. That which God has intended as salvation for him reached him, in accordance with God's will and by his permission (no longer adequately separable in practice), in the *concrete* religion of his actual realm of existence and historical condition, but this fact did not deprive him of the right and the limited possibility to criticize and to heed impulses of religious reform which by God's providence kept on recurring within such a religion. For a still better and simpler understanding of this, one has only to think of the natural and socially constituted morality of a people and culture. Such a morality is never pure but is always also corrupted, as Jesus confirmed even in the case of the Old Testament. It can always be disputed and corrected, therefore, by the individual in accordance with his conscience. Yet, taken in its totality, it is *the* way in which the individual encounters the natural divine law according to God's will, and the way in which the natural law is given real, actual power in the life of the individual who cannot reconstruct these tablets of the divine law anew on his own responsibility and as a private metaphysician.

The morality of a people and of an age, taken in its totality, is therefore the legitimate and concrete form of the divine law (even though, of course, it can and may have to be corrected), so that it was not until the New Testament that the institution guaranteeing the purity of this form became (with the necessary reservations) an element of this form itself. Hence, if there existed a divine moral law and religion in the life of man *before* this moment, then its absolute purity (i.e. its constitution by divinely willed elements alone) must not be made the condition of the lawfulness of its existence. In fact, if every man who comes into the world is pursued by God's grace—and if one of the effects of this grace, even in its supernatural and salvifically elevating form, is to cause changes in consciousness (as is maintained by the better theory in Catholic theology) even though it cannot be simply *as* such a direct object of certain reflection—then it cannot be true that the actually existing religions do not bear any trace of the fact that all men are in some way affected by grace. These traces may be difficult to distinguish even to the enlightened eye of the Christian. But they must be there. . . .

The second part of this second thesis, however, states two things positively. It states that even religions other than the Christian and the Old Testament religions contain quite certainly elements of a supernatural influence by grace which must make itself felt even in these objectifications. And it also states that by the fact that in practice man as he really is can live his proffered relationship to God only in society, man must have had the right and indeed the duty to live this his relationship to God within the religious and social realities offered to him in his particular historical situation.

3rd Thesis: If the second thesis is correct, then Christianity does not simply confront the member of an extra-Christian religion as a mere non-Christian but as someone who can and must already be regarded in this or that respect as an anonymous Christian. It would be wrong to regard the pagan as someone who has not yet been touched in any way by God's grace and truth. If, however, he has experienced the grace of God—if, in certain circumstances, he has already accepted this grace as the ultimate, unfathomable entelechy of his existence by accepting the immeasurableness of his dying existence as opening out into infinity—then he has already been given revelation in a true sense even before he has been affected by missionary preaching from without. For this grace, understood as the *a priori* horizon of all his spiritual acts, accompanies his consciousness subjectively, even though it is not known objectively. And the revelation which comes to him from without is not in such a case the proclamation of something as yet absolutely unknown. . . . But if it is true that a person who becomes the object of the Church's missionary efforts is or may be already someone on the way towards his salvation, and someone who in certain circumstances finds it, without being reached by the proclamation of the Church's message—and if it is at the same time true that this salvation which reaches him in this way is Christ's salvation, since there is no other salvation—then it must be possible to be not only an anonymous theist but also an anonymous Christian. And then it is quite true that in the last analysis, the proclamation of the Gospel does not simply turn someone absolutely abandoned by God and Christ into a Christian, but turns an anonymous Christian into someone who now also knows about his Christian belief in the depths of his grace-endowed being by objective reflection and in the profession of faith which is given a social form in the Church.

It is not thereby denied, but on the contrary implied, that this explicit self-realization of his previously anonymous Christianity is itself part of the development of this Christianity itself—a higher stage of development of this Christianity demanded by his being—and that it is therefore intended by God in the same way as everything else about salvation. Hence, it will not be possible in any way to draw the conclusion from this conception that, since man is already an anonymous Christian even without it, this explicit preaching of Christianity is superfluous. Such a conclusion would be just as false (and for the same reasons) as to conclude that the sacraments of baptism and penance could be dispensed with because a person can be justified by his subjective acts of faith and contrition even before the reception of these sacraments.

The reflex self-realization of a previously anonymous Christianity is demanded (1) by the incarnational and social structure of grace and of Christianity, and (2) because the individual who grasps Christianity in a clearer, purer and more reflective way has, other things being equal, a still greater chance of salvation than someone who is merely an anonymous Christian. If, however, the message of the Church is directed to someone who is a 'non-Christian' only in the sense of living by an anonymous Christianity not as yet fully conscious of itself, then her missionary work must take this fact into account and must draw the necessary conclusions when deciding on its missionary strategy and tactics. . . .

4th Thesis: It is possibly too much to hope, on the one hand, that the religious pluralism which exists in the concrete situation of Christians will disappear in the foreseeable future. On the other hand, it is nevertheless absolutely permissible for the Christian himself to interpret this non-Christianity as Christianity of an anonymous kind which he does always still go out to meet as a missionary, seeing it as a world which is to be brought to the explicit consciousness of what already belongs to it as a divine offer or already pertains to it also over and above this as a divine gift of grace accepted unreflectedly and implicitly. . . .

Non-Christians may think it presumption for the Christian to judge everything which is sound or restored (by being sanctified) to be the fruit in every man of the grace of his Christ, and to interpret it as anonymous Christianity; they may think it presumption for the Christian to regard the non-Christian as a Christian who has not yet come to himself reflectively. But the Christian cannot renounce this 'presumption' which is really the source of the greatest humility both for himself and for the Church. For it is a profound admission of the fact that God is greater than man and the Church. The Church will go out to meet the non-Christian of tomorrow with the attitude expressed by St Paul when he said: What therefore you do not know and yet worship [and yet *worship*!] that I proclaim to you (Acts 17:23). On such a basis one can be tolerant, humble and yet firm towards all non-Christian religions.

JOHN HICK

Religious Pluralism

John Hick (1922–   ) believes that the various world faiths embody different views of Ultimate Reality and thus provide different ways to attain what is called salvation in some religions and liberation or enlightenment or fulfillment in others. To those who object, insisting that Christianity is unique because it was founded by God incarnate in Jesus, Hick replies that God can act through many individuals who are open to God. For Hick, then, Jesus was not uniquely divine but was merely one of many such persons. To those who point out that the different religions provide incompatible descriptions of Reality, he responds that each tradition believes that Reality exceeds our creaturely understanding. Hick explains that each person experiences Reality as it appears to him in his unique cultural situation. In other words, each religious tradition conditions its adherents' understanding of Reality and provides authentic and appropriate ways for them to respond to it.

⌘

Wilfred Cantwell Smith in his work on the concepts of religion and of religions has been responsible, more than any other one individual, for the change which has taken place within a single generation in the way in which many of us perceive the religious life of mankind.

Seen through pre–Cantwell Smith eyes there are a number of vast, long-lived historical entities or organisms known as Christianity, Hinduism, Islam, Buddhism, and so on. Each has an inner skeletal framework of beliefs, giving shape to a distinctive form of religious life, wrapped in a thick institutional skin which divides it from other religions and from the secular world within which they exist. Thus Buddhism, Islam, Christianity, and the rest, are seen as contraposed socio-religious entities which are the bearers of distinctive creeds; and every religious individual is a member of one or other of these mutually exclusive groups.

This way of seeing the religious life of humanity, as organised in a number of communities based upon rival sets of religious beliefs, leads to the posing of questions about religion in a certain way. For the beliefs which a religion professes are beliefs about God, or the Ultimate, and as such they define a way of human salvation or liberation and are accordingly a matter of spiritual life and death. Looking at the religions of the world, then, in the plural we are presented with competing claims to possess the saving truth. For each community believes that its own gospel is true and that other gospels are false in so far as they differ from it. Each believes that the way of salvation to which it witnesses is the authentic way, the only sure path to eternal blessedness. And so the proper question in face of this plurality of claims is, which is the true religion?

In practice, those who are concerned to raise this question are normally fully convinced that theirs is the true religion; so that for them the task is to show the spiritual superiority of their own creed and the consequent moral superiority of the community which embodies it. A great deal of the mutual criticism of religions, and of the derogatory assessment of one by another, has been in fulfilment of this task.

This view of mankind's religious life as divided into great contraposed entities, each claiming to be the true religion, is not however the only possible way of seeing the religious situation. Cantwell Smith has offered an alternative vision.

He shows first that the presently dominant conceptuality has a history that can be traced back to the European Renaissance. It was then that the different streams of religious life began to be reified in Western thought as solid structures called Christianity, Judaism, and so forth. And having reified their own faith in this way Westerners have then exported the notion of 'a religion' to the rest of the world, causing others to think of themselves as belonging to the Hindu, or the Confucian, or the Buddhist religion, and so on, over against others. But an alternative perception can divide the scene differently. It sees something of vital religious significance taking different forms all over the world within the contexts of the different historical traditions. This 'something of vital religious significance' Cantwell Smith calls faith. I would agree with some of his critics that this is not the ideal word for it; for 'faith' is a term that is more at home in the Semitic than in the Indian family of traditions and which has, as his own historical researches have shown, become badly overintellectualised. But I take it that he uses the term to refer to the spiritual state, or existential condition, constituted by a person's present response to the ultimate divine Reality. This ranges from the negative response of a self-enclosed consciousness which is blind to the divine presence, whether beyond us or in the depths of our own being, to a positive openness to the Divine which gradually transforms us and which is called salvation or liberation or enlightenment. This transformation is essentially the same within the different religious contexts within which it occurs: I would define it formally as the transformation of human existence from self-centredness to Reality-centredness. This is the event or process of vital significance which one can see to be occurring in individuals all over the world, taking different forms within the contexts of the different perceptions of the Ultimate made available by the various religious traditions.

These cumulative traditions themselves are the other thing that one sees with the aid of the new conceptuality suggested by Cantwell Smith. They are distinguishable strands of human history in each of which a multitude of religious and cultural elements interact to form a distinctive pattern, constituting, say, the Hindu, Buddhist, Confucian, Jewish, Christian or Muslim tradition. These traditions are not static entities but living movements; and they are not tightly homogeneous but have each become in the course of time internally highly various. Thus there are large differences between, for example, Buddhism in the time of Gautama and Buddhism after the development of the Mahāyāna and its expansion northwards into China; or between the Christian movement in Roman Palestine and that in medieval Europe. And there are large differences today between, say, Zen and Amida Buddhism in Japan, or between Southern Baptist and Northern Episcopalian Christianity in the United States. Indeed, since we cannot always avoid using the substantives, we might do well to speak of Buddhisms, Christianities, and so on, in the plural. A usage consonant with Cantwell Smith's analysis has however already become widespread, and many of us now often prefer to speak not of Christianity but of the Christian tradition, the Hindu tradition, and so on, when referring to these historically identifiable strands of history.

These cumulative traditions are composed of a rich complex of inner and outer elements cohering in a distinctive living pattern which includes structures of belief, life-styles, scriptures and their interpretations, liturgies, cultic celebrations, myths, music, poetry, architecture, literature, remembered history and its heroes. Thus the traditions constitute religious cultures, each with its own unique history and ethos. And each such tradition creates human beings in its own image. For we are not human in general, participating in an eternal Platonic essence of humanity. We are human in one or other of the various concrete ways of being human which constitute the cultures of the earth. There is a Chinese way of being human, an African way, an Arab way, a European way, or ways, and so on. These are not fixed moulds but living organisms which develop and interact over the centuries, so that the patterns of human life change, usually very slowly but sometimes with startling rapidity. But we are all formed in a hundred ways of which we are not normally aware by the culture into which we were born, by which we are fed, and with which we interact.

Let us then enter, with Cantwell Smith, into the experiment of thinking, on the one hand, of 'faith,' or human response to the divine, which in its positive and negative forms is salvation and non-salvation and, on the other hand, of the cumulative religious traditions within which this occurs; and let us ask what the relation is between these two realities—on the one hand salvation/liberation and on the other the cumulative traditions. . . .

However, we may now turn to a second Christian answer to our question, which can be labelled 'inclusivism.' This can be expressed in terms either of a juridical or of a transformation-of-human-existence conception of salvation. In the former terms it is the view that God's forgiveness and acceptance of humanity have been made possible by Christ's death, but that the benefits of this sacrifice are not confined to those who respond to it with an explicit act of faith. The juridical transaction of Christ's atonement covered *all* human sin, so that all human beings are now open to God's mercy, even though they may never have heard of Jesus Christ and why he died on the cross of Calvary. . . . [We omit Hick's discussion of the first answer to the relation between the realities, exclusivism.]

Rahner's is a brave attempt to attain an inclusivist position which is in principle universal but which does not thereby renounce the old exclusivist dogma. But the question is whether in this new context the old dogma has not been so emptied of content as no longer to be worth affirming. When salvation is acknowledged to be taking place without any connection with the Christian Church or Gospel, in people who are living on the basis of quite other faiths, is it not a somewhat empty gesture to insist upon affixing a Christian label to them? Further, having thus labelled them, why persist in the aim of gathering all humankind into the Christian Church? Once it is accepted that salvation does not depend upon this, the conversion of the people of the other great world faiths to Christianity hardly seems the best way of spending one's energies.

The third possible answer to the question of the relation between salvation/liberation and the cumulative religious traditions can best be called pluralism. As a Christian position this can be seen as an acceptance of the further conclusion to which inclusivism points. If we accept that salvation/liberation is taking place within all the great religious traditions, why not frankly acknowledge that there is a plurality of saving human responses to the ultimate divine Reality? Pluralism, then, is the view that the transformation of human existence from self-centredness to Reality-centredness is taking place in different ways within the contexts of all the great religious traditions. There is not merely one way but a plurality of ways of salvation or liberation. In Christian theological terms, there is a plurality of divine revelations, making possible a plurality of forms of saving human response.

What however makes it difficult for Christians to move from inclusivism to pluralism, holding the majority of Christian theologians today in the inclusivist position despite its evident logical instability, is of course the traditional doctrine of the Incarnation, together with its protective envelope, the doctrine of the Trinity. For in its orthodox form, as classically expressed at the Councils of Nicaea and Chalcedon, the incarnational doctrine claims that Jesus was God incarnate, the Second Person of the Triune God living a human life. It is integral to this faith that there has been (and will be) no other divine incarnation. This makes Christianity unique in that it, alone among the religions of the world, was founded by God in person. Such a uniqueness would seem to demand Christian exclusivism—for must God not want all human beings to enter the way of salvation which he has provided for them? However, since such exclusivism seems so unrealistic in the light of our knowledge of the wider religious life of mankind, many theologians have moved to some form of inclusivism, but now feel unable to go further and follow the argument to its conclusion in the frank acceptance of pluralism. The break with traditional missionary attitudes and long-established ecclesiastical and liturgical language would, for many, be so great as to be prohibitive.

There is however the possibility of an acceptable Christian route to religious pluralism in work which has already been done, and which is being done, in the field of Christology with motivations quite other than to facilitate pluralism, and on grounds which are internal to the intellectual development of Christianity. For there is a decisive watershed between what might be called all-or-nothing Christologies and degree Christologies. The all-or-nothing principle is classically expressed in the Chalcedonian Definition, according to which Christ is 'to be acknowledged in Two Natures,' 'Consubstantial with the Father according to his Deity, Consubstantial with us according to his Humanity.' Substance is an all-or-nothing notion, in that A either is or is not composed of the same substance, either has or does not have the same essential nature, as B. Using this all-or-nothing conceptuality Chalcedon attributed to Christ two complete natures, one divine and the other human, being in his divine nature of one substance with God the Father. Degree Christologies, on the other hand, apply the term 'incarnation' to the activity of God's Spirit or of God's grace in human lives, so that the divine will is done on earth. This kind of reinterpretation has been represented in recent years by, for example, the 'paradox of grace' Christology of Donald Baillie (in *God Was in Christ*, 1948) and the 'inspiration Christology' of Geoffrey Lampe (in *God as Spirit*, 1977). In so far as a human being is open and responsive to God, so that God is able to act in and through that individual, we can speak of the embodiment in human life of God's redemptive activity. And in Jesus this 'paradox of grace'—the paradox expressed by St Paul when he wrote 'it was not I, but the grace of God which is in me' (1 Corinthians 15:10)—or the inspiration of God's Spirit, occurred to a startling extent. The paradox, or the inspiration, are not however confined to the life of Jesus; they are found, in varying degrees, in all free human response to God. Christologies of the same broad family occur in the work of Norman Pittenger (*The Word Incarnate*, 1957), John Knox (*The Humanity and Divinity of Christ*, 1967), and earlier in John Baillie (*The Place of Jesus Christ in Modern*

Christianity, 1929), and more recently in the authors of *The Myth of God Incarnate* (1977).

These modern degree Christologies were not in fact for the most part developed in order to facilitate a Christian acceptance of religious pluralism. They were developed as alternatives to the old substance Christology, in which so many difficulties, both historical and philosophical, had become apparent. They claim to be compatible with the teachings of Jesus and of the very early Church, and to avoid the intractable problem, generated by a substance Christology, of the relation between Jesus's two natures. But, as an unintended consequence, degree Christologies open up the possibility of seeing God's activity in Jesus as being of the same kind as God's activity in other great human mediators of the divine. The traditional Christian claim to the unique superiority of Christ and of the Christian tradition is not of course precluded by a degree Christology; for it may be argued (as it was, for example, by both Baillie and Lampe) that Christ was the *supreme* instance of the paradox of grace or of the inspiration of the Spirit, so that Christianity is still assumed to be the *best* context of salvation/liberation. But, whereas, starting from the substance Christology, the unique superiority of Christ and the Christian Church are guaranteed *a priori*, starting from a degree Christology they have to be established by historical evidence. Whether this can in fact be done is, clearly, an open question. It would indeed be an uphill task today to establish that we know enough about the inner and outer life of the historical Jesus, and of the other founders of great religious traditions, to be able to make any such claim; and perhaps an even more uphill task to establish from the morally ambiguous histories of each of the great traditions, complex mixtures of good and evil as each has been, that one's own tradition stands out as manifestly superior to all others.

I think, then, that a path exists along which Christians can, if they feel so drawn, move to an acceptance of religious pluralism. Stated philosophically such a pluralism is the view that the great world faiths embody different perceptions and conceptions of, and correspondingly different responses to, the Real or the Ultimate from within the major variant cultural ways of being human; and that within each of them the transformation of human existence from self-centredness to Reality-centredness is manifestly taking place—and taking place, so far as human observation can tell, to much the same extent. Thus the great religious traditions are to be regarded as alternative soteriological 'spaces' within which, or 'ways' along which, men and women can find salvation/liberation/enlightenment/fulfilment.

But how can such a view be arrived at? Are we not proposing a picture reminiscent of the ancient allegory of the blind men and the elephant, in which each runs his hands over a different part of the animal, and identifies it differently, a leg as a tree, the trunk as a snake, the tail as a rope, and so on? Clearly, in the story the situation is being described from the point of view of someone who can observe both elephant and blind men. But where is the vantage-point from which one can observe both the divine Reality and the different limited human standpoints from which that Reality is being variously perceived? The advocate of the pluralist understanding cannot pretend to any such cosmic vision. How then does he profess to know that the situation is indeed as he depicts it? The answer is that he does not profess to *know* this, if by knowledge we mean infallible cognition. Nor indeed can anyone else properly claim to have knowledge, in this sense, of either the exclusivist or the inclusivist picture. All of them are, strictly speaking, hypotheses. The pluralist hypothesis is arrived at inductively. One starts from the fact that many human beings experience life in relation to a limitlessly greater transcendent Reality—whether the direction of transcendence be beyond our present existence or within its hidden depths. In theory such religious experience is capable of a purely naturalistic analysis which does not involve reference to any reality other than the human and the natural. But to participate by faith in one of the actual streams of religious experience—in my case, the Christian stream—is to participate in it as an experience of transcendent Reality. I think that there is in fact a good argument for the rationality of trusting one's own religious experience, together with that of the larger tradition within which it occurs, so as both to believe and to live on the basis of it; but I cannot develop that argument here. Treating one's own form of religious experience, then, as veridical—as an experience (however dim, like 'seeing through a glass, darkly') of transcendent divine Reality—one then has to take account of the fact that there are other great streams of religious experience which take different forms, are shaped by different conceptualities, and embodied in different institutions, art forms, and lifestyles. In other words, besides one's own religion, sustained by its distinctive form of religious experience, there are also other religions, through each of which flows the life blood of a different form of religious experience. What account is one to give of this plurality? . . .

But if we look for the transcendence of egoism and a recentring in God or in the transcendent Real, then I venture the proposition that, so far as human observation and historical memory can tell, this occurs to about the same extent within each of the great world traditions.

If this is so, it prompts us to go beyond inclusivism to a pluralism which recognises a variety of human religious contexts within which salvation/liberation takes place.

But such a pluralistic hypothesis raises many questions. What is this divine Reality to which all the great traditions are said to be oriented? Can we really equate the personal Yahweh with the non-personal Brahman, Shiva with the Tao, the Holy Trinity with the Buddhist Trikāya, and all with one another? Indeed, do not the Eastern and Western faiths deal incommensurably with different problems?

As these questions indicate, we need a pluralistic theory which enables us to recognise and be fascinated by the manifold differences between the religious traditions, with their different conceptualisations, their different modes of religious experience, and their different forms of individual and social response to the divine. I should like in these final pages to suggest the ground plan of such a theory—a theory which is, I venture to think, fully compatible with the central themes of Cantwell Smith's thought.

Each of the great religious traditions affirms that in addition to the social and natural world of our ordinary human experience there is a limitlessly greater and higher Reality beyond or within us, in relation to which or to whom is our highest good. The ultimately real and the ultimately valuable are one, and to give oneself freely and totally to this One is our final salvation/liberation/enlightenment/fulfilment. Further, each tradition is conscious that the divine Reality exceeds the reach of our earthly speech and thought. It cannot be encompassed in human concepts. It is infinite, eternal, limitlessly rich beyond the scope of our finite conceiving or experiencing. Let us then both avoid the particular names used within the particular traditions and yet use a term which is consonant with the faith of each of them—Ultimate Reality, or the Real.

Let us next adopt a distinction that is to be found in different forms and with different emphases within each of the great traditions, the distinction between the Real *an sich* (in him/her/itself) and the Real as humanly experienced and thought. In Christian terms this is the distinction between God in God's infinite and eternal self-existent being, 'prior' to and independent of creation, and God as related to and known by us as creator, redeemer and sanctifier. In Hindu thought it is the distinction between *nirguṇa* Brahman, the Ultimate in itself, beyond all human categories, and *saguṇa* Brahman, the Ultimate as known to finite consciousness as a personal deity, Iśvara. In Taoist thought, 'The Tao that can be expressed is not the eternal Tao' (*Tao-Te Ching*, 1). There are also analogous distinctions in Jewish and Muslim mystical thought in which the Real *an sich* is called *en Soph* and *al Haqq*. In Mahāyāna Buddhism there is the distinction between the *dharmakāya*, the eternal cosmic Buddha-nature, which is also the infinite Void (*śūnyatā*), and on the other hand the realm of heavenly Buddha figures (*sambhogakāya*) and their incarnations in the earthly Buddhas (*nirmāṇakāya*). This varied family of distinctions suggests the perhaps daring thought that the Real *an sich* is one but is nevertheless capable of being humanly experienced in a variety of ways. This thought lies at the heart of the pluralistic hypothesis which I am suggesting.

The next point of which we need to take account is the creative part that thought, and the range of concepts in terms of which it functions, plays in the formation of conscious experience. It was above all Immanuel Kant who brought this realisation into the stream of modern reflection, and it has since been confirmed and amplified by innumerable studies, not only in general epistemology but also in cognitive psychology, in the sociology of knowledge, and in the philosophy of science. The central fact, of which the epistemology of religion also has to take account, is that our environment is not reflected in our consciousness in a simple and straightforward way, just as it is, independently of our perceiving it. At the physical level, out of the immense richness of structure and detail around us, only that minute selection that is relevant to our biological survival and flourishing affects our senses; and these inputs are interpreted in the mind/brain to produce our conscious experience of the familiar world in which we live. Its character as an environment within which we can learn to behave appropriately can be called its *meaning* for us. This all-important dimension of meaning, which begins at the physical level as the habitability of the material world, continues at the personal, or social, level of awareness as the moral significance of the situations of our life, and at the religious level as a consciousness of the ultimate meaning of each situation and of our situation as a whole in relation to the divine Reality. This latter consciousness is not however a general consciousness of the divine, but always takes specific forms; and, as in the case of the awareness of the physical and of the ethical meaning of our environment, such consciousness has an essential dispositional aspect. To experience in this way rather than in that involves being in a state of readiness to behave in a particular range of ways, namely that which is appropriate to our environment having the particular character that we perceive (or of course misperceive) it to have. Thus to be aware of the divine as 'the God and Father of our Lord Jesus Christ,' in so far as this is the operative awareness which determines our dispositional state, is to live in the kind of way described by Jesus in his religious and moral teaching—in trust towards God and in love towards our neighbours.

How are these various specific forms of religious awareness formed? Our hypothesis is that they are formed by the presence of the divine Reality, this presence coming to consciousness in terms of the different sets of religious concepts and structures of religious meaning that operate within the different religious traditions of the world. If we look at the range of actual human religious experience and ask ourselves what basic concepts and what concrete images have operated in its genesis, I would suggest that we arrive at something like the following answer. There are, first, the two basic religious concepts which between them dominate the entire range of the forms of religious experience. One is the concept of Deity, or God, i.e. the Real as personal; and the other is the concept of the Absolute, i.e. the Real as nonpersonal. (The term 'Absolute' is by no means ideal for the purpose, but is perhaps the nearest that we have.) We do not however, in actual religious experience, encounter either Deity in general or the Absolute in general, but always in specific forms. In Kantian language, each general concept is schematised, or made concrete. In Kant's own analysis of sense-experience the schematisation of the basic categories is in terms of time; but religious experience occurs at a much higher level of meaning, presupposing and going beyond physical meaning and involving much more complex and variable modes of dispositional response. Schematisation or concretisation here is in terms of 'filled' human time, or history, as diversified into the different cultures and civilisations of the earth. For there are different concrete ways of being human and of participating in human history, and within these different ways the presence of the divine Reality is experienced in characteristically different ways.

To take the concept of God first, this becomes concrete as the range of specific deities to which the history of religion bears witness. Thus the Real as personal is known in the Christian tradition as God the Father; in Judaism as Adonai; in Islam as Allah, the Qur'ānic Revealer; in the Indian traditions as Shiva, or Vishnu, or Paramātmā, and under the many other lesser images of deity which in different regions of India concretise different aspects of the divine nature. This range of personal deities who are the foci of worship within the theistic traditions constitutes the range of the divine *personae* in relation to mankind. Each *persona*, in his or her historical concreteness, lives within the corporate experience of a particular faith-community. Thus the Yahweh *persona* exists and has developed in interaction with the Jewish people. He is a part of their history, and they are a part of his; and he cannot be extracted from this historical context. Shiva, on the other hand, is a quite different divine *persona*, existing in the experience of hundreds of millions of people in the Shaivite stream of Indian religious life. These two *personae*, Yahweh and Shiva, live within different worlds of faith, partly creating and partly created by the features of different human cultures, being responded to in different patterns of life, and being integral to different strands of historical experience. Within each of these worlds of faith great numbers of people find the ultimate meaning of their existence, and are carried through the crises of life and death; and within this process many are, in varying degrees, challenged and empowered to move forward on the way of salvation/liberation from self-centredness to Reality-centredness. From the pluralist point of view Yahweh and Shiva are not rival gods, or rival claimants to be the one and only God, but rather two different concrete historical *personae* in terms of which the ultimate divine Reality is present and responded to by different large historical communities within different strands of the human story.

This conception of divine *personae*, constituting (in Kantian language) different divine phenomena in terms of which the one divine noumenon is humanly experienced, enables us to acknowledge the degree of truth within the various projection theories of religion from Feuerbach through Freud to the present day. An element of human projection colours our mental images of God, accounting for their anthropomorphic features—for example, as male or female. But human projection does not—on this view—bring God into existence; rather it affects the ways in which the independently existing divine Reality is experienced.

Does this epistemological pattern of the schematisation of a basic religious concept into a range of particular correlates of religious experience apply also to the non-theistic traditions? I suggest that it does. Here the general concept, the Absolute, is schematised in actual religious experience to form the range of divine *impersonae*—Brahman, the Dharma, the Tao, *nirvāṇa*, *śūnyatā*, and so on—which are experienced within the Eastern traditions. The structure of these *impersonae* is however importantly different from that of the *personae*. A divine *persona* is concrete, implicitly finite, sometimes visualisable and even capable of being pictured. A divine *impersona*, on the other hand, is not a 'thing' in contrast to a person. It is the infinite being—consciousness—bliss (*saccidānanda*) of Brahman; or the beginningless and endless process of cosmic change (*pratītya samutpāda*) of Buddhist teaching; or again the ineffable 'further shore' of *nirvāṇa*, or the eternal Buddha-nature (*dharmakāya*); or the ultimate Emptiness (*śūnyatā*) which is also the fullness or suchness of the world; or the eternal principle of the Tao. It is thus not so much an entity as a field of spiritual force, or the ultimate reality of everything, that which gives final meaning and joy. These non-personal conceptions of the Ultimate inform modes of consciousness varying from the advaitic experience of becoming one with the Infinite, to the Zen experience of finding a total reality in the present concrete moment of existence in the ordinary world. And according to the pluralistic hypothesis these different modes of experience constitute different experiences of the Real as non- or trans-personal. As in the case of the divine *personae*, they are formed by different religious conceptualities which have developed in interaction with different spiritual disciplines and methods of mediation. The evidence that a range of *impersonae* of the one Ultimate Reality are involved in the non-theistic forms of religious experience, rather than the direct unmediated awareness of Reality itself, consists precisely in the differences between the experiences reported within the different traditions. How is it that a 'direct experience' of the Real can take such different forms? One could of course at this point revert to the exclusivism of the inclusivism whose limitations we have already noted. But the pluralist answer will be that even the most advanced form of mystical experience, as an experience undergone by an embodied consciousness whose mind/brain has been conditioned by a particular religious tradition, must be affected by the conceptual framework and spiritual training provided by that tradition, and accordingly takes these different forms. In other words the Real is experienced not *an sich*, but in terms of the various non-personal images or concepts that have been generated at the interface between the Real and different patterns of human consciousness.

These many different perceptions of the Real, both theistic and non-theistic, can only establish themselves as authentic by their soteriological efficacy. The great world traditions have in fact all proved to be realms within which or routes along which people are enabled to advance in the transition from self-centredness to Reality-centredness. And, since they reveal the Real in such different lights, we must conclude that they are independently valid. Accordingly, by attending to other traditions than one's own one may become aware of other aspects or dimensions of the Real, and of other possibilities of response to the Real, which had not been made effectively available by one's own tradition. Thus a mutual mission of the sharing of experiences and insights can proceed through the growing network of inter-faith dialogue and the interactions of the faith-communities. Such mutual mission does not aim at conversion—although occasionally individual conversions, in all directions, will continue to occur—but at mutual enrichment and at co-operation in face of the urgent problems of human survival in a just and sustainable world society.

SUGGESTED READING

Barnes, Michael. *Religions in Conversation*. London: SPCK, 1989.

Byrne, Peter. "John Hick's Philosophy of World Religions," *Scottish Journal of Theology* 35, no. 4 (1982): 289–301.

D'Costa, Gavin. *Christian Uniqueness Reconsidered: The Myth of a Pluralistic Theology of Religions*. Maryknoll, NY: Orbis, 1990.

———. *Theology and Religious Pluralism: The Challenge of Other Religions*. London: Blackwell, 1986.

DiNoia, J.A. *The Diversity of Religions: A Christian Perspective*. Washington, D.C.: Catholic University of American Press, 1992.

Griffiths, Paul. *An Apology for Apologetics: A Study in the Logic of Interreligious Dialogue*. Maryknoll, N.Y.: Orbis, 1991.

Hick, John, and Brian Hebblethwaite, eds. *Christianity and Other Religions*. Glasgow: Collins, 1980.

Hick, John, advisory ed. *Faith and Philosophy* 5, no. 4 (October 1988).

———. *God and the Universe of Faiths*. London: Macmillan, 1977.

———. *An Interpretation of Religion: Human Responses to the Transcendent*. New Haven: Yale University Press, 1991.

———, ed. *Problems of Religious Pluralism*. New York: St. Martin's Press, 1985.

——— and Paul Knitter. *The Myth of Christian Uniqueness: Toward a Pluralistic Theology of Religions*. Maryknoll, NY: Orbis, 1990.

Knitter, Paul. *No Other Name? A Critical Survey of Christian Attitudes Toward World Religions*. Maryknoll, N.Y.: Orbis, 1985.

Nash, Ronald. *Is Jesus the Only Saviour?* Grand Rapids, MI: Zondervan, 1994.

Netland, Harold. *Dissonant Voices: Religious Pluralism and the Question of Truth*. Grand Rapids, MI: William B. Eerdmans, 1991.

Pinnock, Clark H. *A Wideness in God's Mercy*. Grand Rapids, Mich.: Zondervan, 1992.

Rice, Alan. *Christians and Religious Pluralism*. Maryknoll, N.J.: Orbis, 1982.

Sanders, John. *No Other Name! A Biblical, Historical, and Theological Investigation into the Destiny of the Unevangelized*. Grand Rapids, Mich.: William B. Eerdmans, 1992.

Smart, Ninian. *Buddhism and Christianity: Rivals and Allies*. Honolulu: University of Hawaii Press, 1993.

Smith, Wilfred Cantwell. *Towards a World Theology*. Philadelphia: Westminster, 1981.

Vroom, Hendrik. *Religion and the Truth: Philosophical Reflections and Perspectives*. Grand Rapids, Mich.: William B. Eerdmans, 1989.

Yandell, Keith E. "Religious Experience and Rational Appraisal," *Religious Studies* 8 (June 1974): 173–187.

PART TWELVE

RELIGIOUS ETHICS

A great many religious persons maintain that the basic moral principles they affirm have their origin in God, as opposed to human thought or some source totally independent of both. Yet this claim has generated a great number of philosophical debates, some as old as the famed discussion between Socrates and Euthyphro.

One important debate emerges over an apparent dilemma for believers. If believers say that whatever God wills is morally right, then do they mean that *anything*—even rape or torture—could be morally permissible or even obligatory as long as it is commanded by God? This horn of the dilemma seems to make God's morality something alien to our highest ideals. On the other hand, if believers say that God cannot contravene fundamental moral laws, then must they acknowledge that such laws are somehow independent of God and beyond his control? This horn seems to admit something that is binding upon God. Some believers think that they successfully avoid the dilemma by arguing that God's commands must be consistent with absolute moral norms but that these norms themselves have their origin in God's nature.

Many more issues follow upon the heels of the first. For example, if we assume that morality originates in God, we can still legitimately ask whether God's moral perspective should be considered authoritative. And, if we grant that believers can successfully argue that the morality somehow rooted in their God is authoritative, we may still ask hard questions about how believers acquire this ethical insight. Is it a viable option, as some believers think, to claim that God has communicated ethical truth through some form of written revelation—for example, the Bible or the Koran? Or, might they claim, in keeping with the "natural law" tradition, that human reason itself is capable of discovering some divine truth? That is, can they convincingly hold that, although God is the ultimate source of all ethical truth, we humans possess the rational capacities to comprehend those aspects of the ethical standard that has been revealed in nature?

Finally, there are also questions concerning the "moral status" of nonbelievers. For instance, if ethical truth originates in God, does this mean that those who do not believe in God do not have access to such truth or at least cannot appropriate it as fully as can believers? Or is it the case, as some believers maintain, that some of God's truths—including moral truths—are available to all humans whom he has created. In other words, need one acknowledge God's existence to become aware of "God's truths" through ordinary reason or intuition or conscience?

These tough questions and many others continue to make the field of religious ethics a fertile area for philosophical discussion.

ROBERT M. ADAMS

Ethics and the Commands of God

In this reading, Robert Adams (1937–) supports the general divine command thesis: what is right or good is what God commands. But unlike some proponents of divine command theory, Adams does not believe that anything God could command would, for that very reason, automatically be good or right. Adams argues, for example, that it would not be wrong for us to refrain from practicing cruelty, even if we were commanded by God to commit cruel acts. He adds, however, that God is a loving being and therefore that we need not fear God's asking us to act in a capricious, unloving, or unjust manner.

⌘

DIVINE COMMAND THEORY

It is widely held that all those theories are indefensible which attempt to explain in terms of the will or commands of God what it is for an act to be ethically right or wrong. In this paper I shall state such a theory, which I believe to be defensible; and I shall try to defend it against what seem to me to be the most important and interesting objections to it. I call my theory a *modified* divine command theory because in it I renounce certain claims that are commonly made in divine command analyses of ethical terms. . . .

It will be helpful to begin with the statement of a simple, *un*modified divine command theory of ethical wrongness. This is the theory that ethical wrongness *consists in* being contrary to God's commands, or that the word "wrong" in ethical contexts *means* "contrary to God's commands." It implies that the following two statement forms are logically equivalent.

(1) It is wrong (for A) to do X.

(2) It is contrary to God's commands (for A) to do X.

Of course that is not all that the theory implies. It also implies that (2) is conceptually prior to (1), so that the meaning of (1) is to be explained in terms of (2), and not the other way around. It might prove fairly difficult to state or explain in what that conceptual priority consists, but I shall not go into that here. I do not wish ultimately to defend the theory in its unmodified form, and I think I have stated it fully enough for my present purposes. . . .

OBJECTION TO DIVINE COMMAND THEORY

The following seems to me to be the gravest objection to the divine command theory of ethical wrongness, in the form in which I have stated it. Suppose God should command me to make it my chief end in life to inflict suffering on other human beings, for no other reason than that He commanded it. (For convenience I shall abbreviate this hypothesis to "Suppose God should command cruelty for its own sake.") Will it seriously be claimed that in that case it would be wrong for me not to practice cruelty for its own sake? I see three possible answers to this question.

(1) It might be claimed that it is logically impossible for God to command cruelty for its own sake. In that case, of course, we need not worry about whether it would be wrong to disobey if He did command it. It is senseless to agonize about what one should do in a logically impossible situation. This solution to the problem seems unlikely to be available to the divine command theorist, however. For why would he hold that it is logically impossible for God to command cruelty for its own sake? Some theologians (for instance, Thomas Aquinas) have believed (a) that what is right and wrong is independent of God's will, *and* (2) that God always does right by the necessity of His nature. Such theologians, if they believe that it would be wrong for God to command cruelty for its own sake, have reason to believe that it is logically impossible for Him to do so. But the divine command theorist, who does not agree that what is right and wrong is independent of God's will, does not seem to have such a reason to deny that it is logically possible for God to command cruelty for its own sake.

(2) Let us assume that it is logically possible for God to command cruelty for its own sake. In that case the divine command theory seems to imply that it would be wrong not to practice cruelty for its own sake. There have been at least a few adherents of divine command ethics who have been prepared to accept this consequence. William Ockham held that those acts which we call "theft," "adultery," and "hatred of God" would be meritorious if God had commanded them.[1] He would surely have said the same about what I have been calling the practice of "cruelty for its own sake."

This position is one which I suspect most of us are likely to find somewhat shocking, even repulsive. We should therefore be particularly careful not to misunderstand it. We need not imagine that Ockham disciplined himself to be ready to practice cruelty for its own sake if God should command it. It was doubtless an article of faith for him that God is unalterably opposed to any such practice. The mere logical possibility that theft, adultery, and cruelty might have been commanded by God (and therefore meritorious) doubtless did not represent in Ockham's view any real possibility.

(3) Nonetheless, the view that if God commanded cruelty for its own sake it would be wrong not to practice it seems unacceptable to me; and I think many, perhaps most, other Jewish and Christian believers would find it unacceptable too. I must make clear the sense in which I find it unsatis-

factory. It is not that I find an internal inconsistency in it. And I would not deny that it may reflect, accurately enough, the way in which some believers use the word "wrong." I might as well frankly avow that I am looking for a divine command theory which at least might possibly be a correct account of how *I* use the word "wrong." I do not use the word "wrong" in such a way that I would say that it would be wrong not to practice cruelty if God commanded it, and I am sure that many other believers agree with me on this point.

But now have I not rejected the divine command theory? I have assumed that it would be logically possible for God to command cruelty for its own sake. And I have rejected the view that if God commanded cruelty for its own sake, it would be wrong not to obey. It seems to follow that I am committed to the view that in certain logically possible circumstances it would not be wrong to disobey God. This position seems to be inconsistent with the theory that "wrong" means "contrary to God's commands."

A MODIFIED DIVINE COMMAND THEORY

I want to argue, however, that it is still open to me to accept a modified form of the divine command theory of ethical wrongness. . . .

According to this second version of the theory, the statement that something is ethically wrong (or permitted) says something about the will or commands of God, but not about His love. Every such statement, however, *presupposes* that certain conditions for the applicability of the believer's concepts of ethical right and wrong are satisfied. Among these conditions is that God does not command cruelty for its own sake—or, more generally, that God loves His human creatures. It need not be assumed that God's love is the only such condition.

The modified divine command theorist can say that the possibility of God commanding cruelty for its own sake is not provided for in the Judeo-Christian religious ethical system as he understands it. The possibility is not provided for, in the sense that the concepts of right and wrong have not been developed in such a way that actions could be correctly said to be right or wrong if God were believed to command cruelty for its own sake. The modified divine command theorist agrees that it is logically possible[2] that God should command cruelty for its own sake; but he holds that it is unthinkable that God should do so. To have *faith* in God is not just to believe that He exists, but also to trust in His love for mankind. The believer's concepts of ethical wrongness and permittedness are developed within the framework of his (or the religious community's) religious life, and therefore within the framework of the assumption that God loves us. The concept of the will or commands of God has a certain function in the believer's life, and the use of the words "right" (in the sense of "ethically permitted") and "wrong" is tied to that function of that concept. But one of the reasons why the concept of the will of God can function as it does is that the love which God is believed to have toward men arouses in the believer certain attitudes of love toward God and devotion to His will. If the believer thinks about the unthinkable but logically possible situation in which God commands cruelty for its own sake, he finds that in relation to that kind of command of God he cannot take up the same attitude, and that the concept of the will or commands of God could not then have the same function in his life. For this reason he will not say that it would be wrong to disobey God, or right to obey Him, in that situation. At the same time he will not say that it would be wrong to obey God in that situation, because he is accustomed to use the word "wrong" to say that something is contrary to the will of God, and it does not seem to him to be the right word to use to express his own personal revulsion toward an act against which there would be no divine authority. Similarly, he will not say that it would be "right," in the sense of "ethically permitted," to disobey God's command of cruelty; for that does not seem to him to be the right way to express his own personal attitude toward an act which would not be in accord with a divine authority. In this way the believer's concepts of ethical rightness and wrongness would break down in the situation in which he believed that God commanded cruelty for its own sake—that is, they would not function as they now do, because he would not be prepared to use them to say that any action was right or wrong. . . .

OBJECTIONS TO MODIFIED DIVINE COMMAND THEORY

The modified divine command theory clearly conceives of believers as valuing some things independently of their relation to God's commands. If the believer will not say that it would be wrong not to practice cruelty for its own sake if God commanded it, that is because he values kindness, and has a revulsion for cruelty, in a way that is at least to some extent independent of his belief that God commands kindness and forbids cruelty. This point may be made the basis of both philosophical and theological objections to the modified divine command theory, but I think the objections can be answered.

The philosophical objection is, roughly, that if there are some things I value independently of their relation to God's commands, then my value concepts cannot rightly be analyzed in terms of God's commands. According to the modified divine command theory, the acceptability of divine command ethics depends in part on the believer's independent positive valuation of the sorts of things that God is believed to command. But then, the philosophical critic objects, the believer must have a prior, nontheological conception of ethical right and wrong, in terms of which he judges God's commandments to be acceptable—and to admit that the believer has a prior, nontheological conception of ethical right and wrong is to abandon the divine command theory.

The weakness of this philosophical objection is that it fails to note the distinctions that can be drawn among various value concepts. From the fact that the believer values some things independently of his beliefs about God's commands, the objector concludes, illegitimately, that the believer must have a conception of ethical right and wrong that is independent of his beliefs about God's commands. This inference is illegitimate because there can be valuations which do not imply or presuppose a judgment of ethical right or wrong. For instance, I may simply like something, or want something, or feel a revulsion at something.

What the modified divine command theorist will hold, then, is that the believer values some things independently of their relation to God's commands, but that these valuations are not judgments of ethical right and wrong and do not of themselves imply judgments of ethical right and wrong. He will maintain, on the other hand, that such independent valuations are involved in, or even necessary for, judgments of ethical right and wrong which also involve beliefs about God's will or commands. The adherent of a divine command ethics will normally be able to give reasons for his adherence. Such reasons might include: "Because I am grateful to God for His love"; "Because I find it the most satisfying form of ethical life"; "Because there's got to be an objective moral law if life isn't to fall to pieces, and I can't understand what it would be if not the will of God."[3] As we have already noted, the modified divine command theorist also has reasons why he would not accept a divine command ethics in certain logically possible situations which he believes not to be actual. All of these reasons seem to me to involve valuations that are independent of divine command ethics. The person who has such reasons wants certain things—happiness, certain satisfactions—for himself and others; he hates cruelty and loves kindness; he has perhaps a certain unique and "numinous" awe of God. And these are not attitudes which he has simply because of his beliefs about God's commands.[4] They are not attitudes, however, which presuppose judgments of moral right and wrong. . . .

This version of the divine command theory may [also] seem *theologically* objectionable to some believers. One of the reasons, surely, why divine command theories of ethics have appealed to some theologians is that such theories seem especially congruous with the religious demand that God be the object of our highest allegiance. If our supreme commitment in life is to doing what is right just because it is right, and if what is right is right just because God wills or commands it, then surely our highest allegiance is to God. But the modified divine command theory seems not to have this advantage. For the modified divine command theorist is forced to admit, as we have seen, that he has reasons for his adherence to a divine command ethics, and that his having these reasons implies that there are some things which he values independently of his beliefs about God's commands. It is therefore not correct to say of him that he is committed to doing the will of God *just* because it is the will of God; he is committed to doing it partly because of other things which he values independently. Indeed it appears that there are certain logically possible situations in which his present attitudes would not commit him to obey God's commands (for instance, if God commanded cruelty for its own sake). This may even suggest that he values some things, not just independently of God's commands, but more than God's commands.

We have here a real problem in religious ethical motivation. The Judeo-Christian believer is supposed to make God the supreme focus of his loyalties; that is clear. One possible interpretation of this fact is the following. Obedience to whatever God may command is (or at least ought to be) the one thing that the believer values for its own sake and more than anything and everything else. Anything else that he values, he values (or ought to) only to a lesser degree and as a means to obedience to God. This conception of religious ethical motivation is obviously favorable to an *un*modified divine command theory of ethical wrongness.

But I think it is not a realistic conception. Loyalty to God, for instance, is very often explained, by believers themselves, as motivated by gratitude for benefits conferred. And I think it is clear in most cases that the gratitude presupposes that the benefits are valued, at least to some extent, independently of loyalty to God. Similarly, I do not think that most devout Judeo-Christian believers would say that it would be wrong to disobey God if He commanded cruelty for its own sake. And if I am right about that I think it shows that their positive valuation of (emotional/volitional pro-attitude toward) doing *whatever* God may command is not clearly greater than their independent negative valuation of cruelty.

In analyzing ethical motivation in general, as well as Judeo-Christian ethical motivation in particular, it is probably a mistake to suppose that there is (or can be expected to be) one thing only that is valued supremely and for its own sake, with nothing else being valued independently of it. The motivation for a person's ethical orientation in life is normally much more complex than that, and involves a plurality of emotional and volitional attitudes of different sorts which are at least partly independent of each other. At any rate, I think the modified divine command theorist is bound to say that that is true of his ethical motivation.

In what sense, then, can the modified divine command theorist maintain that God is the supreme focus of his loyalties? I suggest the following interpretation of the single-hearted loyalty to God which is demanded in Judeo-Christian religion. In this interpretation the crucial idea is *not* that some one thing is valued for its own sake and more than anything else, and nothing else valued independently of it. It is freely admitted that the religious person will have a plurality of motives for his ethical position, and that these will be at least partly independent of each other. It is admitted further that a desire to obey the commands of God (*whatever* they may be) may not be the strongest of these motives. What will be claimed is that certain beliefs about God enable the believer to integrate or focus his motives in a loyalty to God and His commands. Some of these beliefs are about what God commands or wills (contingently—that is, although He could logically have commanded or willed something else instead).

Some of the motives in question might be called egoistic; they include desires for satisfactions for oneself—which God is believed to have given or to be going to give. Other motives may be desires for satisfaction for other people; these may be called altruistic. Still other motives might not be desires for anyone's satisfaction, but might be valuations of certain kinds of action for their own sakes; these might be called idealistic. I do not think my argument depends heavily on this particular classification, but it seems plausible that all of these types, and perhaps others as well, might be distinguished among the motives for a religious person's ethical position. Obviously such motives might pull one in different directions, conflicting with one another. But in Judeo-Christian ethics beliefs about what God does in fact will (although He could have willed otherwise) are supposed to enable one to *fuse* these motives, so to speak, into one's devotion to God and His will, so that they all pull together. Doubtless the believer will still have some motives which conflict with his loyalty to God. But the religious idea is that these should all be merely momentary desires and impulses, and kept under control. They ought not to be allowed to influence voluntary action. The deeper, more stable, and controlling desires, intentions, and psychic energies are supposed to be fused in devotion to God. As I interpret it, however, it need not be inconsistent with the Judeo-Christian ethical and religious ideal that this fusion of motives, this integration of moral energies, depends on belief in certain propositions which are taken to be contingent truths about God. . . .

MORAL LAW AND GOD

The ascription of moral qualities to God is commonly thought to cause problems for divine command theories of ethics. It is doubted that God, as an agent, can properly be called "good" in the moral sense if He is not subject to a moral law that is not of His own making. For if He is morally good, mustn't He do what is right *because* it is right? And how can He do that, if what's right is right because He wills it? Or it may be charged that divine command theories trivialize the claim that God is good. If "X is (morally) good" means roughly "X does what God wills," then "God is (morally) good" means only that God does what He wills—which is surely much less than people are normally taken to mean when they say that God is (morally) good. In this section I will suggest an answer to these objections.

Surely no analysis of Judeo-Christian ethical discourse can be regarded as adequate which does not provide for a sense in which the believer can seriously assert that God is good. Indeed an adequate analysis should provide a plausible account of what believers do in fact mean when they say,

"God is good." I believe that a divine command theory of ethical (rightness and) wrongness can include such an account. I will try to indicate its chief features.

(1) In saying "God is good" one is normally expressing a favorable emotional attitude toward God. I shall not try to determine whether or not this is part of the meaning of "God is good"; but it is normally, perhaps almost always, at least one of the things one is doing if one says that God is good. If we were to try to be more precise about the type of favorable emotional attitude normally expressed by "God is good," I suspect we would find that the attitude expressed is most commonly one of *gratitude.*

(2) This leads to a second point, which is that when God is called "good" it is very often meant that He is *good to us,* or *good to* the speaker. "Good" is sometimes virtually a synonym for "kind." And for the modified divine command theorist it is not a trivial truth that God is kind. In saying that God is good in the sense of "kind," one presupposes, of course, that there are some things which the beneficiaries of God's goodness value. We need not discuss here whether the beneficiaries must value them independently of their beliefs about God's will. For the modified divine command theorist does admit that there are some things which believers value independently of their beliefs about God's commands. Nothing that the modified divine command theorist says about the meaning of ("right" and) "wrong" implies that it is a trivial truth that God bestows on His creatures things that they value.

(3) I would not suggest that the descriptive force of "good" as applied to God is exhausted by the notion of kindness. "God is good" must be taken in many contexts as ascribing to God, rather generally, qualities of character which the believing speaker regards as virtues in human beings. Among such qualities might be faithfulness, ethical consistency, a forgiving disposition, and, in general, various aspects of love, as well as kindness. Not that there is some definite list of qualities, the ascription of which to God is clearly implied by the claim that God is good. But saying that God is good normally commits one to the position that God has some important set of qualities which one regards as virtues in human beings.

(4) It will not be thought that God has *all* the qualities which are virtues in human beings. Some such qualities are logically inapplicable to a being such as God is supposed to be. For example, aside from certain complications arising from the doctrine of the incarnation, it would be logically inappropriate to speak of God as controlling His sexual desires. (He doesn't have any.) And given some widely held conceptions of God and His relation to the world, it would hardly make sense to speak of Him as *courageous.* For if He is impassible and has predetermined absolutely everything that happens, He has no risks to face and cannot endure (because He cannot suffer) pain or displeasure.[5]. . .

(5) If we accept a divine command theory of ethical rightness and wrongness, I think we shall have to say that *dutifulness* is a human virtue

which, like sexual chastity, is logically inapplicable to God. God cannot either do or fail to do His duty, since He does not have a duty—at least not in the most important sense in which human beings have a duty. For He is not subject to a moral law not of His own making. Dutifulness is one virtuous disposition which men can have that God cannot have. But there are other virtuous dispositions which God can have as well as men. Love, for instance. It hardly makes sense to say that God does what He does *because* it is right. But it does not follow that God cannot have any reason for doing what He does. It does not even follow that He cannot have reasons of a type on which it would be morally virtuous for a man to act. For example, He might do something because He knew it would make His creatures happier.

(6) The modified divine command theorist must deny that in calling God "good" one presupposes a standard of moral rightness and wrongness superior to the will of God, by reference to which it is determined whether God's character is virtuous or not. And I think he can consistently deny that. He can say that morally virtuous and vicious qualities of character are those which agree and conflict, respectively, with God's commands, and that it is their agreement or disagreement with God's commands that makes them virtuous or vicious. But the believer normally thinks he has at least a general idea of what qualities of character are in fact virtuous and vicious (approved and disapproved by God). Having such an idea, he can apply the word "good" descriptively to God, meaning that (with some exceptions, as I have noted) God has the qualities which the believer regards as virtues, such as faithfulness and kindness.

I will sum up by contrasting what the believer can mean when he says, "Moses is good," with what he can mean when he says, "God is good," according to the modified divine command theory. When the believer says, "Moses is good," (a) he normally is expressing a favorable emotional attitude toward Moses—normally, though perhaps not always. (Sometimes a person's moral goodness displeases us.) (b) He normally implies that Moses possesses a large proportion of those qualities of character which are recognized in the religious-ethical community as virtues, and few if any of those which are regarded as vices. (c) He normally implies that the qualities of Moses' character on the basis of which he describes Moses as good are qualities approved by God.

When the believer says, "God is good," (a) he normally is expressing a favorable emotional attitude toward God—and I think exceptions on this point would be rarer than in the case of statements that a man is good. (b) He normally is ascribing to God certain qualities of character. He may mean primarily that God is kind or benevolent, that He is *good to* human beings or certain ones of them. Or he may mean that God possesses (with some exceptions) those qualities of character which are regarded as virtues in the religious-ethical community. (c) Whereas in saying, "Moses is good," the believer was stating or implying that the qualities of character which he was ascribing to Moses conform to a standard of ethical rightness which is independent of the will of Moses, he is not stating or implying that the qualities of character which he ascribes to God conform to a standard of ethical rightness which is independent of the will of God.

NOTES

1. Guillelmus de Occam, *Super 4 libros sententiarum*, bk. II, qu. 19, O, in Vol. IV of his *Opera plurima* (*Lyon*, 1494–96; réimpression en facsimilé, Farnborough, Hants., England: Gregg Press, 1962). I am not claiming that Ockham held a divine command theory of exactly the same sort that I have been discussing.

2. Perhaps he will even think it is causally possible, but I do not regard any view on that issue as an integral part of the theory. The question whether it is causally possible for God to "act out of character" is a difficult one which we need not go into here.

3. The mention of moral law in the last of these reasons may presuppose the ability *to mention* concepts of moral right and wrong, which may or may not be theological and which may or may not be concepts one uses oneself to make judgments of right and wrong. So far as I can see, it does not *presuppose* the *use* of such concepts to make judgments of right and wrong, or one's adoption of them for such use, which is the crucial point here.

4. The independence ascribed to these attitudes is not a *genetic* independence. It may be that the person would not have come to have some of them had it not been for his religious beliefs. The point is that he has come to hold them in such a way that his holding them does not now depend entirely on his beliefs about God's commands.

5. The argument here is similar to one which is used for another purpose by Ninian Smart in "Omnipotence, Evil, and Superman," *Philosophy* XXXVI (1961), reprinted in Nelson Pike, ed., *God and Evil* (Englewood Cliffs, N.J.: Prentice-Hall, 1964), pp. 103–12.

I do not mean to endorse the doctrines of divine impassibility and theological determinism.

KAI NIELSEN

Ethics without Religion

Theists sometimes contend that a world without God necessarily has at least two undesirable characteristics: life can have no meaning and all moral values are totally relative. In this reading, Kai Nielsen (1925–) challenges both claims. Even if there can exist no *ultimate* purpose in a Godless world, he argues, we can still experience a great deal of *personal* meaning and happiness. And even if moral values are purely human inventions, there still exists a sound basis for objective moral standards.

From "Religious Versus Secular Morality," in *Ethics without God* (London: Pemberton Books, 1973).

⌘

I

There are fundamental difficulties and perhaps even elements of incoherence in Christian ethics, but what can a secular moralist offer in its stead? Religious morality—and Christian morality in particular—may have its difficulties, but religious apologists argue that secular morality has still greater difficulties. It leads, they claim, to ethical scepticism, nihilism or, at best, to a pure conventionalism. Such apologists could point out that if we look at morality with the cold eye of an anthropologist we will find morality to be nothing more than the often conflicting *mores* of the various tribes spread around the globe.

If we eschew the kind of insight that religion can give us, we will have no Archimedean point in accordance with which we can decide how it is that we ought to live and die. If we look at ethics from such a purely secular point of view, we will discover that it is constituted by tribal conventions, conventions which we are free to reject if we are sufficiently free from ethnocentrism. We can continue to act in accordance with them or we can reject them and adopt a different set of conventions; but whether we act in accordance with the old conventions or forge 'new tablets,' we are still acting in accordance with certain conventions. In relation to these conventions certain acts are right or wrong, reasonable or unreasonable, but we cannot justify the fundamental moral conventions themselves or the ways of life which they partially codify.

When these points are conceded, theologians are in a position to press home a powerful apologetic point: when we become keenly aware of the true nature of such conventionalism and when we become aware that there is no overarching purpose that men were destined to fulfil, the myriad purposes, the aims and goals humans create for themselves, will be seen to be inadequate. When we realize that life does not have a meaning which is there to be found, but that we human beings must by our deliberate decisions give it whatever meaning it has, we will (as Sartre so well understood) undergo estrangement and despair. We will drain our cup to its last bitter drop and feel our alienation to the full. Perhaps there are human purposes, purposes to be found in life, and we can and do have them even in a Godless world; but without God there can be no one overarching purpose, no one basic scheme of human existence in virtue of which we could find a meaning for our grubby lives. It is this overall sense of meaning that man so ardently strives for, but it is not to be found in a purely secular world-view. You secularists, a new Pascal might argue, must realize, if you really want to be clear-headed, that no purely human purposes are ultimately worth striving for. What you Humanists can give us by way of a scheme of human existence will always be a poor second-best and not what the human heart most ardently longs for.

The considerations for and against an ethics not rooted in a religion are complex and involuted; a fruitful discussion of them is difficult, for in considering the matter our passions, our anxieties, our ultimate concerns (if you will) are involved, and they tend to blur our vision, enfeeble our understanding of what exactly is at stake. But we must not forget that what is at stake here is just what kind of ultimate commitments or obligations a man could have without evading any issue, without self-deception or without delusion. I shall be concerned to display and assess, to make plain and also to weigh, some of the most crucial considerations for and against a purely secular ethic. While I shall try to make clear in an objective fashion what the central issues are, I shall also give voice to my reflective convictions on this matter. I shall try to make evident my reasons for believing that we do not need God or any religious belief to support our moral convictions. I shall do this, as I think one should in philosophy, by making apparent the dialectic of the problem, the considerations for and against, and by arguing for what I take to be their proper resolution.

II

I am aware that Crisis theologians would claim that I am being naïve, but I do not see why purposes of purely human devising are not ultimately worth striving for. There is much that we humans prize and would continue to prize even in a Godless world. Many things would remain to give our lives meaning and point even after 'the death of God.'

Take a simple example. All of us want to be happy. . . . [And] in a purely secular world there are no permanent sources of human happiness for anyone to avail himself of.

What are these relatively permanent sources of human happiness that we all want or need? What is it which, if we have it, will give us the basis for a life that could properly be said to be happy? We all desire to be free from pain and want. [Even masochists do not seek pain for its own sake; they endure pain because this is the only psychologically acceptable way of achieving something else (usually sexual satisfaction) that is so gratifying to them that they will put up with the pain to achieve it.] We all want a life in which sometimes we can enjoy ourselves and in which we can attain our fair share of some of the simple pleasures that we all desire. They are not everything in life, but they are important, and our lives would be impoverished without them.

We also need security and emotional peace. We need and want a life in which we will not be constantly threatened with physical or emotional harassment. Again, this is not the only thing worth seeking, but it is an essential ingredient in any adequate picture of the good life.

Human love and companionship are also central to a happy life. We prize them and a life which is without them is most surely an impoverished life, a life that no man, if he would take the matter to heart, would desire. But I would most emphatically assert that human love and companionship are quite possible in a Godless world, and the fact that life will some day inexorably come to an end and cut off love and companionship altogether enhances rather than diminishes their present value.

Furthermore, we all need some sort of creative employment or meaningful work to give our lives point, to save them from boredom, drudgery and futility. A man who can find no way to use the talents he has, or a man who can find no work which is meaningful to him, will indeed be a miserable man. But again there is work—whether it be as a surgeon, a farmer or a fisherman—that has a rationale even in a world without God. And poetry, music and art retain their beauty and enrich our lives even in the complete absence of God or the gods.

We want and need art, music and the dance. We find pleasure in travel and conversation and in a rich variety of experiences. The sources of human enjoyment are obviously too numerous to detail, but all of them are achievable in a Godless universe. . . .

It is not only happiness for ourselves that can give us something of value, but there is the need to do what we can to diminish the awful sum of human misery in the world. I have never understood those who say that they find contemporary life meaningless because they find nothing worthy of devoting their energies to. Throughout the world there is an immense amount of human suffering, suffering that can be partially alleviated through a variety of human efforts. . . . [And] we can as individuals respond to those people and alleviate or at least acknowledge that suffering and deprivation. A man who says, 'If God is dead, nothing matters,' is a spoilt child who has never looked at his fellowman with compassion.

Yet, it might be objected, if we abandon a Judaeo-Christian *Weltanschauung*, there can, in a secular world, be no 'one big thing' to give our lives an overall rationale. We will not be able to see written in the stars the final significance of human effort. There will be no architectonic purpose to give our lives such a rationale. Like Tolstoy's Pierre in *War and Peace*, we desire somehow to gather the sorry scheme of things entire into one intelligible explanation so that we can finally crack the riddle of human destiny. We long to understand why it is that men suffer and die. If it is a factual answer that is wanted when such a question is asked, the answer is evident enough: ask any physician. But clearly that is no answer to people who seek such a general account of human existence. They want some justification for suffering; they want some way of showing that suffering is after all for a good purpose. It can, of course, be argued that suffering sometimes is a good thing, for it occasionally gives us insight and at times even brings about in the man who suffers an increased capacity to love and to be kind. But there is plainly an excessive amount of human suffering—the suffering of children in hospitals, the suffering of people devoured by cancer and the sufferings of millions of Jews under the Nazis—for which there simply is no justification.

Neither the religious man nor the secularist can explain, that is, justify, such suffering and find some overall scheme of life in which it has some place, but only the religious man needs to do so. The secularist understands that suffering is not something to be justified but simply to be struggled against with courage and dignity. And in this fight, even the man who has been deprived of that which could give him some measure of happiness can still find or make for himself a meaningful human existence.

III

I have argued that purely human purposes—those goals we set for ourselves, the intentions we form—are enough to give meaning to our lives.[1] We desire happiness and we can find, even in a purely secular world, abundant sources of it. Beyond this we can find a rationale for seeking to mitigate the awful burden of human suffering. These two considerations are enough to make life meaningful. . . .

[But] philosophers, and some theologians as well, might challenge what I have said. It could be said that even if we add consciousness as another intrinsic good, there is not the close connection between happiness and self-awareness on the one hand and virtue or moral good on the other that I have claimed there is. That men do seek happiness as an end is one thing; that they ought to seek it as an end is another. As G. E. Moore has in effect shown,[2] we cannot derive 'X is good' from 'people desire X' or from 'X makes people happy,' for it is always meaningful to ask whether or not happiness is good and whether or not we ought to seek it for its own sake. It will be argued that I, like all secularists, have confused factual and moral issues. An 'ought' cannot be derived from an 'is'; we cannot deduce that something is good from a discovery that it will make people happy. My hypothetical critic could well go on to claim that we first must justify the fundamental claim that happiness is good. Do we really have any reason to believe that happiness is good? Is the secularist in any more of a position to justify his claim than is the religionist to justify his claim that whatever God wills is good?

I would first like to point out that I have not confused factual and moral issues. One of the basic reasons I have for rejecting either a natural-law ethics or an ethics of divine commands is that both systematically confuse factual and moral issues. We cannot deduce that people ought to do something from discovering that they do it or seek it; nor can we conclude from the proposition that a being exists whom people call God that we ought to do whatever that being commands. In both cases we unjustifiably pass from a factual premise to a moral conclusion. Moral statements are not factual statements about what people seek or avoid, or about what a deity commands. But we do justify moral claims by an appeal to factual claims, and there is a close connection between what human beings desire on reflection and what they deem to be good. 'X is good' does not mean 'X makes for happiness,' but in deciding that something is good, it is crucial to know what makes human beings happy. Both the Christian moralist and the secular moralist lay stress on human happiness. The Christian moralist—St Augustine and Pascal are perfect examples—argues that only the Christian has a clear insight into what human happiness really is and that there is no genuine happiness without God. But [as I have argued elsewhere] we have no valid grounds for believing that only in God can we find happiness and that there are no stable sources of human happiness apart from God.

I cannot prove that happiness is good, but Christian and non-Christian alike take it in practice to be a very fundamental good. I can only appeal to your sense of psychological realism to persuade you to admit intellectually what in practice you acknowledge, namely, that happiness is good and that pointless suffering is bad. If you will acknowledge this, you must accept that I have shown that man can attain happiness even in a world without God.

Suppose some Dostoyevskian 'underground man' does not care a fig about happiness. Suppose he does not even care about the sufferings of others. How, then, can you show him to be wrong? But suppose a man does not care about God or about doing what He commands either. How can you show that such an indifference to God is wrong? If we ask such abstract questions, we can see a crucial feature about the nature of morality. Sometimes a moral agent may reach a point at which he can give no further justification for his claims but must simply, by his own deliberate decision, resolve to take a certain position. Here the claims of the existentialists have a genuine relevance. We come to recognize that, in the last analysis, nothing can take the place of a decision or resolution. If the end, we must simply decide. This recognition may arouse our anxieties and stimulate rationalization, but the necessity of making a decision is inherent in the logic of the situation. Actually, the religious moralist is in a worse position than the secularist, for he not only needs to subscribe to the principle that human happiness is good and that pain and suffering have no intrinsic value; he must also subscribe to the *outré* claims that only in God can man find happiness and that one ought to do whatever it is that God commands. 'Man can find lasting happiness only if he turns humbly to his Saviour' has the look of a factual statement and is a statement that most assuredly calls for some kind of rational support. It is not something we must or can simply decide about. But the assertion that one ought to do what is commanded by God, like the assertion that happiness is good, does appear simply to call for a decision for or against. But what it is that one is deciding for when one 'decides for God or for Christ' is so obscure as to be scarcely intelligible. Furthermore, the man who subscribes to that religious principle must subscribe to the secular claim as well. But why subscribe to this obscure second principle when there is no evidence at all for the claim that man can find happiness only in God? . . .

IV

The dialectic of our problem has not ended. The religious moralist might acknowledge that human happiness is indeed plainly a good thing while contending that secular morality, where it is consistent and reflective, will inevitably lead to some variety of egoism. An individual who recognized the value of happiness and self-consciousness might, if he were free of religious restraints, ask himself why he should be concerned with the happiness and self-awareness of others, except where their happiness and self-awareness would contribute to his own good. We must face the fact that sometimes, as the world goes, people's interests clash. Sometimes the common good is served only at the expense of some individual's interests. An individual must therefore, in such a circumstance, sacrifice what will make him happy for the common good. Morality requires this sacrifice of us, when it is necessary for the common good; morality, any morality, exists in part at least to adjudicate between the conflicting interests and demands of people. It is plainly evident that everyone cannot be happy all the time and that sometimes one person's happiness or the happiness of a group is at the expense of another person's happiness.

Morality requires that we attempt to distribute happiness as evenly as possible. We must be fair: each person is to count for one and none is to count for more than one. Whether we like a person or not, whether he is useful to his society or not, his interests and what will make him happy, must be considered in any final decision as to what ought to be done. The requirements of justice make it necessary that each person be given equal consideration. I cannot justify my neglect of another person in some matter of morality simply on the grounds that I do not like him, that he is not a member of my set or that he is not a productive member of society. The religious apologist will argue that behind these requirements of justice as fairness there lurks the ancient religious principle that men are creatures of God, each with an infinite worth, and that men are never to be treated only as means but as persons deserving of respect in their own right. They have an infinite worth simply as persons.

My religious critic, following out the dialectic of the problem, should query why you should respect someone, why you should treat all people equally, if doing this is not in your interest or not in the interests of your group. No purely secular justification can be given for so behaving. My critic now serves his *coup de grâce*: the secularist, as does the 'knight of faith,' acknowledges that the principle of respect for persons is a precious one—a principle that he is unequivocally committed to, but the religious man alone can justify adherence to this principle. The secularist is surreptitiously drawing on Christian inspiration when he insists that all men should be considered equal and that people's rights must be respected. For a secular morality to say all it wants and needs to say, it must, at this crucial point, be parasitical upon a God-centred morality. Without such a dependence on religion, secular morality collapses into egoism. . . .

The above argument is enough to destroy the believer's case here. But need we even rely on a historically religious concern as the basis for our moral position? There is a purely secular rationale for treating people fairly, for regarding them as persons. Let me show how this is so. We have no evidence that men ever lived in a pre-social state of nature. Man, as we know him, is an animal with a culture, he is part of a community, and the very concept of community implies binding principles and regulations—duties, obligations and rights. Yet, imaginatively we could conceive, in broad outline at any rate, what it would be like to live in a pre-social state.

In such a state no one would have any laws or principles to direct his behaviour. In that sense, man would be completely free. But such a life, as Hobbes graphically depicted, would be a clash of rival egoisms. Life in that state of nature would be, in his celebrated phrase, 'nasty, brutish and short.' Now if men were in such a state and if they were perfectly rational egoists, what kind of community life would they choose, given the fact that they were, very roughly speaking, nearly equal in strength and ability? (The fact that in communities as we find them men are not so nearly equal in power is beside the point for our hypothetical situation.) Given that they all start from scratch and have roughly equal abilities, it seems to me that it would be most reasonable, even for rational egoists, to band together into a community where each man's interests were given equal consideration, where each person was treated as deserving of respect.

Each rational egoist would want others to treat him with respect, for his very happiness is contingent upon that; and he would recognize that he could attain the fullest cooperation of others only if other rational egoists knew or had good grounds for believing that their interests and their persons would also be respected. Such cooperation is essential for each egoist if all are to have the type of community life which would give them the best chance of satisfying their own interests to the fullest degree. Thus, even if men were thorough egoists, we would still have rational grounds for subscribing to a principle of respect for persons. That men are not thoroughly rational, do not live in a state of nature and are not thorough egoists does not gainsay the fact that we have rational grounds for regarding social life, organized in accordance with such a principle, as being objectively better than a social life which ignores this principle. The point here is that even rational egoists could see that this is the best possible social organization where men are nearly equal in ability. . . .

It is sometimes argued by religious apologists that men will respect the rights of others only if they fear a wrathful and angry God. Without such a punitive sanction or threat, men will go wild. Yet it hardly seems to be the case that Christians, with their fear of hell, have been any better at respecting the rights of others than non-Christians. A study of the Middle Ages or the conquest of the non-Christian world makes this plain enough. And even if it were true that Christians were better in this respect than non-Christians, it would not show that they had a superior moral reason for their behaviour, for in so acting and in so reasoning, they are not giving a morally relevant reason at all but are simply acting out of fear for their own hides. Yet Christian morality supposedly takes us beyond the clash of the rival egoisms of secular life.

In short, Christian ethics has not been able to give us a sounder ground for respecting persons than we have with a purely secular morality. The Kantian principle of respect for persons is actually bound up in the very idea of morality, either secular or religious; and there are good reasons, of a perfectly mundane sort, why we should have the institution of morality as we now have it, namely, that our individual welfare is dependent on having a device which equitably resolves social and individual conflicts. Morality has an objective rationale in complete independence of religion. Even if God is dead, it does not really matter.

It is in just this last thrust, it might be objected, that you reveal your true colours and show your own inability to face a patent social reality. At this point the heart of your rationalism is very irrational. For millions of people, 'the death of God' means very much. It really does matter. In your somewhat technical sense, the concept of God may be chaotic or unintelligible, but this concept, embedded in our languages—embedded in 'the stream of life'—has an enormous social significance for many people. Jews and Christians, if they take their religion to heart, could not but feel a great rift in their lives with the loss of God, for they have indeed organized their lives around their religion. Their very life-ideals have grown out of these concepts. What should have been said is that if 'God is dead' it matters a lot, but nevertheless we should stand up like men and face this loss and learn to live in the Post-Christian era. As Nietzsche so well knew, to do this involves a basic reorientation of one's life and not just an intellectual dissent from a few statements of doctrine.

There is truth in such an objection and a kind of 'empiricism about man' that philosophers are prone to neglect. Of course it matters when one recognizes that one's religion is illusory. For a devout Jew or Christian to give up his God most certainly is important and does take him into the abyss of a spiritual crisis. But in saying that God's death does not really matter, I was implying what I have argued for in this essay; namely, that if an erstwhile believer loses his God but can keep his nerve, think the matter over and thoroughly take it to heart, life can still be meaningful and morality can yet have an objective rationale. Surely, for good psychological reasons, he is prone to doubt this argument, but if he will only 'hold on to his brains' and keep his courage, he will come to see that it is so. In this crucial sense it remains true that if 'God is dead' it does not really matter.

NOTES

1. I have argued this point in considerably more detail in Nielsen, Kai (1964), 'Linguistic Philosophy and "The Meaning of Life"' in *Cross Currents*, vol. XIV, no. 3, pp. 313–34.

2. Moore, G. E. (1903), *Principia Ethica*, Cambridge: Cambridge University Press, chapters 1 and 2.

3. Some of the very complicated considerations relevant here have been brought out subtly by Rawls, John (1958), 'Justice as Fairness' in *The Philosophical Review*, vol. LXVII, pp. 164–94, and by von Wright, Georg (1963), *The Varieties of Goodness*, London: Routledge, chapter 10. I think it could be reasonably maintained that my argument is more vulnerable here than at any other point. I would not, of course, use it if I did not think it could be sustained; but if anyone should find unconvincing the argument as presented here, I would beg him to consider the argument that precedes it and the one that immediately follows it. They alone are sufficient to establish my general case.

THOMAS AQUINAS

Ethics and Natural Law

Even if we assume that theists can justifiably maintain that ethical truth originates in God, this still leaves the question of how such truth is communicated from God to humans. In this reading, Thomas Aquinas (1224–1274) argues that although written revelation is *sufficient* for giving us God's basic moral perspective, it is not always *necessary*. Much of this truth can also be discovered by reflecting upon that which we have been given the rational capacity to learn about the nature of God's world.

⌘

The precepts of the law of nature are related to practical reason in the same way that the first principles of demonstration are to speculative reason. Both are principles that are self-known [*per se nota*]. Now, we speak of something as self-known in two ways: first, in itself; second, in relation to us.

Any proposition is called self-known in itself when its predicate belongs to the intelligible meaning of its subject. However, it is possible for such a proposition not to be evident to a person ignorant of the definition of the subject. Thus, this proposition, *man is rational*, is self-evident in its own nature, since to say man is to say rational; yet, for a person who is ignorant of what man is, this proposition is not self-known.

Consequently, as Boethius says (*De Hebdomadibus*, PL 64, 1311), there are some axioms or propositions that are in general self-known to all. Of this type are those propositions whose terms are known to all; for example, *every whole is greater than its part*, and *things equal to one and the same thing are equal*

From *Summa Theologica*, in *The Pocket Aquinas*, tr. Vernon J. Bourke (New York: Washington Square Press, 1960).

to each other. But there are some propositions that are self-known only to the wise, those who understand the meaning of the terms of these propositions. Thus, to one who understands that an angel is not a body, it is self-known that an angel is not present circumscriptively in place. This is not obvious to uninstructed people, who fail to grasp this point.

A definite order is found among items that fall under the apprehension of men. For, that which first falls under apprehension is *being* [*ens*]: the understanding of it is included in all things whatsoever that one apprehends. So, the first indemonstrable principle is: *It is not proper at once to affirm and to deny*. This is based on the intelligible meaning of being and nonbeing. On this principle all others are founded, as is said in the *Metaphysics* (III, 3, 1005b29).

Now, just as "being" is the first item that falls within apprehension without any qualification, so "good" is the first that falls within the apprehension of practical reason, which is directed toward work: *for every agent acts for the sake of an end*, which has the intelligible meaning of good. Thus, the first principle in the practical reason is what is based on the meaning of "good"; and it is: *The good is what all desire*. This is, then, the first principle of law: *Good is to be done and sought after, evil is to be avoided*. On this all the other precepts of the law of nature are based, in the sense that all things to be done or avoided belong to the precepts of the law of nature, if practical reason apprehends them as human goods.

Now, since the good has the rational character of an end, and evil has the contrary meaning, as a consequence reason naturally apprehends all things to which man has a natural inclination as goods and, therefore, as things to be sought after in working, and their contraries are apprehended as evils and as things to be avoided.

So, the order of the precepts of the law of nature is in accord with the order of natural inclinations. First, there is present in man the inclination toward the good on the level of the nature which he shares with all substances, inasmuch as each substance desires the preservation of its own existence according to its own nature. Now, those things whereby the life of man is preserved, and whereby its contrary is impeded, pertain to the natural law according to this inclination.

Second, there is present in man an inclination toward some more special things, on the level of the nature which he shares with other animals. And on this level, those things are said to belong to natural law "which nature teaches to all animals" (*Corpus Juris Civilis, Digesta*, I, tit. 1, leg. 1), as, for instance, the union of male and female, the upbringing of offspring, and similar things.

Third, there is present in man an inclination toward the good that is in accord with the nature of reason, and this is proper to him. Thus, man has a natural inclination toward knowing the truth about God, and toward living in society. On this level, those things within the scope of this inclination pertain to the natural law; for instance, that man should avoid ignorance, that he should not offend those with whom he must associate, and others of this kind that are concerned with this level.

[The difficulties mentioned at the beginning of the article boil down to this: Why are there many precepts of natural law, when man's nature is one and so is his reason?]

1. All these precepts of the law of nature, insofar as they are referred to one first precept, do have the rational character [*ratio*] of one natural law.

2. All inclinations of this kind, of whatsoever parts of human nature, for instance, of the concupiscible or irascible powers, belong to the natural law inasmuch as they are regulated by reason, and they are reduced to one first precept, as has been said. According to this, there are many precepts in themselves of the law of nature but they share in one common root.

3. Although reason is one in itself, it is directive of all things that pertain to men. For this reason, all things that can be regulated by reason are contained under the law of reason. . . .

Moral rules are concerned with those matters that essentially pertain to good behavior. Now, since human morals are spoken of in relation to reason (for it is the proper principle of human acts), those customs that are in conformity with reason are called good, and those that are in discord with reason are deemed bad. Just as every judgment of speculative reason proceeds from the natural knowledge of first principles, so, too, does every judgment of practical reason issue from certain naturally known principles, as we have explained before.

Now, it is possible to proceed in different ways from these principles in making judgments on different problems. There are some cases in human actions that are so explicit that they can be approved or condemned at once, with very little thought, by reference to those general and primary principles. Then, there are other problems for the judgment of which a good deal of thinking on the different circumstances is required. Careful consideration of such problems is not the prerogative of just any person but of the wise. In the same way, it is not the function of all men to consider the conclusions of the sciences but only of the philosophers. Again, there are still other matters for the judgment of which man stands in need of help by divine instruction, as is so in the case of items of belief.

And so, it becomes evident that since moral precepts belong among the matters that pertain to good behavior, and since these are items that are in conformity with reason, and since every judgment of human reason is derived in some fashion from natural reason, it must be true that all moral rules belong to the law of nature, but not all in the same way.

For, there are some things that the natural reason of every man judges immediately and essentially as things to be done or not done; for example, *Honor thy father and mother*, and *Thou shalt not kill; Thou shalt not steal.* Precepts of this kind belong in an unqualified way to the law of nature.

Then, there are other things that are judged by a more subtle rational consideration, on the part of the wise men, to be matters of obligation. Now, these belong to the law of nature in this way: they of course require instruction, by which less favored people are taught by those who are wise; for example, *Rise up before the hoary head, and honor the person of the aged man* (Lev. 19:32), and other injunctions of this kind.

Finally, there are other matters for the judgment of which human reason needs divine instruction, whereby we are taught concerning matters of divinity; for example, *Thou shalt not make to thyself a graven thing, nor the likeness of any thing. . . . Thou shalt not take the name of thy God in vain* (Exod. 20:4, 7).

SUGGESTED READING

Ewing, A. C. *Prospect for Metaphysics*. London: George Allen and Unwin, 1951.
Frankena, William. *Ethics*, 2d ed. Englewood Cliffs, N.J.: Prentice Hall, 1973.
Gill, Robin. *A Textbook of Christian Ethics*. Edinburgh: TPT Clark, 1985.
Hallet, George L. *Christian Moral Reasoning*. Notre Dame, Ind.: University of Notre Dame Press, 1983.
Hauerwas, Stanley. *The Peaceable Kingdom*. Notre Dame, Ind.: University of Notre Dame Press, 1981.
Helm, Paul, ed., *The Divine Command Theory of Ethics*. Oxford: Oxford University Press, 1979.
Jersild, Paul T., and Dale A. Johnson. *Moral Issues and Christian Response*, 5th ed. New York: Harcourt Brace Jovanovich Publishers, 1993.
Kierkegaard, Søren. *Fear and Trembling*, trans. Howard V. Hong and Edna H. Hong. Princeton: Princeton University Press, 1983.
MacIntyre, Alasdair. *After Virtue*. Notre Dame, Ind.: Notre Dame Press, 1981.
McClendon, James W., Jr., *Ethics: Systematic Theology*, vol. 1. Nashville: Abingdon, 1986.
Quinn, Philip. *Divine Commands and Moral Requirements*. Oxford: Clarendon Press, 1978.
Reichenbach, Bruce. "The Divine Command Theory and Objective Good," in *Georgetown Symposium on Ethics*, ed. R. Porreco. New York: University Press of America: 199–231.
Veatch, Henry. *For an Ontology of Morals*. Evanston, Ill.: Northwestern University Press, 1971.

PART THIRTEEN

PHILOSOPHY AND THEOLOGICAL DOCTRINES

There is a significant historical relationship between philosophy and Christian theology, one that dates back to the early centuries of the church. Although philosophy has gone its own way in much of the modern period, professional philosophers are once again taking a serious interest in a variety of classical Christian doctrines. They are analyzing key theological concepts as well as evaluating how important theological claims interact with other claims that are either part of the same theological perspective or drawn from prevailing philosophical opinion. In recent years, philosophical works have appeared on many topics in classic Christian theology, such as the Trinity, prayer, the Incarnation, forgiveness, revelation, sanctification, and hell.

One fundamental tenet of the Christian faith has been the Incarnation, the belief that God became human in the person of Jesus Christ. Specifically, it is affirmed that Jesus Christ was both fully human and fully divine. However, even some believers in recent years have begun to question not only whether the Incarnation actually occurred but also whether it is even possible. Could one person be fully human and fully divine at the same time? Is it still possible for thoughtful people to accept this doctrine?

Christians have also traditionally held that we are born alienated from God because of the sin of the first humans, Adam and Eve, and can be reconciled to God because of the suffering and death of Jesus Christ. This thinking is related to the doctrine of the Atonement. But exactly what role did Christ's death play in reconciling persons to God? Why was the death necessary? And exactly what was it intended to accomplish?

Along with believers in other religions, Christians believe that prayer somehow links them with or communicates with the divine. They frequently petition God in the sense that they ask God to bring about events that they believe might not occur without direct divine assistance. God is often asked, for instance, to soothe a troubled mind, to help reunite estranged marriage partners, or sometimes even to calm hurricanes or heal diseased bodies. Yet Christians also believe that God is incalculably more knowledgeable and caring than are we. Thus, the question arises: Why do believers feel the need to petition God? If God is the kind of being that Christians say he is—all knowing and perfectly good—would he not already be doing all that can be done? That is, would he not already be meeting all legitimate needs?

Naturally, consensus is seldom reached on issues regarding the above doctrines or other important doctrines. But the philosophical discussion of theological ideas and claims brings additional enlightenment, and allows us to decide more judiciously whether they can be embraced by reasonable persons.

THOMAS MORRIS

Jesus Christ Was Fully God and Fully Human

Historically, the Christian church has held that Jesus Christ was both fully human and fully divine. In this selection, Thomas Morris (1952–) does not attempt to prove that the Incarnation was a matter of fact, or even that all Christians are obligated to believe it to be the case. His main objective, rather, is to demonstrate that none of the standard criticisms of this traditional doctrine are compelling and to show that the main philosophical aspects of the doctrine are indeed coherent. Accordingly, he claims to have established that the orthodox Christian belief that Jesus was God incarnate is rationally justified.

⌘

[Various] contemporary theologians have thought the incarnational claim about Jesus to be patently incoherent and thus absurd in a logical or conceptual sense. From this point of view, it would be possible to believe Jesus to be God Incarnate and to be rational in so believing only if one rationally could fail to see the patent incoherence of the claim. A certain significant degree of ignorance or obtuseness would be required, if this were to be possible at all. A number of philosophers have offered persuasive arguments in recent years to the effect that it is possible rationally to believe the impossible, or necessarily false. However, if 'incoherent' means more than merely 'necessarily false,' if 'patently incoherent' means something more like 'analytically false' or '*a priori* impossible,' then it is less likely, to say the least, that anyone would be able rationally to believe a patently incoherent doctrine, for it is highly unlikely that belief in the truth of an analytically false, or *a priori* impossible, proposition can reasonably be ascribed to a person at all. If a patently incoherent proposition is such that one cannot understand it without seeing it to be false, and it is impossible to believe a proposition to be true without understanding it, and, moreover, it is impossible to believe a proposition to be true while seeing it to be false, then should the doctrine of the Incarnation be patently incoherent, it would not be possible rationally to believe it, because it would not be possible to believe it at all. Furthermore, understood in this way, it is clear that nothing could count as a positive epistemic consideration in favour of the truth of a patently incoherent claim. If the incarnational claim endorsed by traditional Christians had this status, there could be no positive epistemic ground for believing it true. As, for example, Grace Jantzen has said:

> If the claim that Jesus is God incarnate is on an epistemological level with 'Jesus was a married bachelor' then no matter how much evidence we could discover

> for his having said so, his disciples and others having believed it, and the early church having affirmed it, the claim must still be rejected: such 'evidence' would be strictly irrelevant.[1]

And this is certainly correct. Nothing can count as evidence or any other form of epistemic grounding for belief in a proposition the very understanding of which suffices for seeing its falsehood.

The charge of patent incoherence has been repeated in various forms quite often in recent years by critics of the doctrine of the Incarnation. Basically, the sort of argument most of them seem to have in mind is roughly something like the following: On a standard and traditional conception of deity, God is omnipotent, omniscient, incorporeal, impeccable, and necessarily existent, among other things. Moreover, by our definition of 'God,' such properties as these are, so to speak, constitutive of deity—it is impossible that any individual be divine, or exemplify divinity, without having these properties. To claim some individual to be divine without being omnipotent, say, or necessarily existent, would be on this view just as incoherent as supposing some individual to be both a bachelor and a married man at one and the same time. By contrast, we human beings seem clearly to exemplify the logical complement (or "opposite") of each of these constitutive divine attributes. We are limited in power, restricted in knowledge, embodied in flesh, liable to sin, and are contingent creations. Jesus is claimed in the doctrine of the Incarnation to have been both fully human and fully divine. But it is logically impossible for any being to exemplify at one and the same time both a property and its logical complement. Thus, recent critics have concluded, it is logically impossible for any one person to be both human and divine, to have all the attributes proper to deity and all those ingredient in human nature as well. The doctrine of the Incarnation on this view is an incoherent theological development of the early church which must be discarded by us in favor of some other way of conceptualizing the importance of Jesus for Christian faith. He could not possibly have been God Incarnate, a literally divine person in human nature.

As I have addressed this challenge to the doctrine of the Incarnation in great detail elsewhere, I shall give only a relatively brief indication here of how it can be answered.[2] A lengthy response is not required in order for us to be able to see how this currently popular sort of objection can be turned back. A couple of very simple metaphysical distinctions will provide us with the basic apparatus for defending orthodoxy against this charge, which otherwise can seem to be a very formidable challenge indeed.

As it is usually presented, the sort of argument I have just outlined treats humanity and divinity, or human nature and divine nature, as each constituted by a set of properties individually necessary and jointly sufficient for exemplifying that nature, for being human, or for being divine. Such an argument depends implicitly on a sort of essentialist metaphysic which has been around for quite a while, and which recently has experienced a resurgence of popularity among philosophers. On such a view, objects have two sorts of properties, essential and accidental. A property can be essential to an object in either of two ways. It is part of an individual's essence if the individual which has it could not have existed without having it. It is a kind-essential property if its exemplification is necessary for an individual's belonging to a particular kind, for example, human-kind. Human nature, then, consists in a set of properties severally necessary and jointly sufficient for being human. And the same is true of divine nature. The critic of the Incarnation begins with the simple truth that there are properties humans have which God could not possibly have, assumes that these properties, or at least some of them, are essential properties of being human, properties without which one could not be fully human, and then concludes that God could not possibly become a human being. The conclusion would be well drawn if the assumption were correct. But it is this assumption that we must question.

Once a distinction between essential and accidental properties is accepted, a distinction employed in this sort of argument against incarnation, another simple distinction follows in its wake. Among properties characterizing human beings, some are essential elements of human nature, but many just happen to be common human properties without also being essential. Consider for example the property of having ten fingers. It is a common human property, one had by a great number of people, but it clearly is not a property essential to being human. People lose fingers without thereby ceasing to be human. Further, consider a common property which safely can be said to be a universal human property, one had by every human being who ever has lived—the property of standing under fifteen feet tall. Obviously this is not an essential human property either. At some time in the future, an individual might grow beyond this height, certainly not thereby forfeiting his humanity. So it is not a safe inference to reason simply from a property's being common or even universal among human beings that it is an essential human property, strictly necessary for exemplifying human nature.

The relevance of this distinction to the doctrine of the Incarnation should be obvious. It is common for human beings to be less than omnipotent, less than omniscient, contingently existent, and so on. And any orthodox Christian will quickly agree that apart from Jesus, there are even universal human properties. Further, in the case of any of us who do exemplify these less than divine attributes, it is most reasonable to hold that they are in our case essential attributes. I, for example, could not possibly become omnipotent. I am essentially limited in power. But why think this is true on account of human nature? Why think that any attributes incompatible with deity are elements of human nature, properties without which one could not be truly human?

An individual is *fully human* just in case that individual has all essential human properties, all the properties composing basic human nature. An individual is *merely human* if he has all those properties *plus* some additional limitation properties as well, properties such as being less than omnipotent, less than omniscient, and so on. Some examples of this *merely x/fully x* distinction may help. Consider a diamond. It has all the properties essential to being a physical object (mass, spatio-temporal location, etc.). So it is fully physical. Consider now a turtle. It has all the properties essential to being a physical object. It is fully physical. But it is not merely physical. It has properties of animation as well. It is an organic being. In contrast, the gem is merely physical as well as being fully physical. Now take the case of a man. An embodied human being, any one you choose, has mass, spatio-temporal location, and so forth. He is thus fully physical. But he is not merely a physical object, having organic and animate properties as well. So let us say he is fully animate. But unlike the turtle he is not merely animate, having rational, moral, aesthetic, and spiritual qualities which mere organic entities lack. Let us say that he belongs to a higher ontological level by virtue of being fully human. And if, like you and I, he belongs to no higher ontological level than that of humanity, he is merely human as well as being fully human.

According to orthodox Christology, Jesus was fully human without being merely human. He had all properties constitutive of human nature, but had higher properties as well, properties constitutive of deity, properties which from an Anselmian perspective form the upper bound of our scale. What is crucial to realize here is that an orthodox perspective on human nature will categorize all human properties logically incompatible with a divine incarnation as, at most, essential to being *merely human*. No orthodox theologian has ever held that Jesus was merely human, only that he was fully human. It is held that the person who was God Incarnate had the full array of attributes essential to humanity, and all those essential to divinity.

I am suggesting that armed with a few simple distinctions the Christian can clarify his conception of human nature in such a way as to provide for the coherence and metaphysical possibility of the traditional doctrine of the Incarnation. But I am sure it will be objected by many that to use these distinctions to explicate what Chalcedon and the rest of the church has had in mind about Jesus is to land oneself in some well known absurdities. On the Chalcedonian picture, Jesus was omniscient, omnipotent, necessarily existent, and all the rest, as well as being an itinerant Jewish preacher. But this has appeared outlandish to most contemporary theologians. Did the bouncing baby boy of Mary and Joseph direct the workings of the cosmos from his crib? Was this admittedly remarkable man, as he sat by a well or under a fig tree actually omnipresent in all of creation? Did this carpenter's son exist *necessarily*? These implications of orthodoxy can sound just too bizarre for even a moment's consideration.

A couple of ancient claims are sufficient to rid orthodoxy from any such appearance of absurdity. First of all, a person is not identical with his body. Even a modern materialist who holds that all personality necessarily is embodied need not deny this. So the necessary existence of God the Son, with its implications that he cannot have begun to exist and cannot cease to exist, does not entail that the earthly body in which he incarnated himself had these properties. Secondly, a person is not identical with any particular range of conscious experience he might have. With this in mind, we can appreciate the early view that in the case of God Incarnate, we must recognize something like two distinct ranges of consciousness.[3] There is first what we can call the eternal mind of God the Son with its distinctively divine consciousness, whatever that might be like, with its full scope of omniscience. And there is a distinctly earthly consciousness which grew and developed as the boy Jesus grew and developed. It drew its visual imagery from what the eyes of Jesus saw, and its concepts from the languages he spoke. The earthy range of consciousness, and self-consciousness, was thoroughly human, Jewish, and first century Palestinian in scope.

To be as brief as possible here, we can view the two ranges of consciousness as follows: The divine consciousness of God the Son contained, but was not contained by, the earthly range of consciousness. Further, there was what can be called asymmetric accessing relation between the two (think of two computer programs or informational systems, one containing but not contained by the other). The divine mind had full access to the earthly experience being had through the incarnation, but the earthly consciousness did not have such access to the content of the over-arching omniscience of the Logos. This allows for the intellectual and spiritual growth of Jesus to be a real development. It also can help account for the cry of dereliction. We have in the person of Jesus no God merely dressed up as a man. No docetic absurdities are implied by this position. Nor is it Nestorian. Nor Appolinarian. There is one person with two natures, and two ranges of consciousness. He is not the theological equivalent of a centaur, half God and half man. He is fully human, but not merely human. He is also fully divine. There is, in this doctrine, no apparent incoherence whatsoever. Thus, there seem to be no good logical or conceptual grounds for thinking that there can be no rational belief that Jesus was God Incarnate.

But before concluding too hastily that it is at least possible for belief in the Incarnation to be rationally grounded, we would do well to consider briefly a problem which has been raised by Francis Young. Young has said:

> [I]t is now accepted by the majority of Christian theologians that Jesus must have been an entirely normal human being, that any qualification of this implies some element of docetic thinking, and that docetism, however slight, undermines the reality of the incarnation.
>
> I therefore pose the following conundrum:
>
> If Jesus was an entirely normal human being, no evidence can be produced for the incarnation.
>
> If no evidence can be produced, there can be no basis on which to claim that an incarnation took place.[4]

If it is assumed, as I would suspect it is by Young, that the belief that Jesus was God Incarnate cannot be a reasonable or rational belief to hold unless there can be evidence on which to base it, this argument, or conundrum, immediately becomes an argument to the effect that, on a certain assumption concerning what the doctrine of the Incarnation itself requires with respect to the humanity of Jesus, we find that it cannot be reasonable or rational to believe that Jesus was God Incarnate.

It is true that in order to avoid the docetic tendency which some critics have claimed plagues traditional theology, we must maintain the full, complete humanity of Jesus. But Young has a genuine problem here for incarnational belief only if in order to avoid docetism we also would have to hold that Jesus was *merely* human, and thus different from ordinary human beings such as you or me in no metaphysical way which could possibly be empirically manifested. But as we have seen, there is an important distinction to be drawn between being fully human and being merely human. Jesus can be fully human without being merely human. At least, that is the orthodox claim as I have articulated it. His complete humanity is thus compatible with his belonging to the higher ontological level of deity as well, and being such that his deity as well as his humanity is manifest in his life. We need not hold that Jesus was merely human in order to avoid docetism and uphold the doctrine of the Incarnation. If we did hold this, it is clear that we would be fleeing docetism only to fall into the grasp of psilanthropism, and thereby relinquish the doctrine just as certainly, only in a more currently fashionable way. On a careful understanding of the logic and metaphysics of the Incarnation, we can thus see that Young's 'conundrum' cannot even arise. So, once again, we find that what has been taken to be a problem for the traditional position that it is possible for belief in the Incarnation to be rational is in actuality no problem at all. None of the considerations we have examined so far has had the slightest tendency to block in principle the possibility of rationally discerning God in Christ.

But there is one more major sort of objection many recent critics have lodged against the doctrine of the Incarnation, along with the beliefs about divine-human relations it presupposes. The doctrine of the Incarnation is one component in a much larger doctrinal scheme encompassing the themes of creation, fall, and redemption. Contemporary critics of the traditional renderings of these themes often have pointed out that they originally where enunciated and developed in pre-scientific conditions and thus within the context of a very different sort of world-view from the one which modern scientifically minded people have today. They have then usually gone on to suggest that religious claims which may have made a great deal of sense in their original context have lost much, if not all, of their plausibility in the modern age. It is interesting to note that this is a general point made repeatedly in recent years by many prominent professors of Christian theology as well as by critics avowedly outside the communion of the church.

Now, I think we must recognize that many professedly Christian theologians during the past century or so have appeared a bit overly ready to beat a hasty retreat in the face of almost any specious argument or other consideration against the traditional affirmations of the faith they are supposed to be representing. Often they seem inclined to relinquish or "reinterpret'' important doctrines on no better grounds than that those beliefs can appear to some secular critics to be somehow out of step with the march of science. There have been those such as Rudolf Bultmann, for example, who claim to be unable to believe in the literally miraculous while at the same time available themselves of the comforts of modern technology. But of course such cases as these may be of more interest to psychologists than to anyone seeking to determine the objective status, truth value, or rationality of orthodox Christian beliefs. Occasionally, however, an interesting and even challenging philosophical or theological problem can be extracted from the often vague misgivings of such critics of orthodoxy. Let us consider various ways in which such a challenge might be thought to arise here against the doctrine of the Incarnation.

It has been suggested many times during the past two hundred years that this doctrine, which made a great deal of sense to many people living within the geocentric world-picture of Ptolemaic cosmology, is rendered in some sense absurd by modern accounts of the immensity and nature of our universe. The problem seems to be something like this: During the times when the Chalcedonian understanding of Christ was developed and reigned supreme, it was believed by great numbers of people, including the best educated, that we human beings live in a relatively circumscribed universe, the entirety of which has been created for the benefit of human life, which represents the special crowning act of divine creation, situated, appropriately at the hub of the cosmos, around which all else literally as well as figuratively revolves. Within such an overall perspective, it would have seemed in no way incongruous, but rather could have appeared supremely fitting, that the Creator of all take such interest in his human creatures as to step into his world himself and take a part in the human drama, being enacted, as it was, on the center stage of the universe. An anthropocentric world-view provided the cosmological backdrop and framework for a literally anthropomorphic theology—God become a man. The importance of the earth and the importance of humanity rendered this incarnation of deity intelligible and appropriate.

However, during the past few centuries this world-view, and the framework it provided, has been destroyed, chipped away bit by bit by the onslaught of scientific discovery until nothing of it remains. Actually, it is quite a variety of scientific discoveries, assumptions, hypotheses, speculations, and methodological implications which have seemed to many people to have had the net result of demoting human-kind from its traditionally exalted place in the universe to what can appear to be a relatively unexceptional and terribly insignificant role in the cosmic process. I shall not attempt to delineate here the variety of negative effects modern science has been perceived to have on religious doctrine. Numerous books exist which thoroughly document the so-called "history of the warfare between science and theology." But it will be of some interest to at least indicate a couple of points at which scientific developments have been thought to have this de-valuing impact on our view of humanity, and thus on the system of Christian doctrines, including centrally that of the Incarnation, in which the value of human beings seems clearly to be assumed to be great.

Some critics appear to think that the sheer size of the universe renders humanity unimportant in the cosmos, and Christian doctrine thus implausible. Of course, it is not modern novelty to juxtapose the immensity of the universe to the religious emphasis on man. The psalmist, for example, wrote long age:

> When I consider Thy heavens, the work of Thy fingers, the moon and the stars, which Thou hast ordained: What is man that Thou does take thought of him? And the son of man that Thou dost care for him? (Psalm 8:3,4)

This is an expression of an attitude of wonderment, and perhaps astonishment, that amidst the grandeur of the heavens, human beings should be especially valued by God. The attitude of modern critics, however, is that of simple disbelief. Of course, the psalmist was not aware as some of us are today *how* immense the heavens might be. But it is a bit difficult to see exactly what it is about distinctively modern knowledge of the scale of the universe which is thought to show the absurdity of any religious beliefs based on the assumption that the earth and human beings are important to the Creator of all.

Now, it is clear that in many contexts size and value are in direct correlation, the latter depending on the former. For example, all other things being equal, a large army is of greater value than a small one, if one seeks protection of one's country from an enemy. But this dependence of value on size is only relative to some contexts having to do with instrumental value, and clearly does not hold true in either all or even most such contexts. And when it comes to considerations of intrinsic value, the sort of value ascribed to human beings by Christian theology, questions of size or physical magnitude are simply irrelevant. It is just absurd to argue: Small therefore unimportant. Critics often accuse Christian theologians of being anthropomorphic in their thought. But here it seems to be the critics who are anthropomorphizing, or better, anthropopathizing, with the assumption that if there were a God, he would not deign to notice or value anything as small and insignificant on the cosmic scale as the earth and its inhabitants. On the Christian picture, God is sufficiently unlike a man that his attention and care can extend fully to every part of a universe, however large, to the point of being infinite in space and time.

So I think we are safe in concluding that if any discovery of modern science undercuts the Christian belief that God so valued us that he became a man, it will not be any discovery concerning the sheer size of the universe. But as with the link between relative size and value, there have been traditionally believed to be a number of other signs, or even requisites, of human importance which have been undercut by the advance of the sciences. For example, in many primal religions an equation is held between spatial centrality and importance. Anthropologists have found many tribes who hold as a sacred belief the claim that their village, or a fire in the center of the village, is located at the center of the world, or at the center of the entire cosmos. Their importance to the gods is held to be tied to their central location. Such a view also can be seen in the Ptolemaic cosmology and in the many theological and philosophical speculations arising out of that cosmology. In light of this apparently natural equation of importance and spatial centrality, reflected also in non-spatial uses of the notion of centrality, it is easy to understand the resistance many Christian theologians and clerics once felt toward any transition away from a geocentric cosmology. But again, outside a very few contexts of instrumental value considerations, it is simply wrong to think there to be a necessary link between spatial centrality and value. Modern critics who cite the transition from a Ptolemaic to a Copernican to a contemporary cosmology as counting against or as undercutting traditional Christian claims that the earth and humanity are sufficiently important as to render appropriate a divine incarnation on earth are making the same mistake with respect to value theory as the ancients whose views they deride.

There are other lines of reasoning which have been used to support the conclusion that the doctrine of the Incarnation is a cosmologically incongruous claim, but all of them suffer from the same, or similar, sorts of glaring debilities as those two arguments we have just examined. It is a bit surprising to find that a challenge of Christian belief which seems to have such widespread emotional appeal for critics has so little substance when examined closely.

NOTES

1. Grace Jantzen, "Incarnation and Epistemology," *Theology* 83 (May 1983), 171.
2. The challenge is addressed in chapter nine of *Understanding Identity Statements* (Aberdeen: Aberdeen University Press and Humanities Press, 1984), in "Divinity, Humanity, and Death," *Religious Studies* 19 (December 1983), 451–458, and in "Incarnational Anthropology," *Theology* 87 (September 1984), 344–350. It is explored in much greater detail in chapters one through six of *The Logic of God Incarnate* (Ithaca: Cornell University Press, 1986).
3. One contemporary theologian who has hinted repeatedly at the importance of this view is Brian Hebblethwaite. See for example his article, "The Propriety of the Doctrine of the Incarnation as a Way of Interpreting Christ," *Scottish Journal of Theology* 33 (1980), 201–222.
4. Frances Young, "Can There Be Any Evidence," *Incarnation and Myth: The Debate Continued*, ed. Michael Goulder (Grand Rapids: Eerdmans, 1979), 62.
5. Brian Hebblethwaite, "Incarnation—The Essence of Christianity?" *Theology* 80 (1977).
6. Keith Ward, "Incarnation or Inspiration—A False Dichotomy?" *Theology* 80 (1977).
7. Grace Jantzen, "Incarnation and Epistemology," 173, 174.
8. See Richard Creel, "Can God Know That He is God?" *Religious Studies* 16 (June 1980), 195–201.

PHILIP QUINN

The Traditional Understanding of the Atonement Must Be Modified

Historically, many Christians have maintained that Jesus Christ died on the cross to pay the debt we as humans owe to God because of our sins. In the following selection, Philip Quinn (1940–) challenges the contention that one person can absolve another of his or her *moral* debt by volunteering to pay it. Quinn offers instead a model of atonement that he believes is more compatible with our current moral intuitions.

⌘

According to Aquinas, Christ's Passion contributes to man's salvation in many ways that are effective in remedying human sin. It is the price paid to God to redeem us from bondage to the devil, and it removes our debt of punishment by making condign satisfaction for the sins of the whole human race. It also merits grace that aids our efforts to reunite our wills to God's will and so plays a part in cleansing the stain of sin from our souls. And it is a sacrifice that helps to reconcile us to God. One might think of Christ's atonement in a way that includes all modalities in which the Passion works for our salvation; on this understanding of atonement, Christ atones by way of merit, satisfaction, sacrifice, and redemption. Alternatively, one might conceive of Christ's atonement in a way that restricts it to the modality of making satisfaction in order to abolish the debt of punishment for sin; if one thinks of things in this fashion, Christ atones by removing from us a debt of punishment we cannot pay, though his Passion also works for our salvation by way of merit, sacrifice, and redemption. Either way, freeing us from a debt of punishment for sin which we owe but cannot pay by satisfying for our sins has a major role to play in the Thomistic account of Christ's atoning work. It is either the whole or an essential part of what Christ's Passion does to atone vicariously for our sins.

SOURCES OF DISSATISFACTION

There are, however, objections that can be lodged against Aquinas's account of the effects of Christ's Passion. . . . First, many people nowadays find problematic the part Aquinas assigns to the devil in the great drama of sin and salvation. To be sure, the Thomistic account is an improvement on older ransom theories to which the devil justly held sinners in slavery and Christ's Passion was a price paid to him to buy their freedom. Aquinas believes that the devil unjustly holds sinners in bondage and unjustly inflicts suffering on them, and he holds that the price that redeems them from bondage is paid to God rather than to the devil. But he is also committed to the view that there is no injustice in God's permitting the devil to inflict suffering on those sinners who deserve it by way of punishment and to whom Christ's satisfaction has not been applied.

Is this commitment morally acceptable? I think there is something at least slightly unsavory about it. Consider the analogous case of a person who is unjustly enslaved and tortured by a band of brigands, and suppose this person is a convicted criminal who deserves punishment equivalent to what she suffers at the hands of the brigands. Imagine too that the state whose criminal laws this person has broken has the power to free her from the brigands and to inflict on her the punishment she deserves. Would there be no injustice in this state's allowing the brigands to torture the criminal? I doubt it. It seems to me that if we suppose that the state justly allows the brigands to torture the criminal, we are implicitly assuming that the brigands are, as it were, officers of the state who are justly punishing the criminal by torturing her. And, conversely, it seems to me that if we imagine that the brigands are unjustly torturing the criminal so that what they do to her does not count as justly punishing her, then we are implicitly committed to the view that the state does not justly allow the brigands to torture the criminal. Similarly, I can see no way in which the suffering the devil inflicts on the sinners he holds captive could be both unjustly inflicted and justly permitted by God, who has the power to prevent it from being inflicted. It may well be just that such sinners suffer; it does not follow that it is just that they suffer at the hands of the devil. If we suppose that he unjustly inflicts suffering on them, I believe we should hold that it is unjust that they suffer at his hands.

In response to this objection it might be said that Satan is indeed an officer of the divine system of justice because he has been assigned such a role by God. So God justly permits him to inflict suffering on sinners, and the torments to which he subjects them are just in the sense of being proportioned to their deserts. But in another sense he acts unjustly, since he acts from malice rather than for the sake of justice. An analogous case would be the example of a human judge who is called on to pass sentence on his worst enemy and assigns the maximum penalty allowed by law and who is motivated by hatred rather than by a disinterested concern for justice. Though there is a sense in which such a judge acts justly since what he does is legally permissible, there is also a sense in which he acts unjustly because he acts out of partiality or bias.

Two points need to be made by way of rejoinder to this line of argument. First, it appears that there is injustice in a human legal system when its officers administer it in a partial or biased fashion, though such injustice may have to be tolerated in merely human institutions because it is often hard to detect and harder to correct. But since God is presumably not subject so similar limitations, the analogy does not support the claim that he justly permits Satan to torture sinners maliciously. Thus it is far from clear that it would be consonant with divine justice for God to assign Satan the role of administering physical punishment to sinners.

Second, it is not even clear that it makes sense to think of Satan as an officer in a divine criminal justice system. One might, I suppose, imagine that God is like a western sheriff who deputizes a vicious bounty hunter for the purpose of having him track down and execute a condemned criminal. Even if the bounty hunter acts from some unworthy motive such as greed, his killing of the criminal is legal once he has been deputized. But in order to be deputized the bounty hunter has to agree to accept appointment to office and to go through a ceremony of being sworn in or something of that sort, and Satan, who is a rebel against God's system of justice, is unlikely to have agreed to an appointment as God's deputy. Thus it is hard to see what to make of talk of Satan as an officer in a divine system for visiting retributive punishment on sinners. No doubt God can providentially turn Satan's malicious acts of torture to good purposes if he permits Satan to perform such acts, and no doubt it is not unjust for God to permit such acts (if he in fact permits them). But I do not consider it helpful to try to explain this by supposing that Satan serves as God's deputy in an institution whose purpose is to inflict punishment on sinners.

Of course some respond to talk of Satan and his cohorts with incredulity and insist that they are creatures of fiction. I myself do not share the attitude manifested in such responses, and so I have no general objection to assigning the devil a role in the cosmic drama of humanity's dealings with its creator. But I think the particular part Aquinas gives to the devil simply will not play; it seems to me that piety has tempted him into trying to save more of the ransom-theoretic picture than it is necessary or desirable to preserve. The notion of redeeming sinners by paying a price that compensates God for offenses against him can stand apart from the idea of ransoming sinners from sufferings inflicted by the devil. It seems to me feasible to excise the latter idea from the Thomistic account of Christ's atoning work, and I believe the result of doing so would be to enhance its appeal to our moral sensibilities.

A second problem for Aquinas's account of the work of Christ's Passion arises from its insistence both that the debt of punishment for sin will not be removed unless condign satisfaction, which is beyond human power, is made and also that Christ's satisfaction, which is condign, is applied only by means of faith in Christ or the sacraments of the Church. This combination of a doctrine of divine severity and a claim of ecclesiastical exclusiveness has some unattractive consequences that Aquinas has to accept. One already mentioned is that infants who die unbaptized are excluded from heaven altogether because they must endure the loss which is the punishment of original sin. To be sure, there are worse fates: this loss by itself is not so bad as it would be with sensible pain added to it. Still, to be excluded forever from heavenly bliss is to be deprived of a very great good. Another such consequence is that Old Testament Fathers such as Abraham even while they lived had faith in Christ that enabled them to be delivered from actual sins and their penalties and from original sin but not, until Christ descended into hell, its penalty.[1] But this is a view of the worthies of the Old Testament that seems at best strained and at worst wildly implausible; there appears to be no psychological realism at all in the supposition that characters such as Abraham had faith in Christ when they were alive.

If one wished to escape consequences like these, one might modify the Thomistic account either by increasing the ways in which the satisfaction of Christ's Passion can be applied to other humans or by relaxing the demands of divine severity. If one took the former tack, one could still hold that Christ's satisfaction is applied to members of Christian churches through faith in him, while allowing that it is also applied in some other way to those who lack, through no fault of their own, either the ability or the opportunity to have faith in Christ. One could thus continue to insist upon the doctrine of divine severity and maintain that God requires condign satisfaction for the debt of punishment of every sin. But then one would add that Christ's sufficient satisfaction has in some way abolished the debt of punishment of those who, like infants who die unbaptized and the Old Testament patriarchs who never so much as heard of Christ while they lived, lack faith in him through no voluntary fault of their own. On the other hand, if the latter strategy were pursued, one could still hold that Christ's satisfaction is applied only to those who have faith in him to abolish the debt of punishment for their sins, while maintaining that God in his mercy simply does not require condign satisfaction as a precondition of abolishing the debt of punishment of those who lack such faith through no voluntary fault of their own. One could in this fashion hold on to the view that Christ's sufficient satisfaction is efficacious only for those united to him by faith but admit that, in the case of those who lack either the ability or the opportunity to have such faith without thereby being culpable, God sometimes removes the debt of punishment for sin without having first received condign satisfaction.

More would have to be said, of course, about the details of such proposals before we could hope to pass final judgment on their merits. Both strategies raise questions. How, for example, could Christ's satisfaction legitimately be applied to those who, like the Old Testament patriarchs and infants who die unbaptized, lack faith in him? Perhaps it could be said that it is applied to the patriarchs in virtue of their faith in God as he had revealed himself in their times, and maybe one could hold that infants who die unbaptized develop in the afterlife at least to the point at which faith in Christ is a live option for them. Or, on the alternative proposal, why should condign satisfaction be demanded in some cases if it is not required in all cases? Maybe it would be plausible to claim that more is appropriately demanded from those who have been granted the ability and opportunity to share in the kind of intimacy with God characteristic of faith in Christ than from those not so privileged. But since this paper is not the proper place to develop such suggestions in the sort of detail necessary to render them credible, I shall content myself with the observation that either proposal would probably make room for more felicitous accounts of the fates of the patriarchs who died long before Christ was born and of infants who die unbaptized than the stories Aquinas tells about these people.

Aquinas supposes that God can justly exercise severity and insist on condign satisfaction as a condition of abolishing the debt of punishment for sin or can justly exercise mercy and abolish that debt without receiving sufficient satisfaction. If both these options are consistent with perfect justice, as it seems to me they are, then considerations of justice alone will not determine whether or not God has elected to treat sinners with severity. So the most likely sources of information on this matter will be the historical record of God's dealings with sinners and what he has chosen to reveal to us about himself. I take it that there is a strong scriptural case to be made in support of the view that God has shown himself to be severe but just in his dealings with at least some of his human creatures, and so I think it would smack of foolish sentimentality to abandon the doctrine of divine severity if there is a good alternative to doing so. Hence I am tempted to say that there is some way in which Christ's sufficient satisfaction can be applied to those who non-culpably lack faith in him so as to remove their debts of punishment.

But a third difficulty must be faced if we are not prepared to compromise on the issue of divine severity. This is the problem of making sense of the notion of vicarious satisfaction in such a way as to render it morally palatable. Aquinas, of course, would not have felt the force of this problem to the extent we do, for medieval legal codes provided models for vicarious satisfaction. In such codes, the debt of punishment for even such serious crimes as killing was literally pecuniary; one paid the debt by paying monetary compensation. What was important for such purposes as avoiding blood feud was that the debt be paid; who paid it was not crucial. So if a poor killer could not pay to the family of his victim the full compensation specified by law, his rich friends or relatives could voluntarily step in to remove his debt of punishment by paying it for him. One person could therefore satisfy for another at law by voluntarily paying the other's debts of punishment for crimes, since those debts were pecuniary.

It would be natural enough for a medieval thinker to extend this legal model to debts of punishment generally and to think of suffering as a kind of currency that can be used to pay them. Accordingly, a person who voluntarily endures suffering at least as great as what a friend deserves by way of punishment would thus satisfy for the friend by paying his debt of punishment. Similarly, suppose the debts of punishment sinners owe God are such that they must be paid in full, but not necessarily by those who incurred them. Then it is easy to see how one might come to believe, as Aquinas does, that one person can satisfy for another's sins by paying the other's debts of punishment.

But our intuitions about the proper relations of crime and punishment are tutored by a very different legal picture. Though a parent can pay her child's pecuniary debts, a murderer's mother cannot pay his debt of punishment by serving his prison term. If he does not serve his term but his mother, out of love for him, voluntarily remains in prison for a period at least as long as his term, she does not succeed in satisfying for him and his debt of punishment remains unpaid. Admittedly, illness may make it impossible for a murderer to endure the rigors of a prison term, and this could provide grounds for an exercise of executive clemency. But if the murderer is pardoned, then his debt of punishment simply goes unpaid, and no one satisfies for him by paying it for him. So to the extent that we think of serious sins as analogous to crimes and respect the practices embodied in our system of criminal law, we should expect the very idea of vicarious satisfaction for sin to seem alien and morally problematic.

Our intuitions about such matters are, of course, fallible. But if they remain stable under reflection, then we should trust them. Because I take intuition to speak for the view that debts of punishment for serious sins simply cannot be transferred from one person to another, it seems to me rational not to accept the claim that vicarious satisfaction for serious sin is possible.[2] Yet Aquinas insists that Christ's suffering was sufficient and superabundant satisfaction even for his murderers' crime.[3] This objection, then, threatens one of the basic assumptions of the Thomistic account of the effects of Christ's Passion. Indeed, as I see it, it strikes to the heart of any theory of Christ's atoning work that incorporates the element of vicarious satisfaction for the debt of punishment owed on account of serious sin.

In fairness to Aquinas, though, it must be mentioned that he does try to explain how it is possible for Christ's Passion to satisfy vicariously for the debt of punishment of sinners. There is scriptural warrant for thinking of the Church as a mystical body with Christ as its head and others who are united to him by faith as its members.[4] Aquinas uses this organic metaphor to explain how Christ can merit grace for the other members of the Church. Just as in an ordinary human person the action of the head extends in a way to all the members, since it perceives not for itself alone but for all the members, so also the grace Christ merits may extend to others who are members of the mystical body of which he is the head.[5] And Aquinas explicitly applies this figure of speech to the case of satisfaction by claiming that "Christ's satisfaction belongs to all the faithful as being His members"[6]; he supposes this claim is an adequate response to the objection that making satisfaction is the task of the one who commits the sin.

But it is far from clear that this response is adequate. In his discussion of redemption, Aquinas tells us that by his Passion Christ delivered us as his members from our sins in the same way as a man might, by the good industry of his hands, redeem himself from a sin committed with his feet.[7] However, there is no element of vicariousness in the example. The man, not his feet, is the sinner; the feet are merely the instruments by means of which the man sins. And, as Aquinas says, it is the man who redeems himself; his hands are merely the instruments he uses. And, though Christ's flesh is,

Aquinas believes, an instrument of the Godhead, human sinners are not. Indeed, there appears to be no real subject that sins and has both Christ's flesh and human beings as its instruments, and so it seems there is nothing that can be subject to redemption in the way that the comparison suggests. Thus the analogy fails to hold in the right respects, and there is a similar difficulty in the case of satisfaction. The analogy with the organic body of a human agent suggests an agent satisfying for a sin committed using one bodily part as an instrument by performing some good action using some other bodily part as an instrument. But this is not a case of one person making satisfaction for the sin of another; rather, it is a case of an agent satisfying for its own sin.

The comparison of the Church to an organic body therefore does little to aid us in the project of understanding how it is possible for one person who is not a sinner to satisfy for the debt of punishment of another person who is a sinner. If this analogy is to be helpful, it will have to be spelled out in a way that makes its inner workings more evident than does Aquinas's example of the hands and feet. I confess to being skeptical about how much progress can be made along these lines. Like debts of punishment for crime in our legal system, debts of punishment for sin seem to me to be too tightly tied to those who commit the sins for it to be plausible to suppose that one person may remove another's debt of punishment by paying it in full. So I find the very idea of vicarious satisfaction for the debt of punishment of sin hard to swallow.

There is a way to modify the Thomistic theory to avoid having to swallow it. One might suppose that God would have required condign satisfaction for the debt of punishment of all human sin as a condition of abolishing this debt if Christ had not reconciled us to God by his sacrifice, but that God does not in fact require condign satisfaction just because Christ's Passion is such a pleasing sacrifice. On this view, Christ's Passion works by prevailing upon God not to be severe in his dealings with sinners. Its effect is not to remove a debt of punishment for sin by paying it but to forestall the severe demand that the debt be paid in full. Rather than being severe, God is merciful toward some sinners; he forgives that part of the debt of punishment they cannot pay. Such a view also suggests a picture of transactions between the first and second persons of the Trinity that is a bit more edifying than the thought that the Son is paying a penal debt owed to the Father.

Perhaps this can best be brought out by means of a fable. Suppose a great magnate makes his two sons stewards of the two finest farms on his estate. The elder son irresponsibly neglects and thus ruins his farm, but the younger son conscientiously makes his own farm flourish. As a result of his negligence, the elder son has come to deserve punishment at the hands of his father; it would be severe but just for the father to disinherit him if he does not restore the ruined farm to prosperity. Unfortunately, the elder son is not a good enough farmer to accomplish this task, though he could have prevented the ruin of the farm if he had tried.

Then the younger son wonderfully intervenes. Moved by love for his brother as well as by devotion to their father and the welfare of his estate, the younger son undertakes to restore the farm his brother had ruined. This new undertaking requires tremendous sacrifices from him: he now has to maintain one farm and rehabilitate another. But the sacrifices so work upon the father's heart that he is persuaded to be merciful rather than severe toward his elder son. He forgives his elder son for the damage he has done to the estate and does not disinherit him even though the elder son has not himself repaired the damage.

I suppose there is a sense in which one could say that the younger son has paid his brother's debt or righted the moral balance by restoring the farm he ruined, but it seems to me more accurate to say that the father has been moved by his younger son's sacrifices to forgive the debt. For even if the younger son had not succeeded in restoring the ruined farm to its former prosperity but had only been able to make it marginally productive, his sacrifices would still have so moved the father that he would not have disinherited his erring elder son. Or so we may suppose.

Considerations of this sort incline me toward accepting such a revision in the theory, though it is fairly radical, in order to avoid supposing that Christ's Passion works by way of vicarious satisfaction to pay the full measure of the debt of punishment of sin. I am aware, of course, that those who are willing to go along with this radical revision lay themselves open to the charge of foolish sentimentality mentioned earlier by demoting divine severity to merely counterfactual status in at least some cases. But in the end I am prepared to pay this price to relieve the dissatisfaction with vicarious satisfaction I share with other critics of Aquinas.

There are critics prepared to be more radical than I am. Some would object to attributing even counterfactual severity to God and would argue that the revision I propose does not go far enough. My response is to insist that it is a mistake to try to eliminate divine severity from the picture altogether. It is worth remembering that the apostle Paul (in Romans 11:22) juxtaposes the severity of God toward those who fell and his kindness toward those who remain in his kindness. Aquinas tries to strike the same sort of balance. Immediately after speaking of God's severity and referring to that verse, he speaks of God's goodness in delivering up his own Son for us and refers again to the same verse. It seems to me that any account of God's treatment of sinners that does not preserve something of this delicate balance of severity and leniency will not adequately reflect the tension between the claims of strict justice and mercy at the heart of Christian thought about God's response to sin.[8]

NOTES

1. Thomas Aquinas, *Summa Theologica*, III 52, 5, ad 2.

2. I say more on this topic in Philip L. Quinn, "Christian Atonement and Knatian Justification," *Faith and Philosophy* 3 (1986): 440–462.

3. Aquinas, *Summa*, III 48, 2, ad 2.

4. Aquinas, III 8, 1.

5. Aquinas, III 19, 4.

6. Aquinas, III 48, 2, ad 1.

7. Aquinas, III 49, 1.

8. Earlier versions of this paper were read at a meeting of the Philosophy of Religion Society and at the Marquette Conference on Trinity, Incarnation, and Atonement. Richard Purtill and Richard Mouw were my commentators on the first of these occasions; William J. Wainwright was my commentator on the second. I am grateful to them for helpful criticism and to the audiences on those occasions for stimulating discussion. I also owe a debt of gratitude to students and colleagues at Notre Dame for help in understanding Aquinas.

ELEONORE STUMP

Why Petition God?

Many theists have held that God, as an omniscient, omnipotent, perfectly good being, not only *knows* what is best in every context but also *does* everything in his power to bring it about. If this is so, how can we make sense of the standard belief that petitionary prayer changes things in the sense that it influences God to do what he otherwise would not have done? Eleonore Stump (1947–) proposes the view that if God desires to establish a meaningful relationship, then he may at times need to wait to intervene until requested. Otherwise God risks either spoiling us or making the sharing of our innermost desires appear unnecessary.

⌘

Ordinary Christian believers of every period have in general taken prayer to be fundamentally a request made of God for something specific believed to be good by the one praying. The technical name for such prayer is "impetration"; I am going to refer to it by the more familiar designation "petitionary prayer." . . .

Christian literature contains a number of discussions of the problem of how petitionary prayer can be viewed as a useful activity and various attempts to solve it. For the sake of brevity, I want to look just at the proposed solution Aquinas gives. . . . It is the most philosophically sophisticated of the solutions I know; and in the wake of the twentieth-century revival of Thomism, it is the solution adopted by many theologians and theistic philosophers today.[1] Thomas discusses problems of petitionary prayer in his Sentence commentary and in the *Summa contra gentiles,*[2] but the clearest exposition of his views is in the question on prayer in the *Summa theologiae,* where he devotes an entire article to showing that there is sense and usefulness in petitionary prayer.[3] The basic argument he relies on to rebut var-

From *American Philosophical Quarterly* 16, no. 2 (April 1979): 81–90. Reprinted by permission.

ious objections against the usefulness of prayer is this. Divine Providence determines not only what effects there will be in the world, but also what causes will give rise to those effects and in what order they will do so. Now human actions, too, are causes. "For," Thomas says, "we pray not in order to change the divine disposition but for the sake of acquiring by petitionary prayer what God has disposed to be achieved by prayer."[4]

Perhaps the first worry which this argument occasions stems from the appearance of theological determinism in it: God determines not only what effects there will be but also what the causes of those effects will be and in what order the effects will be produced. It is hard to see how such a belief is compatible with freedom of the will. In the preamble to this argument, however, Thomas says he is concerned *not* to deny free will but, on the contrary, to give an account of prayer which preserves free will. So I want simply to assume that he has in mind some distinction or some theory which shows that, despite appearances, his argument is not committed to a thorough-going determinism, and I am going to ignore any troubles in the argument having to do with the compatibility of predestination or foreknowledge and free will.

For present purposes, what is more troublesome about this argument is that it does not provide any real help with the problem it means to solve. According to Thomas, there is nothing absurd or futile about praying to God, given God's nature, because God has by his providence arranged things so that free human actions and human prayers will form part of the chain of cause and effect leading to the state of the world ordained in God's plan. And so, on Thomas's view, prayer should not be thought of as an attempt to get God to do something which he would not otherwise do but rather as an effort to produce an appropriate and preordained cause which will result in certain effects since God in his providence has determined things to be so. Now surely there can be no doubt that, according to Christian doctrine, God wants men to pray and answers prayers; and consequently it is plain that God's plan for the world includes human prayers as causes of certain effects. The difficulty lies in explaining how such a doctrine makes sense. Why should prayers be included in God's plan as causes of certain effects? And what sense is there in the notion that a perfect and unchangeable God, who disposes and plans everything, fulfills men's prayers asking him to do one thing or another? Thomas's argument, I think, gives no help with these questions and so gives no help with this problem of petitionary prayer.

This argument of Thomas's is roughly similar in basic strategy to other traditional arguments for prayer[5] and is furthermore among the most fully developed and sophisticated argument for prayer, but it seems to me inadequate to make sense of petitionary prayer. I think, then, that it is worthwhile exploring a sort of argument different from those that stress the connection between God's omniscience or providence and men's prayers. In what follows I want to offer a tentative and preliminary sketch of the way in which such an argument might go.

Judaeo-Christian concepts of God commonly represent God as loving mankind and wanting to be loved by men in return. Such anthropomorphic talk is in sharp contrast to the more sophisticated-sounding language of the Hellenized and scholastic arguments considered so far. But a certain sort of anthropomorphism is as much a part of Christianity as is Thomas's "perfect being theology,"[6] and it, too, builds on intricate philosophical analysis, beginning perhaps with Boethius's attempt in *Contra Eutychen et Nestorium* to explain what it means to say of something that it is a person. So to say that God loves men and wants to be loved in return is to say something that has a place in philosophical theology and is indispensable to Christian doctrine. Throughout the Old and New Testaments, the type of loving relationship wanted between man and God is represented by various images, for example, sometimes as the relationship between husband and wife, sometimes as that between father and child. And sometimes (in the Gospel of John, for instance) it is also represented as the relationship between true friends.[7] But if the relationship between God and human beings is to be one which at least sometimes can be accurately represented as the love of true friendship, then there is a problem for both parties to the relationship, because plainly it will not be easy for there to be friendship between an omniscient, omnipotent, perfectly good person and a fallible, finite, imperfect person. The troubles of generating and maintaining friendship in such a case are surely the perfect paradigms of which the troubles of friendship between a Rockefeller child and a slum child are just pale copies. Whatever other troubles there are for friendship in these cases, there are at least two dangers for the disadvantaged or inferior member of the pair. First, he can be so overcome by the advantages or superiority of his "friend" that he becomes simply a shadowy reflection of the other's personality, a slavish follower who slowly loses all sense of his own tastes and desires and will. Some people, of course, believe that just this sort of attitude towards God is what Christianity wants and gets from the best of its adherents; but I think that such a belief goes counter to the spirit of the Gospels, for example, and I don't think that it can be found even in such intense mystics as St. Teresa and St. John of the Cross. Secondly, in addition to the danger of becoming completely dominated, there is the danger of becoming spoiled in the way that members of a royal family in a ruling house are subject to. Because of the power at their disposal in virtue of their connections, they often become tyrannical, willful, indolent self-indulgent, and the like. The greater the discrepancy in status and condition between the two friends, the greater the danger of even inadvertently overwhelming and oppressing or overwhelming and spoiling the lesser member of the pair; and if he is overwhelmed in either of these ways, the result will be replacement of whatever kind of friendship there might have been with one or another sort of using. Either the superior member of the pair will use the lesser as his lackey, or the lesser will use the superior as his personal power source. To put it succinctly, then, if God wants some kind of true friendship with men, he will have to find a way of guarding against both kinds of overwhelming.

It might occur to someone to think that even if we assume the view of

God wants friendship between himself and human beings, it does not follow that he will have any of the problems just sketched, because he is omnipotent.[8] If he wants friendship of this sort with men, one might suppose, let him just will it and it will be his. I do not want to stop here to argue against this view in detail, but I do want just to suggest that there is reason for thinking it to be incoherent, at least on the assumption of free will adopted at the beginning of this paper, because it is hard to see how God could bring about such a friendship magically, by means of his omnipotence, and yet permit the people involved to have free will. If he could do so, he could make a person freely love him in the right sort of way, and it does not seem reasonable to think he could do so.[9] On the fact of it, then, omnipotence alone does not do away with the two dangers for friendship that I sketched above. But the institution of petitionary prayer, I think, can be understood as a safeguard against these dangers.

It is easiest to argue that petitionary prayer serves such a function in the case of a man who prays for himself. In praying for himself, he makes an explicit request for help, and he thereby acknowledges a need or a desire and his dependence on God for satisfying that need or desire. If he gets what he prayed for, he will be in a position to attribute his good fortune to God's doing and to be grateful to God for what God has given him. If we add the undeniable uncertainty of his getting what he prays for, then we will have safeguards against what I will call (for lack of a better phrase) overwhelming spoiling. These conditions make the act of asking a safeguard against tyrannical and self-indulgent pride, even if the one praying thinks of himself grandly as having God on his side.

We can see how the asking guards against the second danger, of oppressive overwhelming, if we look for a moment at the function of roughly similar asking for help when both the one asking and the one asked are human beings. Suppose a teacher sees that one of his students is avoiding writing a paper and is thereby storing up trouble for himself at the end of the term. And suppose that the student *asks* the teacher for extra help in organizing working time and scheduling the various parts of the work. In that case I think the teacher can without any problem give the student what he needs, provided, of course, that the teacher is willing to do as much for any other student, and so on. But suppose, on the other hand, that the student does not ask the teacher for help and that the teacher instead calls the student at home and simply presents him with the help he needs in scheduling and discipline. The teacher's proposals in that case are more than likely to strike the student as meddling interference, and he is likely to respond with more or less polite variations on "Who asked you?" and "Mind your own business." Those responses, I think, are healthy and just. If the student were having ordinary difficulties getting his work done and yet docilely and submissively accepted the teacher's unrequested scheduling of his time, he would have taken the first step in the direction of unhealthy passivity towards his teacher. And if he and his teacher developed that sort of relationship, he could end by becoming a lackey-like reflection of his teacher. Bestowing at least some benefits only in response to requests for them is a safeguard against such an outcome when the members of the relationship are not equally balanced.

It becomes much harder to argue for this defense of prayer as soon as the complexity of the case is increased even just a little. Take, for example, Monica's praying for her son Augustine. There is nothing in Monica's praying for Augustine which shows that *Augustine* recognizes that he has a need for God's help or that *he* will be grateful if God gives him what *Monica* prays for. Nor is it plain that *Monica's* asking shields Augustine from oppressive overwhelming by God. So it seems as if the previous arguments fail in this case. But consider again the case in which a teacher sees that a student of his could use help but does not feel that he can legitimately volunteer his help unasked. Suppose that John, a friend of that student, comes to see the teacher and says, "I don't know if you've noticed, but Jim is having trouble getting to his term paper. And unless he gets help, I think he won't do it at all and will be in danger of flunking the course." If the teacher now goes to help Jim and is rudely or politely asked "What right have you got to interfere?," he'll say, "Well, in fact, your friend came to me and *asked* me to help." And if John is asked the same question, he will probably reply, "But I'm your friend; I had to do *something*." I think, then, that because John asks the teacher, the teacher is in a position to help with less risk of oppressive meddling than before. Obviously, he cannot go very far without incurring that risk as fully as before; and perhaps the most he can do if he wants to avoid oppressive meddling is to try to elicit from *Jim* in genuinely uncoercive ways to request for help. And, of course, I chose Monica and Augustine to introduce this case because, as Augustine tells it in the *Confessions*, God responded to Monica's fervent and continued prayers for Augustine's salvation by arranging the circumstances of Augustine's life in such a way that finally Augustine himself freely asked God for salvation.

One might perhaps think that there is something superfluous and absurd in God's working through the intermediary of prayer in this way. If Jim's friend can justify his interference on the grounds that he is Jim's friend and has to do *something*, God can dispense with this sort of petitionary prayer, too. He can give aid unasked on the grounds that he is the *creator* and has to do something. But suppose that Jim and John are only acquaintances who have discussed nothing more than their schoolwork; and suppose that John, by overhearing Jim's phone conversations, has come to believe that all Jim's academic troubles are just symptoms of problems he is having with his parents. If John asks the teacher to help Jim with his personal problems, and if the teacher begins even a delicate attempt to do so by saying that John asked him to do so, he and John could both properly be told to mind their own business. It is not the *status* of his relationship or even the depth of his care and compassion for Jim which puts John in a position to defend himself by saying "But I'm your friend." What protects John against the charge of oppressive meddling is rather the degree to which Jim has freely, willingly, shared his life and thoughts and feelings with John. So

John's line of defense against the charge of oppressive meddling can be attributed to God only if the person God is to aid has willingly shared his thoughts and feelings and the like with God. But it is hard to imagine anyone putting himself in such a relation to a person he believes to be omnipotent and good without his also *asking* for whatever help he needs.

Even if the argument can be made out so far, one might be inclined to think that it will not be sufficient to show the compatibility of God's goodness with the practice of petitionary prayer. If one supposes that God brought Augustine to Christianity in response to Monica's prayers, what is one to say about Augustine's fate if Monica had not prayed for him? And what does this view commit one to maintain about people who neither pray for themselves nor are prayed for? It looks as if an orthodox Christian who accepts the argument about petitionary prayer so far will be committed to a picture of this sort. God is analogous to a human father with two very different children. Both Old and New Testaments depict God as doing many good things for men without being asked to do so, and this human father, too, does unrequested good things for both his children. But one child, who is healthy and normal, with healthy, normal relations to his father, makes frequent requests of the father which the father responds to and in virtue of which he bestows benefits on the child. The other child is selectively blind, deaf, dumb, and suffering from whatever other maladies are necessary to make it plausible that he does not even know he has a father. Now either there are some benefits that the father will never bestow unless and until he is asked; and in that case he will do less for his defective child, who surely has more need of his help than does the healthy child. Or, on the other hand, he will bestow all his benefits unasked on the defective child, and then he seems to make a mockery of his practice with the normal child of bestowing some benefits only in response to requests—he is, after all, willing to bestow the same benefits without being asked. So it seems that we are still left with the problem we started with: either God is not perfectly good or the practice of petitionary prayer is pointless. But suppose the father always meets the defective child's needs and desires even though the child never comes to know of the existence of his father. The child knows only that he is always taken care of, and when he needs something, he gets what he needs. It seems to me intuitively clear that such a practice runs a great risk, at least, of making the defective child willful and tyrannical. But even if the defective child is not in danger of being made worse in some respects in this situation, still it seems plain that he would be better off if the father could manage to put the child in a position to know his father and to frame a request for what he wants. So I think a good father will fulfill the child's needs unasked; but I think that he can do so without making a mockery of his practice of bestowing benefits in response to requests only if putting the child in a position to make requests is among his first concerns.

And as for the question whether God would have saved Augustine without Monica's prayers, I think that there is intermediate ground between the assertion that Monica's prayers are necessary to Augustine's salvation, which seems to impugn God's goodness, and the claim that they are altogether without effect, which undercuts petitionary prayer. It is possible, for example, to argue that God would have saved Augustine without Monica's prayers but not in the same amount of time or not by the same process or not with the same effect. Augustine, for instance, might have been converted to Christianity but not in such a way as to become one of its most powerful authorities for centuries.[10]

With all this, I have still looked only at cases that are easy for my position; when we turn to something like a prayer for Guatemala after the earthquake—which begins to come closer to the sort of petitions in the first half of the Lord's Prayer—it is much harder to know what to say. And perhaps it is simply too hard to come up with a reasonable solution here because we need more work on the problem of evil. Why would a good God permit the occurrence of earthquakes in the first place? Do the reasons for his permitting the earthquake affect his afterwards helping the country involved? Our inclination is surely to say that a good God must *in any case* help the earthquake victims, so that in this instance at any rate it is pointless to pray. But plainly we also have strong inclinations to say that a good God must in any case prevent earthquakes in populated areas. And since orthodox Christianity is committed to distrusting these latter inclinations, it is at least at sea about the former ones. Without more work on the problem of evil, it is hard to know what to say about the difference prayer might make in this sort of case.

I think it is worth noticing, though, that the first three requests of the Lord's prayer do not run into the same difficulties. Those requests seem generally equivalent to a request for the kingdom of God on earth, that state of affairs in which, of their own free will, all men on earth are dedicated, righteous lovers of God. Now suppose it is true that God would bring about his kingdom on earth even if an individual Christian such as Jimmy Carter did not pray for it. It does not follow in this case, however, that the prayer in question is pointless and makes no difference. Suppose no one prayed for the advent of God's kingdom on earth or felt a need or desire for those millenial times strongly enough to pray for them. It seems unreasonable to think that God could bring about his earthly kingdom under those conditions, or if he could, that it would be the state of affairs just described, in which earth is populated by people who *freely* love God. And if so, then making the requests in the first half of the Lord's Prayer resembles other, more ordinary activities in which only the effort of a whole group is sufficient to achieve the desired result. One man can't put out a forest fire, but if everyone in the vicinity of a forest fire realized that fact and on that basis decided not to try, the fire would rage out of control. So in the case of the opening petitions of the Lord's Prayer, too, it seems possible to justify petitionary prayer without impugning God's goodness.

Obviously, the account I have given is just a preliminary sketch for the full development of this solution, and a good deal more work needs to be done on the problem. Nonetheless, I think that this account is on the right track and that there is a workable solution to the problem of petitionary prayer which can be summarized in this way. God must work through the intermediary of prayer, rather than doing everything on his own initiative, for man's sake. Prayer acts as a kind of buffer between man and God. By safeguarding the weaker member of the relation from the dangers of overwhelming domination and overwhelming spoiling, it helps to promote and preserve a close relationship between an omniscient, omnipotent, perfectly good person and a fallible, finite, imperfect person. There is, of course, something counter-intuitive in this notion that prayer acts as a buffer; prayer of all sorts is commonly and I think correctly said to have as one of its main functions the production of closeness between man and God. But not just any sort of closeness will result in friendship, and promoting the appropriate sort of closeness will require inhibiting or preventing inappropriate sorts of closeness, so that a relationship of friendship depends on the maintenance of both closeness and distance between the two friends. And while I do not mean to denigrate the importance of prayer in producing and preserving the appropriate sort of closeness, I think the problem of petitionary prayer at issue here is best solved by focusing on the distance necessary for friendship and the function of petitionary prayer in maintaining that distance.

[It seems to me that any argument against prayer is flawed if it assumes] that it is never logically necessary for God to make the world worse than it would otherwise be and never logically impossible for him to make the world better than it would otherwise be. To take a specific example from among those discussed so far, orthodox Christianity is committed to claiming that the advent of God's kingdom on earth, in which all people freely love God, would make the world better than it would otherwise be. But I think that it is not possible for God to *make* the world better in this way, because I think it is not possible for him to *make* men *freely* do anything. And in general, if it is arguable that God's doing good things just in virtue of men's requests protects men from the dangers described and preserves them in the right relationship to God, then it is not the case that it is always logically possible for God to make the world better and never logically necessary for him to make the world worse than it would otherwise be. If man do not always pray for all the good things they might and ought to pray for, then in some cases either God will not bring about some good thing or he will do so but at the expense of the good wrought and preserved by petitionary prayer.

It should be plain that there is nothing in this analysis of prayer which *requires* that God fulfil every prayer; asking God for something is not in itself a sufficient condition for God's doing what he is asked. Christian writings are full of examples of prayers which are not answered, and there are painful cases of unanswered prayer in which the one praying must be tempted more to the belief that God is his implacable enemy than to the sentimental-seeming belief that God is his friend. This paper proposes no answer for these difficulties. They require a long, hard, careful look at the problem of evil, and that falls just outside the scope of this paper.

And, finally, it may occur to someone to wonder whether the picture of God presented in this analysis is at all faithful to the God of the Old or New Testaments. Is this understanding of God and prayer anything that Christianity ought to accept or even find congenial? It seems to me that one could point to many stories in either the Old or New Testament in support of an affirmative answer—for example, Elijah's performance on Mt. Carmel (I Kings 18), or the apostles' prayer for a successor to Judas (Acts 1:24–26). But for a small and particularly nice piece of evidence, we can turn to the story in the Gospel of Luke which describes Jesus making the Lord's Prayer and giving a lecture on how one is to pray. According to the Gospel, Jesus is praying and in such a way that his disciples see him and know that he is praying. One of them makes a request of him which has just a touch of rebuke in it: teach us to pray, as *John* taught *his* disciples to pray (Lk. 11:1). If there is a note of rebuke there, it seems just. A religious master should teach his disciples to pray, and a good teacher does not wait until he is asked to teach his students important lessons. But Jesus is portrayed as a good teacher of just this sort in the Gospel of Luke.[11] Does the Gospel, then, mean its readers to understand that Jesus would not have taught his disciples how to pray if they had not requested it? And if it does not, why is Jesus portrayed as waiting until he is asked? Perhaps the Gospel means us to understand[12] that Jesus does so just in order to teach by experience as well as by sermon what is implicit throughout the Lord's Prayer: that asking makes a difference.[13]

NOTES

1. See, for example, the articles on prayer in the *Dictionnaire de Théologie Catholique* and *The New Catholic Encyclopedia.*

2. See *In IV. Sent., dist.* XV, q. 4, a.1, and *Summa contra gentiles* I. III. 95–96.

3. See 2a–2ae, q. 83, a.2.

4. See reply, a.2. "*Non enim propter hoc oramus ut divinam dispositionem immutemus: sed ut id impetremus quod Deus disposuit per orationes sanctorum implendum . . .*"

5. Cf. e.g., Origen, *op. cit.*, and Augustine, *City of God*, Bk. V, ix.

6. Plainly, a good deal of skilful work is needed to weave such anthropomorphism and scholastic theology into one harmonious whole. The problem is, of course, given lengthy, detailed treatment in various scholastic writings, including Thomas's *Summa theologiae.*

7. See especially Jn. 15:12–15.

8. I want to avoid detailed discussion of the various controversies over omnipotence. For present purposes, I will take this as a rough definition of omnipotence: a being is omnipotent if and only if he can do anything which it is not logically impossible for him to do and if he can avoid doing anything which it is not logically necessary for him to do.

9. Controversy over this point is related to the more general controversy over whether or not it is possible for an omnipotent, omniscient, perfectly good God to create men who would on every occasion freely do what is right. For a discussion of that general controversy and arguments that it is not possible for God to do so, see Alvin Plantinga's *God and Other Minds* (Cornell University Press, Ithaca, 1967), pp 132–148; I am in agreement with the general tenor of Plantinga's remarks in that section of his book.

10. I have presented the case of Monica and Augustine in a simplified form in order to have an uncomplicated hard case for the view I am arguing. As far as the historical figures themselves are concerned, it is plain that

Monica's overt, explicit, passionate concern for her son's conversion greatly influenced the course of his life and shaped his character from boyhood on. It is not clear whether Augustine would have been anything like the man he was if his mother had not been as zealous on behalf of his soul as she was, if she had not prayed continually and fervently for his salvation and let him know she was doing so. Augustine's character and personality were what they were in large part as a result of her fierce desire for his espousal of Christianity; and just his knowledge that his beloved mother prayed so earnestly for his conversion must have been a powerful natural force helping to effect that conversion. In this context the question whether God could have saved Augustine without Monica's prayers takes on different meaning, and an affirmative answer is much harder to give with reasoned confidence.

11. See, for example, the lessons taught in the two incidents described in Lk. 21:1–6.

12. I have used awkward circumlocutions in this paragraph in order to make plain that it is not my intention here to make any claims about the historical Jesus or the intentions of the Gospel writer. I am not concerned in this paper to do or to take account of contemporary theories of Biblical exegesis. My point is only that the story in the Gospel, as it has been part of ordinary Christian tradition, lends itself to the interpretation I suggest.

13. In writing this paper, I have benefited from the comments and criticisms of John Boler, Norman Care, and Bill Rowe. I am particularly indebted to my friend Norman Kretzmann for his thorough reading and very helpful criticism of the paper. And I am grateful to John Crossett, from whom I have learned a great deal and whose understanding of philosophical problems in Christian theology is much better than my own.

SUGGESTED READING

General

Alston, William. "The Indwelling of the Holy Spirit," in Thomas Morris, ed., *Philosophy and the Christian Faith*. Notre Dame, Ind.: University of Notre Dame Press, 1988.

Baillie, John. *The Idea of Revelation in Recent Thought*. New York: Columbia University Press, 1956.

Feenstra, Ronald J., and Cornelius Plantinga, Jr., eds. *Trinity, Incarnation, and Atonement*. Notre Dame, Ind.: University of Notre Dame Press, 1989.

Goulder, Michael, ed. *Incarnation and Myth: The Debate Continued*. Grand Rapids, Mich.: Eerdmans, 1979.

Hartshorne, Charles. *Man's Vision of God and the Logic of Theism*. Chicago: Willet Clark, 1941.

James, William. *The Varieties of Religious Experience*. New York: Modern Library, 1902.

Keller, James. "Reflections on a Methodology for Christian Philosophers," *Faith and Philosophy* 5, no. 2. (1988): 144–158.

Morris, Thomas. *The Logic of God Incarnate*. Ithaca, N.Y.: Cornell University Press, 1986.

Rossi, Philip, and Michael Wreen, eds. *Kant's Philosophy of Religion Reconsidered*. Bloomington, Ind.: Indiana University Press, 1991.

Wolterstorff, Nicholas. "God Everlasting," in *God and the Good*, ed. Clifton J. Orlebeke and Lewis B. Smedes. Grand Rapids: Eerdmans, 1975.

Prayer

Young, Robert. "Petitioning God," *American Philosophical Quarterly* 11 (1974): 193–201.

Incarnation

Hick, John. "The Logic of God Incarnate," *Religious Studies* 25 (December 1989): 409–423.

Swinburne, Richard. "Could God Become Man?" in *Philosophy in Christianity*, ed. Godfrey Vesey. New York: Cambridge University Press, 1989, pp. 53–70.

Atonement

Swinburne, Richard. "The Christian Scheme of Salvation," in *Philosophy and the Christian Faith*, ed. Thomas Morris. Notre Dame, Ind.: Notre Dame Press, 1988, pp. 15–30.